FEB. 8 2012

TO: MR. MATTHEW BOYLE WITH MY COMPLIMENTS.

P.S. HERE'S HOPING YOU ENJOY THIS BOOK.

ONLY WINNERS WRITE HISTORY
BEST WISHES
Liston B. Monsanto, Sr.

The Extreme Test

By

Liston B. Monsanto, Sr.

authorHOUSE™

1663 LIBERTY DRIVE, SUITE 200
BLOOMINGTON, INDIANA 47403
(800) 839-8640
WWW.AUTHORHOUSE.COM

AuthorHouse™
1663 Liberty Drive, Suite 200
Bloomington, IN 47403
www.authorhouse.com
Phone: 1-800-839-8640

AuthorHouse™ UK Ltd.
500 Avebury Boulevard
Central Milton Keynes, MK9 2BE
www.authorhouse.co.uk
Phone: 08001974150

First published by AuthorHouse 4/4/2006

ISBN: 1-4208-4901-8 (sc)

Printed in the United States of America
Bloomington, Indiana

This book is printed on acid-free paper.

Thus says the Lord: You, son of man, I have appointed watchman for the house of Israel; when you hear me say anything, you shall warn them for me. If I tell the wicked, "O wicked one, you shall surely die", and you do not speak out to dissuade the wicked from his way, the wicked shall die for his guilt, but I will hold you responsible for his death. But if you warn the wicked, trying to turn him from his way, he shall die for his guilt, but you shall save yourself.

-Ezekiel 33:7-9

This book is dedicated to my wife Wilma, my daughter Lorelei, and my son Liston, Jr.

ABOUT THE AUTHOR

Liston B. Monsanto, Sr., the son of Leroy and Othelia Monsanto is an erudite six generation Saint Thomian who has an inborn capacity for doing many things.

In St. Thomas, Virgin Islands where he has lived without limit, he is well known as the Dean of Local Sportscasters, a Taxi Operator, Tour Guide and noted member of "Morgan's Quartet." (i.e., a group of four singers performing together).

Bedridden during his formative and teenage years due to sporadic attacks of asthma, he became a voracious reader – grasping the opportunity to read any available book. In addition, he would take advantage of the facilities of the United States Armed Forces Radio Station whose program format had within it a host of mainland Universities and Colleges competing against each other in various disciplines.

Monsanto began his education at Dober Elementary School in St. Thomas ultimately graduating from Charlotte Amalie High School. Thereafter, by way of fulfilling his military obligation he enlisted in the United States Air Force for a four year tour of duty working as a clerk in the Office of Estimating and Production Control.

Continuing with his education he attended classes at the Universities of Nebraska and the Virgin Islands acquiring credits in a number of disciplines.

In the area of writing for publication, except for the letters appearing in this book, which were authored by him, this is Author Liston Monsanto's initial effort at writing a book.

Author, Liston Monsanto has been married for forty-five years to Wilma Marsh – a marriage that has produced two children, Lorelei and Liston, Jr.

CONTENTS

PREFACE   xiii

CHAPTER I Reuben B. Wheatley   1

CHAPTER II Leroy A. Quinn   31

CHAPTER III Anthony P. Olive   117

CHAPTER IV Edward E. Thomas   357

PREFACE

Living in a Virgin Islands community unrestrained by law and morality, mired in a quagmire of fear and depravity, I (utilizing a true breadth of understanding and being mindful of the fact that as a classified employee of the Virgin Islands Government, protected by the personnel merit system I had, at the inception of my employment, signed a loyalty oath which made it incumbent upon me to uphold the Constitution of the United States and the laws of the Virgin Islands), sacrificed myself and the welfare of my family in making positive inroads into the governmental system—(see Opinion No. 81-1434 of United States Court of Appeals for the Third Circuit). Prior to my achievement, virtually every working person in the United States Virgin Islands, the vast majority of whom worked and continue to work for the Territorial Government, felt that security and safety in numbers took precedence over lawfulness. Unknown to them, their civil rights were constantly being violated. Using altruism and a pledge to deliver my co-workers from all the evil within the Virgin Islands Bureau of Internal Revenue, formerly Tax Division, I undertook the arduous task of reporting and informing an apathetic public through the usage of the very sources (stateside mercenaries, local opportunists, newspaper, radio and television) who were responsible for the existing state of oppression in the Territory and who have since, together with their off-springs, become the beneficiaries of my hard work. Truly, in retrospect, my greatest wrong was always being right when it came to addressing the problems in my workplace.

Today, aware of the fact that current events form the basis for future trends, after much cogitation and actuation as a man of decision, I decided to write for the sake of posterity. As a realist, one who has been at odds with the values of the Virgin Islands power structure, my realism has caused me to dislike fanciful schemes. Because of my thoroughness and other attributes, some of my detractors see me as the devil incarnate while others, due largely to ignorance, see me as a rabble rouser without credibility and consequently not welcomed anywhere. So indentured to the Virgin Islands governmental system are my compatriots, that to say they feel safer among which is familiar, is a massive understatement.

Reflecting the Virgin Islands environment in which they were raised, their deportment, were it legally allowed, would be a constant menace to any well-organized society. A careful review of the many problems endemic in the governmental system plus a long look at my mirror image revealed that most parents in the Virgin Islands prefer not to take disciplinary measures that would improve the overall conduct of their children. Their only concern, sadly to say, is a paycheck and Carnival activities from January to December every year. It is a shame that no one wants to honestly apply the lessons learned in the various institutes of higher learning. They much prefer to live on their knees like most of the disadvantaged people in our small islands. Just imagine rain that would force the closing of the many public schools, would never stop the Carnival.

During my forty years as an employee of the Virgin Islands Government, under the stewardship of Reuben B. Wheatley, Anthony P. Olive, Leroy A. Quinn and Edward E. Thomas, all of whom labeled me restive, I was made to put up with suffering for doing what was right. With these highly paid mercenaries at the helm of affairs from my subordinate positions of: Internal Revenue Officer, Chief of Delinquent Accounts and Returns Branch and later as a Shop Steward representing many employees victimized by unnecessary oppression, I found out after successfully fighting "City Hall" that I could not help people who did not want to help themselves. Today these people, many of them with a vested interest in the system, exerting undue influence over their children, continue to be politically correct, but dead wrong. Rather than relocate elsewhere, as many people have done, over the past several years, I've continued to live in the Virgin Islands where racehorses are glorified and a hand full of decent people despised.

My cynical attitude today in addressing the lifestyle in the Virgin Islands is the same as it was when I became the preeminent force in the Virgin Islands Bureau of Internal Revenue. Although erudite, I'm not one of the signatory powers to the covenant with mediocrity. People in the Virgin Islands who continually complain at the various "nerve centers" and radio talk shows fail to realize that the same system that runs "fools paradise" (i.e. the Virgin Islands), a system that has them where they are, is the same system that's choking off public transportation, sports and everything else. Our government, which is not strict with law enforcement, is headed up by a governor under whose leadership everything falls. Our government, put simply, is not composed of segments. Within the last twenty years the Virgin Islands have been devastated by several hurricanes. "Marilyn" in 1995, for example, resembled the biblical flood experienced by Noah, opening the door to bringing in a new lifestyle in the United States Virgin Islands. Needless to say, it did not happen. Today everything remains status quo.

Over the past several years I've spoken out adnauseam about some of the many problems facing our people and although I've tried my best, the political system has shown me that it's capable of worst. What you are about to read is the absolute truth. It has nothing to do with imaginary people and/or imaginary happenings. It shows you what can happen in any departmental agency of the Virgin Islands Government where the people at the highest levels put politics before principles and ambition before ideas. Additionally, it tells you how employees working in a repressive Virgin Islands governmental system under taskmasters with unrestricted power are treated once they dare to speak the truth. An esoteric style of writing was used on purpose in many of my letters in order to make them shorter (i.e. using fewer words while retaining sense and substance). As a result, the reader's attention is hereby challenged to get away from the dull, commonplace way to which you have become accustomed. Like a vacation, this book has been designed for relaxing. Enjoy!

CHAPTER I
Reuben B. Wheatley

Writing as a pariah spurred on by pride, inspired by opinion #81-1434 of the Third Circuit Court, and encouraged by a motley crowd to shed my inhibitions, I begin this book labeled the "Extreme Test" with a graceful and witty quotation from the famous English essayist Augustine Birrell who wrote:

"It is better to read about a world figure than to live under his rule."

In the United States Virgin Islands, an area of 132 square miles per capita, the elected leaders and their retinue are the most accomplished hypocrites in the world. Through spurious relationships, isolationist policies, a theory of divide and conquer, and a governmental system that's filled to the brim with political patronage, these people take tremendous pride in preying on disadvantaged people. And so you may say, well that happens all over the world. You may with good reason refer to it as man's inhumanity to man, but please bear in mind that I'm speaking of an area of 132 square miles, an area where I was born and raised, and yes an area where just about everybody is (either by blood or through marriage) related to each other. The Governor by virtue of his position as Chief Executive has oversight over all departments, agencies and instrumentalities in the executive Branch of our government. Structurally, the Audit Division of the Inspector General's office from where audits are performed on the various departments, agencies and instrumentalities and the Bureau of Internal Revenue where the local taxpayers file and pay their taxes also fall under his range of operation. Commissioners and Directors requiring senate confirmation are appointed by the Governor and serve at his pleasure. Incidentally, he also appoints judges to the Territorial Court. Put simply, the Governor of the United States Virgin Islands is monarch of all he surveys. He wields more power than any State governor. He can check you, but there is no one to honestly check him.

Money, as you are no doubt aware, is a major source of political power. Taxpayers, many of whom are in the private sector of the Virgin Islands Community, donate money and sponsor a number of worthwhile programs and projects in the territory. Many of them are also responsible for financing the political campaigns of a number of Virgin Islands Politicians. In exchange for their time and money many of the aforementioned taxpayers resort to the quid pro quo operation that exists in the United States Virgin Islands, completely oblivious of the so-called "Mirror Theory," the Internal Revenue Code, or the Internal Revenue Manual. As Plutocrats, some if not all of them came to the Virgin Islands to avoid the United States Federal Tax System after which the Virgin Islands pretend to be mirrored. From time to time these same taxpayers become indebted to the Virgin Islands Government in a variety of ways, one of which is taxes; and yes, these are the same taxpayers on whom the Bureau of Internal Revenue must make a demand for payment. What a predicament!

Headquartered on a sunny island (St. Thomas) among a number of shady people, the guiding principle of the Virgin Islands Bureau of Internal Revenue (formerly Tax Division) when I worked there from May 1960 to November 1992 like a tacit prayer began with these words: "While in fools paradise, one must hear no evil, see no evil or speak no evil. Cooperate with the assembled gentry in doing lots of evil herein."

As a decent, generous and tolerant individual, who was at the time also a classified civil servant of the Virgin Islands Government (pledged through a loyalty oath to uphold the Constitution of the United States and the laws of the Virgin Islands), I knew that I was not at any time during my tenure with the Bureau of Internal Revenue obligated to adhere to the aforementioned principle. Starting from the late sixties and continuing up to the time of my retirement in November of 1992, under the several directors of the Bureau of Internal Revenue, I became persona non grata. Because I dared to do my work in conformity with guidelines established by the Powers that be, I was always being (in the words of my co-workers) "Persecuted for Righteousness Sake." From my subordinate position, I led a precarious life. In order to protect and/or otherwise defend myself, I could not offer inducements such as ice cream and cake to my adversaries. Because of Management's tyrannical authority, serving ice cream and cake would not have done one solitary bit of good. I went for the jugular vein through a series of letters. I selected and weighed the facts carefully and critically, and using my pen judiciously, I saw the burden of my letters achieve a semblance of peace in the workplace. In their strong desire for vengeance, management saw no need to give pity parties which would border on reconciling with me; consequently, I was forced to focus on the positive results rather than the personal pain.

I had been (ever since the first day on the job) for the advancement of the Virgin Islands Bureau of Internal Revenue and not the hindrance of it. As an experienced and compassionate person I had learned during my formative years that (a) to err was human, (b) to forgive was divine, and (c) to exploit was political; but as Management continued to operate under their guiding principle they were from time to time being observed furtively and cautiously haranguing a throng of innocent employees and blind loyalists, who through the acceptance of inducements were forced into a state of delusory happiness which would ultimately lead them down the primrose path to disaster.

But let's not get ahead of ourselves here. Let's start from the beginning. It all started for me in 1960 when I began working as an employee of the Tax Office, which was then the Tax Division of the Department of Finance. I had qualified for the job based on the results of an Inter-Departmental Examination, which I had taken. The little education that I had beyond high school, at the time, consisted of a few college credits. I had been demilitarized - honorably discharged from the United States Air Force where I had spent four years working with civilians and a number of military personnel in the office of Estimating and Production Control.

Prior to that as a civilian I had worked as a Bookkeeper for Mr. Louis Lindquist, a local car dealer. Educationally, I was more or less of the same ilk as Viggo "Mole" Hendricks, Henry Millin, Earle Ottley and Calvin Wheatley to name a few. These men (the record shows) are credited with making positive contributions to the economic growth of the Virgin Islands. They proved like Harry S. Truman (former president of the United States) that it is not always what you know in theory. Anyway, my educational background coupled with my practical knowledge enabled me to fill the vacant position of Chief Trade Tax Clerk in the Tax Division, which at the time was headed by Reuben B. Wheatley. Working in an office and supervising the activities of that office was nothing new to me. I knew what supervisory responsibility was all about. In the past I had supervised the activities of several employees at the Old Virgin Isle Hotel and thereafter I was designated Bay Chief in the United States Air Force where I got the chance to supervise a great number of men for a specific requirement. At the Tax Division, I found Reuben Wheatley to be a very good Administrator. Many of us who worked under his supervision espoused the concept that the man (even up to the date of this publication) was the best Administrator ever to supervise the activities of the Tax Division. (Note: Reuben Wheatley ran the Tax Division at a time when governors of the Virgin Islands were appointed). But as we say in local parlance, "give jack his jacket". Reuben Wheatley was a person most familiar with the overall operation of the Tax Division. As a good manager he would many times condescend to socialize with his lower echelon employees, thereby boosting morale. Personally speaking, I have never worked with anyone who challenged me the way he did. The truth be told, Reuben Wheatley prepared me for the extreme test I was to undergo during my years of employment with the Tax Division and later the Bureau of Internal Revenue. Circumstances it is said do not make a man, they reveal him. When looking back it is safe to say that strong emotions can really make human judgment fallible. Reuben B. Wheatley proved that. With power rooted in his persona, he became selfish and manipulative. This talented man with dominion over the Tax Division would (with the flight of time) go out of his way to prove that he was indeed not perfect. He would find out in the end (in the words of Teddy Roosevelt) that no man is justified in doing evil on the ground of expediency.

The Office of the Tax Division was small in size. It was located on Government Hill in a building sandwiched between the office of the governor and the office of the Lieutenant Governor (nee Government Secretary). Some of the personnel assigned to work therein were Senator Louis P. Hestress, Judge Verne A. Hodge, Marshal Lionel V. Roberts Jr., Joseph Simmonds and Jose Kean. With Reuben Wheatley as our Director, we dutifully did our jobs. There came a time however when the Tax Division would reorganize embodying the idea of the United States Internal Revenue Service. As a result of this reorganization, we were forced (in the interest of finding space) to relocate to larger quarters on lower Main Street # 76 Kronprindsens Gade in downtown Charlotte Amalie. And it was there that Reuben Wheatley would use his plenary powers to flaunt his authority in an effort to inspire intense fear and fearful reverence. The Tax Division had expanded in size threefold. We now had three Branches making up the Tax Division. They were (1) the Audit Enforcement Branch headed up by Louis P. Hestress with supervisory responsibility for the college-trained agents, (2) the Collection Branch also headed up by Hestress in the midst of some half-trained Revenue Officers and (3) the Processing and Accounts Branch headed up by Viggo A. Hendricks surrounded by untrained employees.

I was assigned to the Collection Branch under the job title of Internal Revenue Officer and in the augmentation of personnel that followed, Ernest O. Kean and Rudolph E. Krigger, Sr. joined the Collection Branch and were immediately sent off to Phase I of the Internal Revenue Officer-training program in New York. I was sent to the United States Internal Revenue Service in San Juan, Puerto Rico with orders to watch carefully the workings of the Office Collection Force (OCF) with a view towards systematizing locally. It is noteworthy that when the Tax Division began the process of implementing the enforcement systems of the United States Internal Revenue Service, Mr. Ulric F. Benjamin who had been commissioned as an Internal Revenue Officer in New York and assigned to the Manhattan District returned to the Virgin Islands as an Internal Revenue Agent in the St. Croix Office, acceding to the requests of Wheatley and Governor Farrelly, who at the time was working as an Assistant U.S. District Attorney.

In 1965, (because of his training, experience and ability in the Collection activity) he was designated Chief of the Collection Branch with the responsibility of supervising a group of half-trained Revenue Officers. Benjamin's decision to come back home (good or bad) was a harbinger of things to come. His primary function as Chief of our Branch was to implement a system that would result in the maximum enforcement effort in the Collection of delinquent income and other business taxes and to ensure that delinquent tax returns were filed. This assignment meant moving from St. Croix to St. Thomas where before his death he had established permanent residency.

It was at the Tax Division where I first met Mr. Benjamin. We seemed to have so much in common that we could have been called the Gold Dust Twins. We loved singing, we loved Major League Baseball with a passion, we harbored some sacred terms, we were both trained by the United States Internal Revenue Service and witty as he was, we would engage from time to time in making light banter. And would you believe this? Through his trials and tribulations, unknowingly he taught me the innumerable arts and wiles of office politics. During the period that we worked together (he as supervisor and I as one of his subordinates) we found ourselves at variance every now and then. Because of the overall working conditions, which incidentally succeeded in transforming me into a mal-content, our paths sometimes bristled with difficulties. At times I found myself hoping for the best, but preparing for the worst. Because of hellish temperatures in the workplace the scheme of selling ourselves off as professionals was absolutely mad. The contentious issue of "Rule of Thumb" versus "Rule of Law" permeated the workplace causing our paths to diverge. Mr. Benjamin's fear of Wheatley was evident by his attitude towards his subordinates and this attitude needless to say, affected the overall operations of the Branch.

A cursory reading of what follows provides proof for your edification: In calendar year 1968, Wheatley in a surprise move, named our technical advisor, Mr. Clarence McLaughlin, the Acting Director of the Tax Division. Mr. Benjamin, who heretofore had neglected to inform Commissioner Wheatley of existing injustices and deficiencies in his Branch, immediately wrote McLaughlin a five-page memorandum apprising him of the professional role that the Revenue Officers were required to play in the Tax Division. He went on to compare, among other things, the Revenue Officers to their counterparts in the United States and finally made a proposal for salary increases for the Revenue Officers and himself. At the time that the memorandum was written and up until Benjamin had left the Collection Branch, there were certain individuals on the employee level earning a much higher salary than him and to this he voiced his dissatisfaction, off the record, to his subordinates.

Several times prior to Benjamin's memorandum to McLaughlin, I had seen it fit to write to him about conditions in the Collection Branch and every time that I wrote the results were the same - no response. Nevertheless, it must be noted in all fairness that Benjamin was very sympathetic towards the Revenue Officers cause. Lest you forget, he had worked in the city of New York as a Revenue Officer before coming home to the Virgin Islands and had expressed, on many occasions, mostly off the record, that the Officers were being unfairly treated. But in spite of this, he was still afraid to forward the contents of my memoranda to the Commissioner. Instead, in his informal meetings with Wheatley, he leaked certain information concerning the essentials that were desperately needed for the Branch to function properly. Essentials such as space, partitions, telephone lines, training and transportation, etc. Wheatley (as I later learned from Benjamin) extracted certain information from Benjamin, which prompted him (Wheatley) to ostensibly appoint me as Assistant Chief of the Collection Branch on February 18, 1969. I became suspicious over the manner in which the information naming me Assistant Chief was communicated and immediately asked to see Wheatley. An informal conference was held and two weeks later on March 4, 1969, Wheatley rescinded the appointment giving as his reason that he had not had time to consider and discuss the matter. The Revenue Officers and Benjamin had always given thought to a career plan including a comprehensive training program. We were of the belief that we needed a promotional ladder that would serve as an inducement to remain with the Tax Division.

In May of 1969, Benjamin wrote to Wheatley inquiring about salary increases that had been awarded to certain individuals under his supervision, particularly in the St. Croix office. Wheatley in response to Benjamin's inquiries wrote in part: "I will be very much to the point in stating that it is my prerogative and I have no obligation to explain to any employee, what was the basis for my recommendation of salary adjustments for other employees."

There is more (much more) to say about the Collection Branch with its myriads of problems under the stewardship of Ulric Benjamin, but in order to give you a bird's eye view into the activities of the other two Branches I must put off further information until a little later on in this book.

We move now to the St. Thomas District Audit Enforcement Branch. Aristotle (The Greek Philosopher) said it best. Aristotle said: "Education is the best provision for old age". This quotation is being used as a means of introducing to you a few of the Internal Revenue Agents who were initially assigned to that Branch. They were: Aubrey Lee, Roy Moorehead, Anthony Olive, and Edward E. Thomas, a person with strong ties to the Wheatleys. The Branch was staffed with agents who had furthered their education receiving degrees from the various institutions of learning in which they had matriculated, but because of their servile dispositions and their unwillingness to apply the lessons they had learned in college, an impartial observer would have concluded that they would have preferred to die on their knees rather than live on their feet. Their attitudes and behavioral patterns reminded me of the Chinese Proverb: "A college degree does not change a fool, it merely disguises him." Victims of an inferiority complex, they acted like a bunch of hirelings and these good for nothings (the record shows) are some of the people for whom I would make a vicarious sacrifice.

Reuben Wheatley who was class-conscious favored government by an aristocracy. He had the Internal Revenue Agents programmed into believing that they were the cream of the crop. But as glamorous as they thought they were it did not occur to them that they could not operate in a vacuum. They did not consider the fact that working as a team in the Tax Division would be the only way the Division would be successful and effective and they were oblivious of the fact that they would have to coordinate their work with half-trained and untrained employees in the other Branches. They were (and they had good reasons to be) so proud of being a part of Academia that their servile obedience to the office of the director past unnoticed. Without exaggeration or imagination, the Agents primary function was audits.

In the Processing Accounts Branch where the prime records were stored most of the employees assigned thereto were complaining to a disgusting extent over the way Hendricks was supervising the activities of the Branch. Whenever they'd complain to me about Hendricks I'd ask them to give Hendricks the benefit of the doubt inasmuch as I was no ombudsman and I sincerely felt that he was concerned about the plight of the Tax Division. Because of his loyalty to Wheatley however, the employees considered him a lackey. Reuben Wheatley frustrated Ulric Benjamin's attempts to make inroads into the Virgin Islands Tax Delinquency situation. As his trusted subordinate Benjamin complained adnauseam to me about the obstacles in his path - obstacles he deemed insurmountable. I felt sorry for him but could do nothing legally to help inasmuch as I just happened to be on the employee level where limitations were put on me. Whenever I had questions about any account in my inventory I'd write to Benjamin. The spoken word being ephemeral I was forced to write for the record. What's more, in the Revenue Officers training program we were taught the importance of documentary evidence. Poor Benjamin, he had been backed into a cul-de-sac. Most of my memoranda (formal or informal) that were addressed to him had been ignored and furthermore, he had not shown them to Wheatley until a year or so later when he was forced to disclose their contents. Even though I knew of Benjamin's predicament, I had no choice. In keeping within the chain of authority, I had to deal directly with him. Benjamin was becoming frustrated. He knew that he had the responsibility of supervising the Collection Branch but the needed authority to sign documents, etc., had never been officially delegated to him. He always took the liberty to sign certain documents. What's more many recommendations offered by him were ignored.

Upon learning that all was not well within the Collection Branch Mr. Rudolph Arena, a member of the Assistant Commissioner of the United States Internal Revenue's Staff invited Benjamin to escort him to a meeting with Wheatley in order to evaluate the facts and circumstances surrounding conditions in the Collection Branch. Benjamin accepted the invitation and on the morning of the meeting he came prepared to put his cards on the table. Upon leaving the office (Note: unlike the

Chief of the Audit Enforcement and unlike the Chief of the Processing Branch Benjamin did not have his own private office) he told me, "Look I'm going to be perfectly frank about all that's going on. I'm ripping mad". Well, everything was going just fine and then wonders to behold, in his haste to accompany Arena to Wheatley's office he bumped into Robert 'Bobby' Woods who was himself on the way to the meeting. Woods surmised that something was wrong. He had never seen Benjamin acting so abnormal before. Anyway, cutting to the chase, after learning from Benjamin exactly what he was about to do, Woods reminded Benjamin of his loyalty to Wheatley, thereby resulting in Benjamin being forced to take the blame for the very things which he had despised.

Later in 1969, Wheatley accused Benjamin of encouraging the Revenue Officers to seek affiliation with the Union, and as 1970 rolled around, Benjamin became persona non grata. Wheatley summoned him to his office and outlined to him that he was going to give him one of his so-called "special assignments" which would remove him from the Tax Division. That was the last straw for Benjamin. He envisioned a tempest in a teapot. Through his intuitive knowledge he had reached the conclusion that if he stayed on as Chief he'd be caught in the midst of the storm. And quite rightly he imagined that there would be hopeless confusion. In token of these signs and not desirous of alienating or hurting anyone, Mr. Ulric F. Benjamin decided to bow out graciously, leaving me with his legacy of Chief Delinquent Accounts and Returns Branch (Note: The Collection Branch was now being called the Delinquent Accounts and Returns Branch). Benjamin had wit enough to come in out of the rain. He was hired by the Small Business Development Agency to perform in a less prestigious job. Of prime importance, however, was the fact that the Tax Division had lost another trained employee in much the same manner in which they had lost Aubrey Lee, Juan Sanchez, Jose Ramirez, Claude Molloy, Oscar Hernandez, Verne Hodge, Victor Schneider, Rudolph Krigger, Ernest Kean, Gregory Miller, Juan Centeno, Angel Callwood, Gerald Hodge, Sr. Louis Hestress, Donald Hill, Linda Francis and many others.

The frustration and pain continued. The treacherous Internal Revenue Agents had themselves become disenchanted with what was going on in the entire Tax Division and began discussions dealing with unionization. They wanted to organize themselves in an in-shop union similar to that in the Federal Government. They sought the Revenue Officers out arranging for a meeting of the minds. At the end of the meeting the decision was made to apprise Wheatley of our decision to unionize. It was on October 28th, 1966 that the Revenue Agents and Officers Virgin Islands wide, wrote to Wheatley apprising him that like our counterparts in Puerto Rico and the United States who were members of the National Association of Internal Revenue Employees (NAIRE) we had found it imperative to form an association. He was not receptive to the idea and summoned the members of our Ad-Hoc committee to his office to advise them against any move towards unionization. I was not a member of the Ad-Hoc Committee and consequently, did not attend the meeting. I had known from the beginning that through his theory of divide and conquer, Wheatley wanted to drive a wedge between the Agents and Officers. His demeanor and his modus operandi conveyed a whole lot. He felt that since the Internal Revenue Officers were not college trained that they were lower in rank and importance to the Agents. Reading between the lines of his correspondence and taking into consideration his abrasive attitude one would readily conclude that as far as Rueben Wheatley was concerned the Internal Revenue Officers were "Glorified Bill Collectors." At any rate, due to the fear of reprisals further discussions on the issue were put off for the future. We wanted to live and work together in harmony. Worthy of note nevertheless is the fact that while the agents and officers were mapping out plans for their future through unionization someone faint hearted enough (a mole in our midst) was busy doing unprincipled things so as to gain Wheatley's favor. That person or persons because of my potential ability as a Revenue Officer began smearing my reputation to Wheatley and somehow convinced him that I was one of the ringleaders in opposition to his authority. That was absolutely not true! The rumors and stories not based on facts that he was receiving caused Wheatley to make a number of unilateral decisions. Things were getting very tenuous in the Tax Division. The members of the Ad-Hoc Committee which, had not dissolved, approached me once again with the explanation that Mr. Joseph Simmonds who had been assigned to work along with the agents under the job title of Tax Technician was being treated unfairly. Unlike the agents with whom he was required to work, he had not received any formal training and that due largely to the lack of training his chances for advancement within the Tax Division were very slim.

To say that the Tax Division was made up of men with social natures is a massive understatement. Customarily after work, a group of us would spend the time hob-nobbing at a bar or restaurant to sip on a beer, highball, or cocktail while discussing world affairs and a number of historic and current events. As a newcomer to the Division, Mr. Edward Thomas was invited to join us in perhaps the only time that he ever did. We were at Willie Lewis' Place in the Long Bay Area. And Willie Lewis' Place is where Edward Thomas first made an impression on me with his answer to a question concerning the Virgin Islands and future leadership thereof. In answering the question the word on which he placed his emphasis was exploitation. I looked directly in his direction hoping to respond but a significant nod form Ulric Benjamin warned me not to. Edward Thomas was speaking like Niccolo Machiavelli the Italian Statesman and Writer who advised that rulers use craft and deceit to maintain their authority. It was to my good fortune that I had been made aware that Edward Thomas had designs on being exactly where he is today. His policy was one of pure opportunism. It was for this and other reasons, some of which you've already read in this book that I had begun feeding the members of our Ad-Hoc committee with the proverbial long spoon. They were spineless cowards. Wheatley had himself in a press release to the Daily News of November 1969, stated in part, that, "Many of these people have said they wish to be considered professionals and they are college graduates. But many have said also that they did not feel they should submit themselves to non-professionals."

As a classified employee (Civil Servant) protected by the Personnel Merit System at the time, I was not afraid of what was to come. I had previously told Benjamin that for reasons of security I'd pawn my honor but that I would never be a pawn for anybody. Since we were dissuaded initially by Wheatley from unionizing internally and since our membership Virgin Islands wide had voted for unionization, late in 1969 when just about every Departmental Agency of the Virgin Islands Government had been unionized or were seeking Union representation, the agents and officers once again got together and decided to seek affiliation with the government employees association. The Bargaining Committee to prepare proposals and assist in the negotiations with the Administration's Labor Panel was appointed and included Glen Byron, Juan Centeno, Roy Moorehead, and yours truly Liston Monsanto. We were making several demands among which were the institution of a career plan including a comprehensive training program and the discontinuation of the practice of importing personnel from the outside to handle assignments for which local personnel were qualified. Upon receiving the news, Wheatley became furious, livid with rage. He immediately addressed an envelope dated 11/24/69 to "Liston Monsanto, et al." It was not until I opened the envelope that I recognized his little witticism. The memorandum enclosed therein was addressed to Internal Revenue Agents and Officers and it stated the following: "With reference to your correspondence re your affiliation with the government employees association and the news reports about it, I have always heard that the harder a person works for the average individual the harder that individual will kick him. I hesitate to speculate at your motives, for the record, but misrepresentations and lies have never resulted in a permanent benefit for anyone." He thereafter, according to a report in the local Daily News of December 1, 1969, expressed his strong opposition to unionization on our part. Additionally he wrote a full-paged letter to the editor expanding on his opposition. His letter provoked former Internal Revenue Agent Gregory Miller to anger, causing Miller to express his disapproval and rebuttal in words of bitter scorn in a full-paged article in the local Home Journal of December 12, 1969.

As a follow-up to Miller's Article, Mr. Paul E.M. Iasigi (a Public Accountant on St. Croix) added his voice to our cause pointing out to then Governor Evans that the time had come for us to unionize. Wheatley was hell bent on keeping us out of the Union. He was devoting a lot of time and attention to the matter. He requested and was granted a hearing before Commissioner of Labor Melville Stevens on December 18, 1969. I represented the Revenue Officers and Anthony Olive, the Agent who would ultimately betray the group for a reward, represented the Agents. As witnesses sworn to give honest testimony we answered the several questions asked us by the Union representative Roy Gottlieb. Arnold Selke, an assistant attorney general represented Wheatley who became the object of much attention as he appeared to be little bound by the love of truth. Looking back it is safe to say that the Tax Division had consumed his life. It was his empire. He was always there.

For many years the Department of Finance (with Wheatley as Commissioner and the Tax Division an integral part) had led a precarious existence with Wheatley also acting as the Director of the Tax Division. As has elsewhere been pointed out, in calendar year 1968 Clarence McLaughlin, a state-sider, was designated director of the Tax Division for reasons known only to Wheatley. Reuben Wheatley was fond of boasting. He would always boast of handling six footers during his days in the United States Army and his celebrated expression was: "I've never been known to hurt for an alibi." When it came to training for the employees (Note: Joseph Simmonds who had not been sent for training prior to the hearing before the commissioner of Labor was immediately sent to his training program) he would always offer a cure where there was no disease. He somehow thought that he was doing the employees a favor to send them for required training. And so here he was leading up to the hearing using the gumption for which he was noted in an attempt to divide and conquer the group by: (a) awarding salary increases and (b) sending certain individuals to the mainland for much needed classroom training.

Commissioner Stevens ultimately ruled in our favor only to be reversed by Governor Evans who cited Section 16 of Executive Order #68-1964 as his authority. Prior to the Governor's action however Roy Gottlieb (the Union Representative) in his closing remarks said: "We have heard the Commissioner of Finance say that because there is a petition for an outside organization that he is in favor of the in-shop organization, but we have also heard testimony to the fact that when they sought to form an in-shop organization, he was also opposed to it. This brings to mind only that the Commissioner of Finance only holds himself up to be some type of God and he dislikes the idea of these men being represented by an organization that can meet him as an equal. As long as he can slap down and push around the employees in the agency, everything's all right." Incidentally, if you would re-read the contents of Wheatley's Memorandum of November 24, 1969 to the Internal Revenue Agents and Officers you'll find that the man honestly felt as if he was doing the men a favor in his representative workplace.

The Union now out of his way, he zeroed in on his whipping boy Ulric Benjamin. Under pressure Benjamin had released all of the letters and memoranda that I had written to him critical of the Branch's operation. Wheatley then wrote to me kind of tongue-in-cheek promising to adopt some of my recommendations. He ended his letter by saying that had he been made aware of what was going on in the Branch, he would have done something of a positive nature. (He seemingly had forgotten about the letters that the Revenue Officers had sent him as a group). At that point, Benjamin could take no more.

The election for our first elected Governor was a few months away and he as a Democrat with the charisma of a popular Crucian was quite capable of inspiring great personal allegiance to the party on the island of St. Croix. He would become active in politics; chiefly for his own profit. With him it was security and safety in numbers taking precedence over lawfulness. Ulric Benjamin was departing the Tax Division the place of his forte for greener pastures as elsewhere mentioned in this book. He would leave the Tax Division not desirous of burning his bridges. (He would return to help Wheatley in destroying the standards that were set for admission to the Revenue Officer gentry).

Before leaving presumably as a courtesy he came to me and told me that he had spoken to Wheatley about his plans to resign and that he had recommended me to replace him. I said many thanks, but may I have a copy of the letter wherein you made the recommendation? I never got it.

So Benjamin leaves. The Branch is without a supervisor and would stay without one for about two weeks. I was the senior man, but unlike General Haig, the Secretary of State under President Regan, I was not in charge. Believe you me. I did not want the job as a supervisor under Reuben Wheatley. I had witnessed what Benjamin had gone through and my attitude being what it was, there would be no way that I'd be Wheatley's scapegoat. Two weeks later Wheatley called me to his office and asked me what was going on in the Branch. I told him that after Benjamin had left that I had continued to do the work expected of me as a Revenue Officer and that evidence of this was found in my daily reports which had been placed in one of the drawers of the desk previously used by Benjamin. He then told me that he wanted me to supervise the activities of the Branch. I said ok. Now I knew that the Branch was without an immediate supervisor, but I also knew that I did not want to be the person assuming the responsibility as Chief. But what was I to do? It was a catch twenty-two situation. I couldn't say no I do not want the job. Of course Wheatley would have liked me to say no so that he could tell the powers that be how I was being groomed to be a supervisor and how I had no initiative. Anyway, in the discussion that followed my affirmative answer I told him of my plans and thoughts for the Branch and even went on to tell him that although I was the senior person based on longevity I had never been given an opportunity to complete my training program. I furthermore told him that the training was absolutely necessary in order for me to better handle the technical aspects of the job. He agreed and said he'd send me to training as soon as there was an opening. And so as we emerged from our meeting the decision was made to convey my designation as Chief to the members of the Tax Division with whom I would coordinate my work.

Wheatley had not forgotten what my detractors had told him about my role in our failed Union bid. He was fond of gossip. He wanted to get me. He had a sinister agenda in mind. Through his anonymous accusations, he would punish me. After all, if he could handle six footers who had not been college trained surely he could handle an upstart like me who had come out of the Savan District and whose education like the six footers was limited. As far as he was concerned, Liston Monsanto had been an ingrate, who, like the legendary Swiss hero William Tell had refused to yield to power. Wheatley would use Jens Todman with his vile habits and Edward Thomas his silent partner to systematically oust me from the Tax Division. But as he continued to reason cleverly and falsely (especially with respect to the role that I had played in the Union matter), he completely overlooked the fact the he needed my consent in order to treat me as an inferior person. That consent he or anyone else for that matter would never get. In my lifetime although I carry with me a piece of paper from the school of hard knocks, I've never felt inferior to anybody. As Director of the Tax Division he saw himself as a perfect reproduction of J. Edgar Hoover (former Director of the FBI) and as a consequence felt his power to be absolute.

Due largely to the fact that in November of 1970 the people of the Virgin Islands would elect a governor for the first time, the candidates and their supporters were being seen in every nook and cranny on the islands, so much so that politics became our national pastime. Cyril E. King, a man endowed with firmness of spirit and charismatic enough to fascinate and attract voters had become a most popular candidate for the office of governor. As the conspicuous leader of the Independent Citizens Movement (ICM) and a very good politician, he was sure to get support from the grass roots. Consequently, Wheatley and the opposition had cause to be concerned.

Mr. Rudolph "Lindy" Foy who had returned home from New York was assigned to the Processing and Accounts Branch to be the Chief Cashier in the Tax Division. Foy was the person charged with the responsibility of making the daily deposits to the bank, etc.

Rudolph Foy was a member of the ICM party and by virtue of his membership he was very close to Cyril King. On several occasions Foy had open the doors of the ICM party hoping that I would

9

become a member. I never did however. I was apolitical. Wheatley had a penchant for using third parties as human shields to protect him from meeting his victims face to face. He was in a position where many people found themselves courting his favor. There came a time when Rudolph Foy became the victim of a host of problems in the Processing and Accounts Branch. Wheatley who was always quick to justify Viggo Hendricks' indiscretions wrote to Cyril King on July 24, 1970, explaining to King how Foy had refused to do what Hendricks had requested and what action he (Wheatley) would be forced to take by July 29, 1970, if Foy did not comply. At the time King was not a government employee and Foy over forty years of age was a full-grown adult. Was King supposed to use the art of persuasion in forcing Foy to incriminate himself? On another occasion (one that readily comes to my mind) he sicked Ulric Benjamin on me questioning my part time employment with WSTA Radio as a Sport Editor. He was always seeking out people to do his dirty work.

On May 4, 1970, with a wary eye on Reuben Wheatley, I began working as Acting Chief of the Collection Branch. On May 6, 1970, in my first meeting with the members of the Branch, I circulated the memorandum from Wheatley that designated me Acting Chief of the Collection Branch among the members. I then went on to explain in great detail how I had discussed briefly with the Commissioner some of the existing problems within the Branch. I pointed out to the group that the commissioner was very much aware of our structural needs such as telephone lines, partitions and an air conditioned unit. I stressed the importance of time and attendance, sensitive cases and cooperation with the other Branches. Finally I made a promise to hold periodic meetings.

On May 20, 1970, I traveled to St. Croix for the purpose of addressing my subordinates on that island. I told them that having worked as an Internal Revenue Officer I was very much aware of the Branch's problems but that presently I was about to make the transition from one level to another. I placed heavy emphasis on the importance of operating the office in a business-like manner. I had a sneaking suspicion that Revenue Officer, Christian Begraff, who had an attitude of indifference, was feeding pertinent information to Ulric Benjamin, our deposed Chief. Without accusing him, I cautioned the group against violating the disclosure of information law which was forwarded to us from the Commissioner's Office via a memorandum dated January 28, 1964. The employees of the Collection Branch of the Tax Division Virgin Island wide with me at the helm were now ready and willing to do the job for which they were being paid.

Most of the employees in the Branch before being admitted thereto had never worked in an office before. As a consequence, they were not familiar with the usage of their calendar pads and the other apparatuses in the office. I immediately educated them. I had previously observed under Benjamin that the transmission of authority from superior to subordinate (delegation of authority) and the process of decentralization of authority were absent. The reason for this absence was due to micro managing on the part of Wheatley. Were he not the Commissioner, he could easily have been charged with open intervention into the affairs of the Collection Branch.

I was constantly feeling under attack. There was hardly any oral communication between us. There were countless amounts of hand written memoranda from him to me almost if not all, which began with hearsay statements such as: "It has been brought to my attention." With his assistance I wanted to make the Branch greater in importance. Unlike some of his company men I was not a purveyor of gossip. I wrote to him listing at least seven items which I believed needed his immediate attention. They were Delinquency Investigations, Transportation, Training, Delegation of Authority, Disclosure of Information, Cooperation and Salaries. In an organization requiring a high degree of confidentiality the turnover of employees was abnormal. Rather than asserting their rights with a view towards bringing a semblance of normalcy into the workplace the oppressed employees were leaving and taking with them classified information with respect to taxpayer delinquencies. Our Branch was desperately in need of additional help. I started a recruitment drive through which I was able to augment my staff. And then in order to gain more knowledge and assert myself as Chief I started a course in Evidence and Procedure. I matriculated in the evening program at the then College of the Virgin Islands and became a very busy person.

Four months had gone by since I had been Acting Chief of the Collection Branch and even though Wheatley had promised that he'd send me for my required training, he did not. His toadies were acting in mean and contemptible ways. One morning I'm sitting at my desk immersed in my work when suddenly I heard a sound as if someone was lifting the telephone on my secretary's desk off the hook. I looked up and saw that Edward Thomas was about to use the telephone without permission (there was no one sitting at the desk and he was not assigned to the Collection Branch). What's more, had he asked for my permission to use the telephone, I may have granted it. At any rate, I asked him what was the matter. He told me all he wanted to do was make a phone call. I told him that Mr. Benjamin was no longer here and that in his office which was located about ten feet down the hallway from ours there were many telephones. I then asked him to return the phone to its resting place.

On the afternoon of July 30th, 1970, I met with Wheatley for about fifteen minutes in his office for the purpose of discussing my training program and other incidentals. About twenty minutes later while sitting at my desk I received a hand written memorandum from Wheatley which said: "I have received complaints from some employees and from taxpayers and representatives of taxpayers about what they consider to be an over assertion of your authority and unwillingness or impatience about considering other people's suggestions, proposals etc." In closing he said: "I am leaving this to your judgment. It needs no discussion, but when I hear something concerning one of my supervisors I feel obligated to pass it on."

The next day (July 31, 1970), I sent him a letter, which in part said: "As you well know, people's pocketbooks are highly related to their attitudes. Often, our target is the reduction of the size of the pocketbook. This objective poses special problems. It is unlikely that the members of the Collection Branch will ever be highly welcomed guests. Fortunately, popularity is not our goal. Our goal is to be respected, trusted and believed." In phase I of the Revenue Officer's training program, I was taught not to call on taxpayers or third parties to make friends. And finally I told him: "What puzzles me is the fact that yesterday I spent about fifteen minutes in your office and not once did you mention anything about my behavior. My conscience is clear. I'm no halo wearer, and if I'm guilty of anything, I don't mind being reprimanded. On the other hand, when I'm not guilty, I will not be a scapegoat for anybody." Based on the limited amount of classroom training that I had received from the United States Internal Revenue Service and based on my experience which I had acquired over the years as a member of the Collection Branch I was of the belief that if the Branch consistently performed in ways that convinced the taxpayer (or third parties) that we meant what we said, that we knew what we meant, and we were operating fairly and impartially, we would build the image of the Tax Division. Accordingly, in some cases we would be seen as "Nice Guys," often however, we weren't going to be seen that way. If the showy display of sending us to be trained by the United States Internal Revenue Service meant operating arbitrarily upon completion of that training, then as far as I was concerned the Government of the Virgin Islands was being extravagant.

Wheatley was not satisfied with being boss. He wanted to be bossy. He kept on writing groundless memoranda critical of my operation in the Branch. In one of the rare times that I met with him face to face in his office he tried to placate me to some extent. He inquired of me why (like Viggo Hendricks - Chief Processing and Accountants Branch), I did not visit his office more often. I told him that I had surmised that the duties of his office were onerous, requiring his full attention during the eight-hour working period. I reminded him that this was for me a probationary period as Acting Chief of the Collection Branch and then before leaving his office I told him that in the past and up to now I had sent him a number of periodic reports for his review and that since the reports were designed to convey to him exactly what was going on in the Branch, I saw no reason to engage in small talk about anything else. By now I had seen the general direction Wheatley had begun to take.

As noted previously, I was taking a course offered by the United States Internal Revenue Service in Evidence and Procedure. At the same time, due largely to my urgings, the Revenue Officers were pursuing courses at the College of the Virgin Islands. I had told Wheatley that I was going to stress the importance of these courses since I was very much aware of the fact that a lack of initiative and/or resourcefulness would easily degrade a Revenue Officer faster than any other factor.

The Tax Division, in keeping with the "Mirror Theory" of taxation, was being asked to operate in a vacuum; independent of all the other departmental agencies of the Virgin Islands Government. Although I never discussed the less-than-professional predicament in which the Tax Division found itself mired, I could see why we were being denied our training by a professional organization. There was no way under existing conditions in the Virgin Islands that we could work in a manner reflective of our training by the United States Internal Revenue Service. It evoked memories of the old saying, which goes: "Do not undertake a project unless you can implement it!" It must be borne in mind however, that Wheatley was trying his utmost to systematically remove me from the Tax Division. My honesty was provoking him and so desperate was he that he continued to underestimate me. Wheatley was a mendacious person who was unworthy of trust and belief.

After it had become abundantly clear that I was not going to be sent off for training, I submitted an application on September 23, 1970 for 240 hours of annual leave to commence on September 28, 1970. Wheatley approved my application. However, on Friday afternoon, September 25, 1970, at about 3:00 p.m., Wheatley notified me that I had to be in Boston, Massachusetts on Monday, September 28, 1970 at 8:30 a.m., which was the same date that I was to begin my annual leave. I therefore proceeded to attend the training classes rather than take the annual leave at that time. Before departing for Boston, I had by memorandum (with a copy to Wheatley), assigned Jens Todman the task of supervising the Branch until my return. One week later while in Boston, I called the office and asked Mrs. Gertrude Lewis to call Todman to the phone. She told me that Todman had gone to Oklahoma to play softball. He had used an underhanded trick on me. I could only speculate at the timing of his departure. I could no longer trust a person who was seemingly undermining my efforts while forming an unholy alliance with Wheatley and Edward Thomas for personal gain. He had to have gotten Wheatley's approval to travel to Oklahoma. Right then and there I had found out that doing well for Jens Todman could be disastrous.

While in Boston, I made arrangements with Wheatley to take my annual leave upon completion of my classes there. This was also approved by him and upon completion of the training courses on October 23rd, 1970; I went on approved annual leave until December 4, 1970.

On Monday, December 7, 1970, when I returned to work, Wheatley refused to communicate with me, claiming that I should have returned to work upon completion of my training instead of taking annual leave. I tried in a variety of ways to confer with him: through his office staff, via telephone, through third parties, and through correspondence. All were ignored. Finally, on February 1, 1971, after it had become crystal clear that Wheatley did not want to communicate with me, I wrote asking him to be relieved of the responsibility of acting Chief of the Collection Branch so that I could return to my classified position of Internal Revenue Officer. I cited the fact that there existed a poor rapport between us which was serving only to destroy the Branch.

Wheatley responded to my request on February 4, 1971, saying that I would be relieved of the responsibility of acting Chief of the Collection Branch but that it was not his intention to return me to my former position. Instead he issued instructions that he was removing me from the Tax Division until further notice and that I was to assist the supervisors in the Treasury Division in establishing a comprehensive program for utilization of all of their manpower, etc. He further mentioned that the assignment would begin on Tuesday, February 16, 1971, and that I would be required to submit reports to him on the assignment every two weeks thereafter. I objected to my removal at that time and after various exchange of memoranda, on February 12, 1971, I received another memorandum from Wheatley notifying me that the assignment had been postponed and would begin February 22,

1971 instead of February 16, 1971. He went on to say that his secretary would call to tell me what time he would meet with Mr. Lincoln Watley and me to discuss the assignment. Such a discussion never took place.

Of particular interest however, is the fact that on February 10, 1971, the Revenue Officers, perhaps envisioning themselves as future targets, wrote to Wheatley on my behalf, sending copies of their letter to Governor Evans, Lt. Governor Maas, and Mr. Bruce Delamos. They outlined to him several reasons why they thought that my absence from the Branch would hinder the Collection process. They further pointed out that there was a need within the Branch for a Revenue Officer of my caliber. They concluded by saying that the best interest of the government could be served by allowing me to remain in the Branch and to continue to perform the duties for which I was trained and best suited for.

On February 19, 1971, Wheatley sent me a memorandum directing me to report to Conrado Corneiro of the Audit Division on February 22, 1971. I was to work out of his office on the first phase of the assignment (Note: The assignment was a most frivolous one; one that was designed to throw me out of the Tax Division. Be reminded that Wheatley headed the Tax Division, the Lottery Commission, the Treasury Division, and the Audit Division that served as the watchdog over all the departmental agencies of the Virgin Islands Government. He could check you but without a federal comptroller there would be no one to check him), at the Audit Division where I was to report to Conrado Corneiro together with Gwendolyn Adams and those others, who considered themselves to be blue-blooded and would assume the role of vassals to Wheatley.

Adams for some time had been a delinquent taxpayer as evidenced by recorded liens in the Office of the Recorder of Deeds and Corneiro had become indentured to the governmental system. With them, it was always security and safety in numbers taking precedence over lawfulness.

On February 19th, 1971 these fools would find themselves sucked into the vortex of my struggles. I had started my fight against the Virgin Islands Governmental System. In my struggle, I would be forced to do what the mercenaries in the Virgin Islands Government didn't have the guts to do. Wheatley, in flaunting his authority, had told me in his memorandum that he had already discussed the program with the useless and inefficient Corneiro. I reported to Corneiro as ordered. He told me that I should go back to the Tax Division pending notification from him. I knew that I was now engaged in a type of guerrilla warfare. Reuben Wheatley had become my nemesis.

I went to see then Attorney Verne A. Hodge who had previously worked in the Tax Division under Wheatley, and who at one time was being groomed to take over the helm as director of the Tax Division. He had taken the preparatory courses offered by the Untied States Internal Revenue Service with a view towards being our director but Wheatley for obvious reasons would not surrender the division to Hodge.

In the intervening time, while teetering back and forth between the Audit and Treasury Divisions, Wheatley responded to my former subordinates, the Revenue Officers, in an intimidating way, forcing them through threats and the instillation of fear, to discontinue their support of me. When looking back, it is safe to say that the Revenue Officers' letter of February 10, 1971, was of a perfunctory nature. They, like many people in the Virgin Islands, didn't care one way or the other about me. With the exception of Revenue Officer Mario Lima, they were all spineless bastards. Here was a group of men charged with the responsibility of seizing tangible and intangible assets as well as the responsibility of physically closing the businesses of delinquent taxpayers. Yet when it came to the unnecessary oppression from which they would not be granted immunization, they quickly placed their tails between their legs.

Feeling insulted and somehow believing that a coup d'etat was imminent, Wheatley became a roaring lion. Through the axis of evil that he had formed with people like Edward Thomas and Jens Todman, he zeroed in on Anthony Olive, who as previously mentioned had represented the agents in giving testimony before Commissioner Melville Stevens in the Labor Union affair. Together they succeeded in corralling Olive and ultimately transformed him from a law-abiding citizen into the nominal head of the Virgin Islands Bureau of Internal Revenue. The rules of Government did not apply to Reuben Wheatley.

After I had returned to the Tax Division from Corneiro's office on February 22nd, 1971, I received another memorandum from Wheatley ordering me out of the Tax Division. He explained that he had written to me on February 4, 1971, and that he had expected that I would understand that my reassignment removed me from the Tax Division until further notice. And so once again I reported to Corneiro who explained to me, in a meeting attended by certain supervisory personnel of the department, that because of the type of assignment given to me, he would have to secure written permission from the many departmental agencies of the Government for me to get access to their bills, etc. He spoke specifically of the hospital accounts and stated that he would arrange with Doctor Eric O'Neal to have such permission granted.

As we emerged from the meeting, Mr. Corneiro stated that it was all right for Mr. Lincoln Watley and me to visit the hospital in the interim and launch an investigation there. Watley and I visited the hospital and conferred at length with Mr. Alvin Hammer concerning the hospital accounts with respect to their Collection methods, etc.

Wheatley later wrote saying that he considered it intentional and malicious for me to go to the hospital and leave them, the hospital personnel, with the impression that the Department of Finance was taking over the accounts receivable work of the hospital. I was very surprised, in light of the fact that Corneiro knew that we were going to the hospital. By now Wheatley had become "addle-pated", he knew that his so-called "special assignment" was frivolous but could not admit it. Our private war had escalated into a public exhibition.

In his capacity of senator, then Senator Athniel "Addie" Ottley arranged to meet with Wheatley and myself, to discuss my status with the Tax Division. Nothing was accomplished due to Wheatley's continued interruptions whenever I tried to offer my explanations. Wheatley entertained us in his office merely for the sake of getting rid of Senator Ottley.

Even Rufus Martin, a Reporter for he local Home Journal, wrote an article critical of Wheatley. Wheatley, the man who had continuously displayed a holier than-thou-attitude, was being exposed. I could see the distaste for what was to be done emanating from Corneiro's demeanor and I would make capital of it.

On February 23rd, 1971, I wrote to Wheatley seeking the answers to several questions. He was asked about my status with the Tax Division, a clarification of my assigned duties and the manner in which I was to report on the status of my assignment on a bi-weekly basis. He elected not to answer all the questions and instead outlined to me in his memorandum of February 26, 1971 exactly what he wanted me to do in connection with the assignment. He made it very clear that my assignment would cover only those activities after the billing procedures. He then concluded by saying that written reports were to be sent to him on a bi-weekly basis outlining what had been accomplished as well as any suggestions and recommendations for changes to be introduced in the work of enforcement officers. I acknowledged receipt of his memorandum and told him that I would proceed immediately to complete the project as expeditiously and as thoroughly as possible, submitting reports every two weeks. Incidentally, Wheatley refused to answer my question concerning my status in relation to the Tax Division.

The project got underway and as I had promised, I sent my first bi-weekly report to him on March 4, 1971. Subsequently, the second report was hand delivered to his office on March 18, 1971. In my third report he was notified that work had begun on my final report. Finally, on April 21, 1971, I forwarded my final report to him with a note attached which read: "Should I report to the Tax Division tomorrow or wait until Monday?" In response to my question, Mrs. Berry, Wheatley's secretary, told me that Wheatley's orders were for me to report to the Audit Division and stay out of the Tax Division. By this time, in a show of disrespect and an abuse of his discretionary power, Wheatley had brought in a retired employee from the United States Internal Revenue Service to supervise the same Jens Todman and the other employees who had previously demanded "the discontinuation of the practice of importing personnel from the outside to handle assignments for which local personnel were qualified."

With his patronizing attitude Todman was told by Wheatley to introduce Mr. Robert Wallace, his new supervisor, to the several supervisory personnel with whom he'd be required to work. Why he brought Mr. Wallace into the Treasury Division where I was engaged in conversation with Mr. Watley is not clear. Maybe his conscience pricked him. What is clear is the fact that in my presence he introduced Wallace and Watley to each other and escorted his new boss out the door.

When I had delivered my third report to Wheatley, the report that told him about my final report, he was so preoccupied with Rudolph Foy and Viggo Hendricks that, probably without reading the report, he pushed it aside or deposited it into the waste paper basket. The detailed report that he received was a shocker. It was all encompassing. He never expected it. The end he had in mind had been neutralized. Impulsively, he would once again send me to his human shield, Conrado Corneiro.

On April 22, 1971, I reported to Corneiro who surprisingly expressed his appreciation over my detailed report. He then told me that there was nothing left for me to do in the Audit Division and that Wheatley had promised him that he would send me a letter removing me from the Audit Division to the Treasury Division. And true to form the letter came ordering me to report to Juan Romero in the Treasury Division. Now the pressure was on Romero. It is important to note at this juncture that the Governor, Melvin Evans, and the Lt. Governor, David Maas, having been given copies of the report were aware of what was going on but they allowed Wheatley to continue with his tyrannical ways.

Upon my arrival in the Treasury Division, Mr. Romero in my presence, via telephone, told Wheatley that he did not know what Wheatley wanted me to do. Then on May 3, 1971, he wrote to Wheatley asking him to have me transferred back to the Tax Division citing that there was nothing in the Treasury Division for me to do. He further mentioned to Wheatley that if required, his existing personnel staff could personally implement any of the recommendations listed in the report. Nevertheless, Wheatley insisted on my removal from the Tax Division and ordered Romero to keep me in the Treasury Division. Being completely removed from the Treasury Division and after being sent back and forth from one section to another, I realized that I was being treated unfairly and that Wheatley was trying to do indirectly what he had no basis to do directly – remove me from the Tax Division. After reporting to the Treasury Division, I immediately proceeded to request a hearing before the Director of Personnel pursuant to the provisions of Title 3, Section 452 of the Virgin Islands Code.

At the same time, Wheatley was preparing to take disciplinary action against Rudolph Foy by having all or part of his salary denied in violation of the Virgin Islands Code. He was also effectuating a transfer of Foy from the Processing and Accounts Branch to the Treasury Division - a move to which Foy had agreed. The Chief of the Processing and Accounts Branch, Viggo Hendricks, and Foy were at loggerheads and something had to be done legally to resolve the problem.

Foy joined me in retaining the services of Attorney Verne Hodge. Talk about misery loving company? Now I had company. I knew I was fighting "City Hall". Foy had a much easier case. Wheatley had not given him the "letter of denial" that was legally required to do what he (Wheatley) wanted to do. We had left the spirit of the law in the capable hands of Attorney Verne Hodge. But unknown to him, we would change the whole aspect of the situation through lampoonery.

It was common knowledge throughout the Tax Division that Wheatley was conducting the destinies of the Division in a vicious, dictatorial, dynastic fashion; completely disregarding rules and regulations that had been established for the supervision and direction of the employees. But the public had no idea that this man personified Robert Louis Stevenson's story "Dr. Jekyll and Mr. Hyde." He had to be exposed. Most of the employees in the Department of Finance, which was managed by Wheatley, were saying in private what we were going to say openly. War had been declared. We wrote and delivered several letters to the local newspapers and made a number of calls to the "radio talk shows". Wheatley was forced to react against our lampoonery.

On December 30, 1971, acting like a Milque Toast, he wrote to then Senator Athniel "Addie" Ottley in a glaring attempt to mislead Addie into believing that his frivolous assignment was actually what he claimed it to be. The precursor came on October 15, 1971, when he wrote to me saying: "I continue to receive complaints about you and Mr. Rudolph Foy making loud and disparaging comments across the corridor of our main building about Mr. Viggo Hendricks, and these comments are obviously intended to harass and annoy him and undermine his efforts to perform the duties and responsibilities of his position. I would assume that you are aware that your actions are disrespectful and damaging to Mr. Hendricks. Therefore, they are apparently intended for that purpose and to undermine his ability to maintain the respect and confidence of the employees whom he must supervise. I am now giving you this written notice that I expect these loud disparaging and unwarranted comments against Mr. Hendricks or any other supervisor in this department discontinued immediately. If this type of harassment continues, I will have to conclude that they are positive actions on your part to interfere in the orderly operations of the department and I will initiate whatever actions may be appropriate and necessary to stop them." He sent copies of his letter to the Attorney General, the Director of Personnel, and the Chairman of the Government Employees Service Commission, who I hasten to add, was himself an aristocrat.

I was not daunted by Reuben Wheatley but operating from a subordinate position and appealing to the Government Employees Service Commission, which was made up of some delinquent taxpayers and aristocrats, I knew that there was no way that they were going to rule against him. As far as they were concerned I had nothing to offer. I had been rude to Mr. Wheatley. Anyway, I took his letter to my attorney who immediately addressed a letter to Wheatley.

The letter stated: "I have chosen not to answer your letter of October 12, 1971, because it is not responsive to my letter to you of October 4, 1971 on behalf of Mr. Monsanto. However, I find it necessary to write to you again regarding another letter which you have written to Mr. Monsanto, dated October 15, 1971. In that letter you accused Mr. Monsanto and Mr. Rudolph Foy of annoying Mr. Viggo Hendricks. It appears that you have accepted as true, the alleged complaints without the courtesy of an inquiry to Mr. Monsanto and Mr. Foy. As a commissioner you must surely be aware of the rights of your employees, and that the minimum of due process would guarantee an employee the right to refute such malicious allegations, and to know the name of the persons making such complaints. Unfortunately, you have not only ignored these rights but also compounded your error by sending a copy of your letter to the Attorney General, in an obvious attempt to instill fear and to intimidate Mr. Monsanto. If Mr. Hendricks has a criminal complaint against Mr. Monsanto and Mr. Foy, let him go to the Office of the Attorney General and make the required sworn statements. As long as I am legal counsel for Mr. Monsanto, he will not be coerced or intimidated by anyone who believes that his power is absolute. This is a government of laws, not of men. It is your responsibility to carry out the laws, not to make you own. When those laws give certain rights to employees, they must be respected by you and everyone else. Your continued threats to Mr. Monsanto and recording of these unsupported charges in his personnel file, in your attempt to build a record against him, can only guarantee our continued efforts to resist such autocratic actions. Let's put an end to this continuous harassment and humiliation of Mr. Monsanto."

Again, be reminded, that Governor Evans, Lt. Governor Maas, and all the senators knew what was going on but looked backwards. Wheatley had written to Juan Romero, Director of the Treasury Division, on May 4, 1971, referring to Romero's letter of May 3rd, 1971, wherein Romero had asked that I be transferred out of his division. He wrote in part: "I am more than a little disappointed at the reasons given in your memorandum for your request; after what I wrote and explained to you and after what Mr. Corneiro explained to you about the assignment I cannot understand how you could say that you do know what to do and you can do the job yourself, if the instructions are clear enough!"

Now Romero, who had demonstrated how careful he could be about right or wrong, feared that if he did not do what Wheatley was forcing him to do, he'd be drummed out of his position as Director. He was sandwiched between two aristocrats, Wheatley and Corneiro. Corneiro could not handle me. He was one of Wheatley's lackeys but somehow had managed to persuade Wheatley to remove me from his division to Romero's.

Wheatley was seething with discontent over my final report. As evidenced by the number of letters and memoranda that he was sending me, he was not doing the government's work for which he was being paid. He was acting in a confused, blundering way. On one hand he was saying that my final report was not acceptable while on the other hand he wanted me to implement the recommendations in the report he had adopted. He was placing some rigid restrictions on my movement and communication within and without the department. The question of how to get rid of me occupied his mind. One time he's got me in his "general office" without a desk and yet at another time he has me in Treasury and/or Audit. Wherever he has me I'm without a desk. He wrote me on June 1, 1971. The way the letter was worded one would have thought that he had completed and assignment. He was desperate, telling me exactly what to look for, how to go about looking for it, how to implement it, etc. It was really pitiful. I immediately wrote back to him on June 2, 1971. I said, "First of all, I have never ignored your instructions or any of the division heads regarding the "special assignment" referred to in your letter. More importantly, I have never expressed or implied any untrue or ridiculous remarks regarding the assignment. To the contrary, your remarks that I do not intend to work to earn my salary at any assignment unless it pleases me are totally false and baseless. You know for a fact that I have diligently worked on the assignment and that my final report is proof of this diligence. I find it hard to understand how on the one hand you state that my final report was not acceptable, while on the other hand, you state that the recommendations should be implemented. This is more perplexing in view of the fact that both the director of the Audit Division and the director of the Treasury Division praised the scope and efficiency of the report. Moreover, your criticism at this late date raises a question to its objectivity and fairness; in view of the fact that my report was submitted on April 19, 1971, and because you are well aware that I have charged you with abuse of your discretionary power for which a hearing is pending. It is distressing to note that you continue to accept rumor as fact. This is apparent from your charge that I have ridiculed you and spread lies to encourage disrespect and dissension against you. This is an absolute falsehood. I note, with disappointment, that in your continued attempts to unlawfully exclude me from the Tax Division, you are now assigning me to your general office. As in my prior assignment to the Audit Division and the Treasury Division, this is also being done until further notice. Since my appeal against your unlawful conduct is still pending, I shall continue to cooperate, as always, until a final decision has been made. The abuse and humiliation that I have to endure within the department because of my itinerant status is a small price to pay for the assertions of my legal rights as a classified employee. The restriction that you have placed on my movement and communication within and without the department are clearly discriminatory and is an additional abuse of your discretionary power. Your threats to dismiss me and recommend my removal from the government service with prejudice, shall not intimidate me in any way, and I shall refuse to engage in any conduct which would be unbecoming to a classified government employee."

Wheatley had become a wretched coward. He was afraid to face me. There was always an intermediary. He continued to abuse his authority with impunity, writing letters and memoranda ordering me to migrate between the hospital, which was located next to the Lionel Roberts Stadium, and the Department of Finance (either Audit or Treasury).

It was on April 19, 1971, with the submission of my final report that I had found myself sitting in the catbird seat. I felt confident. The worst was behind me. In one of my many hearings before the Government Employees Service Commission (GESC) which at the time comprised of people like Auguste Rimple, Sr., and Ann Abramson, Wheatley had succeeded in converting Romero into a faceless troll and ordered him to appear before the commission as his representative and although Romero found himself at a loss for words, the invertebrates assumed the role of Pontius Pilate, resulting in my being returned to Romero's office to lean against one of the walls therein. I did not have a desk – a fact brought out in the hearing. I was also not in charge of the Tax Division from where I could grant anybody a favor by way of a quid pro quo. Following the hearing Wheatley delivered an ominous warning which was again without merit. He said, "I have observed from the time cards which are being used as the basis for your salary payments that you have been reporting and being paid for 8 hours on the job although it has been reported to me and I have observed you on the street and in other places where you were obviously not involved or on the way to do the business of the government. It was even rumored that you told people that the reason you were on the streets after checking in is because you had no assignment. I would like to receive an explanation about this." I answered him right away, I said, "I have discussed your memorandum with Mr. Juan Romero, Director of the Treasury Division and many other employees of the Department in an attempt to determine the source of the false and malicious charges made in your memorandum. As I expected, everyone was as surprised as I was to know that you would give credence to such rumors, despite your busy schedule. As a twelve-year employee of the Department of Finance, I have never and will never accept unearned salary payments. This is another obvious attempt on your part to force me to resign or become insubordinate, I will do neither." It is safe to assume that the people with whom Wheatley was surrounding himself were telling him of the glaring abuse of his discretionary power, but as long as he could count on people like Attorney Mario Bryan, Ann Abramson, Auguste Rimpel, Sr. and Chester Williams (all members of the G.E.S.C), to support him in systematically trying to dispose of me, he'd continue to commit his nefarious acts against me.

Earlier in this Chapter, I pointed out to you how the members of the commission had assumed the role of Pontius Pilate (washing their hands) leaving my future hanging in the balance. Incidentally, Albert Commissiong (another aristocrat) was also a member of the G.E.S.C. I knew his face, but his name escaped me when I gave you the composition of the G.E.S.C. They operated like a Kangaroo Court. My unfair trials were a mockery of justice. A classic example of what was going on follows in this letter from Curtis Tatar, Assistant Attorney General, to Auguste Rimpel, Chairman of G.E.S.C. Mr. Tatar wrote on December 5, 1973: "In my capacity as Legal Counsel to the Government Employees Service Commission, I was assigned to defend against the Petition for Writ of Review filed by Liston Monsanto against Reuben B. Wheatley, Commissioner of Finance. It is your Order of March 29, 1973, which the District Court would either sustain or reverse. Commissioner Wheatley is the only named respondent in the court action. The nature of the action makes the Commission an interested party. This letter with copy to Commissioner Wheatley confirms my conversations with you two on November 30, 1973. It is my legal opinion that Judge Christian would ultimately reverse the decision of the Commission, were he to proceed upon a Writ of Review. I have read the Order of the Commission which was drafted by your retained counsel and the transcript of the hearing on July 6, 1972. I opine that the testimony of Juan Romero was insufficient to sustain Commissioner Wheatley's decision upon judicial review. Commissioner Wheatley and Mr. Romero may have had good cause for the decision to suspend Liston Monsanto. However, the record lacks factual testimony of incompetency or inefficiency or lack of cooperation on the part of Mr. Monsanto. Mr. Romero never answered the questions of your Legal Counsel, Mario Bryan, Esq. about specific instances of the alleged failings. Thus, the Commission's findings of fact are not supported by the record. Also, the Order does not specify findings of fact as Judge Christian would require. See his Memorandum and Order in Wheatley v. Foy underline, Civil No. 538/1971 (D.V.I. July 17, 1973). Based on my legal opinion, Commissioner Wheatley has agreed to reinstate Liston Monsanto for the one week he was suspended.

I shall so inform Fred Rosenberg, Esq. whose client will then dismiss the action pending in District Court."

During this period, Attorney Verne A. Hodge was no longer representing me. He had become Attorney General for the Virgin Islands. My attorney for this particular Writ of Review was Fred Rosenberg. When the Assistant Attorney General, Curtis E. Tatar addressed his letter to Rimpel, he sent a copy to Wheatley so that both Rimpel and Wheatley knew what was going on. I did not know until January 11, 1974 when I received a government check (numbered 8775396, dated January 9, 1974) from the Payroll Division in the amount of $196.37. There was no supporting document explaining the check's existence and I was reluctant to accept it. I wrote to Wheatley asking for an explanation and it was then that he wrote to me on January 14, 1974 telling me that "payment was made pursuant to the information in the enclosed letter from Attorney Curtis E. Tatar."

My unlawful removal from the Tax Division which was done under the guise of a special assignment was an ordeal that lasted for three years during which time I was without a desk from which to work, etc. As I write more than thirty years later, what's still fresh in my mind is how I spent my time walking between the Hospital and the Finance Department gathering whatever was necessary to complete frivolous assignments. I solaced myself being in the Treasury Division with Rudolph V. Foy who had already been transferred thereto and the several employees with whom I had established rapport.

Over the years, Wheatley (prominent as he was) had become a most powerful person. For reasons better known to him however, he saw me as a usurper. Judging from his reaction, my letters to him were having an internal impact. Using anybody he could find as an intermediary between him and me, he was stooping to any unscrupulous trick to avoid facing me. The man was living a life of deception and needless to say, when one lives a life of deception, the truth becomes hard to find.

Cyril King and his Independent Citizens Movement with him as their standard bearer had already lost to Melvin Evans in his bid to become the Territory's first elected Governor in 1970. But following his loss, King continued his tireless efforts campaigning for the Office of Governor. In 1972, he made the decision to run for Senator. He would use that office, if elected, as a springboard to the governorship. In January of 1973, on a Saturday afternoon while taking a stroll down Main Street in the area of the Market Square, I heard someone call out to me. I looked up and saw Senator Cyril E. King (he had been elected Senator in November of 1972) waving his arms in a gesture asking me for five minutes of my time. I went over to the side of the street where he was standing and for the very first time he told me that he had become aware of what I was going through in the Department of Finance under Reuben Wheatley. He went on to tell me that he had spoken with Wheatley and that a decision had been made for him and me to appear before Wheatley at 10:00 a.m. on the following Monday. He asked me if I'd meet him outside Commissioner Wheatley's office about five minutes to ten so that Wheatley would have no reason to say that we were late for the meeting. I told him that since Wheatley had approved of our getting together I saw no reason not to be there and so we parted company with the knowledge that we'd meet with Wheatley the upcoming Monday morning. I met Cyril King in the hallway leading to Wheatley's office and together we headed to Wheatley's secretary. King told her about his appointment with the Commissioner after which she offered us a seat and proceeded into Wheatley's office to serve notice on him that we had arrived at the appointed hour. When she came back to us about five minutes later, she told us that Wheatley said he would see us when he was ready and so we waited. Five minutes later the telephone rang and the secretary announced to us that Wheatley was ready to accommodate us. We walked into Wheatley's office, King leading the way. As soon as we sat down, Wheatley started telling King, in a curt way, how busy he was and how he really did not have too much time to devote to him. I sat there listening to Wheatley. King could hardly get a word in edgewise. King would only say, "But Commissioner, you promised you'd see me and Mr. Monsanto this morning and that's why we are here." King was obviously embarrassed. I'll say this much however, Wheatley's blunt and tactless behavior may have brought on some resentment on King's part. Anyway, King looked at me and said, "Let's go, the Commissioner is busy." I got up and we left Wheatley's office. When we got to the hallway, King looked at me still embarrassed and asked me about my reaction to Wheatley. I told him that it was either one of two reasons why Wheatley may have acted the way he did. They were, (1) either to show me how he could handle you, or (2) he wanted me to react vociferously.

Although Wheatley's remarks had a biting edge, I could not allow Senator King, who was then Chairman of the Government Operation Committee of the Senate, to take me before Wheatley merely for the sake of getting rid of his duty. I had always felt that failure sometimes had to be an option, particularly when it came to meeting Wheatley face-to-face in his office. But then on second thought, I surmised it may have been a ruse orchestrated by both men. So in order to clear the air of the mystery surrounding our visit, I immediately wrote to Senator King on January 29, 1973. I sent copies of my letter to Senators Hector Cintron, Elmo Roebuck, Ruby Rouss and Noble Samuel, who were all members of the Senate's Committee on Government Operations. In my letter I referred to King's visit with Wheatley in order to give the members of the committee an awareness of what was going on, presumably unknown to them. I wrote a letter to Senator Claude A. Molloy, then President of the Legislature and a person who had previously worked under Wheatley's directorship as an Internal Revenue Agent. I outlined to Molloy in my letter exactly what was taking place in the Virgin Islands Government's Tax Division. Molloy did as I expected-nothing. I did not want to give anybody in a position of authority a reason to say 'had I known of your situation I would have done something.' They all knew what was going on [the powers that be in the Executive Branch, as well as the powers that be in the Legislative and Judicial Branches]. Again, I was in a fight against "City Hall."

Senator King responded to my letter and scheduled a hearing for me and several of the disgruntled employees in the Tax Division. King was dealing with numbers; he wanted the employees to support him with their votes. At any rate, our grievances were heard and as expected nothing was done to resolve the mystery of Wheatley's special assignment. Other hearings, all before Cyril E. King and his Committee, were thereafter scheduled and recorded for this publication. Following the several hearings, Wheatley, using a holier than thou attitude wrote to King explaining him that he was once again assigning me to work with St. Thomian Edwin Hatchette, who was now Director of the Treasury Division.

Mr. Roland Riguad, a Haitian, who had preceded Hatchette as Director of Treasury had already notified Wheatley that he would not be his pawn in getting involved in what he considered to be petty nonsense. To his credit and unlike Conrado Corneiro, unlike Juan Romero and unlike Edwin Hatchette, Haitian Roland Riguad had been man enough to steer clear of Wheatley who everyone familiar with my situation knew was flaunting his authority. The torturous Edwin Hatchette was tailor-made for Wheatley. As a patsy he could be used as a protective shield for Wheatley the tyrant. He would not have my cooperation, however. Having been drained of strength and energy, Wheatley was worn out and unable to go on. He was repeating the same foolish and wicked things he had done to his toadies Coneiro and Romero and since I had by now become familiar with his modus operandi, it was easy for me to handle both him and Hatchette. I was still without a desk nevertheless.

On February 19, 1974, Hatchette, caught in the crossfire, wrote a memorandum addressed to me with a copy to Wheatley telling me how he had recommended to Wheatley that I be reassigned to the Tax Division inasmuch as there was nothing for me to do in Treasury. Wheatley, who by now had seen Hatchette as his favorite patsy ignored him completely. While Wheatley was using Hatchette in his quest to dispose of me, Cyril E. King had already launched his campaign for Governor. He was going to run against Alexander Farrelly, a democrat, and the incumbent Governor Melvin Evans who was very much aware of Wheatley's behavior through letters and discussions with his Lieutenants Omar Brown and Bruce Delemos. He refused, by his silence, to do anything that would have brought an end to the punishment that I was receiving.

Cutting to the chase, King emerged the winner, beating Alexander Farrelly in the run-off election. Now Cyril E. King had become the Governor elect and needless to say in the Department of Finance a spirit of uneasiness pervaded the office of Reuben B. Wheatley. During the period that we were engaged in our fratricidal struggle, Wheatley had proven to me that he was not a formidable opponent. As mentioned earlier in this publication, Wheatley was very fond of using go-betweens as protective devices to shield him from being hit directly. But now to my good fortune and aided by Cyril King's victory, he was at my mercy. There was no way that I would let him off the hook. Lest you forget, I was not actively affiliated with any political party. I was apolitical all the way. Rudolph Foy who had been at loggerheads with both Wheatley and Viggo Hendricks was a member of the ICM's Territorial Committee and very close to Governor-elect King. Wheatley was very much aware of that fact. King himself did not have to be told about working conditions in the Department of Finance. He already knew. Wheatley was so enamored with the Tax Division that he perhaps regretted that we had become enemies. It was his entire fault, however. He had ignored the first rule of war that says, never underestimate your enemy, and he had given credence to unfounded rumors from every nook and cranny. The time had come for him to pay for his wickedness.

Wheatley took the offensive at once. He wrote, "I have told you several times what I consider to be the areas of your performance which I believe should be improved, but my comments have not been accepted and I will not waste any time and efforts again with you, now or in the future. As I stated to you before, your problem appears to be one of attitude and your refusal to accept the realities of your job position as an employee is not in the best interests of the government and the taxpayers." The man was becoming a most innovative person. He finally restored me to my position as Internal Revenue Officer in the Tax Division.

Then came the issuance of "Service Award" pins on November 20, 1974. His faithful servant, Leroy Quinn, was given the responsibility of distributing the pins to deserving employees. The following letter dated November 22, 1974, addressed to Wheatley is offered here as a means of conveying to you exactly what transpired on that fateful day. "Although I have been carrying out instructions to the letter, over the past few years there has been so much misunderstanding and misrepresentation of the facts that I'm forced by this letter to establish for the record what I consider to be an intolerable situation apparently designed to deceive and confuse most of the employees of the Tax Division.

At the outset however, it is well to mention that for the past several weeks there has been considerable discussion among the employees, surrounding the presentation of longevity pins on November 20, 1974, to those of us meeting certain standards and certainly in view of the many Senate investigations and the continuing investigation being conducted into the affairs of the Department by the Office of the Attorney General. some employees thought that the idea was a very magnanimous gesture, which came at a time when change in the V.I. Government seemed imminent.

Nevertheless, hope springs eternal in the battered eardrums of man or something like that. It is a matter of record that I have been with the Department of Finance for a period in excess of fifteen years during which time I have consistently performed satisfactorily despite many obstacles. In short, I have beyond the shadow of a doubt, earned my fifteen-year service pin. I am quite certain that by now you are aware that I am a person who is strongly opposed to anyone taking divergent views just for their sake. Similarly, you are no doubt aware that when I think that people should be held responsible for what they do, I say it.

Consequently, it is disappointing to note that in ceremonies marking the occasion in the Processing Branch before many of my fellow employees with years of service ranging from five to eighteen years, the official, Mr. Leroy Quinn, presumably acting on instructions from you, passed me over as if I had never been employed by the Department of Finance. His action in this regard appeared petty causing many employees to label the episode a form of harassment.

Although Mr. Quinn offered his apologies the following morning for what he called an "oversight," many employees of the division rejected it. They believe, however, that if in fact it was an oversight, the Department can ill-afford such oversights inasmuch as they can only serve to promote alienation which does very little to bring us together." Copies of my letter were sent to Governor-elect King, Lt. Governor-elect Juan Luis and protocol being what it is, to Governor Evans and Lt. Governor Athniel Ottley.

Wheatley responded at once. He said, "It is unfortunate that during a period of time when everyone who has the best interests of our islands and our government at heart should be concentrating on meaningful and positive actions, you are doing what you can to create problems among some of the employees of the Department of Finance. You must know what I am referring to. I know that there are many "limited" people among us and I fully expected that some of them would think as you have expressed yourself about the presentation of the service award pins, I also recognize the fact that most of the employees are of at least average intelligence (and without all sorts of evil thoughts) and that they would give us the benefit of any doubts.

For your information, Mr. Monsanto, I wrote and otherwise communicated with the division of personnel more than two years ago about the matter of distributing service award pins to our government employees and we made our first effort to obtain the pins more than one year ago. The pins were not distributed before this month for several reasons which may or may not make sense to you. Furthermore, Mr. Monsanto, I do not know why you live with the idea and try to impress people that I find the time to give some special thought and attention to you and your continuing sick attitude.

As I have told you before, I have never done so and I never will do so. It is contrary to my character and to my personality, and most people who know me will acknowledge this. It should be obvious to you that Mr. Quinn and many of us at the Department of Finance are serious individuals who devote very substantial amounts of our time trying to do what is constructive and in the best interest of our islands and we have no time for nonsense and petty foolishness.

What you have said in your letter is in fact insulting to Mr. Quinn and is evidence to everyone that you have respect for anyone in management. It is unfortunate, but yours is a problem of attitude, an attitude that is destructive and harmful, particularly during this period of our development." He added a postscript which said, "Anyone can check my facts, Mr. Monsanto." Needless to say, he sent copies to the same officials to whom I had sent mine. I could tell from his reaction to my letter that he was running scared. I do not believe that he had told Quinn to ignore me. It could have been an honest mistake, a mistake made against the wrong person. As weak as he had become, I had to keep him occupied. So on November 25, 1974, I wrote, "I should really ignore your letter of November 22, 1974, because it is not responsive to my letter of the same date. However, I find it necessary to write to you again regarding certain high opinions that you have expressed in that delicately worded letter seemingly for the review of Governor-elect Cyril E. King.

First of all, let me state that "some people in our government and specifically the Department of Finance, possess a lively imagination and a ready tongue, they can distort facts as smoothly, as fluently and as effortlessly as some of us can recite the multiplication tables, but they don't always get away with their lies. Ironically enough, it is their superb smoothness that makes them suspects; their answers are too quick to be true. Even if they are not caught immediately in their lies, we have learned from unhappy past experience not to suspend out critical faculties when they are talking. We admire their nimble wit, but we listen with a skeptical ear."

You have made the unilateral decision that I'm doing what I can to create problems among some of the employees of the Department of Finance. Mr. Wheatley, "Those who corrupt the public's mind are just as evil as those who steal from the public's purse." Nonetheless, impressive evidence has accumulated over the past several years and I can assure you Sir, that full scale investigations such as the ones conducted by the Senate together with the one presently being conducted by the office of the

Attorney General, will ultimately disclose to the people of the Virgin Islands who is really creating the problems; and speaking about "limited" people among us, let me hasten to remind you Sir, that those are the same people who refused to be intimidated by you and Viggo Hendricks. They possess what many of us refer to as independence of mind.

They firmly believe in the assertion of ones rights and, consequently, will continue to resist the state of oppression that exists in the Department. It has become abundantly clear that theses employees who, for the most part, are taxpayers and voters have lost confidence in your office. Evidence of this was exemplified by their bold appearance before the senate where they gave honest testimony regarding conditions at this most troubled department of our Government. They know for a fact that all things are not equal among them. Furthermore, they believe that it is fine and noble to give trusted subordinates the benefit of the doubt, but they also believe that our government should be of, for and by the people, not for a chosen few as is the case in the Department of Finance. I wonder what their reactions would be to your letter.

It was stated in my letter of November 22, 1974, that Mr. Leroy Quinn was presumably acting on instructions from your office. Your assumption about insulting Mr. Quinn is, to say the least, baseless, malicious and most damaging. For your information, I respect Mr. Quinn very much and he knows it. Sir, respect is a two-way street. To me, being afraid of the boss is not respect. As far as I'm concerned, my record speaks for itself. I know for a fact that I have earned the respect of the majority, including management, within the Department owing to my courage to stand up for what I believe in. It is for this and other reasons which I have previously mentioned in letters to you, that I feel certain that the most important thing that happened during the three-year severe test of my courage was to make hundreds of very decent people, taxpayers and voters, confront the fact that there are many injustices in the Department of Finance, a fact they had been able to ignore heretofore.

Your opinion about my attitude appears to be nothing but platitudes from a glib tongue. A review of my many performance reports which were prepared by local and stateside supervisors and even your so-called draft, which is on record, will attest to the fact that throughout my tenure of service with the Department I have been a model of decorum.

It was these same records that provided you with ample justification for choosing a person with the right attitude to (a) supervise the activities of the Delinquent Accounts and Returns Branch, (b) improve Collections at the hospital and (c) improve the work of the V.I. Treasury Division in order to reduce the receivables of our Government.

Knowing you as well as I do, it would be foolish of me not to believe that you do find time to give some special thought and attention to me. Look at the many letters that we have exchanged over the past years. Look at the notification given me regarding the service pins. I would venture to say that such precious time was never found for any other employee. Finally, as an afterthought, you speak of anyone checking your facts. Your facts sir, I am sure, will be given to the Office of the Attorney General during the period of their investigation. These same facts, no doubt, will aid tremendously in curbing nepotism, ending favoritism and controlling depravity in the Department. (See my letter of July 10, 1974 for a complete listing). P.S. "One may live as a conqueror, a king or a magistrate, but he must die as a man."

At this juncture I'm forced to make a prompt return to the Delinquent Accounts and Returns Branch, the Branch from which I was unlawfully removed under the guise of a special assignment. You may recall that immediately following my ouster, a soldier of fortune, Robert Wallace was hired to replace me without any resistance from the Revenue Officers who had become very weak and timid. The Delinquent Accounts and Returns Branch would never get back to the level where it had been. The unfairness that had befallen me was now a matter of indifference as far as they were concerned. Their apathy after my removal caused the good things that I did to be interred in the records leaving the evil brought against me to ostensibly outlive them. Not necessarily in order of priority I had (a) been instrumental in sending them to complete Phase II of their training program,

(b) taught them the right way to use their calendar pads, (c) structurally I had installed partitions and (d) I had also been responsible for the installation of additional telephone lines. The Internal Revenue Officers were hypnotized by Wheatley. They were being led by their noses so much so that following Wallace's sojourn, Wheatley brought in Robert "Bobby" Woods, an aristocrat, from the Processing and Accounts Branch under Viggo Hendricks to supervise the activities of the Delinquent Accounts and Returns Branch. There was not an iota of Revenue Officer training on Woods' resumé. Where the work of a Revenue Officer was concerned, Woods was a mysterious stranger, a dud, but the one thing that was certain was the fact that the Revenue Officers, servile as they had become, were forced to kneel and touch the floor of the office with their foreheads to show deep respect and submission to him.

As bad as that was, what was even worse was the return of Ulric F. Benjamin to the Delinquent Accounts and Returns Branch from which he had absconded. His arrival in the Branch as a Special Procedures Officer meant that he would be one of Woods' subordinates with the task of undermining the foundation of the Delinquent Accounts and Returns Branch. In the absence of Liston Monsanto, he would strip the Revenue Officers of their ability to do quality work. It was an act lower than the excrement of a whale which, as you are no doubt aware, is located on the bottom of the ocean. After completing his mission (i.e. dropping the standards), Benjamin would become a political prostitute and leave for greener pastures.

All of this took place prior to Cyril E. King's gubernatorial victory in the 1974 elections and my reinstatement. Before my reinstatement and as a person being persecuted, I had written to Governor Melvin H. Evans on July 24, 1974 sending a copy of my letter to Lt. Governor Athniel C. Ottley, which read as follows, "Recently I forwarded to you copies of several letters hoping for the intercession of your office in offering solutions to a most unpleasant situation at the Department of Finance.

The absence of any solutions from your office towards a settlement and my continued requests to departmental officials for an assignment commensurate with my training and experience has caused me, through this letter, to formally appeal to you.

Let me interject at the outset however, that contrary to what you may have heard, it has never been my desire to encroach on the responsibilities of Commissioner Wheatley's office. My respect for law and authority has been such that it may well be the primary reason that I'm still employed at the Department. Briefly, it should be pointed out that for several years, numerous employees of the Department have been victims of the Commissioner's personal vendetta. I have been put upon with sometimes frivolous assignments and set upon by a Commissioner who feels, with good reason so it seems that nothing will be done to him.

In the past and up to now, I have been offered "many studies" of the long-standing problem that continues to plague this most vital Department of our Government; in short, pussy-foot around a little while longer until the Commissioner finds a meaningful assignment for you.

In view of the facts at hand, Governor, many employees of the Department, including myself, feel that we've had enough, more than enough, top echelon tenderness towards injustice and those who bring it on. I therefore request that I be given an opportunity to discuss this serious matter with you at your earliest convenience."

Once again, there was no response from Evans or Addie Ottley. I was being forced to take my case outside of the Virgin Islands where a decent person or a decent group of people would bring me the justice that I was seeking. Instead of using the laws already on the books to discipline the employees of the Virgin Islands Government, the Evans administration was busy sending a bill to the legislature dealing with temporary suspensions of government employees. Being aware of the administration's actions, I immediately wrote to Senator Claude Molloy, then President of the Virgin Islands Legislature. I wrote, "As a government employee who managed to have a suspension revoked after being willfully and maliciously suspended by the Commissioner of Finance, I feel compelled to voice my dissatisfaction over the Governor's bill which provides for the temporary suspension of government employees without pay and without a right of appeal to the government employees service commission. First of all, it should be borne in mind that we live in a democratic society. This means, among other things, that the senate will have to make up its own mind as to how much credibility it wants to attach to a department head. Already government employees have no administrative recourse.

The Government Employee's Commission is comprised of citizens who are all on the affirmative side of the administration. The severe measure now being contemplated by the legislature could play havoc with an already apathetic number of government employees. Furthermore, such a bill, if signed into law, would only serve to (1) give department heads absolute control over lesser public servants and (2) subvert the ambitions of many career employees. I therefore urge you to utilize your good senses and resist this overture."

I continued to work on Wheatley, having been ignored by Governor Evans, the Director of Personnel and everybody else in a position of authority. I knew for certain that I was indeed fighting the governmental system. The extent of my battle with Wheatley was easy to gauge, however. Although I had retuned to the Delinquent Accounts and Returns Branch after a three-year hiatus, Wheatley did not personally welcome me back. My status with the Branch had to be clarified.

On December 13, 1974, I wrote to Wheatley saying, "Since my return to the Delinquent Accounts and Returns Branch as a Revenue Officer on the employee level, I have observed that many of my former subordinates have been promoted to supervisory positions within the Branch. This, as you know, makes me subordinate to them although in reality, my status as the senior Revenue Officer (both in rank and longevity) remained unchanged throughout the period of my absence.

After careful evaluation, I have come to accept the foregoing as the greatest inversion of justice ever perpetrated (as it relates to positions) in the Tax Division and perhaps the Government of the Virgin Islands. Having sufficient justification to appeal this discriminatory matter, I'm by this letter making you aware of my intentions to do so through the Government's Employees Service Commission and then to the U.S. District Court, if necessary". King was given a copy of my letter.

Upon my return to the Delinquent Accounts and Returns Branch, I noticed that the Internal Revenue Officers had become a most opportunistic bunch. They were using every opportunity to their advantage, regardless of right or wrong. I seized the opportunity to capitalize on that (Note: Revenue Officer Mario Lima was an exception, he had witnessed Wheatley's behavior and perhaps envisioned himself as a future target) opportunism. I wrote a letter addressed to Wheatley for their signatures and sent it to the addressee. The letter was dated February 24, 1975, and said, "In order to convey our feelings concerning matters which we consider important, several of us whose signatures appear below in alphabetical sequence, have collaborated in drafting this letter to you. First, we would like to state that now that most of us have finally completed our training programs, we have come to realize that the job of a Revenue Officer is an extremely broad and complex one and therefore should not be belittled. In addition, we have concluded based on production reports, etc., that by now you are aware of the breadth of activities in which we as Revenue Officers are engaged, also the complexities that are involved in the close involvement we have with a variety of taxpayers who are in many social classes and of varying education and financial stability.

Nevertheless, at this writing the Government of the Virgin Islands is caught in a vise, the twin jars of which are inflation and recession. Everything the government does costs more, while income is being impaired by the economic slowdown.

As outlined by Governor Cyril E. King in his state of the territory message, a host of problems are clamoring for immediate attention. Most, if not all of them, can be summed up in a single word, money. We as Revenue Officers are most anxious, provided we are given the latitude to implement our training, to begin the important and arduous task of reducing the high amounts of governmental accounts receivable. This we can assure you would be accomplished by putting together the interaction of theory and practice.

Equally important however and perhaps a major drawback in the Department is the long recognized fact, which deals with our desperate need for a Director of the Tax Division.

The absence of a Tax Director is even more critical at this time than it was nine (9) years ago when the position was abandoned. This vacant position without a doubt continues to be the principal reason for the major problems in the Tax Division.

Furthermore, we feel that the filling of the position of Director of the Tax Division is absolutely essential. The awesome responsibilities of the Commissioner of Finance and the lack of adequate assistance within the Department of Finance, we think, preclude you from devoting the necessary day-to-day time to directing the vital programs of the Tax Division.

As a professional person who has served as acting Governor of the Virgin Islands during the absence of former Governor Evans, we feel certain that you would agree with the statements made herein. At any rate, we would appreciate any comments you may have on the matter." He replied as follows, "This refers to your memorandum of February 24, 1975 regarding the need for a Director of the Tax Division of the Department of Finance. I cannot be sure what you mean when you state that the vacant position, without a doubt, continues to be the principal reason for the major problems in the Tax Division, because the Tax Division has received all necessary supervision from several supervisors on several levels, consulting and working together and with me, whenever necessary, the needs of the division have never been neglected, and my continuing efforts for money and for personnel changes, even with our continuing budget restrictions, have met with fairly good results, including the new building which is being erected for the enforcement Branches. We have, furthermore, been in continuous contact with the national office of the IRS for training arrangements and our employees continue to receive training, although this effort has been severely curtailed in the United States. Even so, for more than one obvious reason, I have recommended in the past that the director position be filled and I made the recommendation, again, to Governor King during the first week of his present term of office."

Now it was my turn to take follow-up action. On February 26, 1975, I wrote to Wheatley once again. I said, "Careful transitions in writing were displayed in your memorandum of February 25, 1975 to the Revenue Officers, which ultimately in the last paragraph agreed with our statement concerning the need for a Director of the Tax Division. Certainly, because of your professionalism, you must know that it is commonplace that absolute power always leads to intolerable abuse.

You may recall that in a letter to you dated December 27, 1973, I mentioned, among other things, the following statement, 'it doesn't take a Rudolph Foy or a Liston Monsanto. Things are now much easier, the resistances less, it does, however, take awareness and decision and above all, an act of decency.' The united effort demonstrated by the Revenue Officers in writing to you about the need for a Tax Director, etc. proves anew that this statement is correct. Also, it should be noted that your famous quotation, 'misrepresentation and lies have never resulted in a permanent benefit for anyone' is really true.

For your information, the revenue agents feel the same way about a director of the Tax Division. The only reason that they have not made their feeling known to you is because they can get what they want by toadying before you in a manner which has resulted in them becoming "trained incapacitance." (i.e. the inability to act other than as required by your office).

Since the job of a Revenue Officer is one that calls primarily for judgment, the Revenue Officers have, over the past several years, taken evening courses at the College of the Virgin Islands. We no longer believe in mediocrity. This is our Government. We want to work and will work, provided we are given the authority to do so.

Your continued attitude of indifference towards this vital Branch of the Tax Division, Revenue Officers being see-sawed from position to position in an effort to divide us, together with your oft repeated explanation which is given in the body of your letter, caused me to make the vicarious sacrifice over the past years for my colleagues and other employees of the Department. Truly I have always felt that no man is justified in doing evil on the ground of expediency."

The momentum had swung my way. I was now on a roll. Next up, a letter from the Revenue Officers to Governor Cyril E. King dated March 14, 1975, the letter read, "As you are no doubt aware, based on reports, letters, legislative hearing, etc., a spirit of disorder has prevailed in the Tax Division of the Department of Finance for many years, appeals notwithstanding. We as professional Revenue Officers had seriously thought that with the flight of time, that the existing situation would have drastically changed and as a result, we would have been able to work harmoniously with each other and in the process increased productivity.

However, owing to the absence of this relationship, we now feel constrained to request a thorough examination into the affairs of the Tax Division, the most essential revenue producing activity of our government.

Such a move, we believe, is urgently needed, especially at this time when the sagging economy of the Virgin Islands Government has caused revenues to decline.

In addition, we strongly feel that outstanding taxes must be collected from all segments of our islands, St. Croix, St. John and St. Thomas, without any curry favor to anyone including the business sector. Also, it should be noted and this is important, that authority now denied, must be delegated to Revenue Officers in order for us to proceed in a manner reflective of our training. Further, we feel that as responsible employees and taxpayers that (1) the responsibility for asserting and waiving penalties should not be unilaterally determined by one person and (2) the present method of selecting returns for audit should be looked into as they both lend themselves to corruption.

This we ask of you as loyal government employees, who throughout the years have witnessed the deterioration of our tax system caused mostly by the demanded mediocrity and leaders in our government who have made a military about face to gross incompetency.

We feel certain that you understand the nature and gravity of the long-standing problems which continue to plague the division, but in order to give you an insight into recent happenings, we have enclosed herewith copies of letters to the Commissioner and a photocopy of the "Code of Ethics for Government Service" which hangs on the wall of our office. These documents should be of great value to you in making a decision.

In order to offer solutions to other problems and those mentioned herein, we would appreciate meeting with you at your earliest convenience." Talk about being opportunistic. One would not believe that these were the same Revenue Officers who had previously forgotten about me. They were very much aware of the fact that the pendulum had swung to my side and consequently would sign any letter designed to tell the world about Wheatley's manner of working. I was forcing Wheatley to write to a disgusting extent. Where he was finding the time was anybody's guess. On March 24, 1975 we received a reaction to our March 14th letter. King, I believe, may have spoken to him. Here's what he wrote to all personnel in the Collection and enforcement Branches, "The Governor, in several pronouncements, has sought to impress all concerned with the present acute financial situation of the Virgin Islands Government. Each department, each employee of the government has an obligation to do everything possible to assist in reducing expenditures. Accordingly, all personnel of the Department of Finance are charged with the responsibility of exercising all economies possible in the use of supplies and equipment. Pencils, paper, forms or paper clips are not natural resources; they are obtained by the expenditure of the taxpayers' money. Now, more than ever, it is vital that the use of supplies, telephones, etc. be restricted to the absolute minimum and all employees will be held strictly accountable for any non-essential use of these. The flow of cash to the government is another critical area. It is vital that taxes due the government be collected as swiftly as possible to the maximum degree permissible. To achieve this goal, it is the responsibility of every agent and officer to close his cases as expeditiously as possible with the highest degree of agreed settlements. This cannot be interpreted to mean that settlements he made or offers accepted which in any way violate the letter or the spirit of the internal revenue laws, the regulations, ruling and policies followed by this office. Conscientious efforts to dispose of cases using your good judgment in identifying issues containing settlement potential will go far to assist in achieving this goal without risk to all of our compliance programs. A supreme effort and nothing short of this, on the part of all personnel in this Department is directed to eliminate waste and to give to your Government a full measure of work each day."

He obviously was trying to forge an alliance with Governor King. In between March 24, 1975 and April 1, 1975, he went back into his bad habit of micro managing. He had always felt that he could do whatever he wanted, whenever he wanted, and consequently he needed to be told that his actions were embarrassing his Revenue Officers and so without soliciting the assistance of Revenue Officers, Alphonse Donastorg, Kenneth Hansen, Roy Malone and Jens Todman, (all ingrates from the Savan District with opportunistic attitudes). I, in no unequivocal language, wrote to him on April 2, 1975. Here is what I said, "I am writing, hoping to advise you that paragraph two (2) of your memorandum of March 24, 1975, which was addressed in part to the personnel of the Collection Branch, has been declared paradoxical by the Revenue Officers following your orders to release a notice of levy against the Kent Company, Inc. after receiving a telephone call from a representative of that company.

Most importantly, however, it should be noted for the record, that your frequent unilateral decisions which are presumably based on discussions held in clandestine meetings with taxpayers and/ or taxpayers representatives, have become a source of annoyance within the Delinquent Accounts and Returns Branch and does absolutely nothing towards boosting the morale of the employees assigned thereto.

Furthermore, during this inflationary period, the records show that your one-sided decisions have had a very telling effect on the economy of the Virgin Islands Government.

This present unilateral decision becomes inexorably complex when consideration is given to whether Revenue Officers will be permitted to make judicious use of the notice of levy. First of all, it is a matter of record that the liabilities against the Kent Company, Inc. were arbitrarily assessed by the processing Branch after the company had failed, as they usually do, to comply with existing laws relating to the filing of tax returns.

Chronologically, Revenue Officer Todman visited the habitually delinquent taxpayers on November 4, 1974, December 19, 1974, February 4, 1975 and March 4, 1975. Each time his demands for payment were ignored. Consequently, Mr. Todman, the Revenue Officer who, because of his ability to utilize judgment, travels to St. Croix every week in order to transform that island's team of Revenue Officers inexperience into accomplishment, and Mr. Robert Woods (Chief, D.A.R. Branch) whose signature validates the document, found that adequate evidence existed regarding the service of a levy.

Hence, the levy was prepared and served. Because of this and other unilateral decisions which you have made heretofore (Tropical Deliveries, et al) coupled with the absence of an organizational chart, are the Revenue Officers now required to consult your office prior to levy?" My postscript was: "For future guidance, I would appreciate any information that you may have relative to what portions of a delinquent taxpayer's liquid assets held by a local bank are earmarked for payroll purposes." A copy of my letter was sent to Governor King.

Then, true to form, Wheatley answered me in his letter of April 4, 1975. He said, "This refers to your letter of April 2, 1975, a copy of which was sent to Governor Cyril E. King, for obvious reasons. Your reference in the letter to "clandestine meetings" is also very obviously another in your continuing efforts at character assassination, but if you do not know it already, you will quickly find out how really serious an individual I am. You should properly go to your supervisor to discuss the matters mentioned in your letter and receive the necessary clarifications, but I will accommodate you with a reply. There is nothing "paradoxical" about my action in the matter involving Kent Company.

My reasons were stated and discussed with the supervisor, and these reasons involved questions of government-wide policy and as I have always stated, using good judgment. If Kent Company or any other tax-exempt business is delinquent in filing required tax returns, the information should be reported as a routine matter with other delinquents to the Department of Law, for any action that may be required under the investment incentive law. Neither I nor anyone else should have to tell you this. If we have an investment incentive program intended primarily to provide employment for our people and our government owes a tax-exempt business under this program a substantial amount of subsidy money, can we really justify spending a substantial amount of time trying to collect a smaller amount than the long-overdue subsidy money they should have received, particularly when most of what we collect is to be returned to them as a subsidy and when we have so many other delinquent accounts? You are misrepresenting the situation when you speak of a lack of an organizational chart because even the taxpayers know that Mr. Woods is the Supervisor, Mr. Malone is the Assistant Supervisor and Mr. Hansen is Special Procedures Officer; and as a matter of fact and records, I have seldom become involved in any of these matters, except at the request of Mr. Woods. With reference to Tropic Deliveries, I believe that the record will ultimately show that we will receive more from that account when it is finally settled, than if it were settled with the sale of the trucks as it was planned. I do not know why you are wasting everyone's time in trying to find issues to try to embarrass me. It is really unnecessary." He added a P.S. which stated, "I will not answer the questions of your P.S. You should know by now that such instructions should be received from the DAR Branch Chief." Needless to say, he sent a copy of his letter to Governor King.

I didn't like the veiled threat in his letter, however. What's more because of its emotional tone and other distractions I felt constrained to answer him. Here I was operating from a subordinate position, very low on the organizational chart, against a man who, in flaunting his authority, had for three years kicked me around like a football from St. Thomas to St. John to St. Croix, wasting government time and money under the guise of a special assignment without any feelings for me or my family. Here was that same man now driven to the wall talking about how quickly I could find out how serious an individual he was. Moreover, because of the frivolous assignments which removed me from the Branch and my subordinates, he was audacious enough to tell me how Woods, his Lackey, was my supervisor and the positions of his two other sheep with an inferiority complex (Kenneth Hansen and Roy Malone).

My persecutor, Reuben Wheatley, had stumbled and as a result did not triumph. I had refused to be guided and used by an influential wrongdoer and so, on April 7, 1975, I addressed a letter to him sending a copy to Governor King. The letter said, "Since it has been established that we are both serious individuals, I will not attempt to question the many assumptions that you have offered in your letter, which is long on emotion and short on reason. Instead, I shall, on the basis of your continued waste of government time and stationary, declare also the first paragraph of your March 24th letter paradoxical. It should be borne in mind sir, that those who exercise significant power usually mask its use claiming that they are acting in the public interest, or following established procedures, or seeking economy, efficiency, justice or some admirable goal. Commissioner, I do not have the technical ability to be a bureaucrat nor do I believe in forwarding copies of letters to our Governor based on the self-fulfilling prophecy. The Governor and the taxpayers already know about the poor working conditions that exist in the Department of Finance, pretentious displays notwithstanding. Lest we forget sir, the Tax Division belongs to the Virgin Islands Government. Therefore, your continued arbitrary interpretations of decisions and letter distributing, especially those to our Governor, serve only to puzzle me, as my letters unlike many of yours are clearly annotated for the Governor. Please be informed sir, that concerning delinquency investigations, the prescribing directive (Part V IRM) will attest to the fact that the Delinquent Accounts and Returns Branch has so many administrative remedies that it does not have to repeatedly interrupt the Department of Law as you believe. Furthermore, following your explanations concerning enforcement action against the Kent Company and Tropic Deliveries, it is safe to say that no one knows the entire tax structure. Moreover, your assumption about taxpayers knowing the position of Mr. Woods and others in the Branch, is tantamount to the many press releases regarding increased and the payment of monthly withholding taxes that taxpayers read and hear about but are never communicated to the employees whose job it is to implement the laws. I suppose that the taxpayers are also aware of the reasons that Anthony Olive, Miss Geraldine Bridgewater and Liston Monsanto hold their present positions. Enough said. Personally, I have never tried to embarrass you, sir. Your many paradoxical letters, the many injustices that you have done to the truth, the lack of an organizational chart, your continued efforts to harass and discriminate against employees through curt letters, etc., have caused many of us to lose confidence in your office and as a consequence, make you vulnerable. Nevertheless, I do believe that we could alleviate many of our problems through oral communication which would afford me the opportunity to find out how serious an individual you are, regular meetings of the various Branches and by acting rather than reacting to situations." "P.S., If the Branch Chief knew the answer to my question, which you have refused to answer, he would never have approved the levy action against the Kent Company." That was the last time Reuben B. Wheatley would ever receive a letter from me.

It was shortly after I had written that letter that he disappeared from the scene. He was one of the most bizarre persons with whom I've ever worked. "The Extreme Test" would continue however, under Leroy Quinn, Anthony Olive and Edward Thomas.

CHAPTER II
Leroy A. Quinn

In 1970 when I was designated Chief of the Delinquent Accounts and Returns Branch for the Virgin Islands, the duties of my office took me to the St. Croix District where the Internal Revenue Officers on that island came under my supervision. On my initial visit to St. Croix I met in a casual meeting with Leroy Quinn who was then the Supervisor of the Agents on that island. On several occasions following that meeting we conferred with each other unceremoniously and without formality. Quinn and Ulric Benjamin were good friends who were very dissatisfied with working conditions in the Virgin Islands Tax Division. Benjamin who was operating out of St. Thomas where, in baseball terminology, the people were born on third base, ninety (90) feet from home plate (because of the harbor), was frustrated in his ambition to work in a manner reflective of his training and ability. Quinn, on the other hand, it bears repeating, was operating out of St. Croix where the Crucians were trying to get to first base somewhat devoid of Reuben Wheatley's wrath. Quinn was, or pretended to be, an advocate for change but was very non-committal when it came to any discussion on the matter. He had a devious agenda that ultimately caused him to be bigger today in death than he was in life.

After Reuben Wheatley's unceremonious departure from the Department of Finance as its Commissioner and Tax Director, being a people's person, I developed a magnanimous attitude towards him. Speaking about attitude, as has been already pointed out here in this publication, Reuben Wheatley was always complaining about my attitude in the absence of anything else with which he could find fault. Didn't he expect my attitude towards the job to change after being formally trained by the United States Internal Revenue Service? Didn't he know that there could be no growth without changed attitudes? The continued failure of Virgin Islanders to apply the lessons learned in the various institutions of higher learning has resulted in the islands being exactly where they are today. "Everybody wants to go to heaven, nobody wants to die." I felt in retrospect that Reuben Wheatley and I were a confrontation of opposites.

As a child growing up in my parents house and later as a member of the United States Air Force, via restrictions, I had experienced what it was like to live in a dictatorship where one person was exercising absolute authority and the truth be told, I was not desirous of going down that road again. I had already been in a trained condition of order and obedience long before my employment with the Tax Division. As public servants, I wanted collaboration.

My devoted friend Rudolph Foy, whom you may recall was a member of the ICM's territorial committee approached me with the idea of asking for a replacement for Wheatley and after thinking it over carefully, I recommended Leroy Quinn for the position. Foy was a professional loner who had no idea about any one attractive enough to replace Wheatley. In recommending Quinn for the position, I took into consideration the fact that he had once served as commissioner pro tempore during the period when governors were appointed. As I look back on the recommendation, I must confess that my expectations were too high. I had deluded myself by offering Quinn's name. You'll see why as you read on. Governor King acted on Foy's recommendation by sending Quinn's name to the legislature for confirmation and it was thereafter ratified. There was no public outrage following the announcement of Quinn's appointment and so Leroy A. Quinn became the new Commissioner of Finance.

The position of Tax Director, which had not been filled for nine years, was still vacant. In 1969, Anthony P. Olive then a fledgling with the Tax Division was chosen by his fellow Revenue Agents to represent them in the hearings before Commissioner Melville Stevens of the Department of Labor. Because of his appearance before Stevens he had to be punished. He was behaving like Liston Monsanto challenging Wheatley's authority. However, unlike Liston Monsanto, Anthony P. Olive was weak and unmanly. He was sent to coventry, ostracized by Wheatley and his co-workers who had misled him into provoking the wrath of Wheatley. He needed to either get back in their good graces or become Tax Director. He became treacherous. He started shamming. He knew that Foy and I were close. He also knew that Foy was very close to Cyril King and so he would lean on me to get to Foy and ultimately to King.

Olive and I, because of our respect for law and authority and because of our appearances before Commissioner Stevens, had developed a close social relationship, but now that he had become persona non grata within his Branch, he had to rid himself of me. I was not a member of the world of scholars and yet a bit too thorough for him to be around. Nevertheless, he needed me as his gateway to Foy to King. He was so transparent I could see right through him. He was making palpable errors via his body language and he had lost whatever little aggressiveness he had. What's more, whenever I'd visit him at his workplace he'd keep me at a distance especially when he felt the eyes of Roy Moorhead and Edward Thomas zeroing in on him. I felt sorry for him. He was lucky though. There were keen hostile feelings between Foy and many of the agents and so by the process of elimination he became our favorite. Foy took his name to Governor King and King graciously obliged by appointing Anthony P. Olive to the position of Tax Director. Now the positions at the highest levels in the Department of Finance and Tax Division were all filled and now the Governor, the new Commissioner and the new Director of the Tax Division all were aware of the existing state of affairs in the workplace.

Two months after both Quinn and Olive had settled down in their positions, Foy asked me if any of the gentlemen had spoken to me. I told him that neither Quinn nor Olive had told me anything and I expanded on my answer by telling him that Olive was giving me a great deal to think about. I told him that in life everybody needs a favor now and then and that I was not granted immunization from asking a favor of anyone if the occasion arose, but that begging was not my forte'. I then told him that with the passage of time, both Quinn and Olive would be controlled by a domineering Edward Thomas.

After five months had gone by and I hadn't heard from either Quinn or Olive on my status, I wrote to Quinn on October 31, 1975. In my letter I stated, "Inasmuch as you are the Commissioner of Finance and due to the absence of an organizational chart, I find it most urgent to write to you concerning the aura of discrimination which has grossly affected me in the Delinquent Accounts and Returns Branch.

At the outset, it should be noted, however, that over the past few years there has been so much misunderstanding and misrepresentation of the facts by your predecessor, that I feel obliged to ask that the contents of this letter neither be misconstrued as an encroachment on the responsibilities of your office nor as a source of annoyance. Instead, I respectfully request that the troubled areas listed on a later page hereof be reviewed and acted upon fairly and impartially.

It is a matter of record that in February of 1971 after I had completed twelve years of satisfactory service with the Department of Finance and working in the capacity of Chief of Delinquent Accounts and Returns Branch, Mr. Reuben Wheatley, in a bizarre move, removed me from the position and exiled me in the Treasury Division because as I later learned, I had fallen out of favor with him owing to my desire to perform the duties of my office in a manner reflective of my training and experience.

After many months in exile, I was restored to my classified position of Internal Revenue Officer on September 3, 1974. I immediately discovered that Mr. Wheatley had committed an unjust act. He had promoted most of my once proud subordinates to various positions within the Branch which was now being headed by Mr. Robert Woods, former Assistant Chief of the Processing and Accounts Branch and a likeable person. In short, the promotions had a very telling effect on my status within the Branch as they in fact made me subordinate to just about everyone and simultaneously stymied my progress. In light of the foregoing, coupled with the fact that I have not been told what the future holds for me, I have listed below, not necessarily in order of priority, certain gray areas which I believe should be clarified as they would be of great benefit in clearing away the cobwebs, (1) chances of advancement within the Branch, (2) eradication of existing injustices especially as they relate to rank, (3) consideration of seniority (17 years), training experience, etc. and (4) consideration with respect to punching time card.

Your paramount and foremost attention to this matter will be highly appreciated." The Commissioner did not respond.

Two weeks later on November 14, 1975, I followed up my letter by telling Commissioner Quinn, "This letter is intended primarily as a reminder as it again respectfully requests answers to the several questions appearing in my letter of October 31, 1975, a copy of which is attached hereto. Kindly accede to my request."

Quinn, a man with several personality disorders and an underachiever, was afraid of me. He knew that I had justifiable reasons for inquiring about my status, but he had been warned by Olive about my law-abiding ways and also by a hardly heralded Edward Thomas whose avid desire for power had allowed him to take the reins from Olive and was operating as defacto Tax Director. Quinn was slow in understanding. He foolishly thought that by ignoring my letters that the problems which he had inherited from Reuben Wheatley would go away. His conduct was not always admirable. He would spend most of his time pretending to be what he was not.

Again, operating from my subordinate position, I knew that I had to say the right thing at the right time. The fraternal brothers were using hope against hope in their carefully designed plans to systematically remove me from the Tax Division and I therefore refused to accommodate them. Actually they were operating as a secret organization of criminals.

Following my reminder to Quinn on November 14, 1975, I made the decision to suspend my letter writing campaign. I did not want to upset Governor King who, eleven months after taking the oath of office, had become inordinately quiet. He hadn't done anything by way of ordering Quinn and/or Olive to come up with a resolution to my long-standing problems.

On December 14, 1976, I met fortuitously with Woods. I did not want Quinn or Olive who seemingly was undergoing an on-the-job training course to tell me that such matters should be discussed with my immediate supervisor before coming to them. In our meeting I could see that Woods was very worried. He knew right away that he had been drawn into a controversial area and that Quinn was using him as his lackey in more or less the same way that Wheatley had previously done.

In the Virgin Islands we were not operating according to Hoyle. In our training, which was given to us by the United States Internal Revenue Service, we were told to use as our authority Part V of the Internal Revenue Manual, together with our Legal Reference Guide and the Internal Revenue Code, but the Government of the Virgin Islands through force of habit, was wasting the employees time and its money sending us to be trained only to come back to the Virgin Islands and act in a perfunctory way. Let's face it. The mere fact that Woods was supervising the activities of the Delinquent Accounts and Returns Branch without any training in Revenue Officer work was an indication that anybody with the exception of Kenneth Hansen, Roy Malone and Jens Todman, could supervise the activities of the Branch. These three gentlemen were all trained by the United States Internal Revenue Service and were now working through the usage of arbitrary power as subordinates of Robert "Bobby" Woods.

Six months later I had not heard from King, Quinn or Olive so I decided to get their attention once again. I started anew by writing to Olive on June 9, 1976. I wrote, "At the risk of being labeled anything but God's child, I take this opportunity to write to you regarding the continuing injustices in the Tax Division.

At the outset however, it is worth noting for the sake of clarity that the primary reason for routing this letter directly to your office is due to the absence of an organizational chart designed in a manner to show the chain of authority within the Tax Division.

Currently, for your information, a large number of the personnel assigned to the Delinquent Accounts and Returns Branch whose academic qualifications compares favorably with that of the Internal Revenue Agents are voicing their overall dissatisfaction with existing conditions which have remained the same, the filling of the position of Tax Director notwithstanding. They have begun to see the special treatment given to agents as if they were prima donnas. Furthermore, right in our midst, we are witnessing an imminent inducement to Revenue Officer Jens Todman who presumably "goes along" with anything contrary to the way we were trained to accomplish our objectives.

Relative to Todman, my reasoning is based on the fact that he was given an assignment to travel weekly to St. Croix in order to improve Collections there where the Crucian Revenue Officers have been malingering for years under the leadership of Mr. Lionel Emanuel. No other Revenue Officer assigned to the St. Thomas office was given the opportunity or perhaps not even considered for the purpose. We now find however, that Mr. Todman is being given an outstanding rating in order to qualify as a recipient for a cash award? Certainly this is not practicing tolerance. It goes without saying that this type of arbitrary action is most damaging to employee morale and should really be discontinued if we truly intend to promote the best interest of the Tax Division."

Then on July 21, 1976, I wrote once more to Olive saying, "My admiration for the multiple skills of Mr. Reuben B. Wheatley which include charm, intelligence and a tremendous sense of wit, plus the fact that I have learned from past unhappy experiences not to suspend my critical faculties when an individual such as Mr. Wheatley is involved, have prompted me to request your permission to review my personnel file, which I believe is stored in Mr. Quinn's office.

Your acquiescence to my request is urgently solicited in light of past attempts at character assassination by Mr. Wheatley, and furthermore, because of the palpable lies charged to him, and corroborated by the record." A copy of this letter was sent to Quinn.

It is rightfully said that the pen is mightier then the sword. My letters which are extant are tangible proof of that. But let's keep the context in perspective here. On August 3, 1976, in the absence of a reply from either Olive or Quinn, I had to, in the interest of being consistent, write to Olive again. This time I wrote, "On July 21, 1976, I wrote and hand delivered a letter to you requesting permission to review my personnel file, which I understand is kept in Mr. Quinn's office. To date, I have not received a reply. Consequently I'm forced to take follow-up action. Of particular importance to my request is the Privacy Act of 1974 (Public Law 93-579), which was designed to place certain restrictions on Government agency record keeping and to give individuals access to records maintained on them by governmental agencies. Many conditions brought about the passage of the act, but principal among them were the fears of abusive use of government power. It is my belief that the secret files kept by Mr. Wheatley symbolized an "enemies list" similar to that of former U.S. President Richard M. Nixon. In addition, I'm curious to know whether or not Mr. Wheatley exceeded his mandate by taking upon himself the duties of keeping a bogus personnel file detrimental to individuals against whom he held a personal vendetta. In view of the foregoing, it is politely requested that you take all necessary measures conducive in granting my request." Once again a copy was sent to Quinn. Their indifference was, I thought, unbecoming.

So at this point I'm forced to write to the man that I had recommended to Rudolph Foy for the position of Commissioner of Finance. Accordingly, I wrote on August 16, 1976. To Quinn I said, "I am writing to you hopefully to defuse a potentially explosive situation and simultaneously to avert a recurrence of the hardships and handicaps endured by many employees during the regime of Mr. Reuben B. Wheatley. Related documents in your possession show that since July 21, 1976, I have been desperately requesting permission to review my personnel file, which is maintained by your office. Thus far however, it is incredible to believe, that my simple request has been completely ignored, thereby necessitating an appeal to your office. Personally, it has always been my feelings that it is error only and not truth that shrinks from inquiry therefore, it is quite possible that the Tax Director may have inadvertently overlooked my request. Nevertheless, the urgent intervention of your office has become necessary and towards this end, I solicit your indulgence." This time a copy was sent to Olive.

What had happened causing Wheatley to return me to the Tax Division and what had happened causing Wheatley's departure, was never told to me. One thing was clear to me, my once proud subordinates, the opportunistic Revenue Officers, under their supervisor Bobby Woods, in a somewhat pseudo Delinquent Accounts and Returns Branch were not to be trusted. At times when it suited their purpose they'd be with management and at times they'd be with me.

I then made the decision to give Olive and Quinn some space and zero in on Woods. On December 17, 1976, I told Woods via a letter that, "Since protocol demands that we give the Tax Director a reasonable time in which to consider and act on our grievances, I believe that it's safe to say, that the upshot of our meeting of Tuesday, December 14, 1976 is still indefinite. This being the case, plus the fact that it is commonplace in the Virgin Islands to cast aspersions on those who deal with truth, I'd like to direct your attention to the record, which shows that I've been a model of decorum throughout my employment with the Government of the Virgin Islands. This, I might add, has been accomplished in spite of obstacles. At any rate, you may recall that owing to our overburdensome workload in the St. Thomas/St. John district, the question surrounding Revenue Officer Todman's frequent visits to St. Croix was raised in the meeting, when it was thought that his continuing visits to that island, despite the presence of a Special Procedures Officer, were not to perform technical work, but instead, presumably devised to embarrass our peers, who have been receiving satisfactory ratings throughout the periods of their employment, for performances rendered satisfactorily, their continued role of malingerers notwithstanding. Today, Mr. Todman is in St. Croix perhaps as a token reward, which incidentally, may lead only to token performances by the silent majority. Inasmuch as there has been some recent developments that have had an intriguing quality about them, I personally feel that Mr. Todman's visits constitute an act of bigotry. The fact that no other Revenue Officer has been given an opportunity to go to St. Croix, fortifies my contention. In addition, it is no secret that I'm the Senior Revenue Officer and although I'm just as zealous as Mr. Todman, I've been completely ignored. Because Todman's visits are usually on Fridays, they have been labeled junkets and have brought intramural hostility as all the Revenue Officers in the Virgin Islands envision his visits and accomplishments, being used as justification for a promotion and/or salary increase. Should management deem it necessary to continue Mr. Todman's visits, I'd like to request that all Revenue Officers on his level be afforded the opportunity to go." Copies of this letter were sent to Olive and all Revenue Officers. Todman had to be stopped. He was making capital of Woods' naivety to travel.

It was now going on two years since Cyril King had been sworn in as Governor of the Virgin Islands. His silence on a matter reminiscent of a tempest in a tea pot and requiring his attention was deafening. He appeared not to be the "no-nonsense" Cyril King that ran for the governorship in 1970. Like Melvin Evans before him, he was protecting the bureaucracy and Liston Monsanto was not going to court his or anybody else's favor. King was fully cognizant of what was going on in the Department of Finance Tax Division. Because I was doing what was good, just and lawful, nobody in a position of authority wanted to come over to my side. I was toxic. Meanwhile, in his own way, Robert "Bobby" Woods was giving in to my demands. He wanted to appease me. He wrote to Olive, who was really a nonentity, on January 24, 1977 asking for parity and salary increases for the Revenue Officers.

On the morning of February 4, 1977, the Revenue Officers addressed a letter to Olive which read as follows, "Because the Revenue Officers of the division have been completely ignored over the last several years, it was most gratifying to read Mr. Woods' letter of January 24, 1977, which was addressed to you. We honestly feel that there is nothing harder than the softness of indifference, especially when we the undersigners, through our own efforts, have enrolled in various courses at the college of the Virgin Islands evening program in a sincere attempt to improve our performances as officers of the Tax Division of which you are the head. We heartily agree with the contents of Mr. Woods' letter and request that you review and consider his proposals with a view towards implementing them. Kindly accede to our request." A copy of the letter was sent to Woods. One of the signatories on that letter was Mrs. Lucia Thomas, wife of the defacto Tax Director Edward Thomas, who, upon her return from maternity leave in March of 1969, had been assigned to work in the Delinquent Accounts and Returns Branch in violation of Title 24, Section 65(1) of the Virgin Islands Code which says, "It shall be an unfair labor practice for an employer to (1) spy upon or keep under surveillance, whether directly or through agents or any other person, any activities of employees or their representatives in the exercise of the rights set forth in Section 64 of this Title."

What's still fresh in my memory is seeing her present at the Branch's meeting on June 9, 1970. That day I asked her was she happy being a member of the Branch. She answered yes.

Quinn who was continuing to ignore me (maybe he was told to do so by King), wrote to Woods on the afternoon of February 4, 1977, with a copy of his memorandum to Olive which said, "Your memorandum dated January 24, 1977, has been referred to me by Mr. Anthony Olive, Director of Tax Division. I appreciate your deep concern for the men working under your supervision and also the recommendations you have made. Having started my career with the Internal Revenue Service as a Revenue Officer, I am aware of some of the problems our Revenue Officers face. As well as the wide discrepancy in salaries when compared with salaries paid IRS Revenue Officers performing similar functions. I am also very mindful of the contribution that these men make to the government revenues by collecting delinquent taxes. Their efforts played a major part enabling the government to balance the budget last fiscal year. The pay scale for Revenue Officers is entirely too low, which as caused problems in recruiting qualified personnel. As you did state in you memo, the government is considering a new pay plan for all government employees. The new plan is intended to establish salaries at levels comparable with private industry. A comparison with existing salaries will show that the minimum increase is $2,972.00. Even though not confirmed, it is expected that this plan will become effective July 1, 1977. In reply to your four recommendations, the following comments are made: (1) by copy of this letter, I am requesting that Mr. Olive review the job specifications of all positions in the DAR Branch and make recommendations for their revisions, if in his judgment revision is needed. (2) I have no objection to creating the position of Revenue Representative, but I would hesitate to hire high school graduates with no experience. The Revenue Representative can work in OCF, thus relieving the Revenue Officers for fieldwork. (3) I see no necessity to change position titles from Revenue Officers I, II, III, IV. (4) You suggest adopting the federal pay scale as of October 1975. I have discussed the new salaries earlier in the memorandum. I doubt very much that the Government of the Virgin Islands can match the salaries paid by the Internal Revenue Service."

Quinn was continuing to use the same lady who had previously served a Reuben Wheatley's secretary as his secretary. The personnel in his general office would continue with him throughout his tenure. The confidentiality and loyalty required from a secretary was notable by its absence.

Mario "Tansy" Lima was an enterprising young Revenue Officer who was always ready to face difficulties. He was a faithful comrade always ready to stand by my side in my struggles, even against heavy odds. Having been raised in a different environment, Puerto Rico, he could readily see that skill and strategy were discouraged in the Tax Division. He knew that I was being persecuted and he, unlike Hansen, Malone and Todman, envisioned himself as a future target of the fraternal brothers and their retinue. He refused to kowtow or otherwise yield to the good-for-nothings through fear and lack of spirit. Mario "Tansy" Lima was to me what "Friday" was to Daniel Defoe's Robinson Crusoe. I am most grateful to him for the role that he played; it is something that I shall never forget.

After joining with the Revenue Officers on February 4, 1977, writing to Olive I felt it incumbent upon me to write to Woods. After all, Olive had passed on Woods' letter of January 24, 1977 to Quinn who had in a showy display responded on February 4, 1977 to Woods.

Against what I considered to be weak opposition (Woods, Olive, Quinn and even Kenneth Hansen who had replaced the "on again/off again" Ulric Benjamin as Special Procedures Officer, they were all profiting from my departure from the Tax Division. They were all enjoying what was going on). I devised a plan that would force Quinn either to call me to his office or write to me the way he had written to Woods. On February 7, 1977, I wrote to Woods (sending copies of my letter to Olive and Quinn) in the following manner:

GOVERNMENT OF
THE VIRGIN ISLANDS OF THE UNITED STATES
CHARLOTTE AMALIE, ST. THOMAS

————— o —————

DEPARTMENT OF FINANCE
TAX DIVISION

February 7, 1977

*Page
54*

Mr. Robert Woods
Chief, D.A.R. Branch
Department of Finance
Tax Division
St. Thomas, Virgin Islands   00801

Dear Mr. Woods:

As a person who suffered vicariously for many of the employees assigned to the Delinquent Accounts and Returns Branch, I'm deeply moved and very encouraged to have a person on your level show such grave concern regarding conditions in the branch. I feel certain that like myself, the revenue officers are most grateful for your manifested concern.

Your letter of January 24, 1977 to Mr. Anthony Olive seemed to have given a clear warning of worsening relations, expecially at a time when many of the revenue officers are making the supreme sacrifice attending evening classes at the College of the Virgin Islands. Additionally, your letter conveyed to me the confidence which you have placed in your subordinates; therefore, as a means of justifying that confidence, virtually all of the revenue officers have written to Mr. Olive echoing your sentiments.

Based on past unhappy experiences however, it is distressing to note that the spirit of altruism which is needed to mold a cohesive unit in the branch is sorely missing. In past administrations, management seemingly offered many of them bribes or perhaps influenced many of them through inducements which were not only ephemeral in nature to the recipient, but as a consequence, continue to haunt the branch. In short, inducements have served only to create the sordid mess in which we find ourselves mired today.

Granted, nobody is perfect, and to me this is exemplified in recommendation (4) section D of your letter, which recommends that the Chief of the branch together with the Assistant Chief and the Special Procedures Officer be placed on the same level. In stating my opposition to you on the matter, I'd like to remind you that there is no organizational chart to indicate the level of the Special Procedures Officer. My experience and training tell me that both the Chief and Assistant Chief are on the side of management and furthermore, there is an old ancient custom which prevails in most societies including the Virgin Islands which seperates the sheep from the goats. So, in order to deliver you from what I believe to be faux pas I'd like to suggest an approach to the matter.

Put simply, the revenue officers have become vassels of the Special Procedures Officer as the position limits completely the activities of the revenue officer when it comes to quality work. Revenue officers are being shut out of any real participation in technical work, thereby (for all intense and purposes) negating them the opportunity to work in a manner reflective of their training and ability.

Because of the curtailment in the revenue officer's activity, and the feeling that the position of SPO (in our small office) encroaches on their responsibilities, one can envision (i.e. after the revenue officers have been completely trained) that a morale problem will pervade and the Special Procedures Officer and the revenue officers will continually be at loggerheads.

It is my belief, that since we are authorized a Technical Advisor whose position is included in the classified service, efforts should be made to utilize his ability to the fullest. Whereas the Special Procedures Section in the United States Internal Revenue Service is called upon to provide technical data on complex matters, we in the Virgin Islands should perhaps give these duties to the Technical Advisor, as he can be reached readily. What's more, in the area of 100% penalties and other related quality work, the record shows that revenue officers who have completed their training were taught how to handle the intricate aspects of these complexities. In other words, please permit the revenue officer to use his brain and earn his salary.

At the moment, revenue officers are restricted to the role of bill collectors which is tantamount to the enforcement officers in the Treasury Division of our department. In order for a revenue officer to be professional and act professional, he must carry his part of the burden in quality work. Isn't this the reason for sending us for training?

It should be noted also, that the failure of management to assign the revenue officers the task of doing his own technical work, could result in the revenue officers forgetting what they learned in training much to the detriment of the Virgin Islands Government.

And lest you forget, the position of Special Procedures Officer is not listed in the current pay plan and for this reason, the person presently holding the position is without a doubt (especially during this period of austerity) in danger of being dropped from the payroll.

It is true that rarely do revenue officers in the Virgin Islands deal directly with bankruptcy cases, and if they did, I would venture to say, that from a legal standpoint, our Technical Advisor and/or the Department of Law would provide assistance. With respect to other quality work such as offers-in-compromise, the more we discourage taxpayers on them, the better. Some taxpayers submit offers as a means of arousing sympathy, etc. But at any rate, I see no reason why each revenue officer could not handle his own assigned offers. We have a handbook and other documents relating to offers. Look at the salaries being proposed. It is incumbent on us to do work commensurate with our training and salary.

Although, as I mentioned earlier, I'm gladdened by the fact that during your brief tenure as Chief of the Delinquent Accounts and Returns Branch you have seen the conditions under which we work, I would like to say in all sincerity, and with conviction, that we do not need outside supervision in the DAR Branch. If the agents are able to handle their own affairs, so too should the revenue officers, especially when one considers the length of time each revenue officer has spent with the branch. In addition, you may recall, that when many of your existing staff sought unionization in CY-1969, grievance number five read as follows: "Discontinuation of the practice of importing personnel from the outside to handle assignments for which local personnel are qualified."

In the interest of avoiding any animosity or repercussions, I do not want you to get the impression that I'm telling you your job. The foregoing suggestions were written with a view towards upgrading the branch.

Sincerely yours,

Liston B. Monsanto
Internal Revenue Officer

LBM/tp

cc: Mr. Leroy A. Quinn
    Commissioner of Finance

    Mr. Anthony P. Olive
    Tax Director

Eight days later I wrote to Quinn:

GOVERNMENT OF
THE VIRGIN ISLANDS OF THE UNITED STATES
CHARLOTTE AMALIE, ST. THOMAS

——— o ———

DEPARTMENT OF FINANCE
TAX DIVISION

February 15, 1977

Mr. Leroy A. Quinn
Commissioner of Finance
Department of Finance
Charlotte Amalie, St. Thomas
U.S. Virgin Islands   00801

Dear Mr. Quinn:

Due to the presence of the position of Special Procedures Officer, it is becoming increasingly apparent that Revenue Officers in the Virgin Islands are underemployed, and their duties impaired.

Accordingly, as Senior Revenue Officer in the territory, and one who formerly supervised the activities of the Delinquent Accounts and Returns Branch, it is my feeling (especially during this period when discussions are being held on the new pay plan) that a lack of initiative or resourcefulness on my part, would serve only to defeat the purpose of our Branch. I therefore submit for your review and consideration, the forthcoming events.

First of all, it is no secret that the position of Special Procedures Officer is an outgrowth of attempts by Mr. Reuben (Benefactor) Wheatley to place Mr. Ulric Benjamin, who had earlier become persona non grata within the Branch, into a position - not in the best interest of the collection process, but certainly commensurate with his training and ability.

It should be noted that there is no Special Procedures Section in the Tax Division and if the person presently holding the position of SPO should become sick or otherwise incapacitated, or even resign, chaos would follow immediately.

In addition, there are many factors to be considered in assessing the value of the Special Procedures Officer. Perhaps not necessarily in order: (a) Should the SPO get an assigned case in which a member of his family, a relative or a close

friend is involved, to whom does he transfer the case? (b) Would the position of
SPO encourage frivolous offers-in-compromise in order to keep him busy?
(c) Does the position indicate that the Revenue Officers training program will be
discontinued?

It is not my aim to annoy you, but since you are aware of the fact that
heretofore Revenue Officers were required to handle cases necessitating a lot
of complex and laborious work, I would venture to say that the abolition of the
position of SPO would grant Revenue Officers the fair competitive opportunity to
prove their ability and simultaneously correct the existing inequities in salaries,
seniority, etc.

Maximum utilization of man-power is most essential, and I must repeat
what I've said so often i.e. I'm not one of those Government employees who enjoy
being paid for doing nothing, and I therefore would like work assigned to me that's
compatible with my salary of $12,000.00.

Finally, should you desire to have me contribute or impart my knowledge
of the collection activity through meetings, etc. I'd be most happy to participate.
I much prefer oral communication.

Sincerely yours,

Liston B. Monsanto
Internal Revenue Officer

LBM/tp

Then on February 25, 1977, Woods acting the role of a milque toast wrote to me sending a copy of his letter to Olive:

GOVERNMENT OF
THE VIRGIN ISLANDS OF THE UNITED STATES
CHARLOTTE AMALIE, ST. THOMAS

———— o ————

DEPARTMENT OF FINANCE
TAX DIVISION

February 25, 1977

Mr. Liston B. Monsanto
Internal Revenue Officer IV
Department of Finance
Tax Division
St. Thomas, V. I.   00801

Dear Mr. Monsanto:

This refers to your letter dated February 7, 1977 concerning the organization of the Delinquent Accounts and Returns Branch and your own connection with the system.

I apologize for not responding to your letter sooner, but the pressures of other work precluded an earlier reply.

In briefly summarizing your comments and recommendations it is concluded that your concern is two-fold:

> 1. The activities or job specifications of the Special Procedures Officer acts to curtail the activities of the Revenue Officers and thus is creating a morale problem.
> 2. Your concern with your present position with respect to seniority with the Branch.

We are all aware of the sequence of events which led to the establishment of the position of Special Procedures Officer. The assignment originally, and the promotion, thereafter, was as in all such cases effected by the Commissioner. As I discussed with you verbally I was not intimately involved or otherwise had no knowledge of the grievances which existed with yourself and management at that time, but hope to assure you that those conditions are non-existant today.

The position of Special Procedures Officer is an intergral part of our organization designed to work within the scope of assigned responsibilities and authority. I am of the opinion that this has worked well for us here and am prepared to defend my stand relative to this position. However, I hasten to point out that while we make recommendations the ultimate authority for organizational changes of any kind rests with the Commissioner.

Obviously your own personnel problems with management and your reassignment to another division played a part in not being considered for elevation to the position, as there is no question as to your seniority or competence. I hope to correct this situation by affording you every such opportunity in the future. The position is in fact budgeted and filled and to the best of my knowledge the incumbent is permanently installed.

The Commissioner of Finance has instructed that a rough draft of a Policy Statement be submitted to his office for final issuance no later than next week. This has long been necessary as the old Policy Statement has never been revised since it's inception in 1968. This Policy Statement will encompass changes in the level of authority of Revenue Officers, as well as, Supervisory employees and will afford the Revenue Officers an opportunity to operate in a manner befitting their experience and training, and thus relieve any moral problem that may exists as a result of such deficiencies.

In conclusion, I appreciate the time and effort that you put into your letter and have considered the various observations and recommendations as objectively as they were written.

The matter of your seniority is recognized and every effort will be made to utilize your experience and training to the fullest in any new assignments that may come up in the future. The Policy Statement when completed will afford guidelines under which all of the officers of the branch will operate and will relieve some of the confusion and doubt that presently exist.

Sincerely,

Robert Woods
Chief, DAR, Branch

RW/gal

cc: Commissioner of Finance
Director - Tax Division

My plan had begun to take effect. Hansen came before me with a guilty look saying that he'd talk to Woods as well as the others, Quinn and Olive, in order to have me placed in a position commensurate with my salary on the condition that I make him my assistant. I told him that as pigeon hearted and insecure as he and the others for whom I had committed altruistic suicide were, there was no way that I would be able to trust him as an assistant. I suggested to him that he ask for a transfer to the Public Assistance Division of the Department of Social Welfare. I somehow could not believe that here was a group of men exposed to danger because of the authority given them to seize a delinquent taxpayer's assets, (tangible or intangible) and here was that same group lacking in confidence and filled with insecurity. It was a most pathetic sight looking at Hansen standing before me like a predatory pirate.

Olive who had become the nominal Head of the Tax Division was looking at Edward Thomas (who incidentally felt that he had a divine right to rule) run most of the affairs of the Tax Division. Unlike Olive, however, Thomas felt no fears in his position of reviewer/classifier in the Tax Division. He was in a very good position where he could check on taxpayers but there was no one really with any authority to check on him.

In April of 1973, according to a house panel report, Governor Melvin Evans had blocked a U.S. audit team from auditing the major sources of revenue in the Virgin Islands. The report, which was prepared by the committee's investigations staff, stated that because of pressure from Governor Evans, the Tax Division of the Finance Department had refused to permit Comptroller Donald Moysey's staff to audit the $76 million in federal income tax returns which account for more than half the local government's annual revenues. According to the report, which was signed by C.R. Anderson, Director of the Appropriation Committee's investigating staff, Moysey wanted access to the returns in order to check on reports that various individuals and businesses were not paying income taxes. The Comptroller said he had no means of checking out such reports without access to the tax returns. Moysey told the house investigators that he was informed that his office could not audit the tax returns because of the Governor's "lack of trust" that the information would be treated in a confidential manner.

I was building a case of which I was sure that, in the process of time, would result in a favorable decision to me. (Note: In an act of contrition several years later, Hansen admitted to me that he was victimized by deliberate misstatements emanating from the mouths of Anthony Olive, Leroy Quinn and Edward Thomas. He said that he had been led to believe that I had wanted him fired from his job and consequently he had to join them in doing evil things to decent people. He also complained to me about the role Ulric Benjamin was playing in an effort to keep things the way they were).

Needless to say, the powers that be were trying desperately to isolate me. As noted earlier, I had written several letters to Olive and Quinn, which were all ignored. I had to get the word out to an apathetic public in order to survive as an employee of the Tax Division and in order to avoid relocating to some other jurisdiction on the U.S. mainland. Locally I could not turn to anybody in a position of authority for help in a matter where I was free from guilt. I had to continue with my plan. Being guiltless I felt certain that it would only be a matter of time before the gutless Leroy Quinn would make his mistake.

On February 28, 1977, Quinn, who had been strangely coy about his plans to meet with me called my office asking that I report to his office for as he called it a "meeting of the minds." I reported to his office and in the discussions that followed, I could tell that he was foolishly judging me by his standards. He punctuated his remarks with gestures intended to make me believe that the reason that he had not seen or written to me before was due to the onerous duties of his office. His story in that regard had a semblance of truth but was really false (Wheatley, Quinn, Olive and Thomas were all mendacious people). Nothing was recorded. I made mental notes with a view towards formalizing what had transpired on February 28, 1977 in Quinn's office.

On March 1, 1977, I wrote to Hansen sending copies of my letter to Olive and Woods. I said, "Since – with the advent of Easter, Mr. Woods has chosen to assume the role of Pontius Pilate, see copy of attached letter, it behooves me to correct the erroneous impressions conveyed by my letter of February 7, 1977. At the outset, it must be made perfectly clear that I feel ambivalent towards nobody. Similarly, it should be noted that I do not believe in causing divergence willfully or maliciously. Of prime importance and certainly worthy of mention, is the fact that in making the transition from the Processing Branch, Mr. Woods, a very nice person, depended on you and many others for advice and direction and for this I would dare say that unlike a lot of other people, he feels grateful and most loyal. Nevertheless, loyalty can be carried to excess and when I wrote to Mr. Woods concerning the position of Special Procedures Officer, I did so in an objective way in order to have him use the power of his office in removing a position which I believe has obstructed completely the Revenue Officers in the performance of quality work. Also, I felt that the position would serve only to subvert the ambitions of many and would further reduce drastically, the salaries proposed by Commissioner Quinn for Revenue Officers, inasmuch as Revenue Officers, are now underemployed.

In the Virgin Islands, honesty has become most provocative and for some strange reason, I feel that a lack of initiative or resourcefulness could easily degrade a Revenue Officer faster than any other factor. I therefore wonder what Mr. Mario Lima's reaction would be if Mr. Ulrie Vialet, a junior Revenue Officer, were to emerge as his supervisor, his satisfactory performances notwithstanding. Morale has long been a problem in our Branch because of our individualistic attitudes. If we are to promote voluntary compliance, we must work together harmoniously. Needless to say, tolerance must be practiced."

Quinn had hired a dearth of promising Revenue Officers to fill the vacancies in the Delinquent Accounts and Returns Branch. I was mortified when I learned that he had foolishly, in an effort to spite me, endorsed the position of Special Procedures Officer, thereby depriving the new Revenue Officers a chance to do the type of quality work that the veterans were trained to do. The presence of a Special Procedures Officer in the Delinquent Accounts and Returns Branch had resulted in the lowering of the standards set initially in the Tax Division's reorganization plans. Using the standards of the United States Internal Revenue Service as a basis of comparison in judging the U.S. Internal Revenue Service and the local Tax Division would have, without difficulty disclosed that the Delinquent Accounts and Returns Branch had become tertiary, exactly the way the powers that be wanted to see it. Woods, appointment as Chief of the Branch and Ulric Benjamin as Special Procedures Officer had changed the composition of the Branch. All the accoutrements that a team of Revenue Officers would expect from a man (Leroy Quinn) who had previously been an Internal Revenue Officer, were taken away from them by that same man who was now putting his own interest first. As indicated earlier in the publication, the way Quinn was addressing the many problems in the Tax Division was a little unorthodox. The man honestly thought that he could easily deceive or cheat me out of the things that I was justifiably requesting.

On March 4, 1977, I wrote him a letter formalizing our meeting of Monday, February 28, 1977. I sent copies of the letter to Woods, Olive and the Director of Personnel who himself was being paid to do what the Tax Division wanted him to do. My letter said:

GOVERNMENT OF
THE VIRGIN ISLANDS OF THE UNITED STATES
CHARLOTTE AMALIE, ST. THOMAS

—— o ——

DEPARTMENT OF FINANCE
TAX DIVISION

March 4, 1977

Mr. Leroy A. Quinn
Commissioner
Department of Finance
St. Thomas, V.I. 00801

Dear Mr. Quinn:

This refers to our meeting of Monday, February 28, 1977 in which I was promised, that serious attention would be given to the existing discriminatory practices in the Delinquent Accounts and Returns Branch, and also to the many reasons which were given in letters to Mr. Robert Woods, Mr. Anthony P. Olive, and yourself, as a means of explaining why I thought that the abolishment of the position of Special Procedures Officer, would be in the best interest of our organization.

Time effaces the memory, and for this reason it has become incumbent upon me to establish for the record, the many points on which we agreed as we emerged from our meeting.

Not necessarily in order, they are:

1. The position of Special Procedures Officer encroaches on the responsibilities of the Revenue Officer, thereby relegating the Revenue Officer to the role of "Glorified Bill Collector" with an extremely high salary.

2. Whereas the Revenue Officer is assigned an inventory of accounts, the Special Procedures Officer - in his quest for work, must encourage frivolous offers in compromise and other complex work.

47

Mr. Leroy A. Quinn
Page 2
March 4, 1977

3. In view of your repudiation of the hardships and
handicaps endured by me under Mr. Wheatley,
efforts would be made either to convert the existing staff to Revenue Officers (which would justify
proposed salaries), or revamp completely the
Branch, in order to restore me to my position as
Senior Revenue Officer in the territory.

4. Abolishment of the position of Assistant Chief, DAR.
in the St. Thomas district in order to have one Assistant Chief, in the Virgin Islands assigned to St. Croix.

5. Efforts will be made to send Mr. Robert Woods to a
supervisory school in the state of West Virginia with
special instructions to observe the operations of the
Delinquent Accounts and Returns Branch while there.
The feeling is, that Mr. Woods has neither been exposed to the workings of a DAR, Branch nationally,
nor formally trained in the collection activity. This,
needless to say, has precluded him from understanding
the activity and more importantly, the role of the Revenue Officer.

6. In Patterson, New Jersey where you once worked as a
Revenue Officer, you were afforded the opportunity to
see a Special Procedures Section at work. There is no
such section in the Virgin Islands, and consequently,
this makes the name Special Procedures Officer a misnomer.

7. The position of Special Procedures Officer has never
been recommended by the U.S. Internal Revenue Audit
Teams. They see no need for it here and have always
felt a "Major Case Program", handled by Revenue Officers,
was the best thing for the Virgin Islands.

Mr. Leroy A. Quinn
Page 3
March 4, 1977

8. The timely manner in which my letters were
    written. This timing gives all concerned ample
    time (i. e. prior to the implementation of the pro-
    posed new pay plan) for discussions, consultations,
    etc. which would ultimately lead to the abolition of
    the <u>position</u> of Special Procedures Officer.

9. It is a matter of record that I once supervised the
    activities of the Delinquent Accounts and Returns
    Branch, with full authority to rate and review the
    performances of those employees, who have now
    advanced ahead of me, due only to the Gross abuse
    of discretionary power on the part of Reuben Wheatley.

Thank you very much for arranging our meeting. I'm most grateful
to you for your confidence. You may be sure I will continue to make every
effort to justify that confidence.

Sincerely,

Liston B. Monsanto
Internal Revenue Officer

LBM/gl

cc: Chief, DAR, Branch
    Director - Tax
    Director - Personnel

Quinn was loaded with dense ignorance. Neither he nor Mr. Leslie Millin, the Personnel Director, acted as if they knew that the only department in the entire Virgin Islands Government to which a Revenue Officer, a specialist, could be lawfully assigned was the Department of Finance's Tax Division. Unlike a clerk typist, for example, who could be transferred from one Department to another, when it came to transferring a Revenue Officer, there was no relativity in the job description anywhere else in the Virgin Islands Government. The foregoing introduces what you are about to read.

On March 7, 1977, I was once again forced to write to Commissioner Quinn about a matter which I labeled "Conduct Unbecoming a Revenue Officer." Here is what I wrote, "I write to you being fully cognizant of the fact that the duties of your office are most onerous in this period requiring your full attention, five days a week, but truth has no special time of its own. Its hour is now…always. A spirit of disorder, contempt for law, order and authority, has broken loose in the Delinquent Accounts and Returns Branch in recent days and as a person who respects law and authority, I feel constrained to bring to your attention a matter that deserves serious consideration, lest the Branch be transformed into a fish market.

The matter of which I speak can be best described as a tirade, inasmuch as it was delivered by, of all persons, a Revenue Officer whose husband is your Reviewer/Classifier. Her glaring churlishness was aimed directly at Mr. Woods (Chief – DAR), who in my opinion is really too nice a person.

Briefly, for your information, here is what happened on March 3, 1977 at about 10:00 a.m.: As if berserk, the Revenue Officer rushed into the Chief's office and began banging hard and noisily on his desk with her fist, while at the same time vehemently making her feelings known. It was an impulsive act performed in the presence of her peers and certain taxpayers. Truly, "nice guys finish last." It is a matter of record that over the past several years, some employees of the Tax Division have been penalized because of their desire to function in a manner reflective of their training and ability. It is also a matter of record that certain individuals currently in positions of authority have condoned wrong and have tried desperately to exonerate them by calling for the proverbial basin of water, ala Pontius Pilate. Nevertheless, one thing appears certain and that is, "esteem cannot be where there is no confidence and there can be confidence where there is no respect." Copies of my letter were sent to Woods, Olive and Revenue Officer Lucia A. Thomas. Quinn was infuriated. I had dared to speak the truth about Mrs. Thomas' behavior. I had to be punished. He summoned me to his office where I found Woods sitting in a chair across from Quinn. Quinn started out by accusing me of spreading a scandal by way of innuendo and I couldn't believe it. I was awestruck when the congenital liar, Woods, agreed with him. Woods said, "Nothing like that which you've written in your letter took place." Mrs. Gertrude Lewis, the Branch's secretary, who had called my attention to the matter, pleaded the fifth amendment of the U.S. Constitution. Quinn, coward as he was, had made an egregious blunder. And now he was about to compound that blunder by writing to his partner in crime, Leslie Millin. Here now is what Quinn wrote to Millin, in his capacity of Personnel Director, on March 8, 1977. "I am writing to request your assistance in transferring Mr. Liston Monsanto, Internal Revenue Officer IV, Tax Division, Department of Finance, to another Department or Agency where he may better get along with his co-workers and supervisors. I am constantly reminded of problems that existed between Mr. Monsanto and my predecessor by his frequent references to Mr. Reuben Wheatley, although he has been out of the Department for almost 2 years. Mr. Monsanto has recently resorted to attacks on various employees of the Tax Division to such an extent that it is affecting the work and morale of the other employees. In addition, he has been writing memorandums regarding abolishing certain positions and classifying all personnel in the section as Revenue Officers. This, he claims, will satisfy his ego. Mr. Monsanto has made it known that he resents the fact that some of the employees he once supervised have been promoted to positions above him and for this reason is creating dissension in the office. As Head of the Department, I cannot tolerate any further distraction and intimidation of our employees because of the negative attitude and vindictiveness of Mr. Monsanto. At a meeting held in my office on Monday, March 7, 1977, with Mr. Monsanto, his immediate supervisor, Mr. Robert Woods and Mr. Anthony Olive, Director of the Tax Division, Mr. Monsanto was informed that he left me no alternative but to seek a transfer to some other Department. I also informed him that because of the animosity he has created among his co-worker, it would be difficult for him to perform at an acceptable level. In accordance with Title 3, 452-133 of the Virgin Islands Rules and Regulations, I recommend the transfer of Mr. Liston Monsanto from the Department of Finance." Quinn sent copies of his letter to the Attorney General, Governor King, Olive and myself. Funny thing is he didn't send a copy to Edward Thomas and/or Lucia Thomas. Quinn was now revealing to me his real intentions. He wanted me out of the Tax Division. He was now going to show his friend Reuben Wheatley how it had to be done. Once again I knew that as long as I did what was lawful, there would be no way that "City Hall" was going to beat me. I had designs on going to the Third Circuit Court of Appeals in Philadelphia, Pennsylvania.

On March 9, 1977 I wrote to Leslie Millin, Director of Personnel,

GOVERNMENT OF
THE VIRGIN ISLANDS OF THE UNITED STATES
CHARLOTTE AMALIE, ST. THOMAS

———— 0 ————

DEPARTMENT OF FINANCE
TAX DIVISION

March 9, 1977

Mr. Leslie A. Millin
Director, Division of Personnel
St. Thomas, Virgin Islands   00801

Dear Sir:

This refers to Commissioner Leroy A. Quinn's letter of March 8, 1977 which was addressed to you, and requested your assistance in transferring me to another governmental department or agency.

At the outset, it is safe to say that it's a good thing for me, that in the Virgin Islands we live under a Democratic form of government. Had I been in Russia or any other country with a like form of government, based on the contents of Mr. Quinn's letter, I would have been treated inexactly the same manner as the Soviet writer Alexander Solzenitsky, who - incidentally, defected to the United States and is currently in the news.

It is axiomatic that there are two sides to a story. Nevertheless, one would never believe this based on the allegations made by the Commissioner. The unilateral conclusions reached therein are baseless, and most damaging to Employee moral, and furthermore, should really be avoided if he truly intends to promote the best interest of the Department of Finance.

Accordingly, I find it necessary to refute (for the record) the allegations made by a Commissioner, who took over a troubled department and has yet to address the employees thereof.

The gist of the Commissioner's letter is: Inability to get along with my Co-workers and Supervisors. This is indeed strange, inasmuch as the record (Performance ratings) shows that I have always been rated satisfactorily on this particular performance factor, and as a matter of fact, I have never been told by anyone (except indirectly in the Commissioner's letter) that my relationship with people was less than satisfactory. I'd be the first person to ask for a transfer, if I thought I could not get along with people.

I wrote to the Commissioner on March 4, 1977 in order to formalize a meeting which was held between us on Monday, February 28, 1977. You were given a copy of the letter which showed the many points on which the Commissioner and myself agreed. It now appears as if his co-operation has evaporated.

Mr. Leslie A. Millin   Page 2
Director, Division of Personnel   March 9, 1977

Subsequently, I wrote to the Commissioner on March 7, 1977 (See attached copy) after it had become crystal clear that an employee, who is the wife of his Reviewer/Classifier, had assaulted our Supervisor, who presumably was afraid to reprimand her out of fear of her husband's presence in the Division, plus his superior position. It was then that Mr. Quinn called me to his office and told me, "I'm going to transfer you".

It is very important to note, that at no time have I told Mr. Quinn anything about satisfying my ego. Everything that has transpired between his office and myself, can be found in the copy of my letter to him of March 4, 1977 which you have in your possession.

In conclusion, I feel that the Commissioner's letter is long on emotion and short on reason. I have been an employee of the Department of Finance for the last eighteen years. My conscience is clear as I much prefer to be right than president.

Should you desire to discuss the matter, I'd be most happy to accomodate you.

Very truly yours,

Liston Monsanto
Internal Revenue Officer

CC:
        Governor
        Attorney General
        Director, Tax Division
        Commissioner of Finance

My removal from the Department of Finance Tax Division was crucial to Quinn's success. For many years the people in positions of authority had been attacking the weak employees while circumventing the stronger ones. Had Leslie Millin, a man who thought he was what he was not, been asked by Quinn to transfer Jens Todman or one of the weaker employees, he would have done so in great haste. As long as I was operating according to Hoyle, there would be no way that I would allow the team of Leslie Millin and Quinn to torment me. With my cheerful countenance Millin's predecessors Charles Lewis and Albert Hugh, together with the team of Ann Abramson, Albert Commissong and Auguste Rimple, Sr. (all members of the G.E.S.C.) would never get the chance to disarrange my personality. They were entitled to feel anyway they wanted, but as far as I was concerned we were all on an equal level.

Quinn was paying scant attention to what I was saying in my letters to him. He had already given in to the same emotionalism that had destroyed Reuben Wheatley. Furthermore, he had become Wheatley's voice of doom. On March 14, 1977, I addressed a short letter to Governor King, which said, "Having been with the Tax Division, Department of Finance for eighteen (18) years, I hereby request the opportunity to discuss my status in the organization with you at your earliest convenience (Saturdays and Sundays included)." On March 15, 1977, Leslie Millin wrote to Quinn with copies to the Attorney General, the Governor, Olive, his assistant Ellen Murraine and myself. He said,

"Receipt is hereby acknowledged of your March 8th letter requesting our assistance in transferring Mr. Liston Monsanto to another Department. Mr. Monsanto is an Internal Revenue Officer IV with a salary of $12,459.00 and because of the high salary level; we anticipate some problems with finding an Agency Head that will be willing to accommodate such a transfer. The situation is further compounded by the fact that Mr. Monsanto's job training and experience is not in demand by any agency outside of the Department of Finance. Nonetheless, we will again attempt to negotiate a transfer with the Department of Health or have Mr. Monsanto administratively reassigned to collect accounts receivables owed to the Department of Health. By copy of this letter, I am assigning your request to Mrs. Murraine, Assistant Director of Personnel. A thorough review of all available vacancies will also be made. Please be assured that every effort will be made to accommodate your request as quickly as possible." Millin's letter, which was loaded with ambiguities, turned out to be a cryptic message to Quinn. Why in the pride of manhood couldn't he tell Quinn that under existing law he could not legally transfer me anywhere?

On March 22, 1977 I received a letter from Leopold E. Benjamin, Administrative Assistant to Governor King. Benjamin wrote, "Governor King acknowledges with thanks, receipt of your letter dated March 14, 1977, indicating that you have been employed with the Tax Division of the Department of Finance for eighteen (18) years and requesting an opportunity to discuss with him your status with the organization. The Governor has referred your letter to Commissioner Quinn for his review and comments and as soon as a response is received from him he will reply to you again about this matter." Either King or his administrative assistant, Leopold Benjamin, was trying to placate me. I had written to King only for the record inasmuch as I did not know whether he had taken the path to deception.

During the period that I was forced to leave the Tax Division under Reuben Wheatley, the organization had recruited a number of Revenue Officers who were new to what they were doing and also a supporting staff whose job was to assist the Chief of the Branch. Among the new Revenue Officers were Terrence Brunn, Alvin Swan, Lucia Thomas and Ulrie Vialet. Although inexperienced and untrained as Revenue Officers, as normal human beings they knew that I had been a victim of an unjust act. The overall ambiance of the office housing the Revenue Officers was such that one could readily see that there was no difference between the Enforcement Officers in the Treasury Division who had not been trained by the United States Internal Revenue Service and the Internal Revenue Officers in the Delinquent Accounts and Returns Branch. With theories abounding about what was going on in my life as an employee of the Branch, like dark clouds foreshadowing a storm, the Revenue Officers struck an attitude that translated into "Liston Monsanto today; the rest of us tomorrow." Moving forward slowly and steadily, I was able by mutual agreement to form an alliance with the new Revenue Officer Gentry. In the absence of an organizational chart I had surmised that we were several steps removed from Commissioner Quinn.

On Friday afternoon, August 26, 1977, the employees of the Tax Division, with my urgings, staged a job action making Quinn so bewildered that he could not think clearly or act sensibly. On Monday morning, August 29, 1977, I wrote to Quinn, "I was shocked and saddened to learn Friday of the demands being made upon you by the employees of the Tax Division. As a concerned employee, I hereby request that you do not attempt to transfer any of the involved employees. They are only asserting their constitutional rights." I sent a copy to Olive and Woods.

The year 1977 was coming to a close. Governor Cyril E. King was hospitalized, moribund and I was still with the Delinquent Accounts and Returns Branch working amiably with my fellow workers.

On December 27, 1977, I received a memorandum addressed to all employees of the Tax Division from the "Entertainment Committee." The memorandum said, "The Entertainment Committee" of the Tax Division extends a cordial invitation to all Tax Division employees to attend a party on Thursday, December 29, 1977 at 5:00 p.m. This party will be held at the Office of the Audit Branch, we are asking for a $2.00 donation to assist us in defraying some of the necessary costs. The menu will include chicken, potato salad, sardine dip and crackers, soup of the day and plenty of beverages. Kindly contact Revenue Agent Verne David at extension 228, as he will be receiving your donation. It is our feeling that since we have worked as a unit for an entire year, we can also share a few moments of fun together." The memorandum was unsigned.

The next day, December 28, 1977, I sent off a memorandum to the Entertainment Committee, which said, "I write to you, at the risk of being labeled cynical, regarding the last paragraph of your unsigned memo of December 27, 1977, as it conveys the false impression about the working relationship in the Tax Division. It is no secret that parties have become a commonplace during the Yuletide for millions of office workers under the American flag who have worked diligently and harmoniously as a unit for an entire year. Unfortunately, for the employees of the Tax Division, however, a line of demarcation has been drawn which serves only to separate us yearly from January 2nd through December 23rd, the inter-relationship of our jobs notwithstanding. Our period of reconciliation is much too short, and furthermore, I believe that if we are to mold a cohesive unit, we must be altruistic and most tolerant with our fellow employees. Finally, since I'm not aware of the existence of an Entertainment Committee within the Tax Division, your memo appears to be a gigantic hoax and a shameful farce."

As presented in this account, the attitudes of indifference displayed by the powers that were, at all levels in the Virgin Islands Government, towards an organization labeled the main income producing arm of the government put the Delinquent Accounts and Returns Branch in a turmoil. I had known all along that the same system that ran the Virgin Islands, a system that had us where we were, was the same system choking off everything else including the Collection of taxes. Through the efforts of Mario "Tansy" Lima who knew that toleration of dishonest official encourages corruption, I had established rapport with my new colleagues. Their games-man-ship was beautiful. Whenever I needed them to join me in sending a message to Olive, Quinn or Governor Juan Luis, who had inherited the Governorship following King's death in 1978, they would cooperate to the fullest.

They had become aware of management's unwritten law, a personification of the "Golden Rule" in a paraphrase that said, "He who controls the gold (i.e. money) makes the rules. Jens Todman perceived to be a purveyor of gossip, had become persona non grata. As a group the Revenue Officers felt insulted by the people in positions of authority who were regularly flouting the laws and due largely to the presence of the Special Procedures Officer, they had become underemployed and consequently obliged to do menial work. And so, lacking in interest and dignity and blessed with the knowledge that I had previously supervised the activities of the Delinquent Accounts and Returns Branch, I became a sight for sore eyes.

On February 17, 1978, we wrote to Governor Luis who already knew about the anomalous situation in our Branch and just would not do anything that would cast a damp over the vexing problem. We told Luis that our morale was being hurt and the Branch as well. We also told him that we were unable to promote voluntary compliance owing to the circumstances that we were bringing to his attention. We blamed Quinn, Olive and the supervisory personnel for everything that had gone wrong. Here are some of the problems we presented to Luis for discussion: "(1) since his appointment as Commissioner of Finance, Mr. Quinn has held one meeting and that came two and one-half years after he had been in office; ironically, only after employees of the Tax Division had made their feelings known that they would stage a sick-out similar to the employees of the Treasury Division. (2) Mr. Anthony Olive, our Tax Director, ignores completely the Revenue Officers and favors only the agents to whom he refers as "my boys." This is done despite the Revenue Officers' role as income producers of the Virgin Islands Government. (3) There are no organizational charts designed to show the chain of authority, although we have been classified as professional employees by management. (4) Revenue Officers are underemployed due to the presence of a Special Procedures Officer. (5) Promotions are awarded based on favoritism and salary increases are given to persons holding positions rather then the positions themselves. (6) The work of the Revenue Officers is not reviewed by the Chief in accordance with prescribed policies. (7) In the absence of a career program and glaring fraternization, senior Revenue Officers are passed over by supervisors in an attempt to win the confidence of junior Revenue Officers. Senior Revenue Officers must strive hard for promotions although their performance rating reflects efficiency. (8) There are no standard operating procedures for usage by the Revenue Officers. The guidelines ostensibly used are taken from the U.S. Internal Revenue Service. (9) There are no group discussions for the purpose of developing the potential of junior Revenue Officers and this has retarded the progress of the Branch. (10) Presently there is an invisible dividing line that separates the employees from their co-workers. As a result, an overall atmosphere of hostility pervades."

Surprisingly, Luis invited us to Government House on the afternoon of February 21, 1978, for discussions on the several grievances that we had listed in our letter. Then presumably in an attempt to put new life into the members of the Delinquent Accounts and Returns Branch and knowing that we had met with the Governor, Olive invited us to his office the next morning. What was said, for the lack of a better word, was uninspiring. When you are dealing with liars, it becomes incumbent upon you to set down in writing for future use, everything that is being said or done and so once again after we had returned to our office, we wrote to Olive on February 22, 1978. We said, "We were awaiting your letter reprimanding us for bringing to Governor Juan Luis' attention the many problems that exist in our troubled Tax Division, but to date we have not received it. This being the case, together with the fact that we have become disenchanted with your office, we have decided to establish, for the record, a statement made by you that really startled us during our meeting with you following our return to the Tax Division from Government House on February 21, 1978. The statement to which we refer may be repeated in substance as follows: "I can, at any time, pick anyone from among you, regardless of his seniority, etc. and elevate him to the number one position in the Branch." This really disturbs us as we can envision ourselves being future targets of your wrath and continued acts of favoritism. As classified employees, we had thought that the law offered us protection in this area, but is has become obvious, on the basis of your statement, that the law does not. Accordingly, you would continue to demoralize the employees until they decide to resign. Finally, the silent majority in the Tax Division is on the verge of duplicating our efforts in order to end the discriminatory practices in the Tax Division."

The next day, February 23, 1978, in another joint effort, we wrote to Revenue Officer Jens Todman. We said, "After reading the contents of Mrs. Jureen Francis Todman's letter to the editor, which appeared in the local Daily News of Saturday, November 5, 1977, plus considering the hardship and handicaps that the Revenue Officers have for so many years endured, it is incredible to believe that you, a senior Revenue Officer, would crawl so low as to play the role of parasite. For your information, Mrs. Todman wrote in part as follows: "Once again 'teachers' as the forerunners of government employees have stuck their heads on the chopping block as they are penalized for taking drastic action toward settlement of a contract with this Government. The wounds are not healed form the last battle with management, but it is somewhat compensating to see that others have taken up arms and joined in the fight. Other government employees, have finally awaken to shoulder their part of the burden and stand up and be counted rather than complacently sitting back and saying 'if the teachers get, we'll get too.' Of course, among each group there are parasites who sit back only to reap the benefits..." We commend Mrs. Todman for expressing her beliefs in all sincerity and with conviction. Furthermore, if many of us, especially the ones with ten or more years of service, in the Delinquent Accounts and Returns Branch had been men instead of soldiers of fortune, many of our long-standing problems would have disappeared. Additionally, it should be borne in mind that we are the employees to whom the responsibilities of bringing about 85-90% of the Virgin Islands Government revenues is charged. If we are unhappy, progress is retarded, thereby causing a drop in revenues that leads to no raises for any government employee, teachers included. You seemingly find it very easy to make demands on poor, uneducated taxpayers, but unfortunately for you, you do not have the guts to assert your rights as a classified employee to whom an injustice was done. Yes, both Kenneth Hansen, who incidentally is a very nice person, even though he is being used by you and management and Roy Malone, who followed you into the Tax Division, have moved ahead of you and now hold superior positions. This, we hasten to add, has been done in spite of your many outstanding performance ratings, all because of glaring favoritism. Stop being a parasite; put the protestant ethic to work! You'll be better for it."

We knew that Governor Luis had perfunctorily invited us to Government House on February 21, 1978. We also knew that we were rocking the boat, but we had to be consistent in our attempts to bring order to the Tax Division. What's more, we did not want Luis to weasel out from his responsibility and so we wrote to him on February 27, 1978 saying, "We would like to express our sincere thanks to you for the manner in which you took time off from your busy schedule to hear our grievances regarding working conditions in the Tax Division of the Department of Finance. While others have decided to turn their backs on existing problems, not only in our Tax Division, but elsewhere in the Virgin Islands, you have conveyed to us that no matter what position the individual holds in our society, or how insurmountable his problem might seem, you will listen and attempt to solve them. We are grateful to you for the confidence that you have placed in us and you may be assured that we will do everything humanly possible to justify that confidence." (Note: Luis, as a Senator, had been made aware of the many problems in the Department via copies of letters from both Reuben Wheatley and me. He had also visited our office as Lieutenant Governor elect in 1974). We were rolling along with the writing of our letters for posterity.

On March 3, 1978, it was Olive's turn, we wrote, "We take this opportunity to let you know that when Governor Juan Luis ordered that you correct the many problems plaguing the Tax Division and implement the proposed salaries, which would bring the pay of both the Processing Branch and the Delinquent Accounts and Returns Branch closer to that of the Internal Revenue Agents, he did not deal with poetic justice. He dealt instead with our substantiative claims, as he thought that they were the primary reasons for the morale problems in the Tax Division. It is no secret that in the past, we have been deceived and confused by your office, and furthermore, it is only because of our willingness to work as responsible employees, that rather than accept another empty promise from you (as you habitually make promises only to break them) we decided to see Governor Juan Luis. In light of the foregoing, we are hereby requesting that you give us a progress report with respect to what action, if any, has been taken since our meeting with the Governor."

To Woods, we wrote, "There was unanimous agreement among us that our meeting at Government House on Friday, February 21, 1978 would have prompted you to call an internal meeting in order to reconcile our differences and at the same time to afford us the opportunity to congratulate you on the stand that you took before Governor Juan Luis.

Needless to say, we were wrong. It was gratifying to hear you refute charges made by Commissioner Quinn with respect to offers in compromise, courtesy investigations, plus other related matters. In addition, we felt very happy to hear you voice your disagreement with Mr. Olive, as we thought and still think that we are being ignored.

Of utmost importance however, is the fact that you recognize the hardships an handicaps that we, as Revenue Officers have endured for so long, and like us, realize that if we are to move forward harmoniously, it is not the position of Chief DARB nor the person holding the position that should be abolished, but the positions of Special Procedures Officer and Assistant Chief DARB in the St. Thomas District.

Again, our heartfelt thanks go out to you for your support at Government House. We now look forward to the abolition of the two positions previously noted as we feel that their absence would inject the much-needed serum thereby motivating us to promote voluntary compliance."

There was much platitudes being spouted from glib tongues. Now it was Adelbert Anduze's, (Executive Assistant to the Governor) turn. He wrote to me on March 6, 1978, sending copies to then Attorney General Ive A. Swan and the Revenue Officers. Anduze wrote, "Your request for re-evaluation and possible abolishment of the positions of Special Procedures Officer and Assistant Chief, Delinquent Accounts and Returns in the St. Thomas Branch of your Department is being considered. The material furnished by you will be forwarded to the Office of the Attorney General in order that a thorough study may be conducted to determine the validity of these positions as applied to the present needs of the Department of Finance. Upon receiving the finding and recommendations of the Attorney General, the Governor will issue a decision. Thank you for your interest in the smooth operations of your Division."

So Mr. Anduze had become pretentiously creative. What was hard for me to believe was here was a group of people (Revenue Officers) complaining on a daily basis to everybody in a position of authority and the same people to whom they were complaining were busy finding ways and means of protecting and defending the Bureaucracy. The Governor, the Lieutenant Governor (Henry Millin, Sr.) and all the powers to which we had written were being exposed to the disadvantaged people of the Virgin Islands. But they just didn't care.

On March 8, 1978, we wrote to our co-workers in the Processing Branch. This is what we said, "Better late than never. Our belated thanks for your support in our quest to put an end to the discriminatory practices in the Tax Division. Your willingness to participate and extend a helping hand to the needy and distressed is heartening. While our Tax Director, Mr. Anthony Olive, has continued to ignore us and treat the agents assigned to the Audit Branch as superior beings, the Revenue Officers are delighted to see that only the employees of the Processing and Delinquent Accounts and Returns Branches realizes that the three Branches are truly representative of the entire Tax Division.

Speaking of the entire Tax Division, the quotation 'you can pick your friends, but not your relatives' really comes into focus when the agents are mentioned. This, we believe, is partly due to the fact that some of the agents have failed to see that our jobs are interrelated and much prefer to consider us inferior. Put simply, they pretend not to see the forest because of the trees. Some of the agents have, for years, complained about working conditions in the Tax Division, but every time that they have been asked to identify the various troubled areas, they have buried their heads in the sand like ostriches. They are always eager to associate with us at social functions, so as to pretentiously display to the public, that all is well in the Tax Division. No wonder they've been getting the gravy for all these years. Because of our united effort, yourselves and us, we were able to see Governor Juan Luis and substantiate our claims before him. If we are to benefit in the manner explained to us by the Governor, chances are that the agents, especially those mentioned heretofore, will realize that a house divided against itself cannot stand. Again, thanks very much for your support. You have demonstrated that the old adage 'United We Stand, Divided We Fall' has merit."

The Revenue Officers led by Lima and I were employing the same strategy of deception being used by the deceitful officials of the Virgin Islands Government. We hadn't forgotten Quinn. We were making certain that none of them could truthfully say, "I did not know what was going on in the Tax Division."

On March 9, 1978, we wrote to Quinn sending copies of the letter to Luis, Henry Millin, Sr. and Olive. We wrote, "Since Mr. Anthony Olive's appointment as Tax Director, there has been a prevailing aura of gross mismanagement throughout the Tax Division. Chaotic circumstances such as the Revenue Officers appearance before Governor Juan Luis and the public declaration by the employees of the Processing Branch in support of the Revenue Officers, which incidentally cited worsening conditions in the division, have all surfaced in recent days and are major factors that make the Office of Tax Director vulnerable. Moreover, Mr. Olive's approach towards his duties has left much to be desired, as he lacks the same leadership qualities that led to his removal as Chief of the

Audit Branch by your predecessor. In addition, he is completely oblivious of us as subordinates and continues to engage in menial work (acts that only the most rank amateur would perform) bringing disgrace to the high office that he holds, consequently, he has subverted the ambitions of many of us, causing us to lose confidence in his office. The fact that Mr. Olive has yet to address us since we met at Governor Luis' office on February 21, 1978, provides tangible proof that Mr. Olive either does not know the magnitude of our morale problem and as a result, does not envision it spreading throughout the Department, or he just doesn't care. Consequently, we feel that the intercession of your office has become necessary in order to eradicate or minimize the vexing problem as it is our belief that these problems may well be the forerunner to a complete collapse of the Tax Division."

On March 10, 1978, not to be outdone, the employees of the Processing and Accounts Branch wrote to Leroy Quinn sending a copy of their letter to Olive. This is what they had to say, "Working conditions in the Tax Division have worsened since the appointment of Mr. Anthony Olive as Tax Director. That he has failed to provide the desired leadership, is evident. As noted earlier, in a letter to Governor Juan Luis, we in the Processing Branch are in full agreement with the Revenue Officers, for we know for a fact that they, like us, have been victimized for too long. The adverse publicity which the Division has been receiving, does not lend itself to a smooth working relationship among the employees who are charged with the responsibility of collecting 85-90% of the Virgin Islands Government revenues. More importantly, the failure of our Tax Director to display his leadership role when our ship is apparently on the verge of sinking, does nothing to help. We are desperately in need of help. Help that our Director seemingly cannot provide. Will you help us?"

After our first gubernatorial election in 1970, I was hoping for periods of marked improvements and a new lifestyle throughout the United States Virgin Islands. However, amid high expectations, we in the Tax Division found ourselves lingering long after the votes had been counted declaring Melvin Evans our first elected Governor. The people making up our local gentry, because of their small numbers, were pushed aside becoming a minority voting bloc, thereby leaving an association of disadvantaged people with common interests to legally decide, through their votes who would be the persons best fitted to lead us in the Executive and Legislative Branches of our Government. Although the gulf between the haves and the have-nots had narrowed somewhat, our lifestyle, albeit more sophisticated, remained status quo.

There were societal changes to which the people were slow in responding and many people in positions of authority were not amenable to the laws. While I had continued to assert my rights as a classified employee (public servant) assigned to work in an organization wrack by unjustness, I had not forgotten my colleagues and the role that they were playing in my ordeal. So once again, I addressed a letter to Leslie Millin, Director of Personnel, sending copies to his father (Lieutenant Governor Henry, Sr.), Governor Juan Luis and Leroy Quinn. I knew that Leslie Millin was fitting himself, by his actions, to the ideas of the wrongdoers, even if he was called upon to fudge the data. I had to deal with him, if only for the purpose of including him in this publication. So I wrote, "On February 21, 1978, the Governor, in a meeting attended by the Commissioner of Finance, the Tax Director, the Chief of Delinquent Accounts and Returns Branch and the Internal Revenue Officers, ordered the supervisory personnel to bridge the gap salary-wise between the employees of the Tax Division. Based on recent developments, we have reason to believe that an attempt is being made to defy the orders of the Governor. Therefore, we are forced to submit for your review and consideration, the following information." I then listed the present and proposed pay ranges and then went on to say, "In addition, we are requesting that favorable consideration be given to the employees of the Processing Branch, as the Governor mentioned that they are grossly underpaid. He felt that because of the unattractive salaries given to these employees', efforts to recruit additional personnel have failed." I finished my letter by saying, "Placing the position of Revenue Officer IV in GS 27 should simplify our continuing efforts to abolish the position of Special Procedures Officer and Assistant Chief DAR, while at the same time making it easier to place the person filling the position of Special

Procedures Officer in Range 27. Incidentally, the position of Special Procedures Officer, although not on a higher level than the position of Assistant Chief DAR, is found in a higher salary range than the Assistant Chief DAR, thereby precluding the person holding the position of Special Procedures Officer from aspiring to become Assistant Chief DARB. Needless to say, this is a gross inequity." The letter was dated March 22, 1978.

On April 14, 1978, I again wrote to Leslie Millin. This time I said, "During this period when the Government of the Virgin Islands is struggling through a severe fiscal crisis, I find it necessary to write to you, not only as a concerned employee, but also as one familiar with the day-to-day operations of the Delinquent Accounts and Returns Branch of the Tax Division, having formerly supervised the activities thereof. Job analysis of the positions of Special Procedures Officer and Assistant Chief DARB which is scheduled for next week, will no doubt disclose that there is no need for these positions in the DARB as it is customary during the Chief's absence to delegate authority to a senior Revenue Officer, who on the basis of his training, etc., becomes an adequate replacement. Currently, the holder of the Special Procedures Officer's position is in a very sensitive spot inasmuch as he is the <u>only person</u> who has the authority to process offers-in-compromise (i.e. taxpayers compromising liabilities for less then the original amount due), thereby leaving himself open to bribery. Nationally, a <u>Special Procedures Section</u> does this type of work as they visualize the danger of placing such a responsibility in the hands of an individual. Noteworthy is the fact that neither the incumbent nor the ostensible proponents, to this day, have given one valid reason as to why the positions should not be abolished. The fact that our Government is in dire need of money, the individuals filling these frivolous positions should be given an inventory of accounts and proceed posthaste to reduce the receivables of the Virgin Islands Government. In conclusion, now that changes have been made with respect to salaries, etc. in the DAR Branch, it is my belief that these positions can be readily converted into essential positions within the Branch, thereby bringing an end to the discriminatory practices therein." (A copy was sent to Governor Luis).

My thoughts then reverted to the figurehead Anthony Olive. On April 20, 1978, I wrote to him sending copies of my letter to Quinn and Woods. I said, "At long last the strife is o'er, admittedly it took a heavy toll in resignations, in hostility, in retarding productivity and in simple human misery. Fortunately for us, it proved in the end that our government of laws works evenly, honestly and swiftly for everybody. Now, as we look towards the future, it is expected that everyone assigned to the DARB will earn their salaries by working together with diligence and in a business-like manner. Such a collaborative effort must be undertaken if we are to accomplish the mission of the DARB and simultaneously promote the best interest of the Virgin Islands Government. I know that the public image of the Tax Division is extremely important and as a consequence, you may be assured that I shall perform my duties as dynamically and with competence and impartiality as I have done in the past, provided I am not restricted from doing so. Despite the above, it is well to mention that in the U.S. Virgin Islands we have a unique tax organization. Our Branch, although powerful, apparently seeks to project an image of amicability within and without the Tax Division, as the same taxpayers continue to be delinquent, if we fail to take enforcement action now. In short, the job is not being done because we do not want it done. For your information, in the United States Internal Revenue Service, after which we are supposedly mirrored, Revenue Officers are seen, in some cases as "nice guys." Often, however, they are not seen that way. Furthermore, not only should we be firm and fair in dealing with taxpayers, but also in our rating the so-called professional employees assigned to our Branch. In light of the foregoing, it is evident that there is no place for a person like me in the top rung of the DARB. It goes without saying, that there is always a place for a person who goes along, but I've never been that way. Accordingly, I will now concentrate on utilizing my ability towards a peaceful design for working with my primary concern being directed towards the promotion of voluntary compliance."

On June 8, 1978, I received a letter from Leslie Millin that said, "Receipt is acknowledged of your letter which communicated certain concerns of the Revenue Officers with respect to the positions of Special Procedures Officer and Assistant Chief DAR. Based on the information received from my classification staff and consistent with the findings of the executed audits, both positions are properly classified and upgrading has been recommended to the Department. Any recommendation from this office to abolish those positions would be arbitrary, capricious and certainly unwarranted in light of the performed job analysis. Besides, our only interest in this matter is to remain impartial in administering the functions of this agency."

My response on June 12, 1978, with copies to his father and Governor Juan Luis follows, "I started to ignore your delicately worked letter of June 8, 1978, which was delivered to me at 4:10 p.m. on June 9, 1978, but after digesting its contents, I decided to accommodate you with a reply. First of all, it is incredible to believe, although not surprising, on the basis of past unhappy experiences, that with all the valid reasons that were forwarded to your office regarding abolition of the positions of Special Procedures Officer and Assistant Chief of the DAR Branch in St. Thomas, that your very abled classification staff would rule in favor of retention, underlining in the absence of one (1) valid reason from the proponents. Ironically, the decision comes, not only in the wake of the budget hearings on increased taxes and the call for much-needed tax Collections, but also at a time when crime has escalated due partly, it is safe to assume, to the continuing poetic justice, such as was handed down by your staff. I hesitate to speculate at the motives of your classification staff, as it is not my intentions to fight the establishment or become hostile towards anyone. Nevertheless, when one is privileged to observe employees in our small office, with fancy job titles, duplicating the duties of Revenue Officers only to stay busy or not doing anything most of the time, one wonders. Furthermore, since we are complaining about the Government's inability to collect money owed, why don't we assign an inventory of accounts to these men so that we may reduce the receivables? Taxpayers have in recent days, and with good reasons, complained about the Tax Division's inability to accomplish their objective. Additionally, Mr. Roy Moorehead and Mr. Dale George, two dedicated, long-time employees, have left the Tax Division since our visit with Governor Juan Luis, owing in part to the organizational structure and the many other long-standing problems of which you are aware. Seriously, I had thought that in light of the rumors and theories that had been circulated, that the truth would have been ascertained by conducting a thorough and independent investigation into the exercise of the positions of Special Procedures Officer and Assistant Chief of the DAR Branch in St. Thomas, positions that have brought on existing morale problems and which the Revenue Officers maintain, with ample justification, are not needed in the DAR Branch. Finally, I appreciate what you've done for the Revenue Officers by way of upgrading, but seriously I, in all sincerity and conviction, question the fairness and impartiality of your classification staff."

Following this letter, I assumed the duties of an ombudsman and on behalf of the Revenue Officers, I wrote once again to Leslie Millin, whose acts like Olive's were seemingly being controlled by an outside force. On June 15, 1978, sending copies to Luis and Henry Millin, Sr., I said, "The Internal Revenue Officers, as authorized by the Privacy Act (Public Law 93-579) hereby request a copy of the report which was prepared by your classification staff and relates to job analysis that were performed on the positions of Special Procedures Officer and Assistant Chief of the DAR Branch in the Tax Division. It is the feeling of the Revenue Officers that since no one from your classification staff deemed it necessary to visit our small office and physically make a comparative analysis of the affected jobs and since they, the Revenue Officers, know that the persons filling the positions are duplicating the duties of Revenue Officers, that the decision made by your staff to retain the positions is arbitrary, capricious and bias. The decision handed down by your staff does nothing to aid a Branch charged with the responsibility of producing income for the Virgin Islands Government and for this reason we ask that you give our request your paramount and foremost attention."

Lest you forget, I was fighting "City Hall" a "City Hall" heavily ladened with liars. On June 26, 1978, I once again wrote to my blue-blooded adversary, Leslie Millin, sending copies to Governor Luis and his father. I wrote, "On the premise that it is error only and not truth that shrinks from inquiry, I wrote to you on June 15, 1978, on behalf of the Internal Revenue Officers, requesting certain information relating to job analysis which was performed by your classification staff. Needless to say, my request was made under the authority of the Privacy Act (Public Law 93-579). Nevertheless, it should be explained, for the sake of clarity, that the Privacy Act was designed to place certain restrictions on government agency record-keeping and to give individuals access to records maintained on them by governmental agencies. Additionally, it is worth noting that many conditions brought about the passage of the Act, but principal among them were fear of abusive use of governmental power. Since my simple request has passed unnoticed and since I am of the belief that there is nothing harder than the softness of indifference, especially during this period when Collections are lagging and the problems in the Tax Division have become more acute, I'm forced to once again ask that you accede to my request." Incidentally, I had also sent a copy of this letter to the American Civil Liberties Union for their edification. It was because of this particular copy, that Millin asked the Attorney General's office to research Public Law 93-579. They were all poltroons.

The Assistant Attorney General (Douglas R. Gardner) wrote to Millin saying, "The primary purpose of Public Law 93-579 is to provide certain safeguards for an individual against an invasion of privacy (Section 2(b)) and should the individual request any information directly concerning him or her, the request specifying the information should be in writing. Section 2 (B)(1) permits an individual to determine what records pertaining to him are collected, maintained, used or disseminated by any such agencies. Agency is defined in 5U, S.C. 551 (1) (C) to include the governments of the Territories or possessions of the United States."

With this information in his possession, Millin wrote to me on July 12, 1978, sending copies of his letter to his father and Governor Luis. He said, "Kindly excuse the delay in responding to your letter of June 26, 1978, wherein you requested copies of desk audits that were performed on the positions of Special Procedures Officer and Assistant Chief of the DAR Branch in the Tax Division. As previously explained to you, I was off-island from June 13th – June 26th therefore, I was unable to respond to your original inquiry that was dated June 15th. Accordingly, there was no deliberate indifference on my part, as you eluded to in your June 26th correspondence. Nonetheless, consideration was given to your request to the extent that I requested an opinion from our staff counsel. On the basis of Attorney Gardner's statement, see attached copy; I am denying your request for copies of desk audit pertaining to other employees of the Tax Division. In conclusion, I wish to emphasize that final authority for classification of positions rests with the Director of Personnel pursuant to Title 3, VIC, Section 492."

The people against whom I was fighting were of the false belief that a person needed a college degree in order to do battle with them. They were operating pursuant to the Department of Finance's golden rule that was cited earlier (i.e. he who controls the money makes the rules). On July 12, 1978, I wrote to Leslie Millin, sending copies to his father, Luis and the ACLU. I said, "It is becoming increasingly apparent to the silent majority that procrastination has become the order of the day, following the Internal Revenue Officers simple request for a copy of your classification staff report that supports your decision to retain the positions of Special Procedures Officer and Assistant Chief of the DAR Branch in the Tax Division. Speaking for the Revenue Officers, I would dare say that none of us are rabble-rousers, nor are we as paradoxical as many of the people in whom we have placed in our trust. Furthermore, it should be noted that when one finds himself mired in a cesspool of moral filth, deception and disgustingly offensive deeds, it becomes incumbent upon that person to locate the documentary evidence needed to identify the responsible source. Heretofore, in an ostentatious move, the Privacy Act was cited as a basis for our simple request, but now that signs of ineptitude have surfaced, it behooves us, under authority of the Freedom of Information Act of July

4, 1967, to make a final request for a copy of the Report. Incidentally, this is the last in a series of letters addressed to you requesting a copy of the aforementioned report; consequently, the Internal Revenue Officers, who are also taxpayers and voters, ask that you, in your capacity as public servant, give consent to our request."

Then came my follow-up of July 14, 1978 to the same Leslie Millin with copies to the Governor and Lt. Governor. I wrote, "Your letter of July 12, 1978, written by way of repartee, is long on emotion and short on reason, to say the least. My respect for law and authority has been such that in none of my letters to you did I questions your discretionary power as you inferred in the last paragraph of your letter. I am very much aware of the primary purpose of Public Law 93-579 as you can readily see from my letter of June 26, 1978. The Freedom of Information Act gives us the authority to review the Report. We've requested a copy of the Report inasmuch as we need it for our records and certainly we feel that no man is justified in doing evil on the ground of expediency."

After Cyril E. King had died in office in January of 1978, Juan Luis assumed the Governorship and thereafter hand picked Henry Millin, Sr. to be his Lt. Governor. Henry Millin, Sr. was a scurrilous political writer diametrically opposed to the existing state of affairs. Using violent and derisive language in his face-to-face discussions and writings he had an invariable habit of denouncing the Virgin Islands Governmental System. But now as Lt. Governor he would stay in step with the administration thereby condoning the very things he had so openly despised.

As already noted, Henry Millin, Sr. was the father of Leslie Millin, Director of Personnel. Looking at their genealogies, they were both seen as aristocrats and so as far as they were concerned, it would have been illusory for Liston Monsanto to believe that they were going to side with him. Based on their abrasive attitudes one could readily tell that they thought that I was playing the legendary William Tell refusing to show subservience to the tyrants in the various positions of authority.

As a law-abiding person there would be no way that I would yield to the power of people who had little or no regard for the law. On July 21, 1978, I continued to provide documentary evidence by writing to Leslie Millin, Director of Personnel, once more sending copies to Governor Luis, Henry Millin, Sr. and the ACLU. I wrote, "There are occasions when the general belief of the people, even though it is groundless, works its effect as sure as truth itself. Fortunately for the Revenue Officers however, your latest display of gumption is not one of those occasions. As trained investigators, the Revenue Officers have ascertained that no report was submitted to you by your classification staff, supporting your decision to retain the positions of Special Procedures Officer and Assistant Chief of the DAR Branch in the Tax Division; consequently, our legal attempts to obtain a copy of a non-existent report proved fruitless. Because of your arbitrary decision to retain the positions, everything in the DARB remains status quo. The salary increases that were awarded to the employees of the Branch are frequently referred to as thirty pieces of silver and the Revenue Officers, who, like most of the employees in the Department of Finance, are taxpayers and registered voters, continue to be concerned about working conditions. Litigation was contemplated as a means of obtaining a copy of the phantom report, but then we thought, why should men of compassion resort to such harsh measures and bring on further embarrassment? Enough is as good as a feast."

With Luis, Millin, Sr. and Leslie Millin receiving copies, I wrote to Olive on July 31, 1978 in this manner, "Forwarded herewith for your review and consideration are copies of correspondence exchanged between Director of Personnel, Leslie Millin and myself. The sequence of events shows that Mr. Millin, like yourself, is desirous of maintaining the status quo in the Tax Division at the expense of the taxpayers of the Virgin Islands. He seems to forget that ours is a government of laws and not of men. Our existing structure which is ostensibly mirrored after the U.S. Internal Revenue Service, is not conducive to the economic growth of a financially troubled Virgin Islands Government. Furthermore, the attitude of indifference displayed by Mr. Millin, coupled with his arbitrary decision to retain the two positions have served only to make his office vulnerable while at the same time demoralizing further the employees of the Tax Division. The attempts of the Revenue

Officers to establish a fair and equitable system in the Tax Division have seemingly proved futile. Consequently, the situation brings to mind the words of Leo Tolstoy, who said, "God sees the truth, but waits…"

Revenue Officer Ulrie Vialet was a problem child. He was always getting into some kind of trouble and being bailed out by me. The end he had in mind was to take advantage of what was going on between those at the highest levels and those on the employee level within the Tax Division. He foolishly mistook my nice virtues for weakness, thereby making capital of the sordid mess in which I had found myself. His penchant for getting into trouble became a source of annoyance for management, especially when it involved me as his representative. Rather than alienate, I had to protect him as one of my allies. I could not afford to lose anybody from my side. When it came to taking disciplinary measures against an employee, Quinn and Olive had difficulty inasmuch as they themselves were not conforming to the accepted standards of the day.

In November of 1978, both Olive and Quinn wanted to suspend Ulrie Vialet but did not really know how to go about with the suspension. Immediately after Olive had started the proceedings, Ulrie Vialet came to me asking for my help. I seized the opportunity to help him by writing a letter to Olive sending copies to Luis, Henry Millin, Sr. and Quinn. I wrote, "Palpable signs of wrath have surfaced in recent days and it causes one to wonder what form of punishment he will receive for the honest testimony that he gave before Governor Luis in February of this year and who has been marked as the next victim of the executioner's picayunish action. Personally speaking, I've become a bit apprehensive at this writing for I've just surmised that based on a recommendation from your office, that a junior Revenue Officer has ostensibly been suspended from duty for a five (5) day period. I'm persona non grata around here owing to my desire to see working conditions improved in the Tax Division. Furthermore, unlike most of my colleagues, I envision that what affects one innocent person can very well affect another; especially when the other person's candor is above reproach. It is no secret that the lack of leadership, which would provide for taxpayer's educational programs, regular group meetings, updates of policy statements wherever necessary, transportation, etc., has been detrimental to the Revenue Officers in the DARB. Junior Revenue Officers go about their duties in a state of bliss not knowing that their lives are in constant danger as they continue to enforce collections from an uninformed public. Fortunately for me, I've been with the division long enough to witness a high degree of insubordination and isolated cases of certain trusted employees attempting to defraud the Virgin Islands Government through the filing of fraudulent income tax returns. Such behavior has been condoned by management for so long, that as a result, we are now surrounded by employees who display a "holier than thou" attitude. Knowing that soon we will be entering calendar year 1979 conjures up memories of 1978 retroactively to 1970 and immediately I get goose bumps as I entertain thoughts of a no-changed attitude towards the sordid mess in which we find ourselves mired. Hopefully, my fears will be short-lived."

Through my letter I was putting Olive and the others on the defensive. They had never been engaged in any thing like this before and consequently didn't know which way to turn. On December 20, 1978, I wrote to Olive again sending copies to the same people to whom I had copied on December 8th. I said, "As a person who respects law and authority, I feel constrained to apprise you of a matter that needs careful handling and tact.

Saying that, I gasped in horror and amazement when Revenue Officer Mario Lima brought to my attention, the fact that two of our professional employees are indebted to the Virgin Islands Government for income taxes is really an understatement. It does however make me shudder to think that employees to whom the responsibility of enforcing the Collection of taxes is delegated would turn right around and defeat that purpose. How Mr. Olive, in the pride of manhood, are we to enforce the tax laws fairly and impartially when we ourselves are guilty of not paying? Are we Liegemen or Internal Revenue Officers? Apathy is not one of my attributes hence I request that you give this serious matter your paramount and foremost attention." What I had been putting in writing was indifferent to everybody from the Governor on down. It is safe to say that they felt that they could get rid of the problems in the Tax Division by running away from them. Any advice that I was offering was unwanted as far as they were concerned. They would pay however.

Ulrie Vialet needed a ghost writer to convey to the Governor and Olive his version of what was going on in the Tax Division with respect to whether he had been officially suspended or not. Again he came to me and gladly I wrote to the Governor sending Quinn a copy. I said, "Constantly feeling under attack and with the threat of a carefully planned suspension hanging over my head, during the month of December 1978 I wrote a series of letters to Commissioner Leroy A. Quinn, of which you have copies, in an effort to ascertain the status of a malicious and deliberate suspension, which is based only on charges trumped up by him. Yesterday, the startling question, "Are you suspended?" by Mr. Robert Woods, my supervisor, who also has copies of the letters referred to above, served only to reaffirm the existence of a perennial communications gap within the Tax Division and told me that in view of the gross mismanagement in the Tax Division, an urgent appeal should be made to you. Although I dislike confrontations of this nature (Commissioner and lower echelon employee), my knowledge that Mr. Quinn is little bound by the love of truth, compels me to seek the intervention of your office so as to avoid a showy display on the part of the Commissioner. In the past, I have participated with the Revenue Officers with whom I work, in order to bring to the attention of the public the injustices that exist in the Tax Division and now that I have become directly involved, I am entertaining thoughts of doing so once more. I therefore ask that you give this most vexing matter your prompt and foremost attention." The letter was dated January 9, 1979.

I had to strike while the iron was hot and so I wrote to Olive. I said, "It is ironic that while Governor Juan Luis and his Lieutenant Governor, Henry Millin, are proclaiming a need for 'drastic change and rapid improvement' in government services, that you in your position as Tax Director of the United States Virgin Islands, would continue to deal with political satire as a means of keeping the present system in tact.

For your information, during the recent inaugural activities, the Lt. Governor used words such as 'fairness, courage, determination and objectivity' to tell us that the recent election showed that people are not satisfied with conditions as they are. He further stated that the new administration would not tolerate dishonesty nor corruption and would not condone incompetence nor ineptness in government.

The Governor declared in part, that we should act quickly and decisively in exploiting the opportunity we now have to achieve progress with divisiveness and to achieve without hatred, preserving valuable differences of opinion, but avoiding the bitter divisions of the past, which have proven so detrimental to our progress.

I do not believe the foregoing to be platitudes from glib tongues. I do know, on the basis of the ruling handed down by the Attorney General's Office, that you ignored both the facts and the law in recommending to Commissioner Quinn that Mr. Ulrie Vialet be suspended from duty presumably in the hope that the suspension would have denied Mr. Vialet the opportunity to attend Phase II of the Revenue Officer Training Program, thereby retarding his progress. (Note: In a conversation with Assistant Attorney General, Douglas Gardner, I had been able to convince him beyond a shadow of a doubt that Vialet was not guilty of the fraudulent charges trumped up against him by Olive and Quinn. I suggested to Mr. Gardner that he write to Quinn asking him to reprimand Vialet. As a result of this action Vialet was absolved). Continuing with my letter which incidentally was dated January 18, 1979, I went on to say, "Some people, like the dodo bird, are fast becoming extinct owing to their desire to behave with reckless duplicity and insincerity. In all likelihood, a moot court would not even have attempted to try the hypothetical case set forth by Mr. Quinn in his letter of December 6, 1978 to Mr. Ulrie Vialet. What's more, there are certain events such as the arbitrary decision that was made to retain the positions of Assistant Chief DARB and Special Procedures Officer which have conspired to subvert the ambitions of many of the employees of the Tax Division and simultaneously hampered the Collection process. For the record, that decision had a telling effect. Employees such as Glen Byron, Audrey Cumbabatch, Alric George, Dale George and Maurice Maynard have all left the Tax Division since that infamous decision.

Finally, I'd like to recommend, for the last time, that efforts be made to wipe out existing factionalism in the Tax Division and an effort made to mold a cohesive unit of which we all can be proud."

Then on January 24, 1979, Ulrie Vialet applied the coup de grace. Through his ghost writer, Liston Monsanto, he wrote: "Now that you've exhausted all unlawful attempts to tarnish or otherwise shatter my image and any resentment that I may have had against management, has been removed. I feel it the duty of management to immediately grant lower echelon employees freedom from bigotry and prejudice in order to meet the objectives of the new administration.

In light of the foregoing, I respectfully request that you reconsider your arbitrary decision to send the brother of the Attorney General, who incidentally still has a tax liability in the files of the Office Collection Force, to Phase II of the Internal Revenue Officers Training Program and instead make a diligent effort to enroll me therein using the same methods you employed while enrolling the wife of our Reviewer/Classifier and Mr. Terrence Brunn.

It is my sincere belief that if we are to function as bonafide Revenue Officers, we must be trained. Moreover, since I'm now at the top rung of the training ladder, a 'first in time, first in right' principle should be the criterion used for sending trainees to school. This principle, I have no doubt, will serve as an incentive for future recruits and myself to make certain sacrifices hoping to develop our potential and ultimately to do a better job. I therefore ask that you give consent to my request."

Quinn was seething with discontent following the Attorney General's decision to reprimand Ulrie Vialet. The Assistant Attorney General, Douglas R. Gardner, had written to him on January 11, 1979, as follows, "The purported suspension is not in keeping with the provisions of the Virgin Islands Code nor the laws of the Virgin Islands. The proper procedure to be used is to make the recommended action for cause which is to be set forth in a letter to the employee and which is to be effective either after the government employees' service commission hearing, if so upheld, or if no appeal is taken by the employee within the ten day period, then upon the expiration of the ten days.

In this matter, it is quite evident that confusion arose from the suspension date being prematurely determined to which no clarification or explanation was transmitted. This being the situation, no suspension is to be recognized and the matter should be resolved by means of a reprimand."

Quinn had always imagined himself to be above the law sitting prettily in a swivel chair in his executive position as a fiscal officer without limits and restrictions.

He found it very had to accept the fact that an unlettered Ulrie Vialet had suddenly risen from a humble position to importance. Through a reprimand, Quinn would be forced to eat humble pie.

He knew the role that I had played in Vialet's vindication and consequently he did nothing. Revenue Officer Ulrie Vialet had gained an easy victory.

On March 16, 1979, I wrote to Olive, sending copies of my letter to Henry Millin, Sr. and Governor Luis after I had received a copy of the minutes of a meeting between Quinn and several employees. In the meeting Quinn displayed his unethical conduct telling the employees that "Olive lacked leadership qualities and trust." He expanded on his criticisms by saying that Olive, who was formerly and agent, did not familiarize himself with the functions of the other Branches and then concluded by asking the employees to bear with Olive while he was learning the various operations of the various Branches."

Nevertheless, in the March 16th letter I said, "With favoritism, ugly nepotism and its retinue, plus glaring attempts on the part of certain top-level employees to injure the highest office in the Virgin Islands Government's Tax Division by subtle, stealthy and insidious means, were I employed by a privately owned business with the same vices, I would have tendered my resignation a very long time ago. As a concerned taxpayer and a firm believer of Government of, for and by the people, however, I feel obligated to stay on.

It is a matter of record that for the last five years the employees of the Delinquent Accounts and Returns Branch have been making earnest appeals to your office for an organizational chart, which would explain to us exactly the chain of authority in the Virgin Islands Tax Division. Nevertheless, hope springs eternal in the battered eardrums of man, or something like that.

At this writing, our simple request has passed unnoticed and chances are, we will never see the make-up of our organizational structure, inasmuch as (a) "certain high level employees cherish the idea of encroaching on the responsibilities of others and consequently would attempt to seize and maintain power by the nicely graduated use of guile, fraud and frightfulness", (b) "these same people are using a common enemy as cement in holding together allies needed in acquiring power who, needless to say, will be liquidated together with rival once power has been acquired", (c) efforts are presently underway to undermine the responsibilities of certain top positions in the Tax Division.

Evidence of this can be found in a recent letter to the Division of Personnel, which requests a change in salary in order to presumably establish dominance over certain peers who, for the most part have developed attitudes of indifference and as a result of the absence of an organizational chart, do not know what position they occupy in the Virgin Islands Government Tax Division. Something smells rotten in Denmark.

Projecting a maverick image, in much the same manner exemplified by the voters of the Virgin Islands in our recent elections, Mr. Ulrie Vialet filed a charge of unlawful seizure of his salary check against you in the United States District Court. Our request, which was denied, to have management conspicuously display an organizational chart in our office, may also result in litigation under authority of the Freedom of Information Act. I therefore request, once again, that out office be given an organizational chart."

Again my letters were having an internal impact. They were confusing and bewildering Quinn and Olive to the point where they were forced to hold meetings on March 19, 1979 and March 23, 1979. It was possible that the Governor and Lieutenant Governor having received so many copies of letters were coming down on Quinn to stanch the bleeding, thereby bringing to an end the letter writing campaign.

On March 23, 1979 a letter addressed to Quinn with copies to the several persons at the highest levels read, "This letter stems from our meeting of Monday, March 19, 1979, where in the presence of Mr. Anthony Olive and Mr. Robert Woods and with acrimony in your voice, you ordered me to stop writing letters to the officials in management (public servants like myself) regarding the poor working conditions in the Virgin Islands Government Tax Division. Were you suggesting that I call the "night line?"

It should be noted that in many of his public appearance, Governor Juan Luis has used the phrase "law and order." This phrase "law and order" has been much abused in recent years, but if law and order means anything, it means that everyone, Rich, Poor, President, Plumber, Chief, Director and Commissioner obey the law; that the law has no favorites; that before it all, men stand equal.

For your information, the record shows that I was the one who requested to be relieved of the responsibilities of acting Chief of the Delinquent Accounts and Returns Branch owing to the same working conditions which exist today. Also, regarding your assumption that I've disassociated myself from certain employees of the Tax Division, let me paraphrase the words of my leader Mr. Leroy Quinn, as he appeared before the Virgin Islands Senate for his confirmation hearing in 1975. Mr. Quinn said, "I do not have to associate with certain individuals after 5:00 p.m. in order to do the job required of me." It is only out of a sincere desire to work in at least an aura of semi-professionalism (a desire voiced by fellow Revenue Officers at a meeting chaired by Mr. Anthony Olive this afternoon) that I've constructively criticized the manner in which we operate. More importantly however, I've offered solutions, which have been deliberately ignored. It appears as if management would prefer to spite Liston Monsanto rather than improve working conditions in the Tax Division.

Honesty has become a very provocative virtue, especially in the Department of Finance and your impulsive order for me to stop writing letters can only be interpreted as an abuse of discretionary power.

In conclusion, it is worth noting that the whole concept of democracy is based upon understanding the other fellow's point of view and of trying to live and be free without encroaching on the freedom of others. For this reason, if it becomes necessary for an employee to express his thoughts in writing, management should never attempt to use fear as a means of discouraging that employee. Such tactics can only result in magnificent obsessions."

By exchanging letters with me, Reuben Wheatley was at least able to counterbalance any difficulty he may have had with my reaction to his phoniness. Quinn and Olive, on the other hand, were apprehensive fearing widespread destruction.

In the intervening time Congressional and Carter Administration officials were toying with the idea of extending the United States Internal Revenue Service to the Virgin Islands to take over the collection of taxes in the territory. The federal officials were dissatisfied over the failure of the Virgin Islands Government to get collection taxes in view of continuing requests for Ad Hoc assistance to Washington. The powers that be in the Virgin Islands became deaf to all suggestions bordering on the proposed federal takeover of tax collections in the territory. Who would be so bereft of their senses that they'd say something like that? It was true that the taxes were not being collected, but Quinn's interest in the job as Commissioner of Finance supervising the activities of the Tax Division jointly with Edward Thomas (lest you forget, Olive was only a figure head) had not waned and furthermore there was no way that the Virgin Islands Government and those people profiting from what was going on would give up the goose laying golden eggs. A carefully designed serpentine plot had to be formed with an eye towards retentiveness.

The Republican Territorial Committee voiced "great shock" at what it called "the tyrannical action of the Democratic Administration," in Washington "in the arbitrary takeover of the Collection of the taxes of the Virgin Islands." They issued a statement saying that they would turn to fellow Republicans in Washington to seek help in "pressing their strong opposition." Then Governor Juan Luis cabled President Carter in an appeal for assistance in stopping "the federal takeover of our income tax Collection."

Luis pointed out that it was the second time that he had brought to the President's attention the fact that "the people of the United States Virgin Islands are vehemently opposed to a federal takeover of our income tax Collections." He furthermore went on to say that a great number of private organizations and many elected leaders had stated their opposition to the move and termed it "colonialism." He also noted that such a move conflicted with federal authorization granted for writing our own constitution, "a move toward greater autonomy and self-determination."

Despite all the heavy blame, Quinn and company operating under their laissez faire principle were hell bent on holding on to the income-producing activity called the Tax Division. Their servility to a governmental system mired in mediocrity and their unwillingness to enforce the tax laws had blinded them into believing that they were indeed a carbon copy of the United States Internal Revenue Service.

By this time, because of the volatile dispositions of certain employees in management and the abnormal turnover of employees in an organization requiring a high degree of confidentialness, the Tax Division had become an alien place for most of us. Personally, I had written a large number of letters which were all designed to bring order to a Tax Division fraught with problems. The Governors (Evans, King and Luis), the Lieutenant Governors (Maas, Addie Ottley, Luis and Henry Millin, Sr.), the Legislature (Earle B. Ottley, Ruby Rouse, et al) had all been made aware of what was going on but indentured as they were to the system, they refused to do anything.

For me, the Tax Division had become a chamber of horrors. My fate was hanging in the balance. Having vowed to use any measure short of violence to support my cause, the time had come for me to reveal my real intentions. I was going to give publicity to everything that I had been exposed to in my fight against "City Hall." I had to strengthen myself just a little bit more before releasing any additional information to a Virgin Islands apathetic public.

On July 31, 1979, I wrote to Quinn sending copies to Luis, Millin and Olive. I said,

GOVERNMENT OF
THE VIRGIN ISLANDS OF THE UNITED STATES
CHARLOTTE AMALIE, ST. THOMAS 00801
———— 0 ————
DEPARTMENT OF FINANCE
TAX DIVISION

July 31, 1979

Mr. Leroy A. Quinn
Commissioner of Finance
Department of Finance
St. Thomas, Virgin Islands 00801

Dear Mr. Quinn:

A recent survey of the employees in our Tax Division has disclosed that we have gone past the days when our organization-with the use of pertinent guidelines, depended upon the joint action of a group of people in which individual interests were subordinated to group unity and efficiency, thereby increasing productivity. So far this year however, there have been a few incidents that seem not just coincidental, but downright eerie, and as a result, forces me to write.

Today, because of poor management and supercilious displays, the Tax Division has declined to the point where no longer are we respected or recognized as the most powerful income producing activity of the VirginIslands Government. Furthermore, the fiscal crises besetting the Territory are due largely to our poor performance.

Today's Tax Division is loaded with personal power plays, sporadic infighting, malingering, spurious relationships, Employees pretending to be overly zealous, and continuing efforts by almost everyone in authority to subordinate the Delinquent Accounts & Returns Branch below the level of the Audit Branch, the Processing Branch, and the Reviewer/Classifier/Conferee, in order to convert the branch's duties (which are now far below the level of the U.S. Internal Revenue Service) into that of a glorified collecting agency.

Some employees of the Branch have been contributing immensely to its decadence. Examples are: (a) Assignment of the Assistant Chief (a position that everyone knows should be abolished) to the Office Collection Force to do the physical work required of a junior Revenue Officer or a potential Revenue Officer (b) Usage of the Assistant Chief as a substitute to prepare simple returns on the island of St. John in lieu of junior Agents and Officers. (c) Sophisticated attitude on the part of certain peers of the Chief to give him instructions as to how the Branch should function, serving only to tarnish the Branch's image, and simultaneously causing subordinates to take the liberty of telling the Chief how to supervise the activities of the Branch.

Yesterday's Tax Division, although in need of improvement, held regular meetings, which were attended by employees possessing intense pride and mutual respect for each other. Cars were readily available for the Revenue Officers use, social functions were held and softball games were played against teams from the Tax Divisions in St. Croix and Puerto Rico, as a means of boosting the morale of the employees. All in all, petty jealousies were held to a minimum.

But lest the foregoing becloud other issues, let me state that we now have an expanded Tax Division, and with the issuance of an organizational chart (the first step in your seemingly reorganizational plans) we should no longer worry about certain opportunistic employees exceeding their authority by taking upon themselves powers that are only vested in management. We must now however, focus our attention on the United States Congress, where at present there is a bill (H. R. 3756), which would not only allow "Federal Officials to assume the responsibility of supervising the tax collection process, but would simultaneously serve as an affront to the Revenue Officers of the Virgin Islands, especially those of us who have brought to your attention-based on our training by the United States Internal Revenue Service, the many troubled areas, which continue to retard or otherwise stymie the collection activity.

In retrospect, reorganizing the Delinquent Accounts & Returns Branch as recommended by the Revenue Officers in letters to you, would have given the Branch a major injection of elan, and furthermore, would have wiped out completely, the moral problem whcih now pervades.

The credit procured by a lie lasts only till the truth comes out, and if the Virgin Islands Government is able to compromise the proposed take-over by the Federal Government by enlisting the services of certain federal agents and Revenue Officers, who incidentally have been trained in the same manner as locals, these same importees (because of their knowledge, skill, experience, etc.) will waste little time in finding out that there exists in the Virgin Islands Tax Division, a moral problem of massive proportion.

The chickens are apparently coming home to roost -much to the detriment of the people of the Virgin Islands. But more importantly, however, unless and until management decides to correct the flagrant injustices within the Virgin Islands Tax Division, it appears certain that the Federal Government will take over the activities thereof. I say this unreservedly.

Very truly yours,

Liston B. Monsanto
Internal Revenue Officer

c.c. Gov. Juan Luis
Lt. Gov. Henry A. Millin
Mr. Anthony P. Olive

On August 3, 1979, I wrote to Olive with copies to Luis, Millin and Quinn. I said,

GOVERNMENT OF

THE VIRGIN ISLANDS OF THE UNITED STATES

CHARLOTTE AMALIE, ST. THOMAS 00801

DEPARTMENT OF FINANCE

TAX DIVISION

August 3, 1979

Mr. Anthony P. Olive
Director-Tax Division
Department of Finance
St. Thomas, V. I. 00801

Dear Mr. Olive:

On the premise that one person with courage constitutes a majority, I take this opportunity to write to you regarding the promises that you made to the Internal Revenue Officers on March 23, 1979 to improve working conditions in the delinquent Accounts and Returns Branch.

Incidentally, even now as I write, Mr. Terrence Brunn, Mr. Kenneth Hansen, Mrs. Lucia Thomas, Mr. Jens Todman, Mr. Ulrie Vialet, and Mr. Robert Woods are all on annual leave from the Branch. Consequently, two men (Lima and Monsanto) must do the work required of the absentees and the prospective Revenue Officers that you contemplate on bringing from the United States Internal Revenue Service. Is it any wonder that we are mired in a fiscal crisis?

Without wandering too far afield however, it is important to note that many of the Revenue Officers present at the March 23rd meeting feel that a tongue in cheek approach was used to convey your feelings, inasmuch as conditions have taken a downward trend since that time.

In order to keep abreast of any developments in the Tax Division (our place of employment), an employee is forced to (a) listen to the news on radio and television, (b) read one of the daily newspapers or (c) adhere to the grapevine. Nothing is said to us in a formal manner. The news of a take-over of the Tax Division by the Federal Government, proves that knowledge is of two kinds. We know a subject ourselves, or we know where we can find it.

Amid all the rumors and conjecture however, the Revenue Officers of the Virgin Islands have good reason to be perplexed as well as disturbed. The Tax Division is the pride of the Department of Finance, thanks to the devoted support of certain Virgin Islands taxpayers. Our enthusiasm wasn't enhanced when we learned of bill H. R. 3756, since a take-over by the Federal Government or the addition of federally affiliated Revenue Officers to our present staff, would serve only as a slap in the face of the local Revenue officer, who has been trained by the same United States Internal Revenue Service.

Truly, justice is effective when it is administered by wisdom, safeguarded by fairness and ever tempered with mercy.

Very truly yours,

Liston Monsanto
Internal Revenue Officer

c. c.   Gov. Juan Luis
      Lt. Gov. Henry Millin
      Mr. Leroy A. Quinn

Mr. Leroy Quinn and Mr. Anthony P. Olive with the blessings of Juan Luis and Henry Millin, Sr., had been impervious to suggestions offered by me hoping to transform inexperience into accomplishment. As a public servant like them, continuing to operate from a subordinate position, I had suggested that a study of the ramifications of the Tax Division be made with a view towards restoring order in the workplace. They had access to a broad array of information but misusing power ostentatiously was their first priority.

The chain of authority was being used in inverse order. Olive was shielding Quinn, Quinn was shielding Millin and Millin was shielding Juan Luis who, without hearing from Ulrie Vialet, had made the unilateral decision to suspend him from duty. These reckless good for nothings had to be exposed for what they really were.

While Quinn and the others were attempting to take the moral high ground, fortuitously I found Fred Clarke through a friend who, like Mr. Clarke lived on St. Croix. Until Fred Clarke had exposed to the public through the contents of my letters exactly what was happening in the Tax Division: "I had no idea that he was doing a weekly five minute radio program in which he would vent his frustrations over what was taking place in our government. I later found Fred Clarke to be a most eloquent speaker with a keen sense of what was going on in the Virgin Islands. He was unlike most Virgin Islanders, unreserved in speech with a flair for the dramatics. I had never met Fred Clarke, but after what he had done in reading my letters I thought it vitally important for me to meet him. I needed to thank him for his help. I launched a minor investigation geared to finding Mr. Clarke. I found him with little difficulty sitting in a bar in Christiansted, St. Croix. Fred Clark felt that serving was far better than self-serving. He told me that he had known what was going on in the Tax Division for some time, but in the absence of documentary evidence he was somewhat restricted from airing what he had been told.

What Fred Clarke had read from my letters was very good fodder to be used against "City Hall" at a time when the federal government was entertaining thoughts of taking over the Tax Collections in the Territory. Here now are some of the actual words used by Fred Clarke in his description of what was happening in the Tax Division: "The Virgin Islands economy is so deep in the red that everybody connected with the financial situation in government just gotta have bloodshot eyes and if what I've been reading is true, this might have been avoided; plus the fact that up in Washington there is a proposal that the Collection of taxes in the Virgin Islands be taken over by the United States Revenue Department. If what I've been reading is true, this might have been unnecessary and there's been a lot of noise about uncollected taxes. More than a couple of dem boys have told Washington we can handle our tax problems. But at least as of now, I ain't heard one single person say that the local government had been forewarned about the mounting amount of taxes that are uncollected and what could be done to, at least, start a steady increase and bring more revenue to the Virgin Islands. I ain't going to go into all the details. There's just too much involved for this program. But I am going to touch on some of the highlights from the many letters that were sent to government officials; copies of which I now have, starting with a letter that was written to the Governor on February 17, 1978, more than one year and a half ago, advising him that unless corrections were made in the operations of the Tax Division the morale of the Revenue Officers was falling so fast that unless corrections were made, the main purpose of the Revenue Officers, promoting voluntary compliance with tax laws, would be defeated. The Governor, apparently, never answered that letter. The Director of the Tax Division was advised, also well over a year ago, that his position regarding the status of Revenue Officers, treating them as Collection Agents and not as trained Revenue Officers, plus advising them that he had the authority to personally promote whomever he chose regardless of seniority or ability was destroying the Division. There were repeated warnings that the establishment of a Special Procedures Officer and an Assistant Chief of the Delinquent Accounts and Returns Branch was completely unnecessary, was a waste of money and manpower and particularly in the area of the Special Procedures Officer, opened up the Tax Division to the possibilities of bribery, in a letter to the Director of Personnel, the Revenue Officers emphasized that the Special Procedures Officer is the only person in the Virgin Islands with the authority to process offers in compromise made by persons trying to compromise their liabilities for lesser than the amount due, nationally, it was pointed out, this type of work is done by a Special Procedures section and there are hints in the letters I have that some Revenue Officers were, in effect, forced out of their jobs. Favoritism became the order of the day and continues to plague the division. Of a most serious note, is a paragraph in a letter written to the Director of the Tax Division on December 8, 1978, in which a veteran Revenue Officer in defending members of the same area of employment stated, and I quote, "Fortunately for me, I've been with the Division long enough to witness a high degree of insubordination and isolated cases of certain trusted employees attempting to defraud the Virgin Islands Government through the filing of fraudulent income tax returns. Such behavior has been condoned by management for so long that as a result, we are now surrounded by employees who display a holier than thou attitude."

An out and out charge of fraud, or attempted fraud, within the Tax Division and no answer to his letter or charges and as recently as a few weeks ago, the Finance Commissioner and the Director of the Tax Division were again advised of the loss of revenues to the government, the strong possibility of the United States taking over the tax Collections despite the fact that the local Revenue Officers were all trained by the United States Revenue Service and have the same training and the same background as any federal officer who would replace them and copies of these letters, I note, were also sent to the Governor and Lieutenant Governor and no responses. Personally, I think the green barn has been listening to the wrong people when they seek the answers to why tax collections are so delinquent in the Virgin Islands. I suggest that dem boys invite some of the Revenue Officers to the floor of the Senate and let them tell where, why and for how long, taxes due have been slipping away from the government and what should be done to stop the leaks."

Quinn was rabid with anger. He was being exposed. He quickly fired off a press release to the Daily News which said: "Commissioner of Finance, Leroy A. Quinn, has taken strong exception to a radio broadcast by Fred Clarke over a St. Croix station on Thursday, August 16th. Clarke purportedly read from letters given him by some unidentified person or persons. In these letters, serious allegations were made against the employees of the Tax Division of the Department of Finance," Quinn said. "I consider it a deplorable form of irresponsibility reporting for Clark to have read these letters before attempting to determine the truth. I categorically reject any attack on my integrity, as well as the integrity of the employees of the Tax Division," Commissioner Quinn stated.

He noted that the Inspections Branch of the Internal Revenue Service periodically checked the operations of the Tax Division and has yet to find any of the problems mentioned by the reporter. The anti-government attitude of Mr. Clarke permeates all his radio programs, Quinn concluded.

Quinn was caught with his pants down. What Inspection Branch was he honestly talking about? The Tax Division had always been unwilling to use the guidelines of the United States Internal Revenue Service - guidelines that were constantly being used by their Inspection Branch as a means of determining whether their personnel was playing the game according to Hoyle. We were operating the Virgin Islands way.

Fred Clarke came back with an answer of his own to Quinn's press release. He said, "Hot damn, we struck a nerve. The normally mild-mannered Mr. Leroy A. Quinn, Commissioner of Finance, has issued a press release in which he accuses me of purportedly reading from some letters from some unidentified person or persons and secondly, of an anti-government attitude that, he says, permeates all of my radio programs. Shucks, the mail delivery must be even slower on St. Thomas than it is on St. Croix. Either that or Mr. Leroy Quinn ain't reading his mail. Let me clear that up a little. On March 10, 1978, a letter tells of the worsening morale in the Department of Finance and Tax Division, it was addressed to, you guessed it, Mr. Leroy A. Quinn, Commissioner of Finance. March 20, 1978, a letter spoke of gross management in the Tax Division and it was addressed to, you're right again, Mr. Leroy A. Quinn. April 20, 1978, a letter addressed to Anthony P. Olive, Director of the Tax Division, discussed, again morale problems in that Division and a copy was sent to, yep, Commissioner Quinn. A letter I quoted a portion of verbatim on this program, dated December 8, 1978, citing cases of certain trusted employees attempting to defraud the Virgin Islands Government through the filing of fraudulent income tax returns, was addressed to Anthony P. Olive, Director of the Tax Division and if you say a copy was sent to Leroy Quinn, you win again. As recently as March 23rd and July 31st of this year, letters again raised the sad morale situation in the Tax Division and they were addressed to, right again, Mr. Leroy A. Quinn, Commissioner of Finance. On August 3, 1979, not three weeks ago, a letter struck out against the sad conditions in the Tax Division, mailed to Anthony P. Olive, Director of the Tax Division and a copy sent to the Governor, the Lieutenant Governor and can you believe it, Mr. Leroy A. Quinn. Now, he says I purportedly read from letters from unidentified person or persons, regarding the allegation that an anti-government attitude permeates this program. I just gotta make a couple of remarks. If Mr. Quinn would qualify his charge by stating I am anti-bad government, I would readily confess. I got this funny habit of putting the welfare of the people first, which is what I always thought was the reason for the Democratic form of government. But I have noticed that ever since the Governor slammed the door of a public meeting in the face of a reporter from the Daily News because he didn't like the way the reporter handled the stories, it has become the custom for all the top government officials in the Virgin Islands to accuse the news media of being anti-government, just for telling the truth. The news media was to blame for the failure of the local government receiving twenty million bucks. It was the news media's fault the hospitals went to hell and on and on. Yes, Mr. Quinn, if making a lot of noise because the people are getting run around the barn is being anti-government, in your opinion, there's damned little hope for any of us. When I addressed myself to these other ills in government, I never heard a sound from you, or any other government official, that I was being anti-government. Once, however, I strike at the ills in the Tax Division, you parrot the remarks made by others currently in government that when things are wrong they are wrong only because of the news media and those in the news media, you knew the information I presented last week was actually from copies of letters, several of which had been mailed to you or you received copies of as recently as weeks ago and as far back as a year and a half ago. You knew who had written and who had signed those letters. If your accusation that an anti-government attitude permeates this program, I can only state that then, the present administration can claim, technically, it is a government of the people and by the people, but it cannot, in any way, address itself as a government for the people."

On August 21, 1979, the Revenue Officers dispatched a letter to the Editor of the Virgin Islands Daily News which stated, "Because the Tax Division is fraught with morale problems, which seemingly the Commissioner is attempting to hide, we (representing 95% of the Internal Revenue Officers assigned to the St. Thomas District), were not at all surprised to read in the Daily news of August 20, 1979 that Mr. Leroy A. Quinn criticized the honest radio remarks that were made by Mr. Fred Clarke and which we believe were designed to give the tax-payers of the Virgin Islands an insight into what is currently going on in their Tax Division.

Mindful of the fact that those who exercise significant power usually mask its use by claiming that they are acting in the public's interest or following established procedures, it behooves us to commend Mr. Clarke very highly for his objectivity in reporting the news and bringing to the public's attention certain contributing factors that have presumably led to the decline in revenues, thereby forcing the federal government to take over the activities of the Tax Division. Yes! There are glaring morale problems in the Virgin Islands Tax Division which, thanks to an objective reporter, have been exposed. In view of these problems, it is our sincere hope that Commissioner Quinn does not blame us for any decrease in government revenues." Signing the letter were Revenue Officers Terrence Brunn, Mario Lima, Liston Monsanto, Alvin Swan and Ulrie Vialet. Revenue Officer Todman was in White Plains, New York receiving a letter from Quinn telling him how impressed he was with the quality of his work and praising him for willingly accepting an assignment to travel to St. Croix to assist in resolving some of the more difficult cases on that island. Thank God we did not need him.

Quinn found himself in a cul-de-sac being beaten out of shape. He had impulsively attacked Fred Clarke for telling the truth and exposing him to the public. I had to take advantage of the situation. So on August 22, 1979, I wrote to him sending copies to Luis, Millin, Olive and Woods. I said, "Like crusaders, who have very definite opinions on such universal subjects as religion, race or politics, many people are spreading rumors and interpreting our existing morale problems in the Tax Division to mean that Liston Monsanto is seeking some admirable goal - Chief of Delinquent Accounts and Returns Branch.

These people, perhaps loyalists and allies to the office, are zealously trying to persuade others to adopt their ideas and falsehoods for reasons better known to them. In light of this however, I feel constrained to clear the air.

At the outset, let me state that my only desire is to see a reorganization of the Delinquent Accounts and Returns Branch as promised by you in our meeting of February 28, 1977, later recorded in a letter to you on March 4, 1977. It would be preposterous of me to entertain any thoughts about being Chief of Delinquent Accounts and Returns Branch.

Furthermore, you may recall that in another letter to you dated March 23, 1979, I stated that I was the one who requested to be relieved of the responsibilities of Acting Chief of the Delinquent Accounts and Returns Branch owing to the same working conditions which exist today. Mr. Quinn, whatever little intelligence I possess tells me that there is no place for a person like me in the top rung of the Delinquent Accounts and Returns Branch. Blind loyalty is not my forte. The Tax Division has become a classic example of the Peter Principle at work. Hierarchies such as ours caused Doctor Laurence Peter to formulate the Peter Principle (i.e. in a hierarchy every employee tends to rise to his level of incompetence).

In conclusion, let me say that I have always advocated working in an atmosphere of harmony and I sincerely feel that if an effort is made to reorganize the Delinquent Accounts and Returns Branch such as you promised in our meeting of February 28, 1977, our existing morale problems would be reduced."

Everybody except Leroy A. Quinn would have thought that the reasonable solution to dismissing the claims of fraud and erasing the notion that the Tax Division was doing things for show would have been an internal investigation and an accelerated Collection drive.

So irrational with rage was he that with the approval of Governor Juan Luis, the appointing authority, who was covertly coaching him, he sent me a letter on August 24, 1979, which said, "I have decided to initiate your dismissal from your position, Internal Revenue Officer IV, in the Tax Division, Department of Finance, Government of the Virgin Islands, pursuant to Title 3 of the Virgin Islands Code, Chapter 25, 'Personnel Merit Systems,' Section 540. I am recommending by copy of this letter to Governor Juan Luis, as appointing authority, that he dismiss you from your employment effective September 14, 1979, at 5:00 p.m. You may appeal the proposed personnel action to the Government Employees' Service Commission within ten (10) days from receipt of this letter, which contains the following statement of charges against you: (1) beginning in October 1975, you have been attempting to tarnish the image of the Tax Division, Department of Finance and the integrity of its employees through a stream of malicious letters. During the weeks of August 13th and August 20th, 1979, you released letters to the media which contained such serious allegations as fraud and the preparation of fraudulent tax returns in an attempt to disrupt the operation of the Department of Finance, its Tax Division, Revenue Officers and employees, (2) beginning with your letter of June 9, 1976 and continuing in your letter of February 7th and 9th, March 16th and 23rd, July 31st, August 3rd and 22nd, 1979, you have been engaged in character assassinations of your co-workers and supervisor who have refused to join you in your disruptive actions, (3) on Monday, March 19, 1979, in the presence of your immediate supervisor, Mr. Robert Woods and the Director of the Tax Division, Mr. Anthony Olive, you were ordered to discontinue using government equipment, supplies and the letterhead of the Tax Division in writing these malicious letters. You were also ordered to discontinue hand delivery of these letters during the regular working hours at this same meeting, but this practice continues, (4) you have failed to devote eight (8) hours each day to our job for which you are being paid, (5) On December 20, 1978, you violated the Disclosure Rules of the Internal Revenue Code, Section 6013, of which you had full knowledge.

As head of the Department of Finance, I feel it incumbent on me to take this action to prevent the further deterioration of the Tax Division. Because of the above-described circumstances, I believe your continued presence at your duty station would be detrimental to the Department and the public interest. I am therefore, hereby relieving you temporarily of your duties with pay. This relief of duties with pay is indefinite and will remain in effect until such time as the Government Employees' Service Commission hears your appeal, if any, and issues and Order. Copies of all correspondence and Notice of Appeal ought to be directed to me."

Quinn's every move since becoming Commissioner of Finance in 1975 had been chronicled by me. He was an arrant liar who did not believe that a man must learn to obey before he can know how to command. His letter of dismissal sounded so surreal that it had me repeating from the Bible the following, "For it is better, if the will of God be so, that ye suffer for well doing than for evil doing." I had become a part of an ugly vicious attack that required legal representation. The extreme test was now magnified. I knew that aristocrats like Albert Commissong and others appointed by the Governor were comprising the Government Employees' Service Commission and I also knew that there was no way that I could be vindicated locally. I had to get my case to the Third Circuit Court of Appeals in Philadelphia, Pennsylvania.

In my search for an attorney I was favored by circumstances rather than mere chance. Attorney Brenda Hollar had just resigned from the staff of the Attorney General's Office and was in the process of setting up her private practice in the Professional Building east of the Emancipation Garden. She was about to unlock the door to her new office when I approached her and introduced myself. I did not know the lady. As a matter of fact, I had never seen her before. At any rate, she invited me into her office where I explained my purpose. I asked her to kindly apply the law to the factual letters that I had in my possession. She made a cursory reading of my letters, nodded in the affirmative and asked me to leave them for her perusal.

From that day, Attorney Brenda Hollar became my attorney. Meanwhile, Governor Juan Luis had all of a sudden become interested in installing a fraud hot-line. On August 29, 1979, he issued a press release which read as follows, "Governor Juan Luis today announced that he will soon install in the Governor's offices on St. Thomas and St. Croix a fraud hot-line for citizens to tip government house on incidents of wrongdoing that may transpire in the various departments and agencies of the Executive Branch. The Chief Executive emphasized that in view of rampant allegations throughout the community, relative to fraud, corruption and illegal practices occurring in the Government, that it is necessary to implement this timely project in an effort to halt such practices. Governor Luis said that citizens will discover that blowing the whistle on waste and fraud in Government is as easy as picking up the telephone and reporting wrongdoing. In defending the soon-to-be installed system, Governor Luis said he 'is optimistic that this service will significantly help to protect taxpayers' dollars and also serve as a deterrent in the Administration's drive against misspending and fraud in Government.' The Governor has recommended that the legislature take steps to implement a similar system."

Led by Mario "Tansy" Lima, my fellow Revenue Officers showed their displeasure with Quinn's spiteful actions by writing to him with copies to Luis, Millin, Sr., the Government Employees' Service Commission and Mr. Leslie Millin. These were the same people to whom Quinn had sent copies of my letter of dismissal.

The Revenue Officers' letter was dated September 10, 1979 and stated, "We, the Internal Revenue Officers of the St. Thomas District, would like to voice our feelings of puzzlement at your recommendation to the Governor for the dismissal of Revenue Officer Liston Monsanto, whom to our knowledge, has committed no sin but that of being vocal, like the rest of us, in voicing the many problems that are causing the massive morale problems that are gradually eroding the Tax Division. Mr. Monsanto, who has twenty-five (25) years of service in the Tax Division, has always been a model of decorum and a source of inspiration to us, his Junior Revenue Officers, not only for his ability in performing his chores, but by the courteous manner in which he exercises the authority vested in him. It is because of these reasons that your recommendation to Governor Juan Luis appears spiteful. Isn't it coincidental that a time when the public's attention is focused on the Revenue's continuing complaints that you've decided to take this action? Because we live in a country of laws, where every individual is afforded certain rights, we as individuals and fellow Revenue Officers will continue to voice our concerns in much the same manner as Mr. Monsanto. Furthermore, your attempts to dismiss Mr. Liston Monsanto will serve only to further increase tensions within the Delinquent Accounts and Returns Branch and further expand the existing morale problems in our Tax Division."

On September 13, 1979, Mr. Norman Chelquist, a retired government employee, wrote to Governor Juan Luis complaining about his past due retirement check. A copy of his letter was sent to the Daily News. What attracted my attention in Chelquist's letter was the part where he stated that, "Recently one of our respected commentators, Fred Clarke, criticized the operations of the Department of Finance and these criticisms were publicly upheld by members of the Department. It has therefore become glaringly obvious that not only something, but a great deal is wrong in the Finance Department. It is also indisputable evidence that the time is overly ripe for the replacement of the Commissioner of Finance. I earnestly trust that your Excellency will see fit to pursue this remedial action."

The people against Quinn's despicable action were showing their strong feelings in press releases and interviews by the local newspaper. On September 17, 1979, Lima and the other Revenue Officers in the St. Thomas District called for the transfer of Anthony Olive to another Department on the grounds that he had failed to demonstrate the leadership or know-how to handle the job. Lima spoke to Penny Feuerzeig of the Daily News staff, telling her, "We have been complaining about conditions in the Tax Division since before 1978 and nothing has been done. Things have worsened instead of getting better." Lima, appearing as spokesman for the Revenue Officers went on to tell Penny that, "It was not anything personal against Olive. It's just that he lacks the leadership to move us ahead. We don't feel he's capable. Our main problem is Olive." Lima expanded his remarks by saying, "We are drifting without any direction. Two Revenue Officers have resigned and haven't been replaced because nobody wants to work there. Some of us haven't resigned because we feel it's our duty to stay there. We are going to continue to fight until they correct the problems. Lagging Collections are because of the lack of leadership on the part of Mr. Olive, mainly."

But I could not repress the urge to laugh when I was shown a copy of a letter dated September 19, 1979, from Lieutenant Governor Henry A. Millin, Sr. to the Revenue Officers. While I had been in the Tax Division writing letters and sending copies to Millin, he had lacked the courage to even approach me. He was running from me because he knew that I was not guilty of any wrongdoing. I could not believe that Henry Millin would take advantage of my absence to finally respond to the Revenue Officers. Here is what he wrote, "Receipt is acknowledged of a copy of your letter dated September 10, 1979 to the Honorable Leroy A. Quinn, Commissioner of Finance. As you probably know, the Department of Finance is not one of the four departments for which I have been delegated some "oversight" responsibility. Personally, and even prior to my return to government service, I have been very concerned over the fact that stated displeasure on the part of Internal Revenue Officers probably results in a loss of considerable revenue which the Territory is entitled to and desperately needs to solve its budgetary problems. From previous correspondence, copies of which have been sent to me, I can only conclude that some of the displeasure on the part of Revenue Officers stems from the fact that they are not allowed to determine the organizational set-up of the Division, which obviously is not their function or responsibility. It is my sincere hope, however, that personnel in the Tax Division will recognize that their role is an extremely important role involving the functions of the Government of the Virgin Islands and that they will strive to perform in a manner becoming persons entrusted with such great responsibility in order that their efforts will redound to the benefit of the Virgin Islands Treasury and consequently to all inhabitants of the Territory. Finally, it is also my hope that if there are other basic causes for what is alleged to be a morale problem with the division, there may be a speedy solution by mans of mutual agreement resulting from the spirit of compromise and understanding."

I had been removed from the Tax Division at the time and therefore had nothing to do with the Revenue Officers response to Millin's letter. They wrote to Millin on September 21, 1979, saying, "We acknowledge receipt of your letter dated September 19, 1979. The Revenue Officers realize that the Department of Finance is not one of the four (4) departments which you have been delegated to "oversight." However, because of the great trust we hold for your high office and realizing that its scope of concern is not limited to those departments only, we have in seeking the best interest of the Government, decided to address our complaints to you on several occasions. On February 2, 1979, and upon your request, we forwarded to you a copy of our letter of February 17, 1978, to Governor Juan Luis. In this letter we did not ask, as we have never asked, to hold any participation in determining the organizational set-up of the Division. We simply stated the various problems that plagued the Tax Division then and continue to do so at this writing. We further would like to stress that we have always been dedicated government employees, aware of our duties and responsibilities and it is not because of us that the government's revenues have been steadily decreasing while visual signs of affluence abound in the private sector. Because of the high degree of respect we hold, not only for your office, but for you as a respected member of our community we thank you sincerely for your concern. We, like you, desire that with a spirit of compromise and understanding the morale problem that is existing in the Tax Division will soon be resolved and if you so desire, we stand ready to further expound on these at your earliest convenience." We never heard from Mr. Millin again.

On Friday, October 12, 1979, the headlines in the Daily News read, "Territorial Officials Attack Fed Tax Collection Proposal." In the details under the headlines it was stated that, "A provision in the proposed omnibus Territories Act for 1980 that would force a federal takeover of income tax Collections in the Virgin Islands and other U.S. Territories drew strong opposition Wednesday, at a hearing of the Senate Energy and Natural Resources Committee." The newspaper mentioned that the Virgin Islands were represented by Governor Juan Luis and Commissioner Leroy A. Quinn (Note: Anthony P. Olive, Tax Director, did not travel with the two men). The newspaper said that the controversial income tax takeover, which would turn local Collections systems over to the Internal Revenue Service was introduced by Rep. Phillip Burton, Democrat from California, Chairman of the House Subcommittee on Territorial Affairs and a long time critic of tax Collection efforts in the territories.

Burton said that the measure, which has already passed the House, would relieve the territories of the $3 million annual cost collecting their own taxes and would provide new tax revenues to ease their chronic fiscal problems. David Rosenbloom, International Tax Counsel, said the entire tax structure in the Territories needs review. He said a federal takeover of Collections would address only a limited part of the problem. Then on Monday, October 29, 1979, once again the headlines said, "Territorial Tax Systems Needing Overhaul, Report Says." In the opening paragraph the paper said, "Territorial income tax systems are functioning poorly and should be overhauled, a report from the U.S. Department of Treasury released here Thursday says." Then in the last paragraph of the news item, the paper closed by saying, "The Government of the Virgin Islands is on record as being opposed to changing the Territory's current systems of taxation.

When Governor Juan Luis commented on the reports of the inter-agency task force, he proposed an alternate option: Improvement of Collections and Enforcement Procedures with Technical Assistance Provided by the Internal Revenue Service."

There was nothing latent about these headlines and surely the members of the Government Employees Service Commission were reading them. This being the case, you would think that they would feel some kind of respect or appreciation for what I had been telling the powers that were in the Virgin Islands Government. They were without honor however.

Quinn was wasting the government's money and time trying to rid the Department of Finance of me. He brought in from the United States Internal Revenue Service a Robert Parkhurst who knew full well that the Tax Division was not operating in the style of the United States Internal Revenue Service. Whether he or any other witness for Quinn was paid off is anybody's guess.

In going before the Government Employees Service Commission I would be exhausting the first rung on the Appellate ladder. Again, my destination was the Third Circuit Court of Appeals in Philadelphia, Pennsylvania. Under the Virgin Islands Governmental System which was loaded with aristocrats and soldiers of fortune, there was no way that Liston Monsanto would be allowed to defeat the system. He had to be taught a lesson. It never occurred to anyone (i.e. Governor Luis, Lt. Governor Millin, Olive and even Quinn) that I had not been given any chance to refute the things with which I was being charged. They just didn't care.

On October 1, 1979, the matter came before Evelyn M. Williams, Albert Comissiong and Jose Garcia, all members of the G.E.S.C. and in an Order dated November 16, 1979, they concluded by saying, "The Commissioner of Finance has requested the dismissal of Mr. Monsanto because of the aforementioned acts, however, this Commission believes, in light of Mr. Monsanto's exemplary performance ratings, such an action would not serve the best interest of the Government of the Virgin Islands; a 90-day suspension without pay should suffice. It is therefore Ordered that Liston Monsanto be suspended for a period of 90 days without pay from his position as an Internal Revenue Officer IV in the Tax Division, Department of Finance of the Government of the Virgin Islands."

I immediately made a request through Attorney Brenda Hollar, that, the Government Employees Service Commission's decision be reversed, totally vindicating me from any wrongdoing. I didn't even bother to find out whether Albert Comissiong and the others were up to date in the filing and payment of their taxes.

On December 8, 1980, I received a political decision from the United States District Court of the Virgin Islands (Division of St. Thomas and St. John). The decision in the form of an Order was labeled Civil No. 79-351 and signed by Almeric L. Christian, Chief Judge. Here is what the Order said, "This case is before the Court on appeal from a November 16, 1979 decision of the Appellee Government Employees' Service Commission (hereinafter "GESC") suspending the Appellant for a period of ninety (90) consecutive days without pay from his position of Revenue Officer IV in the Tax Division, Department of Finance, Government of the Virgin Islands. After reviewing a certified copy of the record of the relevant GESC proceedings, the Brief and Reply Brief for the Appellant, as well as the Brief for the Appellee, this Court has come to the conclusion that the decision of the GESC is supported by "substantial evidence," Turnbull v. Holder, 11 V.I. 93, 98 (D.C.V.I. 1974) and is otherwise correct as a matter of law. The premises considered and the Court being fully advised, it is ordered that the November 16, 1979 decision of the Government Employees' Service Commission, suspending Appellant from his position as Revenue Officer IV in the Tax Division, Department of Finance, for a period of ninety (90) consecutive days without pay be and for the same is hereby, Affirmed."

The Court's decision stunned Lima and the other Revenue Officers who were not as familiar with the governmental system as I was. My indifference towards the legal document was tempered by the knowledge that I had expected the unfavorable decision all along. It was not something inflicted on me that I had found hard to bear. I had been doing the proper diligence with respect to what was going on from the start. Documentary evidence in my possession was proof of that. So in view of the foregoing there was no need for me to enter the realm of demagoguery in order to stir up the Revenue Officers. There was absolutely no need for me to make an appeal to their emotions. I did not have any misgivings. As long as I was being judged legally by "outsiders" such as the judges in the Third Circuit Court who did not know Quinn or myself and as long as I was operating on the thesis that incorruptible judges could not be bribed, I felt certain that I would be vindicated.

Lima and I, our curiosity piqued by the Turnbull versus Holder case that the Local District Court had used in rendering judgment, decided to research the matter. We visited the Public Library where we found the information that we were seeking. As laymen we went over it several times looking for relativity. We just couldn't find any. Mario Lima was such a faithful friend.

Unlike Kenneth Hansen and the others who had worked under my careful supervision, it is safe to say that Lima felt grateful over the way I had improved the overall ambiance of the Delinquent Accounts and Returns Branch. I had made it possible for them to attend their training programs and ultimately won the respect of the other Branch Chiefs who could no longer do to the Branch, the things they were guilty of doing when Ulric Benjamin was in charge. Kenneth Hansen, on the other hand, was an ingrate. Together with Roy Malone and Jens Todman, he would use ploys to gain advantage.

As noted earlier in this publication, Hansen knew that the position of Special Procedures Officer had stripped completely the Revenue Officers of their ability to perform quality work and he also knew that Ulric Benjamin, in order to avoid wandering from place to place, had convinced Wheatley that a Special Procedures Officer was needed. (Note: When Benjamin was the Supervisor of the Delinquent Accounts and Returns Branch supervising the activities of subordinates who were all untrained, he saw no need for a Special Procedures Officer. But after these same subordinates were formally trained with no thanks to him, he came to realize that a Special Procedures Officer was the answer).

Kenneth Hansen was a treacherous fellow. Thinking that I wanted him removed from the Government's payroll he had this pernicious habit of sneaking around the office watching for a chance to take back news to the people at the highest levels whom he foolishly believed had an affinity for him. Blinded by the little pittance that he was receiving on paydays he never suspected that he was being used. In March of 1979, while typing a letter to the Director of Personnel asking for salary increases for Hansen and the others, I made a typographical error that caused me to discard the document in the form of scraps into the waste paper basket. I saw Hansen snooping around the area, but I did not see him when he went into the waste paper basket to retrieve and piece together the fragments of the document. It was only when he appeared as a witness for Quinn that I learned what he had done in order to prove to the good for nothings, comprising the Government Employees' Service Commission that I had not been doing the job for which I was being paid. It never occurred to him that the time that he had spent looking for the pieces in the waste paper basket and putting them together was also time for which he was being paid. Truly, I felt sorry for him.

Brenda Hollar, an attorney with a cheerful outlook on life, was very thorough in her preparation of my case. She stood ready, willing and able to face Quinn and my adversaries in a most corrupted Virgin Islands society. Because I had imposed on her the awesome responsibility of guiding me safely to the Promise Land, I became committed to her legal care. Quinn and company were wrongly judging my actions without considering my motives. I hadn't stolen anything. I hadn't murdered anybody. I was being punished by a group of "closed minded" people (the GESC) by way of quid pro quo. So while I was away on suspension from the office for ninety (90) days without pay, attorney Brenda Hollar did her duty preparing my case for the Third Circuit Court.

Following my departure from the Tax Division, a whole series of events happened. Quinn was still trying to the utmost to get rid of me, but because of my exemplary work performance history he was prohibited. He wanted to use Woods in his capacity of Chief of Delinquent Accounts and Returns Branch as the villain in rating me less-than-satisfactory in order to substantiate dismissal charges. But Woods, for reasons better known to him, would not take the bait. Approximately two-weeks after the GESC had rendered its decision not to dismiss me, Anthony Olive (Quinn's gofer) had signed a performance rating for Woods with comments eluding to the fact that he was not properly supervising his subordinates. The objective of writing those comments was to encourage Woods to erroneously rate me less-than-satisfactory in order to support his future attempts to dismiss me. But Olive's comments notwithstanding Woods, rated me satisfactory in all factors in a performance rating dated February 29, 1980 which was ten (10) days after I had completed my ninety (90) day suspension. As a result of Woods refusing to erroneously rate me, Olive refused to sign my performance rating and instead wrote to me on March 25, 1980. He said, "I am forwarding your employee performance report directly to the Commissioner's Office without my signature as I am not in agreement with the rater. Commissioner Quinn's letter to you, dated August 24, 1979, reflects the many reasons why I cannot concur with the rater. Being aware of my decision, it is anticipated that you will demonstrate a changed attitude and accept the realities of your job position for the best interest of the Government and the taxpayers of the Virgin Islands." No mention was made of my first salary check which management had seized following my return to the Tax Division - a check that was ultimately released to me on March 21, 1980 over a month after I had returned to work.

I had to respond to Olive, if only to show him and the others that I had remained unfazed by their wickedness. On March 26, 1980, I wrote him a letter sending copies to Luis, Millin, Quinn and Woods. I said,

Charlotte Amalie, St. Thomas
U. S. Virgin Islands 00801

March 26, 1980

Mr.   Olive
Direc   vision
Departmen   ance
St. Thomas, V.I. 00801

Dear Mr. Olive:

A glance at your unnecessary, paradoxical, and somewhat ambivalent memorandum of March 25, 1980 which was written on Government time, using Government stationery, and typed by a Tax Division employee, has led me to believe that the memorandum is either a pretentious display designed to harass and/or intimidate me, or you are attempting to amend your life during this lenten period through religious absolution. No matter which is true, I know that politics is like a race horse; hence, a good jockey must know how to fall with the least possible damage.

Based on my personal involvement in or observations of past events, it is distressing to note that certain things in our Tax Division are being made different in details, but not in substance. Favoritism, (as is evidenced by the presence of a number of delinquent accounts in our files, for which certain employees are liable, and the missing name of Kenneth Hansen on the "sign in" and "out" sheet), remains the order of the day, and has forced many dedicated and talented employees to unionize.

The fact that some people in management have been guilty of gross abuse of their positions -or negligence, causes me to remember that it was out of compassion for, and in deference to Governor Juan Luis, who inherited a host of problems that the Internal Revenue Officers decided on July 21, 1978 not to carry on a lawsuit against public servants, who by their appointed positions, had the opportunity to reassess and change policies, but instead chose to extend the programs of previous administrations, thereby resulting in the proposed take over of the Tax Division by the United States Internal Revenue Service.

It is incredible to believe that you would refuse to sign my performance rating after bragging before Senator Athniel Ottley and his Assistant Mr. David Browne on the afternoon of March 19, 1980, that my performance has always been satisfactory.

Furthermore, one would think that the head of any well-run organization given the same particulars, would immediately write to the employee's immediate supervisor reprimanding him for the nine-month delay in making the report available to the employee. Because of the fore-going, I seriously question the sincerity of your memorandum, which follows the seizure of my salary check for the pay period ending March 8, 1980. The unlawful seizure of my salary check was an unfair act causing me and my family a great deal of embarrassment. It was not until my immediate supervisor (Mr. Robert Woods) had intervened that I was able to receive my well-earned check.

It does now seem in retrospect that you could have revealed-perhaps on a most confidential basis, your intentions to seize my check. If you had done so, much of the agitation of the last few days would not have developed. With this latest act of intolerance together with the continuing attitude of indifference displayed by management, one can envision an endless train of lawsuits emanating from employees aggrieved by ill treatment.

With respect to Commissioner Quinn's letter of August 24, 1979 of which you speak, please be reminded that I was subsequently reinstated to my position by the Government Employees Service Commission. And now, since it appears as if the organizational structure was changed during my absence, I would like to request an authentic organizational chart, which would show me that Mr. Woods is indeed my Immediate Supervisor, who works closely with me and who is in a better position to rate me than anyone else in our organization.

Concerning the taxpayers of the Virgin Island to whom you refer in your last paragraph, I wonder how these same taxpayers would rate, or otherwise evaluate the performance of our Tax Division?

Finally, it goes without saying that this latest showy display on the part of top-level public servants (for which incidentally there is not the slightest twinge of guilt), does not coincide with the philosphy of the administration, and leaves a cloud of doubt that may linger throughout your tenure of office. It does, however, bring to mind the words of Mr. Adlai Stevenson as he wrote: "Those who corrupt the public mind are just as evil as those who steal from the public purse."

                    Sincerely,

                    Liston Monsanto
                    Internal Revenue Officer IV

cc: Governor Juan Luis
     Lt. Gov. Henry Millin
     Commissioner Quinn
     Mr. Robert Woods

As far as Quinn and Olive were concerned, Woods had been disloyal. They had been trying to get rid of me for over two years during which time they had initiated dismissal proceedings against me without any success. I had instead been suspended for a ninety (90) day period which resulted in a change in my anniversary date from June 17, 1980 to October 16, 1980. My performance rating was overdue and when Woods, my immediate supervisor, decided to prepare the report he once again gave me a satisfactory rating in every factor. When Olive saw what Woods had done he issued a statement saying, "On August 13, 1980, Mr. Monsanto's performance rating was transmitted to his supervisor, Mr. Robert Woods. In the transmittal it was noted that the employee was on leave without pay from 11/16/79 thru 2/18/80, thus changing his anniversary date from 6/17 to 10/16.

On two occasions, I reminded Mr. Woods that Mr. Monsanto's performance rating was past due. It was finally submitted to Director Quinn on January 19th with a satisfactory rating. On February 4th it was reviewed and reluctantly signed by me. By law I cannot change the rating and it has not been timely submitted. Mr. Monsanto was suspended for 90 days during this period after the Government Employees' Service Commission heard his case in which his dismissal was recommended."

And then Quinn wrote, "I do not concur with the ratings of Mr. Robert Woods, Chief DAR Branch. Mr. Monsanto's dismissal was recommended during the rating period. However, the Government Employees' Service Commission saw fit to instead suspend Mr. Monsanto for 90 days, which was sustained by the U.S. District Court for the Virgin Islands. Thus his work performance was far from acceptable. Since I cannot change the ratings and the fact that the supervisor delayed in processing the rating, I have no choice but to sign the rating which I do with great reluctance."

On the same day that Woods was preparing my satisfactory rating in every factor, Olive had an opening conference with some auditors from the United States Internal Revenue Service wherein he told them that the Delinquent Accounts and Returns Branch was divided into two factors; one with allegiance to management and the other with allegiance to me. He told them of the difficulty he was having in getting rid of me and presumably through some form of a quid pro quo persuaded Robert L. Parkhurst (one of the auditors) to break away from his training and experience thereby putting something derogatory in his report about me.

The law-breaking duo of Olive and Quinn wanted a third-party to write something negative about me in order to use it to substantiate a renewed attempt to dismiss me. Robert L. Parkhurst turned out to be a liar off the same ilk as Olive and Quinn. Without talking to me, without talking to Woods or any of the employees on my level, here is what he entered into his report, "Our review showed that the most experienced Revenue Officer in the St. Thomas office has the smallest workload, a condition that has existed for at least the past two years. During our audit, we observed that this employee spends a lot of time in the office reading newspapers and talking to other employees on non-work related matters. He appears to exert an overall disruptive influence on Collection operations. The St. Thomas Senior Revenue Officer discussed in this memorandum should be assigned a workload commensurate with his grade level and abilities. His performance should be monitored by Bureau Managers for a six-month period. If at the end of this period he has not shown marked improvement, disciplinary action should be taken. The Bureau cannot afford to tolerate "non-producers."

The original report was clearly dated February 11, 1981 but management, in a deliberate attempt to trump up false charges against me, had doctored it to show a date of February 17, 1981 on page one while pages two and three through inadvertence remained dated February 11, 1981. They just couldn't do anything right.

Because Woods had shown management through his aberrant behavior that he was not a company man, Quinn the taskmaster forced him to submit his resignation replacing him through a contract with John Ferrant, a stateside importee in a flagrant violation of the Personnel Merit System. Olive had previously admitted at my dismissal hearing that I was qualified to be Chief of the Delinquent Accounts and Returns Branch, but now he had joined with Quinn to hire Ferrant to erroneously rate me in order to substantiate another attempt to get rid of the man who had played a major role in him filling the position of Tax Director.

Roy Malone was another pitiless and pretentious person who held the position of Assistant Chief of the Delinquent Accounts and Returns Branch. When it came to the enforcement of the tax laws, cowardice enforced him to remain idle. Under Woods stewardship, Malone demonstrated a strong feeling of pleasure arising from a sense of well being, but now that Woods, the neophyte was gone, Ferrant who had previously worked for the United States Internal Revenue Service and understood the method or manner of the work required by the Branch, Roy Malone would become Ferrant's scapegoat.

Not knowing what the results or recommendations were of the Internal Revenue Audit performed by Robert Parkhurst, intuitively I wrote to Malone on April 28, 1981, sending a copy to Ferrant. I said, "An examination of the monthly production reports, St. Thomas District, shows that currently there are ten (10) positions carrying inventories of various sizes in the Delinquent Accounts and Returns Branch. Of the ten (10) positions, seven (7) of the individuals to whom an inventory has been assigned, are either on the top rung of the Delinquent Accounts and Returns Branch or hold top positions in the Revenue Officer classification. As one continually desirous of carrying out my fair share of the Branch's workload, earning my pay and working harmoniously with my colleagues, I took the liberty to conduct a spot-check survey of the accounts in the active and closed files, while simultaneously collating a number of accounts therein. Based on my findings, it appears that certain accounts requiring enforcement action together with other investigations are being assigned to me using seniority as justification. Because of the above, I'd like to know what criterion or criteria is being used in assigning accounts to the other individuals whose ability, experience, advanced training and wages far exceed my seniority. Your prompt response to my inquiry is appreciated." The sneaky Roy Malone had to be brought into the fray. He, like Quinn and Olive, wanted dialogue. He was afraid to write for the record. Now he was being forced to write and demonstrate to Ferrant how aggressive and forceful he could be and so he answered accordingly, "I have read your memorandum of April 28, 1981, one which I find very disturbing as your implications infer that cases are being assigned in other than the manner of directives in the manual. Assignment of cases are made based on dollar value and difficulty of the work as outlined in Section 5100 of the Manual (Exhibit 5100-18). Also consideration has to be given to inventory workloads in the hands of Revenue Officers so as to effect maximum closing of cases in the field. In addition, some higher grade work is assigned to a lower grade Revenue Officer in order to develop and broaden his scope for future advancement. It appears to me that much productive time is lost in the Branch when employees take unnecessary time to make spot-check surveys and write memorandums. If you feel that there is an injustice being done to you, please come in and discuss it with me rather than resort to memoranda. I'm sure matters can be resolved more quickly thereby leaving both of us more time to devote to our daily chores. In conclusion, please be assured that accounts requiring enforcement action, etc. are not being singled out to you or any other individual Revenue Officer. Cases are assigned in a manner that will be effective in the overall objective of the DAR Branch" and he sent a copy to Mr. John J. Ferrant.

I could not repress the urge to laugh after reading that part of his memorandum which said, "If you feel that there is an injustice being done to you, please come in and discuss it with me rather than resort to memoranda." This man had been one of my subordinates before I was unlawfully removed from the Branch. He already knew what was going on but he was profiting while hiding behind Robert "Bobby" Woods. The man was a snake in the grass.

Anyway, I answered his memorandum sending a copy to Ferrant in this manner, "Through the usage of my own stationary, my own valuable time and perhaps the most precious tool available to a Revenue Officer (i.e. documentary evidence), I have decided to answer your letter of April 29, 1981 which incidentally, appears to be long on emotion and short on reason. First of all, I'd like to state that the unique Collection methods utilized in the Delinquent Accounts and Returns Branch continues to send my dull analytical mind back to the basic fundamentals of 'Evidence and Procedure.' This makes it necessary for me at times, to explain certain things in writing. The Branch's policy statement, especially that Section which deals with delegation of authority, will show you that there is no line drawn to separate certain high level positions of authority from lower echelon employees. What's more, it is a matter of record that we use the Internal Revenue Manual only when it suits our purpose. For example, I have yet to find that Section of the Manual which outlines the procedures for assigning accounts directly to the Assistant Chief DARB for Collection. For your information, my experience and training have taught me to use the active and closed files as sources of investigations. This I shall continue to do unless I'm told to do otherwise. Your "open door" policy is fully appreciated. There is a problem that faces this type of policy however. That problem is, although the door stays open, many times the occupant of the office is not in. Finally, the spoken word being ephemeral, I feel certain that Mr. John Ferrant, who sits a hand-shake away from you will, at times, find it necessary to write. Professional people write for the record."

Following that letter no mention was made of my under productivity, Malone had begun acting more shy than he really was. He wanted to silence me but he didn't know how to go about silencing me without losing his lofty position in the catbird seat. He ostensibly preferred being used by Ferrant than agreeing with me that there was no need for the position that he was holding and incidentally, Woods had been demoted to Revenue Officer IV serving as Malone's subordinate.

The place was in a sordid mess, but Roy Malone was trying to the utmost to make an impression on John Ferrant. Trying to appease me and at the same time hoping that it would pass unnoticed, he reintroduced into the Branch, a system used by me during my tenure as Chief of the Delinquent Accounts and Returns Branch. I just could not allow him to steal my thunder. So I wrote to him on May 14, 1981, with a copy to Ferrant. I said, "Now that you have begun your review of the various inventories assigned to the Revenue Officers, I take this opportunity to congratulate you for reintroducing what appears to be the system that worked so effectively for us in the early '70's. For this relief, much thanks." During the above-mentioned period, you may recall, the DAR Branch was held in high regard by the other Branches. Regular meetings were held, similar reviews of the various inventories were made, matching operations (ULC against TDA) were conducted, financial statements were secured and many of the other duties being carried out by the United Stated Internal Revenue Service were performed by us. It is no secret, although distressing to note, that your appointment as Chief, DARB changed the system completely. Many of the Branch's employees were forced to wander into what may be best described as "fool's paradise" their only enforcement tool being the "art of persuasion."

Now that we are seemingly on the way to making inroads into the delinquency situation and promoting voluntary compliance, it is sincerely hoped that an effort would be made to practice tolerance, discourage fraternization and unify the Branch, thereby discontinuing the many appeals which have come before the Government Employees' Service Commission." P.S. "Is Mr. Robert Woods still on the side of management?"

The Carter Administration dissatisfied over the failure of the Virgin Islands Government to collect taxes continued with their plans for the United States Internal Revenue Service to take over the Collection of taxes in the territory. Locally however, the power elite and certain taxpayers who were profiting from the lack of tax enforcement continued to fool themselves into believing that the Tax Division, inferior as it was to the United States Internal Revenue Service, was doing what was prescribed under the rule of law.

Operating under the rule of thumb, Quinn and his good for nothings saw me as a major part of the problem in the troubled Tax Division, while the Carter Administration and the United States Internal Revenue Service continued to see me as the solution. (Audits conducted by the U.S. Internal Revenue Service such as the one conducted by Robert L. Parkhurst were paid for by the local government and conducted at the invitation of the selfsame local government).

The Tax Division had control, authority, influence and right among its many assets, consequently the powers that be were not willing to surrender it to the Federal Government without a fight. But under much pressure in April of 1980, a bill was sponsored by Senators Athniel C. Ottley and Michael Paiewonsky and co-sponsored by then Senate President Elmo D. Roebuck to place responsibility for the Collection of taxes in the hands of a separate agency. They would move the Tax Division from under the Department of Finance, thereby creating the Internal Revenue Bureau. So a bill to provide for the administration and enforcement of tax laws, to create the Virgin Islands Bureau of Internal Revenue was passed on August 13, 1980 and thereafter amended through Act Number 4473 on September 11, 1980. When the Bill became law, Quinn was given the choice of staying in the Department of Finance as the Department's Commissioner where at last he would rid himself of Liston Monsanto, or moving to the newly created Internal Revenue Bureau as its Director. As avaricious as he was however, he chose the latter.

In making the transition from Finance to the Bureau he showed no resentment against what he had criticized as my influence over other employees; influence that he feared would have them standing up for their rights and challenging the arbitrary and capricious personnel action by management.

In creating the Internal Revenue Bureau, the powers that be had done two things: (1) they had changed the name of the Tax Division and (2) the Tax Division was no longer under the Department of Finance. Quinn, Olive and Edward E. Thomas (a person to whom this publication has devoted a chapter) would continue their licentious ways.

Returning from annual leave in October of 1981, I found my performance report on my desk with an overall rating of satisfactory and a note attached thereto asking me to affix my signature. I looked it over and immediately addressed a letter to Mr. Roy Malone (the rater). The letter was dated October 16, 1981 and said, "My ultra paradoxical, albeit satisfactory performance report for the period ending October 16, 1981, prepared and signed by you as the rater, with a preconceived and malicious justification for your evaluation by co-rater Mr. John Ferrant, is returned herewith unsigned. The less than satisfactory rating given in Factors 7, 16 and 17 plus the baseless comments of the co-rater leave much to be desired, as they come in the wake of my charges now before the Government Employees' Service Commission that Mr. Ferrant, through no fault of his own, is filling the classified position of Chief DARB, in violation of the personnel merit system. Lest we forget, ours is a government of laws, not of men. Please be reminded that during the rating period, I was never told by anyone that the subject factors required improvement. As a matter of fact, you may recall that during the period I made arrangements with Mr. Edward Thomas (reviewer/classifier) to assist me in getting my co-workers together; consequently, we proceeded to hold the First Annual Harmonic Meeting, which was attended by co-workers desirous of forming a more cohesive unit, thereby putting to rest the ugly rumors of tension and hostility in the DAR Branch. Forgive my immodesty when I say, I have been a model of decorum from the inception of my employment and since communication is a two-way street, I sincerely hope that employees who do not communicate with each other will not be rated less than satisfactory without first being heard. Unilateral decisions are damaging to employee morale and furthermore, if we truly intend to promote the best interest of the Bureau, I suggest they be discontinued. What's more, they could have the effect of chasing many employees far from the madding crowd. A half truth is nothing else but a lie in full suit. Fortunately for me however, the credit procured by a lie lasts only till the truth comes out. I have never entertained the idea of being a soldier of fortune, inasmuch as I have kept in mind over the years the simple fact that misrepresentation and lies have never resulted in a permanent benefit for anyone.

A survey of all the employees in the Bureau will disclose that my attitude today is the same as it was when I persuaded Commissioner Reuben Wheatley to (1) send you and several other Revenue Officers to school, (2) install push-button type telephones and existing partitions in the DAR Branch and (3) change overall working conditions to include higher salaries, etc. Fear and blind loyalty are the two things that have continued to disrupt the harmony and progress of the DAR Branch. Finally, this being the first time in my career that I have been rated by two persons, I would like to request that you forward the unsigned document through the proper channels so that I may receive my well earned increment." I sent a copy of my letter to their "hit man" John J. Ferrant.

John Ferrant was really not the proper person to join Malone in rating me. He was not even on the island for the six (6) month period covered in the report. In his signed evaluation which was attached to the report he had done for Quinn and Olive what both Woods and Malone were afraid to do. His mission was accomplished or so he had thought.

Quinn and Olive were of the belief that Ulrie Vialet and Paulette Rawlins, the Branch's Secretary, were part of the so-called Monsanto faction of the DAR Branch and they may have given Ferrant his instructions to harass them. Vialet had become a victim of discrimination in the workplace which forced him to file a case with the GESC and Paulette Rawlins had filed a petition to the GESC to get her position reclassified. They had both prevailed and Quinn again was charging me with their success. As far as he was concerned, the only employee with a brain in his head was Liston Monsanto.

Following the submission of the unsigned Performance Report in October of 1981, out of spite and abuse of authority on the part of management, I had not received my increment. I therefore had to write to Ferrant's gofer, Roy Malone, again. On December 4, 1981, I wrote, "This wordy letter is being written in order to convey to you and those persons in management who have been working overtime in an effort to embarrass me and my family, exactly how I feel about the matter. At the outset let me explain that it has been almost two (2) months since (a) I refused to sign my satisfactory rating which I deemed deficient, (b) attempted to get my copy of the document and (c) have been denied my well earned increment. I have been trying to do my best, but it appears as if management is capable of worst. Living on this sunny island and surrounded by so many shady people, I have to admit that I would much prefer to die on my feet than to live on my knees. I realize, perhaps as much as you do, that the job of Internal Revenue Officer is an enormous task necessitating a high degree of complex and laborious work on the part of the person holding the position. It is for this reason more than anything else that I refuse to make the job more difficult by putting obstacles in its path. Noteworthy nevertheless, is the fact that like so many employees assigned to the DAR Branch, I have a family to whom I am deeply indebted; consequently, I refuse to toady before anyone as a means of meeting my family's obligations. Put simply, I believe in making the protestant ethic pay dividends. The foregoing established, I would like to take this opportunity to serve notice on anyone in authority whose desire it is to conspire against me in an effort to remove me from my career occupation, thereby threatening the survival of my family. Such action would be dealt in a way that would be fitting and proper. I take my responsibility to my family very seriously. It goes without saying that in our community, as is the case elsewhere, one is either part of the problem or part of the solution. The record shows that I am part of the solution. Believe me, greater love hath no man for his work. Finally, based on past experiences, I would venture to say that had I signed the faulty Performance Report, I would have by now received my copy and increment. I therefore request, once again, that I be given what is rightfully mine." Quinn, Olive and Ferrant received a copy.

These good for nothings had little or no regard for the law. Following Ulrie Vialet's victory before the GESC he was forced through his ghost writer to write to Quinn sending copies to Governor Luis, Henry Millin, Ferrant and Malone. His letter dated March 1, 1982 said, "Proving that no one is above the law, I have attached hereto a copy of a legal document which <u>orders</u> you to do exactly what the GESC previously <u>ordered</u> you to do. This Order, I hasten to add, should be carried out immediately. The islands recent crime wave and our Governor's continuing efforts to battle it, points up the immediacy for strict compliance with valid orders and furthermore, I'd like to respectfully request that in your position as fiscal officer, authorized by law to enforce the law, that you obey and not defy the order in the manner that you defied the law when it was made clear to you in a letter written by Assistant Attorney General Douglas R. Gardner on January 11, 1979. Over the past few years, you have grossly exhibited your power by: (1) arbitrarily taking my salary check without any regard for my family, (2) embarrassed me by sending an innocent Mrs. Tesla Plaskett, Junior Management Assistant, for Revenue Officer training ahead of me and (3) promoted Mr. Alvin Swan, who had entered the service after me, to the position of Revenue Officer II at a much higher salary than I now receive. Who would have thought that your power was that absolute? The facts outlined above have been the topic of much discussion within the Tax Bureau and as a consequence, hundreds of taxpayers and voters throughout the Virgin Islands have become aware of my plight together with ugly favoritism in our organization. Because of this awareness, presently I have no intentions of going public with the results of my hearing and your subsequent ostensible efforts to have the decision reversed. Incidentally, I have just returned from Phase II of my training program in

Florida and at this time I'm pleased to forward to you for review, the attached certificate and letter of evaluation, which I received upon completion of the training course. With this long overdue piece of training, which comes automatically with the job of Revenue Officer, I'm now better prepared to help promote much needed voluntary compliance in the Virgin Islands, provided I'm allowed to do so."

I had not forgotten about my dismissal hearing which was before the Third Circuit Court in Philadelphia, Pennsylvania. As a matter of fact there was a high degree of optimism about me as I awaited the decision of the Third Circuit Court. Quinn and company had been allowed to do wrong for such a long period of time that it is safe to say that he honestly felt that the real world operated the way we did in the Virgin Islands. My appeal to the Third Circuit Court was the farthest thing from Quinn's mind. I knew that as a soldier of fortune Ferrant was out to get me. I had to say or do anything to keep him off balance. I had to continue to challenge at every juncture what I considered to be injustice on the part of management.

Lima and I had already filed a suit for punitive damages in the United States District Court against the Virgin Islands Government for flagrantly violating the personnel merit system by hiring John Ferrant. Although it was not his fault, as a Quinn loyalist he did not take too kindly to what Lima and I had done. In trying to win me over to his side, Malone had confided in my good faith and perhaps in the process betrayed Ferrant's confidence. Ferrant had come to the realization from the first day on the job that working in the Bureau of Internal Revenue was a far cry from working in the State of Maryland from where he had come. Through a contractual agreement he was locked into a covenant with mediocrity and he was very frustrated. He started exchanging letters of a hostile nature with his secretary and Lima. He had become acclimated to the system and had fallen in love with Quinn's law breaking ways.

On the afternoon of March 3rd, 1982, Lima, Miss Rawlins and I were standing close to my desk discussing the whereabouts of a lien. Their backs were turned to Ferrant while the discussion was going on. I was facing Ferrant as he approached us. I looked him in his face as he angrily walked up to us and shouted, "What's going on here?" He startled both Lima and Rawlins who had not seen him coming. His actions prompted me to tell him to get back to work and earn his pay. Then individually we all wrote to him complaining about his behavior. We sent copies of our letters to Governor Luis, Henry and Leslie Millin, Quinn and Malone. My letter was dated March 4, 1982. It said:

March 4, 1982

News Item: November 18, 1981, - Suit for Punitive Damages filed
              in United States District Court by Revenue Officers
              Mario Lima and Liston Monsanto against the Virgin
              Islands Government for flagrantly violating the Per-
              sonnel Merit System, by illegally placing Mr. John
              J. Ferrant in the classified position of Chief Delin-
              quent Accounts and Returns Branch.

Question: What do Spiro Agnew, Marvin Mandel and John J. Ferrant
              have in common?

Answer: They all hail from the State of Maryland, are monarchs
              of all they survey, and apparently little bound by the
              love of truth.

Mr. John J. Ferrant
Chief, Delinquent Accounts & Returns Branch
Virgin Islands Bureau of Internal Revenue
Charlotte Amalie
St. Thomas, Virgin Islands 00801

Dear Mr. Ferrant:

     Because I feel certain that in the State of Maryland and other states and ter-
ritories under the American Flag (the Chief, DARB is treated like any top level employee with his own private office) that your conduct on Wednesday afternoon (2:06
P.M.) March 3, 1982, would have brought a charge of conduct unbecoming an officer,
I'm forced to voice my displeasure.

     It is pathetic - perhaps infinitely so, that here in the Virgin Islands where
you have presumably entered into a covenant with mediocrity, that you'd resort to
shouting at - by your own admission, Professional Employees, rather than speaking
to them as adult human beings.

     In retrospect, it seems as if everytime something upsets you, you resort to
shouting. Before Wednesday, several employees were critical of you for shouting at
Mr. Ulrie Vialet and Miss Paulette Rawlins in full view of their colleagues. Discretionary power must not be abused as no man is justified in doing evil on the
ground of expediency.

     Wednesday's sequence of events may have been intended to: (a) provoke me
(b) put me to an extreme test or (c) may have been a form of mainland superiority. Only you have the answer to the dilemma.

Letter   -2-   March 4, 1982
Mr. John J. Ferrant

You needn't be suspicious of me. Suspicion creates what it suspects and as a result one should avoid being suspicious. Contrary to what you may have heard from the various crusaders around here, I'm not a Rabble Rouser. The records shows that I'm a law-abiding person, and copies of letter in your possession can attest to that.

And while I'm writing, I'd like to take the opportunity to heavily suggest that action be taken to (1) stop conspiring against me, and instead take the necessary steps to award me my increment which is past due (2) make periodic inquiries to ascertain the status of payment tracers and notice of adjustments that are long overdue (3) collate accounts now in inactive status in order to find out whether audits or other technical work has been completed (4) make attempt to stop buckpassing and making Mr. Malone a scapegoat (5) consult with those in authority in order to make available to Revenue Officers much-needed transportation. Like a desk, transportation is a basic essential tool. "Let us be thankful for the tools but for them the rest of us could not succeed". Also it is further suggested that Contractual Revenue Officer Woods be instructed to stop signing the Government's Transportation Log when he uses his personal car. The Log as we know it, was designed for the use of Government vehicles only. We do not punch a clock and needless to say, our Daily Reports (Form 795) reflect the day's activity.

You need not concern yourself with the collection activity — if you decide to abdicate the Chief's throne and leave the Virgin Islands. Experienced as you are you must know that revenues will get progressively better, especially since more businesses are coming to the Islands and both the tax and interest rates have increased.

Finally, like the Greek Cynic Dyogenes, I'm still looking for an honest man.

         Sincerely,

         Liston B. Monsanto
         Internal Revenue Officer

cc: Governor Juan Luis
     Governor of the Virgin Islands

     Mr. Henry Millin
     Lieutenant Governor

     Mr. Leslie Millin
     Director, Personnel Division

     Mr. Leroy A. Quinn
     Director, V.I. Bureau of Internal Revenue

     Mr. Roy Malone
     Asst. Chief, DAR Branch

On March 12, 1982 Ferrant wrote to me saying, "Paragraphs 2 and 3 of your letter of March 4, 1982, referring to an intended discussion with you and other employees on March 3, 1982 requires a reply. Inquiring as to the subject matter when three employees are gathered at your desk is a duty and responsibility of my position. The mere fact that Ms. Rawlins proceeded immediately to her desk, Mr. Lima held up a slip of paper but started to leave the area was a good indication to me that work-related matters were not being discussed. Your subsequent statements that if I wanted to talk to you I could call you into my office and that I had better get back to work as that is what I am being paid to do was insulting and certainly did not lend any credibility to your constant claim of professionalism. I was working when I questioned a gathering of people that appeared not to be working. For your information and my fortune, some employees of other segments of the Bureau overheard the outbursts of Ms. Rawlins on February 25, 1982. I will leave that to be aired at a later time, if necessary. Needless to say, I do not shout in the performance of my job and have no need to resort to that type of behavior. This can be attested to by the vast majority of our co-workers."

On March 15, 1982 I responded to John Ferrant's letter. I wrote, "Rumor has it that when Mr. Quinn traveled to the mainland in search of a Chief of the Delinquent Accounts and Returns Branch, he sought out a person too tough to be honest and too weak to lead a Branch mired in the profundity of mediocrity. Whether or not you were that person will be determined only with the flight of time. About your vituperative letter of Friday, March 12, 1982, all I can say at this time is if you've got the guts to write a letter using statements involving inferences and loaded with assumptions of certainty, then I've got the guts to answer factually. I know, for obvious reasons, that you are loyal to Mr. Quinn against whom Mr. Lima and myself have filed a suit for punitive damages, but Mr. Ferrant, lest you forget, loyalty can be carried to excess. Liston Monsanto has never ever questioned your discretionary power. The fact is you did shout at us in the manner explained in my letter of March 4, 1982. Perhaps you did it impulsively; your vacuous smile was not exhibited. Now that I've set the record straight, I'd like to offer some more suggestions as follows: (1) regular monthly meetings similar to the ones held by our supervisory personnel, (2) apprise Mr. Luke of a certain Chief Emeritus, who may attempt to run his office by remote control, (3) install a partition around the Chief DARB's desk in order to eliminate distracting office noises, provide privacy and screen out interruptions, (4) alternate our two vehicles in order to accommodate all Revenue Officers and (5) discontinue the practice of exchanging letters with dedicated lower echelon employees who have asserted their rights. These employees are doing their best to earn the money being paid them by the taxpayers of the Virgin Islands. Some people will continue to disrespect law and authority because of their own selfish interest, but blessed are they which are persecuted for righteousness sake; for theirs is the kingdom of heaven."

Following my letter of March 4, 1982, Ferrant realized that he had brought a duck to a cock fight and there was no way the duck would win unless the fight was fixed. He ran to Quinn's office complaining to Quinn that I had compared him to two criminals (Spiro Agnew and Marvin Mandel) in the State of Maryland where he was from. In addition, he told Quinn that I had said that he was dishonest. How little he knew. Had Marvin Mandel and Spiro Agnew been living and working in the Virgin Islands, the crimes for which they were convicted in Maryland would have been treated with reverence here in the Virgin Islands where Ferrant was.

While we were having fun in the Virgin Islands Bureau of Internal Revenue exchanging letters among ourselves the Third Circuit Court of Appeals was busy reversing my ninety (90) day suspension in an Opinion dated March 11, 1982. None of us knew it at the moment, however.

Mr. Quinn felt it an obligation to duty to show Ferrant who was the Head of the Bureau even if it meant flaunting his authority once again.

On December 17, 1982 at approximately 8:00 a.m. a messenger hand-delivered a letter to me from Leroy Quinn which told me the same thing that he had told me on August 24, 1979. In a paraphrase Quinn said, "Liston Monsanto you are fired." One day before Quinn's March 16th letter that was delivered to me on the 17th, by virtue of the Third Circuit Court's decision, I had become the preeminent person in the Virgin Islands Bureau of Internal Revenue. Luis, the Millins, Quinn, Olive and all the others who had been doing things in violation of law in the Virgin Islands had been defeated. What's more, the decision would be used by everybody under the American Flag who found themselves in the position that I had been, including my persecutors and their children.

On March 18, 1982, Attorney Brenda Hollar wrote to Governor Juan Luis on my behalf. She said:

Brenda J. Hollar
Attorney at Law

SUITE 14 ● PROFESSIONAL BUILDING ● P.O. BOX 8897 ● ST. THOMAS ● U.S. VIRGIN ISLANDS 00801 ● PHONE

March 18, 1982

His Excellency Juan Luis
Governor of the Virgin Islands
Government House
Charlotte Amalie
St. Thomas, U.S. Virgin Islands   00801

Re: Recommended Dismissal of
      Liston Monsanto

Dear Governor Luis:

Please be advised that I have been retained (once again) by Liston B. Monsanto to represent him with respect to dismissal action initiated and proposed by Leroy Quinn, the Director of the Virgin Islands Bureau of Internal Revenue.

In that regard, I am writing you this letter to request you to carefully review the attached documents and disapprove said recommended personnel action. Said request may seem quite unusual, however, the circumstances surrounding this particular dismissal action warrant said intervention.

Attached please find a copy of the original dismissal letter dated March 16, 1982 and hand delivered via messenger to my client at approximately 8:00 a.m. on March 17, 1982 at the Virgin Islands Bureau of Internal Revenue.

Also attached please find a copy of the Third Circuit's decision, dated March 11, 1982 reversing a 90 day suspension the G.E.S.C. ordered as a result of a former request by Leroy Quinn to dismss Mr. Monsanto in August of 1979.

Because the Court of Appeals for the Third Circuit held inter alia, that Mr. Monsanto's "letter writing" constituted "protected speech" under the First Amendment to the Constitution of the United States and Section 3 of the Revised Organic Act of 1954 (the Virgin Islands Bill of Rights, 48 U.S.C. section 1561), and that the evidence failed to support that Mr. Monsanto's letter writing had a disruptive effect

His Excellency Juan Luis
Page 2
March 18, 1982

on the operation of the Tax Division, I believe that the present attempt to dismiss Mr. Monsanto on basically the same charges, "flies in the face" of the law of the land as reaffirmed by the Third Circuit.

It is very possible that Mr. Quinn did not have benefit of the decision by the Third Circuit when he initiated the instant dismissal action, however now that it has been rendered and released, I respectfully request its findings and holdings be applied to this and all personnel actions within the Government of the Virgin Islands where an employee is seeking to exercise his inalienable constitutional rights.

Finally, from an economical and practical point of view, I would assume that this is the most crucial season with respect to tax collections. According to the proposed dismissal letter, Mr. Monsanto was relieved of his duties immediately upon receipt of the letter, albeit with pay as required by law. Although said request can only be beneficial to my client, he is quite concerned about the effect it may have on the people of the Virgin Islands.

Using the time schedule of the last dismissal action as a guide, Mr. Monsanto was off, with pay, from August 24, 1979, the day he was served the dismissal letter, until approximately November 23, 1979 when the G.E.S.C. handed down its suspension order. Thereafter he served his 90 day suspension, which now must be paid back, together with costs and attorney fees. I would estimate that said amount will be a substantial sum.

Based upon the aforementioned, I respectfully suggest that the proposed personnel action be disapproved in light of the present Third Circuit decision.

Whatever your decision, kindly advise me so I may be guided accordingly.

With kindest regards,

Brenda J. Hollar

John J. Ferrant, the man brought in as a "hit-man" to systematically fire me had spat in the air and it was falling back in his face. Quinn and all his Lieutenants in the Virgin Islands Bureau of Internal Revenue were smarting from the Third Circuit Court's Decision which said in part: "We do not underestimate the internal unease or unpleasantness that may follow when a government employee decides to break rank and complain either publicly or to supervisors about a situation which he/she believes merits review and reform. That is the price the First Amendment exacts in return for an informed citizenry." Thanks to Opinion Number 81-1434 of the Third Circuit Court I had defeated "City Hall."

For your information, here is a passage taken from Opinion No. 81-1434: "Olive testified that he believed Monsanto would be a "good candidate" to be Chief of the Delinquent Accounts and Returns Branch. Tr.At 128, 153. The GESC did not refer to the specific evidence on which it relied to support its conclusion of disruption. We have accordingly examined the record for evidence to support that conclusion. With regard to whether Monsanto's letter writing had a disruptive effect upon employment relationships among his co-workers and his supervisors and upon the regular operation of the Tax Division in general, the evidence was equivocal. The testimony as to the alleged disruption was in large part conclusory, and non-specific. Commissioner Quinn testified that as a result of a letter written about one co-worker, Lucia Thomas, she went on vacation and requested additional leave time 'because she was unable to cope with the situation, returning to the office, there was so much dissention, (sic) so many problems." Tr.At 25. In addition, Commissioner Quinn referred in unspecific terms to disruption caused when Monsanto wrote about another unnamed employee. 1D. Tax Director Olive, whom Monsanto characterized in his letters as incompetent as Director of the Division and whose removal was requested by Monsanto, Tr.At 87, testified the letters were 'harassing and disruptive' and that they affected him and his work: "the constant flow of letters continues to interfere with the other duties and responsibilities that I have that I'm responsible for in the performance of my daily duties." Tr.At 95. In describing the problems relating to Monsanto, Olive further testified: "the problem is that he has been sending these letters; he is creating disruptiveness. As a result, perhaps fifty or sixty percent of the existing staff continues to find interruptions. They cannot function. They either refuse to work with Mr. Monsanto or they have gone their separate ways." Tr.At 153. He provided no specific example of how reading seventeen (17) letters in four years interfered with his performance of his duties, nor did he particularize any staff interruptions caused by the letters. (Hansen's testimony about his efforts to discover the contents of Monsanto's letters by rummaging through his trash, Tr. (Nov. 9, 1979) At 7-8, must be attributed to Hansen's singular curiosity rather than to Monsanto's disruptive effect). Remarkably, Olive further stated, however, that 'there is currently no animosity between Mr. Monsanto and myself.' Tr. (Nov. 9, 1979) At 19. Robert Woods, Chief of the Delinquent Accounts and Returns Branch characterized his working relationship with Monsanto as 'good,' but stated without specifically citing the letter writing activity as the cause that Monsanto's relationship with other employees was 'strained.' Tr.At 159-60. Lucia Thomas, a co-worker, testified that she was not on good terms with Monsanto and referred specifically to her dissatisfaction over a letter Monsanto had written to Commissioner Quinn concerning an incident between her and Woods. On cross examination, however, Thomas admitted that she had not spoken with Monsanto for many years prior to the date the letter in question was written. Tr.At 3-4 (Nov. 9, 1979). There is no other testimony or evidence to support a finding of disruption caused by the writing or the release to the media of the letters or by playing tapes of the Clarke Broadcast in the office around lunchtime on a day following the broadcast. Monsanto testified that he did not believe his particular letters caused any disruption in the Department and stated that he was not alone in writing letters concerning problems in the Tax Division. Tr.At 238. We do not believe that the above evidence establishes that either the writing of the letters or their alleged release to the media had the effect of materially and substantially disrupting the operations of the Tax Division so as to warrant a conclusion that Monsanto's letters constituted unprotected speech. While there was ample testimony establishing disharmony and discontent among the employees of the Delinquent Accounts and Returns Branch, see Tr.At 169-170, 188, there is only meager evidence establishing that this disharmony and discontent was specifically caused by Monsanto's letter writing activities. The evidence supports

Monsanto's testimony that several of his colleagues shared his views regarding problems in the Tax Division and likewise voiced their discontent in letters to Quinn and Olive. Tr.At 206-207, 234. Thus, much of the discontent appears to have been the result of the very problems in the Tax Division to which Monsanto's letters were directed, rather than a result of Monsanto's letter writing activity itself. Furthermore, although the criticism in Monsanto's letters was directed at identified superiors, there was no evidence that Monsanto's employment relationships with these persons, such as Commissioner Quinn and the Tax Director, were the 'kind of close working relationships for which it can persuasively be claimed that personal loyalty and confidence are necessary to their proper functioning.' Pickering V. Board of Education, 391 U.S. at 570. Monsanto's immediate supervisor, Robert Woods, described his working relationship with Monsanto as 'good' and even Tax Director Olive likewise testified that no animosity existed between himself and Monsanto. Thus, unlike the situation considered in the Sprague case, there was little indication that the effectiveness of close, important working relationships was seriously undermined by Monsanto's activity. The GESC's decision to temporarily suspend rather than permanently dismiss Monsanto indicates that it likewise believed that key employment relationships between Monsanto and others in the Tax Division had not been permanently undermined. It would appear that Monsanto's employers and the GESC may have been more concerned with the volume of Monsanto's letter writing than with its content. The GESC referred to Monsanto's activity as 'pestiferous' speech. However, Monsanto's protected speech did not lose its protection merely because it was persistent. The attention of addressees or listeners can often be attracted in no other manner. Finally, the letters were directed to public officials who had jurisdiction over and legitimate reason for concern about the allegations. Even if they were ultimately released by Monsanto to the media because they were apparently having no internal impact, their first amendment protection is not thereby lost. The timing of Commissioner Quinn's decision to seek Monsanto's dismissal, less than ten (10) days after the radio broadcast, suggests that it was the broadcast rather than the letter writing as such which provoked this controversy. The Appellee, however, produced no evidence to support the GESC's finding of disruption in that intervening ten-day period resulting from the broadcast. Our review of the record convinces us that Monsanto's letter writing concerned issues of public importance and that there is no evidence to support a finding of the Department of Finance. We therefore agree with Monsanto, that his letter writing activity constituted protected speech which could not permissibly furnish the basis for the sanction imposed. Without specifically referring to the Mt. Healthy case, Appellee appears to suggest that Monsanto's other conduct, in writing the letters during regular working hours and utilizing government stationary and secretarial services, was the basis for the imposition of sanctions. We can find nothing in the GESC's findings or opinion to indicate that the letter writing, which it had concluded was unprotected, was not considered in its imposition of the sanction. It is unlikely that the GESC would have imposed the harsh sanction of a ninety (90) day suspension from employment without pay based merely on the other, much more minor charges. We conclude that the letter writing and/or release to the media was a substantial or motivating factor in the sanction imposed. Appellee, of course, had the opportunity to defeat Monsanto's claim by showing that the same action would have been taken even in the absence of the protected conduct. In its third and fourth actual findings, the GESC found that Monsanto wrote the letters during regular working hours using government stationary and secretarial services after being instructed to cease and hand-delivered the letters to the Office of the Commissioner during regular working hours. Monsanto contends that none of the GESC's findings, including these, were supported by substantial evidence. On the basis of our review of the record, we agree that the evidence to support these findings was insufficient to meet Appellee's burden under Mt. Healthy. Each of the letters in question was indeed written on stationary bearing the letterhead of the Tax Division, however, Appellee has not pointed to any regulation which would preclude an employee's use of the Division's stationary in writing to his or her supervisor about matters relating to the operation of the Division. There is little evidence to support the GESC's finding that Monsanto wrote 'numerous' letters utilizing government secretarial services 'during regular working hours.' Monsanto testified that the letters were written or typed either at his home or in the office before or after working hours. Tr.At 237-238, 250. Tax Director Olive verified that Monsanto was very punctual and usually arrived at work early. Tr.At 141. Commissioner Quinn acknowledged that the letter writing could have been done before the start of work or during Monsanto's lunch break. Tr.At 49. Kenneth Hansen testified that on March 22, 1978, he observed Monsanto typing a letter to Leslie Millin at 'around 2 o'clock in the afternoon. Tr.(Nov 9, 1979) at 7-8. Hansen testified that the typing lasted approximately fifteen (15) minutes. Tr.(Nov 9, 1979) At8. The relevance of Monsanto's writing during 'regular business hours' would be its effect on either his production or quality of work. Even if Hansen's testimony were fully credited, as we believe the GESC must have done, a fifteen (15) minute use of working time by Monsanto must be viewed in light of the Appellee's own evidence that Monsanto regularly arrived early and the performance rating showing that his work was characterized by his employer's as exemplary. The only evidence adduced at the Commission Hearing, which was supportive of the finding of the use of secretarial services concerned two letters. Tesla Plaskett testified that during the time she served as administrative secretary for the Tax Division, she typed two of the letters, dated February 7, 1977 and February 15, 1977, for Monsanto during working hours. Tr.At 197-199. This hardly supports a finding of the use of government secretaries for 'numerous' letters. With regard to the GESC's finding that the letters were hand-delivered to the Office of the Commissioner by Monsanto during regular hours, there is no evidentiary support. Commissioner Quinn testified that at least one letter was hand-delivered to his office, but he did not specify by whom. Tr.At 17. There would be some basis for a finding the Monsanto delivered letters to Tax Director Olive since Olive testified that he received the letters during working hours. Tr.At 95. Cecelia Hill, an Administrative Officer in the Tax Division, testified that she had received correspondence from Monsanto for Tax Director Olive during working hours. Tr.At 193-194. And that the letters were hand-delivered by either Monsanto, whose office was 'a few steps away' from hers, or Monsanto's co-worker, Mario Lima. Tr.At 196. As in the case of the fifteen (15) minutes used for letter writing, the interruption in work occasioned by hand delivery of letters to an office a few feet away is obviously minor. We therefore conclude, that the evidence produced by the Appellee to support the GESC's findings with regard to Monsanto's hand-delivery and composition of the letters during working hours and utilization of government secretarial services failed to meet the burden of demonstrating that the ninety (90) day suspension without pay would have been imposed on Monsanto even in the absence of his engagement in protected activity."

The uppity Albert Commisong, Chairman of the GESC, loaded with preconceived notions and still courting the favor of the Bureau of Internal Revenue was all set to dismiss me from my career occupation based only on false and malicious charges trumped up by the scoff-law Leroy A. Quinn. Hung up on tradition and operating as an aristocrat, Albert Commissong foolishly believed that he was what he was not.

Attorney Hollar had written and delivered a letter to him on March 19, 1982, wherein she advised him that the Third Circuit Court had reversed my ninety (90) day suspension imposed by the GESC and affirmed by the District Court as a result of the prior personnel action initiated by Quinn. She further told him of the similar charges in Quinn's letter of March 16, 1982 and asked him to read the twenty-four (24) page decision written by the Court prior to the date my appeal was scheduled. Attorney Hollar was against duplication and waste.

In his decision dated June 1, 1982, presumably intended to soothe or satisfy Leroy Quinn's anger, he wrote, "As previously mentioned, the aforegoing charges were dismissed at the close of government case in Chief. The sole remaining charge, Charge 1, regarding a letter written by the Appellant dated March 4, 1982 and another dated March 15, 1982 was taken under advisement by this Commission. After consideration of the contents of both letters, the deposition of Mr. John Ferrant, testimony of Mr. Anthony Olive and that of the Appellant, Mr. Liston Monsanto, this Commission, for the first time, is hopelessly deadlocked and unable to reach a majority decision. Two (2) members of the Commission are convinced that the Government has met its burden with respect to Charge 1 of the March 16, 1982 letter and that Appellant should accordingly be disciplined. The remaining two (2) members of this Commission are of the contrary conclusion. 3 V.I.C. Section 530 mandates that this Commission render a decision within fourteen (14) days of the conclusion of a hearing in question; failing such, the Appellant is automatically returned to duty with pay. We construe this section to mean that if the Commission should fail to make a determination of the issues involved, even where a conscientious attempt has been made by this Commission to do so, the Appellant must be returned to duty without penalty. This Commission having concluded for various reasons and at the close of the Government's case, that charges 2, 4, 5, 6, 7 and 8 were not sustainable, this Commission hereby dismisses the above-referenced charges. Further, this Commission having failed to render a determination of the issues involved in this proceeding, based upon a majority decision of its members, within fourteen (14) days of the termination of the hearing, the remaining charge, Charge 1, must be dismissed and the Appellant returned to duty as an Internal Revenue Officer IV in the Bureau of Internal Revenue without penalty."

As I look back on the day when I was told what Robert L. Parkhurst, the so-called U.S. Internal Revenue Auditor, had written about me I couldn't help but laugh as his comments called forth the memory of things past; especially as they related to Reuben Wheatley. Reuben Wheatley had told Ulric Benjamin, who in turn may have told Quinn when he brought in Parkhurst that inspection teams from the United States Internal Revenue Service never bothered him inasmuch as he always instructed them on what to look for and what to do.

In his deposition of March 29, 1982, John Ferrant had stated that he wanted to get off the island just as soon as he could. He said he was just fed up with all the harassment that he had taken. Well, John J. Ferrant got his wish. His contractual obligation ended on March 31, 1982 and needless to say, thereafter he left St. Thomas.

At the Bureau of Internal Revenue, formerly Tax Division, everybody assigned to the Delinquent Accounts and Returns Branch was getting a chance as Chief of the Branch to rate each other. At one time there was Ulric Benjamin playing the role of rater, rating those of us assigned to do work in the Branch. Then came Liston Monsanto with the authority to rate Kenneth Hansen and Roy Malone. Next was Woods with the authority to rate Monsanto, Hansen, Benjamin and Malone. Then came Malone with the authority to rate Woods, Monsanto and Hansen. Finally, Hansen with the authority to rate Malone, Monsanto and Woods. At any moment in the Delinquent Accounts and Returns Branch the person holding the position as Chief could be demoted. The place was like a three-ring circus.

But let's go back to Opinion No. 81-1434 of the Third Circuit Court which was argued on December 10, 1981 and thereafter filed on March 11, 1982. Three Circuit Court Judges (Hunter, Van Dusen and Sloviter) of incorruptible integrity who were geographically removed from the Virgin Islands saw what those indentured to the Virgin Islands Governmental System refused to see. Facts and laws reviewed by the Appellate Court revealed a sinister plot designed to systematically remove me from my classified position as civil servant with the Virgin Islands Government for having the courage to do what was just, what was moral and what was right. As a result of my success, the decision of the Third Circuit Court was given little or no consideration by the local press. Put simply, they gave the matter short shrift. The brutish Leroy A. Quinn and company knew through their legal advisers that the Court's decision could not be remedied. They also knew that the employees of the Bureau of Internal Revenue were aware of the landmark decision but because most of them were bound through the existing political patronage, immorally and illegally, there was no way for them to lose confidence in his office. Through Opinion No. 81-1434 of the Third Circuit Court, Quinn had been given another chance to rid himself of Liston Monsanto whom he had labeled a most disruptive person. He could have done exactly what John J. Ferrant had done immediately following the Court's decision, but not Leroy Quinn. There was no way that Quinn would surrender the resources of the Virgin Islands Bureau of Internal Revenue. Rather than leave a place where there was easy gain or profit he started scheming once again in an attempt to isolate me. Now you can clearly see why people like former Vice President of the United States (Spiro Agnew) and former Governor of the State of Maryland (Marvin Mandel) would have been revered in the Virgin Islands.

The first test of my resilience with the Delinquent Accounts and Returns Branch came with the United Steelworkers of America (Local Union No. 8249). Personally speaking, I was not seeking unionization. As far as I was concerned, everybody was searching for his pound of flesh in the United States Virgin Islands and the Union was no exception. But for your edification when the subject of unionization was broached, I had been away from the Bureau of Internal Revenue due to suspension. I was confronted by an employee and asked to participate in an election designed to choose either for or against unionization. I told the employee that unionization meant nothing to me inasmuch as I had just received a favorable decision from the Third Circuit Court which had vindicated me completely from all the lies and innuendos that were emanating from Quinn's office. I told him that I was not looking for adulation and that the favorable decision given me by the Court was an affirmation that I had done the right thing and as we parted I told him that the idea of becoming unionized was a good one that merited careful consideration, not only on his part but by his co-workers. Finally, I told him to count me out. The next day I was forced to give in to his demands when he told me that a plurality of the votes meant that everybody in the shop (whether one voted or not) would become members of a bargaining unit. That he said, was the law. I said fine. It would not hurt me to become a member, a member in good standing only. Again I told him (for it was his desire to submit my name as a member of a negotiating team) that I was not interested in being an official representative for any person, place or thing. My only reason for becoming a member was because of the law. So I became a member of the United Steelworkers of America Local 8249 under the presidency of Luis "Tito" Morales.

Quinn and Olive were continuing to flaunt their authority. They knew and would take advantage of the fact that in the Virgin Islands almost everybody has his moral values mixed up (good as is literally defined means bad and vice versa). I had lost any respect that I may have had for them. How could I have any respect for two liars who were trying to destroy my image while at the same time openly and deliberately disrespecting my family? At least John Ferrant was man enough to leave. Why didn't Quinn leave? After all, he had been defeated. And Governor Juan Luis, couldn't he envision what was going to happen in the Department once I had emerged victorious? Sure he knew. He also knew that Quinn was a little bit more than disingenuous when he accused me of doing the things he had listed in his two letters of dismissal. As the appointing authority, Luis was really the person who was asking for my dismissal.

There was something about Quinn that stuck in the craw of a great number of people. His demeanor was always suspect. Upon my return to duty I was rated "satisfactory" for the rating period June 17, 1981 to June 17, 1982 by Malone out of respect of the Court's decision. Malone sent the document to Quinn for his signature and here is what Quinn wrote for the file on August 10, 1982: "Inasmuch as I recommended dismissal of this employee during this rating period, I cannot agree with the rater's performance ratings, therefore, cannot sign the performance report." I immediately responded to his denunciation. I wrote: "I am writing to you pursuant to the opinion of the United States Court of Appeals for the Third Circuit (No. 81-1434 Liston Monsanto vs. Leroy Quinn) and as an Internal Revenue Officer who is required to obey the law whether his recommendations are adopted or not. I once succinctly explained to you, after earning a modicum of fame in the Third Circuit Court's decision that no one is above the law. I also told you that those among us who are bent on breaking the law doing such things as misleading the politicians by telling them that in the DAR Branch we are authorized a Chief DARB and a Chief Delinquent Accounts and Returns Branch (See '82 Budget), when in fact we are duplicating a particular position, will in time find it most difficult to enforce the law. For your information, it was the Government Employees' Service Commission, sitting in all their pomp and circumstance that dismissed the frivolous charges, which you and Mr. Anthony Olive had trumped up against me. When this same commission ruled against me, I took the next step on the appellate ladder, obeying the law throughout the appellate process.

Your 'memorandum to the file' dated August 10, 1982 surprises me inasmuch as I was of the belief that you as a fiscal and enforcement official, sworn to uphold the law, would abide by the decision of the government's tribunal. It now appears a certainty that there is only one right way, your way. Be that as it may however, this letter is written for the record." Quinn's "memorandum to the file" was an act of a most rank amateur.

The decision of the Third Circuit Court had in itself created a problem. The Court had placed emphasis on my First Amendment right to speak out in a Virgin Islands repressive system but somewhat hidden in the decision was the fact that what I had been saying all along in my many letters had been earnestly believed and was therefore to be taken as a guide for action. Yes, I had been dissatisfied with the operation of the Tax Division. Yes, I had complained that it was poorly managed and that the morale of its employees was low and yes, I had also criticized the structure of the Division; and sought the elimination of certain employment positions and finally I had claimed with good reason that the problems in the Division were impairing the effectiveness of the Division's tax collecting operations. All of this was true and Governor Luis, Quinn and the others knew it but they were not going to reorganize the Bureau so as to put into effect the lawful things I had been addressing in my letters. They were having fun with the status quo and so with the same obstacles in my path, I could do nothing to aid in turning the Bureau of Internal Revenue in the right direction. In the interest of being consistent I had to continue doing the legal things that had gotten me where I was, and this, the power elite knew. I just could not operate in the arbitrary manner to which they had grown accustom. Had I gone over to their side they would have accused me of dilly-dallying from the start.

The Bureau of Internal Revenue, unlike the United States Internal Revenue Service, was not an autonomous agency and therefore found itself in a governmental system mired in mediocrity. As an employee of the Bureau of Internal Revenue however, I was not ready to be used by anybody seeking to gain some advantage.

Thomas Divine is given credit for having said, "It takes courage for government employees to stick their necks out and blow the whistle in time to make a difference." The man was right on target but many people in the Virgin Islands Bureau of Internal Revenue and even Local Union 8249, as apathetic as they were, didn't give a damn about anybody other than themselves.

When I had become a member of Local Union 8249, like many of the other members, there was a desperate desire to put an end to my situation. We wanted to reconcile with the people on the side of management. Smelling smoke we knew there was a fire but we did not know how it was going to affect us. When I had initially visited the offices of Cephus Rogers, the Union's International Representative, and "Tito" Morales, my greatest concern had been legal representation (a lawyer) to replace attorney Brenda Hollar whom I really hated to lose. I was hoping that Rogers and Morales would have told me that somebody like Hollar was their legal advisor. Instead I was told that "Tito" Morales was the person appointed to act or speak legally on behalf of any aggrieved individual in his local union. I honestly thought that they were joking. I couldn't believe that they actually meant what they were saying. I had never heard of Tito's sharpness and quickness in seeing and understanding the legal aspect of any situation and consequently I became apprehensive. I did not want to get in a fight with my newly found union officials whose job it was to represent me. Back at my office I held discussions with Lima over what we considered to be a lack of adequate legal representation to go up against the lawyers working out of the Attorney General's office. Through our membership dues we had become members in good standing; consequently we expected legal representation.

The Union had ushered in an era never before seen in the Virgin Islands Bureau of Internal Revenue. It had opened many opportunities giving new power to the employees who were now ready and willing to assert themselves. Lima and I had to pursue a wise course in order to make our feelings known. We did not want the local officials of the union to join with the unwholesome individuals in management who thought that we were very abrasive. We knew that the attitudes of the union officials at the highest levels in Pittsburg, Pennsylvania and Birmingham, Alabama were by far more business-like than those of Tito Morales and Cephus Rogers and so we made the decision to make an appeal to them for legal representation. Even if we were neither professionals nor amateurs we could see that there was a need for legal advice that only a person with legal knowledge could give. I had been successful in the Third Circuit Court because Attorney Hollar had successfully applied the law to the facts which she had gotten from me and now I felt that the continuous stand-offs between management and me would require a new image of moderation. Had I been present when discussions were being held regarding admission to the Union I would have posed the question with respect to a mouth-piece. Attorney Brenda Hollar who had become familiar with the happenings in the Bureau through my many letters in her possession would have been an ideal candidate for the job. Operating on the thesis that being thoughtful of our local brothers in the Union was the essence of politeness, Lima and I tabled our discussions on the matter until we had given Morales and Rogers a fair chance to say to us on the record that they would not provide us with legal representation.

Our chance came when I needed someone to represent me in a hearing before the GESC. I told Morales about the hearing and once again he told me that he was prepared to represent me. Now that part of our conversation I did not like and so I wrote to Luis "Tito" Morales, "This is to formally request professional assistance (an attorney) to represent me in my hearing, which is due to come before the Government Employees' Service Commission (GESC) in the near future. Past experiences in dealing with the GESC and other such tribunals have prompted my request. Should the Union be unable to provide me with an attorney, I'd be willing to retain one at my expense, provided that Union agrees to it." Morales responded saying, "I must inform you that the Union's position in this step is that the president and the staff representative are quite capable of handling said grievance, as we have done on numerous occasions in the past with such cases. However, if you choose to hire an attorney at this point, I must inform you that it will be at your own expense. The Union's position is that if we have to appeal the GESC's decision that is when we will appoint an attorney and will pay all legal fees that accrue." Now I had on record the Union's legal procedure.

Lima and I would now move to the next rung on the Union's appellate ladder. Lima took the liberty to make a formal request through a petition for the members of the Bureau's bargaining unit. We were going to send the petition to a Thermon Phillips, the Union's District Director, in Birmingham, Alabama for his review and consideration. Among the signatories were Claudette Farrington, Steven "Smokey" Frett, Jens Todman, Ulrie Vialet and Louis "Lolo" Willis. The petition said, "The undersigned employees of the Virgin Islands Bureau of Internal Revenue, members of the United Steelworkers Union, feel that it is the duty of the Union to properly represent its members when grievances are brought against our employer. When an employee of the Bureau files a grievance, he is not only filing a grievance against his employer, but also against the Government of the Virgin Islands, who has at its disposal, the services of the Virgin Islands Attorney General's Office. Thus, the Government has a vast selection of qualified attorney's at its disposal. We do not. Two employees of the V.I. Bureau of Internal Revenue have recently filed grievances and have been told by Mr. Tito Morales, President, Local 8249, that he will represent them and that there is no need for any attorney. Mr. Morales, not being an attorney, would be at a disadvantage when representing an employee under these circumstances. We feel, therefore, that the confidence we have placed on our Union will be in jeopardy unless this situation is corrected immediately."

While all of this was going on I was just another member in good standing of the Bureau's bargaining unit. As noted earlier, I did not want to represent anybody who didn't give a damn about me. As far as I was concerned, through Opinion No. 81-1434 of the Third Circuit Court, I had already made my point.

In the Bureau of Internal Revenue games-man-ship was always the order of the day. From time to time employees would be seen bobbing and weaving between management and labor. It was a most disgusting sight. If the members of our bargaining unit were sincerely concerned about the Bureau's operation, all they had to do was duplicate what I had done. Not one of them would do it. They all wanted to eat their cake and still have it.

At a public hearing at the legislature on the evening of September 2, 1982, conducted by the Government's Operation Committee, chaired by Senator Ruby Simmonds, over three dozen employees of the Bureau on St. Thomas appeared at the Legislature to give testimony relating to the strained relations between management and the workers of the Bureau. The meeting was without a quorum. With the exception of Senator Simmonds and Senator Iver Stridiron, all of the other members of the Committee were absent. Senator Hugo Dennis, a member of the Labor and Veterans Affairs Committee, who was not a member of government operations also attended. At the meeting, a typewritten unsigned letter with the name "Jane Doe" at the bottom was read into the record of the committee. It was a farcical act, needless to say.

We had previously appeared before the Operations Committee on August 24, 1982 and so I was forced to write to Senator Simmonds in the form of a Petition which said, "Fearing a federal takeover of tax collections in the territory and desirous of minimizing the long-standing problems in the Virgin Islands Bureau of Internal Revenue, those of us whose signatures appear below in alphabetical sequence appeared before the Senate's Committee on Government Operations, chaired by you, with co-members William Harvey, Edgar Isles and Iver Stridiron present. Bent Lawaetz was absent on August 24, 1982 and again before you and Senator Stridiron in mock session (i.e. no quorum) on September 2, 1982. On both occasions, clear and convincing evidence was delivered to you for such action as your committee may have taken to determine if violations of law had occurred. We asked you to fulfill your responsibility to us, the taxpayers and voters of the Virgin Islands, by making your findings public and applying yourselves diligently to the urgent task of setting the Virgin Islands Bureau of Internal Revenue in order. To date we have not seen or heard from you. The record shows that over the past several years, many employees have complained to Governor Juan Luis about the overall atmosphere in the Bureau of Internal Revenue. In response, the Governor has done a military about-face. Legislator apathy has also contributed to the status quo and the continuing overtures being made by the Federal Government. This apathy was displayed when the Legislature confirmed the appointment of former Governor Archibald Alexander's protégé, Mr. Leroy A. Quinn, as head of the newly created Bureau, after he had twice failed to produce the desired results as Commissioner of Finance. Finally, we reiterate our contention: If you fail to take positive action in the immediate future or deny the people of the Virgin Islands the right to review your findings, recommendations and conclusions, then it can be predicted as a certainty that many of us will systematically be forced out of the Bureau and the Federal Government will take over tax collections in the Territory."

Kenneth Hansen, the Special Procedures Officer, had been promised the position of Chief of the Delinquent Accounts and Returns Branch by Quinn and so out of his slavish loyalty to Quinn he wrote to Senator Ruby Simmonds saying, "Since I was absent both times, hearings were held (the one on August 26th at the Bureau's office and the other September 2nd), I was certainly not in a position to form or express an opinion one way or the other. For this reason, when your correspondence was presented to me I declined to affix my signature and the fact that I disagreed with the overall connotations of the correspondence. Please be advised that I do not wish to be a party to any constant bickering, exchange of needless correspondence or personality clashes and I thought this should be clarified for the record."

What Kenneth Hansen had said did not square with reality. As members of the same Union we were a group of people being held together by the same interest. Hansen was going around in circles. Prejudice had warped his judgment. I had known from the outset that I was engaged in a fight against "City Hall" and I had also known for many years that the Senators were not going to do anything favorable to me. That was the reason I had been forced to go public with a view towards going to the Third Circuit Court. Senators Belado De O'Neal, John Bell, Lorraine Berry, Virdin Brown, Adelbert Bryan, Hector Cintron, Eric Dawson, Derrick Hodge, Cain Magras, Cleone Creque Maynard, James O'Bryan, Holland Redfield, Paul Shatkin and Iver Stridiron and all the others starting from the year 1970, didn't have the guts to do anything that would have brought a semblance of order to our workplace.

I had written to Senator Ruby Rouss in her capacity of Chairman of the Senate Committee on Finance on April 2, 1975 telling her that, "As an ardent admirer of your continuing acts of altruism on behalf of the people of the Virgin Islands and following your incisive questioning of Mr. Milton Branch, it occurred to me that I should write to you in your capacity as Chairman of the Senate's Committee on Finance in order to shed some light on what appears to be another showy display on the part of the Executive Branch. Our less-than-professional governmental system, which refuses to enforce the laws of the Territory (due largely perhaps to nepotism) while thriving on duplications, etc., has also prompted me to write to you in the hope that you would use the power of your office to deter or otherwise discourage any ostensible attempts designed to make inroads into our delinquency situation. A recent disclosure by the Luis Administration has glaringly revealed that task forces made up of many of the same people who are directly responsible for our fiscal woes, have been formed for the purpose of advising the Governor on how to raise revenues and cut government spending. As shocking as this revelation has been to the public, there exists another dormant seed in our government that of necessity needs exposure. That the Virgin Islands Bureau of Internal Revenue, which supposedly mirrors the United States Internal Revenue Service with all its administrative remedies and powerful enforcement tools, has difficulty reducing its receivables is common knowledge throughout the territory. Yet, the Commissioner of Health expects to reach out to the Bureau in an effort to have them train his employees in bill collecting. Just how much frivolity is involved remains conjectural. One need not be reminded that it was Liston Monsanto in his capacity of Internal Revenue Officer assigned to the Bureau of Internal Revenue, formerly Tax Division, who was given the arduous task of training many of the health employees in their Collection activity during calendar years 1972 and 1973. Needless to say, they could not implement their training because our archaic system of government denied them that opportunity. We are hopelessly trapped in a cul-de-sac. Under present conditions in this society where people are enjoying life based on false beliefs and hopes, we will never ever be able to reduce (significantly) the receivables of the Virgin Islands Government." The taxpayers who were profiting from what was going on in the Virgin Islands Bureau of Internal Revenue were not about to lose it to anybody, least of all me.

David J. O'Connell, perhaps the biggest carpetbagger on the island, operating as an accountant and here only for what the island was doing for him wanted me out of the Bureau of Internal Revenue. He was very concerned about Woods' predicament so much so that he was faced with the dilemma of telling a lie or betraying his friend. And so in a most foolish act designed only to preserve the status quo, he wrote and hand-delivered a letter to Governor Juan Luis dated September 18, 1981. While he may have been a financial contributor to many of the politicians, his letter of desperation really exposed him for what he really was, a big liar. Here's what he wrote, "The enclosed article which appeared in The Daily News on Thursday the 17th of September 1981 concerns me a great deal. Simply put, an honest, hard working, conscientious man seems to be in the process of being overwhelmed by an individual possessing complete opposite attributes. We have dealt with Mr. Woods and his Department on behalf of out clients numerous times over the years. Mr. Woods has always been courteous, tactful and fair in the execution of his responsibilities. He sees the taxpayers before him as proud and dignified human beings who are in the uncomfortable and often embarrassing situation of being delinquent taxpayers. It has been my experience that Mr. Woods exerts a tremendous amount of understanding and patience in these relationships and still effects a reasonable Collection Plan for the government. In my estimation, the value of his expertise far exceeds the compensation he receives. Liston Monsanto has exhibited little or no tact in many of his dealings with the taxpaying public. In one instance, Mr. Monsanto appeared in our client's office threatening foreclosure of their business, loudly proclaiming their tax problem to all who cared to listen and intimidated the owner's wife to a state of tears, all of this while the taxpayers was honestly attempting to quietly resolve the bad business decisions which allowed him to become delinquent and to pay his taxes. In this situation the intervention of Mr. Woods settled the waters and the taxes were collected. In summary, I feel that the absence of Bobby Woods from the Director's position at Collections will be sorely felt, a good man is always hard to replace. Further, Liston Monsanto's arrogance and tactless behavior in the supposed execution of his duties will not enhance the reputation of the V.I. Bureau of Internal Revenue or the government as a whole. Please accept this correspondence in the light that it is offered. We have a great deal of respect and admiration for Bobby Woods and regret the austere and mitigating circumstances surrounding his departure. Please let us know if we can be of any assistance in this matter."

What David J. O'Connell had written was slanderous. Why was he so desperate? Was he hoping for a quid pro quo? He didn't even bother to send me a copy. About nine (9) months later I was assigned an account for one of his clients. I did not want to make a demand for payment inasmuch as I did not want to give him the impression that I was retaliating. Accordingly, I wrote to Malone on June 3, 1982, sending a copy to Olive. I said, "The attached letter authored by local CPA, Mr. David J. O'Connell, who incidentally has always, in his frequent visits to our headquarters, found the time to engage in levity with certain high level personnel, was written by way of lampoonery and partly on behalf of one of his many delinquent clients in an effort to embarrass and humiliate me. Mr. O'Connell's vituperative letter was introduced at my recent hearing before the Government Employees' Service Commission on May 19, 1982 to support one of the many charges trumped up against me by Messrs. Anthony Olive and Leroy Quinn in a glaring attempt to unilaterally dismiss me from my classified position of Internal Revenue Officer IV. Because it appears a certainty that Mr. Olive and Mr. Quinn prefer to destroy the credibility of the Revenue Officer by giving credence to the lies of Mr. O'Connell, thereby impairing the effectiveness of the Revenue Officer, I'm asking that the account of Jane Doe (whom Mr. O'Connell represents) be taken from me and reassigned to another Revenue Officer so that immediate steps may be taken to resolve it. I would hate to work on delinquent accounts and returns without your moral support. Consequently, (unless you've changed the rules to permit harassment on the part of accountants) any thing that may serve as a detriment to morale and mission accomplishment, (such as the Jane Doe case) will be brought to your attention."

Olive returned his copy of the letter to me indicating that he didn't want it. I therefore was forced to write to him on June 8, 1982 sending a copy to Malone. I said, "The return on the carbon copy of my letter of June 3, 1982, which was addressed to Mr. Roy Malone, provides concrete evidence that in the Virgin Islands almost everybody has his moral values mixed up (i.e. good, as is literally defined means bad and vice versa). A classic example of the aforementioned axiom may be found in Mr. David J. O'Connell's letter of September 18, 1982, a copy of which you have in your files. For your information, in the United States Internal Revenue Service, after which we are mirrored, an investigation would have been launched upon receipt of Mr. O'Connell's letter, in order to ascertain the reason(s) for the affinity that he held for Mr. Woods, whom he believed to be Chief of the Delinquent Accounts and Returns Branch. Finally, this letter confirms the statements of fact made in my letter on June 3, 1982. Unlike many people, I see no reason to lie." P.S. "One of man's favorite pastimes – fooling himself."

With the blessings of Governor Juan Luis, the evildoers (Quinn, Olive, et al.) continued with their wicked deeds. In his appearance before the Senate's mock session on the evening of September 2, 1982, Quinn had zeroed in on me telling Senators Simmonds, Stridiron and Dennis that the only way the Bureau would have a chance at being successful would be saying good riddance to Liston Monsanto. In order to get help from any elected official one had to have been out of control and guilty of wrongdoing. I was guilty of neither. None of the Senators on the panel made any attempt to ask Quinn why was I deserving of blame.

The situation continued to be problematic thereby forcing me to continue in a prolonged ordeal. Quinn left the mock session at the senate holding stubbornly to his desire to systematically rid the Bureau of me. In an act bordering on an unfair labor practice, he rewarded Hansen with the position of Chief of the Delinquent Accounts and Returns Branch. (Note: Roy Malone - coward as he was, needed somebody like the artless Kenneth Hansen to shield him from me). As the Assistant Chief he had been exposed to much confusion as John Ferrant's scapegoat. Being aggrieved by Quinn's action I filed a grievance requiring the Union to do for me what they had promised initially. I wrote to Tito Morales on September 27, 1982, telling him, "In a cunningly conceived operation, management has apparently induced two of our members to shift to their side. One happens to be our elected representative, Mr. Kenneth Hansen and the other is Mr. Robert Woods, who received an appointment a few days ago, presumably in violation of the personnel merit system. Mr. Hansen has been with the Delinquent Accounts and Returns Branch for about fourteen (14) years during which time he's been overlooked by management in their quest to find a blind loyalist for the position of Chief of the Delinquent Accounts and Returns Branch. He has witnessed and has vehemently voiced his opposition to the many stateside retirees and junior employees who, at one time or another, has been called upon to supervise the Branch. Mercenaries such as Mr. Robert Wallace and Mr. John Ferrant, plus Robert Woods, a former employee of the Processing Branch, who has yet to be formally trained, have all taken turns as Chief Delinquent Accounts and Returns Branch. Currently, Mr. Roy Malone, who followed Mr. Hansen into the organization, has been given the authority to supervise the activities of our Branch, thereby placing Mr. Hansen in a subordinate position where he enjoys the privilege of not signing in and out the way other employees on his level are required to do. The foregoing clearly shows that under present conditions, Mr. Kenneth Hansen, who does his work so well while exhibiting a "no-nonsense" attitude, will never ever be considered for a supervisory position. It is most unfortunate, for what Mr. Hansen doesn't know about our organization in his capacity as Special Procedure Officer would sell many books."

On July 2, 1982 I had written to Quinn sending copies of my letter to Luis, Millin and Olive. In my letter I had told him, among other things, about the vacant position of Chief of the Delinquent Accounts and Returns Branch. Here is what I wrote:

July 2, 1982

Leroy A. Quinn
Director
Virgin Islands Bureau of Internal Revenue
P.O. Box 3186
St. Thomas, Virgin Islands 00801

Dear Mr. Quinn:

Inasmuch as it has been established that most employees *that* of the Virgin Islands Bureau of Internal Revenue feel security and safety in numbers take precedence over lawfullness, to say that respect for law and authority has been a most powerful weapon in the arsenal of a small minority assigned to the Delinquent Accounts and Returns Branch, is an understatement that deserves the highest degree of publicity.

Armed and blessed with such honor and esteem, plus the landmark opinion filed on March 11, 1982 (81-1434 Liston Monsanto versus Leroy A. Quinn) by the United States Court of Appeals for the Third Circuit, the small minority knows that any unlawful attempt(s) emanating from management and designed to weaken or to exhaust its resources will be a nullity. Moreover, we know that in this government of, for, and by the people, one can afford-like the legendary Swiss Patriot William Tell, not to bow-down to any person, place or thing.

Law-abiding employees see no need to circumuent, restrict, or limit the law as is commonplace in the Bureau of Internal Revenue. Furthermore, the court's opinion referred to in paragraph two of this letter, has opened the door for many aggrieved employees (especially those whose civil rights have been violated) to assert their rights as classified public servants. It has also determined for management exactly what constitutes disruption and libel. In short, the opinion-if followed, will help to bring much-needed order to the Government's Bureau of Internal Revenue, while simultaneously stopping a take-over by the United States Treasury Department.

Equally important however, and perhaps a major drawback in the Bureau, is the long recognized fact, which deals with our desperate need for a Chief of the Delinquent Account and Returns Branch. The absence of a chief is even more critical at this time than it has ever been. This vacant position without a doubt, continues to be the principal reason for the problems in the Delinquent Accounts and Return Branch.

Furthermore, I feel that the filling of the classified position of Chief Delinquent Accounts and Returns Branch is absolutely essential.

It is a common error for public servants (especially those in position of authority) to think that the Government of the Virgin Islands is their personal possession. They fail to see that the mental picture which they have created serves only to make them responsible for certain acts and omissions, while forever making their office(s) open to critisim before the Government Employees Service Commission and the Courts.

If we sincerely intend to improve conditions in the Virgin Islands Bureau of Internal Revenue, and avert a take-over by the Federal Government, we must demonstrate a changed attitude with a willingness to work closely, harmoniously, and ethically with each other. The flaunting of authority by certain personnel in management and the disruptive influence now exerted by certain lower echelon employees over their peers, must cease and be replaced by mutual respect and admiration for each other.

Incidentally, now that I've returned to work after being vindicated of charges trumped up by you and Mr. Anthony P. Olive (see your libelous letter of March 16, 1982), It is hoped that you'd dispense with personalities, as I look forward to working as diligently as I did in the past, with a view towards projecting

an image that best represents the Virgin Islands Bureau of
Internal Revenue. This, I say unreservedly.

Sincerely,

Liston Monsanto

cc: Governor, Juan Luis
      Lieutenant Governor, Henry A. Millin
      Deputy Director, Anthony P. Olive

The Bureau of Internal Revenue was in disarray. Employees who had been quiet for some time were suddenly making noise and Quinn and his Deputy Director Anthony Olive had become restless. Ulric Vialet wrote to Quinn saying, "Once again I'm forced to make an appeal to you asking that you discontinue using what observers have termed an intolerable abuse of power, in your voluntarily stopping monies and the promotion legally awarded me by the Government Employees' Service Commission. As a fiscal officer and head of a professional organization which uses interest (i.e. money paid for the use of money) as a basic essential tool, you must know that your long delay in complying with the order of the Government Employees' Service Commission will ultimately result in our government having to pay an unnecessary accrued interest at the high annual rate of nine percent (9%). This sir, is fiscal imprudence of the highest sort. But above all, perhaps, is the fact that countless employees of the Bureau (taxpayers and voters) have been talking about what they consider to be failure to obey the law on your part and your penchant for suspending their constitutional rights. Accordingly, they have made the decision (predicated on the belief that the law works evenly, honestly and swiftly for everybody) to unionize. These employees have never ceased to be intrigued by management's lack of concern for them. What's more, the silent majority in the Bureau has for some time felt that only a swift and thorough airing of existing conditions and all their ramifications will restore sagging employee's confidence in your office and enable all Branches of the Bureau to focus their energies anew on carrying on the government's business. Furthermore, when referring to your office, they inevitably echo the words of the Greek author Aesop, 'Self conceit may lead to self destruction.' Having won the respect of your office, I take this opportunity to remind you that you've forgotten to return my certificate, which I earned from the United States Internal Revenue Service upon the successful completion of my training program. It was forwarded to your office on March 1, 1982."

In a show of disrespect some employees were posting cartoons on the bulletin boards showing Olive in an exaggerated way while others who were not really qualified for the positions they held were trying to please or otherwise win him over by flattering words and actions.

Time after time Steven Frett had approached me asking that I take over the duties of shop steward and time after time I had refused. Having defeated "City Hall" several times, frankly I didn't give a damn. If through abysmal ignorance the employees wanted to continue down the primrose path to disaster that would be a choice that only they could make. Because of my national pride, an outgrowth of a sincere love for the Virgin Islands and the human beings who occupy them, I had become overly altruistic and like a wary person I had begun to feed individuals and organized groups with the proverbial long spoon. I knew from his demeanor that Frett's intentions were free from pretense but as a realist, cynic and ombudsman with an enviable record, I decided against committing altruistic suicide. I felt sorry over the fact that I had hurt the feelings of Frett. He appeared so honest and enterprising. I really wanted to make common cause with the members of our bargaining unit but the knowledge that I had been bitten several times by ingrates (some of whom were members of the unit) possessing volatile dispositions in the Virgin Islands Bureau of Internal Revenue made me very shy. Grievances were being filed in record numbers. It was a most difficult task for a labor union comprising of manifold shops to throw the greater or more influential portion of its resources in one direction. The Bureau of Internal Revenue, however, was a place of much weight in the Virgin Islands community and we therefore felt that changed attitudes were needed in order to accomplish our objectives.

While we continued to operate in violation of law with the approval of a less-than-professional Virgin Islands society, the silent weight of public opinion was against Quinn ever since I had received my favorable decision from the Third Circuit Court, a decision which had put a halter around his neck. As I look back I feel safe in saying that my kindness (interpreted as stupidity by the wrongdoers) had actuated me to help Kenneth Hansen when he had first entered the government service as a fledgling. He showed promise but turned out to be very opportunistic and like a bull with a ring in its nose could be easily misled down the path of ease leading to wickedness. Kenneth Hansen would betray a friend for a reward in great haste.

As a representative of our bargaining unit he had sold us out for compensation in the form of Chief of the Delinquent Accounts and Returns Branch, a position from where he would aid my detractors in doing to me what the other "hit men" had failed to do. All of a sudden he began writing letters telling me, a man who had been his supervisor and a man who had been labeled "highly desirable" by Ulric Benjamin, that I was taking "short cuts" in the performance of my duties. Then in what appeared to be a zealous effort designed to impress Quinn and the others he instructed me to use the Internal Revenue Code, the Internal Revenue Manual, the Internal Revenue Rules and Regulation and the Virgin Islands Code in the performance of my duties.

In a series of letters beginning March 23, 1983, I responded to Hansen in this manner, "Ordinarily I would ignore a letter written by way of repartee, such as the one you addressed to me on March 22, 1983, but since it would take little time and effort to refute it, I'll accommodate you with an answer. Anyone who confesses to digging through a nasty, dirty garbage can in an attempt to trump up charges that would cause an honest man (especially one who has suffered and continues to suffer vicariously for him) to be fired from his job, is a person worth watching. Reminds you of Judas? My record speaks for itself. Moreover, it is a fact that you have been trying very hard to intimidate me and harass me, even to the point where you've expressed a desire to read the speedometer on my personal car. Other things that you've done in the recent past, plus your letter provide tangible proof of intimidation and harassment. By the way, if you'd read paragraph three (3) of my March 21st letter, you'll find that you've completely misinterpreted its meaning. Also, you may recall, look at the record, that I've been kicked out of our organization several times because I preferred to use the Internal Revenue Code, the Internal Revenue Manual, the Internal Revenue Rules and Regulations along with the V.I. Code, while certain favorites of management used the art of persuasion in collecting. OCF is a classic example. 'A ship with too many pilots sometimes has difficulty reaching port.' Finally, it is an undeniable and true fact of life that misrepresentations and lies have never resulted in a permanent benefit for anyone."

I followed up on March 24, 1983 saying: "A spot check survey of the accounts assigned to our Office Collection Force has disclosed that the personnel assigned to that office have been taking "short cuts" and not using the Internal Revenue Code, Internal Revenue Manual, Internal Revenue Rules and Regulations, along with the Virgin Islands Code as guides in the daily exercise of their duties. Maybe they feel as if they have been granted immunity or is it dereliction of duty? Your part in what has become an obnoxious scenario has been assumed by all knowledgeable observers who feel that a high degree of curryfavor is being shown towards the personnel of OCF. I therefore request that efforts be made to shift your position so that all under your supervision are treated fairly instead of shifting words as you did in your letter of March 22, 1983."

I had to keep Hansen on the defensive. I shot back at him on March 25, 1983. I wrote: "The recent sporadic assignment of accounts, three-fourths (3/4) of which were previously assigned to our Office Collection Force, causes me to wonder exactly what methods are being utilized to assign an account to me for Collection, would you please explain? Accounts coming through OCF do not, in most instances, show: (a) what steps have been taken prior to transfer, (b) whether appropriate form letters were sent to taxpayers, (c) whether a taxpayer is able to pay as evidenced by a completed financial statement or (d) whether follow-up action is being taken. Put simply, OCF is in a sordid mess. For us to pretend that this is not so is tantamount to the reaction given Hans Christian Andersen's naked emperor. You may recall that in a letter addressed to you on January 27, 1983 my cooperation was pledged to work harmoniously with you in trying to accomplish the Branch's objective. You may further recall that after it had become obvious to me that I was being exploited, I again wrote to you telling you that cooperation did not mean emasculation in the hope that you would have changed your modus operandi, but as is so soften said, hope springs eternal in the battered ear drums of man. It seems as if I'm being forced to present another grievance which would change the tongue-in-cheek approach that has become commonplace in our organization. As a sidelight I'd like to state that on March 24, 1983 I was told (off the record) that Mr. Alvin Swan was designated Acting Chief, DAR Branch during your absence from the office, the presence of Lima, Monsanto, Thomas, Todman, Vialet and Woods notwithstanding. All of these officers are Mr. Swan's senior (favoritism again?). Of prime importance is the fact that several taxpayers called for you and being unable to truthfully explain your whereabouts became a source of annoyance. It would therefore be appreciated if you would let us know when you are going to be away from the office and to whom you have delegated the authority to act as Chief." I knew I had gotten to him. He was speechless.

Operating through the usage of double standards was not going to work in the Delinquent Accounts and Returns Branch as long as I was a member. Again, on March 30, 1983, I wrote to Hansen. This time I said, "It has been a long time since you reviewed certain accounts in my inventory (large dollar cases) without issuing any comments. This inaction has left me entangled in a cesspool of uncertainty, inasmuch as I do not know, by your standards, whether or not I'm using the correct approach and explanation in closing the accounts. Our Branch has so many inconsistent qualities about it that objectivity in reviewing a Revenue Officer's caseload has become a most difficult task. On one hand we are given a revised policy statement as an authority for enforcement and on the other hand we are told by you that Mr. Quinn does not want to disturb the business community. Quite a paradox, isn't it? Apart from the foregoing, I'm still awaiting an explanation to the question which I raised in paragraph one of my letter of March 25, 1983. Would you kindly show your mutual cooperation?"

Prior to my writing to Hansen about the Branch's inability to collect taxes from the business community, an editorial appeared in the local Daily News of April 1982 under the caption "Now, More Than Ever." It said, "At times it seems that government and business view each other as natural enemies. This hostile relationship, in many cases, affects the growth of the community in which they exist and this attitude between both parties has an even more damaging effect when the economy is sluggish and poor, a time when both should be seeking a close working relationship. Thus it was with some optimism that we read that Gov. Luis has pledged, once again, to form a partnership between the private sector and the government. The Governor hit the nail right on the head when he remarked that to have a healthy government, we must have a healthy private sector. The Chief Executive told the St. Thomas-St. John Chamber of Commerce that a partnership is needed 'now, more than ever' because of the national and world economic problems and competition faced by these islands for the tourist trade. He also called on the business community to support the government's effort to fight crime, find new ways to promote tourism, develop a home-ownership program and make agriculture a viable industry, in short, to work hand-in-hand with government to improve the quality of life in these islands. Too often in the past we have seen actions by government officials that gave the impression that the private sector is only there to funnel money into the government treasury when it is needed, otherwise the business community is just taken for granted or viewed with hostility. By the same token, we have witnessed an aloofness to the community by some in the private sector in which they give the impression that their only concern is to make as much money as possible, then close up shop and head home with their take. The latest initiative by the Governor and the business community is a positive step toward brining all of us together and utilizing as much of the human resources as we have in the Virgin Islands. We hope also it reflects an atmosphere of sustained cooperation that we will see in other areas with this administration. But above all, we hope it is not merely more empty talk."

I had refused to be guided and used by the influential wrongdoers in the Virgin Islands Bureau of Internal Revenue, something that was being done to Hansen with alarming regularity. As far as I was concerned, on the one hand Governor Juan Luis and the Daily News were publicly saying give the business community a break, while on the other hand the same Governor Luis through Quinn and Hansen was sicking the Internal Revenue Officers on the business community. Through the usage of the rule of thumb, these people intended to do exactly as they pleased when it came to using the employees to do their dirty work.

I continued to build a record against Hansen with a view towards protecting myself. I wrote to him on April 11, 1983 saying: "Abuse of discretionary power, accepting rumor as fact and an overall lack of respect for law and authority have long been deficiencies of management which have served to encourage certain Revenue Officers to take 'short cuts' and even devise a way to get around or through the web of rules, regulation and procedures that serve as guides in the daily exercise of our duties. The accounts of John Doe which were forwarded to me for my review and returned herewith are a classic example of the aforementioned deficiencies. Unlike the accounts of Jane Doe which I recently transferred to St. Croix (after locating the taxpayer and her representative) there is no credible evidence on the history sheet to show where in St. Thomas John Doe can be found. Moreover, the comments made by Chief, DAR Branch on March 26, 1981, clearly indicate that we have exhausted the machinery for Collection under our present system. It is a most unethical thing for the processing Returns and Accounts Branch to engage in buck-passing and it is even worse when in our very own Branch we have Revenue Officers shifting their responsibilities to another Revenue Officer. I therefore ask that you take all steps necessary to correct this inequity."

And yet another letter to Hansen dated April 21, 1983: "When Mr. Quinn first assumed the responsibility of Director of the V.I. Bureau of Internal Revenue (formerly Tax Division), he offered me the position of Special Procedures Officer. I refused it for several reasons. I thought then, as I do now, that we were encouraging certain Revenue Officers to use the Special Procedures Officer as a crutch in carrying out their duties. Additionally, I'm of the honest opinion that malingerers must be told that they are public servants from whom a day's work is expected for a day's pay. What's past is prologue. It is however, well to mention that being Special Procedures Officer in the Virgin Islands requires an apologetic attitude. In short, one must be a milque-toast. I am returning the accounts to you inasmuch as I refuse to be coerced into accepting anything that is designed to incriminate me. I'm also sending copies of the correspondence which relates directly to the matter to the attention of Director Quinn so that he may be made aware of your continuing attempts to harass me and retaliate against me because of the grievance which I've filed. Instead of trying to shift the responsibility for closing the accounts to me, I'd like to suggest that you inquire of the Processing Branch as to whether or not the group promoting horse races at the 'Nadir Race Track' is paying the required five percent (5%) gross receipts tax."

Although it had been a surreal year for Hansen, living in a state of bliss, he just could not see the error of his ways. I had been a pacifist, one opposed to war and favors. The only weapon in my arsenal was a pen. So once again, even though I knew that I was giving unwanted advice, I decided to use it on Mr. Kenneth Hansen. I wrote on June 28, 1983: "Looking through our 'reading file,' by chance I came upon a letter addressed to you from Revenue Officer Ulrie Vialet which released the results of his review of the OCF files. Mr. Vialet's spontaneous review came at a time when he was assigned to OCF and was obviously conducted pursuant to the Guidelines of the United States Internal Revenue Service.

In the United States Internal Revenue Service, allowing a statute to expire is a grievous crime. Revenue Officers found guilty of this violation for the first time are severely reprimanded. Continual infractions however, result in their being expelled from the service. We are lucky to be in the U.S. Virgin Islands where we can flaunt our guilt.

And speaking of the U.S. Virgin Islands, I'd like to remind you of the fiscal crisis in which we have found ourselves. There is not enough money to operate a government whose accounts receivable is very high and the continuous negligence on the part of so-called professional Revenue Officers does nothing to help. Also, bear in mind that the fiscal crisis has closed the door to any kind of employee augmentation. Because the Bureau continues to ostentatiously advertise job vacancies, the inevitable question is: Are we going to continue our status in quo or are we going to get serious about collecting?"

Although my letters had been written directly to Kenneth Hansen, Leroy Quinn received a copy every time that I wrote. On July 14, 1983, I wrote once again to Hansen. I said, "Your continuous assignments of taxpayer delinquent accounts together with an impending review of accounts in my inventory clearly show that despite a meretricious display of holier than thou attitudes, beatific smiles and a serious fiscal crisis demanding urgent attention, management's deportment continues to be a constant menace to the development of the Virgin Islands Bureau of Internal Revenue. Currently, there are certain employees in management who are so mesmerized by pseudo promotions and the sound of a fancy job title, that they have little or no faith in the judgment of their subordinates. Going back to February of this year, the Revenue Officers repeatedly told you the personnel in OCF were operating like a sinecure and that the overall OCF operation required your immediate attention. Yet, without any trace of wangling, you permitted the statute to toll on several accounts in that office.

Review in chronological order the letters that I've written to you and you'll find that the Delinquent Accounts and Returns Branch is not operating according to Hoyle; consequently, you have brought into existence what appears to be a deliberate suspension of my judgment. Mr. Hansen, the record shows that the Internal Revenue Manual is used only when it suits your purpose. Incidentally, some of the accounts that you'll be reviewing are those that were transferred directly from your inventory, after your refusal to take appropriate action. Flouting the law has become commonplace in the Bureau of Internal Revenue. For reasons of security I would pawn my honor, but I doubt (rather seriously) if I'd be a pawn for anybody."

Kenneth Hansen was still masochistic enough to write to me while I was on annual leave saying how ironic it was that I unlike any other Revenue Officer had found what I thought was a reason or several reasons to complain about the absence of established guidelines. He had, with the blessing of Quinn and Olive, become exceedingly accustomed to doing unlawful things that he honestly believed that whatever he was doing was the right thing. But via a method of offset upon my return to work, I responded immediately saying, "Timing is an intrinsic part of any correspondence that is designed to exonerate its author. Whether it is simple or complex, the success of its timing, a memorandum written by the Chief of the Delinquent Accounts and Returns Branch to an employee while that employee is on annual leave to obviously make an impression on the federal auditors, is the key to relieving an individual from an obligation, duty or task. Speaking of irony, here is a bit of it: (a) when Christopher Columbus (one individual) said the earth was round, hardly a person believed him, (b) when Galilei Galileo (one individual) said the velocity of falling bodies was independent of their weight, hardly anyone believed him, (c) when Winston Churchill (one individual) stated that from Stettin in the Baltic to Trieste in the Adriatic an iron curtain had descended across the continent of Europe, hardly a person believed him and (d) when Liston Monsanto proved that the federal guidelines to which you refer in paragraph three of your memorandum, cannot and are not being used (except in certain cases when it suits your purpose), you and others in management talk about my being the only Revenue Officer to complain about the absence of guidelines. One man with courage, Mr. Hansen, constitutes a majority.

As Chief of the Branch and a former Special Procedures Officer, surely you must know that most of the nineteen (19) Revenue Officers to whom you refer, are victims of a governmental system that demands mediocrity. These people do not have the ability to use the guidelines of the United States Internal Revenue Service. I tried to use the provisions of the 'mirror theory' in 1971 and 1979 and both times I was ousted from my position. Ask Mr. Quinn and Mr. Olive. The trouble with the Bureau, is an unwillingness on its part to accept the philosophy of the mirror theory.

Since your appointment as Chief, DARB, I have written you several letters which explain in detail my sincere feelings about working conditions in our Branch. Hence, I suggest you immediately review them as your memorandum of October 7, 1983 is nothing but a diversion to cloud the real issue." My letter was dated October 11, 1983.

Hansen was keeping me busy writing letters. As a person who had done me a lot of wrong, I felt free from mean or petty feelings against him but I felt it necessary to protect myself. They were out to get me and I was not too certain about the Union's ability to give me the protection that I required. On January 30, 1984, I wrote to Hansen in this manner: "Since it appears as if you have assumed the role of figure-head, I'd like to (in the interest of giving you an insight into the affairs of our local tax system) ask that you ponder the following statements of fact: (a) owing to the political system in the Virgin Islands, you've been appointed Chief of the Delinquent Accounts and Returns Branch, (b) owing to the political system in the Virgin Islands, after nearly a quarter of a century as an employee of the Bureau of Internal Revenue (formerly Tax Division), I'm still an Internal Revenue Officer, my seniority and qualifications notwithstanding, (c) in spite of our positions, neither you nor I can do any more than the political system allows us to do. I fully understand the system and its myriad of problems. Rather than play hocus pocus however, as part of the solution I go about my daily task as legitimately as possible. That is why I'm able to sleep at night and get to work on time the next day. Those who are part of the problem and pretend not to see the forest for the trees, have been doing wrong for so long that they have reversed completely the meaning of good to mean bad and vice versa. That is why they are unable to sleep at night and continue to be late for work. Although I've seen the system work for me, I did not design or promote it. What's more, it is a matter of record that you, in defiance of the system and on your own volition, submitted to the College of the Virgin Islands a thesis on 'The Mirror Theory' which supported my contention that the Delinquent Accounts and Returns Branch is without a standard or principle by which to make a judgment.

So this brings to issue our desperate need for guidelines. Please re-read your thesis keeping in mind that the only difference between the U.S. Tax System and ours is the fact that the monies collected in the Virgin Islands stay in the Virgin Islands. After you've re-read the document you will agree that our way of doing things in the Bureau does not coincide with the contents of your thesis. In short, Revenue Officers are glorified bill collectors without guidelines. On another matter, please be reminded that horse races have been scheduled for Sunday, February 5, 1984 at the Nadir Race Track. I believe that the five percent (5%) gross receipts tax is in order."

Quinn and Olive were enjoying what was going on. Hansen had become their shield, the shield that they had always wanted. They would not get away from me, however. I would address them both a little later because of the positions they held in the Bureau. Olive had always been a non-entity and Edward Thomas was continuing to usurp the power of both men, a fact of which I was aware.

On February 2, 1984, I aimed with precision towards Olive sending copies of my letter to Luis and Hansen. I said: "Late in 1971, following my introduction of certain innovations (which included Revenue Officer participation in Phase II of their training program, higher wages and appearances before the Department of Labor as a representative for you, Mr. Hansen, et al) into an inferior tax system, I was removed from the then Tax Division by way of ostracism, thereby resulting in an unproductive effort similar to that of today. A direct report on my present status was forwarded to you on January 27, 1984, after you had received several copies of letters addressed to Mr. Hansen. As of this writing, everything remains status quo and inasmuch as you've refrained from recognizing any of my letters, I can only conclude that the existing condition or state of affairs surrounding the matter has been sanctioned by you. This being the case, I would like to notify you once more that I'm without an assignment. It is most embarrassing and humiliating to be in this unproductive position during this period when the V.I. Government is struggling through a financial crisis and when my services are so badly needed as an Internal Revenue Officer IV for which I have been specially trained and which has been my career occupation. Finally, I repeat, I am not one of those government employees who enjoy being paid for doing nothing; hence, I request that I be immediately given an assignment that is commensurate with my salary of $25,000.00 per annum."

Then I went back to Hansen on February 6, 1984. I wrote: "I've told you before and I repeat in substance as follows: You cannot fairly evaluate my performance according to the Internal Revenue Manual. Many of us (including yourself) would not be in our positions were we in fact a carbon copy of the United States Internal Revenue Service. You can review my accounts and 795 (daily report) anytime you deem it necessary, but as long as we have no guidelines, I doubt very much if you can cite any source as the authority for your review and comments. Again, let me state that the things that you are now attempting to implement are the same things that I tried to implement during my reign as Chief of the Delinquent Accounts and Returns Branch. Do you know what happened? I was removed from the position, a statesider (who would do exactly what the system required) was brought in and once again the ambitions of the Delinquent Accounts and Returns Branch were subverted. Ask Mr. Anthony Olive."

Lest you forget I was now a member of the Bureau's bargaining unit and not in a position to represent anybody in the unit. Our shop steward was Miss Vashti Gumbs, an employee assigned to work in the Delinquent Accounts and Returns Branch. I was trying my best through my letters to make available to the Union any information that they might need to represent me. On February 8, 1984, in a letter to Hansen I said: "Our exchange of correspondence (with copies to Mr. Anthony Olive, who remains silent), tells me that you have attained the rank of Director Defacto of the Virgin Islands Bureau of Internal Revenue. Your memorandum of February 8, 1984 indicates that you are not understanding my letters; consequently, it behooves me to inform you that I was the first Internal Revenue Officer IV in the entire Virgin Islands. I was also present at the negotiating table (after you had betrayed us) as a union representative when management (through Mr. Olive, et al.) accepted a contract that they now choose to ignore in much the same manner as you've ignored 'examples of work' on the job specification. Management has no respect for law and authority. Evidence of disrespect may be found in your so-called authoritative source (IRM 5(14) 13 Sections 4 and 5) which ironically authorized me to do exactly what I did in returning certain accounts to you. Why, in the absence of guidelines would you want to continue your double standards? Once again, I ask that you read and digest all the letters that I've sent to you, keeping in mind, all the while, that the position of Chief of the Delinquent Accounts and Returns Branch is still open and goes before an arbitrator on February 23, 1984. Speaking of tools, please arrange for cars, adding machines, briefcases and other basic essentials to be delivered to our Branch. We've been without them since your inheritance of the position as Chief of the Delinquent Accounts and Returns Branch. 'Let us be thankful for the tools; but for them the rest of us could not succeed'."

February 29, 1984, another letter to Hansen: "In a memorandum dated February 15, 1984 (one day after you were accused of being habitually late for work) you were asked a question relating directly to our work. To date it has not been answered. If the Bureau of Internal Revenue sincerely intends to educate the taxpayers of the Virgin Islands (prior to enforcing) Revenue Officers must be given appropriate answers to their questions. I therefore ask that you answer the question."

Then Olive, acting in a perfunctory way, called a meeting placing emphasis on professionalism. There was nothing about overall working conditions in the Bureau of Internal Revenue that distinguished the methods of a professional from those of an amateur. He was really using the self-fulfilling prophecy. I immediately wrote to Olive saying: "Already following your meeting, the analysts are coming up with various explanations as to why you continuously used the art of dissuasion in denying us the opportunity to discuss any job-related matter with you, but inasmuch as you admitted to Revenue Officer Louis Willis in your October 25th meeting with the Revenue Officers and Miss Paulette Rawlins that the phrase 'mirror theory' is a misnomer and that to implement the mirror theory would result in a change of personnel, I feel it my duty to provide documentary evidence for the future. It is well to mention that with the change of each Director, (Note: Leroy A. Quinn had departed the Bureau in May of 1984) in the past, we have seen competent personnel at the Bureau of Internal Revenue hampered because they were subjected to orders from less competent people, who happened to be pawns and scapegoats of the Directors in our less than professional governmental system. These incompetents exerted such great influence that currently it poses a serious threat to the overall operations of the Bureau of Internal Revenue. It therefore goes without saying that if we continue along our chartered course, the future collapse we all are trying to deter may be upon us before we know it. And with respect to the professionalism of which you speak, let me, for the sake of clarity, explain that the Governor by virtue of his position as Chief Executive has oversight over all the Departments, Agencies, Bureaus, Instrumentalities, etc., in the Executive Branch of our government; consequently, it is very doubtful that he would permit trained employees (as is ostensibly the case in the Bureau) to channel their work through half-trained and untrained employees in the other Departments, etc. Finally, I reiterate my contention to wit: 'The trouble with the Bureau is an unwillingness on its part to accept the philosophy of the mirror theory'."

CHAPTER III
Anthony P. Olive

Anthony P. Olive had moved up from Deputy Director to Director in May of 1984. Edward Thomas was still a member of the shadow cabinet using his influence with the power elite to control things in the Virgin Islands Bureau of Internal Revenue. Olive would be at his mercy for some time after his pseudo appointment. The thought of being the Chief shop steward suggested that I would be in a very good position to see and hear what was going on with the management team selected to represent the Bureau at the negotiating table. So once again at the suggestion of Steven Frett, I relented and became Chief Shop Steward of the Bureau's bargaining unit. I had been put in a position where I would have to choose between trying and failing or doing nothing and succeeding.

Together with members of a shadow cabinet, the Bureau's management team had been operating with reckless abandon for many years. Many employees in the bargaining unit with time in grade ranging from one to five years were not as familiar with the overall operations of the Bureau as I was. The older employees such as Kenneth Hansen, Roy Malone and Jens Todman were not trustworthy and had already proven that they could be bought. At any rate, two days after I had been elected by the members of my bargaining unit, negotiations were being held at the office of the Chief Negotiator. I had prepared myself for the negotiations inasmuch as I would come face to face with Anthony Olive and Edward Thomas, among others.

On the day of the negotiations, Steven Frett and I walked into the room where the management team was sitting awaiting our team's arrival. They did not expect to see me and became speechless with surprise. They immediately held a caucus which out of a sense of desperation and the usage of the flimsy excuse that they were not told that I had been elected to represent the employees, resulted in a cancellation of the negotiations. They carried no burden of shame at all and needless to say, where there is no shame there is no honor. They were, unknown to them, fulfilling my expectations right in front of Frett thereby leaving me in a state of wonderment. It was for me an eventful day. Frett himself was infused by their cowardly action. Why did they have to be told about me as a representative? Where representation was concerned, it did not matter to our side, who they would choose to represent them. In retrospect, it would have been illusory to think that my presence at the negotiating table was a welcomed one.

Edward Thomas and all the others on the side of management knew that it was an unfair labor practice under Title 24, Section 65(1) of the Virgin Islands Code to have his wife working on the employee level while he was working on the other side. How could we exclude Mrs. Lucia Thomas from any meeting we may have called dealing with a job action? Olive who was at the highest level in the Bureau of Internal Revenue and the officials in Local 8249 didn't have to be told about this violation. They knew it existed. Something like this, the lack of legal representation (a lawyer), plus an overall aura of union apathy made working conditions more or less the same way it had been prior to the Union's entry.

There is an old saying that goes: "Shake any family tree and a few nuts are bound to fall." This particular saying was used to introduce Roy Vanterpool, an employee assigned to the Processing Branch. He was a degenerate character very proud of his academic life and regularly carried a gun in the workplace holstered to his right leg, something that Olive knew and ignored completely. Through Civil Number 1984/37, three (3) female employees (June Blyden, Donna Phillips and Marilyn Turner) were each awarded $2,000.00 together with interest after Vanterpool had been charged, among other things, with sexually harassing them. Roy Vanterpool took tremendous pride in taking advantage of disadvantaged people. He couldn't put his ego on the side long enough for anyone without a college degree to say anything to him. The man was one of the most bizarre supervisors in the entire Virgin Islands. For his subordinates there was nothing more disquieting then to go to work knowing that your supervisor was armed and dangerous. To the employees' credit, however, they were not afraid of Roy Vanterpool.

On August 4, 1982, one of his subordinates (Rickheild Thomas) wrote to Vanterpool (after Vanterpool had thrown one of his juvenile temper tantrums) telling him: "As the only predominantly black territory under the United States Flag, we as a people were expected to do a great deal in promoting American Democracy for the greatest nation on earth. In short, we were expected to serve as a model for black people the world over, by simply showing them that only through hard work will one achieve success. Instead, our selfish leaders (political and otherwise) using selfishness and the instillation of fear, conveyed to the United States Government just how sophomoric, greedy, immature and subservient, they and other Virgin Islanders preferred to be, thereby failing the test. Washington D.C. knows that even a mosquito does not get a pat on the back unless he works.

A supervisor returning a letter to an employee with the word "garbage" written in capital letters could be construed as the work of a most rank amateur and is a sordid act lower than the excrement of a whale, which is found on the ocean floor. The lack of sincerity and compassion in the Processing and Accounts Branch, plus the absence of periodic meetings, make it most difficult for management to know how an employee feels. I do not have an inferiority complex and I'm definitely not a loafer. Finally, I'm sending copies of this letter to the officials as indicated below so that they may be made aware of the pettiness surrounding the work in our Branch." P.S. "I have no doubt that you read my letter before labeling it 'garbage,' but I will again enclose a copy herewith with an envelope should you desire to return it."

On February 18, 1986, Mr. Clyde George, another subordinate of Roy Vanterpool wrote to him saying, among other things, "as a law-abiding individual who does not have to keep a gun on his person the way you do at work and as an elected representative of the Employees Bargaining Unit, which is seeking to negotiate an agreement between the Bureau and the United Steelworkers of America, I have received new encouragement in our recent meetings inasmuch as I've seen (as I'm sure you have) that new alliances and a contract are currently in the spotlight." Mr. George followed up his letter by writing to Olive about Vanterpool's behavior. Here is what it said, "I am writing to you in the hope that you would give serious attention to what is happening between a difficult Mr. Roy Vanterpool and me, with a view towards improving communication in the Processing and Accounts Branch of the V.I. Bureau of Internal Revenue.

Perhaps hoping that his paycheck would grow, Mr. Vanterpool worked overtime, sometime last week, trumping up charges against me and subsequently cautioned me that I'd be disciplined if I did not correct the fraudulent charges listed in a letter addressed to me from him. I responded to Mr. Vanterpool's letter which was dated February 14, 1986 on February 18, 1986 and sent you a copy refuting most of his charges and asking for clarification on others. After reading my letter, Mr.

Vanterpool, obviously frustrated, tore it to bits. He then placed the pieces in an envelope addressed to me and walked into the file room where I was and where my desk is located and promptly placed the envelope thereon. Is this a new trend? If not, what do we do when taxpayers react the same way? Maybe you can offer some valuable advice, but as far as I'm concerned, Mr. Vanterpool should be charged with conduct unbecoming an Officer. Had I done to him what he did to me when I received his worthless letter, he may have used his gun to shoot me. I therefore ask that you give this matter your utmost attention."

Liston Monsanto was not the only employee complaining about working conditions in the Virgin Islands Bureau of Internal Revenue as you can readily see. Agent Vashti Gumbs on May 21, 1986 wrote to Olive as follows: "While passing your suggestion box today, several suggestions came to mind. It is my sincere hope that you would take suggestions seriously; they will not only improve conditions in the Bureau but save the Bureau embarrassment and money as a result of future lawsuits. The suggestions are as follows: (a) instruct management personnel to spend more time in their office doing the work for which they are being paid; rather than trying to harass and intimidate their employees, (b) inform management personnel that this is an office filled with adult professional people; and not a concentration camp, (c) direct management personnel to behave in a manner befitting that of a professional and not that of sniveling weaklings always looking for someone to fight their solicited battles, (d) remind management personnel that there is a disclosure act and that information obtained in the Bureau is not to be broadcast in bars in Frenchtown, Banks, etc."

Edward Thomas had already made an attempt on May 15, 1984 to stir up the employees by appealing to their emotions and prejudices in order to get more power and further his own interests. He had written to a timid Anthony Olive saying: "I am very disturbed at the article in today's newspaper in which you imply that you had to bring in retired U.S. employees to get more revenue and get more taxpayers to file and comply with the law. You specifically mention that Mr. Wharton along with Mr. Riley will work on forty (40) cases. Let me remind you that every one of those forty (40) cases was worked by a local revenue agent. You also failed to mention the under-reported income program which was commended in the audit report and is all being done by local people. You also failed to mention that Collections are up substantially and this is all being done by local people. As you seek confirmation to the position of Director, I think that you have made a serious blunder in slighting the very people that you must depend on for your success. I think that apologies are in order."

Olive continued to operate as a figure head. He couldn't control Vanterpool, he couldn't control Thomas and he couldn't control the lower echelon employees. Together they all had a strangle-hold on him.

The shadow cabinet had proven to be a powerful force, so powerful that even the Governor didn't give a damn about the income producing arm of the Virgin Islands Government being in turmoil. It was a most disgusting thing. There was a fiscal crisis and the apathetic people of the Virgin Islands could care less. They just did not know what was going on. Like the others, Olive was afraid of the truth and knowing that he was not guaranteed the protection from the shadow cabinet ala Thomas and Vanterpool, he quietly stayed in his office hoping for his share of the milk and honey. Every now and then he would write a letter telling us about equipment, etc.

On November 5, 1984, I wrote to him in this manner: "I read with keen interest your somewhat platitudinous and vituperative letter (featuring what appears to be a frivolous equipment request exhibit) of October 31, 1984 and it reminded me of the many times that I have served notice on Mr. Kenneth Hansen (through letters with copies to you) about the Bureau's unwillingness to accept the philosophy of the 'Mirror Theory,' the absence of guidelines and the need for equipment. Previously your silence and insensitiveness toward the aforementioned letters took effect moments after you became certain that they were not directly addressed to you. You took a tremendous delight in not responding to them and as a consequence, you did exactly what you were trying to achieve in your meeting with the Revenue Officers on October 25, 1984, i.e. extricate yourself from the long-standing problems (a la Pontius Pilate) in the Delinquent Accounts and Returns Branch, while simultaneously shifting the responsibility for wrong and/or corrective action to Mr. Kenneth Hansen, the Division Personnel, the United Steelworkers Union and the Virgin Islands Legislature. Your letter of October 31, 1984 has an implicit message of encouragement, but fails to provide any meaningful or useful means to accomplish the stated goal."

It had become routine for Olive and his evildoers, through their vitriolic criticism of me to claim that the Virgin Islands Bureau of Internal Revenue was outdoing any records that it may have had previously. This was very easy to do inasmuch as the media (perhaps looking for favors), the Legislature and an apathetic public would conveniently overlook what was going on. Then too, our Union had become a horse of a different color. While Olive and the Union were headed down the primrose path to prosperity, I had taken to the path of much resistance. Several times I was forced to write either to the local president, the public employees Relations Board and Thermon Phillips (the Union's Regional Director) about the Union's role in the Bureau of Internal Revenue. The Union's only concern, due largely to the employees attitudes was that portion of our bi-lateral contract that dealt with salaries. Nobody cared about job security, education or training which were but a few of the articles making up our contract. Even the Union didn't seem to care about membership dues. I couldn't understand their lackadaisical behavior. I was overwhelmed with wonder. I had to know the reason. I had spoken with Tito Morales and Cephus Rogers about the matter without any success and so I wrote to the Public Employees Relations Board: "Because I suspect that certain members of the bargaining unit of the V.I. Bureau of Internal Revenue are paying dues far in excess of that required by Title 24, V.I.C. Section 370, due largely perhaps to those members who have not been paying their fair share since their admission to the United Steelworkers of America more than two years ago, I hereby request that an investigation be launched into the matter forthwith. In a related matter, several weeks ago I requested from Local 8249 (United Steelworkers of America) a copy of the rules covering their strike and defense fund, together with a copy of a current analysis of the local's income and expenses, for my edification. To date, no word has been received in response to my request. I therefore ask that you take whatever action you deem necessary in seeing that the documents are forwarded to me."

I then wrote a letter to Tito Morales saying: "I am writing to you in compliance with Article X of our By-laws to inform you that you have (perhaps inadvertently) violated Title 24, Section 370 of the V.I. Code and Article XIV of our Constitution which relates to finances and specifically unpaid dues by certain members of our bargaining unit. You have also failed to provide me (under authority of the Freedom of Information Act) with copies of the rules covering our Strike and Defense Fund and a current analysis of Local 8249 (USWA) income and expenses. Your prompt attention to this matter is highly appreciated."

From my experiences I knew that these people were all the same but as Chief Steward representing a Bargaining Unit I had to write, if only for the record. I would not give any employee any reason to say that they were not being represented. And so having been ignored by the Public Employees Relations Board and the Union, I again wrote to PERB: "Several members of the bargaining unit of the Virgin Islands Bureau of Internal Revenue are not paying union dues as required by Title 24, Section 370 of the Virgin Islands Code. Letters hand-delivered to Mr. Luis "Tito" Morales (President of Local 8249) in an attempt to have him rectify the situation have fallen on deaf ears. Having exhausted the machinery for appeal at this particular level, I request the intercession of your office in (1) taking the necessary steps to see that all members pay their dues as required and (2) helping me to secure a copy of the rules covering the local's Strike and Defense Fund, plus a copy of a current analysis of the local's income and expense. Your attention to this very important matter is highly appreciated."

As far as our bargaining unit was concerned, the Union had become a fortunate circumstance. We felt free, far from being in captivity or confinement. As Shop Steward representing the members of the unit I had the power to do, say or think as I felt. I had always had a commitment to truth. As a child growing up in my parents house I had come about my honesty the hard way and throughout my ordeal I had flatly refused to have it impugned. As told to you earlier, management was operating in a rascally manner. There was talk of corruption among officials, indifference and veil threats which were all preventing serious investigations and now I had become worried and perplexed over the Union's behavior.

Negotiations were about to begin with a view towards putting in place a new contract wherein our emphasis would be placed on training. When it came to that portion of our bi-lateral contract dealing with training, management was shamming. They knew that specialized skills were needed in order to work in the Bureau of Internal Revenue and they also knew that training for such skills were being offered by the United States Internal Revenue Service, but they were always using excuses when it came to sending the employees to be formally trained. Of course it is worth mentioning again that once the employee(s) had been trained by the United States Internal Revenue Service they would not be able to apply it anyway.

Our style of negotiating with the Bureau's management team was rather unique. Edward Thomas, a vessel of wrath who because of his absolute authority in carrying out his duties had threatened to touch me up (he didn't say how) during the negotiations, was enjoying life. This evildoer had found himself sitting on the other side of the table in a unique situation wherein he was being called upon to negotiate his wife's salary. Olive who had been victimized by Miss Cheryl McMillan, a lower echelon employee assigned to the Delinquent Accounts and Returns Branch, was also at the table. Furthermore, on management's side all of the Branches were represented with the exception of the useless Kenneth Hansen to whom I had written a letter about Miss McMillan's behavior. I said: "Although she didn't leave any distinguishing marks on November 20, 1984, Revenue Officer Cheryl McMillan's overt hostility towards Director Anthony P. Olive and the subsequent profane discussion in which you participated, caused her to leave an indelible mark in the Virgin Islands Bureau of Internal Revenue. So influential was she on November 20, 1984, that in COF where she is presently assigned, accounts requiring her immediate attention and the securing of waivers, as shown on Form VI 2-T107 for the period ending September 30, 1984, are transferred (in buck-passing fashion and with your approval) to other Revenue Officers in the Delinquent Accounts and Returns Branch. (See delinquent accounts of John Doe and Jane Doe, which you attempted to transfer to me on, January 24, 1984). It is axiomatic for accounts coming from COF to be collated and assigned to Revenue Officers based on their training and experience.

One cannot honestly expect Junior Revenue Officers (especially recruits) to adequately handle the same technical accounts as a higher level Revenue Officer. Furthermore, to have any Revenue Officer operate as Chief De Facto and overtly engineer transfers from COF (as is presumably the case in our Branch) is a most serious matter. In the absence of guidelines, it is heavily suggested that we find ways and means of putting our talents or specialized knowledge to good use. Calendar year 1985 (fifteen years away from the year 2000 appears to be the appropriate time to clear out clutter and proceed with our primary objective of voluntary compliance. Because of the fact that there are thousands of taxpayers indebted to the Virgin Islands Government against whom enforcement action is long overdue, I will refrain from sending copies of this letter to the press. A word to the wise is sufficient, however, you cannot do anymore than the system allows. Furthermore, by now you should recognize that you will get more support if you put first things first."

Since I had become involved with the evildoers in the Bureau of Internal Revenue one of the few remarks coming from the mouth of Kenneth Hansen with which I had agreed was: "The responsibility for asserting and waiving penalties should not be unilaterally determined by one person and the present method of selecting returns for audit should be looked into as they both lend themselves to corruption." Hansen was of course speaking about people like Anthony Olive and Edward Thomas.

But let's not get too far ahead of ourselves here once again. Let's back up a bit to 1984 when the transfer of ownership or control from Quinn ostensibly to Olive took place. Being undermined by Edward E. Thomas, Olive's appointment would be a thing that would cause much horror. After he had been given a favorable recommendation from the Senate Rules and Nominations Committee sometime in May of 1984, Olive thereafter appeared before the Virgin Islands Legislature for his confirmation hearing for Director of the Bureau of Internal Revenue. Although the silent majority with the Bureau of Internal Revenue were diametrically opposed to his confirmation, the local Daily News embraced it. In a news item dated May 18, 1984, they sang Olive's praises telling the public how Olive had been Assistant Director of the Bureau since its creation in 1980 and how he was groomed by Leroy Quinn to succeed him as Director. They even took the time to devote half of their editorial comments to him under the caption: "Good Man For IRB." The editorial stated the following: "Anthony Olive's unanimous confirmation by the Legislature to be the Territory's second Director of the Internal Revenue Bureau is an outstanding vote of confidence. It appears to be well deserved. Olive has the training, experience and character to handle this job in the even-handed fair manner that's essential to success. He has the strength to withstand any pressure to politicize the tax-Collection process and we have every confidence that he'll exercise that strength if pressure is applied. But Olive can't do the job alone. He needs back-up held from trained and experienced tax collectors and tax prosecutors. An investment in both areas will bring multiple returns. It will be up to the same legislature who confirmed him to make sure Olive has the assistance he needs in both areas." The employees of the Bureau of Internal Revenue had listened to the hearing with skeptical ears. They had heard Senator Hugo Dennis prefaced his remarks with a statement of his support for Olive's nomination when he told Olive: "Your nomination has sparked some morale problems with the Bureau." But Olive, feeling anxiety over his confirmation, had told Senator Milton Frett that he intended to continue the practice of promoting from within while supporting training programs for Bureau employees.

In supporting Anthony Olive the Daily News had obviously accepted the empty promises from a man who habitually made promises in order to break them. Read on, you'll see the injustice that Olive had done to the truth on the day of his confirmation hearing when it came to that portion of our contract dealing with training. At the Legislature (all fifteen Senators) knew that Olive was waffling. There was nothing haphazard about his confirmation. Everybody knew beforehand that Anthony P. Olive who could be used would be confirmed through a unanimous vote.

At the Virgin Islands Legislature on the day that Olive was confirmed to be Director of the Bureau of Internal Revenue, it was, put simply, birds of a feather flocking together. Nevertheless, Olive's confirmation had created an unsettled Bureau of Internal Revenue. The fish had started stinking from the head down.

After long deliberations I had concluded that because of Opinion No. 81-1434 of the Third Circuit Court, as long as I stayed with the Government of the Virgin Islands and especially with the Bureau of Internal Revenue I would have a strangle hold on the system. Through that record which was being suppressed by the shadow cabinet I had made a tremendous contribution to the Virgin Islands and its people and what's more, the power elite was still smarting from it. They were trying desperately to rewrite and further simplify what appeared to be cumbersome guidelines. Kenneth Hansen, the man with the bedside manners of a gnat, had risen to a higher place than he was fit for as Chief of the Delinquent Accounts and Returns Branch. He had completely forgotten that at one time I had been his supervisor with full authority to evaluate his performance, among other things. His notion that he was being supported by Anthony Olive and company was ridiculous. These people had an intense dislike for me and needed a person stupid enough to do their dirty work.

On March 11, 1985, Hansen, in an ostentatious move, really designed to flex his muscles and show me how forceful he could be initiated a program designed to have me accept certain accounts which had become the butt of stale jokes and stories. I immediately returned the accounts to him under the law of caveat emptor. He was so stressed up by emotion and anger over what I had done that he sent me a memorandum saying: "The reasons given for returning the attached accounts are not acceptable. The accounts are being returned to you and you are directed to make every effort to resolve them. Continued refusal to accept the assignment is cause for disciplinary action. As a reminder, you are being paid to work eight (8) hours each work day, beginning at 8:00 a.m. to 12:00 noon and 1:00 p.m. to 5:00 p.m."

I wrote back to Mr. Hansen immediately. I said: "Your intuition is very active and your powers of persuasion continue to be strong, but as one who seldom engages in levity, I'm forced to take issue with your ostentatious memorandum of March 11, 1985, which tells me to accept a number of "off island" accounts (in violation of the law of caveat emptor) transferred to me by Revenue Officer Louis Willis, who has just returned from the final phase of his Revenue Officer training program. The subject accounts are being returned to you owing to the very restrictions experienced by Mr. Willis. Furthermore, it is suggested that they be given to COF where letters can be prepared and sent to the taxpayers in an effort to resolve them. Your standing in the Branch rises when you take a stand on important matters. Reminding Liston Monsanto of the government working hours at this point in time is not as important as reminding Mr. Kenneth Hansen to be to work on time. When it comes to time and attendance I'm the envy of many." Hansen was disturbed and confused. He promptly returned the accounts listing the names of the delinquent taxpayers on a memorandum with a copy earmarked for Tito Morales (President of Local 8249). His memorandum said: "The above-referenced accounts are being returned to you for the second time and you are hereby ordered to pick up the accounts and to make every effort to resolve them. As a Grade IV Revenue Officer you should be aware of the legal procedures to follow in resolving any tax case. Disciplinary action for insubordination will be initiated if these accounts are not picked up on your daily report and every effort made to resolve them." His memorandum was dated March 12, 1985.

Now he was testing my patience. I fired back saying: "When Mr. Leroy A. Quinn decided to fill the position of Chief, DARB, he looked for a person too tough to be honest and too weak to lead a Branch which has become so licentious over the past several years, that it has difficulty reducing its receivables. Whether or not you are that person will be determined only with the flight of time. Threats to an employee (who has and continues to ask for guidelines as a means of providing a chartered course) do not serve to better the situation. I'm sure that if you were using Part V of the Internal Revenue Manual you would see that an employee has a right (American Democracy) to do exactly what I did. Your accounts are returned inasmuch as they do not belong to me."

I didn't stop there. I sent him a letter dated March 13, 1985, wherein I said: "March 12, 1985 (three days before the ides) was apparently (for you) an excellent day for pursuing a new interest. Without consulting the experts about mapping out a better course of action, you made an impossible demand upon me, thereby disclosing the names of several delinquent taxpayers to Mr. Luis "Tito" Morales, who if need be, can spread the word about them. In the Delinquent Accounts and Returns Branch where we have so many sensitive cases, covered by a disclosure law and so many Revenue Officers looking to us for inspiration, we must avoid being too assertive around the many critical people outside of the organization, whose desire it is to expose the Branch's utter disregard for strict rules of correctness. It must be borne in mind that it takes more than a letter or memorandum to impersonate me. What it takes (pride, honesty, intestinal fortitude, etc., as evidenced by Opinion No. 81-1434 of the Third Circuit Court) you haven't got."

Hansen, through blind loyalty, was always being used as a defensive shield for Olive and Leroy Quinn and because I was keenly aware of what was going on it had become easy for me to penetrate Olive's line of defense. As I had done in the past, sometimes I would write to Hansen and/or anyone who was overtly serving as a shield or I'd write directly to Olive.

On March 18, 1985, I wrote to Olive in this fashion: "Whereas the Delinquent Accounts and Returns Branch has become so licentious characterized by a high degree of superficiality and routine work. Whereas the Delinquent Accounts and Returns Branch has become so licentious resembling a tempest in a teapot. Whereas the Delinquent Accounts and Returns Branch has become so licentious that Mr. Kenneth C. Hansen freely discloses information previously concealed, and in violation of the Government's disclosure law. Whereas the Delinquent Accounts and Returns Branch has become so licentious that Mr. Kenneth C. Hansen allows the statutory period for Collection to expire on certain accounts in its office Collections. Whereas the Delinquent Accounts and Returns Branch has become so licentious that (a) Mr. Kenneth Hansen is always late for work, (b) his whereabouts (whenever he's absent) are never known and (c) no one is delegated authority to act during his many absences. Whereas the Delinquent Accounts and Returns Branch has become so licentious that it deceives and confuses many of its employees. Whereas the Delinquent Accounts and Returns Branch has become so licentious that it is without enforcement tools and guidelines to perform its function as the major revenue producing arm of the Virgin Islands Government. Whereas the Delinquent Accounts and Returns Branch has become so licentious that taxpayers galore have become indebted to the Virgin Islands Government for the taxes which it is responsible to collect. Whereas the Delinquent Accounts and Returns Branch has become so licentious that Director Anthony P. Olive condones the many wrongs which continue to serve as the forerunner to the Virgin Islands Government's fiscal woes. Whereas the members of the sixteenth legislature have been asking about sources, from which money can be derived to balance the budget. Whereas, a lack of initiative or resourcefulness on my part, could defeat the purpose of the Delinquent Accounts and Returns Branch. Now therefore, I, Liston B. Monsanto, seeing that many employees are lacking in interest and enthusiasm and relying on the foregoing as a basis for my concerns, submit them to you, as they are either nuisances or blessings in disguise contributing immensely to the pervasion of a poor working atmosphere in the Delinquent Accounts and Returns Branch. We cannot afford to take our job responsibilities lightly if we are hoping to promote the best interest of the Virgin Islands Bureau of Internal Revenue."

Any change or changes being made in the Virgin Islands Bureau of Internal Revenue were made for one of the following reasons: (a) to spite Liston Monsanto or (b) to do what Liston Monsanto said. Kenneth Hansen himself had become a by-product of my efforts to rid the Bureau of John Ferrant and Olive was in his position because of me. Both men were addle pated. What I had been doing to them was not stimulating them to work hard. They couldn't as long as I was involved. They were operating quasi-officially and I was forcing them to operate in accordance with existing law. The Governors, the members of the shadow cabinet and the Legislature all knew that for Olive and his bunch of law-breakers, it was a life containing many troubles. It was not something that I relished or enjoyed going through. I had to look at things for the long haul.

Over the years, because of the cosmopolitan aura existing in the Virgin Islands Bureau of Internal Revenue there were many people of diverse interests clamoring for attention. In a disorganized governmental system headed by mercenaries and opportunistic people, the so-called "outsider" once he became eligible to vote had the political and other advantages over many of the hypocritical indigenous people who were without knowledge of evil and who found themselves indentured to the system through political patronage. "Outsiders" who were coming to the VI for what the islands could do for them were really not concerned about the indigenous people whose only claim to fame was the fact that they were born here. They were influenced more by the expediency of making money than by the needs of the indigenous population. Put simply, "outsiders" with common interests who knew that ultimately they were going to return to their places of origin would easily combine for the purpose of creating a voting bloc strong enough to attract the attention of the local politicians.

Wherever they came from in the world did not matter. One thing was certain however, they did not come to the VI to change a life style which offered them the milk and honey that they had always dreamed of.

Mr. Anthony Attidore, a native of Dominica, who worked with us in the Virgin Islands Bureau of Internal Revenue as Budget Control Officer, was a classic example of a so-called "outsider" who would always be found meddling in someone's business. I can recall an incident in 1985 when he openly intervened into the affairs of Mr. Clyde George of the Processing and Accounts Branch without knowing that I was Shop Steward. He foolishly thought that he could do to the members of our bargaining unit what Olive and his bunch of good-for-nothing persons could not do. He was dead wrong. Here is what I wrote to him on April 4, 1985: "I am writing to you in my capacity of Shop Steward in order to let you know that a copy of your memorandum to Mr. Clyde George, which is dated March 13, 1985 arrived at my desk at 12:30 p.m. today and following a careful evaluation of the record, I've concluded that it is either by intention or through ignorance that you have chosen to write Mr. George imputing dishonesty to him while amplifying the same picayune charges of negligence and unwariness, which he previously denied. It is incredible to believe that while the employees of the bargaining unit are cautiously trying to bring order to an organization rife with nepotism, unlawfulness and daily abuse of discretionary power, that you in your capacity of Budget Control Officer would resort to the "self-fulfilling prophecy" in an obvious attempt to prove to Mrs. Joyce Petersen and Mr. Roy Vanterpool that you, in the existing power struggle, can coerce Mr. George into saying exactly what you believe that they would want to hear. For your information, the employees of the bargaining unit feel that the bilateral contract (including Title 3, Chapter 25 V.I.C.) which they recently negotiated with management is not a hazardous one. In fact, they view it as an avenue whereby management and themselves can reconcile their differences with an eye towards improving productivity. Why then would you (at a time when the count down for the ratification of our contract has begun) want to wantonly break up an organization which is headed in a new direction? Truly misrepresentation and lies have never resulted in a permanent benefit for anyone.

As a person inflated with pride, Attidore's reaction was not surprising. He had written to Clyde George in a mean contemptible way hoping to instill fear in him while at the same time showing off his new position to anybody privileged to read his letter. At the Department of Conservation and Cultural Affairs, where he had been previously employed, a few artless employees had been receptive to his tutelage. He did not appreciate my candidness and as a consequence he found himself mixed in the affairs of the Union and management when he impulsively responded to my letter telling me about his position and the duties thereof. It was an awkward moment as far as I was concerned. Here was a newcomer to the Bureau of Internal Revenue, totally green (i.e. not trained, inexperienced and not mature enough in judgment) telling a member of my bargaining unit how he should behave.

I wrote to him as follows: "Anyone intrepid enough to write the ignominious memoranda which you've written in the past several days is indeed worthy of a reply. It is becoming increasingly apparent to all concerned that in your short tenure (less than one (1) year) as Budget Control Officer desirous of showing "the office" where your loyalty lies, that you have perhaps not read the Opinion No. 81-1434 of the United States Court of Appeals for the Third Circuit, which was filed on March 11, 1982. One cannot afford to ignore new trends and if the Third Circuit Court which is located in Philadelphia and whose judges are physically removed from the Virgin Islands can see (based on the tangible evidence provided to them) the many wrongs being done and the accusatory statements being made against the same employees whom you've adjudged to be guilty of wrong doing, then it should not be difficult for you, in your capacity as Budget Control Officer with an office in our building, to understand what's happening. So, it is with a deep sense of obligation to duty that I've enclosed herewith a copy of the Court's decision. The trouble with the Bureau of Internal Revenue is its unwillingness to accept the philosophy of the mirror theory. Finally, organizational charts are not conspicuously posted in the Bureau and as you are completely removed from the day-to-day activity of the Delinquent Accounts and Returns Branch, I believe that your memoranda have infringed on the floor leadership of Mr. Kenneth C. Hansen."

Mr. Attidore promptly answered back saying: "Ms. Vashti Gumbs is the Shop Steward for the employees in the Bargaining Unit and communicating with her on ways of dealing with abuse of the coffee break and non-productivity as a means of improving services is not ignoramus (sic). Your deep sense of obligation to duty quoted is well taken. Your cooperation is expected." And finally I wrote: "The spirit of disorder which continues to exit in the Bureau of Internal Revenue has been brought about by some people in management who take pride in usurping the authority of others even if they do so during their probationary period. Your memorandum to me is not responsive to my letter which was designed to bring light to readers darkened by ignorance. Your open intervention into the internal affairs of the Delinquent Accounts and Returns Branch (a deed vehemently denounced by me) is shocking to say the least. Always remember that a ship with too many pilots sometimes has difficulty reaching port." Since I had been sending copies of my letters to Olive and Hansen, they may have told Mr. Attidore that his actions were futile.

Having paid the sum of $750.00 for legal representation, I watched like a sentry while Local Union 8249 headed by Luis "Tito" Morales maintained as true that the Union would provide an attorney only if it became necessary to appeal a decision coming from the Government Employees' Service Commission. I knew that the Union was greedy for wealth in a Virgin Islands society fond of careless and lavish spending but personally I found it unfair as a member of the union, in good standing, that I would have to take money from my pocket in order to get a lawyer to legally express any sentiments or opinions I may have had. Publicly I had begun to say little or nothing. Privately, however, I had become a silent and thoughtful man saying to myself, "Unionization without representation is tyranny."

I felt certain that Tito was not serving as a legal mouthpiece representing the various bargaining units on his own volition. His authority, I surmised, was derived from an unwritten policy statement issued by the regional office in Birmingham, Alabama through Thermon Phillips; accordingly, I wrote to Mr. Phillips once again seeking a reimbursement. I wrote: "I wrote to you on April 15, 1985, in my capacity as Internal Revenue Officer (in good standing with the United Steelworkers of America) requesting a reimbursement of the $750.00 which I was forced to spend on attorney fees for my defense against the high degree of office politics, which I sought to avoid when I became a member of your prestigious Union. You've ignored by letter reminiscent of your reaction to a letter of February 27, 1984 (copy enclosed) which was addressed to you and signed by a number of employees (Union members) of the Virgin Islands Bureau of Internal Revenue and which requested legal assistance similar to that given to your members on the U.S. mainland. Because you have decided to ignore my request for reimbursement, I am today forwarding all information in my possession (including your returned receipt of my certified letter of April 15, 1985) to my attorney for his review and consideration. As a wage earner and family man, I cannot afford to be a member of a union that offers no legal assistance."

I had known even before I had written to Thermon Phillips that I was not going to be reimbursed. Tito (to his credit) had already told me beforehand that the financial burden would be on me. I was hoping however, that the union upon the urgings of Tito and Cephus Rogers who were both familiar with my persecution would have struck a magnanimous attitude, thereby making me an exception to the rule. I had become a victim of Union avarice, however. The only sensible course was to drop the subject. I did.

During my tenure of service with the Virgin Islands Government I had written so many letters (some laudatory, some critical) that when I made the decision to write this book I found little or no problems in gathering my material. In many of my letters I had succeeded in exposing the once unheralded bosses who were enslaving their subordinates by lies, deception and the assistance of a disclosure law. But despite my letter writing activity, events in the Virgin Islands Bureau of Internal Revenue failed to take a different course to that chartered originally by Reuben Wheatley.

Following my plea for pity from Thermon Phillips, I continued to write letters to Olive and anybody whenever I deemed it necessary to do so. Vividly I recall sending copies of my letters to Senators Lorraine Berry, Hector Cintron, Eric Dawson, Derrick Hodge, Cleone Creque Maynard,

Jimmy O'Bryan, Ruby Rouss, Iver Stridiron and a host of others whose names appear on a later page of this book.

Repeating my contention in most of my letters to Quinn and Olive that the Bureau of Internal Revenue was poorly managed and that the problems in the Bureau were impairing the effectiveness of the tax collecting operations I found no reason to expose them all to ridicule. Initially I had carefully reviewed the sequence of events leading up to my decision to publish this book. I had collated my letters deleting those I considered duplicitous and therefore not worthy of mention herein.

Unionization had forced the personnel merit system to become obsolete in the Bureau. The merit system's obsolescence had been replaced by the Union contract. Whereas under the personnel merit system, an employee needed an overall rating of satisfactory to qualify for an increment, due to unionization that same employee would qualify for an increase come rain or shine. This meant for all intents and purposes that employee performance reports were being prepared only for the record. It was safe to say, however, that too many performance reports with less-than-satisfactory ratings would result in a dismissal of the employee.

Because I had foreseen that management, evil as they were, would rate me consistently less-than-satisfactory in order to get rid of me, while negotiating our contract we had adopted Title 3, Chapter 25, of the personnel merit system. Put simply, we had the best of both worlds.

On July 8, 1985, Olive with the help of Kenneth Hansen rated me less-than-satisfactory, completely ignoring our bilateral contract which offered me the protection that we had negotiated and agreed upon at the negotiating table. I immediately refused to sign the document and attached to the report a statement, which explained my reason for not signing. I met with Olive in the manner prescribed by our contract knowing full well that he was not going to change the rating. He thereafter wrote: "I reviewed your performance report for the period which ended June 17, 1985, unsigned by you along with your accompanying statement, your letter to the Director of Personnel dated July 10, 1985, his reply of July 12, 1985 and your Grievance Report of July 15, 1985. As stated in my meeting with you this morning, based on my review of the documents on file dealing with your work assignments, I support the rating that improvements are required in your performance. The report is being forwarded to the Division of Personnel as completed by your Supervisor. Article XVII of the Collective Bargaining Agreement which deals with evaluation and personnel record does not require the Agency to give automatic satisfactory ratings. In the case of Article XXV which you cited in your Grievance Report, there has not been any discrimination in rating you. It is expected that you will improve on these areas during the next performance period."

My immediate response was: "Without any warning and twenty-five (25) years after the first day on the job as an employee of the Virgin Islands Bureau of Internal Revenue, I've been told (through a delinquent performance report), in defiance of Title 3, Chapter 25 of the Personnel Merit System, as amended, that my overall performance as an Internal Revenue Officer for the period ending June 17, 1985 was less than satisfactory. The report has become the umpteenth in a series of farcical acts on the part of the rater Mr. Kenneth Hansen. In rating me less than satisfactory for the first time in my illustrious career, Mr. Hansen completely forgot that what small chance there was of him illegally rating me the way he did was destroyed simultaneously by Article II, Section 4, of the agreement between the Virgin Islands Bureau of Internal Revenue and the United Steelworkers of America.

Some folks in the Bureau of Internal Revenue (most of whom are detractors of Liston Monsanto) refuse to see people and situations as they really are. They prefer to see them as they would like them to be. A strained relationship will continue to deteriorate unless you (in your capacity as Director) take the first step to patch things up. I say this unreservedly. I therefore request that you take immediate steps to correct the situation."

I then wrote him another letter which said: "Your delicately worded letter dated July 17, 1985, was received this afternoon at 3:07 and truthfully speaking, I was almost swept away by your nebulous recollection and negative reaction to what has become a simple matter. Sending copies of your letter to the Director and Assistant Director of Personnel, who by law are required to file and pay their taxes and being cognizant of the fact that both the Division of Personnel and the Bureau of Internal Revenue fall directly under the kindly patronage and guidance of the Governor's Office, should provide positive proof that you have once again violated instruction number 3, as shown on the reverse side of the fraudulent Performance Report and Title 3, Chapter 25, as amended, of the Personnel Merit System.

It is beyond my imagination to understand how a person in your position, sworn to obey the law, (especially as it applies to tax filing deadlines and fraudulent tax returns) can, on the basis of the Bureau's guiding principle (see attachment to the subject report) ignore the law that covers an employee's performance rating. If you'd take time out to re-read the attached memorandum which was sent to you by Mr. Kenneth C. Hansen on September 6, 1983, you'd notice that contrary to paragraph 3 thereof, Mr. Hansen (the same Chief of the Delinquent Accounts and Returns Branch, who has a proclivity for disclosing pertinent taxpayer information and who also works as a part time accountant in violation of the Bureau's Code of Ethics) has risen up against me in doing evil pursuant to the Bureau's guiding principle. In short, Mr. Hansen has done a military about-face by condoning the very thing he once justifiably condemned. So without belaboring the point, I'd like to add that the carefully reasoned theories of Liston Monsanto go drifting down empty alleys, but he is not discouraged because he knows it is only a matter of time until the philistines of today are the Monsanto disciples of tomorrow.

As for you sir, failing to do what is legally and morally right and continuing to flaunt your authority through the usage of your guiding principle, will result in unproductive efforts, massive layoffs and ultimately your being judged harshly by Virgin Islands history. Finally, if I'm forced to comment further on this simple matter which you have blown completely out of proportion in your quest to discredit me, the people of the Virgin Islands will hear about it through the press. Who knows, maybe it needs airing."

But let us gravitate back to the negotiation of 1985 between the Union and the Bureau of Internal Revenue which ultimately led up to a "strike" in 1986 for, of all things, training or better yet, the lack of it. Bear in mind that during his confirmation hearing for the Directorship, Olive had told the Legislature that he was committed to training the employees of the Bureau. That he was lying was evidenced by our strike.

At the negotiating table where the faint-hearted Edward Thomas sat, someone had sent him an anonymous letter voicing their displeasure with his way of doing things. He took umbrage and immediately told me that he would touch me up. I couldn't repress the urge to laugh when he said that to me. Thomas, for the moment, may have thought that I was one of his ordinary subordinates who would scare easily. I had to show him through documentary evidence that I was not afraid of him or anyone else for that matter. I went back to my office and wrote: "This letter, albeit concise, stems from your artless behavior at the ongoing negotiations between the Virgin Islands Bureau of Internal Revenue and the United Steelworkers of America, which took place at the Chief Negotiator's office on Monday, November 25, 1985 and where you impulsively threatened to "touch me up" in response to, of all things, an anonymous note criticizing you which you believed to be authored by me. Anonymous letters, Mr. Thomas, are not new to the Bureau of Internal Revenue. Liston Monsanto has received a number of them, two of which are enclosed herewith for your review. The fact that you are the only person in the Bureau of Internal Revenue with the authority to unilaterally decide whose income tax return should be selected for audit does not give you a license to express your intention to inflict some form of punishment on a particular taxpayer. I have been audited before and will gladly submit to another provided some of the many delinquent taxpayers shown on our records are made to do the same. Finally, it is well to remember that there are lots of peninsulas in the human race, but no man is an island."

During the negotiations there were a number of distractions which served to interrupt the sessions. Worthy of note here was the Luis/Stridiron pas-de-deux, a dance loaded with gyrations and absurd actions which allowed Luis and Stridiron to engage each other in a squabble over drug testing. Stridiron had openly issued a challenge to Luis to accompany him to Puerto Rico where they were both tested for drugs.

Then there was the Ulrie Vialet accident that caused Olive to ground him and further trouble him by repeated attacks which forced Vialet to address him on January 17, 1986 in this manner: "In one of his latest decisions, District Court Judge Almeric Christian has ordered Commissioner Roy L. Schneider to formally give up one of his dual responsibilities by February 28, 1986, owing to the fact that Schneider wields too much power. I am neither a pundit nor a student of law, but somehow my dull analytical mind tells me that if the honorable jurist was called upon to render a decision relating to the organizational structure of the Virgin Islands Bureau of Internal Revenue, he would find (by way of consistency) that you and a few of your trusted subordinates are weighing a considerable amount of power and therefore, for the good of the Virgin Islands Government he'd have to duplicate his order.

Where else (under the American Flag) can a Director and a few trusted subordinates file an income tax return free from audit, while reserving the power to audit any taxpayer's return, including the Judge's? And what makes you think that you can interfere with the police's investigation of the accident so as to weaken or change it for the worst. I will not, as ordered, drive any of the vehicles that are assigned to the Virgin Islands Bureau of Internal Revenue during the period that you have decided to tamper with the police's investigation. I will, however, define the word accident according to Webster's New World Dictionary: 'A happening that is not expected, foreseen or intended.'

At the negotiating table we had reached a "Gentlemen's Agreement" on wages and a number of other issues. The contentious issues of training and a clause in our contract saying Title III, Chapter 25 of the Virgin Islands Code, which detailed that the Personnel Merit System should be adopted brought us to a panorama of the history of the Bureau of Internal Revenue. Both issues were discussed at length without progress. It was a harrowing story. It must be noted, however, that Olive and company did not rule out training completely. They cited what they thought to be legitimate reasons such as lack of funds and classroom space to accommodate Virgin Islanders hoping to dissuade us. They were very adamant in voicing their refusal to give us the training necessary for the performance of our assigned duties and/or proposed assignment.

Through captious arguments, etc. our side (which included Steven Frett) envisioned a job action designed to force compliance with our demands. The shock of management's negative attitude towards training had unsettled our minds. What management was waiting for, or hoping for, was left to speculation. Olive and his team were beginning to look more noble than smart. And so rather than go after the symptoms on March 3, 1986, we went after the disease by going on strike. It was a defining moment in the history of the Bureau of Internal Revenue. Management's attitude had confirmed every misgiving I had about them. They had lost sight of the fact that the virus of fear which had pervaded the workplace for many years and many of the things that had poisoned the minds and/or morals of the employees had been reduced to the point where they were not afraid to strike; not for money but for training. Yes, we did not stop working to get higher wages or shorter hours. We were on strike for the training that Anthony Olive had promised the Legislature he would provide.

And so with a battle cry of "train and retain" resonating on the picket line together with the presence of several spies in our midst swinging like a pendulum from the side of management to that of labor we succeeded in accomplishing our objective. In summary it was safe to say that the overall attitudes of the members of our bargaining unit and management's intransigence were the two circumstances that made our strike a great success.

Sometime before our job action, Olive had chided Louis "Lolo" Willis (a lower echelon employee several steps removed from the Director's office) about the "constant discussions" around his desk which were attracting many of his co-workers. Mr. Willis was a young man with pretensions to the highest level in the Delinquent Accounts and Returns Branch. He had been rejected by John Ferrant initially and now that he was on the payroll he had become a most opportunistic person.

What he may have promised Olive in their meeting may have surfaced during our job action. His inability to hold his tongue together with his body language branded him a fifth columnist. The memory of his prying still rankles in my mind. There were others in our midst far from trustworthy and as expected there were a few scabs. The irregular behavior of our members made me the villain.

We were in an election year. Juan Luis (the incumbent Governor) was finishing up his final term in office and Alexander Farrelly would replace him in January of 1987. The end Olive had in mind was retention. The Bureau of Internal Revenue headed by him was scoring dismally (all things considered) and a scapegoat was necessary. It would be a facile task to charge Liston Monsanto with disruption. The shadow cabinet and his fickle friends in the business community all wanted me out of the Bureau of Internal Revenue. One man with courage (Liston Monsanto) had become a majority.

The power elite and the members of the shadow cabinet all saw the employees of the Bureau as sheep-sheep being led to the slaughter house by me. They were wrong in their analysis however. It was a formal expression of our members through a vote that had resulted in our job action.

We were about to ratify our contract when in a showy display Hansen addressed two memoranda to "all Revenue Officers" one accused us of malingering and the other reminded us of his "objectives and policies." In a letter dated April 28, 1986 I told Hansen: "After reading your editorial comments which appeared in a memorandum of April 24, 986 to all Revenue Officers, I've concluded that you are (perhaps innocently) in violation of the Fifth Amendment of the U.S. Constitution as it relates to double jeopardy* and at the same time you have placed the proverbial wedge between management and certain employees of our Bargaining Unit at a time when (as Mr. Olive and the members of his negotiating team will truthfully tell you) the count down for the ratification of our contract has begun. The sequence of events which led up to your memorandum shows that certain people in management continue to believe that they are inculpable. Unfortunately for them however, their preconceived judgments and opinions which form the basis for your memorandum do nothing to end the pettiness and personality conflicts that have prevailed in the Bureau of Internal Revenue for the past several years. If you believe or otherwise know that someone under your supervision is guilty of reading a magazine as you have implied in your memorandum, I suggest you issue a cease and desist order to that individual before casting aspersions on the professional character of the Revenue Officers to whom the memorandum was sent. And regarding your "objections and policies" of which you have reminded us in a separate memorandum, I've already made my feelings known in a number of letters to you. Consequently, it is not my intention at this time to magnify them. I therefore request that you review the files with a view towards going over my position on the matter. In conclusion, let me say that nobody wants to enforce any more than the Revenue Officers do. We know that (a) education and enforcement mean a reduction of the receivables and (b) a reduction of the receivables means that the Internal Revenue Officers would have justified their long awaited salary increases.

*Mr. Olive had already absolved Mr. Willis of the "constant discussions" at his desk." Olive was caught in an odd fancy. He had taken a turn for the irrational worst. The man had given to cursing loudly on the telephone whenever he thought it necessary to do so. During my ordeal I had remained optimistic that Olive would have seen the error of his ways and amended his life accordingly. As I look back I feel safe in saying my expectations were too high. Even though he and many others had managed to climb the career ladder at my expense, thanks to my upbringing which had within it an air of altruism I had taken great comfort in knowing that qualified locals were filling the various vacancies in the Virgin Islands Bureau of Internal Revenue.

There was enough evidence to reach the conclusion that Olive feared losing his job in the event Farrelly won the election. He found solace in the fact that Thomas (a disciple of Farrelly) would conciliate him only because Thomas himself would be vulnerable in the event Farrelly was removed from office four (4) years later. As devastating as a strike led by Liston Monsanto could be on the psyche, it paled in comparison to knowing that Anthony P. Olive was vulnerable to Farrelly. 1986 had become a surreal year for him.

On August 4, 1986, I called Olive on the telephone to make arrangements for a meeting. He picked up the phone and shouted, "Monsanto you can kiss my ass." I immediately sent him a letter which said: "'Monsanto you can kiss my ass!' These are words which impulsively emanated from your mouth in our conversation (at 3:45 p.m.) on Friday, August 1, 1986. They confirmed my suspicions that there are some people in the Bureau of Internal Revenue who don't like me. And frankly speaking, I don't have any problems with that inasmuch as I don't like them anymore than they like me. My primary concern is to do the job for which I'm being paid by the taxpayers of the Virgin Islands. In this gubernatorial election year things have suddenly become a bit tenuous in the Bureau of Internal Revenue. I know that attitudes and belief do not necessarily predict behavior, but I also know that it is on the "sound education of the people that the security and destiny of every nation chiefly rest". Rather than trying to blacken Liston Monsanto's character, however, management would do well to use its many legitimate appeals to encourage employees in a positive way. How can management ignore my personnel file and surrender it to Satan? Can't you see what a terrific force you can make Liston Monsanto for good and against evil?"

I had been a pacifist, one opposed to war in the workplace and it was because of this attitude that I had never entertained the thought of physically hurting anyone. I was of the feeling that one cannot defeat wicked people like Olive with a gun. You've got to use the pen inasmuch as it's mightier than the sword. You may kill wicked people but not the idea or furthermore their ideology.

Olive's ability to function as Director had been severely disrupted by the spate of letters and grievances criticizing his management style. Anthony Attidore knew that Olive had his hands full with trouble of his own making. Attidore had been drinking from the trough for sometime because of Olive and the existing government. He therefore felt a sense of loyalty to the office of Director and would defend the bureaucracy even if he had to lie. Attidore believed Kenneth Hansen to be a person of little or no importance and would make capital of this belief. (Note: Attidore was a member of Olive's negotiating team. Kenneth Hansen was not).

Farrelly and Adelbert Bryan had become opponents in a run-off election scheduled for November 18, 1986 and so on November 13th Mr. Attidore in usurping Hansen's authority called a meeting of the members of the Delinquent Accounts and Returns Branch presumably to feel the political pulse of the Branch. In a show of resentment I wrote to him on November 14, 1986 saying:

GOVERNMENT OF
THE VIRGIN ISLANDS OF THE UNITED STATES

---o---

VIRGIN ISLANDS
BUREAU OF INTERNAL REVENUE
P. O. Box 3186
Charlotte Amalie, St. Thomas, U.S.V.I. 00801

November 14, 1986

Anthony Attidore
P.O. Box 3186
St. Thomas, V.I.   00801

Dear Mr. Attidore,

Perhaps desirous of spreading Hansen's desease throughout the Bureau of Internal Revenue, you invited the Employees of the Delinquent Accounts and Returns Branch into the office of Mr. Kenneth C. Hansen on the morning of November 13, 1986 to tell us among other things, the outright lie that you had told me about a meeting which incidentally never took place (the way you wanted us to believe) at the Office of the Chief Negotiator.

Knowing about the inborn Greed, Super-Ambition, intolerance and snobbishness of many a man and woman, man's inhumanity to man is not just a mere poetic phrase to me. In addition, I know how volatile the Supervisory Personnel in the Bureau can be when it comes to respecting law and authority. If legislation is currently being considered by the Legislature to award salary increases to Non-Union Employees, why then are we the only Government Employees being denied our fair share?

From time to time, I have accused you of open intervention into the internal affairs of the Delinquent Accounts and Returns Branch and have further asked that rather than emulate a self-seeking flatterer that you give Article XX Section 6 of our Contract your utmost attention and full compliance. Example Sir, is not the main thing in influencing others. It is the only thing.

With the coming of the Gubernatorial Run-Off Election (Tuesday November 18, 1986) wispering hope remains the order of the day among the Supervisory Personnel. Some Supervisors find themselves in a Cul-De-Sac while others(many with a vested interest in the status Quo) are praying that their hopes end in fruition.

Mr. Anthony Attidore
Page 2.
November 14, 1986

We in the Delinquent Accounts and Returns Branch desirous of working in a manner reflective of our training and abilities are looking forward to working for a Governor who will Delegate authority and give us Supervisors with orders to rate us based on performance and not bias.

For the past several years, the professional attitude of the Bureau of Internal Revenue has been completely decimated by a Governmental System that demands mediocrity. During this "Lame Duck" period however, we are quite satisfied with Mr. Hansen as our Supervisor. We do not need a Surrogate Father!

Sincerely,

Liston B. Monsanto
Shop Steward

cc: Mr. Anthony P. Olive
     Mr. Kenneth Hansen
     Luis "Tito" Morales
     Mr. Cephus Rogers

The die had been cast in 1970 when Melvin Evans (a Republican) became our first elected Governor. Evans began by charting a course for his successors to follow, their political persuasion notwithstanding. Cyril King as a member of the Independence Citizens Movement (ICM) succeeding Evans had extended Evans' program and Juan Luis who operated as an independent further extended it. Being elected to the Office of Governor by a majority of disadvantaged voters (Democrats for the most part) compelled our governors to reward those voters with jobs while at the same time granting favors to their financial supporters hoping that they'd be re-elected four (4) years later.

Alexander A. Farrelly had emerged victorious over Adelbert Bryan in the gubernatorial elections of 1986 and while many people were of the opinion that it was doomsday for Anthony Olive, as one of Farrelly's confidants Edward E. Thomas knew better. He did not want to see Olive leave. Because of Olive's presence he would continue in his position as Director de facto. He enjoyed operating behind the scenes where he was not vulnerable. He could afford to wait until 1991, when he had enough time for retirement and when he was sure that Farrelly had prevailed in November 1990.

I watched with wary pride as Farrelly and his bunch of merciless friends (all Democrats indentured to the governmental system) took their turn at extending Evans' program, continuing to take advantage of disadvantaged people. Skill and strategy had already been replaced by arbitrary power. Now collaborating in tandem with each other, they would contrive and arrange by agreement to place underachievers and unlettered people in key positions, thereby creating a less-than-professional atmosphere throughout the Territory. The principle of letting people do as they pleased (Laissez Faire) would become the order of the day. Throughout it all Edward Thomas continued to whisper to himself: "Discretion is the better part of valor."

On January 20, 1987, Olive called a meeting of the Delinquent Accounts and Returns Branch. Due to illness I did not report to work on that particular day and consequently I wrote him a letter dated January 21, 1987, sending copies to Farrelly and Derek Hodge the new Lieutenant Governor. I said:

January 21, 1987

Mr. Anrhony P. Olive
Director
Virgin Islands Bureau of Intenral Revenue
Charlotte Amalie
St. Thomas, Virgin Islands 00801

Dear Mr. Olive:

Owing to the infirmities of age, I was unable to attend the meeting of the Delinquent Accounts and Returns Branch which was held on January 20, 1987 as the forerunner (hopefully) to the many more scheduled for Calendar Year 1987.

I understand that the meeting was one wherein you as incumbent Director began flexing your political muscles (without any statutory basis) in full view of the members who were present.

This showy display coming early in Governor Farrelly's Administration is needless to say, a continuation of the licentious behavior of Mr. Anthony P. Olive, who operated with a high degree of flippancy and was always impervious to suggestions during the Luis Administration.

Just as responsible parents are solicitous for their children's progress, so too am I solicitous of the plight of the Virgin Islands Government's Bureau of Internal Revenue. I am, therefore, mortified that you would prolong the existing state of affairs especially after reading Governor Farrelly's State of the Territory Address which he delivered before the Seventeenth (17th) Legislature on January 16, 1987.

It has always been my contention that the Bureau of Internal Revenue – under your leadership, has operated continually in violation of law. Evidence of my contention may be found in the accompanying documents – some of which were previously reviewed by you during Mr. Juan Luis' tenure of office.

A comparison of the documents with Mr. Farrelly's Address will disclose that he has echoed my sentiments and that all along I've been wanting to work in a manner reflective of my training and ability. Are you willing to change your modus operandi?

Best wishes,

Liston B. Monsanto
Shop Steward

Enclosures:

cc: Governor Alexander Farrelly

Lieutenant Governor Derek Hodge

Mr. Kenneth C. Hansen, Chief, DAR Branch

Mr. Anthony Attidore, Budget Control Officer

134

In a move intended to impress the new Governor, Olive quickly responded on January 22, 1987 saying: "In response to your letter of January 21, 1987, and the various attachments, I hereby request that your resignation from the Bureau of Internal Revenue be submitted to me no later than 5:00 p.m., January 23, 1987." War had been declared. I wrote back on January 23, 1987:

RECEIVED
DIRECTOR'S OFFICE

JAN 23 1987

V.I. BUREAU OF INT. REV.
ST. THOMAS, V.I.

January 23, 1987

Mr. Anthony P. Olive
Director
Virgin Islands Bureau of Internal Revenue
Charlotte Amalie
St. Thomas, Virgin Islands 00801

Dear Mr. Olive:

After reading your letter of January 22, 1987, which was seemingly designed to put me to the extreme test, one would have to conclude that Liston Monsanto had committed the perfidious crime of high treason.

I can vividly recall that in August of 1985 you did the same thing to Mr. Henry O. Millin, Jr.

Based on my observations in this Government of, for and by the People, I do not believe that our new Governor will tolerate the existence of an empire within his Administration. Lest you forget, the territory is in shambles.

For your information, I am not seeking a fight, but if one is forced upon me, I will be ready, willing and able.

I, therefore, ask that you discontinue your past practices so that we may proceed with our mission of promoting voluntary compliance.

With all due foundness and respect,

Liston B. Monsanto
Shop Steward

cc: Honorable Alexander Farrelly
     Governor of the Virgin Islands

I followed up on January 28, 1987 with the following letter:

January 28, 1987

Mr. Anthony P. Olive
Director
V.I. Bureau of Internal Revenue
St. Thomas, Virgin Islands 00801

Dear Mr. Olive:

Your letter to Mr. Henry O. Millin, Jr., wherein he was denied permission to meet with Governor Farrelly at this point in time, was forwarded to me in my capacity of Shop Steward and after reading its contents, I decided to respond to wit:

Entering Calendar Year 1987 conjures up memories of 1986 retroactively to 1976, and immediately (with your retention as Director of the Bureau apparent) I get goose bumps as I entertain thoughts of a no-changed attitude towards the sorid mess in which we find ourselves.

Granted, nobody is perfect, and to me this was amply demonstrated by your performance during Governor Juan Luis' administration. In view of this, I feel obligated to ask that the contents of this letter neither be misconstrued as an encroachment on the responsibilities of your office nor as a source of annoyance. Instead, I respectfully request that the troubled areas listed on a later page hereof be reviewed and acted upon fairly and impartially.

First of all, what must become a reality is our apparent need to use all laws, policies, rules, regulations, executive orders, memoranda etc., not formerly used in carrying out our duties. If you fail to use the prescribing directives during your next four (4) years in office, you will certainly run the risk of exceeding your mandate by taking upon yourself certain duties detrimental to our Bargaining Unit. In short, you must allow the Bureau to operate according to Hoyle.

And now as promised, listed below - not necessarily in order of priority, are certain long-standing problems that require your immediate attention:

1. Avoid spurious relationship which could untimately end in someone holding a preeminent position with absolute power.

2. Curb the high degree of nepotism in this income producing activity especially in the many cases where you have close relatives split between management and the Bargaining Unit. It should be borne in mind that the Bureau is not a monarchy.

Letter   –2–   1/28/87

Anthony P. Olive, Director

3. Palpable lies corroborated by the record and the issuance of curt letters must cease. Careful handling and tact must be utilized on sensitive matters.

4. Owing to a system that demands mediocrity Revenue Officers are underemployed and their duties impaired. Please take corrective action.

5. Discontinue existing discriminatory practices and vitriolic talk. Rate employees based on performance and not bias.

6. Dealing with political satire will serve only to promote the present system. Politics must be left to the politicians.

7. Stop being a Perfunctory Director; consider giving employee(s) assignments who are now without.

I admire your intentions with respect to employee augmentation, but the continued use of vindictiveness as exemplified by your recent farcical acts (firings of Graciano Petersen and Michael Degraff plus your request for my resignation) and failure to enforce collections will definitely result in conditions that may be best termed inert.

Incidentally, you have forgotten to do what you promised in reaching an agreement with the United Steelworkers of America on October 1, 1985. Can we expect another empty promise?

The foregoing are matters that – I believe, need the attention of a third party (our Governor), but in any event, we stand ready to appear before you and ultimately Governor Farrelly.

Very truly yours,

Liston B. Monsanto
Shop Steward

cc: Honorable Alexander Farrelly
Governor of the Virgin Islands

P.S. I did not receive a copy of the minutes of your meeting of January 20, 1987.

Olive's back was to the wall. I eased off until March 2, 1987, sending him another letter with a copy to Mr. Roy Vanterpool who continued to show off his academic life. I wrote: "This morning I witnessed Miss Yvonne Phipps working in her capacity as Secretary Pro-Tem to the Chief Processing Accounts and Returns Branch and it occurred to me that Miss Phipps was busy concentrating on documents which contained information whose unauthorized disclosure could be prejudicial to the Bureau's interest. Coincidentally, I was in the process of reviewing Perb's "Decision and Order" Numbers UC82-12 and UC87-1 and to say that I gasped in horror and amazement upon seeing Miss

Phipps operating as a confidential secretary is really and understatement. As a person who respects law and authority, I would like to remind you that Perb acting favorably on petitions filed by the Bureau of Internal Revenue, excluded several secretaries from our Bargaining Unit because of the confidentiality of their work. Needless to say, this included the secretary to the Chief Processing Accounts and Returns Branch. Based on the foregoing, I hereby request the immediate removal of Miss Yvonne Phipps from the confidential duties assigned her and further ask that she be replaced by Mrs. Hill, Mrs. Moron, Mrs. Faulkner, Miss Vessup, Miss Lee or Miss Adams. In giving consent to my request, the Bureau would have put to rest the criticisms of many of the employees in our Bargaining Unit who feel (with good reason) that the Bureau is trying to get the best of both worlds."

Olive did not respond but Roy Vanterpool did. Playing the role of psychiatrist, Roy wrote: "This letter should be used by the writer himself to support his request for an examination to determine if he is a victim of the defect of dementia praecox."

Promoted too quickly and believing that he was a person of high rank or great importance, Roy Vanterpool had become overbearing. I classified his letter as junk mail and entertained thoughts of ignoring him, but since he was of the belief that a recipient of a college degree automatically became intelligent I decided to write to him in this manner: "You are a perplexing man! An air of sarcasm was detected in your letter of March 2, 1987 and it immediately reminded me of the old adage which says, 'Throw an old shoe in a pack of dogs; the one that gets hit will always holler.' For your information, my letter was sent to Mr. Olive after he had failed to stand by his undertaking as outlined in a stipulation dated January 28, 1987, between the Union and the Bureau of Internal Revenue. Maybe you ought to investigate the veracity of the Stipulation (PERB ULPC-87-5). My brain (although miniscule) is being used to help (as evidenced by Opinion No. 81-1434 of the Third Circuit Court) an oppressive people, who have entertained thoughts of violence against management for several years. Some people in management are trained incapacitance(s) and so programmed that if their brain(s) was placed in a bird, the bird would fly backwards. Men such a Viggo Hendricks, Earle Ottley and Calvin Wheatley have proven that it is not what you know in theory, but what you do on the job that counts. Always remember that no man is justified in doing evil on the ground of expediency."

In the Virgin Islands Bureau of Internal Revenue an employee working in a manner reflective of his training and ability had to be exceptionally strong or exceptionally stupid. The workplace was in a sordid mess, something Farrelly and his cohorts knew but to them and many other people working in the Bureau, loyalty was more important than honesty especially since the people of the Virgin Islands were indifferent to corruption.

As a paragon of efficiency there was no way that I was going to allow Olive and his cronies to deprive our members the training that he had agreed to at the negotiating table. He had to be reminded. On April 21, 1987, I wrote:

April 21, 1987

Mr. Anthony P. Olive
Director
V.I. Bureau of Internal Revenue
Charlotte Amalie
St. Thomas, Virgin Islands 00801

Dear Mr. Olive:

Owing to the existing state of confusion and the high degree of deception in the Virgin Islands Bureau of Internal Revenue – perhaps due largely to the ludicrous requirement that trained, half-trained and untrained employees, coordinate their work arbitrarily and capriciously, the Union together with the Bureau of Internal Revenue reached an Agreement on June 18, 1986, which required you to send unconditionally ("within twelve (12) months after acceptance") newly-promoted or newly-hired employees to formal training conducted by United States Internal Revenue Service Instructors either on or off island.

The deadline of June 18, 1987, is rapidly approaching and rather than reacting the way most people in the Virgin Islands do, through this letter I'd like to serve notice on you that several Members of our Bargaining Unit, who are desperately in need of training are anxiously awaiting your compliance with Article XIX of our Contract. They know – like you do, that in order to increase productivity and promote voluntary compliance, training that would improve their technical skills must be given.

For your information, many employees have taken umbrage at the fact that the personnel in the highest levels of management who are called upon to enforce the tax laws etc., are always the first to violate them together with other rules and regulations, expecially those to which they have agreed after thoughtful consideration.

Instead of dutifully complying with anything not in violation of law, management continues to make a mockery out of a Bilateral Contract which they regard as an object of ridicule and/or scorn. In short, flouters in management have – by their scornful behavior, labelled our Contract the laughing – stock of the Bureau of Internal Revenue.

Like the folks in management, employees of the Bureau of Internal Revenue must be trained so that they may act together in a smooth concerted way. We must

Letter   -2-   April 21, 1987

Mr. Anthony P. Olive

all be thankful for the tools, were it not for them the rest of us could not succeed. Furthermore, it must be borne in mind that the battle cry of our Strike in 1986 was: "Train and Retain."

Sincerely,

Liston B. Monsanto
Shop Steward

cc: Mr. Cephus Rogers
International Representative

Mr. Luis "Tito" Morales
President, Local 8249

Mrs. Alda M. Monsanto
Chief Negotiator

I had become a gadfly trying to goad Olive to action by simply reminding him of our agreement. But guess what, I had to write to him again on June 8, 1987. I wrote:

June 8, 1987

RECEIVED
DIRECTOR'S OFFICE

JUN 8 1987

VIRGIN ISLANDS BUREAU OF
INTERNAL REVENUE
St. Thomas, V.I.

Mr. Anthony P. Olive
Director
Bureau of Internal Revenue
Lockhart Gardens #1A
St. Thomas, V. I.   00802

Dear Mr. Olive:

Trying to forget the past and seeking to get down to the more mundane problems facing the Government of the Virgin Islands, The Union-during our 1985-1986 negotiating sessions, broached the very important, but somewhat controversial subject of training.

Your strong exception to the subject, resulted in a Job-Action by the members of our Bargaining Unit, which forced management to enter into an agreement to send Unconditionally ("within twelve (12) months after acceptance") Newly-Promoted or Newly-Hired Employees to formal training conducted by United States Internal Revenue Instructors either on or off Island.

At this writing (10 days before the June 18th deadline), it appears as if our side was given a false sense of assurance inasmuch as you have either by omission, silence, or past practice, failed to live up to your promise. Maybe you felt that once the publicity of our Job-Action died down, we'd become apathetic.

This Sir is not the case. It is no secret (and records in your possession would corroborate this fact)that over the past several years I have spoken Ad-Nauseam about the poor working conditions under your Stewardship. These conditions-needless to say, have contributed immensely to the overall decline of our Government. In addition, They have caused the United States Internal Revenue Service (time after time) to entertain thoughts of collecting our taxes.

If we are to improve working conditions and increase productivity, like the Personnel in Management Employees of the Virgin Islands Bureau of Internal Revenue must be trained.

Since it is becoming increasingly apparent that you are once again attempting toviolate the law, I must admonish you that a Breach of Contract on your part will result in still another grievance being filed by us. It therefore behooves you to ponder over the best way to get out of this scrape.

(2)

Sincerely,

Liston Monsanto
Shop Steward

cc: Luis "Tito" Morales
Cephas Rogers
Mrs. Alda Monsanto

Farrelly was being kept abreast of what was going on in the Bureau of Internal Revenue via copies of letters that I had sent to Olive, now it was his turn to hear from me.

I wrote to Governor Farrelly on June 30, 1987. Here is what I said:

June 30, 1987

Honorable Alexander Farrelly
Governor - U.S. Virgin Islands
Office of the Governor
Charlotte Amalie
St. Thomas, Virgin Islands 00801

Dear Governor Farrelly:

After several years of service as an ombudsman in the Virgin Islands Bureau of Internal Revenue (formerly Tax Division), I took over the responsibility of Chief Shop Steward with the serious pledge to implicitly defend the members of our Bargaining Unit against the many injustices therein.

I assumed – what has become a most arduous responsibility, knowing full well that manifold problems – such as the ones in the Bureau of Internal Revenue, would not be solved by simply running away from them.

In addition, I discovered that if we were looking for perfection in our less than professional governmental system under your predecessor, we would not find it in the V.I. Bureau of Internal Revenue.

Striving for perfection, nevertheless, and knowing that no gains would be made without pains, during Calendar Year 1986 we negotiated with management a Bilateral Contract (which expires on September 30, 1987) placing emphasis on education and training.

For your edification, our Contract also contains a Grievance Procedure which from its inception has legitimately served as our authority to file a number of Grievances. This – I hasten to add, is to our good fortune inasmuch as disorder reigns so rampant in the Bureau of Internal Revenue that Mr. Anthony P. Olive (our Director) finds himself before an Arbitrator more often than any other department head in the Virgin Islands Government. Although our grievances have been valid, many of them were systematically resolved.

Inherited by your administration, the existing Contract stipulates - among other things, that newly-hired and newly-promoted employees must be given formal training by United States Internal Revenue Service Instructors on or before June 18, 1987. This was not done, thereby necessitating the filing of yet another grievance.

There are a number of ingrates and scoff-laws in management who are steadfastly opposed to fromal training for lower echelon employees. When it comes to our Contract, management has an innate tendency to believe that one cannot practice law by the books all of the time as sometimes there are extenuating circumstances.

Letter
Hon. Alexander Farrelly
Governor of the V.I.

      Why management continues to violate our Bilateral Contract is among the Bureau's best kept secrets. Accordingly, the urgent intervention of your office has become necessary, and towards this end, I solicit your indulgence.

Sincerely,

Liston B. Monsanto
Shop Steward

cc: Luis "Tito" Morales
       President, Local 8249

       Mr. Cephus Rogers
       International Representative

    My letters were all ignored. While this was going on however, my counterpart on the island of St. Croix notified me that Revenue Officer Jens Todman (yes the same Jens Todman that you've read so much about) and another Revenue Officer had been selected to attend a training program somewhere in the United States. Todman had been on the picket line with us during our job action. Todman was working in the same office with me, sitting at a desk directly behind me to boot. He never uttered a word to me about his training classes. But that was Jens Todman.

On July 17, 1987, I wrote to Olive once again:

July 17, 1987

Mr. Anthony P. Olive
Director
V.I. Bureau of Internal Revenue
St. Thomas, Virgin Islands 00801

Dear Mr. Olive:

Some members of our Bargaining Unit have become utterly miserable and puzzled over the very important matter of training – a topic excoriated by management in discussions with us and subsequently magnified in letters from me, which have served as the forerunner to Grievance Number 7-87 dated June 19, 1987.

For some inexplicable reason, Revenue Officers Martinez and Todman (two veterans) were selected to attend a training program somewhere in the United States on July 20, 1987.

We must have incurred the wrath of your office because unless these men were "newly promoted," there is absolutely no legitimate reason for their selection – especially since we have in our midst an untrained employee, who recently received her Masters Degree from the University of the Virgin Islands.

And speaking about training, by now it must be quite obvious to you that your latest act (see paragraph two) towards this critical issue has compounded your error, inasmuch as it borders on unfair labor practice. Frankly, I'm bemused.

Since you made the decision to send the two veterans to training, I have had numerous visits from concerned employees of our Bargaining Unit, who feel with good reason that you are still trying to divide and conquer them, while continuing to ignore our Contract.

For anyone to think otherwise is ludicrous. Furthermore, it is safe to say that with the emergence of the Bureau of Internal Revenue and all its broad powers, abuse of discretionary power became the eight deadly sin of the world.

It saddens me to see how things in this most sensitive area of our Government have gone awry under your stewardship. Allowing yourself to fall prey to the many vessels of wrath (internally and externally) after being highly recommended by me to fill the position of Tax Director is something that brings me strong regret. Your ambitions – I believe, have been subverted. You have so much to offer.

Letter   -2-   7/17/87
Mr. Anthony P. Olive
Director

       In light of the foregoing, I politely request that you put the Labor/ Management Committee to work as agreed to in our Contract.

       Kindly accede to my request.

                                    Sincerely,

                                    Liston B. Monsanto
                                    Shop Steward

cc: Honorable Alexander Farrelly
      Governor of the Virgin Islands

      Mr. Kenneth C. Hansen
      Chief, Delinquent Accounts & Returns Branch

      Mr. Cephus Rogers
      International Representative

      Mr. Luis "Tito" Morales
      President Local 8249

      Mr. Jose McGregor
      Shop Steward (St. Croix)

       Roy Vanterpool was a hemorrhoid. He was always trying to instill fear in his subordinates and were it not for the Union and its Shop Steward (Liston Monsanto), he may have succeeded. Vanterpool operated with great pomp, always showing off. With Olive pretending to be in charge of the Bureau of Internal Revenue, Roy Vanterpool with the blessings of the shadow cabinet could do anything he wanted. A classic example of what I'm talking about took place on October 5, 1987. Vanterpool wrote the following memorandum to two lower echelon employees through their supervisor. He wrote: "Through you, by this memorandum, the below assignment and scheduling of the numbering of the subject returns are to commence today (10/5/87). Rickhield Thomas (Mondays, Wednesdays, Fridays), Judith DeCastro (Tuesdays, Thursdays, Fridays). On each of the days scheduled, each named employee is to be given a reasonable amount of returns to be numbered and with an acceptable amount to be completed. This agreement has been discussed with the Director and it is expected to be carried out as is outlined herein. Article IV of the Contract is invoked and any further delay of this assignment, employees named herein will be cited for insubordination and disciplinary action such as suspension with loss of pay or could be asked for their resignation letters. Note: This assignment was originally made September 17, 1987."

In a footnote in one of my letters he had said to me, "As a person who is academically qualified to be your mentor, I have decided to dignify the construction of this letter by applying a grade. Grading is in the area of (1) thought processes, (2) diction and (3) fair grammar. On a scale of 1 to 10 with 10 being the high, I generously grade this .02." I loved it when Roy Vanterpool tried to get satirical with me. It would always fill me with derisive laughter in the preparation of my response.

On October 5, 1987, I sent him my response. I wrote:

RECEIVED
PROCESS, & ACCT. BRANCH

OCT 05 1987

VIRGIN ISLANDS BUREAU OF
INTERNAL REVENUE ST. CROIX   October 5, 1987

r. Roy A. Vanterpool
nief, Processing & Accounts Branch
.I. Bureau of Internal Revenue
t. Thomas, V.I. 00801

ear Mr. Vanterpool:

What's going on here? Are you trying to circumvent Article XI of our ontract?

I have just received a copy of your October 5th memorandum which was os-ensibly written to Mrs. Rosalind Scipio directing Mr. Rickhield Thomas and rs. Judith DeCastro (under the threat of Article IV of our Contract) to do xactly what management has categorically and deliberately refused to do, .e., adhere to the Agreement between the Bureau of Internal Revenue and the nited Steelworkers of Ameirca. (See copy of Grievance 7-87 dated June 19, 987, which is attached hereto).

Careful transistions in writing must be utilized when it comes to com-municating with you, inasmuch as (judging from your reaction to my letter even (7) months ago) you are hearing my voice every time I write.

Yes sir! I became petrified upon reading your footnote on my March 4, 987 letter (copy attached) which had you - through the usage of the self-ulling prophecy, declaring yourself "academically qualified" to be my mentor. n your enthusiasm, however, you criticized my diction in - of all things, a on-verbal instrument.

We have now entered Fiscal Year 1988 and the deficiencies and inade-uacies that I have spoken about adnauseam are still prevalent. Additionally, ne same attempts to instill fear and a continuation of the harassment which ne employees of the Bargaining Unit have endured in the past, is about to .. esume.

As you are no doubt aware, this harassment has already taken a heavy toll n resignations, in hostility, in retarding productivity and in simple human isery. "We are all for progress unless it involves change", has become the attle cry of the Bureau of Internal Revenue.

Letter   -2-   10/5/87
Mr. Roy A. Vanterpool
Chief, Processing & Avvts. Br.

extent, but cooperation does not mean emasculation.

Sincerely,

Liston B. Monsanto
Shop Steward

cc: Mr. R. Thomas

      Mrs. J. DeCastro

      Mr. A.P. Olive

      Mrs. J. Petersen

      United Steel Workers of America
         (Local 8249)

Vanterpool was really swellheaded. He quickly responded in an attempt to show Olive how easy it was to handle Liston Monsanto. On October 6, 1987, he wrote me a letter and a memorandum. In his letter he said:

GOVERNMENT OF
THE VIRGIN ISLANDS OF THE UNITED STATES

---o---

VIRGIN ISLANDS
BUREAU OF INTERNAL REVENUE

---o---

Lockharts Garden No. 1A
Charlotte Amalie, St. Thomas, U.S.V.I. 00802

October 6, 1987

Mr. Liston Monsanto
Shop Steward
V.I. Bureau of Internal Revenue
St. Thomas, Virgin Islands   00801

Dear Mr. Monsanto:

This is in response to your, October 5, 1987, letter to me regarding my memorandum of instruction to, Mrs. Scipio.

This needs only to be brief. It is clear that you, as Shop Steward, may not have been explained fully as to why my memorandum. You made reference to Article XI of the agreement. This however, does not apply as a new nor a temporary assignment. This task has been done by this same unit over the years. At this point in time, they feel that they no longer want to do it. To be brief again, I am sure you now see the difference and also understand why Article IV of the agreement is invoked.

Further, the possible disciplinary action mentioned is in concert with the necessity to give warning before action. I am sure you would agree, for this is part of the process. Can you be fair in a few things? We do not want to take such actions. However, at the same time, it is not our position to abrogate Article IV and I am sure you will not want to do the same with other articles therein. Fair isn't it?

I am sure that you would want to explain to the employees involved the difference between what the facts are and what they may desire.

Thank you.

Roy A. Vanterpool
Chief, Processing & Accounts Branch

RAV/dma

cc: Mr. A. Olive
    Mr. J. Petersen
    United Steel Workers - Local 8249

149

And in his memorandum he said: "For some reason, I believed that by this time (after 7 months), I could improve the .02 rating. Please help yourself to score higher by marking your copy book to show. Diction "choice of words" etc. (It does not have to be verbal). Footnote – an explanation, commentary, etc. (I only rated your masterpiece. Again, your diction continues to be very poor). I do feel that in time, there will be improvement. You can do it. Try harder."

I had given Roy Vanterpool unwanted advice. And so I wrote to him once again on October 7, 1987. My salutation started with: "O ye of little faith." And then I wrote: "Because you have apparently taken to copycatting, it behooves me to tell you (without a trace of banter and by way of accentuating the positive) that it takes more than a letter or memorandum to impersonate Liston Monsanto. What it takes (pride, honesty, intestinal fortitude, etc. as evidenced by Opinion Number 81-1434 of the Third Circuit Court of Appeals) you haven't got. You see, good habits are the mentors that regulate our lives. When you cross the great divide your degree of which you boast will be interred in your grave. When I cross the great divide my record will be outliving me so that the living may be afforded the opportunity of using it. With all the talented and decent people in the Processing and Accounts Branch, Director Quinn made the decision to fill the vacancy created therein by Mr. Viggo Hendricks' retirement, by looking for a rank amateur too tough to be honest and too weak to lead the employees of a Branch, rife with charges of sexual harassment and embezzlement. Whether or not you were that person, will be determined only with the flight of time. Based on my observations it should be noted that it was presumably with an overabundance of vigor and enthusiasm plus new encouragement received by my letter of October 5, 1987, that prompted you to assume the role of "milque toast" in your apologetic letter of October 6, 1987. But instead of ending the exchange of correspondence with a mark of some quality, you had to go on to prove, through the issuance of a most preposterous memorandum, that aberration is truly the hallmark of homosapiens. Some people are naturally savvy, the rest can't learn. How in God's name do you expect one side (our Bargaining Unit) to obey a Contract that has become the laughing-stock of the Bureau of Internal Revenue and the United Steelworkers of America? If the people are trained and permitted to use their training, a lot would be accomplished."

Roy Vanterpool may not have known it, but perfection was not a part of his job description. The only person taking as much heat as Roy Vanterpool was the Farrelly administration through Anthony P. Olive who was receiving copies of any letter addressed to Roy Vanterpool from me.

Without any warning, Kenneth Hansen passed away in September 1987, leaving an aching void in Olive's heart. That Olive had been treating the work of the Delinquent Accounts and Returns Branch with indifference would surface. The day-to-day supervision of the Branch was in jeopardy. He could not turn to me for help inasmuch as I had been banished by ostracism by Edward Thomas and the shadow cabinet. Mr. Jerome Ferdinand (a Crucian assigned to the St. Croix office as Assistant Chief of the Branch where he had been programmed to see no evil, hear no evil or speak no evil) was always willing to do lots of evil given the chance. Olive would give him his chance to become his pawn.

Mr. Ferdinand called a meeting on October 8, 1987 to tell the assembled gathering that he had been designated Acting Chief of the Branch. In telling us of his new position and duties, not once did he tell us that Olive or anybody else for that matter would come before us in order to corroborate what he was saying. I thought it very unorthodox and so I wrote to Mr. Ferdinand on October 13, 1987 saying:

October 13, 1987

Mr. Jerome A. Ferdinand
Assitant Chief
Delinquent Accounts & Returns Branch
V.I. Bureau of Internal Revenue
Hamilton House Building
56 & 56A King Street
Christiansted, St. Croix, V.I.   00820

Dear Mr. Ferdinand:

I am writing to you in my capacity of Shop Steward fully conscious of the fact that office politics is a nasty game (especially the awful brand played in the Virgin Islands Bureau of Internal Revenue by people with volatile dispositions) during which bad people do evil things to innocent, decent people.

Cutting a path through this network of politics however, is documentary evidence - the most powerful weapon in the arsenal of the Internal Revenue Officer.

The foregoing established, it is worth noting that in our meeting of October 8, 1987, not once did we see or hear you read from any correspondence from Mr. Anthony P. Olive (Director of the Bureau) designating you Acting Chief of the Delinquent Accounts & Returns Branch, nor did we see any information communicating to the supervisory personnel in the Bureau that you had in fact been authorized (by Mr. Olive) to act as Chief, Delinquent Accounts & Returns Branch.

Since his appointment as Director, games-man-ship has been Mr. Olive's forte'. He used it on you when he (a) failed to designate you Acting Chief, Delinquent Accounts & Returns Branch (b) conveniently forgot to pick you up from the airport and (c) fooled you into believing that he'd be on hand to formally introduce you to the assembled gathering at our meeting.

Because of his artlessness, Mr. Kenneth C. Hansen was not considered good enough to be a part of Management's Negotiating Team, but was ostensibly good enough to carry out multiple duties of (1) Chief, Delinquent Accounts & Returns Branch (2) Super Revenue Officer as attested by his last seizure and sale in July of this year (3) Speical Procedures Officer defacto and (4) Scapegoat (at times) for management and certain scoff-laws in trying to rid the Bureau of a law-abiding Liston Monsanto. Needless to say, these were duties not in the best interest of the Bureau of Internal Revenue.

As a clairvoyant person who told both Mr. Quinn and Mr. Olive that chaos and/or havoc would someday reign supreme (see enclosed letters) in the Delinquent Accounts & Returns Branch, I take this opportunity to tell you - as you

Letter   -2-   10/13/87

Mr. Jerome A. Ferdinand
Asst. Chief, BARB (STX)

consider your ascension to the highest level in the Delinquent Accounts &
Returns Branch, that you can do no more than the system allows. You have
my cooperation.

                                        Sincerely yours,

                                        Liston B. Monsanto
                                        Shop Steward

cc: Mr. Anthony P. Olive
      Director

I had reasons for my madness and Ferdinand knew that my concerns were justified. He also knew that I had opened the doors to Olive's office allowing him to tell Olive that some form of communication was needed to formalize his designation. He wrote to me on October 24, 1987. He said: "This refers to your letter, dated October 23, 1987. First, I would like to thank you for the pledge of cooperation in my capacity as Acting Chief, Delinquent Accounts and Returns Branch. In briefly summarizing the comments of your letter, particularly in paragraph 3), it appears you are seeking clarification and/or information from the Head of the Bureau, Mr. Olive, concerning the designation of authority for my title position of Acting Chief of the Branch. Your concerns have been taken into consideration by the undersigned and I trust they can be addressed for the benefit of all concerned employees of the Delinquent Accounts and Returns Branch in St. Thomas."

And then Olive, with the passive obedience of a slave, did last what he should have done first. He wrote to all employees on October 28, 1987 saying: "Effective October 17, 987, Mr. Jerome Ferdinand has been designated Acting Chief of the Delinquent Accounts and Returns Branch. Mr. Ferdinand will be responsible for all DAR Branch activities. It is expected that he will identify support staff to assist him in carrying out his additional duties and responsibilities. For performing these additional duties and responsibilities, the Acting Chief will receive additional compensation."

Olive appeared to be reorganizing. He wrote another memorandum to his subordinates on October 28, 1987 saying: "In order to remove any doubt and improve lines of communications, Mr. Graciano Belardo, Supervisor, Audit/Enforcement Branch, has had and continues to have oversight responsibility for the Bureau's St. Croix operation. In Mr. Belardo's absence, this responsibility is delegated to Mr. Jerome Ferdinand, Acting Chief, DAR Branch. It is expected that Mr. Belardo and Mr. Ferdinand will coordinate their activities in such a manner that it will provide for the orderly flow of all operations on St. Croix. Mr. Jerome Ferdinand will continue to be responsible for the cars and will coordinate reporting requirements with Mr. Anthony Attidore."

Jerome Ferdinand was useless and inefficient, a real dud. Everything he did appeared to be more symbolic that tangible. He lived on St. Croix, completely removed from the computers and tax records. He didn't commute to St. Thomas on a daily basis for the purpose of conducting reviews, etc. and as a consequence appeared to be a perfunctory Supervisor running the Branch by remote control. The employees knew that he was shamming and that there was no one qualified and in a position of authority to supervise their work while evaluating their performance; hence they were malingering and having a glorious time at the expense of the taxpaying public. The designation of Jerome Ferdinand as Acting Chief of the Delinquent Accounts and Returns Branch was a gigantic hoax and a shameful farce.

Amid surreal developments I remained busy representing the members of the Bargaining Unit. Roy Vanterpool was at it again trying desperately to usurp Olive's throne by leading him astray. Here is what Olive wrote to Mr. Clyde George on October 23, 1987: "Your Performance Report for the period ending 4/1/87 has been in your possession since April 23, 1987. By request, it was sent to my office on October 15, 1987. On April 23, 1987, Mr. Roy Vanterpool gave you your Performance Report and asked that you sign it and return it to him. You did not comply and it has been in your possession since that time. In the Report, deficiencies were cited for time and attendance, compliance with rules and volume of acceptable work. Since that time I have talked with you regarding your performance. Mr. Vanterpool has again cited you for unauthorized leave and you continue to do as you please. The purpose of this letter is to give you final notice regarding your total disregard for our rules and regulations and disrespect for authority. Unless there is a substantial improvement in your time and attendance, productivity and decorum, I will recommend that you be dismissed from the Bureau of Internal Revenue."

On the same day he wrote to Mr. Rickhield Thomas, another subordinate of Roy Vanterpool. He said: "This is to notify you that you are hereby cited for insubordination and as a result suspended one week without pay, effective 8:00 a.m., October 26, 1987. You were given oral and written assignments September 17, 1987 at which time you refused to carry out. Again on October 5, 1987, not having complied, you were again in writing given the same assignment (numbering St. Croix returns) with a warning of possible disciplinary action. To date you still refuse to carry-out this task." He wrote a similar letter to Judith DeCastro.

Liston B. Monsanto, Sr.

As Shop Steward I received copies of the letters and immediately wrote to Olive. I said:

October 26, 1987

Mr. Anthony P. Olive
Director
V.I. Bureau of Internal Revenue
St. Thomas, Virgin Islands 00801

Dear Mr. Olive:

What a cheap shot! Your memorandum dated October 23, 1987, to Mrs. Judith DeCastro and Mr. Rickhield Thomas proves anew that management who has been charged with willful disobedience and open disrespect for our Bilateral Contract, loves to attack those employees they consider weak while circumventing the strong ones.

In your memorandum you have (based only on exparte evidence and perhaps through the usage of your guiding principle which is attached hereto) systematically suspended both employees from an organization rife with nepotism and abounding with a number of employees unable to submit to office discipline. (see attached correspondence establishing the validity of my statements).

"Train and Retain" - the battle cry of our strike in 1986 told the world that we (including Mrs. DeCastro and Mr. Thomas) have consistently been clamoring for much-needed training in order to better perform our work. Unlike most Government Employees, we did not strike for money. We want to work   - a fact corroborated by Opinion No. 81-1434 of the Third Circuit Court of Appeals. The system, of which you are an integral part, does not want the job done.

Four Internal Revenue Agents and one Revenue Officer have left the employment of the Bureau of Internal Revenue over the past twelve (12) months and with the abnormal turnover of employees in an organization requiring a high degree of confidentiality in these tiny islands, it becomes incumbent upon me to ask that you not be swept away by Mr. Roy Vanterpool's emotional pleas to harass and intimidate the members of the Bargaining Unit. Let's get the Labor/Management Committee together for the purpose of reducing by analysis the long-standing problems that are serving only to destroy the Virgin Islands Bureau of Internal Revenue.

Sincerely,

Liston B. Monsanto
Shop Steward

RECEIVED
DIRECTOR'S OFFICE

OCT 26 1987

V.I. BUREAU OF INT. REV.
ST. THOMAS, V.I.

cc: Mrs. Judith DeCastro
Mr. Rickhield Thomas
Mr. Luis "Tito" Morales
Mr. Cephus Rogers
Mrs. Rosalind Scipio
Mr. Roy Vanterpool
Mrs. Joyce Petersen

Olive responded right away by submitting to me the names of several employees whom he said would represent him on the Labor/Management Committee. It appeared as if he could only function when told to do so by me. I had some unfinished business relating to Clyde George to whom you may recall Olive had written on October 23, 1987. Here is what I wrote to Olive:

RECEIVED
DIRECTOR'S OFFICE

OCT 27 1987

V.I. BUREAU OF INT. REV.
ST. THOMAS, V.I.

October 27, 1987

Mr. Anthony P. Olive
Director
Virgin Islands Bureau of Internal Revenue
St. Thomas, Virgin Islands 00801

Dear Mr. Olive:

Just when it appeared that we had normalized relations between Management and Labor in the Bureau of Internal Revenue, I received a copy of a vague memorandum which was sent to Mr. Clyde George by you under a date of October 23, 1987.

Judging from its contents, the inference is clear that once again - based only on exparte evidence, you have cautioned Mr. George (a competent employee) that he'd be dismissed from the Bureau of Internal Revenue for, all things, his total disregard for rules and regulations plus disrespect for authority. Isn't this the same thing of which management is guilty?

The nature and gravity of the problem stems from the fact that Mr. Roy Vanterpool - a super incumbent bent on showing his subordinates who's boss, continues to misinterpret the language contained in Article IV of our Contract. As far as Mr. Vanterpool is concerned, employees have no rights. His part in what has become a personality conflict has been assumed by all knowledgeable observers.

This being the case, I'm asking that you steer clear of what may be best described as a potentially explosive situation.

On several occasions Mr. George has written to the supervisory personnel in the Processing Branch with copies to you explaining his part in a most obnoxious scenario. What's more, he wrote directly to you on February 19, 1986, (copy of letter attached) seeking the intercession of your office so as to avoid the very things you've deemed it necessary to accuse him of in your memorandum.

Again, if we are to normalize relations and stop singing "We Shall Overcome," efforts must be made to put the Labor/Management Committee to work. I, therefore, ask that you accede to my request.

Sincerely,

Liston B. Monsanto
Shop Steward

cc: Mr. Luis "Tito" Morales
    Mr. Clyde George
    Mr. Roy Vanterpool
    Mrs. Joyce Petersen
    Mrs. Albertha Sprauve

155

February 19, 1986

Mr. Anthony P. Olive
Director
V.I. Bureau of Internal Revenue
St. Thomas, V.I.   00801

Dear Mr. Olive:

I am writing to you in the hope that you would give serious attention to what is happening between a difficult Mr. Roy Vanterpool and me, with a view towards improving communication in the Processing and Accounts Branch of the V.I. Bureau of Internal Revenue.

Perhaps hoping that his paycheck would grow, Mr. Vanterpool worked overtime – sometime last week, trumping up charges against me and subsequently cautioned me that I'd be disciplined if I did not correct the fraudulent charges listed in a letter addressed to me from him.

I responded to Mr. Vanterpool's letter which was dated February 14, 1986 on February 18, 1986, and sent you a copy refuting most of his charges and asking for clarification on others.

After reading my letter, Mr. Vanterpool obviously frustrated, tore it to bits. He then placed the pieces in an envelope addressed to me and walked into the File Room where I was, and where my desk is located and promptly placed the envelope thereon. Is this a new trend? If not, what do we do when taxpayers react the same way?

Maybe you can offer some valuable advice, but as far as I'm concerned, Mr. Vanterpool should be charged with conduct unbecoming an officer. Had I done to him what he did to me when I received his worthless letter, he may have used his gun to shoot me.

I therefore ask that you give this matter your utmost attention.

Sincerely,

Clyde George
Senior Tax Record Clerk

cc: Mrs. Joyce L. Petersen
     Mr. Luis "Tito" Morales
     Mr. Liston Monsanto ✓
     Personnel File

The Bureau of Internal Revenue was a hornet's nest of dissatisfied employees. Olive was wavering between siding with me or doing as he had been instructed to do by Vanterpool and while he continued to waver, somebody in the spirit of Thanksgiving had playfully posted a picture of a home-cooked turkey with Olive's face serving as the turkey's on the bulletin board. Seeing the lovely butterball turkey with his face, Olive went wild with rage. He found himself in such a frantic condition that he could not think clearly or act sensibly. He started shouting in loud and very emotional tones without identifying anyone as the culprit.

Ever so often by way of disrespect a stunt such as the turkey would rear its ugly head. The employees did not respect Olive and both Farrelly and Edward Thomas knew this.

After a short time of relief and rest I wrote to Olive on December 7, 1987 saying:

RECEIVED
DIRECTOR'S OFFICE

DEC 7 1987

VIRGIN ISLANDS BUREAU OF
INTERNAL REVENUE
St. Thomas, V.I.

December 7, 1987

Mr. Anthony P. Olive
Director
V.I. Bureau of Internal Revenue
St. Thomas, V.I. 00801

Dear Mr. Olive:

Wary members of our Bargaining Unit (aware of your games-man-ship) have considered your ploy to send certain borderline veterans and fifth columnists within their ranks to formal training, as one designed to win friends while gaining influence over them.

With the sometimes arrogant manners of a dictator, you have offended the employees through your anonymous accusations, your invasion of their breathing space, which has been polluted by the profanity emanating from your glib tongue, and perhaps above all, your continued violation of Bill Number 16-0515, which was passed by the Sixteenth Legislature on August 11, 1986. The employees have come to realize that circumstances do not make a man, they reveal him.

Forced over the past several years to assume the role of cynic and operating on the thesis that a person wanting peace must work for justice I feel it an obligation to duty to remind you that the less than professional governmental system fought successfully by me under former Governors Evans, King and Luis, is the same system with which I previously worked and which previously worked against me. A system - I hasten to add that to date continues to work beautifully for me and the members of our Bargaining Unit as well.

As you are well aware, there is absolute bedlam on the floor of the Virgin Islands Bureau of Internal Revenue. The cesspool is running over. The man chosen to deliver us from all the evil in our orgainzation has abandoned us. Today (because of my Third Circuit Court Decision) it dosen't take a Liston Monsanto. Things are now much easier, the resistances are less. Saying you can't do anything to improve working conditions, is an abdication of leadership and an affront to the people of the Virgin Islands.

Selfishness and a high degree of spite which have within itself insolence and the sometimes farcical act on the part of certain employees in management to shred (after reading) letters addressed to them before returning the pieces to the author have become commonplace in the Bureau. Who would believe that people in whom the authority is vested to prepare and send letters to taxpayers would resort to such nonsense.

Liston B. Monsanto, Sr.

Letter   -2-   12/7/87

Mr. Anthony P. Olive
Director

    Because you are a haughty person, you have become most unpopular with many of
your once blind loyalists in the Bureau. What's more, your negative reaction to
the picture of a lovely butterball turkey, which appeared on the bulletin board on
November 25, 1987, borders on conduct unbecoming an officer. Behavior such as you
displayed is unacceptable and really has no business in a place mirrored off the
United States Internal Revenue Service.

    You owe it to your subordinates. At this writing I'm hard pressed to find a
reason for your not holding periodic meetings in the Bureau. Why can't we know
what course you have chartered? Please tell us what you expect from us.

                                              Sincerely yours,

                                              Liston Monsanto
                                              Shop Steward

cc: Honorable Alexander Farrelly
     Governor of the Virgin Islands

     Mr. Edward Thomas
     Reviewer-Classifier

     Mr. Jerome Ferdinand
     Acting Chief,
     Delinquent Accounts & Returns Branch (STX)

     Mr. Anthony Attidore
     Budget Control Officer

     Mr. Luis "Tito" Morales
     President, Local 8249

     Mr. Cephus Rogers
     Staff Representative

Showing thanks by sharing

By PHILIP HARRIGAN
Daily News Staff

Thanksgiving is a time to be grateful for life's blessings. And starting today, at least two groups on St. Thomas are reaching out to share those blessings.

The recently formed Downstreet People club will feed the homeless in a luncheon starting at 11 a.m. today at To God Be The Glory Mission on Harwood Highway, across from Western Cemetery.

"This is our first major project," said Renaa Rhymer, recording secretary of Downstreet People. "Some of those people may not have had a home-cooked meal in a long time."

Rhymer said the Thanksgiving lunch idea came about after she read in the paper "about organizations donating this and

Daily News Photo by HILLARY HODGE

On December 10, 1987, the Daily News carried a news items captioned "IRB Agents in Training" the item said: "Six Internal Revenue Agents from the Virgin Islands are attending a six-week training session in Miami, Florida, sponsored by the U.S. Internal Revenue Service. Anthony Olive, Director of the V.I. Bureau of Internal Revenue announced the training session Wednesday saying it is 'in keeping with the Farrelly Administration's commitment to train its employees.' Olive has come under fire for not providing more training to IRB employees. Recently, Gov. Alexander Farrelly said the issue is one reason why he has not reappointed Olive to the Directorship." Farrelly was shamming. His comments became nothing more than a footnote to my letter of December 7, 1987. Lest you forget, Olive was still serving as Director by virtue of his appointment by Farrelly's predecessor, former Governor Juan Luis.

I had not forgotten the "Drug Store Cowboy" (Jerome Ferdinand) however. I wrote to him on December 14, 1987 as follows:

Liston B. Monsanto, Sr.

December 14, 1987

Mr. Jerome A. Ferdinand
Assitant Chief
Delinquent Accounts & Returns Branch
V.I. Bureau of Internal Revenue
Hamilton House Building
56 & 56A King Street
Christiansted, St. Croix, V.I. 00820

Dear Mr. Ferdinand:

Following discussions with Mr. Anthony P. Olive (in which you participated) on December 8, 1987, and based on the attached "Daily News" item of December 10, 1987, I find it necessary to respond in some measure to the critical issue of training – an issue that has been given too much notoriety already.

Mr. Olive – for some strange reason, believes that the employees of the Bureau of Internal Revenue can work on a par with their counterparts anywhere under the American Flag without the appropriate training. He conveniently fails to understand how half-trained and untrained employees feel, after meeting with a sophisticated tax-payer or his representative. Under Juan Luis Mr. Olive and you (by your silence) be-came "Companymen" much to the deteriment of the Virgin Islands people.

Throughout the years, I've spoken out to a disgusting extent over management's will-ful disobedience and open disrespect for Article XIX (education and training) of the ex-isting Bilateral Contract between the United Steelworkers of America and the Virgin Islands Bureau of Internal Revenue. I was even forced to submit a Grievance on June 19, 1986.

Credible evidence of my speaking out in an attempt to have your side comply duti-fully with the Contract, surfaced in our strike of 1986 with our slogan of "Train and Retain". This was followed by letters decrying management's modus operandi – some of which I've enclosed herewith.

The wave of euphoria (brought about by abysmal ignorance) which under the Luis Administration pervaded the halls of the Virgin Islands Bureau of Internal Revenue is being replaced by employees willing and ready to work. Employees who are not content to accept poor workmanship.

As a pundit committed to excellence, Governor Alexander Farrelly (in eleven months) has shown that he truly says what he means and means what he says. This attitude Mr. Ferdinand, is a far cry from the less than professional attitude exhibited by the Luis Administration.

160

Letter   -2-   12/14/87

Mr. Jerome Ferdinand
Acting Chief, DAR Br.

        As a reactionary Mr. Olive had to wait until Alexander Farrelly became Governor to be told publicly by Mr. Farrelly that training is one reason why he has not been re-appointed. The inevitable question to Mr. Olive (by copy of this letter) thus becomes: Is Grievance Number 7-87 dated June 19, 1987 settled?

                                      Merry Christmas and Happy New Year

                                      Liston B. Monsanto
                                      Shop Steward

cc: Mr. Anthony P. Olive
     Director

     Mr. Cephus Rogers
     Staff Representative

     Mr. Luis "Tito" Morales
     President, Local 8249

1987   The Daily News, Thursday, December

Short reports

Holder appointed: Senate President Iver Stridiron has appointed Alphonso Holder to serve on the three-member government reorganization panel.

At the same time, Gov. Alexander Farrelly sent a proposal to the Legislature asking it to extend the deadline for the panel to make its report about how well the reorganization is working.

The current deadline is the end of this month, but the panel has yet to be established much less started its work.

Farrelly is asking to postpone the report to March 31.

Holder served as commissioner of Property and Procurement in former Gov. Melvin Evans' administration and as the first executive director of the Muncipal Council, the forerunner to the Legislature.

Health care assured: All government employees covered by Blue Cross/Blue Shield will continue to receive all necessary care at the territory's hospitals and clinics despite the impasse between the company and the government.

"We at the Department of Health will continue to honor the insurance cards until we are notified of any change in the insurance agreement or the insurance carrier," Health Commissioner Deborah McGregor said.

Persons holding Blue Cross cards need not worry that they will be denied care or will be required to pay in full for services, she added.

Blue Cross suspended its payment of claims at 5 p.m. Friday in an attempt to force the government to pay or at least guarantee payment of more than $6 million the company claims it owes.

Teacher paychecks: Teachers in the Education Department's adult education program should have paychecks by next week, St. Thomas-St. John Schools Superintendent Gaylord Sprauve said Wednesday.

Sprauve said 24 adult education teachers at Charlotte Amalie High School hadn't been paid since the school year began in September.

Sprauve, who said he met with the teachers Tuesday night, said teachers were awaiting retroactive and regular paychecks, but couldn't get them because of a problem with paper work.

"There are a lot of steps that have to be followed," Sprauve said, explaining that adjustments were made to continue the payroll because Education is operating under last fiscal year's budget and "no provisions had been made to include the adult education program."

Sprauve said the checks are currently being processed and should be ready by the end of next week.

IRB agents in training: Six Internal Revenue agents from the Virgin Islands are attending a six-week training session in Miami, Fla., sponsored by the U.S. Internal Revenue Service.

Anthony Olive, director of the V.I. Internal Revenue Bureau, announced the training session Wednesday, saying it is "in keeping with the Farrelly administration's commitment to train its employees."

He also announced that special agent Steven Frett has successfully completed a seven-week training session in special agent investigative technique.

Olive has come under fire for not providing more training to IRB employees. Recently, Gov. Alexander Farrelly said the issue is one reason why he has not reappointed Olive to the directorship. Olive is still serving by virtue of his appointment by Farrelly's predecessor, former Gov. Juan Luis.

The agents currently receiving training are Janis Callender, Alonzo Brady and Roosevelt Davis from the St. Thomas office, and Naomi Phillip, Joe McGregor and Thomas Black Jr. from St. Croix.

Those who successfully complete this course, Phase I of revenue agent training, will have the opportunity to take Phase II next year, Olive said.   *12/10/87*

Through the usage of body language, Olive was on his knees begging Farrelly to appoint him. He was willing to do anything, even attempting to mislead me into believing that he'd make me Chief of the Delinquent Accounts and Returns Branch. Before responding to the Daily News on December 10, 1987, he had invited me to his office on December 9th where, in the presence of the "Drug Store Cowboy," he made an exaggerated appeal to my emotions offering me the position of Chief of the Delinquent Accounts and Returns Branch and then by way of telling the world of his offer, he wrote to me on January 11, 1988 in this manner: "On December 9, 1987, you met with Mr. Jerome Ferdinand and myself in order to discuss various problems in the Delinquent Accounts and Returns Branch. During our discussion you stated that you had no interest in being Chief, DAR, and in fact did not want to be Chief, DAR Branch. In a certification of eligible candidates from the Division of Personnel dated December 14, 1987 your name appears as an eligible candidate. Based on your remarks as stated above, it appears that we now have a conflict. In order to complete the selection process, please indicate whether or not you wish to be considered for the position of Chief, DAR Branch. Your approved annual leave is scheduled to end on 1/14/88 at 10:00 a.m., thus, if you wish to be considered, an appointment is being confirmed for you on January 25, 1988."

On January 12, 1988 I fired back at Olive saying:

GOVERNMENT OF
THE VIRGIN ISLANDS OF THE UNITED STATES

——◊——

VIRGIN ISLANDS
BUREAU OF INTERNAL REVENUE

——◊——

Lockharts Garden No. 1A
Charlotte Amalie, St. Thomas, U.S.V.I. 00802

January 12, 1988

Anthony P. Olive
Acting Director
Bureau of Internal Revenue
St. Thomas, V.I.   00801

Dear Mr. Olive:

In a strong attempt to amend your law-breaking ways obviously to conform to the rules of the Farrelly Administration, you wrote to me (for the record) on January 11, 1988, a letter which has been described as an excercise in utterly bad taste.

Flighty people often have volatile dispositions, but honestly, you have never ceased to amaze me-especially now that you have suddenly decided to show your impeccability as Director of the Bureau of Internal Revenue.

The record shows that at an arbitration hearing held on February 23, 1984, you testified before Lois Rappaport (Arbitrator) that: "Mr. Leroy Quinn (Former Director) made his position known that as Director of the Bureau of Internal Revenue he had in fact followed the procedures as prescribed by the Personnel Merit System, and had thus appointed Mr. Kenneth Hansen as Chief of the Delinquent Accounts and Returns Branch. He (Mr. Quinn) always maintained that position."

You continued by saying: The Director of Personnel is required by law to certify a list of eligibles for a position, and it was that procedure that was utilized in promoting Mr. Hansen to Chief.

Concluding that particular portion of your testimony, you stated: "Out of the eligibles that personnel transmits to me, I make a selection."

It is therefore incredible for me to believe that during this period (87-88) when Mr. Gary Hart has changed his mind and re-entered the Democractic Primary, and during this period when Senator Iver Stridiron changed his mind about not wanting to be Senate President, and during this period when even Mr. Farrelly changed his

Mr. Anthony P. Olive
Page 2.
January 12, 1987

mind and decided to give the run for the Territorial Governorship another try, that you would allow our meeting of December 9, 1987 to confuse you. Gosh, it was five (5) days later on December 14, 1987 that you received the Certification of Eligible Candidates from the Division of Personnel. Truly, some people don't grow when they get responsibilities, they just puff up.

You have an empire without a title. You also have my record and resume'. There is no "conflict." Do what you have to do in completing your selection process and utimately you'll find that you've <u>changed</u> your modus operandi.

Sincerely,

Liston B. Monsanto
Internal Revenue Officer

I followed up with another letter on January 26, 1988 wherein I said: "As a law-abiding person desirous of projecting an image conducive to the growth of the Bureau of Internal Revenue, thereby promoting voluntary compliance, I find it necessary to issue a terse report concerning my interview of January 25, 1988. <u>Under present conditions</u>, I refuse to be considered for the position of Chief of the Delinquent Accounts and Returns Branch. To accept the position would change me into a recalcitrant to be used by everybody and respected by none. In short, due to my thoroughness, I refuse to supervise a Branch whose activities have been criticized by me over the past several years. I will not now condone the things that I've deemed condemnatory."

In a systematic fashion, Roy Vanterpool was still trying to enhance my letter writing capabilities through puckish remarks, etc. to his subordinates. On January 29, 1988, he addressed Mrs. Ilean Forbes: "This is to document your performance and your pugnacious attitude on the job. Two weeks prior to this date, I had to contact you concerning reports coming to my desk that the office at the airport was "closed." The time reported was within scheduled working hours. You did not deny the existence of the sign and destroy it. Your response to me was 'If you want it moved, come down here and move it yourself.' Rude; very much disrespectful. Further, I have been receiving numerous calls or complaints from persons clearing shipment wherever you are assigned. In this regard, please be reminded that it is your job to assist persons who are new to the procedure or unsure as to filling out the form properly. It should not depend on your evaluation of the person nor how you feel today. Reasonable people would have no difficulty in doing these things. It is my suggestion that you control yourself during working hours and not project a bad image of all government employees, the Bureau and Government. This I do not feel that you want to continue. I feel that this does put an end to this matter and that no further communication is necessary."

Mrs. Forbes brought the memorandum to me for my review and consideration. She further asked me to draft a letter for her signature and this I did on February 1, 1988. She told Mr. Vanterpool: "Because I've always prided myself on being a person who respects law and authority, over the past several weeks I've become tired of your false accusations and unsubstantiated charges. You knew the moment you had written it that your memorandum of January 29th was loaded with half-truths. This was corroborated by the fact that you put distance between yourself and the Union by not notifying them (by copy) of my so-called 'performance and pugnacious attitude on the job.' As a low echelon employee assigned to the Bureau of Internal Revenue, I shudder to think that I work for an organization wherein certain top-level personnel go about their daily duties with the arrogant manners of a dictator. They can conduct investigations, etc. into the affairs of certain people without having to worry about being investigated themselves. In order to promote harmony in the Virgin Islands Bureau of Internal Revenue, we must do away with most of our past practices. Mutual respect between management and labor is urgently needed and periodic meetings now discouraged must be encouraged. While you felt that your memorandum ended the matter and that no further communication was necessary, I felt that the people to whom you sent copies were treated to an ambiguous document thereby prompting my refutation."

Then I wrote to Vanterpool in my capacity as Shop Steward:

GOVERNMENT OF
THE VIRGIN ISLANDS OF THE UNITED STATES

VIRGIN ISLANDS
BUREAU OF INTERNAL REVENUE

Lockharts Garden No. 1A
Charlotte Amalie, St. Thomas, U.S.V.I. 00802

February 1, 1988

Mr. Roy Vanterpool
Chief, Processing & Accounts Branch
V.I. Bureau of Internal Revenue
St. Thomas, V.I. 00801

Dear Mr. Vanterpool:

I don't mean to suggest that you are lying, but inasmuch as I have information beyond your memorandum of January 29, 1988 to Mrs. Ilean Forbes, I feel that your reprimand was written out of necessity or compassion and proves anew that some people don't grow when they get responsibilities, they just puff up.

Amid a high degree of nepotism and the farcical act on the part of management to shred (after reading) letters addressed to them before returning the pieces to the author, you continue to display a holier than thou attitude in an organization abounding with charges of embezzlement (which incidentally has landed one man in jail) and sexual harassment.

Incidentally, may I have the names of the persons from whom you have been receiving "numerous calls or complaints?"

The image of the Virgin Islands Bureau of Internal Revenue has been eroded for some time. And-I repeat, "since Mr. Anthony Olive has not shown any interest in the fact that the Rules, Laws, Regulations, Etc. are being violated, how can he go about disciplining any employee. Example is not the main thing in influencing others. It is the only thing." Mr. Olive himself is guilty of telling me to kiss his ass.

Speaking of Mr. Olive, however, reminds me of the old derisive question that people ask when someone tries to elbow himself up front in an office, a schoolyard or a barroom debate. It goes: "Hey, who departed and left you boss?"

Mr. Roy Vanterpool
Page 2.
February 1, 1988

We know at this writing that Governor Farrelly has not reappointed Mr. Olive. As Shop Steward, I also know however, that the members of our Bargaining Unit do not need you as a surrogate father. I deplore your actions and abrasive attitude.

The Virgin Islands Bureau of Internal Revenue is in great turmoil. Private little wars have turned into public exhibitions as evidenced by opinion 81-1434 of the U.S. Court of Appeals for the Third Circuit and our big strike of 1986.

It is my belief that unless and until Management introduces certain innovations into a system which now results in mediocre performances, we will never ever be able to accomplish anything in the future.

Finally, Mrs. Ilean Forbes is not the problem in the Virgin Islands Bureau of Internal Revenue. Management is.

For the umteenth time I ask that we put the Labor/Manangement Committee to work. It is a useful avenue through which may of our problems can be solved. Let's sit down at the table of reasoning.

Sincrely,

Liston Monsanto
Shop Steward

cc: Anthony Olive, Director
    Mr. H. Brathwaite, Supervisor, Excise Tax
    Mrs. J. Petersen, Asst. Chief, Proc. & Accts. Branch
    Ms. J. David, Asst. Chief, Proc. & Accts. Branch

Vanterpool, feeling embarrassed, responded to my letter by way of digression questioning my ability to function as Shop Steward and declaring me to be crazy. I answered him on February 2, 1988 saying: "Ordinarily I would ignore an arcane and malicious letter such as the one you addressed to me today, but since it would take little time and effort to issue a reply, I'll accommodate you with an answer. Your letter is nothing but a diversion to cloud the real issue. Nothing sticks in my craw with more irritation than a disoriented supervisor who in the wake of a governmental reorganization would waste precious time on the job in order to assume the dual role of neurologist and psychiatrist. Your deportment continues to be a constant menace to the development of the Virgin Islands Bureau of Internal Revenue. In your cycle of reprisals and retaliation, you have forgotten that you have a whole lot of work to do. Work, such as the issuance of credit and debit advices, taxpayer refunds,

168

taxpayer extensions, a matching operation and the overall supervision of the Processing and Accounts and Returns Branch. It is my profound hope that you'd do the work for which you are being paid by the taxpayers of the Virgin Islands always remembering that a person who believes that his power is absolute has no right in a democratic form of government."

For me there were many issues to grapple with including the issue of the battle with Jerome Ferdinand. In St. Thomas, the Delinquent Accounts and Returns Branch was devoid of leadership, leadership that Ferdinand could not provide. On February 11, 1988, he addressed a memorandum to the Revenue Officers in the St. Thomas Branch that read: "The Taxpayers Assistance Program for the District of St. John will commence on February 17, 1988. The hours of operation will be from 9:00 a.m. to 4:00 p.m. (every Wednesday and 14 & 15 of April 1988) at the Administrator's Office in Cruz Bay, St. John. The attached schedule covers the entire period of the program. Please adhere to the schedule and by all means be on time at your place of duty. If for any reason you are unable to report for work, please notify the Supervisor immediately. Ms. Cecilia Hill will provide the transportation tickets for your travel to and from St. John. Please furnish to me by phone the number of returns filed at the end of the workday or the following day."

I responded in this manner on February 16, 1988:

Liston B. Monsanto, Sr.

February 16, 1988

Mr. Jerome A. Ferdinand
Acting Chief, DAR Branch
V.I. Bureau of Internal Revenue
Christiansted, St. Croix
Virgin Islands 00820

Dear Mr. Ferdinand:

Knowing about the inborn greed, super ambition, intolerance and snobbishness of many a man and woman, man's inhumanity to man is not just a mere poetic phrase to me. Instead, it has been magnified to such a degree in the Virgin Islands Bureau of Internal Revenue, that the scoff-laws assigned thereto have the predonderance.

After reading your startling memorandum of February 11th, which seeks to augment the Taxpayers Assistance Program with certain erudite Revenue Officers, and after carefully examining your recent decision to assign those same Revenue Officers to the Office Collection Force, I have concluded that because of your strong desire to be Chief of the Delinquent Accounts and Returns Branch, thereby preserving the status quo, you have joined with Mr. Anthony Olive and others - to whom I've made reference in paragraph one of this letter, in simultaneously ignoring and disrespecting the Agreement between the Bureau of Internal Revenue and the United Steelworkers of America plus (and this very improtant) Opinion Number 81-1434 of the Third Circuit which was filed on March 11, 1982. (For more on the Opinion and the telling blow that it struck at the Bureau, I've attached hereto a copy of a letter from Liston Monsanto to Leroy Quinn. I suggest you read it in order to better understand my position).

Now that you have presumably read my letter, I ask you: Have you no honor? If you would pay attention to what I'm saying, you would find that the Virgin Islands Bureau of Internal Revenue is in disarray. It is collasping!

Lest you forget, Circuit Judges Hunter, VanDusen and Sloviter agreed with Liston Monsanto that the Bureau of Internal Revenue is not now, and has not been operating according to the rules for a long time. And this is the underlying reason for my not wanting to be considered for Chief, Delinquent Accounts and Returns Branch. Additionally, I'm not one desirous of living on my knees, thereby obligating myself to some people and certain ingrates who believe that the Bureau of Internal Revenue is their little empire.

If John Ferrant (a mercenary) could get the message after reading and digesting the Third Circuit Court's Opinion, Why can't you? Stand up for what you know to be right. Who knows, a splendid new opportunity could arise.

While you are desperately trying to run the Delinquent Accounts and Returns Branch by remote control from St. Croix your subordinates are having a glorious time.

Letter   -2-   2/16/88

Mr. Jerome A. Ferdinand

    Some of them were directed to attend a seminar at the University of the Virgin Islands in order to ostensibly prepare them for the Taxpayers Assistance Program. Upon completion of their participation in the seminar, however, flimsy excuses were given by management so that they could assign the task of preparing returns to those employees who were never given the opportunity to attend the seminar.

    The foregoing brings to issue the following excerpt from a government house report which appeared in the Daily News on Thursday, December 10, 1987: "Olive has come under fire for not providing more training to IRB employees. Recently, Governor Alexander Farrelly said the issue is one reason why he has not reappointed Olive to the Directorship."

    During this period the Bureau must give serious thought about how it chooses a Chief of the Delinquent Accounts and Returns Branch. As a person who seldom engages in levity, I believe that a serious study is essential to our future.

    Under present conditions, I will not hold you to the letter of the law. That's impossible. I only ask that you read and digest the message sent to Mr. Leroy Quinn in my letter of July 2, 1982, with a view towards full compliance.

                                  Sincerely,

                                    Liston B. Monsanto
                                    Shop Steward

cc: Mr. Anthony P. Olive
      Director

      Ms. Cecilia I. Hill
      Tax Coordinating Officer

Liston B. Monsanto, Sr.

July 2, 1982

Leroy A. Quinn
Director
Virgin Islands Bureau of Internal Revenue
P.O. Box 3186
St. Thomas, Virgin Islands   00801

Dear Mr. Quinn:

Inasmuch as it has been established that most employees of the Virgin Islands Bureau of Internal Revenue feel security and safety in numbers take precedence over lawfullness, to say that respect for law and authority has been a most powerful weapon in the arsenal of a small minority assigned to the Delinquent Accounts and Returns Branch, is an understatement that deserves the highest degree of publicity.

Armed and blessed with such honor and esteem, plus the landmark opinion filed on March 11, 1982 (81-1434 Liston Monsanto versus Leroy A. Quinn) by the United States Court of Appeals for the Third Circuit, the small minority knows that any unlawful attempt(s) emanating from management and designed to weaken or to exhaust its resources will be a nullity. Moreover, we know that in this government of, for, and by the people, one can afford-like the legendary Swiss Patriot William Tell, not to bow-down to any person, place or thing.

Law-abiding employees see no need to circumvent, restrict, or limit the law as is commonplace in the Bureau of Internal Revenue. Furthermore, the court's opinion referred to in paragraph two of this letter, has opened the door for many aggrieved employees (especially those whose civil rights have been violated) to assert their rights as classified public servants. It has also determined for management exactly what constitutes disruption and libel. In short, the opinion-if

followed, will help to bring much-needed order to the
Government's Bureau of Internal Revenue, while simultaneously
stopping a take-over by the United States Treasury Department.

Equally important however, and perhaps a major drawback
in the Bureau, is the long recognized fact, which deals with
our desperate need for a Chief of the Delinquent Account and
Returns Branch. The absence of a chief is even more critical
at this time than it has ever been. This vacant position
without a doubt, continues to be the principal reason for the
problems in the Delinquent Accounts and Return Branch.

Furthermore, I feel that the filling of the classified
position of Chief Delinquent Accounts and Returns Branch is
absolutely essential.

It is a common error for public servants (especially
those in position of authority) to think that the Government of
the Virgin Islands is their personal possession. They fail to
see that the mental picture which they have created serves
only to make them responsible for certain acts and omissions,
while forever making their office(s) open to criticism before
the Government Employees Service Commission and the Courts.

If we sincerely intend to improve conditions in the Virgin
Islands Bureau of Internal Revenue, and avert a take-over by
the Federal Government, we must demonstrate a changed attitude
with a willingness to work closely, harmoniously, and ethically
with each other. The flaunting of authority by certain personnel
in management and the disruptive influence now exerted by certain
lower echelon employees over their peers, must cease and be
replaced by mutual respect and admiration for each other.

Incidentally, now that I've returned to work after being
vindicated of charges trumped up by you and Mr. Anthony P. Olive
(see your libelous letter of March 16, 1982). It is hoped that
you'd dispense with personalities, as I look forward to working
as diligently as I did in the past, with a view towards projecting

an image that best represents the Virgin Islands Bureau of
Internal Revenue. This, I say unreservedly.

Sincerely,

Liston Monsanto

cc: Governor, Juan Luis
     Lieutenant Governor, Henry A. Millin
     Deputy Director, Anthony P. Olive

And then serving as ghostwriter for Ulrie Vialet, I addressed another letter to Ferdinand on February 17, 1988.

February 17, 1988

Mr. Jerome A. Ferdinand
Acting Chief, DAR Branch
V.I. Bureau of Internal Revenue
Christiansted, St. Croix
Virgin Islands 00820

Dear Mr. Ferdinand:

This letter is not intended to be rude or insubordinate. It is instead designed to formally notify you that I do not have the practical education that's needed to participate in this years Taxpayers Assistance Program.

In the spirit of cooperation and my desire to stand-by to serve in any way needed, over the past several years I've used my formal training as a Revenue Officer to make a positive contribution to the Taxpayers Assistance Program – expecially as it applies to the Island of St. John.

This year, because of the Tax Reform Act of 1986 which made sweeping changes to our tax system, special orientation and training were made available to – I would dare say, all employees under the American flag authorized to prepare 1987 returns, except myself and maybe a pariah or two in our organization.

In the past and up to now my presence has been felt at boxing and wrestling matches, horse racing, carnival activities and all other events held after our regular working hours, and requiring the payment of Entertainment Taxes. Why I was not given the formal training to prepare me for the assignment of which you speak in your February 11th memorandum really puzzles me. I do not consider myself a "bypass specialist." If top-notch Revenue Officers in the United States are required to prepare themselves preliminarily to administering taxpayer assistance, who am I to go blindly before taxpayers without training? No, I'm aufully sorry. I do not intend to embarass myself and the Virgin Islands Bureau of Internal Revenue.

Being physically removed from St. Thomas where the records are kept may have caused you to overlook Revenue Officers Lima, Monsanto and Vialet, in choosing the various people to attend the training seminars. Nevertheless, I give you the assurance (provided I'm trained) that I'll continue to help the Bureau as much as I possibly can.

Sincerely,

Ulrie Vialet

Ulrie Vialet
Internal Revenue Officer

cc: Mr. Anthony P. Olive
    Director

    Ms. Cecilia I. Hill
    Tax Coordinating Officer

I was really an ombudsman appointed by many disadvantaged people in the Bureau of Internal Revenue to receive and investigate grievances against a bunch of pigeon-hearted supervisors.

For some time Miss Paulette Rawlins, the Branch's Tax Coordinating Secretary, had been assigned certain duties foreign to her job description without any financial compensation. This, needless to say, was in violation of our Contract. Management knew that they were in violation but they just didn't care. When Miss Rawlins approached me with her complaint I felt it an obligation to duty to represent her in a letter to Olive. I wrote on February 24, 1988:

February 24, 1988

RECEIVED
DIRECTOR'S OFFICE

FEB 24 1988

VIRGIN ISLANDS BUREAU OF
INTERNAL REVENUE
ST. THOMAS. V.I.

Mr. Anthony P. Olive
Director
V.I. Bureau of Internal Revenue
St. Thomas, Virgin Islands 00801

Dear Mr. Olive:

I have just received from Miss Paulette Rawlins (Tax Coordinating Secretary 11) a copy of her February 23rd letter which is addressed to you.

In her letter Miss Rawlins complains about being stripped of all duties, after she had served notice on you that she was in fact serving as Assistant Chief pro-tem without any financial compensation.

This reaction on your part conjures up memories of an extraction from Opinion No. 81-1434 of the Third Circuit which goes: "The timing of Commissioner Quinn's decision to seek Monsanto's dismissal, less than ten (10) days after the radio broadcast, suggests that it was the broadcast rather than the letter writing as such which provoked this controversy."

Miss Rawlins went on to notify both you and Mr. Ferdinand that she is presently without an assignment. This, I hasten to add, is not an oddity in the Bureau, and is one of the many reasons why you are scoring dismally among the employees.

We are moving in an orbit around the hostile confines of the Virgin Islands Bureau of Internal Revenue and whatever secret plans or thoughts you may have had about the Bureau (such as those appearing in the attached December 17, 1985 clipping from the Daily News) have been upstaged by recent events which have revealed the irony of calling a stupid plan clever.

Granting "Peace Officer Status" to those employees worthy of it, is one way through which you can accomplish the very thing that you have stated in the clipping.

Your staunch supporter, Senator Lorraine Berry, has conveniently pointed to nepotism in the Department of Health as exemplified by yet another clipping (which is attached hereto) from the Daily News of January 23, 1988. She has completely forgotten - it seems, that the Virgin Islands Bureau of Internal Revenue has become a citadel for nepotism.

Although we know that looking ahead has not been one of the Bureau's attributes, you should consider the problems listed herein as each is crucial to its future.

Sincerely,

Liston Monsanto
Shop Steward

cc: Mr. Jerome Ferdinand
    Ms. Paulette Rawlins
    Mr. Mario Lima

176

On March 24, 1988 the Daily News, under the headline: "Problems Tax IRB, Audit Says" detailed that the Virgin Islands Internal Revenue Bureau is so strangled by a lack of funds that it cannot collect $14 million in delinquent taxes according to an audit by the U.S. Department of the Interior's Inspector General's Office. One of several examples of how little money the IRB has, according to the audit released Wednesday: The IRB cashier's office on St. Croix did not have a cash register for at least seven years. The audit cites a high level of non-compliance with income tax laws but it adds because of problems at IRB in processing and filing income tax returns, there was no absolute certainty that specific taxpayers in our sample did not file."

In his response to the audit, IRB Director Anthony P. Olive wrote to Governor Alexander Farrelly that many of the problems are solved or are being solved. "By working together and supplying the ingredients, the (IG's) recommendations will be adopted and implemented." Olive wrote. "The top priority of the Bureau is full computerization. Manpower and funding are the needed ingredients. We have requested funding and salary increases to attract needed, competent staff. The train is on the track as it moves through the Bureau."

On April 1, 1988, the Daily News came out with an editorial under the caption: "Evading the Taxman." In the editorial they opened with the following lines: "In case anyone had any doubts about how many Virgin Islanders are evading the taxman, they should ask for a copy of the latest audit by the Interior Department's Inspector General's Office."

As you can readily see by now, I'm writing through a chronological method of organization in order to make it easy for me to walk the reader through the garden path leading to my extreme test.

Anthony Olive had a facility for accepting rumor as fact and using the rule of thumb as a basis for doing many things. In another of his foolish undertaking he wrote to Clyde George on April 8, 1988 notifying him that he had recommended his dismissal from the Bureau through a letter to Governor Farrelly. He went on to tell Mr. George that he had a poor performance record and that on December 21, 1987, he was very rude and disrespectful to employees in the Processing Branch. He concluded by saying: "The Director, the Chief of Processing and your immediate Supervisor have written to you and have spoken with you; yet, no noticeable change has resulted." And there was an afterthought which said: "As of April 7, 1988, there has been no communication from you regarding your whereabouts. Based on your poor past performance record, you have no sick leave and no annual leave."

On April 12th when Mr. George learned of Olive's recommendation, he wrote to Vanterpool (Chief-Processing): "Having told my supervisor (Mrs. Albertha Sprauve) on Monday, March 7, 1988 that I was on my way to see a doctor, I now find it necessary to notify you that since that time I have been undergoing a series of physical examinations at a medical center in Washington, D.C. As soon as the examinations are completed, like you, following your brief illness in 1987, I shall return to the Bureau of Internal Revenue with a view towards resuming my duties."

For the sake of clarity I followed George's letter to Vanterpool by writing to Olive on April 13, 1988. I wrote: "Seven days after the attached editorial appeared in the Daily News of April 1, 1988, you wrote (in what appears to be the absolute in frustration) a paradoxical letter (as attested by the first and last paragraph) to Mr. Clyde George, which has me in a quandary and forces me to ask: Must Mr. George await the word from Governor Farrelly to whom your recommendation was sent or must he file a grievance based on a recommendation that has yet to be adopted? An answer to this very important question is requested inasmuch as your letter is simply an opinion formed without taking time and care to judge Mr. George fairly. How can you allow one unfortunate experience to prejudice you against Mr. George? Records in your possession show that the supervisory personnel in the Processing Branch and Mr. George have aired their acrimonious differences time after time without any intervention from your office. The records also show (a fact corroborated by your letter) that Mr. George is in poor health presumably due to the fact that he works in a building where there is: (a) an inevitable malfunction of the air-conditioning unit, (b) frequent power outages, (c) a combustion chamber in the ceiling and (d) an obnoxious smell of tar that continues to invade our breathing space. Because Mr. George's records are carbon copies of those in your files, you ought to go over them once again. A review will undoubtedly disclose that your letter of recommendation to Governor Farrelly bespeaks prejudice against Mr. George." Now it was Vanterpool's turn. On April 21, 1988 he wrote to Mr. George in a letter filling me with irrepressible laughter. Here's what he wrote: "This will acknowledge receipt of your April 12, 1988 letter. In response to same, please note that I was informed by the Director that he has recommended termination of your services. You no longer work for the Bureau. Any further communication is to be made with the Director."

I felt compelled to answer Vanterpool. And so I did on April 25, 1988. I wrote:

April 25, 1988

RECEIVED
PROCESS & ACCTS. BRANCH
APR 25 1988
V.I. BUREAU of INTERNAL REVENUE

Mr. Roy Vanterpool
Chief-Processing & Accounts Branch
Bureau of Internal Revenue
St. Thomas, Virgin Islands   00801

Dear Mr. Vanterpool:

Truly, you are a perplexing man! With the advent of the Farrelly Administration, almost everybody under your supervision was foolish enough to believe that you would get rid of your old thought patterns, with a view towards promoting harmony in the Virgin Islands Bureau of Internal Revenue. Needless to say, they were wrong.

Your letter of April 21, 1988 to Mr. Clyde George - which was just brought to my attention, tells me that you are still on a roller coaster headed in the wrong direction.

Praying and hoping that Mr. George would be discharged from his duties, you made a manifest error of prematurely notifying him that he no longer works for the Virgin Islands Bureau of Internal Revenue.

How - after reviewing the record, did you unilaterally conclude that Mr. George is no longer employed by the Bureau of Internal Revenue? Is Mr. Anthony Olive the appointing authority for the V.I. Government? When was Mr. George discharged by Governor Farrelly? When did Mr. George find out about Mr. Olive's recommendation to Governor Farelly? Where did Mr. Olive get the supreme authority to discharge Mr. George? How did Mr. Olive arrive at his April 22nd date as the end of Mr. George's ten-day period?

Ponder the foregoing questions and please stop abusing whatever little discretionary power you may have.

The Virgin Islands Bureau of Internal Revenue inherited by Governor Farrelly, continues to operate "in violation of law, and without rhyme or reason". My best advice to you and the scoff-laws in management: When all else fail, follow directions. Apologize to Mr. George.

Sincerely,

Liston Monsanto
Shop Steward

cc: Mr. Anthony P. Olive
     Mr. Clyde George
     Mr. Tito Morales
     Mr. Cephus Rogers

179

My letter dampened their enthusiasm so much that the matter became moot. Working in a less-than-professional atmosphere surrounded by a large number of disadvantaged people was problematic. Some of our matured college trained employees through fear, lack of ability and spurious relationships were operating in conformity with the unwritten guidelines bequeathed to them by Reuben Wheatley and the Union leaders themselves could not be trusted inasmuch as they were backers of many of the prominent politicians in the Territory.

Two weeks after I had done away with the Clyde George matter an event occurred that would have a significant impact on the Bureau's future. Louis "Lolo" Willis, a known fifth columnist on his way up the rungs of the career ladder, in order to spite Liston Monsanto, was illegally placed in the position of Acting Assistant Chief of the Delinquent Accounts and Returns Branch. Learning about this unjust act I immediately wrote to Tito Morales on May 13, 1988 sending copies of my letter to Olive and Willis. I said:

May 13, 1988

Mr. Luis "Tito" Morales
President-Local 8249
United Steelworkers of America
St. Thomas, Virgin Islands 00801

Dear Mr. Morales:

In a cunningly conceived operation, Mr. Anthony P. Olive (Director of the Bureau of Internal Revenue) has induced one of our members, who has been with the Delinquent Accounts and Returns Branch for about four and one-half years, to shift to his side as <u>Acting</u> Assistant Chief of the Delinquent Accounts and Reutrns Branch.

The member-Mr. Louis Willis, is the designated successor to Mr. Kenneth C. Hansen. Mr. Willis is an Internal Revenue Officer 1, who no doubt has many talents and endearing qualities. There is nothing to indicate, however, that he is in the former chiefs league when it comes to vision, analytical powers and - to a degree, independence of mind.

Nor is he, as the kind of "team" player Mr. Olive values, likely to go along with everything he (Mr. Olive) and his Revenue Officer gentry tells him to do in violation of law.

The timing and nature of Mr. Willis' appointment as <u>Acting</u> Assistant of the DARB virtually lead me to conclude that Mr. Olive is awfully eager to release information slapping the members of management on their backs, while illegally preparing Mr. Willis to meet the requirements to legally fill the position of Assistant Chief Delinquent Accounts and Returns Branch.

Incidentally, I've been on the Personnel List of Eligibles for the position since it was first advertised in 1983.

This latest act on the part of Mr. Anthony Olive borders on an unfair labor practice, as he seeks to reduce our numbers through circumvention of the agreement between the Bureau of Internal Revenue and the United Steelworkers of America.

I therefore ask that you take all steps conducive so as to prevent Mr. Olive from violating our agreement.

Very truly yours,

Liston B. Monsanto
Shop Steward

c.c. Mr. Anthony P. Olive
Mr. Louis M. Willis
Mr. Cephus Rogers
Mr. Anthony Attidore

The Union's silence on the matter was deafening. Willis was an upstart. Ferdinand was bad enough, but Willis' appointment was nightmarish causing me to file a grievance while addressing a letter to Olive and Thomas who I know had something to do with what was going on. My letter began with the salutation "Gentlemen" and said:

```
                    RECEIVED
                 DIRECTOR'S OFFICE


                  MAY 23 1988              May 23, 1988
               V.I. BUREAU OF INT. REV.
                  ST. THOMAS, V.I.
```

Mr. Anthony P. Olive (Director)
Mr. Edward E. Thomas (Acting Director)
V.I. Bureau of Internal Revenue
St. Thomas, Virgin Islands 00801

Gentlemen:

The final blow to our once proud organization was struck on May 10, 1988 when, at a critical moment Mr. Louis Willis (an Internal Revenue Officer I, and a member of our Bargaining Unit), was designated Acting Assistant Chief of the Delinquent Accounts and Returns Branch.

Mr. Willis is a nice person, but I know of no particular reason why he was suddenly qualified for the position of Acting Assistant Chief of the Delinquent Accounts and Returns Branch. As noted in my May 13th letter to Mr. Luis "Tito" Morales (copy to you), there is nothing to indicate that Mr. Louis Willis is in the former chiefs league when it comes to vision and analytical powers.

As an Internal Revenue Officer I, he could not qualify for the higher level positions of Internal Revenue Officer II, III, or IV in a Branch teeming with trained and experienced Revenue Officers, whose tenure of service range from seven to twenty-eight years. He has however moved with alacrity to the top where he can ostensibly lead the Veterans. In short, Mr. Louis Willis has become a perfunctory supervisor.

In the past, the rising tide of mediocrity resulted in many talented people in our Branch being afraid to assume the responsibilities of Chief and Assistant Chief. Prospective candidates (with the exception of Liston Monsanto) for the top positions became withdrawn and spoke only in monosyllables; consequently, the Branch's spirit sank to zero, and prompted your latest mayday in the month of May.

My own concern about the impact of the problems in the Delinquent Accounts and Returns Branch is greater than ever. Having been educated along practical lines, it is my sincere belief that imminent defeat can be turned into victory if we plan our moves carefully. I know as I'm sure that you know that the DAR Branch cannot survive without adequate space and supervisors who can circulate their innovative ideas while looking for constructive ways to handle situations.

Since my letter of January 26, 1988 (a copy of which is attached hereto), I've seen palpable signs of change in the Delinquent Accounts and Returns Branch. At the moment, I'm being persuaded and furthermore told by several members of your management team that they would support and/or draft me for the vacant position of Chief Delinquent Accounts and Returns Branch.

Messrs Olive & Thomas
May 23, 1988   2

      It is my belief that one should take advantage of any opportunity that comes his way, especially when so many people in management are desirous of seeing me in the position of Chief DARB.

      So, in order to restore sagging employees confidence in your office, and in order to make it possible for the Delinquent Accounts and Returns Branch to work itself out of the doldrums, I find it necessary to serve notice on you that I now stand ready, willing and able to assume the responsibility of Chief DARB.

      If the Chinese could normalize relations with the United States, why can't we? The olive branch is lying directly in front of us. Let's go for it!

c.c.   Mr. Cephus Rogers
       Mr. Luis "Tito" Morales
       Mr. Louis Willis

Sincerely,

Liston B. Monsanto
Shop Steward

January 26, 1988

Mr. Anthony P. Olive
Director
V.I. Bureau of Internal Revenue
St. Thomas, V.I. 00801

Dear Mr. Olive:

As a law-abiding person desirous of projecting an image conducive to the growth of the Bureau of Internal Revenue, thereby promoting voluntary compliance, I find it necessary to issue a terse report concerning my interview of January 25, 1988.

Under present conditions, I refuse to be considered for the position of Chief, Delinquent Accounts and Returns Branch.

To accept the position would change me into a recalcitrant to be used by everybody and respected by none.

In short, due to my thoroughness I refuse to supervise a Branch whose activities have been critcized by me over the past several years. I will not now condone the things that I've deemed condemnatory.

Sincerely,

Liston Monsanto
Internal Revenue Officer

After meeting with a sanctimonious Edward Thomas on the 24th of May, he wrote to Tito Morales on May 25th saying: "A hearing was granted to you and Mr. Liston Monsanto on Tuesday, May 24, 1988, with regard to the cited grievance. You presented your case in an acceptable fashion basically indicating your displeasure with the naming of Mr. Louis Willis as Acting Assistant Chief of the DAR Branch. I have reviewed and evaluated all the evidences submitted and decided to deny your appeal. I see no merit in your argument that Mr. Willis, a college graduate, employed as a Revenue Officer for almost five years is not qualified to supervise the Secretary and Revenue Officers under general and technical supervision from the acting Chief, Mr. Ferdinand." An erudite Calvin Wheatley, a subordinate of Edward Thomas at the West Indian Company, would say sometime later that, "The central government could learn from WICO's example. At WICO, it's business. You have fun times, but the bottom line is getting things done. That's something that's so lacking in government. The difference is like east to west, and that's a lot of miles." Wheatley was correct in his comparison. What he had failed to mention, however, was the fact that Edward Thomas had contributed immensely to the poor performance of the central government by holding kangaroo courts and placing upstarts in supervisory positions for which they were not qualified.

Following my meeting with Thomas, I wrote Tito a letter sending copies to Thomas and Olive. I extracted a passage from an article written by a Marilyn Mackay which served as the opener to my letter. The passage was as follows: "Here in the Virgin Islands, blaming our problems on outsiders is a copout. It's time we face the real culprit: leaderless leaders in government." I then went on to say: "In the Virgin Islands and specifically St. Thomas, the failure of the college graduate to make the contributions expected of him continues to result in sub-par performances to the detriment of the masses. Just as the Olive decision to appoint Mr. Louis Willis (an employee not even on the journey-man level), as Acting Assistant Chief was surprising, the reaction from Edward Thomas (Acting Director) was predictable. When one considers the fact that during an erudite Mr. Ervin Dorsett's (Supervisor of our Audit Branch) absences from the Bureau of Internal Revenue, Mr. Joseph Simmonds (the most qualified senior person) acts as Supervisor over a number of college graduates, the inevitable question becomes: Why can't Liston Monsanto, whose status is the same as Simmonds', supervise the activities of the Delinquent Accounts and Returns Branch during this critical period?"

Most of us have heard about brutality and abuse of power on the part of some police in the Virgin Islands but in the Bureau of Internal Revenue, Olive and Thomas like their predecessors, wielded great personal power which they found necessary to misuse from time to time. Working in the Bureau of Internal Revenue where there was no one to audit their returns or those of their friends, relatives and associates they did whatever they wanted. And any employee daring to speak the truth about anything that would expose them to the public would be charged with disclosure of information and thereafter dismissed.

In an incident very reminiscent of what happened to Clyde George in April of 1988, Olive addressed a letter to Mrs. Diane Tyrell on May 2, 1988 telling her: "For the reason stated below, you are suspended from duty effective May 3, 1988. Your suspension shall be in effect and continue until your dismissal become final. The cause for your suspension is as follows: two (2) counts of alleged unauthorized disclosure of tax information pursuant to Title 33, Section 1532, Virgin Islands Code. Based on the evidence relating to the unauthorized disclosure of tax information, it has been recommended that you be criminally prosecuted."

On the 3rd of May, I wrote to Olive saying: "I have just received my copy of your May 2, 1988 letter which is addressed to Mrs. Diane Tyrell (Tax Revenue Clerk) and which will, according to you, serve as the forerunner for her dismissal from the Virgin Islands Bureau of Internal Revenue. This is a most anomalous situation that borders on imperialism. In suspending Mrs. Tyrell for an indefinite period, you have asserted (without proof) that she is in violation of Title 33, Section 1532 of the Virgin Islands Code. Could it be that you are trying to systematically remove her from the Bureau of Internal Revenue? At any rate, since her suspension temporarily bars her from the office with a right to financial compensation, a grievance will be filed as required in order to hopefully discontinue the relentless infliction of cruelty deliberately brought about by management against certain members of our Bargaining Unit."

I had found Olive's action to be another undeserving charge against one of my members and therefore it became incumbent upon me to force him to do what he eventually did. I wrote to him on May 5th as follows: "This is to notify you that Mrs. Diane Tyrell will be returning to work on Monday, May 9th, 1988 as she continues to fight what she believes to be an abuse of discretionary power on your part in suspending her for an indefinite period. You may recall that in March of 1985, Mr. Kenneth C. Hansen was found guilty of the very thing for which Mrs. Tyrell has been accused. He was allowed, however, to report to work on a regular basis until the matter was presumably resolved. (See copies of correspondence attached hereto for information on Mr. Hansen). Ignoring this letter will be construed as acceptance of Mrs. Tyrell on May 9th. If you decide to respond, a specific time for her suspension must be given. No one wants to be held in suspense while on suspension. There are still too many double standards in the Virgin Islands Bureau of Internal Revenue. Compare Hansen's case with Mrs. Tyrell's."

That Olive had read my letter was evident. He hurriedly wrote back to me on May 6th. He said: "Relative to your May 5, 1988 letter regarding Mrs. Diane Tyrell's suspension, please refer to the grievance procedure as outlined in our Contract. You have followed that procedure in the past and if your position is to contest Mrs. Tyrell's suspension, I am prepared to proceed accordingly." In turn, I said: "Your letter of this morning (received by me at 9:45 a.m.) is not responsive to my letter of May 5, 1988. Accordingly, Mrs. Diane Tyrell will be reporting for work at 8:00 a.m. Monday, May 9, 1988." And finally Olive did what I wanted. He said: "Be advised that a hearing has been scheduled for 9:00 a.m. on Monday, May 9, 1988, at the Director's office regarding the Tyrell matter."

As an upstart, Olive had a penchant for placing notoriety over character. As the person who had brought the charges against Mrs. Tyrell, Olive had enough impudence to sit as the hearing officer in his kangaroo court. But such was life in the Virgin Islands Bureau of Internal Revenue.

The United Steelworkers of America (Local 8249) to which we belonged was still under scrutiny. Day after day in the workplace the employees were complaining about what they considered to be prolonged Union apathy. From time to time they would approach me asking about the status of their grievances. Because I did not have the authority to tell Tito or Cephus when they should be present at a hearing or who I had single-handedly chosen as an arbitrator, I could not answer their questions. Tito and Cephus were busy people who had to concern themselves with several Bargaining Units negotiating contracts and attending hearings. Our members knew that Tito, Edward Thomas and Governor Farrelly were all bosom buddies, but whether or not these friends would let their professional allegiances get in the way of their personal lives was not known.

Four members of our Bargaining Unit (Judith DeCastro, Mario Lima, Paulette Rawlins and Rickhield Thomas) decided to write to Mr. Thermon Phillips (Director – District 36) on May 17, 1988. They wrote:

May 17, 1988

Mr. Thermon Phillips
Director District 36
United Steelworkers of America
1825 Morris Avenue
Suite B
Birmington, Alabama   35203

Dear Mr. Phillips:

The undersigned, members of United Steelworkers of America Local 8249, St. Thomas, United States Virgin Islands, and more specifically employees of the Virgin Islands Bureau of Internal Revenue, have decided to bring to your attention a very trying situation which is severely hampering the prestige of not only the United Steelworkers of America, but of the labor movement in general.

Because of the Union's failure to take the initiative in resolving various grievances filed by the undersigned, the members of our Bargaining Unit are seriously questioning the practicality of maintaining membership in an organization that appears to have a laissez-faire attitude towards management's transgressions and disregard for our Contract.

We write as members in good standing and as a result demand serious representation on the part of our Union.

As of this writing the Union has not made a serious assertive motion to resolve the grievances mentioned heretofore. (The earliest was filed in February 1987).

We anxiously await a prompt solution to this problem.

Very truly yours,

Judith P.C. DeCastro
Judith P.C. DeCastro

Mario Lima
Mario Lima

Paulette Rawlins
Paulette Rawlins

Rickhield Thomas
Rickhield Thomas

cc: Mr. Lynn R. Williams
International President

Mr. Luis "Tito" Morales
President, Local 8249

Mr. Liston B. Monsanto
Shop Steward
V.I. Bureau of Internal Revenue

Mr. Cephus Rogers
Union Representative

In support of my people I addressed a letter to Mr. Phillips which read as follows:

Liston B. Monsanto, Sr.

May 23, 1988

Mr. Thermon Phillips
Director District 36
United Steelworkers of America
1825 Morris Avenue
Suite B
Birmington, Alabama 35203

Dear Mr. Phillips:

This letter is a follow up to a May 17th petition, which was addressed to you from several members of our Bargaining Unit complaining of union apathy.

I'm in total agreement with the position of our Members. Our Local Union challenges management - it seems, only on matters relating directly to money.

I don't know whether the local officials of the United Steelworkers of America (specifically 8249) are mentally prepared to grapple with the many problems in the Virgin Islands Bureau of Internal Revenue, but because I envision myself and certain Members of our Bargaining Unit as future targets of management's wrath, as Shop Steward I feel compelled to forward to you, the enclosed case histroy of the circumstances surrounding the plight of Mrs. Diane Tyrell.

After reading and digesting the information contained in the several letters which are to be used as evidence, you must conclude that Mrs. Tyrell has committed nothing worthy of an indefinite suspension. Mr. Anthony P. Olive (you will see) indicated beforehand in the first paragraph of his May 2nd letter, that Mrs. Tyrell would be dismissed from the Bureau of Internal Revenue.

The record goes on to show that Mr. Olive has assumed the roles of judge, jury and executioner in persecuting Mrs. Diane Tyrell while our Union sits back observing one of its paying members suffer through an indefinite suspension, which really narrows down to a dismissal with pay. Why haven't they filed a temporary restraining order with a view towards returning the lady to work?

Apathy on the part of the United Steelworkers of America is causing a number of employees to lose confidence in its operations. Accordingly, the urgent intercession of your office has become necessary, and towards this end, I solicit your indulgence.

Sincerely,

Liston B. Monsanto
Shop Steward

cc: Mr. Luis "Tito" Morales
President, Local 8249

Mr. Cephus Rogers
Union Representative

Despite their differing profiles, Olive and Roy Vanterpool were regarded as comparable talents. On June 17, 1988, Mr. Roy Vanterpool was at it again. He wrote to Mr. Rickhield Thomas accusing him of goldbricking without even the courtesy of hearing from Mr. Thomas. Vanterpool wrote:

Internal Revenue Service
memorandum

date: June 17, 1988

to: Mr. Richheild Thomas
Teller III

from: Roy A. Vanterpool
Chief, Processing & Accounts Branch

subject: Goldbricking – June 17, 1988

This is the second day in a row in which I must bring to your attention, the urgency of your assigned tasks preparing remittances for deposit.

After making several cursory check to ascertain that the deposits are moving I personally discovered that you are spending long lenghts of time from your desk. Today you spent over one (1) hour outside the building talking with an associate while the other employee worked. You have for too long impeded the deposit function here in the Bureau. Is this the examples set by a long time employee? Is this the kind of performance that will enhance your desire for a promotion or higher wages?

By this memo, please be notified that other than break period times, time spend away from your work will be charged leave without pay.

I urge you to arrange to change this kind of behavior.

Thank you.

RAV/dma

cc: Mr. A. Olive
    Mrs. R. Scipio
    Mrs. J. Petersen
    Ms. J. David
    Shop Steward ✓

     As an experienced and caring person, I had to protect and defend the members of our Bargaining Unit from the priggish Roy Vanterpool. And so in keeping with my modus operandi I wrote to him on June 17, 1988 saying:

Liston B. Monsanto, Sr.

June 17, 1988

Mr. Roy A. Vanterpool
Chief-Processing & Accounts Branch
Bureau of Internal Revenue
St. Thomas, Virgin Islands 00801

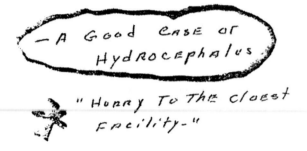

" Do not be afraid to take a stand in
what you believe in, even if it is
unpopular, a man or woman will be judged by the caliber of his enemies as
(well as) by his friends. Do not follow the counsel of the fearful who
seek certainty in an uncertain world,
who see change not as a challenge but
as a threat, and who dream of yesterday rather than tomorrow".

—Elmo Roebuck

Dear Mr. Vanterpool:

Trying to be the voice of reason, I'm writing to you concerning your
malicious memorandum of today to Mr. Rickhield Thomas, wherein you have sought
to treat him as a wanton child while accusing him of goldbricking.

On April 26, 1988, Mr. Thomas wrote to Mrs. Rosalind Scipio (his supervisor) with a copy to you - which you have presumably ignored, revealing in
chronological order certain historical facts which at the time, he deemed worthy
of mention for the edification of her and the others to whom copies were sent.
(see attached correspondence).

On May 28, 1988, Mr. Elmo Roebuck, through an article appearing in the
Daily News(attached hereto), gave a clear warning of worsening conditions in the
Bureau of Internal Revenue and cautioned Senator Lorraine Berry -to whom he wrote,
that the financial health of the government would be in serious disarray if corrective action was not taken.

It is therefore incredible to believe that a person like you - cognizant of the aforementioned information would take the time out from your seemingly busy schedule to write to Mr. Thomas charging him with goldbricking without even hearing his side of the story.

The members of our bargaining unit, especially those assigned to your
Branch have been filing grievances on an average of about one a month, and if

190

Mr. Roy A. Vanterpool   -2-
Chief-Proc. Branch
June 17, 1988

that does not convey to you their dissatisfaction with existing conditions,
I honestly don't know what will.

It is my sincere hope however that you would consider taking a little bit more time from your somewhat busy schedule to call a meeting with a
view towards addressing the many employees under your supervision.

It is grossly unfair to charge Mr. Thomas with goldbricking at a time
when he is seriously considering Mr. Roebuck's criticisms.

Sincerely yours,

Liston B. Monsanto
Shop Steward

c.c. Mr. A. Olive
     Mrs. R. Scipio
     Mrs. J. Petersen
     Miss J. David
     Mr. Rickhield Thomas

Upon receiving my letter, Roy Vanterpool flipped his lid writing across the document, "A good case of hydrocephalus, hurry to the closest facility." Vanterpool's vulnerability was growing more and more. He appeared to grow more agitated following each one of my letters.

On June 21, 1988, Rickhield Thomas hand-delivered a letter to him which read as follows:

Liston B. Monsanto, Sr.

June 21, 1988

Mr. Roy A. Vanterpool
Chief, Processing Returns & Accts. Branch
V.I. Bureau of Internal Revenue
St. Thomas, V.I. 00801

Dear Mr. Vanterpool:

This is in response to your malicious memorandum of June 17, 1988 wherein (in the absence of an investigation) you unilaterally decided to charge me with "goldbricking" on the job.

Lest you forget, my job is exactly like yours, in that it confines me to the office. Neither one of us is required to do field work, so that there is no need for any of us to be away from the office for any protracted length of time, under normal circumstances.

For your information, the record and the employees with whom I work on a day-to-day basis will - if need be, give honest testimony before any tribunal regarding the fact that I'm not a goldbricker. Furthermore, like most of my fellow employees in the Processing and Accounts Branch, I can honestly say: Greater love hath no man for his work.

Finally, It is well to mention that unless and until present trends are dramatically reversed, we will continue to have serious problems (such as the ones publicized by Mr. Elmo Roebuck) in the Virgin Islands Bureau of Internal Revenue. One thing is certain, however. I'm no dead beat!

Sincerely,

Rickhield Thomas
Teller II

cc: Mr. Anthony P. Olive
     Mrs. Rosalind Scipio
     Mrs. Joyce Petersen
     Ms. Janice David
     Mr. Liston Monsanto ✓

Then on June 24, 1988, after receiving a complaint from Miss Barbara Magras (one of Vanterpool's subordinates), I was forced to address a letter to Vanterpool once again. Accordingly, I wrote:

192

June 24, 1988

Mr. Roy A. Vanterpool
Chief, Processing & Accounts Branch
V.I. Bureau of Internal Revenue
St. Thomas, Virgin Islands 00801

Dear Mr. Vanterpool:

Although you've demonstrated over the past several months that you are capable of being a neurologist and/or psychiatrist when it comes to rejecting letters, I find it necessary at this particular time, to write to you as it concerns Miss Barbara Magras' health.

Miss Magras has complained to me about your abrasive attitude towards her since her return to duty on June 21, 1988, after being on Sick Leave from June 13, 1988 to June 17, 1988 inclusive.

She contends that upon her return to duty, she presented to you - as required, a "Leave Slip" signed by Doctors Aguas and Fallaria which you immediately frowned upon. (I have decided to attach a copy of the Leave Slip hereto for your enlightenment).

Being belligerent and accepting one side of a story is not my forte'. I would, therefore, appreciate hearing from you.

Sincerely yours,

Liston Monsanto
Shop Steward

cc: Miss Barbara Magras

Certificate to return to work or school

Mr.
Mrs. _Barbara_ _Magras_
Miss

has been under my care from _6/0_ to _6-17-88_

and is able to return to work/school on _____

Remarks _____

Dr. _Fallaria_ Phone _68311_

Address _STT Hsp_ Date _____

Eli Lilly and Company • Indianapolis, Indiana 46285

60-PJ-9625-0 PRINTED IN U.S.A. 001134-3080100 SEPTEMBER, 1980

Name _MAGRAS BARBARA_ Date _6-21-88_
   (Print or type—Last, First, Middle Initial)

Organizational Unit _IRS_

TYPE of LEAVE
☐ Annual ☐ Without pay
☑ Sick* ☐ Compensatory
☐ Other (specify)

No. of hours _40_ to begin _6-10-88 8_ a.m. To end _6-17-88 5_ p.m.
(Month, date, time)

NOTE: Annual leave authorized in excess of that to your credit will be charged to leave without pay.

*I certify that this absence was due to ☐ illness (nature) _____
which incapacitated me for duty;
☐ medical, dental, or optical treatment by _____
(Name of Practitioner)

(If absence was for 2 or more consecutive days or on a day immediately preceding or immediately following any weekend or legal holiday, practicing physician must complete form on back.)

_____ (Approving Officer)   _Barbara Magras_ (Signature of Employee)

Form VI-135   APPLICATION FOR LEAVE

At times, as you can readily see, I had to deflect my attention from Vanterpool to Olive in a circular motion. These people were lawbreakers. Vanterpool did not answer my letter of June 24, 1988, which caused me to take follow-up action in a letter dated July 5, 1988. I said:

July 5, 1988

Mr. Roy A. Vanterpool
Chief, Processing Returns & Accts. Branch
Virgin Islands Bureau of Internal Revenue
St. Thomas, Virgin Islands 00801

Dear Mr. Vanterpool:

Nobody will win the battle of the sexes. There is too much fraternizing with the enemy.

Since Mr. Anthony P. Olive's reappointment as Director of the Bureau of Internal Revenue, you have returned with renewed vigor, seeking once again to instill fear in your subordinates - many of whom have vowed to use any measure short of violence against you.

Because you have ignored my letter of June 24, 1988, which was inspired by a convalescing Barbara Magras and which was designed - at the same time, to hear your side of the story, I find it necessary to admonish you - to wit: You have in your possession an authentic Leave Slip signed by two Doctors which provides tangible proof that Miss Magras was in fact sick during the period June 13 1988 to June 17, 1988. What more do you require?

Personally speaking, I'm hard pressed to think that you are in fact questioning the Doctors integrity. If you are, I suggest you challenge them. At the moment, all I ask is that you allow Miss Magras to do the work for which she's being paid. Encourage her.

Your reaction to Miss Magras' valid Leave Slip as explained to me by her, was an excercise in utterly bad taste. Why don't you in your capacity and with the aid of our Bargaining Unit try to promote harmony in the Bureau of Internal Revenue?

You can do no more than Director Olive allows; consequently, I've decided to send a copy of this letter together with a copy of the one mentioned in paragraph three (3) herein for his attention, so that he may be made aware of the ongoing pettiness in the Bureau of Internal Revenue.

Sincerely,

Liston Monsanto
,Shop Steward

cc: Mr. Anthony P. Olive
     Director

     Miss Barbara Magras

The Rickhield Thomas and Barbara Magras matters became moot following my letters. Meanwhile, motivated by malice forty (40) miles away on St. Croix and amid his continuous pleas and urgings to have me assume the responsibility of Chief of the Delinquent Accounts and Returns Branch, Jerome Ferdinand did a military about face on June 17, 1988 galvanizing me. Ferdinand made a series of statements that as they stood, contradicted fact, common sense and even themselves; yet suggested a truth or at least a half truth. Factors listed on my performance report were not enough, so he had to add items 24 and 25, thereby contradicting some of the factors he had considered satisfactory.

Because I had asked him a question on December 2, 1987 relating to my status, Ferdinand concluded that my attitude was negative. He had forgotten that long before he had joined the Bureau of Internal Revenue, Liston Monsanto was serving levies and enforcing the tax laws. As a matter of fact, Liston Monsanto at one time supervised the activities of the Delinquent Accounts and Returns Branch.

Liston Monsanto (the record showed) had been dismissed on two occasions for doing his work. It was the Third Circuit Court of Appeals who rendered Opinion 81-1434 on March 11, 1982, vindicating him of all the false and malicious charges that were trumped up against him by Mr. Leroy Quinn, et al. Quoting from Malcolm X, I told Jerome Ferdinand: "One of the first things to learn is to think for yourself. If you form the habit of going by what you hear others say you will be walking west when you think you're going east. If you form the habit of taking what someone else says about a thing without checking it out for yourself, you'll find that you (will be) hating your friends and loving your enemies. Our people have made the mistake of confusing the methods with the objectives. As long as we agree on objectives, we should never fall out with each other just because we believe in different methods to reach a common objective."

Olive had developed an intense dislike for me. He found it hard to believe that I was getting the better of him and his top Lieutenants from a subordinate position in an organization controlled by Farrelly and his shadow cabinet. A classic example of Olive using his position to deal directly with a plutocrat who owned a business on Main Street, St. Thomas, took place between June 14, 1984 and July 26, 1988 when the taxpayer's delinquent account showing an unpaid balance of $5,151.85 was given to me for collection. On June 14, 1984, Olive wrote to the taxpayer's accountant (Mr. Foster L. Baynes) as follows: "I have received your request to have the penalties waived for the above-named corporation. Based on my investigation, I have established that all three returns were filed on December 16, 1983, thus indicating that the taxpayer was in fact delinquent in filing and paying its taxes. Had the corporation filed timely, the misconception on its subsidy grant would have been clarified at the time of filing its first return. No estimated tax returns were filed and based on your erroneous interpretation of the subsidy grant; no payments were remitted when the returns were filed. In order to resolve this matter, I am requesting that the corporation remit payment for the Section 6654(A) penalty and the Section 6651(A)(2) penalty. Upon receipt of payment, I will proceed to have the late filing penalties waived." A copy of Olive's letter reached me on July 6, 1984 at 9:00 a.m.

I wrote to Olive on July 8, 1988 after finally getting the green light to collect the unpaid amount. I wrote: "The delinquent corporation agrees with the last part of your June 14, 1984 letter which is attached hereto. Nevertheless they want to pay the unpaid amount of $5,151.85 in installments. Was this the purpose of your letter?" Before Olive could answer my letter, the taxpayer sent him a letter dated July 14, 1988 saying: "As per our phone conversation, please find enclosed a check in the amount of $1,151.85. I promise it will be followed each month by a check of $1,000.00 till our debt of $5,151.85 is paid off. At the time of our conversation I was unaware of our delinquency of corporate taxes. It was only upon confronting Foster Baynes on the matter that he informed me of the situation. His reason being that he was waiting for the IDC matter to be resolved. Believe me Mister Olive, I was not aware of it, but now that I am I'll see to it that everything is put in order as quickly as possible."

Olive responded right away by addressing a memorandum to me which said: "The President of the subject corporation called on July 12, 1988 seeking permission to liquidate the account on an installment plan. I requested that his proposal be submitted in writing at which time you can make a recommendation. Please make a full compliance check to insure all required tax returns are filed to date." In a footnote I said to Olive: "We are duplicating out efforts in trying to resolve a simple matter. The last paragraph of your June 14, 1984 tells the corporation's President what should be done. Where do I come in? We've got to say what we mean and mean what we say." Olive came back with a memorandum of his own addressed to me wherein he said: "In response to your note of July 14, 1988, please comply with my memorandum to you of July 14, 1988."

His reaction to what was going on gave me a queasy stomach. Olive had found himself in a cul-de-sac but I had to make certain that he could not wiggle out in any form or fashion. I paid a visit to the President of the corporation and demanded payment of the account. Receiving a negative response, I returned to the office and in a memorandum dated July 19, 1988, I told Olive: "The President of the subject corporation has advised me that he has reached an agreement with you and that he mailed a letter and check to you following the agreement. This action on your part reminds me very much of Mrs. Lucia Thomas' letter of August 3, 1984 wherein she said to Kenneth Hansen (with a copy to you), 'There are several cases which have been assigned to me for Collection which the Director, Mr. Anthony P. Olive, have met with their representatives and formulated certain plans. As Director, he is privileged to do so, however, being a Senior Revenue Officer it becomes increasingly difficult and frustrating to do the 'correct thing' when these practitioners feel that I would take orders from them, given by Mr. Olive, while in the meantime he gives you messages as to what should be done. These cases are large dollar cases and in the future, as I, as a Senior Revenue Officer cannot be present at these meetings to secure 'first hand information and instructions,' the case can be transferred to someone else who might prefer such actions. This job can be very frustrating at times, but if there is cooperation between managers and their employees, the work would flow smoothly and the Collection process would be greatly enhanced.' Should I return the account to you?"

Olive replied the same day. He simply said: "You are wrong. The President of the corporation called. I told him to write. Please act like a Revenue Officer IV should." In my reply of July 26, 1988, I wrote: "Acting like a Revenue Officer IV should, I'm enclosing herewith copies of correspondence which prove anew that the credit procured by a lie lasts only till the truth comes out. In observance of Bastille Day (July 14, 1988), you departed from the truth by issuing a memorandum wherein you requested (beforehand) a recommendation from me, knowing full well that you had already reached an agreement with the President of the subject corporation, whereby he'd make monthly payments of $1,000.00. Because of your actions, I'm now forced to stand with Mrs. Lucia Thomas, whose letter of August 3, 1984 to Mr. Kenneth Hansen adequately pointed out what trained and experienced Revenue Officers are up against as they try to do the work for which they are being paid."

On July 29, 1988, obviously embarrassed, Olive shot back. He said: "In response to your July 26, 1988 letter, it is clear that you are trying to create issues and unnecessary interruptions in the orderly flow of our operations. You wrote to me on July 8, 1988. I responded on July 14, 1988 indicating that the President had called on July 12, 1988 and he was instructed to put his proposal in writing. His letter of July 14, 1988 confirms his calling me. If your July 19, 1988 statements are correct, why did he write his July 14, 1988 letter? Why did he acknowledge that the corporation was delinquent in filing corporate tax returns? Why is he asking for patience if he had an agreement? As a trained Revenue Officer IV, you should have made your decision without writing to me on July 8, 1988. You should have ascertained the facts, determined whether the taxpayer was in full compliance and proceed accordingly. Your performance in this case proves that you are performing below standards." In conclusion I ended it by simply saying to Olive: "Your delicately worded letter of this afternoon is a showy display and an indication of a convoluted style with emphasis on the self-fulfilling prophecy. Accordingly, I feel it an obligation to duty to note in a paraphrase that I may disagree with what you have written, but I would defend to the death, your right to say it. One thing appears certain: What unites us if far greater than what separates us. We must never allow taxpayers such as the subject corporation to divide us."

Olive knew no limits and had no shame. He had become a recalcitrant being used by everybody. I was doing what I knew was right. Being apolitical, diplomatic immunity was not mine and since Olive had a tendency to remain in a fixed condition without change he would continue to ignore the rule of law. As the Bureau's Shop Steward, I had established a time table in dealing with the Union and their representatives outside of the Virgin Islands. Whereas they had grown accustomed to the lackadaisical life style that existed in their various shops throughout the Virgin Islands, I was bent on showing Mr. Thermon Phillips that our Bargaining Unit was not the type that he envisioned. I was not in any way going to second guess the experts at the highest levels in the United Steelworkers of America, but as members in good standing we wanted the representation that we were promised.

My letter of May 23, 1988 was ignored by Thermon Phillips causing me to write to him once again on July 11, 1988. I wrote:

July 11, 1988

Mr. Thermon Phillips
Director District 36
United Steelworkers of America
1825 Morris Avenue
Suite B
Birmingham, Alabama 35203

Dear Mr. Phillips:

I have always heard that misrepresentations and lies have never resulted in a permanent benefit for anyone, but at this writing, I'm hard pressed to think that the United Steelworkers of America could be guilty of misrepresentation, especially after reading the attached publication which features the official USWA Ring as a symbol of commitment to Union ideals, traditions and brotherhood, while placing emphasis on pride, strength and togetherness.

Before joining USWA, prospective members of our Bargaining Unit - victimized by a high degree of office politics, were mired in a most difficult situation. We were being put upon - with empty promises - and set upon by a Director and certain crusaders who knew - for reasons which were obvious, that nothing would be done to them.

Since joining USWA, working conditions in our office have worsened. Recently, (for example) there have been some developments which - based on prima-facie evidence, have had an intriguing quality about them. Our Contract has become a laughing-stock of the office. Employees are being harassed, suspended and systematically removed from their jobs. Grievances have been filed only to be shelved by management. What's going on? Are our local officials members of the Virgin Islands cartel Why are we paying Union Dues? Is this the same USWA that promised to implicitly defend us?

At the moment a melancholic scene exists in the offices of the Virgin Islands Bureau of Internal Revenue. Members of our Bargaining Unit have sensed that they've been forsaken by USWA; consequently, they are clinging to whispering hope as their only weapon against the "crusaders for management" whispering campaign and games-manship.

At a recent meeting, the employees silently warned USWA beforehand, that the United Steelworkers of America's burning belief that they (the Union) can continue to misrepresent us is an illusion of reality.

Many employees - including myself, feel that we've had enough - more than enough top officials tenderness towards injustice and those who bring it on. We are all hoping for our hopes to end in fruition.

Letter   -2-   July 11, 1988
Mr. Thermon Phillips

   Finally, the time has come for some positive action on tha part of our Union. Representation now denied to members in good standing, must be granted. We have been clamoring for attention and much needed representation for too long.

            Sincerely yours,

            Liston B. Monsanto
            Shop Steward

cc: Mr. Luis "Tito" Morales
   President, Local 8249

   Mr. Cephus Rogers
   Staff Representative

   Mr. Lynn R. Williams
   International President

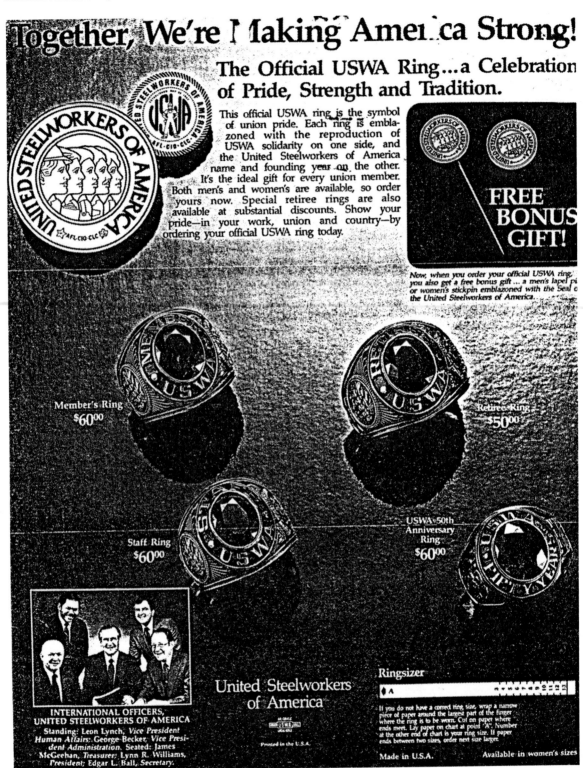

In retrospect it is safe to say that the Farrelly years were marked by behavior more aberrant that that of any other administration, as Governor Farrelly was being kept abreast of what was going on in the Bureau of Internal Revenue via copies of letters sent to Olive, Thomas, Vanterpool and all the rest. He did nothing.

Operating on the thesis that one man's pleasantry is another man's pain, I wrote to Olive on August 1, 1988, reminding him of things he had presumably forgotten and extended the proverbial Olive Branch in an attempt to increase my productivity and that of the Internal Revenue Bureau. Here is what I wrote:

RECEIVED
DIRECTOR'S OFFICE

AUG -1 1988

VIRGIN ISLANDS BUREAU OF
INTERNAL REVENUE
ST. THOMAS, V.I.

August 1, 1988

Mr. Anthony P. Olive
Director
V.I. Bureau of Internal Revenue
St. Thomas, V.I.   00801

Dear Mr. Olive:

Following my defeat of the Virgin Islands "less than professional" governmental system, (see Opinion 81-1434 of the United States Court of Appeals for the Third Circuit) you immediately assumed the role of Isolationist, bent - with the aid of certain Virgin Islands cartel members, on isolating Liston Monsanto from an oppressed number of employees (some gone, some still on board) assigned to the Bureau of Internal Revenue. At the moment, however, you seem to have reverted to man's original wild and untamed state, in desperately trying to convince everyone that you should stay on as Director of the Bureau of Internal Revenue.

Throughout your role-playing activity, I have remained calm. I have repressed my feelings and have ignored the pressures under which you continually put me, only to force me to change my mind into violating existing laws.

Who would have thought that you (the person recommended by me to fill the position of Director) would have the temerity to harm Liston Monsanto unjustifiably.

I have now ferreted out new evidence which indicates that you have become a person of shallow changeable character. Your isolationist policies show that you are telling us one thing and doing something entirely different (see Mrs. Lucia Thomas' letter of August 3, 1984, which is attached hereto).

Your political theory of divide and conquer has resulted in: (a) Blocking my path to a promotion (b) an invitation to Union Officials Morales and Rogers to participate in a private meeting of the Delinquent Accounts and Returns Branch (c) pseudo promotions and (d) the settlement of certain grievances without any notification to the aggrieved employees or the Shop Steward.

As I write, it is worth noting that over the past several years you have read more into my attitude than I have meant to convey. Look at my frivolous performance reports with their unfounded and malicious entries. Those unsigned reports with my attachments, continue to make the raters and yourself seem little and unimportant to many a reader.

And what are you doing about Mr. Roy Vanterpool's unacceptable behavior? Is he going to continue to usurp your authority? Are you overlooking the crazy letters that he has addressed to me in my capacity of Shop Steward?

Liston B. Monsanto, Sr.

Mr. Anthony P. Olive
Director

There are two (2) sides (Labor and Management) working for one side (namely
the Government of the Virgin Islands) in the Bureau of Internal Revenue. Operating from a position of spite and trying to isolate Liston Mansanto from the employees he represents will result only in unproductive performances. People with
contagious diseases should be isolated. People like me should be allowed to make
a contribution towards the economic growth of the Virgin Islands. Let's all get
together and do the work expected of us. Lest you forget, we are all taxpayers.

Sincerely,

Liston B. Monsanto
Shop Steward

cc: Luis "Tito" Morales
    President, Local 8249

    Cephus Rogers
    Staff Representative

GOVERNMENT OF
THE VIRGIN ISLANDS OF THE UNITED STATES

VIRGIN ISLANDS
BUREAU OF INTERNAL REVENUE
P. O. Box 3186
Charlotte Amalie, St. Thomas, U.S.V.I. 00801

August 3, 1984

Mr. Kenneth C. Hansen
Chief, Del. Accts & Returns Br
Charlotte Amalie
St. Thomas, V.I. 0801

Dear Mr. Hansen:

There are several cases which have been assigned to me for collection which the director, Mr. Anthony Olive, have met with their representatives and formulated certain plans.

As director, he is privileged to do so, however, being a senior revenue officer, it becomes increasingly difficult and frustrating to do the "correct thing" when these practitioners feel that I would take orders from them — given by Mr. Olive — while in the meantime, he gives you messages as to what should be done.

These cases are large dollar cases, and in the future, if I, as a senior revenue officer cannot be present at these meetings to secure "first hand information and instructions", the case can be transferred to someone else who might prefer such actions.

It would be noted that when Mr. Quinn received a request to meet with a practitioner to discuss a tax liability he always notified and requested us to brief him on the particular case. There were no second and third hand information given, therefore there was always a meeting of the minds.

This job can be very frustrating at times, but if there is cooperation between managers and their employees the work would flow smoothly and the collection process would be greatly enhanced.

Sincerely,

Lucia Thomas

cc: Mr. A. Olive
    Director

On August 12th, after ignoring my letter, Olive wrote three letters to Tito Morales explaining to Tito how he had denied the settlement requested in grievances filed by Mrs. Judith DeCastro, Mr. Rickhield Thomas and myself. Sending the letters to Tito for consideration was a charade. All along Olive had been screamish over what was going on in the workplace now given a chance at reconciliation he preferred to be uncompromising. I just had to get back at him. On August 15, 1988 I wrote: "Your letters of August 12, 1988 addressed to Mr. Luis "Tito" Morales (President of Local 8249 USWA) contain remarks that are obviously calculated to hurt the feelings of Mrs. Judith DeCastro, Mr. Rickhield Thomas and myself. There is no fair-minded person in this whole wide world who would (given the information that you have in your possession) continue to fiddle while the Bureau of Internal Revenue burns, by using rigmarole as his instrument. I can only hope that when your head finishes turning, that your face is to the front again. Why must you depart form the truth? Through your rustic manners and your inability to produce documentary evidence to support the position stated in your letters, you have failed to bring the Virgin Islands Bureau of Internal Revenue into the right relationship with its surroundings. No matter how thin you slice the contents of your letters, they are still baloney. Love your enemies, it really gets on their nerves."

Olive had a great short term memory. Remember the role he played in dealing directly with the plutocrat who operated a business on Main Street, St. Thomas? Well, he was back at it again with another company's President in violation of the Bureau's policies. Here is what happened: I was given a delinquent account on August 31, 1988, which bordered on a "jeopardy assessment." I immediately called the president of the company and made a demand for payment. The man found himself in a state of perplexity and uncertainty over my call and explanation. Right away he told me that he would write a letter to Olive who was aware of his delinquency and his willingness to satisfy his liability. On September 1, 1988, the President wrote to Olive sending me a copy of his letter. He said, "Through the good office of the Commissioner of Finance, John DeJohngh, we met in your office late in June of this year to discuss my company's gross receipts problem. At that time I submitted to you returns due without payment. In our second meeting of that same month in which we met to review 1987's and first quarter 1988 returns, it was decided that an account be set up to which you would turn over the forms that I left with you. Since that conversation I have not heard anything from you except for a phone call from Mr. Monsanto on 8/31/88. I requested then and I am still requesting now that you consider waiving the penalties and interest. We are a small and new business with a cash flow problem because of the fact that we are an inventory incentive business. In our discussion I also proposed that payment of the balance be made within 24 months. Thank you for lending a listening ear and I anticipate your favorable consideration in the matters discussed above."

Immediately upon receiving my copy of the taxpayer's letter, I wrote to Olive. I said: "You have done it again! Mrs. Lucia Thomas was absolutely correct about your direct involvement in the collection activity. You and former Director Mr. Leroy Quinn have so much in common, it's a phenomenon. Based on the contents of the President's letter (copy attached hereto), one can only conclude that a gentlemen's agreement was made between you and him (in your office) sometime late in June of this year, a gentlemen's agreement on which you seemingly reneged. The record shows that Mr. Louis Willis, in his pseudo position of acting Assistant Chief, had no private or secret knowledge of the June meeting and the upshot thereof. As the person to whom the company's accounts have been assigned, I ask you: What's left for me to do?"

I then wrote to Willis on September 2nd with copies to Olive and Ferdinand. I said: "Due to an unholy alliance with certain delinquent taxpayers who have failed or otherwise neglected to do what duty or law requires, Mr. Anthony P. Olive has placed himself in an awkward position as he finds himself entering into payment agreements with many of these same people (e.g., plutocrat on Main Street and the President of the company mentioned in my letter of September 1st, 1988) to our Branch's detriment. As a result of his strange participation in the collection process and manifold problems (which include the pseudo position you now occupy). it has become apparent that Revenue Officers in the Delinquent Accounts and Returns Branch are underemployed and their duties impaired. Blind loyalty together with our individualistic attitudes has contributed immensely to the sordid mess in which we find ourselves. As a member of our Bargaining Unit which prides itself on solidarity, I must caution you against creating schism in our ranks. If we are to promote voluntary compliance, we must work together harmoniously. Needless to say, tolerance must be practiced."

Olive was provoked to anger, he wrote me a memorandum on September 2, 1988 wherein he said: "The President of the company met with me in late June to discuss tax problems. He was reacting to a recommendation by Commissioner John DeJohngh. At this meeting his tax problems were discussed. Various returns that were already prepared were given to me without payment. Based on what was presented, it was determined that certain returns were still missing. The President of the company said he had left them in his office and he would have them submitted. At the second meeting the missing returns were delivered. I explained to the President that the returns would go to the Processing Branch and that he would be billed. I told him that upon receipt of the bills he should contact Mr. Willis, the Acting Assistant Chief of the DAR Branch and at that time he would have an opportunity to arrange for an installment plan based on the facts and circumstances. No action was taken on his request to have the penalties waived as I told him his request should be in writing stating the reasons why the returns were late. Interest is statutory and cannot be waived. All returns were transmitted to the Processing Branch for appropriate action. Mr. Monsanto, as a Revenue Officer IV, to whom the company's accounts have been assigned, I expect you to do your job. Based on your training and years of experience, you must make your own decisions in accordance with the relative facts and circumstances. This is the second time you have chosen this route in the last two months. It clearly shows that your performance, attitude and judgment continue unsatisfactory." He sent a copy of his internal memorandum to the taxpayer.

I fired back on September 6, 1988. I said: "Inasmuch as you continue to demonstrate that you are a person who favors reaction, your confusing memorandum, addressed to me, dated September 2, 1988 (wherein you glibly explained your part in a secret meeting with an ingenious company president who, I would dare say, had never thought of being suspicious of what was said in the meeting), immediately reminded me of a well-known proverb which goes: Better late than never. In writing this letter, I will not (as you have done) attempt to wash the Bureau's dirty linen in public by sending a copy to the company's president. After all, we are covered by a disclosure law. Aren't we? As confusing as your memorandum is, in the final analysis, it does coincide with the president's version of what happened at the summit meeting of June 1988. At the meeting, the company president (a big dealer in housing material) may have decried the use of concrete for houses, but the contents of his letter show that he knows (without a doubt) that to betray a friend is ignoble. Once again you are caught in a cul-de-sac! And now, since it has been established that you do favor reaction, it is expected that you'd react to this letter by simply allowing the Revenue Officers to do the work for which he's being paid."

Instead of writing an apology, in contrite words Olive responded on September 7th saying: "Your letter to Mr. Louis Willis, Acting Assistant Chief DAR Branch, dated September 2, 1988, is another attempt to harass the Director's Office. I pointed out to you that your performance in the first and second cases was unsatisfactory and proves that as a Revenue Officer IV, you were performing below standards. For the past three months you have deliberately launched an attack on my office with emphasis on destroying the DAR Branch. You have criticized Mr. Jerome A. Ferdinand and Mr. Louis M. Willis in order to be disruptive and antagonistic. Your daily collection activities reports are evidence of your inferior collection activity. Your behavior, attitude and lack of support for the Bureau of Internal Revenue are dramatized in your hateful letters. How can you find happiness in destroying others? Were you happy in the Air Force or was it that experiencing that changed your life? As you review the past three months you will agree that an improvement is necessary."

It never occurred to Olive that I could do the things that I was doing from my subordinate position because he was in violation of law. Governor Alexander Farrelly knew that I was not guilty of any wrong. I could tell from his letter, however, that he was still pleading with Farrelly to keep him on as

Director. He didn't' have to worry. As long as he could be used by Edward Thomas he would stay on.

On September 12, 1988, I answered his letter saying: "During your Stewardship as Director of the Virgin Islands Bureau of Internal Revenue, you have treated the members of our Bargaining Unit as underachievers who are vain and empty-headed for the most part. You have tried to the utmost to divide our unit into hostile groups by bringing false and outrageous charges against people like Mr. Liston Monsanto and Mr. Levi Farrell. Through extravagance and by your frivolous behavior, you have succeeded in making an innocent member of our Bargaining Unit (Mr. Louis M. Willis) believe that you two are palsy-walsy and that he has been legitimately appointed Acting Assistant Chief of the Delinquent Accounts and Returns Branch. What Mr. Willis does not know, is that Liston Monsanto and Anthony P. Olive like Damon and Pythias, were the alter egos of each other until Mr. Anthony P. Olive was elevated to the position of Director. Your bias opinions which appear in your letter of September 7, 1988, show that you have become desperate due largely perhaps to the modicum of fame currently being enjoyed by Mr. Levi Farrell, whom you tried unsuccessfully to put behind bars and your thoughts of having our government to make cash awards to Miss June Blyden, Mrs. Donna Phillips and Miss Marilyn Turner, as a result of their being sexually harassed by one of your Supervisors. And regarding my military service of which I'm very proud, I would venture to say, had you (and many others in the Bureau) been in the Air Force or any other Branch of the United States Armed Forces, your method of operation, especially as it relates to leadership, would have been greatly enhanced. Because of the baneful effects (lies, spite, sexual harassment, embezzlement, etc.) you are having upon the Virgin Islands Bureau of Internal Revenue, like Gregory Rasputin who prided himself on licentiousness, your licentiousness will in time destroy the Bureau of Internal Revenue. Liston Monsanto is too far down on the employee level to launch any attack on your office. Self-conceit may lead to self-destruction."

Working as an employee in the Virgin Islands Bureau of Internal Revenue was easy if you just went along. Because I was following established guidelines it was never easy for me, however. I was desperately trying to show Olive the error of his ways. He had been doing wrong for so long without being challenged that he thought he was carrying out his duties the right way. I wrote to him on September 14, 1988 saying:

September 14, 1988

Mr. Anthony P. Olive
Director
V.I. Bureau of Internal Revenue
Lockhart Gardens #1A
St. Thomas, Virgin Islands 00801

Dear Mr. Olive:

I'm writing to you cognizant of the fact that I'm neither a meteorologist nor a storm Petrel. I'm an Internal Revenue Officer IV (Employee of the Virgin Islands Government) assigned to work in a storm center headed by you, and generally called the Virgin Islands Bureau of Internal Revenue.

This letter is furthermore dedicated to you and certain people in management with their intrigues, double-talk and lies, who in spite of weather conditions are insistent on creating trouble.

During Calendar Year 1988 - by the irony of fate, here in the Virgin Islands we have had much rain when (at times) all we needed was a little sun to put us in a prominent or favorable position.

The year is coming to a close and we are practically home. But behold! The black clouds lingering over the offices of the storm center portend a storm - a storm that may be best described as a tempest in a teapot.

Such an atmosphere has been created because for some strange reason(s) you continue to believe that you are playing an impeccable role in carrying-out your duties as Director. You have complained quite a lot, but none of your complaints have been compelling. You have proven by. way of meaningless talk and open discrimination against Liston Monsanto that licentiousness is a Director's preponderant characteristic.

It is ironical that you, in your capacity of Director, would try or otherwise pretend to protect Mr. Jerome Ferdinand and Mr. Louis Willis who have both been saying one thing and doing something entirely different (see the attached corrospondence for proof).

We, in the Delinquent Accounts and Returns Branch have yet to have an index card matching of TDA's and there has been absolutely no explanation from Mr. Ferdinand as to why. As for Mr. Willis, he lied to us on August 31, 1988, when he said he'd be in St. Croix on September 1, 1988.

Letter   -2-   9/14/88

Mr. Anthony P. Olive
Director

Let's face it. You have an empire but no title. To say that you take pleasure in ignoring my letters and my attachments to my Performance Reports is an understatement. Look at the abuse of discretionary power on your part in willfully and deliberately denying Mr. Levi Farrell (a family man) his salary checks. You know, without a doubt that this denial is in violation of our Bilateral Contract.

What's more, in using the power of your office which you believe to be absolute, you took it upon yourself to dismiss Mr. Farrell from duty after the Governor had presumably failed to respond to your recommendation. Now I ask you: Who's being disruptive and antagonizing?

Because I have echoed the sentiments of Mrs. Lucia Thomas about your behind-the-scenes activity with certain taxpayers, you've taken umbrage.

The Government of the Virgin Islands is a Government of, for, and by the people. It's our Government - one to which I've pledged my allegiance and one towards whose economic growth I would love to contribute. You are fully aware of this. If you aren't, I suggest you go over the many letters and employee grievances in your possession.

If present trends continue in this storm center, (called the Virgin Islands Bureau of Internal Revenue) I can predict as a certainty that you will find it necessary to deputize Mr. Louis Willis (my union brother) as one of your storm troopers akin to those used by Adolph Hitler in his private army in the 1920's. Your troubles (petty or otherwise) will continue.

My speaking of storm troopers and the impending storm, points up the immediacy for me to barricade myself through the usage of storm doors and windows in the hope that I'll be able to weather the storm. Please stop operating in violation of law.

Sincerely,

Liston Monsanto
Shop Steward

cc: Jerome Ferdinand

     Louis Willis

At 9:25 a.m. on September 19, 1988, I hand-delivered a letter to his office written by me which said:

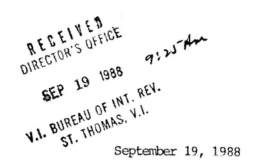

September 19, 1988

Mr. Anthony P. Olive
Director
V.I. Bureau of Internal Revenue
Lockhart Gardens #1A
St. Thomas, V.I. 00801

Dear Mr. Olive:

Your violation of Article XI of the Agreement between the United Steel-workers of America and the Virgin Islands Bureau of Internal Revenue, plus your continuing discriminatory practices against Liston Monsanto (see Roberts vs. Department of Health) together with your latest gem (i.e., awarding Mr. Louis M. Willis an Internal Revenue Officer I in Grade 6 a salary of $26,542.00) have brought about yet another disparity in our pay schedule.

Prompted by your actions and led by Miss Jean Liburd (a Tax Examiner III with twenty (20) years of meritorious service in Grade 7 of the pay schedule) several Members of our Bargaining Unit filed Grievance Number 18-88 on September 16, 1988, for your review and consideration.

Today, I'm amending that grievance to include the entire Bargaining Unit retroactive to the date when Mr. Willis was first awarded his new and unlawful salary of $26,542.00.

Honestly, I do not like what is happening in our organization. The Bureau of Internal Revenue is in disarray! There is just too much turmoil in this most sensitive area of our Government, and like a civil war, nobody wins.

Based on recent events, however, I can safely say that a renaissance is imminent. Having vowed to use any measure short of violence in order to bring a semblance of order to the Bureau of Internal Revenue, it is not my desire to end whatever bitterness or contention that we may have had (over the years) in donny-brook fashion. My purpose from the beginning has been to protect myself, my family, and the people I represent. I have never ever thought of destroying the Bureau of Internal Revenue.

My proudest achievement in life - like the Reverend Martin Luther King, must be a peaceful design for living

    With this in mind, I ask (for the umpteenth time) that all concerned pre-pare to sit down at the table of reasoning for discussions that would pave the way for a settlement of our differences.

    I still feel that what unites us is far greater than what seperates us.

                                 Sincerely,

                                 Liston B. Monsanto
                                 Shop Steward

cc: Cephus Rogers
       Staff Representative

       Luis "Tito" Morales
       President, Local 8249

    After Olive had written to me on September 7, 1988, I had stayed focused forgetting somewhat his less-than-professional behavior in the cases of the two plutocrats. I had to keep things in perspective by looking through the windshield. I was therefore made speechless with surprise when on September 19th I received a letter from Olive which said: "In response to your letter of September 6, 1988, be advised that my memorandum is not confusing nor glibly. My meeting was not secret, it was requested by the taxpayer. You are required to tell the President of the subject company the truth; as the taxpayer he has his rights in accordance with the disclosure provisions of the Internal Revenue Code and the Tax Reform Act of 1986. He should know how insubordinate you are. In your third paragraph you concede that the taxpayer's version of what happened coincides with the facts as stated in my letter. In paragraph four you state that the contents of his letter shows that he knows that to betray a friend is ignoble. What are you insinuating? Are you saying that the taxpayer offered me a bribe? Are you calling for an investigation into this matter? The taxpayer can speak for himself. Mr. Monsanto, as you continue to fabricate stories and behave in an unprofessional manner, how can you aspire to become a Supervisor or a Chief. To lead you must find solutions. Your anger and hate is evident in your daily transmittals."

    Olive was desperate, he had continued to exhibit a holier than thou attitude which compelled me to write to him on September 20, 1988. I said: "I was of the opinion that my letter of reconciliation dated September 19, 1988 would have brought us closer together, but after receiving your most recent letter (also dated September 19, 1988), I must admit that my judgment was wrong. All things considered, I feel it an obligation to duty to respond in some measure to your letter which is long on emotion and short on reason. As a matter of fact, it is not the contents of the letter so much as the tone that has shocked and dismayed my person. Accordingly, for your sake, I will explain to you in the most grandiose terms that ours is a government of laws, not of men. It is your responsibility to carry out the laws, not to make you own. When these laws give certain rights to employees, they must be respected by you and everyone else. Your meeting with the subject taxpayer, as explained by you, was a manifest error and a variation from the norm. You are misrepresenting the situation when you speak of bribes and investigations. Did you answer Mrs. Lucia Thomas when she wrote to Mr.

Kenneth Hansen (copy to you) on August 3, 1984, regarding other taxpayers with whom you'd met? Insubordination: to be insubordinate is to be disobedient. A person who does not submit to authority is insubordinate. Had you been a member of the United States Air Force, you certainly would have known this. You, Mr. Olive, are disobedient when it comes to doing what the laws, rules, regulations, etc. require you to do (see Opinion 81-1434 Third Circuit Court of Appeals). I can provide proof about everything I've said to you. You should apologize to the people of the Virgin Islands for being insubordinate to them. As for me being a Supervisor or a Chief, my record speaks for itself. If you'd turn to page sixteen (16) of Opinion 81-1434 you'd find that even you testified that Monsanto would be a 'good candidate' to be Chief of the Delinquent Accounts and Returns Branch. With you however, 'Bible is Testimony, but Testimony is not Bible.' Forget about the subject taxpayer. What's past is prologue. Let's start working to get our house in order. At the moment, there is a wide disparity in our pay schedule as outlined to you in my letter of September 19th. Let's start life anew."

The Bureau of Internal Revenue and especially the Delinquent Accounts and Returns were in need of leadership. Steps had to be taken to satisfy its most urgent demands. Discriminating against Liston Monsanto was not the answer as Olive would ultimately learn.

On September 20, 1988, Louis M. Willis began feeling his oats. He wrote a memorandum to two of his union sisters (Ms. Evelyn Hodge and Ms. Paulette Rawlins) accusing them of abusing break periods and tampering with the time cards. He was acting exactly like Anthony P. Olive. On September 21, 1988, when it was brought to my attention, I immediately wrote to Willis in this manner:

September 21, 1988

Mr. Louis M. Willis
Acting Asst. Chief, DAR Branch
V.I. Bureau of Internal Revenue
Lockhart Gardens #1A
St. Thomas, Virgin Islands 00801

Dear Mr. Willis:

This is in response to your memorandum of September 20, 1988, wherein you have chosen - either by intention or through ignorance, to attack two (2) of your Union Sisters (Mrs. Evelyn Hodge and Miss Paulette Rawlins) based only on hearsay.

As a half-trained Internal Revenue Officer you should know that documentary evidence is always needed for future reference. Do not allow spite (which I believe is listed among the seven deadly sins) to get the best of you in dealing with certain employees.

Mr. Willis, you have no authority to do what your memorandum states. Instead of concentrating on the money aspect, you should read the language in our Bi-lateral Contract and/or confer with Mr. Olive and Mr. Ferdinand who are both in possession of certain letters from me relating to the subject. Why must you be a salmon swimming up stream?

Vindictiveness will get you no where. For your information, I've attached hereto a copy of Mr. Edward Thomas' letter of May 26, 1988, which shows that Miss Paulette Rawlins has filed a grievance with respect to your pseudo position of Acting Assistant Chief Delinquent Accounts and Returns Branch. Is this your reason for attacking her?

A word to the wise is sufficient. The next time that you find it necessary to accuse any of your Union Brothers or Sisters, of wrongdoing, kindly include the name of the complainant.

Generalities such as "it has been brought to my attention" will not work on our group of which you are a part.

Finally, until Mr. Olive makes a positive move to correct the injustices in the Bureau of Internal Revenue and until a decision is reached with respect to Grievance No. 12-88, I'm asking that you leave the Members of the Bargaining Unit alone.

Sincerely,

Liston Monsanto
Shop Steward

cc: Mr. Anthony P. Olive
     Mr. Jerome Ferdinand
     Miss Paulette Rawlins

Ms. Rawlins followed up my letter by writing one of her own to Willis. She said:

September 22, 1988

Mr. Louis M. Willis
Acting Asst. Chief, DAR Branch
V.I. Bureau of Internal Revenue
Lockhart Gardens #1A
St. Thomas, Virgin Islands 00801

Dear Mr. Willis:

On September 14, 1988, Mr. Liston Monsanto (our Shop Steward) wrote a letter to Mr. Anthony P. Olive (copy to you) wherein in the penultimate paragraph he stated. "If present trends continue in this storm center, (called the Virgin Bureau of Internal Revenue) I can predict as a certainty that you will find it necessary to deputize Mr. Louis Willis (my union brother) as one of your storm troopers akin to those used by Adolph Hitler in his private army in the 1920's. Your troubles (petty or otherwise) will continue."

Recent events show that, since the issuance of that letter and the several grievances that have been filed against Mr. Olive, you have displayed a most arrogant, abrasive and belligerent attitude – an attitude I hasten to add, that borders on conduct unbecoming an officer.

As a dedicated and long time employee of the Virgin Islands Bureau of Internal Revenue, I cannot and will not go home to sleep during duty hours the way you confessed to doing in your meeting in May of this year.

Mr. Monsanto's latest letter to you (dated September 21, 1988) asked you to leave us alone pending a decision on Grievance No. 12-88. Can't you see the reason for this? Mr. Olive can.

While some people take pleasure in pretending, I much prefer to be respected.

Sincerely,

Paulette Rawlins
Tax Coordinating Secretary

cc: Mr. Anthony P. Olive
    Director

    Mr. Liston Monsanto ✓
    Shop Steward

Forgetting about his officious interference into the affairs of several taxpayers with delinquent accounts and fueled by letters coming from Ms. Rawlins and myself, Mr. Olive, acting like my immediate Supervisor sent me a letter dated September 30, 1988. He said: "Your performance as an Internal Revenue Officer IV for the months of June and July continues to be unsatisfactory. Your daily collection activities reports and the monthly production reports clearly demonstrate your lack of performance. It is expected that you will work on your assigned cases from 8:00 a.m. to 12:00 noon and 1:00 p.m. to 5:00 p.m. on a daily basis. Time charged to Union activities must be in accordance with our contract and must be properly reflected on your 795. I will be reviewing your performance in the months ahead and I expect to see an improvement in your work."

Upon receiving his letter I thought to myself, the more you try to help people, the less it is appreciated. I had never been a victim of the virus of fear and so in no unequivocal language, I wrote to him on October 3, 1988 saying: "Somebody has brought a duck to a cock fight! Here we are in the Delinquent Accounts and Returns Branch preparing to submit several frivolous reports to Mr. Jerome Ferdinand for the period ending September 30, 1988 and there you are writing about June and July 1988 in your September 30th letter which is addressed to me. Mr. Olive, if I'm not doing the work required of me, why do you continue to assign me work? And why don't you take some more time (since you seemingly have time to concentrate on me) to digest the many letters that you've received from me. Read them again and you'll see that you'll have no legitimate reason to question my work. One thing is certain, work in our Branch is a two-way street (up and down). If Revenue Officers do not work, the Chief or his designee does not work and since the jobs are interrelated in the Bureau of Internal Revenue, nobody works. Let's begin at the top!"

On December 9, 1987, Special Agent Steven "Smokey" Frett had written to Olive with copies of his letter to Edward Thomas and Liston Monsanto telling Olive: "This letter is in reference to the vacant position of Chief of the Delinquent Accounts and Returns Branch. The vacancy should be filled by no other than Liston Monsanto. Mr. Monsanto not only has the seniority and qualification necessary to do the job, but he is very articulate, punctilious, has good penmanship and communication skills, has the respect of the majority of the employees in that section and has the leadership abilities to move that stagnated section. I know, given the opportunity, he will show his iridescence. He will accomplish this by piloting the Delinquent Accounts and Returns Branch to new heights by increasing productivity ten-fold the present level and by bringing the long lost respectability eluding that section for so many years. I write this letter to you solely thinking only on what's best for the Bureau."

In trying to show Louis Willis how aggressive he could be, Olive may have secretly hired a prompter to show him how to take the offensive. Without any warning he wrote to me on October 3, 1988 saying: "With respect to your September 6, 1988 letter regarding Miss Paulette Rawlins' Grievance No. 11-87, your facts were created according to your standards. Why not provide the truth according to the files. Mr. Monsanto, as Shop Steward you must learn to deal with the truth. All of the employees that you have represented in the past have left the Bureau because of the environment and image of the union that you have created. They lost confidence in your modus operandi."

Olive was looking in the mirror shouting "Liar! Liar! Your pants are on fire." His bold rudeness caused me to write and deliver to him two letters on October 4, 1988. He received one at 1:20 p.m. and the other at 1:30 p.m. In the first letter he was told:

October 4, 1988

Mr. Anthony P. Olive
Director
Virgin Islands Bureau of Internal Revenue
Lockhart Gardens #1A
St. Thomas, Virgin Islands   00801

Dear Mr. Olive:

"When he came into office in January 1987, Governor Alexander Farrelly galvanized the Virgin Islands with his strong words, his honest assessment of the state of the territory and his invitation to all to "climb on the train of progress, the train of freedom, the train of fairness."

"He described the Government he inherited as "in a shambles: Bankrupt in its legal meaning, dispirited, often in violation of law, and operating often without rhyme or reason, benefiting neither the persons for whom services are to be provided, nor fairly and fully compensating those who are to provide the services." All true. But not much has changed.

At the time (October 3, 1988) that I received your letter of September 30, 1988, I was not mentally prepared to give you a detailed response relating to my job performance. But since your letter singles me out the way Mr. Leroy Quinn singled me out when he fired me for doing my work in 1979, I find it necessary once again to respond in some measure.

On October 26, 1987, you were told the following: "Train and retain" - the battle cry of our strike in 1986 told the world that we (including Mrs. DeCastro and Mr. Thomas) have consistently been clamoring for much-needed training in order to better perform our work. Unlike most Government Employees, we did not strike for money. We want to work - a fact corroborated by opinion No. 81-1434 of the Third Circuit Court of Appeals. The system, of which you are an integral part, does not want the job done."

On December 14, 1987, in a letter addressed to Mr. Jerome Ferdinand (copy to you), I wrote: "The wave of euphoria (brought about by abysmal ignorance) which under the Luis Administration pervaded the halls of the Virgin Islands Bureau of Internal Revenue is being replaced by employees willing and ready to work. Employees who are not content to accept poor workmanship."

The subject of work in the Virgin Islands Government and especially the Bureau of Internal Revenue (my post of duty) must be treated with a measure of caution, inasmuch as working in an environment where loyalty is more important than honesty and where just about everyone is indifferent to corruption does nothing to enhance the credibility of that environment.

Because your letter appears to be nothing but a perversion and a distortion, it becomes incumbent upon me to list (for your review) several areas where action of a positive nature must be taken by your office:

1. Donna Phillip, June Blyden and Marilyn Turner v. Government of the Virgin Islands, et al., <u>D.C.V.I. St. T. and J., Case No. 37/1984</u>. $2,000.00 is due each individual from our Government because of their charges of sexual harassment.

2. PERB-ULPC-87-5 Stipulation dated January 28, 1987, wherein you agreed not to change the actual job duties of any employee who was or became a member of our Bargaining Unit. (clarify status of Debra Adams and Cynthia Faulkner).

3. Start working - as ordered, to correct disparity brought about by your violation of section 552 (a) Virgin Islands Code in the Callender vs Virgin Islands Bureau of Internal Revenue case.

4. Make available to PERB any information concerning my refusal of the temporary position of <u>Acting</u> Assistant Chief of the Delinquent Accounts and Returns Branch.

Because you are a carry-over from the Luis Administration, which was according to Governor Farrelly "often in violation of law," you may even find it difficult to understand what is generally accepted (based on consensus) as right and wrong.

Finally, on May 23, 1988, I wrote: "So, in order to restore sagging employees confidence in your office and in order to make it possible for the Delinquent Accounts and Returns Branch to work itself out of the doldrums, I find it necessary to serve notice on you that I now stand ready, willing and able to assume the responsibility of Chief, Delinquent Accounts and Returns Branch." Isn't this an indication of a man wanting to work?

Let's sit down and talk.

Sincerely,

Liston Monsanto
Internal Revenue Officer

cc: Cephus Rogers
     Luis "Tito" Morales
     Louis M. Willis
     Jerome A. Ferdinand

In the other letter he was told: "You have become most desperate and perplexing in your attempts to block my path to a promotion. Never mind the platitudes emanating from your glib tongue with respect to Miss Paulette Rawlins. We (Paulette and I) know, based on our experiences that you are trying to build a case against us. You are such a scoff-law however, that we feel certain that if our cases are heard by an arbitrator, that that arbitrator will once again find that you are violating our contract. When it comes to saying anything about Liston Monsanto you suddenly become little bound by the love of truth. Can't you see that you are being exposed? With respect to my duties as Shop Steward, a word of caution: Stop tampering with the members of our Bargaining Unit lest you be charged with an unfair labor practice. Finally, if you would focus your attention on the contents of my letter which I hand-delivered to you moments ago, you'd find that there is much work to be done in the area of setting our house in order."

I had become the target of Olive's ire for many months. For a period of time (February 24, 1988 to May 9, 1988, through Olive's games-man-ship the Delinquent Accounts and Returns Branch had been held motionless by some strange power. St. Thomas was without a Supervisor or anyone to act as liaison between Ferdinand and the Revenue Officers. Our tax coordinating secretary (Ms. Paulette Rawlins) was given the additional task of filling in as Ferdinand's Assistant Chief in violation of our contract. Aware of what was happening, Ms. Rawlins filed a grievance seeking financial compensation for the additional duties. The sight of the grievance paralyzed Olive with horror. Without delay, Olive reviewed the situation, conferred with Ferdinand and immediately stripped Ms. Rawlins of the additional duties.

Olive was coming to his senses as evidenced by his invitation to Steven Frett (who had recommended to him that I be given the job as Chief) and me to come to his office on February 16, 1988, where he would hold discussions relating to the filling of the vacant position of Chief of the Delinquent Accounts and Returns Branch. At the outset of the meeting he showed great warmth of feelings. From his gestures I apprehended his desire to have me fill the vacancy but the Director Defacto (Edward Thomas) with Farrelly's blessings, anxious about his future two or three years down the road, had seen me demonstrate a form of mental power to do things well and therefore wanted no part of anyone with the unusual ability to do the job as Chief of the Delinquent Accounts and Returns Branch. Mid-way through our talks, Olive shifted to the opposite attitude saying that he already had someone in mind to take over the activities of the Branch. Olive had found himself between a rock and a hard place in his desire to impress upon Farrelly that he was worthy of being retained.

Flexible as I can be at times, had he called me to his office and presented to me a list of do's and don'ts for my review and consideration once I had accepted his guidelines I would have shifted my loyalty to his side and at the same time I would have been made compelled to relinquish the Shop Steward's throne.

Except for unionization, nothing had changed in the Bureau of Internal Revenue since Rueben Wheatley's departure in 1975. I was still fighting City Hall. As noted earlier, Governors were coming and going but the governmental system which demanded mediocrity remained intact. The Public Employees Relations Board (PERB) which was made up of a group of members appointed by Governors were like the Government Employees Service Commission beholden to the Governor. Through their legal counsel (Dennis Heilman, Esq.) they conducted what may be best described as kangaroo trials meting out kangaroo justice. The political patronage in government had welcomed aboard a number of hirelings who had no interest or pride in the work for which they were being paid. Fighting City Hall was not their forte. I had made, for the record, several appeals to PERB knowing full well that they were not going to agree with me. Members such as Mr. Vargrave Richards, Mr. Leo Petersen, Mrs. Rosalie S. Ballentine, Mr. Luis S. Llanos, Sr. and Mr. Keith A. Husbands were all on board when I submitted several letters and documents charging Olive with an unfair labor practice in designating Louis Willis as Assistant Chief of the Delinquent Accounts and Returns Branch.

After appearing before Attorney Heilman in an informal hearing on August 22, 1988, I was forced to address him on September 7, 1988. I wrote: "I have enclosed herewith for your information, a concise statement of the main points of my case. You may recall, and the record will show that Attorney Denise Reovan was told at our informal hearing on August 22, 1988, that in the absence of evidence to corroborate her testimony, the Public Employees Relations Board (PERB) would give her an extension of time to September 6, 1988, in order to submit a brief for my review. As Petitioner, I know that there is no evidence to support Attorney Reovan's claim that I refused the position of Acting Assistant Chief of the Delinquent Accounts and Returns Branch. I therefore ask that you act on my Petition as expeditiously as possible so as to avoid schism in our Bargaining Unit." Then I continued as follows:

September 7, 1988

Whereas Respondent, the Virgin Islands Bureau of Internal Revenue (led by Mr. Anthony P. Olive) embraces a wide range of activities, chiefly among which is licentiousness.

Whereas the employees of the Bureau of Internal Revenue have been grieved and burdened by the Bureau's licentiousness and wanton disregard for their Labor Agreement.

Whereas Petitioner, Liston Monsanto, (an Internal Revenue Officer IV) forced by circumstances, took upon himself the role of cynic, vowing to use any measure short of violence in order to bring a semblance of order to the Bureau.

Whereas the Bureau of Internal Revenue through its Director, Mr. Anthony P. Olive, takes pleasure in discriminating against Liston Monsanto.

Whereas Mr. Anthony P. Olive on May 10, 1988, resorted to his political theory of "divide and conquer" by designating Mr. Louis M. Willis Acting Assistant Chief of the Delinquent Accounts and Returns Branch.

Whereas Respondent on August 22, 1988, given orders from the Public Employees Relations Board (PERB) through its Representative Attorney Dennis Heileman, to submit a brief, which would include documentary evidence that Petitioner refused to accept the position of Acting Assistant Chief of the Delinquent Accounts and Returns Branch.

Whereas Respondent has failed to meet deadline of September 6, 1988, due to absence of any documents to support his contention.

Now, therefore, I, Liston Monsanto, aware of the foregoing incidents, and desirous of promoting harmony within the offices of the Virgin Islands Bureau of Internal Revenue makes plain the crux of my argument insofar as it relates to Mr. Willis' appointment.

Mr. Willis is an Intenral Revenue Officer I, and a member of the Bureau's Bargaining Unit. He started work with the Bureau of Intenral Revenue on July 25, 1983. His biography - somewhat abridged, was submitted to the Public Employees Relations Board (PERB) together with a number of other pertinent documents at an informal hearing on August 22, 1988.

Petitioner, Liston Monsanto, has been employed by the Government of the Virgin Islands for a total of thirty-five (35) years - twenty-eight (28) prominently with the Bureau of Internal Revenue (formerly Tax Division) where, during his tenure of service, he was called upon (prior to Mr. Olive's stewardship) to supervise the activities of the Delinquent Accounts and Returns Branch on several occasions

Petitioner is also Chief Shop Steward of the Bureau's Bargaining Unit by virtue of his membership with the United Steelworkers of America (hereinafter referred to as USWA) - Local 8249. Local 8249 is not a Company Union and, therefore, not dominated by Respondent.

Prior to joining USWA, Petitioner served as ombudsman for an oppressed number of employees - many of whom had encountered manifold problems such as the ones previously given to PERB on August 22, 1988, and manified by Mr. Elmo D. Roebuck (former Post Auditor of the Virgin Islands Legislature) in an article appearing in the local Daily News of May 28, 1988.

Unlike Respondent who prefers to fiddle by way of rigmarole and sometimes repartee (e.g., Mr. Olive May 31st smoke screen in response to the Daily News' article of May 28, 1988, succeeded in beclouding the issue and shifted the focus of the readers attention from a real to an imagined issue) while the Bureau burns, Petitioner filed an Unfair Labor Practice with the Public Employees Relations Board (PERB) on July 21, 1988, for several reasons:

1. In order to quell ugly rumors of collusion between Management and Labor.

2. In order to put to rest idle talk of Management's attempts to bust USWA.

3. In order to avoid a private little war turning into a public exhibition.

4. In order to avoid the services of an outside arbitrator so as to resolve the matter through the quickest and cheapest means.

Petitioner contends that he has become a victim of Mr. Anthony P. Olive's discriminatory and isolationist policies and that presently there is no need for the pseudo position of Acting Assistant Chief of the Delinquent Accounts and Returns Branch. Petitioner further contends that his May 13th letter to Mr. Luis "Tito" Morales (copy in PERB'S possession) virtually tells the story, and furthermore, that there is a desperate need for a Chief - Delinquent Accounts and Returns Branch - a position for which he is qualified as attested by the appearance of his name on the Personnel List of Eligibles.

Respondent, on August 23, 1988 - in a bizarre move - testified before the Senate's Finance Committee that the search was on for a local person to fill the vacent and classified position of Chief Delinquent Accounts and Returns Branch - the same position previously occupied by Petitioner who was removed therefrom sometime in 1971 because of a fiscal crisis, which required his expertise and immediate attention.

Petitioner is cognizant that Respondent has full responsibility and authority in carrying out the duties of his office. Petitioner is also cognizant of the existence of a Bilateral Contract which clearly states under Article XI Section 1(c) that "Temporaty Assignment shall be assigned to the most qualified senior person."

With respect to grievances previously filed and the deceptive trick now being used by Respondent, Petitioner submits that subject grievances do not duplicate his charge of Unfair Labor Practice inasmuch as:

(a) The Unfair Labor Practice is intended to prevent schism in the Bureau's Bargaining Unit

(b) Grievance No. 12-88 was filed by several Members of the Bargaining Unit after it had become abundantly clear that Respondent was violating the Labor Agreement and

(c) Grievance No. 13-88 was filed by Petitioner after he had determined that Mr. Louis M. Willis had been designated Acting Assistant Chief with a salary of $26,542.00.

Petitioner has submitted a preponderance of the evidence which clearly shows that things have become a bit tenuous in this most sensitive area of the Virgin Islands Government. Owing to his failure to grapple with the many problems in the Bureau of Internal Revenue, Respondent has been caught in a cul-de-sac. What is the panacea? Petitioner wants peace; hence he's working for justice.

My Local Union (8249) was keeping me busy representing members of our Bargaining Unit inside and outside the workplace. On September 15, 1988, on behalf of Paulette Rawlins, I again wrote to PERB. I wrote:

September 15, 1988

Attorney Dennis W. Heileman
Public Employees Relations Board
#17 Church Street
Bolero Building 2nd Floor
Room 3
Christiansted, St. Croix, V.I. 00820

Dear Attorney Heileman:

Submitted herewith for your review and consideration is my amended version of PERB U1-81 (1) and (2).

Items B and C under section three (3) (Basis of Charge) have been changed in order to fully comply with your order.

Very truly yours,

Liston Monsanto
Shop Steward

cc: Attorney Denise Reovan

RECEIVED

SEP 15 1988

OFFICE OF
COLLECTIVE BARGAINING

SEP 16 1988

Man's inhumanity to man was amply demonstrated at our informal meeting of September 14, 1988, when Union Officials Morales and Rogers (perhaps because of guilt) made the silly and inappropriate remark that PERB ULPC 88-24 Rawlins and Bureau of Internal Revenue, is a matter that requires a petition for unit clarification.

Granted, nobody is perfect, but the sophisticated Officials have known this ever since PERB first issued a decision and order (PERB UC 82-12) on February 16, 1983, which amended our Bargaining Unit to exclude therefrom the Secretary to the Director, the Secretary to the Deputy Director, the Secretary to the Reviewer/Classifier Conferee and the Secretary to the Chief of the Processing Accounts and Returns Branch, who incidentally were all (at the time) Tax Coordinating Secretaries and who (in defiance of maximum utilization of time), strangely type material in conjunction with negotiations for several different supervisors who supposedly are part of a cohesive unit called Management.

Our Representatives, the United Steelworkers of America, acting like a Company Union did nothing to indicate that they would - in fact, file a petition with PERB for Unit Clarification. And this is, therefore, the reason that Miss Paulette Rawlins (a union member in good standing) was forced to spend $25.00 in order to be heard (as an individual) before the Public Employees Relations Board.

Re: PERB ULPC 88-24 Paulette Rawlins and
     Virgin Islands Bureau of Internal Revenue.

Miss Paulette Rawlins is Secretary to the Chief Delinquent Accounts and Returns Branch. She is classified as a Tax Coordinating Secretary II.

The Chief Delinquent Accounts and Returns Branch supervises the Bureau's Revenue Officers both by providing work assignments and instructions and by reviewing and evaluating their work.

As his Secretary, she critiques and types the Chief's Job Performance Evaluations of each Officer. These evaluations are seen only by the Director and Deputy Director, and are used to select candidates for specialized training and promotions.

Revenue Officers-like the other subordinates of the various supervisors, are bonafide members of our Bargaining Unit; consequently, should the occasion arise, Miss Rawlins would be called upon to type material prepared by her Supervisor in conjunction with negotiations.

Revenue Officers are involved in the processing of Offers-in-Compromise, Transferee Assessments, 100% Penalty Assessments, Decedents Estates and investigations requiring collaboration with Special Agents. Miss Rawlins types all the relative reports.

Information relative to Fraud Referral emanating from the Delinquent Accounts and Returns Branch and earmarked for the Special Agent is typed by Miss Rawlins.

In order for the branches within the Bureau to function harmoniously, completed investigations are normally transferred to Revenue Officers by way of Miss Paulette Rawlins - some of which are deemed sensitive.

Miss Rawlins also receives and screens incoming mail and prepares outgoing correspondence.

One can hardly blame Paulette Rawlins for not being in the secretarial positions that are presently excluded from our Bargainint Unit. As noted heretofore, Miss Rawlins is a Tax Coordinating Secretary II who was never given the opportunity to apply for one of the positions. With her years of service which date back to August 23, 1977, she most certainly would have qualified. After all, they are all Tax Coordinating Secretaries (some Miss Rawlins' junior) working as Secretaries to the various Supervisors.

In light of the foregoing, I'm forced to list several questions for which the Public Employees Relations Board should provide answers:

1. PERB UC 82-12 list among those excluded from our Bargaining Unit the names of Lourde M. Blyden and Joyce L. Peterson. Blyden no longer works for the Bureau. Peterson has long been promoted. What is the status of their replacements?

2. PERB UC-87-1 specifically deprives Ms. Janice M. Lee of union character. Ms. Lee no longer works for the Bureau. What is the status of her successor?

3. And now after reading Exhibit I (attached hereto) the inevitable though disturbing question must be asked: What happens when these secretaries who are now excluded from our Bargaining Unit go on leave or is otherwise absent from the Bureau? Who replaces them?

4. What happens if the people - now excluded from our Bargaining Unit, are promoted to a position not in management, but paying a higher salary?

There is unanimous agreement that there is a need for a Unit Clarification - a clarification that may be brought about only through the efforts of our Local Union.

In the absence of any movement on their part, however, I feel it an obligation to duty as Shop Steward to represent Miss Paulette Rawlins in her quest to be excluded from the Bargaining Unit.

The information contained herein provides tangible proof that like many of the secretaries who are now excluded from our Bargaining Unit, Miss Paulette Rawlins qualifies for exclusion.

GOVERNMENT OF
THE VIRGIN ISLANDS OF THE UNITED STATES

—◊—

VIRGIN ISLANDS
BUREAU OF INTERNAL REVENUE

—◊—

Lockharts Garden No. 1A
Charlotte Amalie, St. Thomas, U.S.V.I. 00802

March 2, 1987

Anthony P. Olive
Director
Bureau of Internal Revenue
St. Thomas, V.I.   00801

Dear Mr. Olive:

This morning I witnessed Miss Yvonne Phipps working in her capacity as Secretary pro-tem to the Chief Processing Accounts and Returns Branch, and it occured to me that Miss Phipps was busy concentrating on documents which contained information whose unauthorized disclosure could be prejudicial to the Bureau's interest.

Coincidentally, I was in the process of reviewing Perb's "Decision and Order' numbers UC82-12 and UC87-1 and to say that I gasped in horror and amazement upon seeing Miss Phipps operating as a confidential secretary is really an understatement.

As a person who respects law and authority, I would like to remind you that PERB acting favorably on petitions filed by the Bureau of Internal Revenue, excluded several secretaries from our Bargaining Unit because of the confidentiality of their work. Needless to say, this included the secretary to the Chief Processing Accounts and Returns Branch.

Based upon the foregoing, I hereby request the immediate removal of Miss Yvonne Phipps from the confidential duties assigned her and further ask that she be replaced by either Mrs. Hill, Mrs. Moron, Mrs. Faulkner, Miss Vessup, Miss Lee, or Miss Adams.

In giving consent to my request, the Bureau would have put to rest the criticisms of many of the employees in our Bargaining Unit who feel (with good reasons) that the Bureau is trying to get the best of both worlds.

Very truly yours,

Liston B. Monsanto
Shop Steward

This letter should be used
by the writer himself to
support his request for an
examination to determine if
he is a victim of the defect
of dementia pracox.

cc: PERB
     Mr. Cephus Rogers
     Mr. Luis "Tito" Morales
     Mr. Roy Vanterpool

And so you might ask how I found the time to write so many letters to so many people. The simple explanation is: The Third Circuit Court's decision and my role of Shop Steward had provided me with a solid foundation and the unfettered right to write my letters. Through their letters and memoranda, Olive and his bunch of unscrupulous good-for-nothings were pressing me to join them in breaking the law. For me to have joined with them in their law-breaking ways would have been a slap in the faces of the three judges in the Third Circuit Court who had already ruled that I was inculpable. Lest you forget, I had been using the legal guidelines established by them when I was unlawfully removed from my position by Reuben Wheatley and thereafter dismissed by Leroy A. Quinn and Juan Luis. I had to be consistent.

Louis "Lolo" Willis felt uneasy over his Union brothers and sisters' decision to file grievances asking for his removal from the position of Assistant Chief. After all, he had done what he had promised to do during our job action in 1986 and there would be no way that he would allow anybody to take away what he considered to be a legal reward. Prompted by apparent frustration over reforms, Willis who had become a "pit bull" for Olive and Thomas, foolishly threatened me with his fists in the presence of several employees in the workplace believing I was afraid of him. The date was September 16, 1988. Willis wanted to show Olive and Thomas exactly how college graduates behaved when caught working in concert with evildoers. As far as Louis "Lolo" Willis was concerned, muscular strength and the use of guns in the workplace was the answer to the turmoil in the Virgin Islands Bureau of Internal Revenue. Anyway, I reported the incident to the Department of Justice headed by Godfrey DeCastro (another Farrelly appointee) where it died. On October 11, 1988, I wrote to Olive once again. I said:

Liston B. Monsanto, Sr.

October 11, 1988

Mr. Anthony P. Olive
Director
V.I. Bureau of Internal Revenue
Lockhart Gardens #1A
St. Thomas, V.I. 00801

Dear Mr. Olive:

On Friday, September 16, 1988, a haughty and artless "college graduate" (now occupying the pseudo position of Acting Assistant Chief of the Delinquent Accounts and Returns Branch) under tremendous pressure from your office, threatened to use his fists on me. Being educated along practical lines, however, I immediately used my miniscule brain to report the incident to the Department of Justice, where I'm hopeful that appropriate action will be taken.

The contents of the above paragraph serves as my introduction, but in order to arrive at the gist of this letter, let me begin by saying that if a third party (completely unaware of the stormy whather in our storm center) was privileged to read your recent letters, placing emphasis on your billetdoux of October 3, 1988, that third party would conclude that I was either a bigot or a person showing the effects of drinking alcoholic liquor; consequently, I feel it's of the utmost importance that I list - for your review, certain incidents that have become a mirror of the life of the employees in the Virgin Islands Bureau of Internal Revenue.

(a) Early in 1986 you were told that a certain Supervisor was carrying a gun while on duty.

(b) On August 1, 1986, you made a churlish reply to wit: "Monsanto you can kiss my ass!"

(c) In June of 1987 you became "very arrogant and insultive" to Mr. Luis "Tito" Morales during a telephone conversation.

(d) Later in the year, (November 25th) you became a most vocciferous person in displaying your negative reaction to a picture of a thanksgiving turkey on our bulletin board.

(e) In May of this year, Mr. Louis Willis admitted to going home (on a number of occasions) during duty hours and was rewarded with his token position of Acting Assistant Chief.

(f) On October 5, 1988, Mr. Roy Vanterpool (a Supervisor whose behavior on the job has resulted in our government having to pay $2,000.00 each to three (3) of the employees mentioned in the last paragraph of your October 3rd letter) issued two (2) memoranda recommending the termination of Marva Brathwaite and Rickhield Thomas.

Because of the aforementioned incidents, I'm mortified that you would complain in item three (3) of your October 3rd letter that Miss Paulette Rawlins was loud and rude to Mr. Ferdinand. Example, Mr. Olive, is not the main thing in influencing others. It is the only thing.

In the Virgin Islands Bureau of Internal Revenue the phrase "law and order" has been much abused in recent years, but if "law and order" means anything, it means that everyone – rich man, poor man, president, governor, judge, senator, arbitrator and Director of the Bureau of Internal Revenue, obey the law; that the law has no favorites; that before it all men stand equal.

The foregoing established, I'd like to remind you that the employees comprising our Bargaining Unit are bonafide members of Local 8249 of the United Steelworkers of America. Local 8249 is not a company union and, therefore, not dominated by you or any of your company men.

For the past several months, you have openly discriminated against me in violation of our Bilateral Contract. You have become repulsive to some people, inasmuch as everytime that you talk and/or write anything about Liston Monsanto their perception becomes clear, that like the puppet pinocchio, your nose grows longer.

You have conveniently forgotten that you were the one – who on January 16, 1986, deputized me Shop Steward to represent the same people, whom you are not pretending to defend in the last paragraph of your letter of October 3, 1988.

Because I made the vicarious sacrifice for you and a number of ingrates in the Virgin Islands Bureau of Internal Revenue (formerly Tax Division), I suppose you thought that the least you could do to repay me would be to court the Virgin Islands favor, by making a desperate appeal to the emotions and prejudices of the members of our Bargaining Unit and others, in order to retain your power and further your own interest.

This brings to issue the matter of improper solicitation. I, therefore, offer the following in a paraphrase: Government officials should not solicit favors from the people that they are paid to serve. To do so becomes a kind of compensation racket: Help me and you'll get something in return (i.e., quid pro quo), don't and see what happens (use your imagination).

In your cycle of reprisals and retaliation against me, you continue to confuse my methods with my objectives and you seemingly have forgotten that on July 19, 1986, you were told that: "The carefully reasoned theories of Liston Monsanto go drifting down empty alleys, but he is not discouraged, because he knows it is only a matter of time unitl the philistines of today are the Monsanto disciples of tomorrow."

Most members of our Bargaining Unit now know that there can be no growth without change. What's more, with protective devices such as Opinion 81-1434 of the Third Circuit Court of Appeals and the recent decision which was handed down by Arbitrator David Helfeld in the pay disparity case, (Grievance No. 02-87 dated January 28, 1987) they are no longer receptive to outside impressions or influences.

Letter   -3-   10/11/88
Mr. Anthony P. Olive

Because you are hung up on tradition, you are going to find difficulty in trying to grapple with the many problems in the Virgin Islands Bureau of Internal Revenue. Due to double talk and lies, the chickens are steadily coming home to roost. While I'm busy singing "the party's over", the employees are having a glorious time at the expense of the taxpayers of the Virgin Islands.

To distract attention from your office, you have relied on ruses which over the years have completely reversed your moral values.

The decadence of morals was one of the causes of the fall of Rome. Tooth decay is accelerated by failure to brush the teeth. Liston Monsanto's greatest wrong is always being right when it comes to addressing the many problems in the Bureau.

Mr. Olive, The Virgin Islands Bureau of Internal Revenue is being destroyed! You have no evidence to support your contention that I refused the pseudo position of Acting Assistant Chief of the Delinquent Accounts and Returns Branch. Why are you sitting back waiting for another unfavorable decision? Let's sit down and talk. I'm ready.

Sincerely,

Liston Monsanto
Shop Steward

cc: Mr. Cephus Rogers
  Mr. Luis "Tito" Morales
  Miss Paulette Rawlins

Jerome Ferdinand had remarkable enthusiasm as evidenced by his letter of 10/11/88.

GOVERNMENT OF
THE VIRGIN ISLANDS OF THE UNITED STATES
———o———
VIRGIN ISLANDS
BUREAU OF INTERNAL REVENUE
———o———
HAMILTON HOUSE BUILDING
No. 56 — 56A King Street
Christiansted, St. Croix, U.S.V.I. 00820

October 11, 1988

Mr. Liston B. Monsanto
Internal Revenue Officer
V.I. Bureau of Internal Revenue
St. Thomas, Virgin Islands   00802

Dear Mr. Monsanto:

I'm in receipt of your letter, dated October 3, 1988. I have decided to respond because I am a competent manager having a mind and a record of my own.

The attack you have made on my leadership ability is malicious, and slanderous which again demonstrates your continuous lack of respect for authority.

Your statements are demonstrably false because you are aware that the Semi-Annual Physical Inventory of Delinquent Accounts, etc, is a requirement and have been customary each year during the rein of the former Chief, Delinquent Accounts and Returns Branch. I intend to keep it alive. In 1987, an inventory was not accomplished due to his untimely passing on September 18, 1987. Also, in August 1987, I had requested a matching with the ULC (unit ledger card). To that end, it is pure nonsense for you to assessed my judgment and action as being "showy" or to impress a third party.

I would like to remind you that the functions of the entire Delinquent Accounts and Returns Branch is my responsibility. I will carry out the duties of my office to the best of my ability in spite of your harrassment and the constant attempts to interdict.

My leadership role is one that I'm proud of and comfortable with. Since assuming my position you have been talking about having an inventory and a matching. On several occasions you made complaints to me about higher ups in the Bureau that you felt were advising taxpayers on their accounts assigned to you. Those matters were settled expeditiously and with fairness to your satisfaction. I came aboard to the then Tax Division with leadership experience attained from many years of military service in the United States Air Force which provided the training and schooling in leadership, management and self discipline. In addition, my studies toward higher education with the University of Maryland and University of the Virgin Islands gave me the foundation to be a leader. Where is the beef?

Letter to Liston B. Monsanto
Page 2
October, 11, 1988

In your letter of May 23, 1988 to the Director (Mr. Olive) you stated that you stand ready, willing and able to assume the responsibility of Chief, Delinquent Accounts and Returns Branch. While you proclaim, I maintain that you ought to seek the position on your own record and refrain from applying wrongful tactics on my leadership.

Finally, I call upon you to let us work together to get the job done.

Sincerely,

Jerome A. Ferdinand
Acting Chief, Delinquent Accounts
and Returns Branch

JAF:celw

cc: Mr. Anthony P. Olive
Director

What he had said in his letter may have been politically correct but in the real world where I lived and operated it was poppycock.

Using a quotation from Mr. Randall Johns, I answered forthwith:

October 24, 1988

Mr. Jerome A. Ferdinand
Acting Chief DARB
V.I. Bureau of Internal Revenue
Christiansted, St. Croix, V.I. 00820

> "The Virgin Islands problems will not im-
> prove unless there is a greater sense of
> right and wrong amongst the people."
>
> --Randall Johns

Dear Mr. Ferdinand:

Your letter of October 11, 1988 was hand-delivered to me this morning, and following a careful evaluation of its contents, I reached the sad
conclusion that in spite of your prerequisites of which you boast, that you
are hung up on tradition.

In your letter you have demonstrated that your loyalty towards Mr.
Anthony P. Olive is of an unquestioning kind. You have indicated a desire to
continue a system and process that is a proven failure; consequently, you
have prompted me (by copy of this letter) to suggest to Mr. Olive that he save
himself some pain by doing what is right.

The automobile has grown tremendously since it was first invented.
Today's car is an improvement over yesterday's. Mr. Ferdinand, we cannot
have growth without change! Can't you see that?

You have exacerbated my cynical feelings by defending the very people to whom Governor Farrelly referred in his inaugural address when he stated that he'd inherited a government "often in violation of law."

My letter of October 4, 1988 to Mr. Olive-a copy of which you have,
should give you an insight into the problems facing the Virgin Islands Bureau of Internal Revenue.

If it does not, then I ask that you turn to page 23 of Opinion 81-
1434 of the Third Circuit Court of Appeals. Written thereon by Circuit Judges Hunter, Van Dusen, and Sloviter is the following: "We do not underestimate the internal unease or unpleasantness that may follow when a government
employee decides to break rank and complain either publicly or to supervisors about a situation which s/he believes merits review and reform. That is
the price the first Amendment exacts for an informed citizenry."

Because you are desperately trying to make me out as the Villain in an environment where loyalty is more important than honesty, I'm standing with what I said in my letter of October 3rd, 1988.

Truly, honesty is a most provocative thing. I now ask (once again) that we sit down and discuss the future of our organization.

Sincerely yours,

Liston B. Monsanto
Internal Revenue Officer

c.c. Mr. Anthony P. Olive

The members of our Bargaining Unit were hoping that unionization would have kept management within bounds but instead we were left with feelings of no hope. We had written to Tito Morales and Cephus Rogers locally and also the District Director, Thermon Phillips, whose office was located in Birmingham, Alabama. Our pleas for representation had fallen on deaf ears. As far as these people were concerned, the people of the Virgin Islands were without systematic training and learning and would be satisfied only with pay increases.

On October 26, 1988, I wrote to Tito Morales: "Through his silence, Mr. Thermon Phillips (District Director) has deliberately disregarded our correspondence (copies of which you have) and furthermore refused to consider the many complaints launch against Local 8249 of which you are President. As members in good standing, we honestly cannot allow what is taking place in the Virgin Islands Bureau of Internal Revenue to continue. Accordingly, I'm serving notice on you that it is my intention (if need be) to invoke Article IX of the By-laws for the Local Union with a view towards invoking Article X. May we see some movement please?"

I had surveyed the situation. I knew that PERB was an ally of the Virgin Islands Government. I knew that the Bureau of Internal Revenue was operating like the sword of Damocles. I knew that the Union (because of its member's attitudes) wanted to get their money through Union dues and thereafter ship it to the mainland. I knew that Tito (the Local Union's President) and Governor Alexander Farrelly were friends and I knew that we were not getting the representation that had been promised by the Union. When you find yourself in a workplace where you have no recourse and no appellate rights, you don't take chances. I hurriedly made the decision to take another route.

On December 7, 1988, I wrote to Attorney Dennis Heileman (counsel to PERB). I wrote:

December 7, 1988

Attorney Dennis W. Heileman, Esq.
Counsel to the PERB
P.O. Box 148
St. Thomas, Virgin Islands 00801

> "It takes courage for government employees
> to stick their necks out and blow the whi-
> stle in time to make a difference."
>
> — Thomas Divine

Dear Attorney Heileman:

With the coming of calendar year 1989 and the continuous stand-off's between management and myself, I feel that the time has come for me to promote a new image of moderation.

Before doing so however, I find it of the utmost importance (in view of the numerous rumors and theories that have been circulated) to write to you in order to formally solicit your assistance and that of the PERB in evaluating certain facts and circumstances surrounding working conditions at the Virgin Islands Bureau of Internal Revenue.

These conditions I hasten to add, have within themselves certain deficiencies and inadequacies that have retarded the overall collection program of the Virgin Islands Government.

Desiring to promote harmony in our organization and looking for the greatest good for the greatest number, over the past several years I tried in a variety of ways and through a number of channels to convey to management our urgent need to discontinue our bitter contention and repeated unfriendly attacks.

Having failed in my efforts to reconcile with management and as a civil servant not wanting to play the role of Mr. Roan Creque's alter ego, I would like to request that you exert whatever influence and/or power you may have in arranging for a meeting between management and myself with you in attendance.

Because the employment relationships between myself and others in the Bureau of Internal Revenue has not been permanently undermined, I feel certain that we can settle our differences around a table even if we must compromise. Compromise is not defeat.

Your prompt attention to this matter is greatly appreciated.

Sincerely,

Liston B. Monsanto
P.O. Box 2763
St. Thomas, V.I. 00803

```
c.c.     Mr. Anthony P. Olive
         Attorney Denise Reovan
```

Meanwhile, two years had elapsed since Alexander A. Farrelley had taken the oath of office as the fourth elected Governor of the United States Virgin Islands. Familiar with my status in the government, he refused to show any firmness in bringing to an end, the sordid ordeal in which I had found myself. The man just didn't care.

As an attorney engaged in private practice, Farrelley had for sometime sat in his office looking with wistful eyes at Government House. Through informal discussions and the usage of body language, he had conveyed to his so-called friends and associates, a heart and mind that yearned for the disadvantaged people of the Virgin Islands.

Based on what he had told me in a private conversation, I knew that some of my repugnant views were shared by him. But I also knew that as the incumbent Governor he had formed an alliance with Edward Thomas and many of my detractors who were courting his favor. What Governor Alexander Farrelley had told me as a private citizen was critical to my decision to write. And so with the advent of the New Year (1989), I made the decision to exploit what I thought to be his weakness by addressing him in this fashion:

188

P.O. Box 2763
Charlotte Amalie
St. Thomas, V.I. 00803

January 20, 1989

Honorable Alexander Farrelly
Governor - U.S. Virgin Islands
Office of the Governor
Charlotte Amalie
St. Thomas, Virgin Islands 00801

Dear Governor Farrelly:

After reviewing and finally digesting the contents of your Inaugural Address and your State of the Territory Message, which you delivered before the Seventeenth (17th) Legislature on January 16, 1987, I have decided to write to you (in my capacity of civil servant) in the same fashion that I would want you to write to me if I were Governor.

First and foremost, I'd like to say that over the past several years Mr. Anthony P. Olive (the man that I recommended for the position of Director of the Bureau of Internal Revenue) has read more into my attitude than I've meant to convey.

Mr. Olive knows that I'm right when I speak of unfairness and the poor working conditions in the Virgin Islands Bureau of Internal Revenue, but because of his aberrant behavior and his strong feelings, where emotionalism is concerned in a sensitive place such as the Bureau of Internal Revenue, "right" does not matter. It now appears a certainty that there is only one right way in the Bureau of Internal Revenue - Mr. Olive's way. I'm trying my best, but Mr. Olive is capable of worst.

Even as I write, the Virgin Islands Bureau of Internal Revenue is in disarray. It has become an absolute disgrace. Working therein has become (for the lack of a better description) an occupational hazard.

I'm no halo wearer, and the record will show that I'm definitely not a usurper. I'm fully aware of the fact that Mr. Olive has full responsibility and authority in carrying out the duties of his office, but his flagrant abuse of discretionary power plus the wrath that he expresses have been such that they have created a line of demarcation, which is serving only to block my path to a promotion and limit me from contributing - in a positive way, to the overall growth of the Bureau.

I've seen the system work against me and I've seen the system work for me. Now I'd like to be given a fair chance to work with the system. That's all I ask. Greater love hath no man for his work.

On August 23, 1988, Mr. Olive went before the Seventeenth (17th) Legislature and in a bizarre move, testified that the search was on for a local person to fill the vacant and classified position of Chief Delinquent Accounts and Returns Branch - the same position previously occupied by me before I was removed sometime in 1971 because of a fiscal crisis which required my expertise and immediate attention. To date, the position remains open.

Mr. Olive is still smarting over my landmark decision of 1982. At the time he was a part of a triumvirate who tried to fire me systematically.

For your information, it is worth noting that on March 11, 1982, the United States Court of Appeals for the Third Circuit filed Opinion Number 81-1434 which completely vindicated me from any wrong in openly complaining about Mr. Olive's poor managerial skills, while at the same time openly criticizing the Bureau's organizational structure.

Following the Court's decision, Mr. Olive immediately assumed the role of despot using isolationist policies bent on discriminating against me and geared to isolate me from the overall operations of the Bureau. In short, Mr. Olive has removed me from participating in the complex activities of the Virgin Islands Bureau of Internal Revenue.

Throughout his role-playing activity however, I have remained calm. I have repressed my feelings and have ignored the pressures under which he continually puts me.

Several years ago, speaking out in the Virgin Islands was a novelty; today it is a commonplace for top officials - especially in your administration, to turn private wars into public exhibitions. I do not want to be forced by circumstances to go public once again.

Admittedly, I have fought and won some battles that other people might have lost, but please forgive my immodesty when I say that I'm not one who thrives on playing the role of aggressor.

In spite of the fact that Mr. Olive has been scoring dismally in the Bureau of Internal Revenue, the employment relationships between myself and many others have not been permanently undermined. In fact, I would venture to say that what unites Mr. Olive and myself is far greater than what divides us.

As a classified employee with an unblemished record and thirty five (35) years of governmental service, I feel that serving my government is far better than self-seeking.

Governor, I'm wounded of heart. For the past two (2) years I have protected the bureaucracy in deference to your attributes and the wishes of your dear ally and loyalist, who incidentally feels that there is nothing harder than the softness of indifference.

188

Letter   -3-   January 20, 1989

Honorable Governor Farrelly

    I have now begun to feel the intensity of the circumstances in which I live, and because I'm not desirous - at this time, of using the press to air whatever acrimonious differences Mr. Olive and myself may have, I'm appealing to you in the hope that you'd use the power of your office to settle once and for all our differences - not favoring either side especially.

    Finally, I am not suggesting that you dispose of Mr. Olive. I'm merely asking for an end to the hostilities in the Virgin Islands Bureau of Internal Revenue. I'm on the verge of retiring from the service and somehow I feel that we do not need a third party such as the Union to handle the matter. By now Mr. Olive should understand that greater power brings greater scrutiny.

    Your paramount and foremost attention to the matter will be highly appreciated.

                        Sincerely,

                        Liston B. Monsanto
                        Internal Revenue Officer

On April 3, 1989, after Farrelly had ignored my letter, I wrote to him once again using a quotation from Mark Twain which said:

April 3, 1989

Honorable Alexander A. Farrelly
Governor-U.S. Virgin Islands
Government House
St. Thomas, Virgin Islands 00801

"Do what is right for it
will gratify some people
and astonish the rest."

-Mark Twain

Dear Governor Farrelly:

In spite of what you may have been told by some people in the highest levels of management in the Bureau of Internal Revenue, and in spite of what some of the crusaders of these same people may tell you, the Virgin Islands Bureau of Internal Revenue is an absolute abomination.

As a person not guilty of the perfidious crime of treason and therefore not desirous of courting your favor, I wrote to you on January 20, 1989 seeking the intervention of your office into the critical state of affairs in the Virgin Islands Bureau of Internal Revenue.

Today — forced by circumstances and utter exasperation, I feel oblige to write to you once more—and without a lot of explanation and commentary, in order to inform you that I'm preparing to make public the many injustices that have been brought about by nepotism and discrimination in the Bureau of Internal Revenue.

I say this unreservedly for I have played the role of pariah for too long.

Sincerely,

Liston B. Monsanto
Internal Revenue Officer

Members of Farrelly's shadow cabinet were not going to allow Farrelly to do what was right. They were afraid that in doing what was right, Farrelly may have killed the goose that was laying the golden eggs for them. On May 26, 1988, Edward Thomas had sent me a tacit message saying that as an erudite person of the same ilk as Viggo Hendricks (former Chief Processing Branch), Earle B. Ottley and Calvin Wheatley, I was without a license to join him and the evildoers in the Bureau of Internal Revenue in their wickedness.

Amid chaos in the workplace there was a lot of work ahead for me. The most vocal critic in the Bureau (other than me) continued to be my friend and co-worker, Mario Lima. Through the grapevine and several letters to the editor, the public had been made aware of my sad plight in the Virgin Islands Bureau of Internal Revenue. There was no outcry from them and I saw no need to lose my rationality over what I considered to be public apathy. For the definitive answers I was seeking I would have to appeal to the American Civil Liberties Union (ACLU), the Equal Employment Opportunity Commission (EEOC) or perhaps Governor Alexander Farrelly. There was an urgent need for me to overpower my rivals. I still held out hope that an outside organization (either the ACLU or the EEOC) would come to my rescue.

My condemnation by Edward Thomas had made me an outcast. He was so afraid of me that he was willing to condemn me to eternal punishment. He would say or do anything to me through Olive or members of the shadow cabinet hoping to keep me off balance. Being deceitfully underhanded, my honesty was too transparent for him to take. You'll be reading more about Edward Thomas in another chapter of this book.

On April 17, 1989, I addressed a letter to Mr. Edward Mercado of the New York District Office (EEOC) after learning through the local Daily News of February 8, 1989, that the EEOC had set right an unfairly injured employee's claims that he had been discriminated against. Mr. Mercado telephoned to inform me that he had assigned my case to Mr. Richard Turer (one of his investigators) under Charge Number 160-89-1628. That was indeed a positive step.

My appeal to the EEOC caused Olive to panic. He ran to the Department of Justice where he conferred with Attorney Treston Moore, a person who had found living in the Virgin Islands to his liking. Treston Moore would do anything as a carpetbagger to stop me from introducing any kind of innovations into the governmental system. He was benefiting from what was going on in the Virgin Islands and had no desire to change it. Treston Moore had the effrontery to tell the EEOC that I operated a taxi on government time. He had joined Olive in his lying ways.

With respect to the position that I wanted it was my recollection that Ambassador Terrance Todman at one time had said: "Just imagine the difference it would make to our great country and to the world if young men and women were to be identified and prepared for the professions in the same way now that is done for spectator sports, or those who are already prepared could be placed into positions where their abilities could be fully utilized." Things were becoming a bit tenuous in the Bureau. I didn't know whether or not bribery was being used or practiced but from what was going on, Treston Moore was sending to the EEOC a number of documents that were completely off the subject. One of the major drawbacks in dealing with the EEOC in New York was the absence of face-to-face meetings.

Treston Moore had represented the Bureau of Internal Revenue many times. He didn't have to be told about the turmoil therein, he already knew. On June 9, 1989, I wrote to Attorney Moore. I stated:

Liston B. Monsanto, Sr.

June 9, 1989

Treston E. Moore, Esq.
Assistant Attorney General
V.I. Department of Justice
St. Thomas, U.S. Virgin Islands 00801

Dear Attorney Moore:

On November 12, 1987 (representing the VirginIslands Bureau of Internal Revenue where -incidentally, the noblest form of leadership comes not by example, but through nepotism and discrimination), you entered into an agreement with Plaintiffs June Blyden, Donna Phillip, Marilyn Turner, and the Law Office of John R. Coon (Civil No. 1984/37), which provided that judgement in the amount of $7,500.00 be entered in favor of them and against the Defendant Government of the Virgin Islands.

Since the aforementioned agreement, things have become a bit more tenuous in the Offices of the Bureau of Internal Revenue. Under the stewardship of Mr. Anthony P. Olive, the Bureau has ungraciously refused to atone for its transgressions and continues its journey down the primrose path to disaster.

The existing tension in the Bureau has been heightened by abuse and disorder in the working place and simultaneously has caused Mr. Olive and many of his subordinates to become (for the lack of a better phrase) a confrontation of opposites.

Speaking about tension, it is important to note that on Friday, September 16, 1988, I filed a complaint (in my capacity of civil servant) with your office charging that Mr. Louis Willis (an Internal Revenue Officer I with the Bureau) had threatened to use his fists on me. As I write, it is distressing to note that I have yet to receive word from your office regarding your investigation.

Today-operating on the thesis that good Lawyers have insight into the problems of ordinary people, I'm forced to put to you several queries concerning your long delay in .completing the appropriate investigation into the Willis matter plus the case of Mr. Urdley Smith. (The enclosed letter and a conference with Attorney Michael Lee will give you an insight into the Smith matter).

Having stated my case, I now present to you -in your capacity of Assistant Attorney General and civil servant, the several questions to which I'd like honest answers.

1. Do you have a vested interest in the status quo?

Letter Atty. Treston Moore   -2-   June 9, 1989

2. Do you believe that security and safety in numbers take precedence over lawfulness in the U.S. Virgin Islands?

3. Are you sincerely concerned with the affairs of the United States Virgin Islands?

4. Are you handling the cases (i.e. Willis and Smith) in a perfunctory way?

Recently, there has been some developments that have had an intriguing quality about them, and as a person who respect law and authority, I shall appreciate hearing from you in the immediate future, for I want no doubt in my mind as to your position on the subject cases.

Sincerely,

Liston B. Monsanto
P.O. Box 2763
St. Thomas, V.I. 00803

c.c. Atty Gen. Godfrey DeCastro

Then on June 26, 1989, I wrote to then Attorney General Godfrey DeCastro saying:

June 26, 1989

Godfrey DeCastro, Esq.
Attorney General U.S. Virgin Islands
Virgin Islands Department of Justice
St. Thomas, U.S. Virgin Islands 00801

Dear Attorney DeCastro:

On the premise that it is error only, and not truth that shrinks from inquiry, I wrote and hand-delivered a letter dated June 9, 1989 to Assistant Attorney General Treston Moore (copy to you), wherein I sought answers to the several questions listed therein.

To date, I have not received any response from Attorney Moore; consequently, the urgent intervention of your office has become necessary, and towards this end I solicit your indulgence.

Sincerely,

Liston B. Monsanto
P.O. Box 2763
St. Thomas, Virgin Islands 00803

c.c. Atty. Treston Moore
Atty. Michael Lee

242

Then I followed-up with another letter dated July 17, 1989 to Decastro which stated:

July 17, 1989

Mr. Godfrey DeCastro. Esq.
Attorney General — U.S. Virgin Islands
Virgin Islands Department of Justice
Charlotte Amalie, St. Thomas V.I. 00801

Dear Attorney DeCastro:

Because you work for an administration which teaches that the word virtue is synonomous with keeping away from evil while being absolutely independent, I was of the belief that you would use the power of your office to at least respond to my letter of June 26, 1989.

Instead, it appears that by asking several incisive questions of an apathetic Attorney Treston Moore, I have drawn on your patience and consequently, been silently declared guilty of a rarity.

Having invoked the fifth amendment as a basis for your silence conjures memories of the old adage which goes: Justice delayed is justice denied. But now that my cases have been recorded, I have every reason to believe that Attorney Treston Moore as a member of your staff, adds grandeur to all your efforts.

Finally, the Willis case proves anew that ours is still an unjust system that lets a Commissioner serve as Prosecutor, Judge, and Jury.

Sincerely,

Liston B. Monsanto
P.O. Box 2763
St. Thomas, V.I. 00803

c.c. Attorney Treston Moore

Attorney Michael Lee

While Attorney Treston Moore and Anthony Olive (a political appointee, who was defeated in an epochal battle on March 11, 1982) were praying and hoping with intensity to deceive and confuse the EEOC by trying to make them believe that Ferdinand and Willis were both filling the vacant positions of Chief and Assistant Chief of the Delinquent Accounts and Returns Branch, I found myself forced to rely on my strong Christian beliefs and the facts at my fingertips to correct any erroneous impressions conveyed by their exhibits. I wrote to Richard Turer on August 28, 1989 in this manner:

August 28, 1989

Mr. Richard Turer
Investigator-EEOC
New York District Office
90 Church Street – Room 1501
New York, New York 10007

Re: Charge No. 160-89-1628
    Monsanto vs Bureau of
    Internal Revenue.

Dear Mr. Turer:

I have just received a copy of Attorney Treston Moore's letter (dated August 19, 1989) which is addressed to Mr. Marc J. Weisenfield (copy to you) and which—as anyone can see, is another deceptive trick designed to delay your investigation, while continuing the discriminatory practices at the offices of the Virgin Islands Bureau of Internal Revenue.

The opinion advanced by Mr. Moore (and seemingly the conclusion reached) that I operate a Taxi on government time for which I'm compensated, compares favorably with the suspicions of certain employees in the Bureau, who feel that because of the presence of nepotism and embezzelment plus the absence of a system of checks and balances similar to that in the United States Internal Revenue Service, that many top-level employees and their cronies are being granted special favors with the blessings of Mr. Anthony P. Olive, who believes that his power is absolute. (Opinion No. 81-1434 - a copy of which you have in your possession,shows that one must seek justice outside the Virgin Islands).

I am really amazed at Attorney Moore's and Mr. Olive's desperate attempts to becloud the issue. Their reasoning is so unsound that it obviously is a glaring attempt to shift the focus of one's attention from a real to an imagined issue.

What does the diatribe in his letter has to do with a person whose civil rights are being violated? Why the hocus-pocus? If an employee is guilty of wrong doing-including operating a Taxi on government time, why not bring the appropriate charges against him?

And as far as case number 1330-0304-83 (the one introduced by Mr. Moore in his letter) is concerned, that decision (the record shows) was made based on the language in a contract that has long expired.

The positions of Chief Delinquent Accounts & Returns Branch (the position that I'm currently seeking) and Assistant Chief Delinquent Accounts & Returns Branch are both open. Why doesn't Mr. Olive fill them legitimately?

Finally, I ask that you re-read my letter of September 7, 1988, which is addressed to Attorney Dennis Heilman. Therein you'll find the important facts

Letter   -2-   August 28, 1989

Mr. Richard Turer
Equal Employment Opportunity Commission

that I've deemed necessary in helping you to complete your investigation.
This does not mean that you should ignore the other documents in your po-
session however.

Sincerely,

[signature]

Liston B. Monsanto
Civil Servant

c.c. Attorney Treston Moore
      Mr. Anthony P. Olive
      Mr. Cephus Rogers

Throughout my employment with the Virgin Islands Government I had been a model of decorum and I dare anyone to prove otherwise. The questionable methods that Treston Moore was using in addressing the inquiries of the EEOC told me that he was afraid of a transformation of the Virgin Islands Governmental System. Here's why: Under existing conditions in the Virgin Islands the so-called "outsider" has the advantage. Most of them are in the Virgin Islands for what the islands can do for them and will at some future time return to the place whence they came. They don't give a hoot about whether the Bureau of Internal Revenue is violating our Contract by illegally placing Jerome Ferdinand and Louis Willis in vacant positions. What's more, they could care less about an incumbent governor or any governor for that matter, as long as that governor continues to extend his predecessor's programs. Operating as a voting bloc, they combine to serve notice on any aspiring politician seeking the office of governor that they exist. To their good fortune they are more enlightened and politically astute than the disadvantaged people in the Virgin Islands and consequently they exploit with joy the existing political patronage which envelops the island, a political patronage that the indigenous population has difficulty living without.

Olive had never anticipated that I would appeal to the EEOC for help. He had been doing everything possible to prevent another appeal to the Third Circuit Court when out of the blue came the EEOC. My appeal to the EEOC was not something that I reveled in. It was done in order to stop the onslaught of illegal activities emanating from Olive's office. (A little more on that later).

We return now to our chronological sequence which was broken abruptly in order to accommodate the Equal Employment Opportunity Commission.

On April 25, 1989, Olive was once again back to making unilateral decisions based on information he was receiving from Roy Vanterpool. I was forced to address a letter to him which read:

Liston B. Monsanto, Sr.

April 25, 1989

Mr. Anthony P. Olive
Director
V.I. Bureau of Internal Revenue
St. Thomas, V.I.   00801

Dear Mr. Olive:

Instead of intensifying your efforts to end the civil war in the Bureau of Internal Revenue, you are once again (based only on exparte' evidence from a fault-finding Mr. Roy Vanterpool, who works in an organization requiring a high degree of investigatory work) on the verge of abusing your discretionary power by threatening to suspend Miss Daisy Williams for her sincerity in exposing Mr. Vanterpool in Case Number 37/1984 of the United States District Court of the Virgin Islands.

While President George Bush is placing emphasis on cooperation, you continue to promote confrontation internally through reaction - especially on a subject matter into which you should have intervened long before its escalation.

This being the case, I'm asking that you consider this letter an essential first step in Miss Williams' defense.

Because his conduct (as reflected in Case No. 37/1984 and his carrying a gun while on duty) and conversation differed from each other, Mr. Vanterpool was told sometime ago that no one would win the battle of the sexes inasmuch as there was just too much fraternizing with the enemy.

Mr. Vanterpool has been on an extended hiatus ever since the date of his last blunt and tactless reply to me. Prior to that reply, he had demonstrated his curtness in a number of letters (copies in your possession) - some of which are included herewith for your immediate review.

Miss Daisy Williams is a model of decorum. She has an unblemish record and is relatively intelligent. Are you and Mr. Vanterpool trying to erode her image by sending her to Coventry?

For your information, Mr. Roy Vanterpool (like most people in management) has proven through his aberrant behavior and abrasive attitude that he's not in-culpable.

And speaking about not being inculpable, who can forget Mr. Edward Thomas' (your Reviewer/Classifier) letter to you (copy enclosed) of May 15, 1984, where-in he vehemently voiced his dissatisfaction with your abnormal way of doing things.

246

Letter   -2-   4/25/89

Mr. Anthony P. Olive
  Director

    We are faced with a most anomalous situation in the Virgin Islands Bureau of Internal Revenue. Because you refuse to treat lower echelon employees fairly and justly, working in this most sensitive area of our Government has become an occupational hazzard.

    I say unreservedly that it is time for all of us to bury the proverbial hatchet and start doing the work for which we are being paid. The accounts receivable of our Government are very high.

                   Sincerely,

                   Liston Monsanto
                  Shop Steward

cc: Daisy Williams

     Luis "Tito" Morales

     Mr. Cephus Robers

     Miss Jacqueline Brown

GOVERNMENT OF
THE VIRGIN ISLANDS OF THE UNITED STATES
—o—

VIRGIN ISLANDS
BUREAU OF INTERNAL REVENUE
P. O. Box 3186
Charlotte Amalie, St. Thomas, U.S.V.I. 00801

May 15, 1984

Mr. Anthony P. Olive
Acting Director
Bureau of Internal Revenue
St. Thomas, Virgin Islands   00801

Dear Mr. Olive:

I am very disturbed at the article in today's newspaper
which you imply that you had to bring in retired U.S. employ
to get more revenue and get more taxpayers to file and compl
with the law.

You specifically mention that Mr. Wharton along with Mr
Riley will work on forty (40) pending cases. Let me remind
you that every one of those forty (40) cases was worked by a
local revenue agent. You also failed to mention the under-
reported income program which was commended in the audit rep
and is all being done by local people. You also failed to
mention that collections are up substantially and this is al:
being done by local people.

As you seek confirmation to the position of Director, I
think that you have made a serious blunder in slighting the v
people that you must depend on for your success. I think tha
apologies are in order.

Sincerely,

Edward E. Thomas
Reviewer/Classifier

cc: Mr. Roy Vanterpool
     Mr. Ervin C. Dorsett
     Mr. Kenneth Hansen
     Mr. Irwin H. Wharton
     Mr. William Whaley
     Mr. Graciano Belardo
     Mr. Jerome Ferdinand

EET/dar

248

On July 26, 1989, at 2:30 p.m., I received a letter of admonition from Ferdinand which really irritated me. Ferdinand was conveying to me that whatever I had been telling him was going in one ear and coming out the other. Here is what he wrote:

GOVERNMENT OF
THE VIRGIN ISLANDS OF THE UNITED STATES

——o——
VIRGIN ISLANDS
BUREAU OF INTERNAL REVENUE
——o——

HAMILTON HOUSE BUILDING
No. 56 — 56A King Street
Christiansted, St. Croix, U.S.V.I. 00820

Rec'd
7/26/89
7:30 P.M

July 25, 1989

MEMORANDUM

To: Mr. Liston Monsanto
                Internal Revenue Officer

From: Mr. Jerome A. Ferdinand
                Acting Chief, Delinquent Accounts & Returns Branch

Re: Liston Monsanto

On July 21, 1989, you were asked to appear in my office, and by your request the time was set for 1:30 p.m.

At approximately 1:45 p.m., I notified you that I would be reviewing the large dollar amount tax cases assigned to you. In our discussion you take decisive action by declining to work on any of your accounts. Further, that you would relate the same to the Director (Mr. Olive) and the Governor.

The reasons given for your action are as follows:

(1) That you (Monsanto) had been fired before for doing your job.

(2) That an arbitration proceeding in your (Monsanto) behalf is pending.

(3) That Mr. Louis M. Willis, who possess no job knowledge or leadership has been appointed Acting Assistant Chief, Delinquent Accounts and Returns Branch.

(4) The need for the matching of accounts between the Processing Branch and the Delinquent Accounts and Returns Branch to establish the accuracy of the delinquent accounts.

249

Liston B. Monsanto, Sr.

Memo to Mr. Liston Monsanto
Page 2
July 25, 1989

I have determined that the circumstances does not present any cause for your refusal or in delaying the collection of the delinquent taxes in your inventory. Therefore, I'm directing you to devote eight (8) hours each day to your job for which you are being paid. The collection of revenues and protecting the interest of the government is your primary duty and responsibility.

Request your acknowledgement of this memorandum.

Jerome A. Ferdinand

250

Liston Monsanto
V.I. Bureau of Internal Revenue
lA lockharts Garden
St. Thomas, U.S.V.I.   00802

Office of the Govern
V. I. Bureau of Internal Revenue
Hamilton House Building
56 - 56A King Street
Christiansted, St. Croix, V.I.   **00820**

HAND-DELIVERED

251

On July 26, 1989, I wrote two letters. The one to Olive dealt with an investigation into the United States Internal Revenue Service by the House of Representatives. The other written to Ferdinand on July 27, 1989, by simply saying:

RECEIVED
DIRECTOR'S OFFICE

JUL 27 1989
July 27, 1989

VIRGIN ISLANDS BUREAU OF
INTERNAL REVENUE
ST. THOMAS, V.I.

Mr. Jerome Ferdinand
Acting Chief DARB
V.I. Bureau of Internal Revenue
Christiansted, St. Croix, V.I. 00820

Dear Mr. Ferdinand:

Because I recognize the little witticism in your memorandum of July 25, 1989, and because I'm hard pressed to believe (unless you suddenly became disoriented) that you'd hand deliver to me a dead memorandum at 2:30 P.M. on July 26, 1989 after reading (in front of me) your copy of my July 26th letter to Mr. Anthony P. Olive at 11:30 A.M., I have decided to expand my letter to you of July 26, 1989.

At the outset it is worth noting that your memorandum —although dead, was a personification of a cheap shot and was presumably designed to deliver you from misuse of authority while at the same time serving notice on the many scoff-laws in management that you are indeed made to order to meet the particular conditions for chief of the Delinquent Accounts and Returns Branch. Maybe you remembered that Mr. Olive testified several months ago that Liston Monsanto would be a "godd candidate" for Chief DARB. (see bottom of page 16 of opinion no. 81-1434 of the U.S. Court of Appeals for the Third Circuit).

Incidentally, your conduct and conversation do not coincide at all. You are saying one thing and doing something entirely different. It has become obvious to me and some people in the Bureau that there is a difference in our philosophies when it comes to office decorum.

While I would not want to anticipate negatives, I would like to use this letter to admonish you as follows: The burning belief that you can continue to work overtime in an effort to erode my image is an illusion of reality.

At the moment, the most serious problem for the Virgin Islands Bureau of Internal Revenue is its failure to atone for its transgressions.

The next most serious problem the Bureau faces is its unwillingness to accept the philosophy of the mirror theory.

Finally, after you had read the copy of Mr. Olive's letter to which I referred in the first paragraph of this letter, you should have immediately sent your memorandum to the dead letter office.

Sincerely,

Liston B. Monsanto
Internal Revenue Officer

c.c. Mr. Anthony P. Olive

252

Were it not for the letters which appear in this publication, it would have been highly improbable for me to write this book which to a degree exposes many people who heretofore had been labeled sacrosanct. In a letter designed to discredit Olive, I wrote to him on July 31, 1989 as follows:

```
RECEIVED
DIRECTOR'S OFFICE

JUL 31 1989 AM        July 31, 1989

VIRGIN ISLANDS BUREAU OF
    INTERNAL REVENUE
    ST. THOMAS. V.I.
```

Mr. Anthony P. Olive
Director-Bureau of Internal Revenue
Charlotte Amalie,
St. Thomas, Virgin Islands 00801

Dear Mr. Olive:

When I made the strong recommendation for you to become Director of the Virgin Islands Bureau of Internal Revenue (formerly Tax Division), I knew that you had earned a reputation for moodiness and violent outbursts, but it had never ever occurred to me that you could be as unruly and ungrateful as you demonstrated on July 28, 1989, when you attempted to temporize action on the many grievances which came before us at the office of the Chief Negotiator.

Really, I could not believe that a simple review of documents could warrant such rudeness. You were a personification of a tempest in a teapot as you successfully proved that circumstances do not make a man. They only reveal him.

The record shows that while you continue to harbor resentment of criticisms, I (as a civil servant whose civil rights are constantly being violated) have made vain attempts to foster tolerance as exemplified by Opinion number 81-1434 of the Third Circuit Court of Appeals wherein three judges agreed with Liston Monsanto that all's not well in the hostile confines of the Virgin Islands Bureau of Internal Revenue.

I do not know whether the local officials of the United Steelworkers of America are mentally prepared to grapple with the many problems in the Bureau of Internal Revenue. Our local union (as is the case with just about everybody else in the Virgin Islands) challenges management only on matters relating to money.

Of prime importance is the fact that management and labor are currently on the verge of making some extremely important decisions that must be tempered with the realization that Federal Investigators from the Equal Employment Opportunity Commission are on their way to St. Thomas for the purpose of providing a system of checks and balances, which would aid them in conducting an impartial investigation into the affairs of our government's Bureau of Internal Revenue, where unfortunately, the noblest form of leadership comes not by example, but through nepotism and discrimination.

The Investigators were reluctantly invited to St. Thomas by me after several years of speaking out to a disgusting extent about our long-standing problems. In addition, I thought that inviting them to the Island would be an admirable way of convincing you that ours is a government of laws. It is not that I love Mr. Anthony P. Olive less, but that I love the Virgin Islands more.

As a civil servant I have become a victim of much aggression emanating from your office. The fact that I have always extended the olive branch in a sincere effort to normalize relations with you and the Aggressors, should in some way indicate to you that its time to move towards reducing the receivables of our government.

So without belaboring the matter, and before the Investigators arrive to make public their findings, I'd like to make a last-ditch effort to reconcile our differences post haste.

Knowing that you are a person that's long on emotion and short on reason, I ask that you do not allow spite and/or irascibility to interfere with what has to be done.

The Third Circuit Court has already found the Bureau guilty of my many criticisms. What's more, it should be noted that in a civil war such as ours, nobody wins. Furthermore, with all the notoriety given to conditions in the Bureau, I fear that a Federal investigation could result in talks of a Federal takeover of Tax Collection in the Territory.

I therefore request that you consider my impassioned plea for reconciliation. The settling of matters in the Bureau would make for an exciting page in the history of the Virgin Islands Government.

At this point, it is worth noting (if only for the record) that the employment relationships between myself and others in the Bureau have not been permanently undermined. Have no fear. Forget the past. Let's settle down to work.

The Chief of the Delinquent Accounts and Returns Branch (the position currently sought by me before my retirement from the V.I. Government), like the Governor and members of his cabinet, must work out of the capital city of St. Thomas.

Treat me fairly and justly. I'm ready to come over to your side. "Happy is the house that shelters a friend".

Sincerely,

Liston B. Monsanto
Shop Steward

c.c. Gov. Alexander Farrelly

Ten days later (August 10th), by way of placating me, Willis sent me a copy of my Employee Performance Report with an overall rating of satisfactory. There was nothing on the Report to indicate that I had not been doing the work for which I was being paid. Willis had taken the path of least resistance breaking away from Olive and Ferdinand who had been lying about my performance. I returned the document to Willis unsigned inasmuch as I knew that as a Junior Revenue Officer he did not have what it took to rate me. My letter that accompanied the Performance Report back to Willis said:

RECEIVED
VIRGIN ISLANDS BUREAU
INTERNAL REVENUE

AUG 10 1989

ST. THOMAS, VIRGIN ISLANDS
COLLECTION BRANCH

August 10, 1989

Mr. Louis M. Willis
Acting Asst. Chief, DAR Branch
V.I. Bureau of Internal Revenue
St. Thomas, V.I. 00801

Dear Mr. Willis:

I do not know whether my Performance Rating Report for the period ending June 17, 1989, is an action or maneuver that's intended to outwit or disconcert me, but as an Internal Revenue Officer IV with over a quarter of a century of service, I cannot and will not accept a rating from a figure head or any soldier of fortune who is below me in rank, power or importance.

Honor is the greatest asset in the world. It beats money, power and influence.

Your rating me satisfactorily is greatly to my honor and a tacit confession that: (a) You are aware of the injustices in the Delinquent Accounts and Returns Branch and (b) the Branch is without a standard or principle by which to make a judgment.

In all my years as an altruistic employee of the Virgin Islands Bureau of Internal Revenue (formerly Tax Division) it had never ever occured to me that anyone - especially an employee on your level, could be so systematized.

Sincerely,

Liston Monsanto
Internal Revenue Officer IV

cc: Mr. Anthony P. Olive
     Director

     Mr. Jerome Ferdinand
     Acting Chief, DAR Banch (STX)

     Mrs. Majorie Roberts
     Technical Advisor

GOVERNMENT OF THE U.S. VIRGIN ISLANDS

(CLERICAL & ADMINISTRATIVE)
EMPLOYEE PERFORMANCE REPORT
(READ THE REVERSE SIDE BEFORE FILLING OUT)

Rec'd 8/10/89

EMPLOYEE NAME	JOB CLASSIFICATION	DEPARTMENT
Liston Monsanto	Int. Rev. Officer IV	Bur. of Int. Revenue St. Thomas, V.I.

REASON FOR EVALUATION DATE (1) _____ (2) _____

RATING PERIOD FROM: 6/17/88 TO: 6/17/89

*PROBATION ☐   FINAL PROBATION ☐   ANNUAL ☒   SPECIAL (EXTENSIONS, ETC.) ☐

SECTION A—FACTOR CHECK LIST Immediate Supervisor Must Check Each Factor in the Appropriate Column	A Not Satisfactory	B Requires Improvement	C Meets Standards	D Exceeds Standards	E Does Not Apply
1 Observance of Work Hours			✓		
2 Attendance			✓		
3 Grooming and Dress			✓		
4 Compliance With Rules			✓		
5 Safety Practices			✓		
6 Attitude Towards Public			✓		
7 Attitude Towards Employees			✓		
8 Knowledge of Work			✓		
9 Work Judgments			✓		
10 Planning and Organizing			✓		
11 Job Skill Level			✓		
12 Quality of Work			✓		
13 Volume of Acceptable Work			✓		
14 Meeting Deadlines			✓		
15 Accepts Responsibility			✓		
16 Accepts Direction			✓		
17 Accepts Change			✓		
18 Effectiveness Under Stress			✓		
19 Appearance of Work Station			✓		
20 Operation and Care of Equipment			✓		
21 Work Coordination			✓		
22 Initiative					
23 (Additional Factors)					
24					
25					
26					
27					
28					
29					

FOR EMPLOYEES WHO SUPERVISE OTHERS

30 Planning and Organizing					
31 Scheduling and Coordinating					
32 Training and Instructing					
33 Productivity					
34 Evaluating Subordinates					
35 Judgments and Decisions					
36 Ability to Motivate Employer					
37 Operational Economy					
38 Supervisory Control					
39 (Additional Factors)					
40					
41					

(PRELIMINARY EVALUATION)

RATED BY: _____ DATE: _____

DEPT. HEAD: _____ DATE: _____

Checks in Column (A) Must be explained in Section E

SECTION B— Record job STRENGTHS and superior performance incidents.

SECTION C— Record PROGRESS ACHIEVED in attaining previously set goals for improved work performance, or career development.

SECTION D— Record specific GOALS or IMPROVEMENT PROGRAMS to be undertaken during next evaluation period.

SECTION E— Record specific work performance DEFICIENCIES or job behavior requiring improvement or correction. (Explain checks in Column A.)

SUMMARY EVALUATION— Check Overall Performance—

( ) Satisfactory   ( ) Requires Improvement   (✓) Effective Meets Standards
( ) Not
( ) Exceeds Standards

RATER   I certify this report represents my best judgment.
( ) I do ( ) Do not Recommend this employee be granted permanent status.
(For Final probation reports only)

(Rater's signature) _____ (Title) Acting Ast. Chief (Date) 8/9/89

Department Head: Anthony P. Olive-Director

REVIEWER: (If None. So Indicate)
(Reviewer's Signature) _____ (Title) _____ (Date) _____

EMPLOYEE: I certify that this report has been discussed with me. I understand my signature does not necessarily indicate agreement.

Comment

(Employee's Signature) _____ (Date) _____

— SEE INSTRUCTIONS ON REVERSE SIDE —

PERSONNEL COPY

256

On August 18, 1989, I addressed a letter to two actors (Ferdinand and Willis) who were trying to force me into accepting certain delinquent accounts. I wrote:

```
          RECEIVED
VIRGIN ISLANDS BUREAU
  OF INTERNAL REVENUE

    AUG 18 1989                          August 18, 1989

ST. THOMAS, VIRGIN ISLANDS
    COLLECTION BRANCH
```

Mr. Jerome A. Ferdinand
<u>Acting Chief Delinquent Accounts & Returns Branch</u>
Mr. Louis M. Willis
<u>Acting Ass't Chief Delinquent Accounts & Returns Branch</u>
Virgin Islands Bureau of Internal Revenue
St. Croix, V.I. 00820 & St. Thomas, V.I. 00801

Gentlemen:

If I didn't know better and had to use the appellations underlined above as a basis, I would come to the sad conclusion that the Virgin Islands Bureau of Internal Revenue had been transformed into one of Hollywood's Repertory Theaters.

Gentlemen, for your information, the verdict came in on March 11, 1982, when a Three-Judge panel (Hunter, VanDusen, and Sloviter) of the Third Circuit Court of Appeals ruled unanimously in favor of Liston B. Monsanto, the people of the Virgin Islands, and the many decent employees of the Bureau of Internal Revenue, who have a nice sense of what is right and proper and who have been for sometime, desirous of putting the protestant ethic to work. Mr. P.T. Barnum had absolutely nothing to do with the decision.

Mr. Leroy A. Quinn (our former Director) was a villain, but admittedly he had some virtues. Rather than ignore completely the Court's decision, and rather than paying strict attention to my letter of July 2, 1982 which stated my position with sweeping clarity, (see attached copy) he completely avoided me and the small minority to whom I referred in paragraph one (1) of the letter.

Seven (7) delinquent accounts totalling $19,629,078.87 have just been given to me - I assume, for my review and consideration.

I have made the decision (following my review) to return the accounts herewith for the reasons previously given to both of you and Mr. Anthony P. Olive. (You may need to review the several letters previously sent you).

The Bureau of Internal Revenue has steadfastly refused to atone for its transgressions. The people in management joined by certain actors and drug store cowboys, continue to flaunt their authority to the detriment of the V.I. Government.

Until and unless the Delinquent Accounts and Returns Branch is given a chartered course to follow, we are going to have a most difficult task closing our accounts.

Sincerely yours,

Liston B. Monsanto
Internal Revenue Officer

c.c. Mr. Anthony P. Olive

Liston B. Monsanto, Sr.

July 2, 1982

Leroy A. Quinn
Director
Virgin Islands Bureau of Internal Revenue
P.O. Box 3186
St. Thomas, Virgin Islands   00801

Dear Mr. Quinn:

Inasmuch as it has been established that most employees
of the Virgin Islands Bureau of Internal Revenue feel security
and safety in numbers take precedence over lawfullness, to say
that respect for law and authority has been a most powerful
weapon in the arsenal of a small minority assigned to the Delinquent
Accounts and Returns Branch, is an understatement that deserves
the highest degree of publicity.

Armed and blessed with such honor and esteem, plus the
landmark opinion filed on March 11, 1982 (81-1434 Liston Monsanto
versus Leroy A. Quinn) by the United States Court of Appeals
for the Third Circuit, the small minority knows that any unlawful
attempt(s) emanating from management and designed to weaken or to
exhaust its resources will be a nullity. Moreover, we know
that in this government of, for, and by the people, one can
afford-like the legendary Swiss Patriot William Tell, not to
bow-down to any person, place or thing.

Law-abiding employees see no need to circumvent, restrict,
or limit the law as is commonplace in the Bureau of Internal
Revenue. Furthermore, the court's opinion referred to in
paragraph two of this letter, has opened the door for many
aggrieved employees (especially those whose civil rights have
been violated) to assert their rights as classified public
servants. It has also determined for management exactly what
constitutes disruption and libel. In short, the opinion-if

followed, will help to bring much-needed order to the
Government's Bureau of Internal Revenue, while simultaneously
stopping a take-over by the United States Treasury Department.

Equally important however, and perhaps a major drawback
in the Bureau, is the long recognized fact, which deals with
our desperate need for a Chief of the Delinquent Account and
Returns Branch. The absence of a chief is even more critical
at this time than it has ever been. This vacant position
without a doubt, continues to be the principal reason for the
problems in the Delinquent Accounts and Return Branch.

Furthermore, I feel that the filling of the classified
position of Chief Delinquent Accounts and Returns Branch is
absolutely essential.

It is a common error for public servants (especially
those in position of authority) to think that the Government of
the Virgin Islands is their personal possession. They fail to
see that the mental picture which they have created serves
only to make them responsible for certain acts and omissions,
while forever making their office(s) open to criticism before
the Government Employees Service Commission and the Courts.

If we sincerely intend to improve conditions in the Virgin
Islands Bureau of Internal Revenue, and avert a take-over by
the Federal Government, we must demonstrate a changed attitude
with a willingness to work closely, harmoniously, and ethically
with each other. The flaunting of authority by certain personnel
in management and the disruptive influence now exerted by certain
lower echelon employees over their peers, must cease and be
replaced by mutual respect and admiration for each other.

Incidentally, now that I've returned to work after being
vindicated of charges trumped up by you and Mr. Anthony P. Olive
(see your libelous letter of March 16, 1982). It is hoped that
you'd dispense with personalities, as I look forward to working
as diligently as I did in the past, with a view towards projecting

an image that best represents the Virgin Islands Bureau of Internal Revenue. This, I say unreservedly.

Sincerely,

Liston Monsanto

cc: Governor, Juan Luis
     Lieutenant Governor, Henry A. Millin
     Deputy Director, Anthony P. Olive

Through many of my letters I was trying to reconcile with the good-for-nothings, who were being supervised by the shadow cabinet in doing unprincipled things. I wrote to Olive on September 5, 1989, once again extending the Olive Branch. Here's what I said:

SEP 5 1989

VIRGIN ISLANDS BUREAU OF
INTERNAL REVENUE
St. Thomas, V.I.

September 5, 1989

Mr. Anthony P. Olive
Director-V.I. Bureau of Internal Revenue
Charlotte Amalie
St. Thomas, Virgin Islands 00801

Dear Mr. Olive:

In the past and furthermore up to now (thru emissaries and letters, and even in formal discussions around the negotiating table), I have made several requests for us to sit down together and talk with a view towards reaching an amicable settlement of our differences.

You have also been warned of the dire consequences that would result if you continued the extremely dangerous practice of disrespecting law and authority, but for reasons known only to you, my warnings have been completely ignored.

Today the in-fighting continues unabated in the offices of the Virgin Islands Bureau of Internal Revenue, and although it would be very easy for me to dwell on the negatives of our organization in this letter, I wouldn't. The Bureau -you see, stands as a constant reminder of the seven deadly sins of the world.

The criminal activity herein aided by nepotism and discrimination in this most sensitive and income-producing arm of our government, exceeds all bounds of decency - the Administration's motto of "Fairness for all" notwithstanding.

At issue at the moment, is Miss Paulette Rawlins' letter of September 1, 1989 - a letter I would venture to say, that has become an arresting experience for me. Since Miss Rawlins' letter is a recent piece of history, I will not-in this letter, attempt to magnify it anymore than is necessary.

I'd like to say however, that Miss Rawlins is not finding fault without good reasons. In her letter she indicates (perhaps apprehensively) that she's losing confidence in our law enforcement system and is therefore desirous of presenting her case before the Equal Employment Opportunity Commission, which as you are no doubt aware, is an agency of the Federal Government.

The lady's letter was obviously motivated by two aged grievances (one of which was filed two years ago), Union apathy, and vindictiveness on the part of management. How many more employees will appeal to the Federal Government for help, remains conjectural.

You may recall that on May 23, 1988, I reminded you in a letter that China and the United States had normalized relations. Now as I write, Poland (after forty -five years) is turning towards democracy. Other countries such as Angola, Iran, Iraq, and Nicaragua are now living somewhat peacefully.

What's wrong with us? Are we (by our behavior) asking the Federal Government to takeover tax collections in the territory? When are we going to learn that there can be no growth without change?

In order to protect your power you have become increasingly licentious. Because of nepotism and discrimination plus your unwillingness to do what is right, you are making your predecessor, who had a proud bearing, look better today in death than he was in life.

As public servants who know the truth about our problems far better than anybody else, surely we must know that the Delinquent Accounts and Returns Branch cannot operate in a vacuum—without any concern for other policies and programs of our entire government.

The fate of the Bureau of Internal Revenue is hanging in the balance, and it is very vital during this period in our history, that we get together for the express purpose of molding a cohesive unit. With all the remarkable talent in the Virgin Islands Bureau of Internal Revenue, you could glamorize the workplace by dropping the appelations of "Acting Chief DARB" and "Acting Assistant Chief DARB" replacing them with enterprising people and authentic job titles, thereby creating an organizational structure of which we all can be proud.

All along we've known that the employment relationships between myself and others have not been permanently undermined. Now we know that what unites Mr. Anthony P. Olive and Liston B. Monsanto is far greater than what divides them; consequently, I'd like to offer a solution to our morale and managerial problems.

The solution sir, is altruism. Altruism is the only vehicle and incentive that I can readily think of that would keep our hopes within bounds, and ultimately aid us in defusing what has become a potentially explosive situation.

We must work harmoniously together in an effort to save the Virgin Islands Bureau of Internal Revenue from destruction and/or a Federal takeover. Let's accentuate the positive and leave a legacy of which we all can be proud.

Sincerely,

Liston B. Monsanto
Shop Steward

c.c. Chief Negotiator
      Mr. Cephus Rogers
      Mr. Luis "Tito" Morales

It had been close to twenty years since I had been fighting "City Hall" and going through the extreme test and although I had come a long way, I still had a long way to go before retiring. I began to focus my attention on a possible retirement plan while trying my best to improve strained relations in the Virgin Islands Bureau of Internal Revenue.

The incoming employees with whom I would be required to work were mostly contemporaries of my children and Olive through his law-breaking ways was pressing me to delay my planned retirement. I knew deep down in the innermost part of myself that a decision by the EEOC would take some time and so as Olive and Treston Moore braced for a report from the EEOC, by way of opening the door to a resolution, I wrote to Mr. Richard Turer (EEOC Investigator) on September 7, 1989. I said:

                                        September 7, 1989

Mr. Richard Turer
Equal Employment Opportunity Commission
New York District Office
90 Church Street - Room 1501
New York, New York 10007

                        Re: Charge No. 160-89-1628
                            Monsanto vs USVI Bureau of
                                Internal Revenue

Dear Mr. Turer:

        As an Internal Revenue Officer and trained Investigator like yourself, based on our telephone conversation of today I got the feeling that you were playing "Devil's Advocate" as the final step in completing your investigation.

        If I did not know that I was being discriminated against (for whatever reason), I would never have entertained the thought of filing the charge now in your possession.

        As I indicated to Mr. Bream and Mr. Hoxie (even before the case was assigned to you) the documentary evidence that I would make available to your office would make it very easy for you to conclude that I am in fact being discriminated against.

        I have not seen any of the information submitted to you by the other side. I know for a fact however, that the positions of Chief Delinquent Accounts and Returns and Assistant Chief DARB are both still open.

        My goal is to become Chief and then retire from the Service. Am I asking for too much?

                                        Sincerely,

                                        Liston B. Monsanto
                                        Internal Revenue Officer

My record was as intimidating as my letters. Whatever Treston Moore had been saying to Richard Turer was not known. What was known was the tangle of contradictory statements that I was receiving from Turer which led me to believe that something was rotten in Denmark. What's more, we were in the hurricane season and winds from an approaching storm called Hurricane Hugo were about to be felt territory wide and it would create somewhat of a chaotic situation in the Virgin Islands Bureau of Internal Revenue.

Because it was time to bring life back into our mausoleum, Revenue Officer Juanito Maduro and the Acting Assistant Chief squared off to do physical battle in the workplace on September 14, 1989. Here according to Maduro is what took place:

RECEIVED
DIRECTOR'S OFFICE

SEP 15 1989

VIRGIN ISLANDS BUREAU OF
INTERNAL REVENUE
ST. THOMAS. V.I.

September 15, 1989

Mr. Anthony P. Olive
Director
V.I. Bureau of Internal Revenue
Lockhart Gardens No. 1A
St. Thomas, Virgin Islands 00802

Dear Mr. Olive:

Yesterday afternoon I came into the office for the sole purpose of arranging my delinquent accounts in an orderly manner so that I'd be able to start work anew today.

As I started the task of sifting through my new accounts, I came upon a memorandum addressed to me from Mr. Louis Willis (Acting Assistant Chief DAR Branch) that he had written on August 29, 1989, while I was on official leave from the office.

Seeing that the contents of his memorandum was baseless, I got my thoughts together and immediately wrote him a letter refuting his allegations. (I have attached a copy hereto for your enlightenment).

After writing the letter, I started up the hallway for Mr. Willis' office. My intention was to deliver the document for his review.

Upon seeing my letter, Mr. Willis got loud and abusive and impulsively, I found myself quarrelling with him.

We fussed and quarrelled before our tempers flared causing us to (for the lack of a better word) fight it out in the corridor of the building.

It is to be noted (because of its importance) that we did not fight in Mr. Willis' office nor did we exchange blows.

Although Mr. Willis was the aggressor in the brawl of yesterday, I'd like to apologize to you and all the employees of the Bureau for the part that I played.

Letter   -2-   9/15/89

Mr. Anthony P. Olive

    I'm here for the sole purpose of working, and as I have noted in my letter of September 14, 1989, I'm not guilty of any worng doing.

Sincerely,

Claude Maduro
Internal Revenue Officer

cc: Mr. Liston Monsanto

     Mr. Jerome Ferdinand

     Mr. Cephus Rogers

     Mr. Luis "Tito" Morales

As an eye-witness and Shop Steward I immediately wrote Olive a letter of admonishment on September 15, 1989 which also spoke to my exceptional insight into the affairs of the Virgin Islands Bureau of Internal Revenue. I wrote:

```
              RECEIVED
           DIRECTOR'S OFFICE

            SEP 15  1989 September 15, 1989

        VIRGIN ISLANDS BUREAU OF
            INTERNAL REVENUE
             ST. THOMAS, V.I.
```

Mr. Anthony P. Olive
Director
V.I. Bureau of Internal Revenue
Lockhart Gardens No. 1A
St. Thomas, Virgin Islands 00802

Dear Mr. Olive:

Victimized by office politics and forgetting that the pen is mightier than the sword, two (2) Members of our Bargaining Unit squared-off in what may be best described as a fracas in the hallway of the new building which houses the Delinquent Accounts and Returns Branch.

Brother Louis Willis (now a full-fledged Actor) and Brother Claude Maduro (a Ham in a place which at times is called a repertory theater) finished up the working day in donnybrook fashion on September 14, 1989, only because of your laissez faire attitude towards the entire Bureau.

One Year ago (September 14, 1988) I wrote one of my many letters wherein the Bureau was described as a storm center (see attached copy) - a center of trouble and turmoil.

Yesterday afternoon (September 14, 1989) the passions of Brother Willis and Brother Maduro overcame their reasons and as a result, there was a strong outburst of emotion and excitement in our Branch.

I'm also including herewith a copy of my October 11, 1988, letter which should give you some indication of the anomalous working conditions in our workplace.

Willis and Maduro may have been storm-proof inasmuch as they both weathered the storm, but once again I find myself asking you to sit down with us so that we may discuss the future of the Bureau. Please do not allow the radio stations to dedicate the song "stormy weather" to us.

Sincerely,

Liston Monsanto
Shop Steward

cc: Mr. Jerome A. Ferdinand

    Mr. Cephus Rogers

    Mr. Luis "Tito" Morales

266

September 14, 1988

Mr. Anthony P. Olive
Director
V.I. Bureau of Internal Revenue
Lockhart Gardens #1A
St. Thomas, Virgin Islands 00801

Dear Mr. Olive:

I'm writing to you cognizant of the fact that I'm neither a meteorologist nor a storm Petrel. I'm an Internal Revenue Officer IV (Employee of the Virgin Islands Government) assigned to work in a storm center headed by you, and generally called the Virgin Islands Bureau of Internal Revenue.

This letter is furthermore dedicated to you and certain people in management with their intrigues, double-talk and lies, who in spite of weather conditions are insistent on creating trouble.

During Calendar Year 1988 -- by the irony of fate, here in the Virgin Islands we have had much rain when (at times) all we needed was a little sun to put us in a prominent or favorable position.

The year is coming to a close and we are practically home. But behold! The black clouds lingering over the offices of the storm center portend a storm - a storm that may be best described as a tempest in a teapot.

Such an atmosphere has been created because for some strange reason(s) you continue to believe that you are playing an impeccable role in carrying-out your duties as Director. You have complained quite a lot, but none of your complaints have been compelling. You have proven by way of meaningless talk and open discrimination against Liston Monsanto that licentiousness is a Director's preponderant characteristic.

It is ironical that you, in your capacity of Director, would try or otherwise pretend to protect Mr. Jerome Ferdinand and Mr. Louis Willis who have both been saying one thing and doing something entirely different (see the attached corrospondence for proof).

We, in the Delinquent Accounts and Returns Branch have yet to have an index card matching of TDA's and there has been absolutely no explanation from Mr. Ferdinand as to why. As for Mr. Willis, he lied to us on August 31, 1988, when he said he'd be in St. Croix on September 1, 1988.

Liston B. Monsanto, Sr.

Mr. Anthony P. Olive
Director

Let's face it. You have an empire but no title. To say that you take pleasure in ignoring my letters and my attachments to my Performance Reports is an understatement. Look at the abuse of discretionary power on your part in willfully and deliberately denying Mr. Levi Farrell (a family man) his salary checks. You know, without a doubt that this denial is in violation of our Bilateral Contract.

What's more, in using the power of your office which you believe to be absolute, you took it upon yourself to dismiss Mr. Farrell from duty after the Governor had presumably failed to respond to your recommendation. Now I ask you: Who's being disruptive and antagonizing?

Because I have echoed the sentiments of Mrs. Lucia Thomas about your behind-the-scenes activity with certain taxpayers, you've taken umbrage.

The Government of the Virgin Islands is a Government of, for, and by the people. It's our Government - one to which I've pledged my allegiance and one towards whose economic growth I would love to contribute. You are fully aware of this. If you aren't, I suggest you go over the many letters and employee grievances in your possession.

If present trends continue in this storm center, (called the Virgin Islands Bureau of Internal Revenue) I can predict as a certainty that you will find it necessary to deputize Mr. Louis Willis (my union brother) as one of your storm troopers akin to those used by Adolph Hitler in his private army in the 1920's. Your troubles (petty or otherwise) will continue.

My speaking of storm troopers and the impending storm, points up the immediacy for me to barricade myself through the usage of storm doors and windows in the hope that I'll be able to weather the storm. Please stop operating in violation of law.

                                        Sincerely,

                                        Liston Monsanto
                                        Shop Steward

cc: Jerome Ferdinand

     Louis Willis

Internal Revenue Service
memorandum

date: August 31, 1988

to: Mr. Anthony P. Olive
           Director

from: Acting Asst. Chief, DAR Br.

subject:

On the days of September 1st and 2nd, 1988, I will be working in the DAR Branch on the Island of St. Croix upon the request of Mr. Jerome Ferdinand, Acting Chief, DAR Branch.

I will return to the St. Thomas office on September 6, 1988.

Louis M. Willis

cc: Employees DAR Branch

October 11, 1988

Mr. Anthony P. Olive
Director
V.I. Bureau of Internal Revenue
Lockhart Gardens #1A
St. Thomas, V.I. 00801

Dear Mr. Olive:

On Friday, September 16, 1988, a haughty and artless "college graduate" (now occupying the pseudo position of *Acting* Assistant Chief of the Delinquent Accounts and Returns Branch) under tremendous pressure from your office, threatened to use his fists on me. Being educated along practical lines, however, I immediately used my miniscule brain to report the incident to the Department of Justice, where I'm hopeful that appropriate action will be taken.

The contents of the above paragraph serves as my introduction, but in order to arrive at the gist of this letter, let me begin by saying that if a third party (completely unaware of the stormy whather in our storm center) was privileged to read your recent letters, placing emphasis on your billetdoux of October 3, 1988, that third party would conclude that I was either a bigot or a person showing the effects of drinking alcoholic liquor; consequently, I feel it's of the utmost importance that I list - for your review, certain incidents that have become a mirror of the life of the employees in the Virgin Islands Bureau of Internal Revenue.

(a) Early in 1986 you were told that a certain Supervisor
     was carrying a gun while on duty.

(b) On August 1, 1986, you made a churlish reply to wit:
     "Monsanto you can kiss my ass!"

(c) In June of 1987 you became "very arrogant and insultive"
     to Mr. Luis "Tito" Morales during a telephone conversation.

(d) Later in the year, (November 25th) you became a most voc-
     ciferous person in displaying your negative reaction to a
     picture of a thanksgiving turkey on our bulletin board.

(e) In May of this year, Mr. Louis Willis admitted to going
     home (on a number of occasions) during duty hours and was
     rewarded with his token position of Acting Assistant Chief.

(f) On October 5, 1988, Mr. Roy Vanterpool (a Supervisor whose
     behavior on the job has resulted in our government having
     to pay $2,000.00 each to three (3) of the employees men-
     tioned in the last paragraph of your October 3rd letter)
     issued two (2) memoranda recommending the termination of
     Marva Brathwaite and Rickhield Thomas.

270

Because of the aforementioned incidents, I'm mortified that you would complain in item three (3) of your October 3rd letter that Miss Paulette Rawlins was loud and rude to Mr. Ferdinand. Example, Mr. Olive, is not the main thing in influencing others. It is the only thing.

In the Virgin Islands Bureau of Internal Revenue the phrase "law and order" has been much abused in recent years, but if "law and order" means anything, it means that everyone - rich man, poor man, president, governor, judge, senator, arbitrator and Director of the Bureau of Internal Revenue, obey the law; that the law has no favorites; that before it all men stand equal.

The foregoing established, I'd like to remind you that the employees comprising our Bargaining Unit are bonafide members of Local 8249 of the United Steelworkers of America. Local 8249 is not a company union and, therefore, not dominated by you or any of your company men.

For the past several months, you have openly discriminated against me in violation of our Bilateral Contract. You have become repulsive to some people, inasmuch as everytime that you talk and/or write anything about Liston Monsanto their perception becomes clear, that like the puppet pinocchio, your nose grows longer.

You have conveniently forgotten that you were the one - who on January 16, 1986, deputized me Shop Steward to represent the same people, whom you are not pretending to defend in the last paragraph of your letter of October 3, 1988.

Because I made the vicarious sacrifice for you and a number of ingrates in the Virgin Islands Bureau of Internal Revenue (formerly Tax Division), I suppose you thought that the least you could do to repay me would be to court the Virgin Islands favor, by making a desperate appeal to the emotions and prejudices of the members of our Bargaining Unit and others, in order to retain your power and further your own interest.

This brings to issue the matter of improper solicitation. I, therefore, offer the following in a paraphrase: Government officials should not solicit favors from the people that they are paid to serve. To do so becomes a kind of compensation racket: Help me and you'll get something in return (i.e., quid pro quo), don't and see what happens (use your imagination).

In your cycle of reprisals and retaliation against me, you continue to confuse my methods with my objectives and you seemingly have forgotten that on July 19, 1986, you were told that: "The carefully reasoned theories of Liston Monsanto go drifting down empty alleys, but he is not discouraged, because he knows it is only a matter of time unitl the philistines of today are the Monsanto disciples of tomorrow."

Most members of our Bargaining Unit now know that there can be no growth without change. What's more, with protective devices such as Opinion 81-1434 of the Third Circuit Court of Appeals and the recent decision which was handed down by Arbitrator David Helfeld in the pay disparity case, (Grievance No. 02-87 dated January 28, 1987) they are no longer receptive to outside impressions or influences.

Because you are hung up on tradition, you are going to find difficulty in trying to grapple with the many problems in the Virgin Islands Bureau of Internal Revenue. Due to double talk and lies, the chickens are steadily coming home to roost. While I'm busy singing "the party's over", the employees are having a glorious time at the expense of the taxpayers of the Virgin Islands.

To distract attention from your office, you have relied on ruses which over the years have completely reversed your moral values.

The decadence of morals was one of the causes of the fall of Rome. Tooth decay is accelerated by failure to brush the teeth. Liston Monsanto's greatest wrong is always being right when it comes to addressing the many problems in the Bureau.

Mr. Olive, The Virgin Islands Bureau of Internal Revenue is being destroyed! You have no evidence to support your contention that I refused the pseudo position of Acting Assistant Chief of the Delinquent Accounts and Returns Branch. Why are you sitting back waiting for another unfavorable decision? Let's sit down and talk. I'm ready.

Sincerely,

Liston Monsanto
Shop Steward

cc: Mr. Cephus Rogers
    Mr. Luis "Tito" Morales
    Miss Paulette Rawlins

The Maduro/Willis scuffle, as I look back, became the precursor of what was to come. Two days later (September 17, 1989) Hurricane Hugo devastated the Territory. The ferocity of the winds knocked out power and seriously damaged the building housing the Bureau causing a suspension of work therein. The storm, arresting as it was, may have brought about a temporary disorder of Claude Maduro's mind as he had taken a turn for the worst following his altercation with Willis on September 14th. I hadn't seen Maduro since the 14th. The hurricane struck on the following Sunday.

On Friday morning, September 22, 1989, while walking through the parking lot leading to the doors of the Bureau of Internal Revenue I was cut off by Mr. Harold Brathwaite (an employee of the Bureau) who in his excitement told me that Olive and Edward Thomas needed me to help to unravel what was going on in the building. He went on to say that the inside of the building was a mess and that Maduro had brought to bay some of the people at the highest level in our organizational structure.

With the commitment to turn things around I started running towards the Bureau. When I entered the door what I saw was a corroboration of Brathwaite's charges. Eight cowards were standing facing Maduro looking as submissive as ever with no desire to rebel against Maduro who was lecturing. My arrival relieved Thomas of the tremendous pressure under which he had found himself. He shouted: "Aha, Monsanto is here, he's going to help us." Turning his exclamation against him I said in sharp reply: "I'm not here to help you. I'm here to help Maduro." Then turning to Maduro, I said: "Maduro, you are asking for trouble. Please leave the premises."

Maduro did a military about-face and started out the door when all of a sudden Olive in an unprovoked attack started moving with alacrity after Maduro while at the same time shouting: "Get out of here and stay out!" Maduro reversed his tracks and impulsively headed back towards the building from which I had taken extreme care to remove him. Maduro was acting with sudden and rash energy, as he returned to the building everybody scattered. I had already done what I was supposed to do. I no longer had a hand in the matter.

As I began my walk towards my office, Thomas in a panic shouted: "Monsanto you are the cause of this, I ought to blow your head off." I turned around, looked at him and laughed. I said: "You are a coward, you wouldn't know how to start blowing my head off, but in the event you'd like to try it, I'll be in my office." On the way to my office I heard noises that reminded me of the commotion of the marketplace. I looked in the direction from where the somewhat violent movement was coming from and there I saw Olive's and Thomas' pit bull (Louis "Lolo" Willis) and Maduro trying to take cover from each other in a gun-fight. They chased each other into (nearby) grand union supermarket where the shoppers ran amok. I later learned that the police were called to the scene. What happened after that I couldn't say. I had gotten my paycheck and left by then.

I could not allow Thomas to get away with his threat to blow my head off. He had been playing a cat and mouse game with the employees for too long. He had to be put on record. I filed a criminal complaint against him with the Department of Justice where a hearing took place on Monday, November 27, 1989. The report on the hearing follows:

<u>CONCISE REPORT ON HEARING BEFORE ATTORNEY</u>
<u>NELSON JONES IN CONFERENCE ROOM OF THE</u>
<u>DEPARTMENT OF JUSTICE — ST. THOMAS VIRGIN</u>
<u>ISLANDS ON MONDAY NOVEMBER 27, 1989.</u>

In attendance was Mr. Liston Monsanto, Sr., together with Mr. Edward Thomas, Sr., against whom Monsanto had filed a criminal complaint charging that Thomas had (on Friday, September 22, 1989) threatened to blow his head off in the presence of eight (8) people among whom were Mr. Anthony Olive, Mr. Ervin Dorsett, Mr. Roy Vanterpool and Mr. Anthony Attidore.

Also in attendance was Mr. Ray Chesterfield (Investigating Officer for the Department of Justice) and Attorney Nelson Jones who served as Hearing Officer and voice of reason.

Inasmuch as Mr. Monsanto refused to have Mr. Thomas brought before a court of law for prosecution and inasmuch as both parties in a spirit of goodwill shook hands as they emerged from the table, this reporter is averse to detailing verbatim, exactly what transpired at the hearing as it relates to testimony.

For his defense Mr. Thomas brought along a cassette and player which had been used in 1986 to record the voice of Liston Monsanto as he spoke about Thomas' profound impact on the taxpaying public, while occupying certain sensitive positions carrying a high degree of latent power.

Mr. Thomas (it turned out) was using the tape (which he claimed had been given to a reporter during the strike of 1986 so that it could be made a part of his news broadcast for that particular day) in an obvious attempt to justify his threats against Monsanto on September 22, 1989.

<u>CONCLUSION AND RECOMMENDATION</u>

As Reviewer/Classifier with the Bureau of Internal Revenue and one who sits in the catbird seat, Mr. Edward Thomas, Sr., went perforce to the hearing to meet face to face with Mr. Liston Monsanto - a lower echelon employee and member of the Bureau's Bargaining Unit, thereby creating a most anomalous situation.

-2-

It is to be noted at this time that some employees express dismay privately when speaking about the Bureau's organizational structure, but are very apprehensive when it comes to going public with their complaints and/or criticisms, owing only to their false belief that the disclosure act would have an effect on whatever they say about the many injustices in the Bureau of Internal Revenue. Members of the press - especially the newspaper gentry, are loathe to criticize the Virgin Islands abode of devils, which is affectionately referred to as the Virgin Islands Bureau of Internal Revenue.

This behavior without a doubt, points up the immediacy for the introduction of a system of checks and balances within the Government of the Virgin Islands which would be a specific remedy for the Virgin Islands Bureau of Internal Revenue.

The knowledge that there is no one to check the checker puts the checker in an enviable position, where at times he can make threats against lower echelon employees indicating his intentions of inflicting harm on them without having to worry about being reprimanded or even prosecuted. Furthermore, he could become an extortionist.

Finally, as noted by Kenneth C. Hansen, et al on March 14, 1975: "The responsibility for asserting and waiving penalties should not be unilaterally determined by one person and the present method of selecting returns for audit should be looked into as they both lend themselves to corruption."

For additional information on the matter, please refer to Liston Monsanto, Virgin Islands Bureau of Internal Revenue, Lockhart Gardens #1A, St. Thomas, Virgin Islands 00802.

December 4, 1989

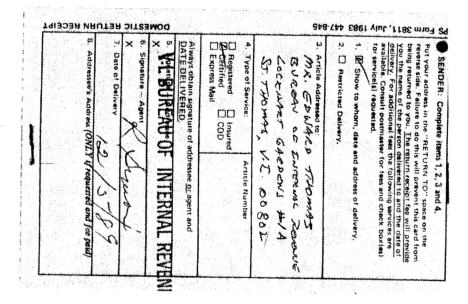

On Friday, September 15, the Daily News had reported in part that a man in Louisville, Kentucky had killed seven of his co-workers as he went from floor to floor at a printing plant. I didn't know whether Olive and his bunch of good-for-nothings was aware of this violent act, but as so-called leaders who were leading a number of oppressed employees, I thought it wise to let them know what could take place in the Bureau.

On September 26, 1989 I wrote to Olive. I said:

September 26, 1989

Mr. Anthony P. Olive
Director - Bureau of Internal Revenue
Lockhart's garden #1
St. Thomas, Virgin Islands 00801

Dear Mr. Olive:

The way the mere mention of his name calmed the preponderance of employees in the Delinquent Accounts and Returns Branch on Friday September 15, 1989, one would have thought that Mr.Claude Maduro had laid siege to the Virgin Islands Bureau of Internal Revenue. The workplace was so peaceful, that it reminded me of the calm preceeding Hurricane Hugo.

But the calmness came about as a result of the correlation between the Louisville, Kentucky massacre wherein seven co-workers were shot to death by a disgruntled employee (as attested by the attached clipping), and the fracas in which Mr. Maduro participated in the corridor of the new building housing the Delinquent Accounts and Returns Branch.

Your carelessness deserves the blame for many of the mistakes in the Virgin Islands Bureau of Internal Revenue. It is distressing to note that you-in your capacity of Director, has joined with most Virgin Islanders who favor reaction. In addition, you continue to accept rumor as fact in the same way that some people have surmised that you have been catching and selling fish on government time.

Your penchant for accepting such rumors is apparent from the silly charges that you have enumerated in your letter accusing Mr. Claude Maduro of being "The Heavy" while suspending him from an organization rife with nepotism and abounding with a number of employees unable to submit to office discipline (see my letter of January 28, 1985 and Mr. Edward E. Thomas' of June 24, 1986 - both of which are attached hereto. It must be noted that Miss Cheryl McMillan - a member of your minority group while in St. Thomas, was not charged with being "loud and rude" to Mr. Anthony P. Olive).

Those of us who were trained by the United States Internal Revenue Service in Investigative Principles and want to use that training for its intended purpose, could tell by your demeanor and your letter suspending Mr. Maduro that as a Director with plenary power and one who had read about the Louisville massacre, that you had to suspend him if only to allay the fears of yourself and those employees who would be cowed by Mr. Maduro's continued presence in the workplace.

Based on the reasons given in Mr. Maduro's report of September 15, 1989 and based on what I saw on the afternoon of September 14, 1989, I'd have to say that both Mr. Maduro and Mr. Louis Willis (his union brother) became violently angry on that particular day. I was there. In short, I was an eye witness.

And speaking about Mr. Willis (the half-trained Internal Revenue Officer I, who has become a victim of much exploitation emanating from your office), gives rise to the inevitable question: What are you going to do to this poor "soldier of fortune" who through inexperience and tact made a manifest error, by leaving his office to do battle with Mr. Maduro?

The fate of the Virgin Islands Bureau of Internal Revenue continues to hang in the balance. As Shop Steward-sworn to implicitly defend the members of our Bargaining Unit, I feel it an obligation to duty to promote solidarity within our ranks. The fact that I know that there are two sides (management and labor) in the Bureau of Internal Revenue working for one side (the Virgin Islands Government) I cannot allow you to divide us.

I am still desirous of meeting you face to face for the purpose of settling all disagreements. You can contact me at extension 216 or if you prefer, you may call Miss Paulette Rawlins (who in spite of Mr. Maduro's presence in the workplace did not join the exodus on Friday September 15, 1989) at extension 233. Miss Rawlins is always cool, gracious, and serene and will deliver any message that you may have for me.

Incidentally, Miss Paulette Rawlins is the same Paulette Rewlins that you take pleasure in discriminating against, and whom you've charged (in your letter of October 3, 1988) with being "loud and rude" to Mr. Jerome Ferdinand.

Today you are pretending to care so much about Miss Rawlins and even Miss Jean Liburd by accusing their union brother (Mr. Claude Maduro) of being "loud and rude" to them. Tell me, did you meet with those two ladies to ascertain the facts? Unlike Ms Cecelia Hill who suddenly finds herself in the middle as a hostile witness, neither Miss Rawlins nor Miss Liburd were given a copy of your letter.

By your own admission, you had a chance to speak with Mr. Maduro at about 4:30 P.M. on September 13, 1989. Why didn't you get his side of the story? If you had, chances are you would have halted what took place on the following day.

Your suspending Mr. Maduro may have opened a Pandora's box that may ultimately prove to be your waterloo. Did you pay attention to what he was saying about a certain woman in our organization on September 22, 1989?

This letter was written in the aftermath of Hurricane Hugo and with the usage of lamplight (lucubration?) because on Friday September 22, 1989, Mr. Edward Thomas (your Assistant) became delirious (he really lost his head) and in front of several people which included Mr. Anthony Attidore, Mr. Ervin Dorsett, Mr. Roy Vanterpool, and yourself, he was "loud and rude" to me threatening to blow my head off.

This is not the first time that I have been threatened by Mr. Thomas. You may recall that on November 25, 1985 at the office of the Chief Negotiator, he also threatened to "touch me up". Have you done anything about these threats?

Liston B. Monsanto, Sr.

    In alphabetical order, we had Hurricane Hugo, which ravaged many miles of the Territory. Following Hugo, we were threatened by Tropical Storm Iris. Now Hurricane Juanito has surfaced in our Storm Center. What are we going to do?

    I know that in the past (perhaps up to now) you've been impervious to suggestions, but since it appears a certainty that we must start life anew in the Virgin Islands Bureau of Internal Revenue, I suggest you call a general meeting.

Sincerely,

Liston B. Monsanto
Shop Steward

c.c. Mr. Jerome Ferdinand
      Ms. Cecelia Hill
      Mr. Claude Maduro
      Mrs. Alda Monsanto
      Mr. Luis "Tito" Morales
      Mr. Cephus Rogers
      Mr. Louis Willis

Sunken treasure worth is put at up to $1 billion

LOUISVILLE, Ky. (AP) — A man with an AK-47 assault rifle mowed down co-workers as he went from floor to floor at a printing plant Thursday, killing seven people and wounding 12 before taking his own life, police said.

The gunman, Joseph T. Wesbecker, had been on permanent disability and was described by Police Chief Richard Dotson as a disgruntled employee. One worker called him paranoid and said he had a fixation with guns.

"I told them I'd be back. Get out of my way, John. I told them I'd be back," Wesbecker told fellow Standard-Gravure Co. employee John Tingle, who approached him during the shooting spree.

Tingle and other employees nearby then ran into a bathroom and locked the door.

Police searched every floor of the three-story Standard-Gravure building for victims. Two were found as officers led Mayor Jerry Abramson through the building, adjacent to The Courier-Journal newspaper.

"We also found a fellow sitting in a corner that was just shuddering in fear," Abramson said. "He hadn't been shot, but he was in shock."

Five of the wounded were in critical condition with multiple gunshot wounds, hospital officials said. One person who was not wounded suffered a heart attack and was taken to a hospital.

"It looks like a battle zone ... with the blood and the people involved there," Abramson said. "There were bodies lying across staircases. It was just frightening."

Wesbecker entered the building at 8:30 a.m. with a duffel bag, an AK-47 rifle and a 9mm semiautomatic pistol and randomly fired at people with the rifle, using ammunition clips of about 25 rounds.

"He was loaded for bear," Dotson said. The gunman had six to eight clips, but it was unclear how many shots he fired.

"It started on the first floor," Dotson said. "By the time our officers arrived he had gone up to the third floor ... and he eventually ended up in a pressroom in an annex area, which is where he killed himself."

Dotson described Wesbecker, 47, as a disgruntled employee of Standard-Gravure, which prints newspaper inserts and Sunday newspaper supplements. He was on permanent disability, although the nature of his disability was not immediately known.

Man kills 7 fellow workers, self

WASHINGTON (AP) — President Bush, prodded by congressional leaders to do more for the new Polish government, announced Thursday he will double

is separate from a $119 million package of economic assistance to Poland previously announced by the White House.

Senate Minority Leader Bob Dole, R-Kan., who visited Poland last month with his wife, Transportation Secretary Elizabeth

Liston B. Monsanto, Sr.

January 28, 1985

Mr. Kenneth C. Hansen
Chief, D.A.R. Branch
V.I. Bureau of Internal Revenue
St. Thomas, V.I. 00801

Dear Mr. Hansen:

Although she didn't leave any distinguishing marks on November 20, 1984, Revenue Officer Cheryl McMillan's overt hostility towards Director Anthony P. Olive and the subsequent profane discussion in which you participated, caused her to leave an indelible mark in the Virgin Islands Bureau of Internal Revenue.

So influential was she on November 20, 1984, that in COf where she is presently assigned, accounts requiring her immediate attention and the securing of Waivers - as shown on Form VI 2-T107 for the period ending September 30, 1984, are transferred (in buckpassing fashion and with your approval) to other Revenue Officers in the Delinquent Accounts and Returns Branch. (See delinquent accounts of Caleb Whims and Michael and Susan Zwick, which you attempted to transfer to me on January 24, 1984.)

It is axiomatic for accounts coming from COf to be collated and assigned to Revenue Officers based on their training and experience. One cannot honestly expect Junior Revenue Officers (especially recruits) to adequately handle the same technical accounts as a higher level Revenue Officer. Furthermore, to have any Revenue Officer operate as chief defacto and overtly engineer transfers from COf (as is presumably the case in our Branch) is a most serious matter.

In the absence of guidelines, it is heavily suggested that we find ways and means of putting our talents or specialized knowledge to good use. Calendar Year 1985 (fifteen (15) years away from the Year 2000) appears to be the appropriate time to clear out clutter and proceed with our primary objective of voluntary compliance.

Because of the fact that there are thousands of taxpayers indebted to the Virgin Islands Government against whom enforcement action is long overdue, I will refrain from sending copies of this letter to the press. A word to the wise is sufficient however: You cannot do anymore than the system allows. Furthermore, by now you should recognize that you will get more support if you put first things first.

Sincerely,

Liston B. Monsanto
Internal Revenue Officer

cc: Anthony P. Olive, Director

Vashti M. Gumbs, Shopsteward

280

GOVERNMENT OF
THE VIRGIN ISLANDS OF THE UNITED STATES

—————◊—————

VIRGIN ISLANDS
BUREAU OF INTERNAL REVENUE
P. O. Box 3186
Charlotte Amalie, St. Thomas, U.S.V.I. 00801

June 24, 1986

MEMORANDUM

TO   : Mr. Anthony P. Olive, Director

FROM   : Mr. Edward E. Thomas
             Reviewer-Classifier

This memorandum has been long in coming, but yesterday's actions brought it to a head.

I was attempting to advise an elderly, soft-spoken taxpayer on the telephone about 4:00 p.m. when the noise emanating from the general secretarial stations of the DAR Branch prohibited same. I placed the caller on "hold" and asked for some quiet from those persons gathered there. The situation was worst than the proverbial "market square."

The problem here stems from the fact that almost daily an employee in the DAR Branch leaves her station up front and sets up shop for hours at the Secretarial stations. This employee should remain in her assigned station and make telephone contacts 8 hours a day attempting to have persons pay their outstanding obligations to the Government.

One should not criticize unless he is able to make constructive suggestions and therefore I am proposing the following:

(1) Ensuring that employees work at their assigned stations at all times. Some persons like to state that we are a "mirror image" of the Internal Revenue Service. Well, you know that in the Service Centers and National Offices persons cannot wander from station to station without proper authorization. This is done for security reasons-securing the confidentiality of tax return information.

(2) Immediate rearrangement of the office set-up so that the audit and collection branches be moved to the front of the building. This would enable the DAR Supervisor to completely supervise his entire office and at the same time have easy access for the public to the Agents and Officers.

There was without a doubt a need for a sweeping overhaul of the Bureau of Internal Revenue. Farrelly and company, like all the other governors and their retinue were fully aware of what was going on, but again, who would kill the goose that was laying golden eggs for a few.

Liston B. Monsanto, Sr.

Hurricane Hugo had interrupted communications between the EEOC and me and consequently I was forced to direct my attention to the Virgin Islands legislature. I didn't want to give anybody a reason for saying I did not know what was going on in the Bureau of Internal Revenue or had I known what was going on I would have investigated. On October 6, 1989, I wrote to the Honorable Allen Paul Shatkin (Chairman on Government's Operation Committee). I said:

Received
APS 10/6/89

October 6, 1989   2:20 p.m.

Honorable Allan Paul Shatkin
Senator - 18th Legislature
Chairman - Committee on Government's Operation
Charlotte Amalie
St. Thomas, Virgin Islands 00801

Dear Senator Shatkin:

A spirit of disorder-contempt for law, order and authority (as evidenced by threats from supervisors against lower echelon employees, gun-toting employees, charges of sexual harassment, embezzlement, and rumors of pay-offs and kickbacks) has broken loose in the Virgin Islands Bureau of Internal Revenue over the past several years, and Mr. Anthony P. Olive (our Director)-his gumption notwithstanding, seems unable to handle the problem tactfully.

On October 4, 1989, in recommending to the Governor that Mr. Claude J. Maduro be dismissed from duty and in agreeing with my version of things(see paragraph one), Mr. Olive issued a proclamation which announced in part that Mr. Maduro's (who has now become the villain) disruptive behavior had caused stress, fear and anxiety among the employees in the Bureau.

He went on to repeat some of the same charges that he had previously trumped up on September 15, 1989, when he suspended Mr. Maduro for a two-week period and further asked the Governor to outlaw, ban, or otherwise restrict Mr. Maduro from working in the Virgin Islands Bureau of Internal Revenue.

The Bureau of Internal Revenue has become a center of trouble and turmoil. The dictum of the employees and Mr. Olive is that somebody is going to get hurt in the workplace.

This being the case, I'm forced to appeal to you and your committee asking that you take a dispassionate look into what has become a sordid mess in this income-producing activity of the Virgin Islands Government.

Sincerely,

Liston B. Monsanto
Internal Revenue Officer

c.c.   Sen. Williams
        Sen. Tutein
        Sen. Berry
        Sen. Puritz
        Sen. Lawaetz

While Senator Shatkin was contemplating a decision to respond to my letter, in the interim (November 27, 1989) I wrote to Ferdinand once again in his acting capacity. I said:

November 27, 1989

Mr. Jerome A. Ferdinand
Acting Chief, DAR Branch
V.I. Bureau of Internal Revenue
Christiansted, St. Croix
Virgin Islands 00820

Dear Mr. Ferdinand:

Webster's Collegiate Dictionary defines the professional as one who belongs to one of the learned professions or is in an occupation requiring a high level of training and proficiency: One with sufficient authority or practical experience in an area of knowledge or endeavor to resemble a professional.

"A layman's understanding of the professional is exemplified through criteria giving status to employees in teaching, engineering, chemistry, biology, geology, economics, statistics, medicine, psychology, law, accounting and similar vocations (but not limited to those mentioned)." What typifies the professional employee?

  (1) He dislikes administrative and supervisory duties unless
       the supervision is directly connected with his profession.

  (2) He reflects the environment in which he was trained.

  (3) He emphasizes perfection and precision in his daily work;
       he is inclined to argue over minute points.

  (4) He desires professional recognition as a specialist and the
       prestige that accompanies this recognition.

  (5) He works best by himself, but often works well in a team of
       other professionals.

  (6) He respects a fellow professional who is a leader.

The failure of Revenue Officers in the United States Virgin Islands to conform to the technical and ethical standards of their profession has become a disaster for the territory.

Here in the Virgin Islands where the word integrity is defined as doing the right thing when no one is looking, "glorified bill collectors" - cast in their leader's mold, continue to masquerade as professionals while serving as mercenaries under the pseudonym of Internal Revenue Officer. There is no professional polish to their work.

Local Revenue Officers are controlled by elitism and have been demoted to ranked amateurs. The "less than professional" governmental system - with its political influence continues to work its unfortunate effects on the attitude of Virgin Islands Revenue Officers.

Certain supervisors - working with the characteristic of a parvenu continue to assign delinquent accounts (in buck-passing fashion) to Revenue Officers. Needless to say, the Branch's record of doling out TDA's to Revenue Officers is depressing. At the moment, they are being asked to make a convincing debut as a professional in the "less than professional system."

When it comes to emergencies, etc., a state-side Revenue Officer because of his ability, training and other prerequisites can be readily transferred from one state to another or even a territorial possession - save the Virgin Islands. He is inhibited in the Virgin Islands because of an inferior tax system.

An NCO in your career field for example can be transferred to any United States Military Installation where his services are needed without hurting or otherwise being a liability to his new organization. Unites States NCO's are professional soldiers.

With respect to the several reports (Semi Annual report of inventory of TDA's and Investigation, Waiver Determination Report and Large Dollar Tax Case Report) which were due on October 3, 1989, I have decided to forward for your review and consideration certain comments from an audit report which was made for the period October 1, 1968 through September 30, 1969.

      (1) Voluntary compliance from the tax paying public as a whole cannot be obtained unless assurance is given that all taxpayers are required to comply with the tax laws.

      (2) All larger balance deferred accounts be transferred to field Revenue Officers in cases where taxpayers have defaulted in agreements, refused to furnish adequate financial statements or are not filing timely returns and paying their taxes with their returns.

(3) Chronic delinquent cases remain in the hands of Field Revenue Officers until it is definitely determined that these taxpayers file all required returns timely with remittance and pay off their delinquent liabilities as quickly as they are financially able. If the taxpayers refuse to cooperate, immediate enforcement actions should be taken including seizure of assets, bank accounts or businesses. It was agreed that measures must be taken to assure compliance with tax laws by all taxpayers and to assure the general public of evenhanded treatment of taxpayers regardless of their position or wealth.

(4) It was agreed that ULC accountability records should be established and the the Chiefs of the Collection and Processing Branch should attempt to reconcile the differences desclosed by the matching of ULC's and TDA's.

(5) The purpose of the unit ledger card is to maintain an accountable control over taxpayer delinquent accounts. These records are the official record of delinquent taxes. As is the case with any accounting system, subsidiary records should be balanced to the control accounts periodically to assure the accuracy of postings and the validity of the accounts.

A full score has passed since the issuance of the report. And over those twenty (20) years, everything has remained status quo - our submission of various reports notwithstansing.

In order for us to increase productivity and show any meaningful changes in the various reports, arbitrary power must be replaced with skill and strategy, thereby removing all doubts that any one of us in the Delinquent Accounts and Returns Branch has a vested interest in the status quo or is acting for a special interest group.

Sincerely,

Liston B. Monsanto
Internal Revenue Officer

Then I got back to Senator Shatkin who hadn't responded to my letter in nearly two months. My letter was dated November 29, 1989. It said:

Received
11/29/89

November 29, 1989

Honorable Allan Paul Shatkin
Senator-18th Legislature
Chairman-Committee on Government Operations
Charlotte Amalie
St. Thomas, Virgin Islands 00801

Dear Senator Shatkin:

Because I agree with Senator Elmo D. Roebuck that the people have a right to know what's going on in their government, I wrote to you on October 6, 1989 (in your capacity as Chairman of the Committee on Government Operations with copies to the other members) asking you and your committee to take a dispassionate look into the "sordid mess" in the Virgin Islands Bureau of Internal Revenue. Needless to say, my letter has been ignored.

Today as I write, I am seriously toying with the idea of using my retroactive salary check to purchase ads in the San Juan Star, the Washington Post and the New York Times so that whomever may read of the employees plight would respond.

In addition, I find myself entertaining thoughts of placing a sound system on the roof of my car for the purpose of driving throughout the Island in order for the many Taxpayers and Voters to better understand what is happening in their government.

To quote Senator Roebuck in a paraphrase, the Bureau of Internal Revenue is having personnel problems and there are serious abuses of discretionary power on the part of supervisors.

I therefore ask (once again) that you take whatever steps you deem necessary in order to alleviate existing pressures.

Sincerely,

Liston B. Monsanto
Internal Revenue Officer

c.c. Sen. Williams
     Sen. Tutein
     Sen. Berry
     Sen. Puritz
     Sen. Lawaetz
     Sen. Roebuck
     Sen. White
     Sen. Brown
     Sen. Hansen
     Sen. Belardo
     Sen. Redfield

(Note: Every time that I wrote to a member of the Eighteenth Legislature headed by the Honorable Bent Lawaetz, every Senator received a copy of the letter).

On December 6, 1989, I addressed a letter to Senators Elmo D. Roebuck (Chairman – Committee on Labor and Veterans Affairs) and Lorraine Berry (Chairman – Committee on Finance). I started the letter with a passage from Roebuck himself which said: "There are serious problems in the Virgin Islands Bureau of Internal Revenue that threaten our revenue Collection system. Because of internal personnel problems, the recording of government revenues has come to a virtual standstill." That was said on May 28, 1988. I also included a terse statement from the Department of Interior of December 5, 1989 which said: "In the Virgin Islands, $14.3 million in delinquent taxes might not be collected because the Bureau of Internal Revenue could not effectively administer the income tax laws and collect delinquent taxes." Then the letter said:

DEC 06

L. Berry

December 6, 1989 9:40

Honorable Elmo D. Roebuck
Chairman
Committee on Labor & Veterans Affairs

Honorable Lorraine Berry
Chairman
Committee on Finance
Legislature of the Virgin Islands
St. Thomas, Virgin Islands 00801

"There are serious problems in the Virgin
Islands Bureau of Internal Revenue that
threaten our revenue collection system.
Because of internal personnel problems,
the recording of government revenues has
come to a virtual standstill".

-Elmo D. Roebuck 5/28/88

"In the Virgin Islands $14.3 million in
delinquent taxes might not be collected
because the Bureau of Internal Revenue
could not effectively administer the Income tax laws and collect delinquent taxes".

-Dept. of Interior 12/5/89

Dear Sir and Madam:

In view of your control and authority, I have decided to write simultaneously to both of you with copies to your many colleagues (pursuant to instructions received from Senator Allan Paul Shatkin and under the authority of the rules
of the 18th Legislature - specifically sections 515(d) and 518) in order to solicit
the assistance of your committees in delivering the employees of the Virgin Islands
Bureau of Internal Revenue from all the evil therein.

It is no secret that the Virgin Islands Bureau of Internal Revenue has
become an abode of devils. Furthermore, documentary evidence in your possession -
provided by me since October 6, 1989, provides tangible proof that the Bureau of Internal Revenue is an abomination.

In the Bureau of Internal Revenue, the noblest form of leadership comes
not by example, but through nepotism and discrimination. Personally, I have come
to realize that because of its unlimited powers that there is no unanimous hatred
of the Bureau of Internal Revenue in the Virgin Islands Legislature. Yet, it goes
without saying Sir and Madam that if the Bureau continue along its chartered course,
the future collapse we are all trying to deter may be upon us before we know it.

288

Letter to Senators Roebuck & Berry   -2-   December 6, 1989

         I therefore ask that you use the power vested in your offices to
bring an amicable ending to a situation that has become a grim sordid mess.

                              Sincerely,

                              Liston B. Monsanto
                              Internal Revenue Officer
                              V.I. Bureau of Internal Revenue
                              Lockhart Gardens #1-A
                              St. Thomas, V.I. 00802

c.c. All Senators

These people were inherently fooling the people of the Virgin Islands. I had to calibrate my every response. At times I was forced to turn my attention from one person to another in order to convey to them that they had not been forgotten. With this in mind, I wrote a short letter to Olive on December 6, 1989 which said: "Just a reminder to let you know that unlike calendar year 1989, when no one in the Delinquent Accounts and Returns Branch was sent off island for their training, I expect that during calendar year 1990 many of them will be given the opportunity to attend classes on the mainland. Governor Farrelly's long delay in formally reappointing you to your position was based on your unwillingness to train your employees. So let's kick it off in January or February by sending Mr. Louis Willis and the others for training." In going through the extreme test and fighting "City Hall," I had to do a terrific job.

One week following Hurricane Hugo's visit to the Territory I had the distinct advantage of making public the credible evidence in my possession which would show the whole wide world what was going on in the Virgin Islands Government headed by Alexander Farrelly. On September 26, 1989, I hand-delivered to General Manager Ronald Dillman, of the Daily News, several copies of documentary evidence designed to win the Daily News a Pulitzer Prize and to support my contention that all was not well in the Virgin Islands Bureau of Internal Revenue. Dillman was not yet ready to win a Pulitzer Prize, however, and so while making a wry face to show his disgust, he adopted a business as usual mode asking me to leave the documents for his review.

Farrelly, Olive and Thomas had all failed to make the adjustments that were necessary to play the game according to Hoyle. They were furious over the fact that I was making public what was going on, but coped well because of Dillman's games-man-ship. On October 13, 1989, after mustering enough humility to listen to Dillman's lame excuses for not publishing the documents, I handed over to him my Scotia Bank check number 3542, made payable to the Daily News in the amount of $138.08. Dillman was in an awkward position. He didn't have the guts to publish the truth even though I was paying for it voluntarily. One month after I received the cancelled check from the bank of Nova Scotia which had been deposited by the Daily News for services not rendered. They did refund my money, however.

On December 1, 1989, after I had already written to Senators Berry and Roebuck, Senator Shatkin responded to my letter of November 29th as follows:

Liston B. Monsanto, Sr.

ALLAN PAUL SHATKIN
SENATOR

Legislature of the Virgin Islands

Capitol Building, Charlotte Amalie
P. O. Box 477
St. Thomas, Virgin Islands 00801
————————0————————

December 1, 1989

(809) 776-5566
(809) 774-0680
FAX (809) 774-7310

Mr. Liston B. Monsanto, Internal Revenue Officer
Internal Revenue Bureau
Lockharts Garden No. 1A
Charlotte Amalie
St. Thomas, VI 00802

Dear Mr. Monsanto:

I am in receipt of your letter dated November 29, 1989, about the "sordid mess", as you call it, that is the Virgin Islands Internal Revenue Bureau. Permit me to edify you and direct your concerns appropriately.

The Rules of the 18th Legislature, Section 515 (d) states that the Committee on Finance shall "review and investigate as it deems necessary the operations of the Department of Finance, the Bureau of Internal Revenue and the Office of Management and Budget." Note that I am neither the Chairman nor a member of the Committee on Finance.

On the other hand, if the problems you are concerned about at IRB are not structural in nature, do not directly relate to the collection of revenue, but are of the more classic labor-management relations type, the Rules of the 18th Legislature, Section 518 clearly states that matters pertaining to "labor, collective bargaining....training and retraining programs...and all matters pertaining thereto" rest in the jurisdiction of the Committee on Labor and Veterans Affairs. Note that I am neither the Chairman nor a member of this Committee. As you have repeatedly paraphrased Senator Elmo D. Roebuck in your letter, I assume you know that my colleague chairs this Committee and should be able to assist you.

It is my hope that you will secure the help you need from the above recommended sources and will therefore not feel the necessity to invest your hard-earned retroactive salary check, as you indicated you would, in advertisements in off-islands newspapers to highlight your concerns.

With best wishes, I remain

Sincerely yours,

ALLAN PAUL SHATKIN
Chairman
Committee on Government Operations

xc: All Senators

290

On December 7, 1989 I received a copy of a letter sent to Olive by Senator Berry worded as follows:

LORRAINE L. BERRY
MAJORITY LEADER

Chairman
Committee on Finance

Co-Chairman
Commission on Status
and Federal Relations

Legislature of the Virgin Islands

Capitol Building
Charlotte Amalie, St. Thomas, U.S. Virgin Islands 00804
(809) 774-2696 / 774-0880 • Home 774-7767 • Fax: 774-7310

COMMITTEES
Rules
Government Operations
Housing, Parks and Recreation

December 7, 1989

THE HONORABLE ANTHONY OLIVE
Director
Bureau of Internal Revenue
Lockhart Gardens No. 1-A
Charlotte Amalie
St. Thomas, USVI 00801

Dear Director Olive:

I have enclosed herewith a copy of a letter dated December 6, 1989 over the signature of Mr. Liston B. Monsanto, Internal Revenue Officer, Bureau of Internal Revenue in which he alleges (a) that the Bureau has become an abode of devils (sic); (b) that in the Bureau, the noblest form of leadership comes not by example, but through nepotism and discrimination; and (c) that if the Bureau continues along its chartered course, its future collapse may be upon us before we know it.

It is my understanding that the United Steel Workers Union is the collective bargaining agent for the employees of the Bureau of Internal Revenue, that a contract exists between the Union and the Bureau, and that Mr. Monsanto is a member of the Union.

In view of the foregoing, I would appreciate it very much if you would let me know whether Mr. Monsanto's complaints have been processed as grievances under the Union contract.

I would appreciate it very much also, if you would provide me with a general evaluation of Mr. Monsanto's letter and a detailed response to his complaints and/or criticisms.

Your cooperation in this matter will be greatly appreciated.

With every good wish, I remain,

Very truly yours,

Lorraine L. Berry
Majority Leader

LLB/kdw

Enclosure

pc: All Senators
Mr. Liston B. Monsanto
Mr. Cephus N. Rogers

On December 11th (although I knew he was being told my Thomas and the members of his shadow cabinet) I wrote to Farrelly in this manner:

December 11, 1989

Honorable Alexander Farrelly
Governor of the Virgin Islands
Charlotte Amalie
St. Thomas, Virgin Islands 00802

Dear Governor Farrelly:

Just when Moscow (headed by an innovative Mikhail Gorbachev) is allowing democracy to make inroads into Eastern Europe by way of reforms and Civil Rights, here in the United States Virgin Islands the Bureau of Internal Revenue (headed by a malaise Anthony P. Olive and a vindictive Edward E. Thomas) keeps on struggling amid internal dissension.

Lately, the tension in the workplace has been heightened by the after-shocks of (a) The Maduro/Willis disgraceful show of tempers on September 22, 1989 (b) The unbecoming behavior of Mr. Edward E. Thomas (see the enclosed report) and   (c) The recent Jones/St. Juste pas de deux.

In another related matter, Mrs. Diane Robles-Tyrell - violated Mr. Olive's unwritten law which goes: "When in fools paradise, one must hear no evil, see no evil, or speak no evil. Cooperate with the assembled gentry in doing lots of evil herein. The receivables of the Virgin Islands Government will continue to escalate with reckless abandon, while the possibility of layoffs hangs threatenly over the heads of Government Employees not assigned hereto."

She so much provoked Mr. Olive's wrath that he recommended her dismissal at the same time with Mr. Claude J. Maduro.

But while Mr. Maduro (who like Mr. Levi Farrell and Mrs. Tyrell was recommended for dismissal) continues to be paid, both Farrell and Tyrell are being denied salary checks - a classic example of man's inhumanity to man.

The Bureau of Internal Revenue is in disarray! I fully realize that it cannot operate in a vacuum -- without any concern for other policies and programs of our entire Government, but I also realize that something has to be done to put an end to all the hostilities herein.

I'm, therefore, asking for your help.

Sincerely,

Liston B. Monsanto
Internal Revenue Officer

293

CONCISE REPORT ON HEARING BEFORE ATTORNEY NELSON JONES IN CONFERENCE ROOM OF THE DEPARTMENT OF JUSTICE - ST. THOMAS VIRGIN ISLANDS ON MONDAY NOVEMBER 27, 1989.

In attendance was Mr. Liston Monsanto, Sr., together with Mr. Edward Thomas, Sr., against whom Monsanto had filed a criminal complaint charging that Thomas had (on Friday, September 22, 1989) threatened to blow his head off in the presence of eight (8) people among whom were Mr. Anthony Olive, Mr. Ervin Dorsett, Mr. Roy Vanterpool and Mr. Anthony Attidore.

Also in attendance was Mr. Ray Chesterfield (Investigating Officer for the Department of Justice) and Attorney Nelson Jones who served as Hearing Officer and voice of reason.

Inasmuch as Mr. Monsanto refused to have Mr. Thomas brought before a court of law for prosecution and inasmuch as both parties in a spirit of goodwill shook hands as they emerged from the table, this reporter is averse to detailing verbatim, exactly what transpired at the hearing as it relates to testimony.

For his defense Mr. Thomas brought along a cassette and player which had been used in 1986 to record the voice of Liston Monsanto as he spoke about Thomas' profound impact on the taxpaying public, while occupying certain sensitive positions carrying a high degree of latent power.

Mr. Thomas (it turned out) was using the tape (which he claimed had been given to a reporter during the strike of 1986 so that it could be made a part of his news broadcast for that particular day) in an obvious attempt to justify his threats against Monsanto on September 22, 1989.

CONCLUSION AND RECOMMENDATION

As Reviewer/Classifier with the Bureau of Internal Revenue and one who sits in the catbird seat, Mr. Edward Thomas, Sr., went perforce to the hearing to meet face to face with Mr. Liston Monsanto - a lower echelon employee and member of the Bureau's Bargaining Unit, thereby creating a most anomalous situation.

It is to be noted at this time that some employees express dismay privately when speaking about the Bureau's organizational structure, but are very apprehensive when it comes to going public with their complaints and/or criticisms, owing only to their false belief that the disclosure act would have an effect on whatever they say about the many injustices in the Bureau of Internal Revenue. Members of the press - especially the newspaper gentry, are loathe to criticize the Virgin Islands abode of devils, which is affectionately referred to as the Virgin Islands Bureau of Internal Revenue.

This behavior without a doubt, points up the immediacy for the introduction of a system of checks and balances within the Government of the Virgin Islands which would be a specific remedy for the Virgin Islands Bureau of Internal Revenue.

The knowledge that there is no one to check the checker puts the checker in an enviable position, where at times he can make threats against lower echelon employees indicating his intentions of inflicting harm on them without having to worry about being reprimanded or even prosecuted. Furthermore, he could become an extortionist.

Finally, as noted by Kenneth C. Hansen, et al on March 14, 1975: "The responsibility for asserting and waiving penalties should not be unilaterally determined by one person and the present method of selecting returns for audit should be looked into as they both lend themselves to corruption."

For additional information on the matter, please refer to Liston Monsanto, Virgin Islands Bureau of Internal Revenue, Lockhart Gardens #1A, St. Thomas, Virgin Islands 00802.

December 4, 1989

Now I was ready to respond to the copy of Senator Berry's letter which she had sent me. Then I answered Berry's letter saying:

December 12, 1989

Honorable Lorraine Berry
Chairman-Committee on Finance
Legislature of the Virgin Islands
St. Thomas, Virgin Islands 00804

"Do not be afraid to take a stand in what
you believe in, even if it is unpopular,
a man or woman will be judged by the caliber of his enemies as (well as) by his
friends. Do not follow the counsel of the
fearful who seek certainty in an uncertain
world, who see change not as a challenge
but as a threat, and who dream of yesterday rather than tomorrow".

    -- Elmo D. Roebuck

"Here in the Virgin Islands, blaming our
problems on outsiders is a copout, it's
time we face the real culprit: Leaderless
leaders in government".

    -- Marilyn Mackay

Dear Senator Berry:

First of all let me say, that I'm not picking a fight with you, but if
one is forced upon me, I'll be ready willing and able to defend myself.

Over the past several years Mr. Anthony P. Olive (Director of the Bureau
of Internal Revenue) has habitually made the mistake of confusing my methods with
my objectives and using his political theory of "divide and conquer", he continues
to attack the weak while circumventing the strong.

Your letters of December 7, 1989 which were addressed to Mr. Anthony P.
Olive and Mr. Cephus Rogers seem calculated to delay action on the facts supplied
to you by Senator Elmo D. Roebuck and myself.

So -- if only in the interest of expediency, I'd like to suggest that
we start working on the facts while Mr. Olive and Mr. Rogers are busy working on
the allegations. A public hearing may not be a practical option for a week or two
since the holiday season is upon us.

Early in calendar year 1988 you chided Miss Deborah McGregor (former
Commissioner of Health) at a public hearing for hiring members of her family. Lately, you have been chiding and scholding Mr. Bruce N. Hadley (former V.I. District
Director of Customs and Mrs. Janice Jarrett (Acting V.I. District Director of Customs) for the allegations made by Mr. Melvin Williams in his letter to Mrs. Jarrett.

In addition, you have voiced your dissatisfaction with the secrecy provision which is embodied in the V.I. Police Contract as it relates to the Magdalin Jerson case. Your comments follow: "The public has a right to know. Whatever crime they're being accused of should be known to the public. The public pays their salary and has a right also to protect themselves; there may be some cowboys walking around".

The Cowboys are indeed walking around (you may want to ask Mr. Olive to give you an account of what happened between Mr. Claude Maduro and Mr. Louis Willis on the morning of September 22, 1989) in the Virgin Islands Bureau of Internal Revenue, and unless and until present trends are dramatically reversed, we will continue to have serious problems in the Virgin Islands Bureau of Internal Revenue.

"It is error only; and not truth that shrinks from inquiry".

Sincerely,

Liston B. Monsanto
Internal Revenue Officer

c.c. All Senators

In response, Senator Berry wrote on December 12th: "I have the honor to return herewith, without comment, your letter dated December 12, 1989. With every good wish, I remain, Sincerely, Lorraine L. Berry – Majority Leader." Draw your own conclusions.

Olive's turn came again when I wrote to him on December 14, 1989. I said:

December 14, 1989

Mr. Anthony P. Olive
Director
V.I. Bureau of Internal Revenue
St. Thomas, Virgin Islands 00802

Dear Mr. Olive:

It's like a phantasmagoria! When will it end?

At a time when the world is getting ready to usher in Calendar Year 1990 and at a time when many decent people are contemplating what resolutions can be made as to future actions, you have – through the usage of your law-breaking ways (and with the arrogant manners of a Dictator), issued an aggressive memorandum dated December 11, 1989, ordering all employees to use authorized government vehicles only.

No thought was given to our existing Contract or the Executive Order under which the employees are now operating their vehicles. Your memorandum Mr. Olive, sadly to say is an exercise in utterly bad taste.

On August 18, 1989, I addressed a letter to Mr. Jerome A. Ferdinand (Acting Chief, Delinquent Accounts and Returns Branch) and Mr. Louis M. Willis (Acting Assistant Chief, Delinquent Accounts and Returns Branch) wherein I spoke about their pseudo job titles and even hinted that the Virgin Islands Bureau of Internal Revenue had become the express image of a reperatory theater.

As I write – aware that early farces were used to fill interludes between acts in theaters, and as I reflect on what was said in the foregoing paragraph, I can only conclude that Mr. Jerome A. Ferdinand has finally insinuated himself into your favor. Existing conditions being what they are, however, (the same conditions that chased Mr. John Ferrant, and Mr. Roy Malone and the same conditions that may have led to Mr. Kenneth Hansen's and Mr. Robert Woods' death) forces me to ask: What can Mr. Ferdinand do now that he could not do before in his acting capacity?

In order to promote harmony in the Virgin Islands Bureau of Internal Revenue, we must do away with most of our past practices. Mutual respect between management and labor is urgently needed and periodic meetings now discouraged must be encouraged.

Sincerely,

Liston Monsanto
Shop Steward

cc: Mr. Jerome A. Ferdinand
         Chief, DAR Branch

299

Then it was Ferdinand's turn. December 18, 1989, I wrote to him in this manner:

December 18, 1989

Mr. Jerome A. Ferdinand
Chief, DAR Branch
V.I. Bureau of Internal Revenue
#7B Estate Diamond
Christiansted, St. Croix, V.I.   00823

Dear Mr. Ferdinand:

Because I know the truth of our problems far better than anyone else in our organization, and because I know that my astringent letters continue to bring fear to the lawless, I wrote to Mr. Anthony P. Olive on December 6, 1989, reminding him to do exactly what you said he'd consented to do, about the Revenue Officers training program in your meeting of December 15, 1989.

Now, just as parents are solicitous for their children's progress, so too am I solicitous for the progress of my Union Brothers and Sisters. People in management become exasperated owing to my willingness to help a fallen brother or sister. They seem to forget that Anthony P. Olive, et al were placed in their current position only because Liston Monsanto had committed altruistic suicide.

As a matter of fact, I was of the opinion that you (knowing my role in the reperatory theater) had called the meeting to heap praises on me for the important part that I had played in the various promotions. That was not the case however.

On December 11, 1989, Mr. Olive in practicing a little extracurricular czarism, was all set to use you as his procurator. His notion — I believe, was predicated on the belief that you were a person who cared little about contracts, guidelines, methods of government or even the paramours with whom we must work on a daily basis. Since these lovers are kissing and telling, I feel certain that you know them.

When I told him on December 14, 1989 (see the copy of my letter which is now in your possession) that as a Director with a high degree of plenary power he lacked the authority to unilaterally change our Contract, he fed you to the wolves by immediately refusing to introduce you to your subordinates as Chief, Delinquent Accounts and Returns Branch in our December 15th meeting.

He also forced you to change your agenda without even notifying Brother Louis Willis, who incidentally, had thought that he was being promoted when you derisively said. "First shall be last and last shall be first."

Letter   -2-   12/18/89

Mr. Jerome A. Ferdinand

Unaware of what was going on, Brother Willis almost blew the whole thing by forcing you to say something about a jeep. You could not elaborate on Mr. Olive's memorandum which called for us to use government cars only in the performance of our duties, because earlier in the morning you had discovered (via my letter) that Mr. Olive was once again attempting to violate our Contract.

Your spurious relationship with certain miscreants coupled with your attempts to gain the favor of certain incompetents resulted in your becoming disoriented during the meeting as you completely forgot that you were on the side of management. Fraternizing can do that for you.

Finally, it is beyond my imagination to understand how you could be such an about face from a proud professional career soldier to a civilian life that borders on that of a soldier of fortune.

                                      Sincerely,

                                      Liston Monsanto
                                      Shop Steward

cc: Mr. Anthony P. Olive
      Director

      Mr. Louis M. Willis
      Acting Asst. Chief, DAR Br.

      Daily News.

Then it was back to Senator Roebuck. In a letter dated December 27, 1989 I wrote:

RECEIVED
DEC 27, 1989
Sharon Turnbull

RECEIVED DEC 27 1989

December 27, 1989

Honorable Elmo D. Roebuck
Chairman-Committee on Labor & Veterans Affairs
Legislature of the Virgin Islands
St. Thomas, Virgin Islands 00801

"Do what is right for it will gratify
some people and astonish the rest."

—Mark Twain

Dear Senator Roebuck:

In the aftermath of Hurricane Hugo (which prior to today produced loud
cries from several quarters on St. Croix for local government and showy displays
by Senator Lorraine Berry on St. Thomas), you and your senatorial colleagues have
by your silence, refused to dedicate yourselves to those who voted for you and the
people whom you represent.

Your silence has ben such, that it has exasperated the silent majority
in the Virgin Islands Bureau of Internal Revenue to the point, where they feel
contempt for a coward.

While many people in the Virgin Islands are of the belief that security
and safety in numbers take precedence over lawfulness, your silent refusal to do
what is right tells me that you are of the belief that strategy is more important
than numbers when it comes to attacking the "serious problems" facing the employees in the Virgin Islands Bureau of Internal Revenue.

A word of caution is therefore in order: Your burning belief that a
hands-off attitude can automatically right the wrongs in the Bureau is nothing
but an illusion of reality.

Surely you and your colleagues must know that problems are never solved
by running away from them. What's more, your silence won't diminish my efforts to
go public-especially now that I've learned about the public's right to know. You
may rest assured Senator, that I will keep my promise.

You may recall that you were the one (sitting in all your pomp and circumstances) who in May of 1988, rightfully reported to Senator Lorraine Berry that
the serious problems in the Bureau of Internal Revenue were threatening our revenue collection system.

As if terrified by the enormity of the problems and using the written
word as a vehicle of communication, an angry Senator Lorraine Berry-in one of
her farcical acts, issued a blunt and tactless reply to me on December 12, 1989.
(See the copy of her letter in your possession).

Her refusal to be held responsible for conducting even a minor investigation into the affairs of the Virgin Islands Bureau of Internal Revenue has giv-
en some employees cause to feel disgust.

Letter - Sen. Elmo D. Roebuck   -2-   December 27, 1989

Because she's scoring dismally with these same employees, and because she was on the brink of defeat in our last elections of 1988, I shouldn't wonder if she loses her seat in November of 1990.

Senate apathy and your discourtesies have challenged my manhood while putting my patience to the extreme test. What started out as a simple request for order in the Bureau of Internal Revenue, has gathered ferocity to the point where talks of a federal takeover of the Bureau could be resurrected.

If we are to avert talks of a federal takeover in the territory, we must put our house in order. Employees now being persecuted by people in positions of authority must be given a feeling of happiness and bodily well-being.

My astringent style of writing should tell you that I'm not desirous of courting your favor. I'm on the verge of retiring from government and would like very much to bow out graciously. The Bureau is in disarray, and as you well know, no one can work in a state of confusion.

In order to give you a bird's eye view into the seriousness of the problems in the Bureau, I have included herewith a recent report which gives an accurate if unflattering description of how supervisors are haranguing employees with threats, etc. The report is not loaded with allegations.

Since my letter of December 6, 1989 (which was addressed to Senator Berry and yourself) relations have worsened in the Bureau. Some positive action has to be taken by our elected officials to minimize existing problems in the workplace. To continue along our chartered course is going to result in even more chaos.

And this is why - especially during this period of peace on earth goodwill to men, we must sit down and reconcile with each other. Finally, I ask you: Wouldn't that be an admirable way to start the new year?

Happy New Year!

Liston B. Monsanto
Internal Revenue Officer

c.c. Senator Lorraine Berry
     All other Senators

<u>CONCISE REPORT ON HEARING BEFORE ATTORNEY
NELSON JONES IN CONFERENCE ROOM OF THE
DEPARTMENT OF JUSTICE - ST. THOMAS VIRGIN
ISLANDS ON MONDAY NOVEMBER 27, 1989.</u>

In attendance was Mr. Liston Monsanto, Sr., together with Mr. Edward
Thomas, Sr., against whom Monsanto had filed a criminal complaint
charging that Thomas had (on Friday, September 22, 1989) threatened
to blow his head off in the presence of eight (8) people among whom
were Mr. Anthony Olive, Mr. Ervin Dorsett, Mr. Roy Vanterpool and
Mr. Anthony Attidore.

Also in attendance was Mr. Ray Chesterfield (Investigating Officer for
the Department of Justice) and Attorney Nelson Jones who served as
Hearing Officer and voice of reason.

- Inasmuch as Mr. Monsanto refused to have Mr. Thomas brought before a
court of law for prosecution and inasmuch as both parties in a spirit
of goodwill shook hands as they emerged from the table, this reporter
is averse to detailing verbatim, exactly what transpired at the hearing
as it relates to testimony.

For his defense Mr. Thomas brought along a cassette and player which
had been used in 1986 to record the voice of Liston Monsanto as he
spoke about Thomas' profound impact on the taxpaying public, while
occupying certain sensitive positions carrying a high degree of latent
power.

Mr. Thomas (it turned out) was using the tape (which he claimed had
been given to a reporter during the strike of 1986 so that it could be
made a part of his news broadcast for that particular day) in an obvious
attempt to justify his threats against Monsanto on September 22, 1989.

<u>CONCLUSION AND RECOMMENDATION</u>

As Reviewer/Classifier with the Bureau of Internal Revenue and one who
sits in the catbird seat, Mr. Edward Thomas, Sr., went perforce to the
hearing to meet face to face with Mr. Liston Monsanto - a lower echelon
employee and member of the Bureau's Bargaining Unit, thereby creating a
most anomalous situation.

-2-

It is to be noted at this time that some employees express dismay privately when speaking about the Bureau's organizational structure, but are very apprehensive when it comes to going public with their complaints and/or criticisms, owing only to their false belief that the disclosure act would have an effect on whatever they say about the many injustices in the Bureau of Internal Revenue. Members of the press - especially the newspaper gentry, are loathe to criticize the Virgin Islands abode of devils, which is affectionately referred to as the Virgin Islands Bureau of Internal Revenue.

This behavior without a doubt, points up the immediacy for the introduction of a system of checks and balances within the Government of the Virgin Islands which would be a specific remedy for the Virgin Islands Bureau of Internal Revenue.

The knowledge that there is no one to check the checker puts the checker in an enviable position, where at times he can make threats against lower echelon employees indicating his intentions of inflicting harm on them without having to worry about being reprimanded or even prosecuted. Furthermore, he could become an extortionist.

Finally, as noted by Kenneth C. Hansen, et al on March 14, 1975: "The responsibility for asserting and waiving penalties should not be unilaterally determined by one person and the present method of selecting returns for audit should be looked into as they both lend themselves to corruption."

For additional information on the matter, please refer to Liston Monsanto, Virgin Islands Bureau of Internal Revenue, Lockhart Gardens #1A, St. Thomas, Virgin Islands 00802.

December 4, 1989

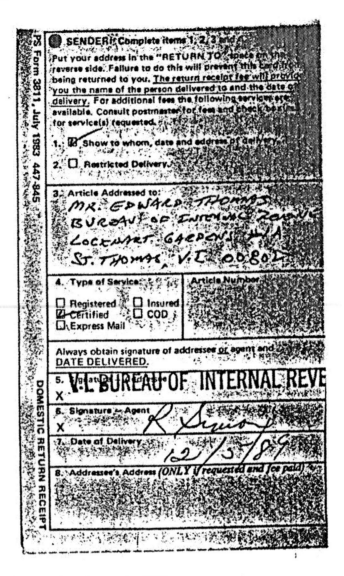

That was the last letter written by me in 1989.

But with the advent of the New Year, knowing that I would write this book, I was back at it once more. I wrote to the Honorable Lorraine L. Berry. I said:

RECEIVED JAN 0 2 1990   *Rec By: Sharon June*
1-2-90
11:30 Am

January 2, 1990

Honorable Lorraine Berry
Chairman-Committee on Finance
Legislature of the Virgin Islands
St. Thomas, Virgin Islands 00801

Dear Senator Berry:

On October 4, 1989, Mr. Anthony P. Olive (in attempting to rid the Virgin Islands Bureau of Internal Revenue of Mr. Claude J. Maduro) wrote the following: "On Friday, September 22, you returned to the Bureau and again your behavior was atrocious. You assaulted three employees and Police were required. You were subsequently arrested and that matter is pending with the Department of Public Safety."

Were it not for the Police blotter of September 22, 1989. I would have (for your edification) expanded on Mr. Olive's charge to include the fact that Mr. Claude Maduro and Mr. Louis Willis (literally armed and dangerous) staged an exhibition by running amok through the workplace, outside into the parking lot, and down through the aisles of the Grand Union Super Market, where frightened shoppers ran wild with fear for their lives.

When looking back at the other Louis Willis/Claude Maduro pas de deux of September 14, 1989, I recall (quite vividly) that I made available to all Senators certain pertinent information which provided you and your committee of finance (from inception to interment) the facts with which to dig a grave. I note with disappointment however, that the employees have yet to see any movement on your part for a safe workplace. In fact, it appears as if you and your colleagues are hiding behind the old adage which goes: "Politics make strange bedfellows."

But inasmuch as you seem to have a nice sense of what is right an proper and inasmuch as your position with respect to apartheid in the Republic of South Africa shows that you understand clearly that justice is justice anywhere on our Planet, I feel certain that you'll find it of the utmost importance to review and investigate the operations of the Virgin Islands Bureau of Internal Revenue pursuant to section 515 (d) of the rules of the 18th Legislature.

Your wild idea of writing to Mr. Olive and Mr. Cephus Rogers (our Union Boss) runs counter to common sense. Olive and Rogers do not need us to tell them about the turmoil in the Bureau. They already know – even before you. Unfortunately however, they like you and the other oppressors have formed an unholy alliance to the detriment of the people they are being paid to serve.

While our elected leaders continue to spout platitudes from glib tongues with their grandstand plays, the employees inside the building which houses the Bureau of Internal Revenue are in a dangerous predicament due only to your cold unwillingness to show mercy to them.

According to the United States Department of Interior, $14.3 million in delinquent taxes might not be collected because the Bureau of Internal Revenue cannot effectively administer the Income Tax Laws and collect taxes.

Why we need to tbe told (everytime) about our ineptness and inefficiencies by Washington, D.C. is beyond my imagination. Are we products of fancy?

The time has come for reconciliation. At the moment, I'm prepared to meet with you and/or any Senator (since they all know what is happening) in order to amicably resolve all our doubts. With the advent of calendar year 1990. let's resolve to do better work.

Happy New Year

Liston B. Monsanto
Internal Revenue, Officer

c.c. Senator Elmo D. Roebuck
     All other Senators

On January 12, 1990, I wrote to the Honorable Bent Lawaetz (President – 18th Legislature) using this lead-in by Franklin D. Roosevelt: "The Country needs bold, persistent experimentation. Take a method and try it; if it fails admit it and try another. But above all, try something." 1989 was a year that took more turns for the worse than for the better.

While our surroundings had remained the same, Olive had made suspensions and terminations of lower echelon employees the signature of a troubled Virgin Islands Bureau of Internal Revenue. As the villain, he was always trying to entangle the lower echelon employees in evil schemes. He stood ready to punish any employee whom he believed had ideas of blocking his path to retention by Farrelly. On January 19, 1990, Olive sent a letter to Lorraine St. Juste advising her that he was recommending to Farrelly that she be terminated from her position as Tax Revenue Clerk. Here's what he wrote: "My recommendation to the Governor is based on: (1) On January 12, 1990, you and Ms. Suzanne Stout were involved in a verbal altercation. You spoke loudly and used obscene language. Your behavior was unbecoming and distracted other employees in the Bureau. (2) This matter was brought to your attention by management at which time you continued to be rude and shouted obscenities of the four letter type. (3) On other occasions you have had continued persistent outbursts and have caused several disturbances with the Bureau. (4) On November 28, 1989, you were issued a warning for disturbing another employee within the Bureau by the Department of Justice. (5) On August 25, 1989, your office conduct was such that it showed complete disrespect for your fellow employees and other office personnel. Be advised that in accordance with Article V, Section II, of the Collective Bargaining Agreement you have ten (10) working days from receipt of this notice to appeal your discharge. Your termination becomes effective ten (10) working days after receipt of termination notice and there is no appeal."

As far as I was concerned, Olive's letter to Miss St. Juste defied common sense. The man was actually in agreement with me. I wrote to him on January 23, 1990 saying:

January 23, 1990

Mr. Anthony P. Olive
Director
V.I. Bureau of Internal Revenue
Charlotte Amalie
St. Thomas, V.I. 00802

Dear Mr. Olive:

You are a perplexing man! Your amazement is without cease. If what you have written about Miss Lorraine St. Juste's deportment (in your letter of recommendation which is dated January 19, 1990) is true, then all of us (Senator Elmo Roebuck, Anthony P. Olive and Liston Monsanto) are now in accord in our concerns over the "serious problems" in the Virgin Islands Bureau of Internal Revenue. I take great comfort knowing that.

Employees assigned to the Bureau of Internal Revenue have become blatant in their disrespect for each other. They have found themselves mired in an organization that's rife with rumors of pay-offs and kick-backs, plus charges of sexual harassment and embezzlement, which incidentally has landed one man in jail.

One does not have to be a soft-on-crime bleeding heart, or even a member of the Bureau's Bargaining Unit to detect the undercurrent of animosity and fustration in the workplace.

But in case anyone has any doubts about what's going on in the Bureau, they should ask for a copy of this letter.

The facts are disheartening:

(1)   November 20, 1984 - Cheryl McMillan (office clerk) chides Anthony P. Olive (Bureau's Director) for carelessness.

(2)   November 25, 1985 - Edward Thomas (Reviewer Classifier) abuses his authority as a member of management's negotiating team and threatens to "touch up" Revenue Officer Liston Monsanto.

(3)   August 1, 1986 - Director Anthony P. Olive tells Revenue Officer Liston Monsanto: "Kiss my ass".

(4)   Later in 1986 Mr. Graciano Petersen is found guilty of embezzlement.

(5)   June 1987 - Director Olive insults Mr. Luis "Tito"
      Morales (President - Local 8249) in a long vehement
      speech.

(6)   November 12, 1987 - Civil No. 1984/37 settled with
      three (3) ladies being awarded $2,000.00 each.
      Case against defendant Roy Vanterpool is dismissed
      with prejudice.

(7)   November 25, 1987 - In his negative reaction to the
      picture of a turkey on the bulletin board, Mr. Olive
      gives a long scolding speech wherein "obscenities of
      the four letter type" are used.

(8)   May 1988 - Mrs. Diane Tryell is suspended by Mr. Olive
      for alledgedy violating the Bureau's Disclosure Law.

(9)   Later in 1988 Mr. Levi Farrell is aquitted in Territo-
      rial Court from charges of embezzlement. To date
      Mr. Olive is still smarting from the Court's decision.

(10) July 28, 1989 - Speaking with anger and acting like an
      erupted volcano, Mr. Olive breaks loose at the office
      of the Chief Negotiator.

(11) September 14, 1989 - Employees Claude Maduro and Louis
      Willis breaks the stillness in the office with a
      noisy quarrel in which objects are thrown.

(12) September 22, 1989 - Part II of Maduro and Willis starts
      in the workplace and ends in Grand Union Super Market.

(13) September 22, 1989 - Mr. Edward Thomas threatens to blow
      Monsanto's head off.

(14) Mr. Olive suspends Ms. Suzanne Stout for conduct unbe-
      coming an employee.

Because of the hellish temperatures in the Virgin Islands Bureau of
Internal Revenue and because we now know that unless and until present
trends are dramatically reversed we will continue to have serious problems, I'm sending copies of this letter to every Senator in the Virgin
Islands Legislature so that they may review the happenings and thereafter fashion a solution in an informed and deliberate way.

Letter   -2-   1/23/90
Mr. Anthony P. Olive

    The Virgin Islands Bureau of Internal Revenue is an absolute dis-
grace.

                                Sincerely,

                                Liston Monsanto
                                Internal Revenue Officer

cc: All Senators
      Eighteenth Legislature

      Miss Lorraine St. Juste

**GOVERNMENT OF
THE VIRGIN ISLANDS OF THE UNITED STATES**

---◆---

**VIRGIN ISLANDS
BUREAU OF INTERNAL REVENUE**

---◆---

**Lockharts Garden No. 1A
Charlotte Amalie, St. Thomas, U.S.V.I. 00802**

January 19, 1990

Ms. Lorraine St. Juste
Tax Revenue Clerk
V.I.Bureau of Internal Revenue
Lockhart Gardens No. 1A
St. Thomas,Virgin Islands 00802

Dear Ms. St. Juste:

By copy of this letter to the Governor of the Virgin Islands, I am recommending that you be terminated from your position as Tax Revenue Clerk in the Virgin Islands Bureau of Internal Revenue, Government of the Virgin Islands.

My recommendation to the Governor is based on:

(1). On January 12, 1990, you and Ms. Suzanne Stout were involved in a verbal altercation. You spoke loudly and used obscene language. Your behavior was unbecoming and distracted other employees in the Bureau.

(2). This matter was brought to your attention by management at which time you continued to be rude and shouted obscenities of the four letter type.

(3). On other occasions you have had continued persistent outbursts and have caused several disturbances within the Bureau.

(4). On November 28, 1989, you were issued a warning for distrubing another employee within the Bureau by the Department of Justice.

(5). On August 25, 1989, your office conduct was such that it showed complete disrespect for your fellow employees and other office personnel.

Be advised that in accordance with Article V, Section 11, of the Collective Bargaining Agreement, you have ten (10) working days from receipt of this notice to appeal your discharge. Your termination becomes effective ten (10) working days after receipt of termination notice and there is no appeal.

Sincerely,

Anthony P. Olive
Director

cc: Honorable Alexander A. Farrelly
     Mrs. Alda Monsanto
     Mr. Luis "Tito" Morales

On February 9, 1990, after Farrelly and the powers that be had ignored everything that I had said to them, I sent a number of documents to the Inspector General's Office in Washington, D.C. for their perusal. Then on February 12th I wrote to the Office of the Inspector General (Department of the Interior) in this manner:

February 12, 1990

Office of the Inspector General
Department of the Interior
18th and C Street N.W.
Washington, D.C. 200240

Gentlemen:

Under the stewardship of Mr. Anthony P. Olive, things have gone awry in the Virgin Islands Bureau of Internal Revenue Service. Documents forwarded to your office on February 9, 1990 serve to corroborate this fact.

Most of the employees of the Bureau (although members of the United Steel Workers of America) are fearsome of danger in the workplace, and even fearful of anything they say or do that they believe would bring on repercussions from Mr. Olive's office.

Through inducements, Union apathy, and a high degree of quid pro quo, they (the employees) have become blind loyalists and toadies of many of the Oppressors in management.

Greedy, mistrustful and power-hungry Politicians (aware of the passive behavior of their constituents) have become politically bold in their methods of operation. Off the record however, they – like the many Sidewalk Analysts in the Virgin Islands, have regarded the Virgin Islands Bureau of Internal Revenue as an inviolable sanctuary.

Mr. Olive is a mendacious person whose games-man-ship is well known to the people in positions of authority. With his trusted aides, the Virgin Islands communication media (my negotiable check dated October 13, 1989, in the amount of $138.08 in payment for an advertisement to be given publicity on October 16, 1989, was returned by the Virgin Islands Daily News after they had refused to publish the ad), and Local Union No. 8249 of the United Steel Workers of America they have all joined in concert against me and the people of the Virgin Islands in an attempt to get their pound of flesh, while the Bureau continues to operate in a less than professional manner.

Due to the absence of an aggressive collection program and mired in a governmental system that demands mediocrity, the Virgin Islands Bureau of Internal Revenue finds itself in yet another fiscal crisis. Governmental receivables continue to escalate, while the Bureau – through its Delinquent Accounts and Returns Branch, heads down the primrose path to disaster.

Liens on file at the Office of the Recorder of Deeds accurately tell a Taxpayer conducting a records search that the Bureau of Internal Revenue is unable to make inroads into the large quantity of Taxpayer Delinquent Accounts.

Incidentally, of prime importance is the fact that the Virgin Islands Bureau of Internal Revenue like the local Departments of Health, Education, and Welfare falls directly under the kindly patronage and guidance of the Governor's Office. And because it is the income-producing arm of the Virgin Islands Government, the Bureau can ill-afford to operate in a laissez-faire manner.

The time has come for the employees of the Bureau who were trained by the United States Internal Revenue Service to reflect the environment in which they were trained. Enforcement action must be taken in order to reduce the high amounts of receivables.

Finally, since it appears as if I'm alone against all in this most sensitive area of the Virgin Islands with no one to turn to here in the Territory, I respectfully request that you consider this letter an impassioned plea for the intervention of your office into what has become a most disgusting situation in the Virgin Islands Bureau of Internal Revenue.

Kindly accede to my request.

Sincerely,

Liston B. Monsanto
Internal Revenue Officer
P.O. Box 2763
St. Thomas, Virgin Islands 00803

What the Farrelly Administration was doing was beneath contempt. My letters spoke volumes and Farrelly himself was in possession of a great number of them. As a Governor seeing and smelling smoke, he knew there was a fire, but guess what, he never invited me for any discussion on the matter. He knew I was right. What was he going to say to me. One thing appeared certain. Were it not for the Third Circuit Court which is geographically removed from the Virgin Islands, there would be no way that I would be exonerated from the charges which were trumped up against me by Leroy A. Quinn and Juan Luis.

Anyway, I had to continue with my mission. On March 20, 1990 I wrote to Olive as follows:

March 20, 1990

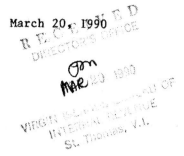

Mr. Anthony P. Olive
Director-V.I. Bureau of Internal Revenue
Lockharts Gardens #1-A
St. Thomas, Virgin Islands 00801

Dear Mr. Olive:

Over the past several years training has been a topic of much discussion and a matter of so much discontent that it has given most of our employees cause for complaining.

You may recall and as a matter of fact, the record shows that in 1986 there was a job action in the Virgin Islands Bureau of Internal Revenue to protest working conditions with the emphasis on training.

Governor Alexander Farrelly in a published report appearing in the Daily News of December 10, 1987 made his feelings known by voicing his displeasure with your attitude towards training.

Then frustrated and somewhat humiliated in his acting position, Mr. Louis M. Willis (a babe in the woods) sometime in 1989 made a preliminary sketch of a piece of writing (see the attached) wherein he begged you earnestly as a kindness or favor, to send him to his training program.

Hearing Mr. Willis' cries for help and knowing that the personnel in the Delinquent Accounts and Returns Branch needed to be trained so as to make them more proficient and qualified for their mission, I wrote to you on December 6, 1989 asking (once again) that Mr. Willis and his co-workers be sent to training.

Today as I write, I'm supremely happy to see that as a matured individual that you have made an adjustment of your mental activity in order to meet the unavoidable demands of our environment.

You are now facing the facts as they relate to the training provision of our contract and at the same time being practical rather than imaginative or visionary.

This attitude-needless to say, is a source of satisfaction to me and the others whose desire it is to see an improved Bureau of Internal Revenue.

Thanks very much for affording the untrained employees the opportunity to be trained.

Sincerely,

Liston B. Monsanto
Shop Steward

315

Mr. Anthony P. Oline
Director
Virgin Islands Bureau of Internal Revenue
Lockhart Garden #1A
St. Thomas V.I. 00801

On May 10, 1988, I was designated as Acting Assistant Chief of Delinquent Accounts and Returns Branch. Since that commencing commencement date, I have try tried to do the job to my best of my ability permits me to do.

But I have noticed that certain things within the DAR Branch have to be rectify if the DAR Branch will is to be more productive.

In order for me your Acting Assistant Chief to be more productive Mr. Oline, I have to attend Officer School. The schools that I have to attend are Revenue Officer School Phase II, Advance Training Group Manager School and Special Procedure School. I feel by going adding Special Procedure School I will be able to supervise Mrs. Santana and also can carry home that knowledge *to better assist her.*

Mr. Oline, I see these schools as an asset to my career as I feel I can be an integal or effictive effective Manager. The bottom line is that I need trainning to proform my job and I need trainning school.

Mareover, Our Branch is in need for four additional officers. At this present time, Our active inventory of our St. Thomas units units on the Island of St. Thomas is at

On the morning of March 5, 1990, while walking towards the entrance of the Bureau of Internal Revenue, accompanied by Mario Lima and Alvin Swan, a belligerent Roy Vanterpool approached me with his hand in his pocket speaking in a loud and emotional manner. Via the usage of obscenities, he threatened to put me away. I ignored him completely and continued on to my desk from where I immediately filed a complaint against him for the review of the Territorial Court and the Department of Justice.

At this juncture, I find it of the utmost importance to show you exactly how Local 8249 operated in providing legal representation to their members. On April 20, 1990, an arbitrator had given me an unfavorable decision which I had to appeal. There was no way given the facts of the case that he could honestly rule the way he did. When we received the decision, Cephus Rogers was heard to say: "Somebody paid him off." While preparing for my appeal, I noticed that records in my possession relating to the hearing were incomplete and so I wrote to Cephus Rogers on May 22, 1990. I said:

Liston B. Monsanto, Sr.

May 22, 1990

Mr. Cephus Rogers
International Representative
United Steelworkers of America
Medical Arts Complex
Charlotte Amalie,
St. Thomas, Virgin Islands 00801

Dear Mr. Rogers:

With time running out on me, I have decided to retain the services of an Attorney for the purpose of appealing my unfavorable decision which was received by you from Mr. Marc Weisenfield (Arbitrator) on April 20, 1990.

In order for me to be properly represented however, my Attorney needs to know what was submitted by the Virgin Islands Bureau of Internal Revenue that formed the basis for Mr. Weisenfield's decision.

In view of the foregoing, I hereby request that you furnish me immediately with a copy of the Bureau's brief for my Attorney's perusal.

As a member of the United Steelworkers of America in good standing, I'm relying on the Union to pay my Attorney fees.

Your prompt attention to this matter is greatly appreciated.

Sincerely,

Liston B. Monsanto
Chief Shop Steward

c.c. Mr. Luis "Tito" Morales

318

Rogers did not respond forcing me to address him again on August 1, 1990. I said:

Received 8/1/90
MaB

August 1, 1990

Mr. Cephus Rogers
International Representative
United Steelworkers of America
Medical Arts Complex
St. Thomas, Virgin Islands 00801

Dear Mr. Rogers:

As a member of USWA in good standing, and as a Chief Shop Steward who continues to suffer vicariously for the members of our Bargaining Unit in the VIrgin Islands Bureau of Internal Revenue, I wrote to you on May 22, 1990, apprising you of the fact that I had retained an Attorney for the purpose of appealing my unfavorable decision of April 20, 1990.

Working against time, I also noted my expectations and reliance on USWA to pay my Attorney fees.

Your silence on the matter and the fact that prior to my May 22nd letter I had written to you (upon your request) outlining the particular areas where I believed the Arbitrator had erred in making his decision indicates Union approval.

I am therefore attaching hereto a photo-copy of my check number 3586 which is dated May 24, 1990 and served as my deposit towards my Attorney fees.

Kindly take the necessary steps to see that I'm reimbursed.

Sincerely,

Liston B. Monsanto
Chief Shop Steward
Bureau Internal Revenue

c.c. Mr. Luis "Tito" Morales

Liston B. Monsanto, Sr.

As you can readily see, based on the contents of my letters to Rogers, I had retained the services of an attorney expecting the Union to satisfy the attorney fees. Again, there was no response from Rogers. I wrote to him once more on August 27, 1990 saying:

August 27, 1990

Mr. Cephus Rogers ,
International Representative
United Steelworkers of America
Medical Arts Complex
St. Thomas, Virgin Islands 00801

Dear Mr. Rogers:

Because of your impending retirement as International Representative of the United Steelworkers of America, and because of my past unhappy experiences with the Union and the Virgin Islands Government, I'm forced to write to you hoping that you'd do whatever is necessary in providing payment of my Attorney fees.

The canard that the Union's District Director is reviewing the matter must be replaced by the following facts:

1. Your urgings that I make available to you (on a timely basis) the particular areas of the decision in dispute.

2. I (as a member of USWA) am without the wherewithal to pay for my defense.

3. I am a member in good standing.

Please contact Mr. Archie Jennings (my Attorney) for the purpose of making the arrangements for payment.

The reimbursement of my $800.00 payment (as shown on my check number 3586 of May 24, 1990) should be mailed to me through P.O. Box 2763, St. Thomas, U.S. Virgin Islands 00803.

Sincerely,

Liston B. Monsanto
Chief Shop Steward
Bureau-Internal Revenue

c.c. Mr. Luis "Tito" Morales

Cephus Rogers was acting more shy then he really was. He forced me into writing Thermon Phillips in Birmingham, Alabama on September 4, 1990. I said:

September 4, 1990

Mr. Thurman Phillips
Director-District 36
United Steelworkers of America
1825 Morris Avenue, Suite B
Birmingham, Alabama 35203

Dear Mr. Phillips:

Aware of the fact that Brother Cephus Rogers' impending retirement has hampered his ability to effectively communicate with me, I'm forced through this letter to ask for a helping hand.

Sincere as he might be, Brother Rogers' verbal promises have not been enough and has prompted me to forward to you my record of recent events as they relate to the payment of my Attorney fees.

As a practical person and member of USWA in good standing, I'm wary of becoming financially entangled with my friends or a lending institution for the purpose of footing the bill.

So in the character of a Unionist - sworn to protect and promote the interest of the United Steelworkers of America, I respectfully request that you give a little more thought to protecting and promoting our members interest, while providing for our security.

You may feel free to contact Mr. Archie Jennings (my Attorney) at (809)776-1577 in order to better understand what's taking place.

Sincerely,

Liston B. Monsanto
Chief Shop Steward
Bureau of Internal Revenue
St. Thomas, Virgin Islands 00801

The Union had proven that their only reason for being in the Virgin Islands was money. They knew full well that they could not help people who didn't want to help themselves.

On September 21, 1990, Frederick T. Kukendall, III, out of Alabama, addressed a letter to me which said:

LAW OFFICES

COOPER, MITCH, CRAWFORD, KUYKENDALL & WHATLEY

JEROME A. COOPER
WILLIAM E. MITCH
THOMAS N. CRAWFORD, JR.
FREDERICK T. KUYKENDALL, III
JOE R. WHATLEY, JR.
FRANKLIN G. SHULER, JR.*
GLEN MARSHALL CONNOR
PATRICIA GUTHRIE FRALEY
JAY SMITH
CANDIS A. McGOWAN
ANDREW C. ALLEN+
WILLIAM Z. CULLEN

SUITE 201-409 NORTH 21ST STREET
BIRMINGHAM, ALABAMA 35203
——
(205) 328-9576
FAX (205) 328-9669

September 21, 1990

*ALSO ADMITTED IN FLORIDA
AND SOUTH CAROLINA
+ALSO ADMITTED IN MISSISSIPPI

Mr. Liston B. Monsanto
P. O. Box 2763
St. Thomas, U. S. Virgin Islands 00803

Re: September 4, 1990 Correspondence

Dear Mr. Monsanto:

I have been asked to respond to your letter to Director Phillips dated September 4, 1990.

As you have been informed, the United Steelworkers of America is not in a position to offer you financial assistance in the handling of an appeal of Arbitrator Weisenfeld's decision in your case. I trust you will recall our telephone conversation wherein I informed you of this. My recollection is that this telephone conversation was initiated from Cephus Rogers' office and was prompted after Mr. Rogers had informed you that the Union was not in a position to take any additional action on your behalf with regard to the arbitration, and further, would not offer you assistance in defraying any legal expense and/or costs associated with your initiating such action on your own behalf.

Moreover, pursuant to your direction, I wrote your counsel, Mr. Jennings, a letter which made clear that, among other things, the Union was not in a position to participate in any appeal of the subject arbitration award.

Very truly yours,

Frederick T. Kuykendall, III

FTK/mtl

I then addressed a letter to Thermon Phillips on September 28, 1990 using a paragraph from one of his letters as my lead-in.

Liston B. Monsanto, Sr.

Then I wrote:

September 28, 1990

Mr. Thermon Phillips
Director-District 36
United Steelworkers of America
1825 Morris Avenue, Suite B
Birmingham, Alabama 35203

> "It is not true that this Union does not
> furnish legal assistance to our members
> where necessary. As a matter of fact,
> thousands of dollars have been spent for
> legal representation in the Virgin Islands
> area, representing claims where we thought
> it necessary to have legal representation.
> We do not as a matter of policy provide an
> Attorney to handle grievances and arbitra-
> tion cases;that is the function of the lo-
> cal union and the staff representative as-
> signed to each local union".
>   —Thermon Phillips

Dear Mr. Phillips:

Mr. Frederick T. Kuykendall's letter of September 21, 1990 is not responsive to my letter of September 4, 1990; hence I'm forced to repeat my call for reimbursement of my $800.00 plus any additional fees that may accrue.

It is clear to me that you did not make available to Mr. Kuykendall the
several documents addressed to Mr. Cephus Rogers which were simultaneously delivered to you with my letter.

It is also crystal clear that Mr. Kuykendall's preconceived notions formed the basis for his conclusions. He did not even consider a compromise.

In any event, as a member of USWA in good standing I'm still looking forward to the payment of my Attorney fees.

Sincerely,

Liston B. Monsanto
Chief Shop Steward
P.O. Box 2763
St. Thomas, Virgin Islands 00803

Then I sent him another letter on October 16, 1990 which said:

October 16, 1990

```
Mr. Thermon Phillips
Director-District 36
United Steelworkers of America
1825 Morris Avenue, Suite B
Birmingham, Alabama  35203

Dear Mr. Phillips:

      This is a final word from Liston Monsanto, the Chief Shop Steward,
who struggled, struggles, and will continue to struggle on behalf of the
United Steelworkers of America for his Union brothers and sisters.

      For the past several years, Liston Monsanto has been USWA's voice
of reason in the Virgin Islands Bureau of Internal Revenue. He has paid, pays,
and will continue to pay his membership dues in order to get the representa-
tion he rightfully deserves.

      Because his conscience does not sanction stealing and/or usurpation,
Monsanto went out of his way (as attested by the enclosed documents) to se-
cure the services of a Lawyer and the subsequent payment of his legal fees.

      It was presumably because of Monsanto's attitude and overall conduct
that he received the approval of the United Steelworkers of America (through
Mr. Cephus Rogers) to retain a Lawyer.

      Noteworthy is the fact that Mr. Rogers - without any form of coer-
cion and in a timely manner, made the records available to Monsanto's Law-
yer in order to assist him with the preparation of his brief.

      At this writing it is important to note, that the Grand Jury (a new
avenue of appeal for the oppressed) has been impanelled in the United States
Virgin Islands, thereby making it possible to investigate the many individu-
als and organizations who heretofore were granted immunization from wrong do-
ing.

      Like a conspicuous billboard, a conspiracy is afoot to ostracize Lis-
ton Monsanto for his part in the United Steelworkers of America. And this fact
together with the foregoing information causes him to ask that you intercede
so as to bring about an amicable settlement of a long-standing problem.

                                             Sincerely,

                                             Liston Monsanto
                                             Chief Shop Steward

c.c. Mr. Richard Davis
     Mr. Homer Wilson
```

I had lost confidence in the Union. Thermon Phillips through his letters was suggesting to me that Tito Morales had the legal acumen to go up against the lawyers in the Attorney General's Office.

And maybe he did, politics being what it is in the Virgin Islands. The Union found doing business in the Virgin Islands profitable. The principle of laissez-faire that's so prevalent in the islands pays handsome dividends to businesses like the unions whose headquarters are located off-island. With a game plan designed to make money, there is no way that the Union or anybody else for that matter is going to be innovative.

On November 9, 1990, I addressed a letter to Homer Wilson (Assistant District Director). I wrote:

November 9, 1990

Mr. Homer Wilson
Assistant District Director USWA
5401 Kirkman Road-Suite 490
Orlando, Florida 32819

Dear Mr. Wilson:

Not knowing that Mr. Thermon Phillips had retired as District Director, I made vain attempts to contact him through the several letters now in your possession.

In his letter of September 21, 1990 (also in your possession) Mr. Frederick T. Kuykendall never - in any way, shape, or form, indicated to me that Mr. Phillips had retired. His refusal to pay my Attorney fees was merely a gesture. In short, Mr. Kuykendall's letter was more symbolic than tangible.

As a Shop Steward parexcellence and one who has endured a high degree of vicarious punishment for the many bewildered employees of the Virgin Islands Bureau of Internal Revenue, I would hate to feel that I've worked in vain for a futile cause.

Because of the foregoing and the several reasons listed in my letters, I respectfully request that you use the power of your office to intercede with a view towards persuading those in whom the authority is vested to fulfill their responsibility to me. As a member of USWA in good standing, my $800.00 reimbursement is long overdue.

Sincerely yours,

Liston B. Monsanto
Chief Shop Steward
P.O. Box 2763
St. Thomas, Virgin Islands 00803

Looking back it is safe to say that the only advantage enjoyed by me as a member of the Union was the position of Shop Steward, a position from where I could freely write to the oppressors without being insubordinate. And incidentally, copies of all the letters in my possession were either stamped received by the addressee or sent certified mail. None of the addressees could honestly say that he was unaware that he had received the letter intended for him.

On December 12, 1990, I again wrote to Homer Wilson. I said:

December 12, 1990

Mr. Homer Wilson
Assistant Director
District 36
5401 Kirkman Road-Suite 490
Orlando, Florida 32819

Dear Mr. Wilson:

Acting upon your word, I have awaited the reimbursement of my $800.00 for over a week, and inasmuch as many hours have elapsed since you gave me the assurance (via telephone on December 4, 1990) that USWA would make reparations for the $800.00 previously paid by me for legal representation, I feel duty-bound (through my membership) to ask that you take immediate follow-up action to insure repayment.

There is no solidarity in our Bargaining Unit which falls under the auspices of Local Union 8249 because the wrongdoers in management working with the assistance of certain representatives of USWA continue to be an elusive enemy. Several aged grievances (some four years and older) have yet to be processed and disposed of.

Mr. Thermon Phillips (former district director) who seems beleaguered with annoyances in his notorious court case failed while in office to take stern measures or swift disciplinary action against the President of Local Union 8249 and the International Representative in the St. Thomas District.

The Levi Farrell case with which you are familiar together with the fact that Mr. Tom Clancy must travel from Pittsburgh, Pennsylvania for the express purpose of negotiating our contract, while our local representatives look on, should give you an indication of the type of representation that we receive from USWA in these United States Virgin Islands.

So once again, I politely ask that you take whatever action you deem necessary in returning my $800.00 payment. Christmas is around the corner.

Merry Christmas

Liston Monsanto
Chief Shop Steward
P.O. Box 2763
St. Thomas, VIrgin Islands 00803

The several letters between the Union and me were put on display in this publication in order to give the reader a bird's eye view of what unionization in the United States Virgin Islands under existing conditions is all about.

You may recall that earlier in this chapter I told you about Roy Vanterpool's stupid threats against me on March 5, 1990. Well, on September 7, 1990, we appeared before Judge Ishmael Meyers of the Territorial Court. Here now for your enlightenment is what happened:

September 10, 1990

Attorney Henry Thomas. Esq.
P.O. Box 6576
Charlotte Amalie
St. Thomas, Virgin Islands 00804

Dear Attorney Thomas:

Enclosed herewith are two (2) copies of the September 7th Conciliatory Hearing before the Honorable Ishmael Meyers (Judge of the Territorial Court).

Kindly forward a copy to your client (Mr. Roy Vanterpool) for his records.

Very truly yours,

Liston B. Monsanto, Sr.
P.O. Box 2763
St. Thomas, Virgin Islands 00803

SYNOPSIS OF CONCILIATORY HEARING OF
SEPTEMBER 7, 1990 BEFORE THE HONOR-
ABLE ISHMAEL MEYERS (JUDGE OF THE
TERRITORIAL COURT OF THE V.I.

The guiding principle in the Virgin Islands Bureau of Internal Revenue which
goes: "When in Fools Paradise one must hear no evil, see no evil, or speak no
evil. Cooperate with the assembled gentry in doing lots of evil herein", has
caused a fratricidal struggle among a number of oppressed employees.

Certain people in management-frustrated in their ambitions to attain rank and
influence and thwarted by the Third Circuit Court of Appeals through opinion
81-1434 from ridding the Virgin Islands Bureau of Internal Revenue of Liston
Monsanto, they are desperately trying to misinform and distort his image.

To date however, Liston Monsanto in his capacity of Nationalist and Altruist
(moving prudently rather than precipitously) continues to provide strong opposition against the Bureau's licentiousness.

Monsanto knows that if one wants peace, he must work for justice. And operating on this thesis, on March 5, 1990, he brought charges of threats and disturbing the peace against Mr. Roy Vanterpool (Chief-Processing Accounts Branch)
who on several occasions (prior to March 5, 1990) had insulted him with churlish replies to his letters of inquiry which were all written in the performance
of his duties.

Acting like a person of low birth and flouting the law, Mr. Vanterpool on January 25, 1990 issued a veiled threat to Monsanto which formed the basis for his
aberrant behavior on the morning of March 5, 1990.

Then, forgetting that justice delayed is justice denied, the Department of Justice working in conjunction with the Territorial Court, reduced Monsanto's
Court case (without any notification to him) to a conciliation which bordered
on a Kangaroo Court, before the honorable Ishmael Meyers (Judge of the Territorial Court) at 3:00 P.M. on September 7, 1990.

Monsanto found himself in an awkward position inasmuch as (and this was told to
the assembled gathering which included the Judge, Mr. Roy Vanterpool, Attorney
Henry Thomas, Attorney Orin Alexis and himself) he knew that the Judge's son
(Ishmael, Jr.), who had been previously employed by the Bureau was also related to Mr. Edward Thomas (the Bureau's Reviewer/Classifier and the same person
who had on September 22, 1989 threatened to blow Monsanto's head off).

Monsanto also knew that Mr. Roy Vanterpool was the brother of Ms. Viola Smith
(the Clerk of the Territorial Court) and yes, Monsanto also knew that Mr. Alvin
Swan - the witness who heard and saw Vanterpool assault him, was the brother of

Territorial Court Judge Ive Swan. Poor Alvin (timid as always) assumed the role of Pontius Pilate and begged to be excused rather than tell the truth.

Using haughty words and exhibiting a superiority complex, Mr. Vanterpool completely forgot that no one can make another feel inferior without their consent. He pleaded guilty when he said that his behavior on the morning of March 5, 1990 against Liston Monsanto (the same man who had sufferred vicariously for him and everybody else under the American flag through opinion 81-1434) was a reaction to an action.

As a conformist, he took exception (with much acrimony in his voice) to the legal channels used by Monsanto in his (Monsanto's) desire to bring order to the Bureau of Internal Revenue.

Mr. Vanterpool bragged about his academic achievements and the fact that he was called upon to supervise most of the employees in the Bureau - most of whom believe (like him) that security and safety in numbers take precedence over lawfulness.

He went on to explain how he had accepted rumor as fact and spoke negatively of Monsanto's many appeals to the Virgin Islands Legislature (Public Officials) completely oblivious of the fact that late in 1989 and early in 1990 Monsanto made these same Senators kowtow before him. Caught in the maze of quid pro quo, etc. they refused to right the wrongs in the Virgin Islands Bureau of Internal Revenue.

He amply demonstrated that he was unfamiliar with the workings of the organization when he sought to rule out maximum utilization of time by asking that he be left alone and that Monsanto communicate with him through a third party.

It never occurred to him that because of his abrasive attitude that the solution to his problem would be a transfer from the Bureau of Internal Revenue.

At the moment Mr. Vanterpool appears to be filled with remorse for any worry he may have caused his allies and relatives. His academic achievements and supervisory responsibilities notwithstanding, he is worried and perplexed by an erudite Liston Monsanto's behavior because what it takes to do what Monsanto has done (pride, honesty, intestinal fortitude, etc.) he hasn't got. Monsanto gave new meaning to the old adage:"Good habits are the mentors that regulate our lives".

CONCLUSION AND RECOMMENDATION

Working in the VIrgin Islands Bureau of Internal Revenue where the noblest form of leadership comes not by example but through nepotism and discrimination makes Mr. Roy Vanterpool feel as if he's above the law. He has completely forgotten that ours is a government of laws and not of men.

He could glamorize the academic achievements of which he boast by displaying a changed attitude towards his co-workers. He must erase from his mind the belief that the Virgin Islands Bureau of Internal Revenueis his personal possession.

With his attributes and his claim of supervising most of the employees in the Bureau of Internal Revenue, He should channel his abilities to bring order rather than cause trouble.

For additional information on the matter, please refer to Liston Monsanto, P.O. Box 2763, St. Thomas, Virgin Islands 00803.

September 10, 1990

Louis "Lolo" Willis, acting like a member of the lowest class of supervisory personnel on the morning of August 30, 1990, sent me a memorandum which stated: "You are hereby requested to prepare the annual taxpayer delinquent account inventory report. The ending balances of taxpayer delinquent accounts should reflect the balances as of September 30, 1990. In addition, the following other reports will be included: (1) Waiver Determination Report, (2) Large Tax Dollar Cases Report ($10,000.00 and over). The format and guidelines for the reports are the same as previous years. Finally, this report is due October 3, 1990." I had to laugh at Willis. He did not understand the reason or reasons that I had been challenging management over the years that he had been with the Bureau. It meant nothing to him that I once held the position of Chief of the Delinquent Accounts and Returns Branch with full authority Virgin Islands wide. My unblemished record meant nothing to him. What's more, it did not occur to him that I was being victimized and that one day he himself could become a victim of the evildoers with whom he had joined forces. Willis just didn't care. All he wanted was a fancy job title and fat pay check.

Anyway, that same afternoon (August 30th) I gave him my response. I said:

August 30, 1990

Mr. Louis M. Willis
Acting Asst. Chief, DAR Branch
V.I. Bureau of Internal Revenue
St. Thomas, V.I. 00802

Dear Mr. Willis:

Your memorandum of today (together with Form 2268 and V.I. Form 2-T107) — like my Performance Report for the period June 17, 1989 to June 17, 1990, has a noisome odor about it and consequently, compels me (morally and legally) to forward to you (for your edification) a copy of my letter of November 27, 1989 to Mr. Jerome Ferdinand — the man whose alter ego you've become.

Mr. Ferdinand and the powers that be in the Virgin Islands Bureau of Internal Revenue — believing that our government is their personal possession, have set me apart from the rest. In short, they have isolated me. Didn't they tell you?

Did they tell you that collection forms which serve as a basis for enforcement action (such as the 433 series) are no longer being ordered for the St. Thomas district inasmuch as their unwritten policies and our past practices have discontinued their use?

Of course you know that periodic reviews of the accounts in a Revenue Officer's inventory have been discarded, thereby leaving the Revenue Officers to wonder if Group Supervisors are earning their salaries.

Mr. Ferdinand who knows what's taking place in the Delinquent Accounts and Returns Branch also knows that he can use you as a shield to protect him. Why then should he bother to right the wrongs?

Until and unless it is explained to me what course has been chartered for the Delinquent Accounts and Returns Branch by the people in whom the authority is vested, I'm forced to return your memorandum with all its attachments.

Sincerely,

Liston Monsanto
Internal Revenue Officer

REC'D BY ADDRESSEE
4:10 P.M.
8/30/90

Willis was in a period of preparation before becoming whatever Olive and Thomas had promised him for being a fifth columnist during our strike of 1986. Nevertheless, if Mr. Willis really thought he was being wise in a keen practical way, he had chosen the wrong person to practice on. He was not shrewd enough. Willis came back at me again on September 6, 1990. He wrote: "This memo is to reinforce my memo dated August 30, 1990 which relates to the preparation and deadline of the annual inventory of taxpayer's delinquent accounts is still in effect along with the other reports previously listed. I resubmit the forms for you to prepare."

I was having fun with Mr. Willis who had no idea of what supervisory responsibility was all about. I wrote to him on September 7, 1990. I said:

September 7, 1990

Mr. Louis M. Willis
Acting Assistant Chief
Delinquent Accounts & Returns Branch
Bureau of Internal Revenue
St. Thomas, Virgin Islands 00801

Dear Mr. Willis:

Rather than ignore the last paragraph of my letter of August 30, 1990, I ask that you review and answer it.

This is no time for flippancy. At a time when the young people of our community are being asked to make positive contributions into our somewhat antiquated system, I ask that you stop allowing yourself to be used by the many law-breakers and opportunistic people with whom you have surrounded yourself.

Your forms are being returned herewith for the simple reason that unlike the hypocrites who pretend to accept you in your acting position, I would like to be informed of the facts before I can possibly believe them.

Finally, why don't you ask Mr. Jerome Ferdinand to do what you are hopelessly trying to do?

Sincerly yours,

Liston B. Monsanto
Internal Revenue Officer

c.c. Mr. Anthony P. Olive

Mr. Jerome Ferdinand

*Rec'd by addressee
2:23 p.m. 9/7/90*

334

Willis ran to Ferdinand for help and Ferdinand, the great soldier of fortune, wrote to me on September 14, 1990 requesting in the last paragraph of his letter that I hand-deliver to Willis the subject reports. Ferdinand wrote:

**GOVERNMENT OF
THE VIRGIN ISLANDS OF THE UNITED STATES**
———o———
**VIRGIN ISLANDS
BUREAU OF INTERNAL REVENUE**
———o———

7B Estate Diamond, Sunny Isles
Christiansted, St. Croix, U.S.V.I. 00820

**TEL: (809) 773-1040
FAX: 809 773-1006**

September 14, 1990

Mr. Liston Monsanto
Internal Revenue Officer
V. I. Bureau of Internal Revenue
Lockhart Gardens #1A
St. Thomas, V.I. 00802

Dear Mr. Monsanto:

Your memorandums of August 30, 1990 and September 7, 1990 addressed to Mr. Louis M. Willis, Acting Assistant Chief, Delinquent Accounts and Returns Branch have been brought to my attention.

My memorandum (attached) dated August 28, 1990 directed Mr. Willis to disseminate to all Revenue Officers in the St. Thomas Office that an Annual Inventory of Taxpayer Delinquent Accounts will be prepared as of September 30, 1990, the ending fiscal year.

In your reply to Mr. Willis's memorandums of August 30,1990 and September 6, 1990 you have refused to comply with his official directive, and have also returned his memorandums.

I would like to remind you that Mr. Willis is my assistant and also your immediate supervisor. It is demonstrable that you have not shown any respect for Mr. Willis's position of authority. This is a very disturbing and unpleasant situation that cannot and will not be condoned.

Therefore, I urge and encourage you to put aside your differences and accept your responsibilities, and act professionally to get the job done for which you are being paid.

I expect you to have the Annual Inventory Reports completed as requested by Mr. Louis M. Willis, Acting Assistant Chief, Delinquent Accounts and Returns Branch.

Liston B. Monsanto, Sr.

Letter to Mr. Liston Monsanto
Page 2
September 14, 1990

Request you hand delivered the reports to Mr. Willis by the deadline
date of October 3, 1990.

Sincerely,

Jerome A. Ferdinand
Chief, Delinquent Accounts
and Returns Branch

Enclosure

cc: Mr. Anthony P. Olive
     Director

     Mr. Graciano Belardo
     Deputy Director

     Mr. Tito Morales
     President, LU 8249

Internal Revenue Service
memorandum

date: August 28, 1990

to: Mr. Louis M. Willis
        Acting Asst. Chief, DAR Branch

from: Mr. Jerome A. Ferdinand
        Chief, DAR Branch

subject: Annual Inventory of Taxpayers Delinquent Accounts

      The annual inventory of TDAs will be prepared by all Revenue Officers as of September 30, 1990.

      In addition, the following other reports will be included:

      Waiver Determination Report

      Large Tax Dollars Cases Report
         ($10,000.00 & over)

      The format and guidelines for the reports are the same as previous reports.

      Request this information be promptly disseminated with your instructions. The annual reports should be submitted to me no later than October 3, 1990.

Enclosures

cc: Mr. Anthony P. Olive
      Director

On September 17, 1990 I answered Ferdinand in this fashion: "Your request of September 14, 1990 is denied. I'm not one to join the weak side. My record which is continuing to grow, shows that I'm a strong person among the many people with whom you've chosen to ally yourself. Why don't you join me in doing what is right? Rising from a low to a high stratum of society among scoff-laws will do neither you nor Mr. Willis any good. The grand jury system is coming to the Virgin Islands. Stop breaking the law." Ferdinand was embarrassed. He had tried unsuccessfully to show Willis how the matter should be handled. He would not stop however.

Liston B. Monsanto, Sr.

On September 19, 1990, he wrote me again. He said:

Internal Revenue Service
memorandum

date: September 19, 1990

to: Mr. Liston Monsanto
Internal Revenue Officer

from: Mr. Jerome A. Ferdinand
Chief, Delinquent Accounts and Returns Branch

subject: Annual Inventory Report
Waiver Determination Report
Large Tax Dollar Cases Report

This is in reference to your memorandum of September 17, 1990, hand delivered by you to me on September 17, 1990.

You have stated your denial to comply with my request as stated in my memorandum of September 14, 1990. I'm hereby reiterating my request that you prepare the above mentioned subject reports by the deadline date of October 3, 1990.

It is your responsibility and duty to prepare the annual reports just like all other Revenue Officers.

I trust that you will give this matter the utmost consideration.

Jerome A. Ferdinand

cc: Mr. Anthony P. Olive
Director

Mr. Graciano Belardo
Deputy Director

Mr. Luis (Tito) Morales
President, LU 8249

338

Poor Ferdinand, he honestly thought (with his moral values reversed) that he could frighten me into doing wrong. I wrote back to him on September 24, 1990 saying:

September 24, 1990

Mr. Jerome A. Ferdinand
Chief, Delinquent Accounts & Returns Branch
V.I. Bureau of Internal Revenue
St. Thomas, Virgin Islands 00801

> "When the dicision was made to fill
> the vacant position of Chief, De-
> linquent Accounts & Returns Branch,
> the Recruiters looked for a person
> too tough to be honest and too weak
> to lead."
> —Liston Monsanto

Dear Mr. Ferdinand:

I have given your request for a frivolous report – which according to you is due on October 3, 1990, much consideration, and needless to say, my position remains as negative today as it was on September 19, 1990.

It has become increasingly apparent over the past several years – my writing of letters notwithstanding, that you have shown little or no faith in my judgement. Because I work in strict compliance with the law, I've become the pre-eminent force in the Virgin Islands Bureau of Internal Revenue. For your information, there are lots of advantages when one operates within the law.

Management's deportment continues to be a constant menace to the development of the Virgin Islands Bureau of Internal Revenue.

Going back to the inception of your employment and even up to now, your office has been repeatedly told that because they do not really care about their work, the Revenue Officers are acting in a perfunctory way.

You were also told that the personnel in the Collection Office Force (COF) were operating like a Sinecure and that the overall COF operation required your immediate attention. (You may want to refer to Mr. Ulrie Vialet's letter of June 27, 1983 for corroboration).

Yet, without any trace of wangling and with Annual Inventory Reports, etc., in your possession, you permitted the statutory period for collection to toll on several accounts in our office.

With rampant rumors of pay-offs and kick-backs in the Virgin Islands now-adays, allowing the statutory period on accounts to toll is a most serious offense. It is one that warrants dismissal from the Unites States Internal Revenue Service.

Because I know that time effaces the memory and because I know that the usage of spite and coercion in carrying out our duties can result in chaos, it may be of interest to note some of my accomplishments following Opinion No. 81-1434 of the Third Circuit Court.

1. I won the respect of the powers that be throughout the Virgin Islands.

2. I prolonged Mr. Anthony P. Olive's stewardship.

3. I stopped the importation of mercenaries to do jobs for which locals are qualified.

4. I forced Mr. Olive to place you illegally in the position of Chief, Delinquent Accounts and Returns Branch where you have no real authority.

5. I forced Mr. Olive to go against his will when he inserted a servile Louis Willis in his acting position.

6. With the exclusion of fakirs I imbued the office force with the ambition to succeed.

7. Through stateliness I was able to subdue the many supervisors who were excercising absolute authority.

8. With rampant anarchy in the Bureau of Internal Revenue, I helped to bring about the impanel-ment of the Grand Jury system making it possible to check the Checkers.

Although I've been sent to Coventry, I've managed to keep abreast of the wrong being perpetrated against the people of the Virgin Islands by the people with whom you have chosen to associate.

As long as you operate within the law my kindness and obligation to duty will actuate me to cooperate.

Under present conditions, however, I'm standing with Voltaire who once said:" I may disagree with what you say but I'd defend to the death your right to say it.

Sincerely,

Liston Monsanto
Internal Revenue Officer

cc: Mr. Anthony P. Olive
Director

Mr. Graciano Belardo
Deputy Director

Mr. Louis M. Willis
Acting Asst. Chief, DAR Br.

Mr. Luis "Tito" Morales
President, LU 8249

Liston B. Monsanto, Sr.

I wasn't finished. I wrote to him again on October 3, 1990 saying:

October 3, 1990

Mr. Jerome A. Ferdinand
Chief, DAR Branch
V.I. Bureau of Internal Revenue
#7-B Estate Diamond
Christiansted, St. Croix, V.I. 00823

Dear Mr. Ferdinand:

Aroused by the Bureau's guiding principle and conscious of the fact that prior to the impanelment of the Grand Jury in the Virgin Islands, that there was no one to check the Checker, certain members of the Bureau's management team (in their desire for vengeance) launched into a violent attack on Liston Monsanto - abusing his civil rights and inspiring false stories about the one and only employee hero, who had suffered vicariously for them and succeeding generations as evidenced by Opinion Number 81-1434 of the Third Circuit Court.

The continued misuse of power by the wrongdoers has been made easy only because they are working in concert with some Officials and a host of Fifth Columnists in the Labor Union.

Also aiding them in their atrocious acts, are the Public Employees Relations Board and a group of opportunistic people, who through their servile dispositions and moral numbness, are forced to yield to the evil Taskmasters whose broad powers border on absolutism.

The Director of the Bureau (Mr. Anthony P. Olive) appears to be in a virtual state of prolonged unconsciousness. His intransigence and aberrance have done nothing to improve conditions in the workplace. In short, his modus operandi transcends disbelief.

Mr. Olive's atrocities in the workplace have caused widespread indignation. Through turmoil and the maze of confusion, my simple requests for employee training and my many letters of admonition (some of which are attached hereto) have fallen on deaf ears.

Adding to my woes is the fact that unlike you, blind loyalty is not my forte.

With tongue in cheek, you have boasted about the fact that Mr. Louis M. Willis is your assistant and my immediate supervisor. If this is so, why don't you use your military experience of 21 years, 8 months, and 4 days to help him? Can't you see he's sophomoric?

Letter
Mr. Jerome A. Ferdinand   -2-   October 3, 1990

Were it not for my efforts (please refer to letters of December 6, 1989, and March 20, 1990) Mr. Willis may never have been sent to his Training Program. Some people never grow with responsibility however, they just puff up.

This has been the hottest summer within my memory, and with the waiver determination dates dwindling on a number of accounts (not to mention those accounts whose statutory period for collection has expired) we must take all steps necessary to avoid their expiration.

With rampant rumors of pay-offs and kick-backs, so far we have been very lucky to be in the United States Virgin Islands where we can flaunt our guilt.

Instead of challenging my manhood and delaying my retirement while receiving a salary check for non-performance, I suggest that you get together with the Chief of the Processing and Accounts Branch for the sole purpose of conducting a matching operation which would update the status of the many payment tracers and notice of adjustments previously forwarded to his Branch. Lest you forget, we are dealing with money.

And now I respectfully ask that you shift your position so that the employees who are ostensibly under your supervision are treated fairly instead of shifting words the way you usually do.

Moreover, I ask that you start doing some work (reflective of your training for which our government paid) so that the lower echelon employees can do the work for which they are being paid. If Management does not work, Labor cannot work.

Sincerely,

Liston B. Monsanto
Internal Revenue Officer

c.c. Mr. Anthony P. Olive
Mr. Louis M. Willis

Rec'd By Assessor
11:59 A.M. 10/3/90

Liston B. Monsanto, Sr.

August 18, 1989

Mr. Jerome A. Ferdinand
<u>Acting Chief Delinquent Accounts & Returns Branch</u>
Mr. Louis M. Willis
<u>Acting Ass't Chief Delinquent Accounts & Returns Branch</u>
Virgin Islands Bureau of Internal Revenue
St. Croix, V.I. 00820 & St. Thomas, V.I. 00801

Gentlemen:

If I didn't know better and had to use the appellations underlined above as a basis, I would come to the sad conclusion that the Virgin Islands Bureau of Internal Revenue had been transformed into one of Hollywood's Repertory Theaters.

Gentlemen, for your information, the verdict came in on March 11, 1982, when a Three-Judge panel (Hunter, VanDusen, and Sloviter) of the Third Circuit Court of Appeals ruled unanimously in favor of Liston B. Monsanto, the people of the Virgin Islands, and the many decent employees of the Bureau of Internal Revenue, who have a nice sense of what is right and proper and who have been for sometime, desirous of putting the protestant ethic to work. Mr. P.T. Barnum had absolutely nothing to do with the decision.

Mr. Leroy A. Quinn (our former Director) was a villain, but admittedly he had some virtues. Rather than ignore completely the Court's decision, and rather than paying strict attention to my letter of July 2, 1982 which stated my position with sweeping clarity, (see attached copy) he completely avoided me and the small minority to whom I referred in paragraph one (1) of the letter.

Seven (7) delinquent accounts totalling $19,629,078.87 have just been given to me - I assume, for my review and consideration.

I have made the decision (following my review) to return the accounts herewith for the reasons previously given to both of you and Mr. Anthony P. Olive. (You may need to review the several letters previously sent you).

The Bureau of Internal Revenue has steadfastly refused to atone for its transgressions. The people in management joined by certain actors and drug store cowboys, continue to flaunt their authority to the detriment of the V.I. Government.

Until and unless the Delinquent Accounts and Returns Branch is given a chartered course to follow, we are going to have a most difficult task closing our accounts.

Sincerely yours,

Liston B. Monsanto
Internal Revenue Office

c.c. Mr. Anthony P. Olive

July 2, 1982

Leroy A. Quinn
Director
Virgin Islands Bureau of Internal Revenue
P.O. Box 3186
St. Thomas, Virgin Islands 00801

Dear Mr. Quinn:

Inasmuch as it has been established that most employees
of the Virgin Islands Bureau of Internal Revenue feel security
and safety in numbers take precedence over lawfullness, to say
that respect for law and authority has been a most powerful
weapon in the arsenal of a small minority assigned to the Delinquent
Accounts and Returns Branch, is an understatement that deserves
the highest degree of publicity.

Armed and blessed with such honor and esteem, plus the
landmark opinion filed on March 11, 1982 (81-1434 Liston Monsanto
versus Leroy A. Quinn) by the United States Court of Appeals
for the Third Circuit, the small minority knows that any unlawful
attempt(s) emanating from management and designed to weaken or to
exhaust its resources will be a nullity. Moreover, we know
that in this government of, for, and by the people, one can
afford-like the legendary Swiss Patriot William Tell, not to
bow-down to any person, place or thing.

Law-abiding employees see no need to circumvent, restrict,
or limit the law as is commonplace in the Bureau of Internal
Revenue. Furthermore, the court's opinion referred to in
paragraph two of this letter, has opened the door for many
aggrieved employees (especially those whose civil rights have
been violated) to assert their rights as classified public
servants. It has also determined for management exactly what
constitutes disruption and libel. In short, the opinion-if

followed, will help to bring much-needed order to the Government's Bureau of Internal Revenue, while simultaneously stopping a take-over by the United States Treasury Department.

Equally important however, and perhaps a major drawback in the Bureau, is the long recognized fact, which deals with our desperate need for a Chief of the Delinquent Account and Returns Branch. The absence of a chief is even more critical at this time than it has ever been. This vacant position without a doubt, continues to be the principal reason for the problems in the Delinquent Accounts and Return Branch.

Furthermore, I feel that the filling of the classified position of Chief Delinquent Accounts and Returns Branch is absolutely essential.

It is a common error for public servants (especially those in position of authority) to think that the Government of the Virgin Islands is their personal possession. They fail to see that the mental picture which they have created serves only to make them responsible for certain acts and omissions, while forever making their office(s) open to criticism before the Government Employees Service Commission and the Courts.

If we sincerely intend to improve conditions in the Virgin Islands Bureau of Internal Revenue, and avert a take-over by the Federal Government, we must demonstrate a changed attitude with a willingness to work closely, harmoniously, and ethically with each other. The flaunting of authority by certain personnel in management and the disruptive influence now exerted by certain lower echelon employees over their peers, must cease and be replaced by mutual respect and admiration for each other.

Incidentally, now that I've returned to work after being vindicated of charges trumped up by you and Mr. Anthony P. Olive (see your libelous letter of March 16, 1982). It is hoped that you'd dispense with personalities, as I look forward to working as diligently as I did in the past, with a view towards projecting

an image that best represents the Virgin Islands Bureau of
Internal Revenue. This, I say unreservedly.

Sincerely,

Liston Monsanto

cc: Governor, Juan Luis
     Lieutenant Governor, Henry A. Millin
     Deputy Director, Anthony P. Olive

Liston B. Monsanto, Sr.

December 6, 1989

Mr. Anthony P. Olive
Director
V.I. Bureau of Internal Revenue
Lockhart Gardens #1A
St. Thomas, V.I. 00802

Dear Mr. Olive:

Just a reminder to let you know that unlike Calendar Year 1989 when no one in the Delinquent Accounts and Returns Branch was sent off island for their training, I expect that during Calendar Year 1990 many of them will be given the opportunity to attend classes on the mainland.

Governor Farrelly's long delay in formally reappointing you to your position was based on your unwillingness to train your employees.

So let's kick it off in January or February by sending Mr. Louis Willis and the others for training.

Sincerely,

Liston B. Monsanto
Shop Stewart

December 18, 1989

Mr. Jerome A. Ferdinand
Chief, DAR Branch
V.I. Bureau of Internal Revenue
#7B Estate Diamond
Christiansted, St. Croix, V.I.   00823

Dear Mr. Ferdinand:

Because I know the truth of our problems far better than anyone else in our organization, and because I know that my astringent letters continue to bring fear to the lawless, I wrote to Mr. Anthony P. Olive on December 6, 1989, reminding him to do exactly what you said he'd consented to do, about the Revenue Officers training program in your meeting of December 15, 1989.

Now, just as parents are solicitous for their children's progress, so too am I solicitous for the progress of my Union Brothers and Sisters. People in management become exasperated owing to my willingness to help a fallen brother or sister. They seem to forget that Anthony P. Olive, et al were placed in their current position only because Liston Monsanto had committed altruistic suicide.

As a matter of fact, I was of the opinion that you (knowing my role in the reperatory theater) had called the meeting to heap praises on me for the important part that I had played in the various promotions. That was not the case however.

On December 11, 1989, Mr. Olive in practicing a little extracurricular czarism, was all set to use you as his procurator. His notion — I believe, was predicated on the belief that you were a person who cared little about contracts, guidelines, methods of government or even the paramours with whom we must work on a daily basis. Since these lovers are kissing and telling, I feel certain that you know them.

When I told him on December 14, 1989 (see the copy of my letter which is now in your possession) that as a Director with a high degree of plenary power he lacked the authority to unilaterally change our Contract, he fed you to the wolves by immediately refusing to introduce you to your subordinates as Chief, Delinquent Accounts and Returns Branch in our December 15th meeting.

He also forced you to change your agenda without even notifying Brother Louis Willis, who incidentally, had thought that he was being promoted when you derisively said. "First shall be last and last shall be first."

Letter   -2-   12/18/89
Mr. Jerome A. Ferdinand

Unaware of what was going on, Brother Willis almost blew the whole thing by forcing you to say something about a jeep. You could not elaborate on Mr. Olive's memorandum which called for us to use government cars only in the performance of our duties, because earlier in the morning you had discovered (via my letter) that Mr. Olive was once again attempting to violate our Contract.

Your spurious relationship with certain miscreants coupled with your attempts to gain the favor of certain incompetents resulted in your becoming disoriented during the meeting as you completely forgot that you were on the side of management. Fraternizing can do that for you.

Finally, it is beyond my imagination to understand how you could be such an about face from a proud professional career soldier to a civilian life that borders on that of a soldier of fortune.

                                   Sincerely,

                                   Liston Monsanto
                                   Shop Steward

cc: Mr. Anthony P. Olive
       Director

       Mr. Louis M. Willis
       Acting Asst. Chief, DAR Br.

       Daily News.

In November of 1990 Farrelly was reelected Governor and prepared himself for four (4) more years of not conforming to the accepted standards and/or guidelines of his administration. Through a congratulatory letter to him on January 18, 1991, I wrote in part: "Happy days are apparently here again! And to say that I'm pleased and gratified over your acceptance of Mr. Anthony P. Olive's resignation as Director of the Virgin Islands Bureau of Internal Revenue is really an understatement. Many thanks. Your recent designation of Mr. Edward Thomas as our Acting Director demonstrates to me that your administration, in keeping with its slogan "the best is yet to come," found it of the utmost importance to install a person familiar with the overall operations of the Bureau and one with whom (I believe) the employees can deal with successfully. Speaking about our Acting Director evokes memories of my fratricidal struggles with Mr. Olive and his retinue. Due to the little affectations and bellicose statements emanating from the mouth of Mr. Thomas while in his capacity of reviewer/classifier, we grappled in combat many times. I told Farrelly in my letter that "now that the hostilities have presumably ended and our long-standing dispute has been settled (shall we say) through peaceful means, I feel that the time has come for Mr. Thomas and his subordinates to join together in singing the refrain from an old song which goes: 'let bygones be bygones forever.' There is much to be done in the Virgin Islands Bureau of Internal Revenue. As a former Chief of the Delinquent Accounts and Returns Branch, all I ask is that you give me a fair chance to make a positive contribution before my retirement. World-wide the Cold War came to an end in an amicable way. Locally however, the inevitable question remains: Why can't we as fun-loving humans living on these tiny islands (where just about everyone is related either by blood or through marriage) normalize relations? Governor, as a long time civil servant and one who has felt and expressed my admiration for you, it behooves me to let you know that the Bureau of Internal Revenue is fraught with morale problems. Due largely to Mr. Olive's lassitude and vindictiveness, Mr. Louis Willis (an Internal Revenue Officer I) has been designated Acting Assistant Chief of the Delinquent Accounts and Returns Branch, where he's ostensibly being called upon to supervise the activities of a number of higher level Revenue Officers. Mr. Willis' designation as acting Assistant Chief is an abuse of discretionary power. It was a very wicked act perpetrated by Mr. Olive and one of the many costly mistakes he made during his tenure of office. As a young Revenue Officer, Mr. Willis is an upstart, who has only an empirical knowledge of the Collection activity. He has yet to make his initial appearance as a field Revenue Officer, moving swiftly from the lowest to the highest level in one fell swoop. Mr. Willis makes stupid and careless mistakes such as the ones he made between September 15th and 22nd, 1989, when he got involved with one of his subordinates whom he ultimately chased (armed to the hilt) into the parking lot and through the aisles of the Grand Union Supermarket. No telling what would have happened if the police had not appeared on the scene. Because I'm an altruistic and sweet tempered person (note my cheerful disposition and vow to use any measure short of violence throughout my civil war with Mr. Olive and his allies) on the verge of retiring from the Virgin Islands Government, I feel extremely bad over the sordid mess created by Anthony Olive's isolationist policies and overall intransigence. The designation of Mr. Willis as Acting Assistant Chief of the Delinquent Accounts and Returns Branch had done violence to my principles, inasmuch as it requires me to work as a subordinate to a Junior Revenue Officer. Today, as I write, the fate of the Bureaus is hanging in the balance. It is fully realized that it cannot operate in a vacuum without any concern for the other policies and programs of our entire government. But because many employees have in the past relied on arbitrary power in making their decisions, some observers are predicting as a certainty that everything will remain status quo in the Virgin Islands Bureau of Internal Revenue. Since every decision will be sifted through the Office of the Director, if Mr. Thomas is not impervious to suggestions and hopes to turn the aura of ignorance which envelops our workplace into a reservoir of understanding, I'd like to suggest that he make a study of the ramifications of our organization with a view towards restoring order into what has become a most complex structure. Finally, by removing Mr. Anthony P. Olive from office, you have delivered the employees from most of the evil in the Virgin Islands Bureau of Internal Revenue. Again, many thanks and Happy New Year."

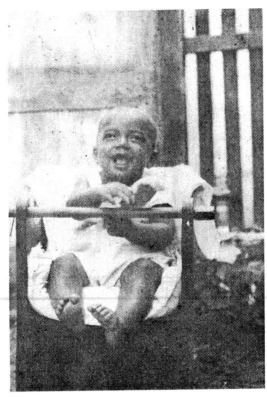

AUTHOR AS BABY

AUTHOR (FAR RIGHT) WITH SIBLINGS

AUTHOR (RIGHT) WITH
BROTHER AT YOUNG AGE

AUTHOR AS AN AIRMAN IN USAF

AUTHOR AS EMPLOYEE OF TAX DIVISION

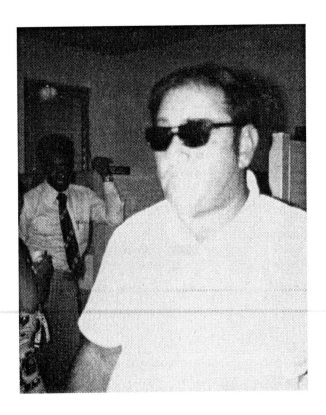

ROBERT "BOBBY" WOODS IN THE FOREGROUND
WITH AUTHOR LISTON MONSANTO

AUTHOR (IN LONG SLEEVES) FLANKED
BY ULRIC BENJAMIN ON HIS RIGHT
AND RUDOLPH FOY ON HIS LEFT.

AUTHOR WITH FELLOW EMPLOYEES MARIO LIMA (FAR RIGHT) AND TERRENCE BRUNN

AUTHOR AND WIFE

AUTHOR PICTURED DINING WITH WIFE TO HIS RIGHT

AUTHOR AND WIFE

AUTHOR WITH WIFE

CHAPTER IV
Edward E. Thomas

Olive was removed from the Virgin Islands Bureau of Internal Revenue and replaced with Edward Thomas, not because of me but because of the need to create an underworld organization. Greedy for wealth as they were, Farrelly needed a confidant, a person he could trust with his secrets and private affairs. The Government of the Virgin Islands, hostile to the law through its disclosure law in the Bureau of Internal Revenue was operating as a secret organization. Olive could not fill the bill as Director in Farrelly's second term owing to his alliance with certain opponents of Farrelly. He had always seen the reality of his relationship with Farrelly and Thomas, but as one indentured to the governmental system, a system he had helped to create through an unholy alliance with Reuben Wheatley, Leroy Quinn and Edward Thomas, he had been fooled into a life of subjugation to falsehoods becoming a masochist only to be used and abused by Farrelly and his shadow cabinet. In the end, his dissolute past had brought suffering to himself and many others. Like his predecessors, however, he didn't say goodbye. Edward Thomas was a mixture of a drug store cowboy (a phony) and megalomaniac with an insatiable appetite for power. With these attributes he became the most celebrated disciple of Farrelly. Thomas knew no limits and had no shame. He took great pleasure in being at variance with the facts, but through this publication he would find out that he couldn't do whatever he wanted whenever he wanted. A coward follower of the political theory of Machiavelli, the treacherous Thomas with treachery always lurking behind his smooth manners consummated his ambition when he became Director of the Virgin Islands Bureau of Internal Revenue. Edward E. Thomas is a person not on my list of favorite people.

True to form, the moment he had assumed the responsibility of Director, with Farrelly's blessings, he incited Willis to write to me on March 8, 1991 saying: "I would like to meet with you in my office on Monday, March 11, 1991 at 10:00 a.m." I had never accepted Willis as acting Assistant Chief of our Branch for the many reasons that I've listed before, plus the others that you'll read about on a later page of this publication. The ink hadn't dried on Willis' memorandum when I answered him on the same day. I said:

357

Liston B. Monsanto, Sr.

March 8, 1991

Mr. Louis Willis
Acting Asst. Chief, DAR Branch
V.I. Bureau of Internal Reveue
St. Thomas, V.I. 00802

Dear Mr. Willis:

Before starting to act like an Iraqi-Terrorist with a scud missile in his hand, and before getting into dichotomies which would create domestic confusion and ultimately resurrect the infamous cases of Liston Monsanto vs Edward Thomas and Liston Monsanto vs Roy Vanterpool, I suggest you take inventory of yourself with a view towards assisting our Acting Director with the fairness of which he spoke before the Rules Committee of the Nineteenth Legislature on March 7, 1991.

Additionally, I ask (if you have not already done so) that you confer with Mr. Edward Thomas to whom I made my feelings known (on January 18, 1991) about the past, present and future conditions, of the Virgin Islands Bureau of Internal Revenue.

For your information, supervisory responsibility is not as simple as you perceive it to be. Sometime last year, an audit by the Interior Department Inspector General's Office disclosed (among other things) that there was an urgent need for experienced people to fill vacancies in crucial technical positions in the Virgin Islands Bureau of Internal Revenue.

If Mr. Anthony P. Olive who was not in sync with his employees and the man to whom you were indentured had a blue ribbon program (i.e. designating the best in the Bureau) a soldier of fortune such as yourself, would never have been placed in your temporary position of Acting Assistant Chief, Delinquent Accounts and Returns Branch.

As your Shop Steward and Union Brother it behooves me to tell you that your memorandum of March 8, 1991, is an exercise in utterly bad taste. Furthermore, it is stupid and morally atrocious. But because you are obviously fond of power and authority, I am not a bit suprised at your loutish behavior.

It would do you well to remember, however, that tolerance must be practiced in order to bring our itinerant and wayward employees into the right relationship with their surroundings.

No lower echelon employee (for example) should be put in charge of a superior officer. (ask Mr. Jerome Ferdinand whose military career spanned over twenty years). Then consider Mr. Edward Thomas reaction (were he a classified employee) if some classified lower echelon employee (e.g. Mr. Ervin Dorsett) was put in charge of him. Lower echelon employees Mr. Willis, cannot charge their superiors with insubordination.

Letter   -2-   2/8/91

Mr. Louis Willis

The tone of this letter is harsh because it was meant to be. Nevertheless, it is worth noting that beneath the harsh exterior of Liston Monsanto is a strong desire (before retiring and provided he's treated fairly) to help not only the bewildered employees, but also those in the various positions of authority within the Bureau of Internal Revenue.

It is my firm belief that management's goal is to transform inexperience into accomplishment, thereby burying any memories of the dark ages which came under the stewardship of Mr. Olive.

As a young man in a hurry, you have shown a very great desire for money. Blinded by avarice, you have failed to see that most of the Revenue Officers whose tenure of service range from fifteen to thrity years are on a much higher level than you.

Neither does it occur to you that if Governor Farrelly was satisfied with Anthony Olive's dismal performance as Director, he would never have removed him from the Virgin Islands Bureau of Internal Revenue. Now that you've gotten the message, I ask that you forget the Olive years. Anthony P. Olive was a scofflaw of the highest sort.

I fully realize that I've been highly critical of you, but admittedly I have tempered my criticisms with reason.

No, I will not be meeting with you on Monday, March 11, 1991.

                                Sincerely,

                                Liston Monsanto
                                Chief Shop Steward

cc: Mr. Edward E. Thomas
      Acting Director

Thomas, who had been challenging my judgment behind the scenes, was forced to come forward in order to show Willis that unlike Olive, he would use his college degree to handle me. He addressed a memorandum to all managers and employees (usurping Farrelly's authority as the appointing authority), which told everybody that he (Edward E. Thomas) had appointed Willis Assistant Chief of the Delinquent Accounts and Returns Branch. Here's what he wrote:

GOVERNMENT OF
THE VIRGIN ISLANDS OF THE UNITED STATES

---o---

VIRGIN ISLANDS
BUREAU OF INTERNAL REVENUE

---o---

Lockharts Garden No. 1A
Charlotte Amalie, St. Thomas, U.S.V.I. 00802

March 11, 1991

<u>MEMORANDUM</u>

TO   : All Managers and Employees

FROM   : Mr. Edward E. Thomas
            Acting Director

RE   : Appointment of Louis M. Willis

Please be advised that Mr. Louis M. Willis is now formally installed as the Assistant Chief of the Delinquent Accounts and Returns Branch for the District of St. Thomas-St. John.

This appointment accomplishes the following:

1. Mr. Willis is no longer a member of the United Steel Workers of America Local 8249 Unit.

2. Mr. Willis is a member of the Management team with all rights and responsibilities as outlined in Article IV of our Collective Bargaining Agreement.

It is anticipated that all other managers will accord Mr. Willis the same courtesies desired. It is expected that all subordinates will comply with all directives issued by Mr. Willis as these directives have the initial authorization from me.

Edward E. Thomas
Acting Director

EET/cef

cc: Mr. Luis A. "Tito" Morales
    President
    Local Union 8249 - USWA

The lingering effects following the Olive years had surfaced. I immediately filed a grievance in order to protect myself against the evil Edward Thomas. He wrote back on March 11, 1991, pretending to aid me in the preparation of my Grievance and reached out to me asking me to deal with Willis and Ferdinand. Here is what he wrote:

GOVERNMENT OF
THE VIRGIN ISLANDS OF THE UNITED STATES

VIRGIN ISLANDS
BUREAU OF INTERNAL REVENUE

Lockharts Garden No. 1A
Charlotte Amalie, St. Thomas, U.S.V.I. 00802

March 11, 1991

MEMORANDUM

TO   : Mr. Liston Monsanto
           Revenue Officer

FROM   : Mr. Edward E. Thomas
           Acting Director

RE   : Your Grievance No. 1-91

      Returned herewith is subject document since it violates the provisions of Article V of our collective bargaining agreement. Section 3 of Article V provides for the steps to be followed before a grievance reaches the office of the Director.

      For your information, I have attached a copy of the pertinent section of our agreement for your review. Further, your immediate supervisor (since 1988) is Mr. Louis M. Willis and the Division Head is Mr. Jerome Ferdinand, Chief of the Branch.

Mr. Edward E. Thomas
Acting Director

EET/cef

cc: Mr. Luis A. "Tito" Morales
    President
    Local Union 8249 - USWA

    Mr. Louis M. Willis, Asst. Chief, DARB
    Mr. Jerome Ferdinand, Chief, DARB

ARTICLE V

GRIEVANCE AND ARBITRATION PROCEDURE

Section 1:

For the purpose of this Agreement, a grievance is defined as a complaint, dispute or controversy between the parties, as to the interpretation, application or compliance with the provisions of this Agreement. The following procedure, including arbitration, may be initiated by either party and shall be the exclusive means of settlement of all grievances arising under this Agreement, except for those involving classification matters which shall be processed pursuant to Title 3, Chapter 25, Sub-Chapter 3, of the Virgin Islands Code.

Section 2:

Reasonable work time spent by the Employee-grievant in the filing, discussion, investigation and processing of a grievance shall be with pay.

Section 3:

Should an employee believe he has a justifiable complaint or request under the terms of this Agreement, the complaint or request shall be handled in the following manner:

A. **Step 1** The employee shall discuss the complaint or request with his immediate supervisor. The employee may elect to have a member of the Grievance Committee present during this discussion should he desire. The supervisor shall, within three (3) workdays of said discussion, advise the employee and, where appropriate, the Grievance Committee member of his decision.

B. **Step 2** If the matter has not been resolved by the employee and his immediate supervisor in Step 1, it must be reduced to writing by the employee or the Union within ten (10) workdays and presented to the Division Head in order to be considered further. A meeting between the Division Head, the grievant and a member of the Grievance Committee shall be held to discuss the grievance

-8-

within five (5) workdays after it has been presented. Within five (5) workdays after this meeting has been held, the Division Head shall advise the grievant and the Chairman of the Grievance Committee, in writing, of his decision.

C. <u>Step 3</u> If the Division Head's decision is not acceptable to the Union, then the Union, within five (5) workdays after receiving the answer in Step 2, shall appeal the decision to the Commissioner in writing. A meeting between the Commissioner, the Representative of the International Union, the grievant and the Chairman of the Grievance Committee shall be held to discuss the grievance within ten (10) workdays after it has been appealed to the Commissioner. It is recognized that to accommodate the work schedule of the Representative of the International Union and the Commissioner, it may be necessary to extend the time limits for this Step 3 meeting. Therefore it is agreed that should it be necessary to extend the time limit of this Step 3 meeting, said time shall not be extended for more than twenty (20) workdays from receipt of the Union's filing at Step 3. Within ten (10) workdays after this meeting has been held, the Commissioner shall advise the Representative of the International Union, the grievant and the Grievance Committee Chairman of his decision in writing. The decision shall contain a brief summary of the proceedings and the statement of the Commissioner's position. In the event of arbitration for the sole reason that the Employer has failed to observe the time limit of this Step 3, the Arbitrator's compensation and expenses shall be borne completely by the Employer; liability for such compensation and expenses shall begin upon execution of this Agreement.

<u>Section 4:</u>
Grievances which allege violations directly affecting a large group of employees may be initiated by the Union at the Step 3 level of the grievance procedure outlined in this Article.

Section 5:

A grievance submitted in writing shall contain a clear and concise statement of the grievance, the issue involved, the relief sought, the date the violation took place, and the specific Article and/or Sections of this Agreement involved.

Section 6:

All grievances shall be presented promptly and in no event later than ten (10) workdays after the employee or employees knew or should have reasonably known of the occurrence or non-occurrence of the incident which gave rise to the grievance.

Section 7:

The time limits set forth in this Article shall be binding on the parties unless extended in writing and the processing of a grievance to arbitration shall not waive the rights of a party to assert before the Arbitrator that the grievance was untimely processed.

If the Union fails to process a grievance within the time limits provided, the grievance shall be considered disposed of on the last answer of the Department. The Union may withdraw a grievance at any step in the procedure by notifying the Department in writing. If the Department fails to process its response to a grievance within the time limits provided, the Union shall have the right of automatic appeal. If the Department initiates the grievance, the role shall be reversed.

Section 8:

In the event a grievance remains unsettled under the foregoing procedures, the Representative of the International Union may, by written notice to the Commissioner within ten (10) workdays of receipt of the latter's decision, appeal the matter to arbitration.

The Arbitrator shall be selected by mutual agreement of the parties. For the purpose of selecting an impartial Arbitrator, the parties shall, within five (5) workdays after the date of written designation of the grievance for arbitration, request from the Public Employees Relations Board a list of names and addresses of local impartial persons. The parties shall then make every effort to agree to one of the local persons on the list as the Arbitrator.

In the event the parties are unable to agree on a local Arbitrator within ten (10) workdays of the exchange of lists, the parties acting jointly shall request the Federal Mediation and Conciliation Service to provide to the parties a panel of seven (7)) arbitrators in accordance with the rules and procedures of the Service.

Each party, commencing with the one seeking arbitration, shall alternately strike one (1) name from the list and the name of the person last appearing on the list shall be designated as the Arbitrator and his appointment shall be binding on both parties.

The Arbitrator's compensation and expenses shall be shared equally by the parties, except as otherwise provided for in this Article.

The Arbitrator shall have no jurisdiction or authority to add to, detract from, or alter in any way the provisions of this Agreement.

The decision of the Arbitrator shall be final and binding on both parties to this Agreement and the grievant. It shall be rendered in writing within thirty (30) days of the last hearing or submission of facts as provided herein.

Section 9:

A grievance not processed to arbitration or a grievance withdrawn from arbitration by the Union, or the grievant, shall be deemed settled on the basis of the written answer submitted by the Department.

Section 10:

All time limits set forth in this Article may be extended by mutual agreement. Whenever used in this Article, the term "working day" means a calendar Monday through Friday, exclusive of holidays.

Section 11:

No employee shall be suspended or discharged except for just cause. In the event an employee is suspended or discharged, the Employer shall give such Employee, and the representative of the Union a written notice setting forth the cause for suspension or discharge.

Grievances arising from suspension, demotion or discharge may be appealed in writing directly to the Commissioner within ten (10) workdays of notice of such action. Such grievance shall be heard by the Commissioner within ten (10) workdays and a written decision shall be submitted to the Union within three (3) workdays. In the event the grievance remains unsettled, the Representative of the International Union may, by written notice to the Commissioner, within ten (10) workdays of receipt of the latter's decision, appeal the matter to arbitration as set forth in Section 8 of this Article.

If an employee is suspended or discharged for cause, his right to compensation shall remain unaffected until a grievance challenging the suspension or discharge has been finally disposed of or the time in which to file a grievance has expired, whichever occurs earlier.

SPECIAL NOTE

In those Agencies of the Government that do not have a Division Head or Commissioner, grievances shall be appealed at Step 2 and 3 to the representatives of the Employer who have been designated to hear grievances at such steps.

There was no difference between Olive and Thomas. They were both law-breakers and therefore easy targets. There was no way that I was going to do what Thomas had suggested in his memorandum. Now I had the chance to deal with him directly and I would not allow him to get away. First I had to get Willis who was running interference out of the way. Willis was acting like a child with a new toy. He didn't want to move out of the Office of Assistant Chief from where he could be seen strutting like a proud peacock. Through cryptic statements he wrote to me on March 9, 1991, in defense of a taxpayer. I immediately wrote back to him saying: "Stop! Look! Listen! Anthony P. Olive is gone and gone with him is his guiding principle of 'While in fool's paradise, one must hear no evil, see no evil or speak no evil, but cooperate with the assembled gentry in doing lots of evil herein.' Having been bitten once by the aforementioned principle, I am now twice shy. And it is for this reason that I have decided to issue a reply to your memorandum concerning Jane Doe which is dated March 9, 1991. The cryptic statements therein fail to bring into view any evidence of a letter written to Liston Monsanto by Jane Doe. What's more, your assertion that the lady tried unsuccessfully to contact me regarding her delinquent accounts is without merit and furthermore a falsehood. Through this letter it is not my intention to bring you to your knees. It is instead my intention to bring you to your senses in my capacity of Chief Shop Steward. Unilateral decisions are damaging to employee morale and must be discontinued if we truly intend to promote the best interest of the Virgin Islands Bureau of Internal Revenue. You can learn a lot by starting at the bottom and working your way up."

On March 12, 1991, I wrote to Thomas using as my lead-in a quotation from Marcus Garvey which said:

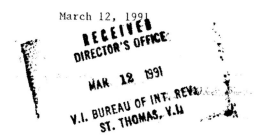

March 12, 1991

Mr. Edward E. Thomas
Acting Director
Virgin Islands Bureau of Internal Revenue
Lockhart's Garden #1
St. Thomas, Virgin Islands 00801

"If we must have justice, we must be
strong; if we must be strong, we
must come together; if we must come
together, we can only do so through
the system of organization."

- Marcus Garvey

Dear Mr. Thomas:

When Circuit Judges Hunter, VanDusen, and Sloviter ruled in Opinion No.81-1434
that the Bureau of Internal Revenue (formerly Tax Division) was overrun with problems
and had in fact violated Liston Monsanto's first amendment rights, they did so on the
basis of the evidence presented to them and moreover, they relied on several events-one
of which appears on page 20 of the Opinion and reads as follows: "The timing of Commissioner Quinn's decision to seek Monsanto's dismissal less than ten days after the radio
broadcast, suggests that it was the broadcast rather than the letter writing as such
which provoked this controversy".

I have not seen any tangible evidence from the appointing authority (i.e. the
Governor of the Virgin Islands) which would indicate to me that Mr. Louis Willis, because of his attributes, has moved with deliberate speed from an Internal Revenue Officer I (the lowest level falling below the levels of Revenue Officer II, III, and IV)
to Assistant Chief of the Delinquent Accounts and Returns Branch ahead of several higher level Revenue Officers including your wife - Mrs. Lucia Thomas.

When will it end? In the Virgin Islands Bureau of Internal Revenue, there is
a persistent, abnormal, and irrational fear of Liston Monsanto.

Recently, I wrote two letters to Mr. Louis Willis. One on March 7, 1991, and
the other on March 8, 1991 (see the attached copies). The latter I surmised, may have
prompted you to serve notification on the employees about Willis' promotion - less
than ten (10) days after you had read either letter.

Now comes your negative reaction to grievance number 1-91, which was filed by
me on March 11, 1991. Do you really expect me to discuss the matter with Mr. Willis,
who is directly affected?

And since you are presumably not aware, through this letter I'd like to serve
notice on you that litigation has been underway for sometime with respect to the unlawful act committed by Mr. Olive in naming Mr. Jerome Ferdinand Chief of the Delinquent
Accounts and Returns Branch. So you see Sir, I could not in all fairness discuss my
plight with him.

Also attached hereto are two letters (one from Edward Thomas to Mr. Luis "Tito" Morales dated May 26, 1988 and the other from Liston Monsanto to Mr. Luis "Tito" Morales dated May 26, 1988) which show that as second in command to Mr. Anthony P. Olive, you were fully aware of the injustices in the Delinquent Accounts and Returns Branch.

Here in the Virgin Islands, integrity is defined as doing the right thing when no one is looking. Not aware of this, I was of the stupid belief that Olive's departure had given me the legacy of freedom needed to better communicate with my co-workers. That's not the case however.

Because of the litigation of which I spoke earlier, I'm forced to return your copy of grievance number 1-91 (dated March 11, 1991). As for me, I shall remain as dormant as a TDA in our inactive files pending the courts final decision.

Meanwhile, an Arbitrator (should one become necessary) will have to decide if in fact I have violated the provisions of Article V of our Agreement.

Sincerely,

Liston B. Monsanto
Chief Shop Steward

c.c. Mr. Luis "Tito" Morales

Mr. Jerome Ferdinand

Mr. Louis M. Willis

Another letter to Willis followed on March 15, 1991, wherein I stated:

March 15, 1991

Mr. Louis M. Willis
Assistant Chief DARB
V.I. Bureau of Internal Revenue
St. Thomas, Virgin Islands 00801

Dear Mr. Willis:

Although I have been trying my best (as evidenced by my letter of January 18, 1991 to Governor Farrelly with a copy to Mr. Edward Thomas) to promote harmony among a peaceful gathering in the Virgin Islands Bureau of Internal Revenue, you have continued - perhaps due to the fact that our Acting Director Mr. Edward Thomas' wife (who as an Internal Revenue Officer IV was on a higher level than you) works with us, to prove that you are capable of worst.

Owing to the lackadaisical attitudes of the Revenue Officers assigned to the St. Thomas District, of the Delinquent Accounts and Returns Branch, the Bureau has been riddled with inefficiency for more than a decade. It is demonstrably guilty of unfairness and vindictiveness.

As trained individuals, our Revenue Officers lack the courage and aggressiveness to take issue or engage in direct action with many taxpayers including your contemporaries

Those in positions of authority within the Bureau are playing deaf to my pleas for unity and fairness. They much prefer - it seems, to brazen it out among a number of timid Revenue Officers and certain underachievers.

As noted previously (see my letter to Mr. Edward Thomas which is dated March 12, 1991) litigation similar to grievance 2-87 (Calendar/Attidore or pay disparity case) has been underway for sometime appealing the inversion of justice perpetrated on me by an Arbitrator sometime last year.

With the continued confusion and bewilderment in our Branch over your somewhat pseudo appointment and the fact that you'd be directly affected in any grievance challenging the appointment, I saw no need to confer with you on the matter. What's more, it is my firm belief that you've been placed in your position in order to protect certain employees from me. Why are they afraid?

I am not about to lose out on a technicality and since I'm now aware of the fact that Mr. Jerome Ferdinand is to become the Assistant Commissioner of Finance, I ask that you consider this letter the first step in Article V of our grievance procedure.

Sincerely

Liston B. Monsanto
Chief Shop Steward

369

Then showing how stupid he could be, Louis "Lolo" Willis sent me a memorandum on March 19, 1991, which said: "I have set a date for you to hear your grievance. I will meet with you on March 22, 1991, at 4:00 p.m."

Thomas was trying his best to have me focus my attention towards Willis and/or Ferdinand. He wrote to me on March 21, 1991 talking about a "Collection Plan." He wrote: "Attached for your information is an updated statement which clearly defines our mission and your role. You are being assigned to Zone 4 on the island of St. Thomas—this zone covers a line west of Tri-Mart at Nisky to include the Nisky Shopping Center, Cyril E. King Airport and west to the end of the islands as shown on the attached map. You will receive further detailed information and working tools from Mr. Willis and Deputy Director Graciano Belardo."

On March 22, 1991, using as my lead-in a quotation from former Major League Baseball Commissioner, Happy Chandler, which said

March 22, 1991

Mr. Edward E. Thomas
Director
V.I. Bureau of Internal Revenue
St. Thomas, Virgin Islands 00802

> "For twenty-four (24) years the
> record will show that my prede-
> cessor said, "If you're black,
> you can't play." Why? Because
> that's what the owners wanted
> him to do. Landis has a reputa-
> tion as an independent Commissioner
> that he doesn't deserve."
>
> --Happy Chandler (Former
> Baseball Commissioner
> April 1945)

Dear Mr. Thomas:

This letter is being written in secret and without the knowledge of anyone
else, so as to avoid an internal uprising against any pronouncement(s) from your
office dealing with the introduction of any new policies in the Virgin Islands
Bureau of Internal Revenue.

Prefatory note: Murphy's Law (i.e., If anything can go wrong it will) has
interposed in your latest pronouncement!

Before explaining the above remark, I'd like to state that as a civil servant
(victimized by man's inhumanity to man) I'm employed by the Virgin Islands Bureau
of Internal Revenue for the express purpose of assisting the Office of Director in
carrying out its duties and simultaneously to aid our Government (within the frame-
work of existing law) in accomplishing its primary objective - that of voluntary
compliance.

In order to better serve the Office of Director and in order to erase all
vestiges of the Olive years, I have decided to promote a new image of moderation.
Any other image - I believe, would serve only to militate against the success of
the Virgin Islands Bureau of Internal Revenue.

Some people have a purpose in life; others just drift. And unlike many of
our employees who believe that security and safety in numbers take precedence
over lawfulness, the record shows - and anyone with credibility would invariably
say, that during this period of your Directorship I have steered clear from anything that would neutralize the efforts of our organization, thereby taking us
down the primrose path to disaster as was the case under Olive's stewardship.

Letter   -2-   3/22/91

Mr. Edward E. Thomas
Director

As I write, it is my honest belief that what unites Edward E. Thomas and Liston Monsanto is far greater than what divides them; consequently, I have drawn a conclusion from the facts known and as presented by you earlier today, and I now feel compelled to caution you against the interposition of Murphy's Law in your future decisions, especially if such decisions would produce a change foreign to the Agreement between the Bureau and the United Steelworkers of America.

After scrutinizing your Collection Plan which you outlined in your memorandum of March 21, 1991, and after comparing the language therein with our Contract, I have concluded that your Collection Plan and our Contract are not congruent.

While it is fine and dandy to make yourself well acquainted with that portion of our Contract which deals with Grievances, it would also be fine and dandy for you to familarize yourself with the entire Contract, especially as it relates to what you are desirous of doing.

We cannot change the rules in the middle of the game. In order for you to legally accomplish what you are trying to do, we must renegotiate the Contract.

It is not my intention to interfere with your operations which incidentally are laudable, but since I'm challenging the positions of Chief and Assistant Chief of the Delinquent Accounts and Returns Branch, like Mr. Anthony Attidore, who is still on board awaiting a final decision in the pay disparity case (Grievance 2-87) I find myself in limbo while awaiting a final decision on my court cases.

Incidentally, the initial decision made on Grievance 2-87 by then Arbitrator Ives A. Swan was reversed by David M. Helfeld and subsequently appealed to the Territorial Court where currently Judge Ives A. Swan sits.

Now that I have (shall we say) spoken with a clear voice, I would like to end this letter by substituting the words of Happy Chandler's quotation which appears on page 1. The substitution follows: For the past several years Liston Monsanto's exemplary record will show that your predecessors said in a paraphrase, "If Monsanto is serious about his work and intends to work with diligence while acting with decorum, he cannot work for the Bureau of Internal Revenue." Why? Because that's exactly what the business community doesn't like. Send him to Coventry they say.

Sincerely,

Liston Monsanto
Chief Shop Steward

On March 25, 1991, with the faint-hearted Thomas on my mind, I wrote to him using a quotation from Alexis Detocqueville. Then I wrote:

March 25, 1991

Mr. Edward E. Thomas
Director-V.I. Bureau of Internal Revenue
Lockhart Garden #1
St. Thomas, Virgin Islands 00801

"When an opinion has taken root amongst
a democratic people, and established
itself in the minds of the bulk of the
community, it afterward subsists by itself and is maintained without effort,
because no one attacks it. Those who
first rejected it as false, ultimately
receive it as the general impression;
and those who will dispute it in their
hearts, conceal their dissent; they
are careful not to engage in a dangerous and useful conflict".

            Alexis DeTocqueville

Dear Mr. Thomas:

Because I would hate to think that what's happening under your stewardship
is a pious fraud being committed by a charitable, humble, and devout christian, I
have decided to write to you in the same fashion that I would want you to write to
me if I were Director.

First and foremost, I'd like to remind you of some of our past experiences.
Experiences which I had hoped would remain dormant — never ever to be resurrected.

Take — for example, the morning of November 25, 1985, at the Office of the
Chief Negotiator. Do you remember?

Well, following your threat to touch me up on that particular morning, I
recorded the incident in a letter to you which reminded you in the last paragraph
of the following: "There are lots of peninsulas in the human race, but no man is
an island".

Then you came back with renewed vigor on September 22, 1989, threatening
to blow my head off. In a fit of passion you ended your temper tantrum with a most
coherent statement on that very special day. You cautioned me against complaining
to anyone about your aberrant behavior, saying that my complaints would fall on
deaf ears.

But in taking you before Assistant Attorney General Nelson Jones on your
threats to blow my head off, I completely ignored that portion of your tirade
which dealt with complaining, inasmuch as I had thought that in the aftermath of
Hurricane Hugo and in the absence of your unctuous manner of operating, that you
were performing under stress.

Now as I look at your organizational structure showing the various people filling the various positions in the Bureau, I suddenly find myself giving credence to what you were saying on that day.

Yes sir, the bellicose statements emanating from your mouth on September 22, 1989, tie in beautifully with the Public Officials and your fellow Cabinet members who both have relatives working for you as trusted subordinates. Politics, it is said makes strange bed-fellows.

In the United States Virgin Islands we occupy 132 square miles of land - a fact reminiscent of small town America, where just about everybody is related.

Because of my experiences with many kinds of people, I have developed great powers of intuition. And since I see this letter as a most potent weapon in my arsenal, it behooves me to list (for the edification of a third party) the many key people with whom we must work. Starting with you, the list follows:

1. Mr. Edward E. Thomas (Director of the Bureau of Internal Revenue)

2. Mrs. Lucia Thomas - Wife of Mr. Thomas. Assigned to work in DARB where there is much turmoil.

3. Ms. Cynthia Faulkner - Sister of Commissioner Eric Dawson and Secretary to Mr. Edward Thomas.

4. Ms. Joyce Petersen - Sister of Commissioner Eric Dawson and Cynthia Faulkner. Works as Assistant Chief Processing and Accounts Branch.

5. Mr. Roy Vanterpool - Brother of Commissioner Rudolph Krigeer. Works as Chief Processing and Accounts Branch.

6. Mr. Alvin Swan   -   Brother of Judge Ives A. Swan. Assigned to work in DARB under the supervision of a lower level Revenue Officer.

7. Mrs. Janice Callender - Wife of Senator Malcolm Callender. Works as Agent while awaiting Court's decision in pay disparity (Grievance 2-87)

8. Mr. Louis Willis   -   Cousin of Senator Malcolm Callender. Position unclear?

Because you have shown that you are impervious to suggestions, I will not make any with respect to the above listing. To do so would only upset you. It is my belief that you are still smarting from Opinion 81-1434 of the Third Circuit Court of Appeals.

And this brings to issue the matter of Mr. Louis Willis' sppointment. Since the human race is guilty of breaking God's ten commandments, I feel certain that I speak for both of us when I say that given the opportunity, members of the human race would also break man-made laws.

It is incredible to believe nevertheless, that you would-through great warmth of feeling, promote Mr. Willis (a man guilty of fighting in the workplace with a lower echelon employee and a man who is also guilty of chasing a lower echelon employee fully armed out into the parking lot and into the Grand Union Super Market) from the bottom of the totem pole (Internal Revenue Officer I) to the second highest level (Assistant Chief DARB) in the Delinquent Accounts and Returns Branch - not only ahead of former Chief Liston Monsanto and several Veterans, but also ahead of your wife, who has both the seniority and qualification over Mr. Willis.

I believe that Governor Farrelly is sincerly concerned about the Bureau of Internal Revenue and I also believe him when he says that the best is yet to come. But as noted in my letter of March 12, 1991, I have not seen any tangible proof from the appointing authority (i.e. the Governor) that Mr. Willis has in fact been appointed Assistant Chief.

In the past and up to now, the Bureau of Internal Revenue has been guilty of an intolerable level of abuse.

There has been a number of grievances filed as the result of unfairness. Many of these grievances have been held motionless by some strange power. Incidentally, could that strange power be the source of your September 22, 1989 statement? (see paragraph 5 of this letter).

For your information it is worth noting that at 4:05 P.M. on Friday, March 22, 1991 I met withMr. Louis Willis for the purpose of complying with Step 1 of the Grievance Procedure.

Once again however, I have no proof from the Governor's Office showing that Mr. Willis has been actually promoted and this Mr. Thomas, leaves me in a quandary.

The rule of law being effectively applied, I ask that you make available to me the desired information. I would hate to feel that there is a conspiracy of officials afoot.

Having made my point with respect to the continuing events in the Virgin Islands Bureau of Internal Revenue, I have now made the decision to stay "Far from the madding crowd ignoble strife." While Mr. Anthony Attidore, Mrs. Janice Callender, and Mr. Louis Willis remain in their positions pending decisions from the Courts, Liston Monsanto will continue to do what he's been doing until a final decision is made. This - needless to say, will retard productivity.

Finally, Mr. Willis' situation reeks of vindictiveness!

Sincerely yours,

Liston B. Monsanto
Chief Shop Steward

What was going on in the Virgin Islands Bureau of Internal Revenue was not a new trend. The trend had been set in 1970 when we were given the opportunity to elect our governor for the first time. In a Virgin Islands Bureau of Internal Revenue marked by allegations of backstabbing and shady tax settlements, Thomas continued to extend Olive's management style to help ensure that everything remained a secret. Farrelly, as Governor, aware of what was going on in our workplace, continued to do to Thomas what Thomas had been doing to Quinn, Olive, Ferdinand and a power-hungry Louis Willis. Thomas' behavior showed his utmost consideration for Farrelly. None of them had the guts to come forward as leaders and talk to a subordinate who had broken rank and was exposing them.

I wrote to Willis on March 26, 1991 in this manner:

March 26, 1991

Mr. Louis M. Willis
Assistant Chief DARB
V.I. Bureau of Internal Revenue
St. Thomas, Virgin Islands 00801

Dear Mr. Willis:

As a concerned taxpayer and citizen of the Virgin Islands and one of the many people who pay your salary, I have been desperately trying (since March 12, 1991) to get information from Mr. Edward Thomas (our Director) relating to your status.

I know - based on my past unhappy experiences, that there is a high degree of games-man-ship in the Bureau of Internal Revenue, but it has become a most difficult thing for me to believe (without any information from the Governor) that anyone through games-man-ship would promote you from an Internal Revenue Officer I to Assistant Chief over a number of higher ranking Officers.

At any rate, while I'm awaiting the information on your status from Mr. Thomas, who has once again violated our agreement, I ask that you consider this letter as Step 1 of Article V of the Grievance Procedure.

I have decided to discuss Mr. Thomas' deviation from the Agreement between the Bureau and the United Steelworkers of America with you only because of my respect for the Office of Assistant Chief Delinquent Accounts and Returns Branch.

Sincerely,

Liston B. Monsanto
Chief Shop Steward

I was in a way apprising Willis of my respect for law and authority as evidenced by the Grievance that I had filed in compliance with our Contract. Then I cleared the next hurdle by writing to Ferdinand on April 2, 1991. I said:

377

Liston B. Monsanto, Sr.

April 2, 1991

Mr. Jerome A. Ferdinand
Chief-Delinquent Accounts & Returns Branch
Bureau of Internal Revenue
Christiansted, St. Croix, V.I. 00820

Dear Mr. Ferdinand:

Because of the state of confusion and deception which pervades the sacred halls of the Virgin Islands Bureau of Internal Revenue, Management – given the highest degree of poetic license, has been characterized as experts with always a perfect reason for the wrong results.

Bordering on the principle of this somewhat vague axiom is the following unanswered questions:

1. Is Mr. Louis M. Willis really the Assistant Chief of the Delinquent Accounts and Returns Branch?

2. Was Mr. Louis M. Willis appointed by Governor Alexander A. Farrelly?

3. Is Mr. Edward E. Thomas (under the authority of the Freedom of Information Act) going to make available to me a copy of Mr. Willis' appointment papers for my review?

After meeting with Mr. Louis Willis on March 22, 1991, the matter of my grievance relating to Mr. Thomas' unlawful appointment of Mr. Louis M. Willis as Assistant Chief of the Delinquent Accounts and Returns Branch remains unresolved.

For this reason, I ask that you consider this letter as a prelude to Step 2 of Article V (Grievance and Arbitration Procedure) of the Agreement between the Bureau of Internal Revenue and the United Steelworkers of America.

A copy of this letter is being sent to Mr. Thomas in order to keep him abreast of what's going on in this most troubled Branch of the Virgin Islands Bureau of Internal Revenue.

Sincerely,

Liston B. Monsanto
Chief Shop Steward

c.c. Mr. Edward E. Thomas

378

I was showing Thomas that there was more than one way to skin a cat. Thomas' turn came on April 2ⁿᵈ also when I wrote:

RECEIVED
DIRECTOR'S OFFICE

APR 2 1991

V.I. BUREAU OF INT. REV
ST. THOMAS, V.I.

April 2, 1991

Mr. Edward E. Thomas
Director-V.I. Bureau of Internal Revenue
Lockhart's Garden #1-A
St. Thomas, Virgin Islands 00801

Dear Mr. Thomas:

Because I have surmised that your actions during the 1991 Lenten season were taken under color of an edict proclaimed by the highest authority in the Virgin Islands Bureau of Internal Revenue and therefore violated the existing Agreement between the Bureau of Internal Revenue and the United Steelworkers of America, as Chief Shop Steward and an aggrieved civil servant-aware of the fact that there is no one to check the Checker in the Bureau, I find it of the utmost importance to take follow-up action on my grievance.

At the outset I'd like to state that whether or not Mrs. Lucia Thomas (your wife) stays with the Bureau of Internal Revenue during your tenure of office, does not bother me at all.

But inasmuch as the majority of your subordinates are whispering in private what they should be saying to your face, I decided to break rank in order to let you know that Mrs. Thomas' employment on the employee level puts her within the realm of labor and therefore constitutes an unfair labor practice within the true meaning of Title 24, Section 65(1) of the Virgin Islands Code.

In an event which seems of little importance to you, please be reminded that Step 2 of the Grievance Procedure (i,e, Article V, of the Agreement between the Virgin Islands Bureau of Internal Revenue and the United Steelworkers of America) says in part: "A meeting between the Division head, the Grievant and a member of the Grievance Committee shall be held to discuss the grievance within five (5) workdays after it has been presented."

Mr. Jerome Ferdinand, who cannot reverse any decision(s) made by you, but is considered the Division head and furthermore, the person to whom I sent a letter today (copy to you) requesting a review of my complaint, is based on St. Croix and presently-I've been told, somewhere in the United States.

In light of the foregoing, I'd like to inform you that in processing my complaint, I'll be giving strict compliance to the time limits set forth in Step 2 of our Agreement.

When Liston Monsanto, "et al" filed Grievance number 12-88 wherein they complained of Mr. Louis Willis' unlawful designation of Acting Assistant Chief of the Delinquent Accounts and Returns Branch, the positions of Chief Delinquent Accounts and Returns Branch (check the record) and Assistant Chief Delinquent Accounts and Returns Branch were both vacant.

Willis was (according to you) promoted from an Internal Revenue Officer I-ahead of several Revenue Officers II's, III's, and IV's, to Assistant Chief on March 11, 1991. Ferdinand (the record shows) was named Chief-also in violation of our Agreement, after Grievance number 12-88 was filed. How Mr. Marc Weisenfeld (the Arbitrator) could rule the way he did in his Decision, has me overwhelm with wonder.

Some dishonest person had to use his influence in persuading Mr. Weisenfeld to do what he did. What a shame!

By unlawfully promoting Mr. Louis Willis to the position of Assistant Chief, you are stretching something beyond its proper limits and demonstrating in the process that you are no Machiavellian. The palpable errors that you are making are beginning to mirror those of your predecessors.

There have been many managers and a manager defacto, who before you became Director felt themselves superior to me and showed it by treating me with cold indifference and scorn.

My many evil-minded nemeses such as Reuben Wheatley, Leroy Quinn, Robert Woods, Anthony Olive, John Ferrant, Roy Malone, and Kenneth Hansen-through their evil plans and schemes, all found Liston Monsanto to be their waterloo.

I fully realize that it is a most difficult thing to reconcile oneself to a long standing quarrel. I also know that problems are never solved by running away from them. But if we are to accomplish anything in the Virgin Islands Bureau of Internal Revenue (such as playing the soft-ball games of which you spoke before the Rules Committee of the Legislature) we must reconcile with each other. Looking at me with an evil eye and extending the evil doings of your predecessors will result only in your destruction.

Let us therefore start life anew in the Bureau by reconciling with each other. I can be reached readily in the Delinquent Accounts and Returns Branch where I will be awaiting your call.

It is my honest belief that history will judge us harshly if we fail to meet in an atmosphere of serenity where we can settle once and for all, our differences.

Sincerely,

Liston B. Monsanto
Chief Shop Steward

c.c. Mr. Luis "Tito" Morales
     Pres. Local Union 8249

380

Then I returned to Ferdinand on April 4, 1991 when I wrote:

April 4, 1991

RECEIVED
DAR BRANCH
APR 4 1991
V.I. Bureau of Internal Revenue

Mr. Jerome A. Ferdinand
Chief, DAR Branch
V.I. Bureau of Internal Revenue
#1DA Estate Diamond
Christiansted, St. Croix
Virgin Islands 00821

Dear Mr. Ferdinand:

Since March 12, 1991, I have been inquiring for information concerning what I believe to be a pseudo-promotion given to Mr. Louis Willis by Mr. Edward Thomas, who seems to have little knowledge in the area of governmental appointments.

Due largely perhaps to some overpowering fear, I have not yet received any conclusive evidence from Mr. Thomas which would establish the truth that Mr. Willis has in fact been promoted by Governor Alexander A. Farrelly - the government's only appointing authority.

In a related matter, during the intervening time, Mr. Thomas (on March 22, 1991) once again violated the Agreement between the Bureau of Internal Revenue and the United Steelworkers of America, when he introduced a new Collection Plan into the Delinquent Accounts and Returns Branch.

On March 26th, Mr. Willis was alerted of Mr. Thomas' violation pursuant to Step 1 of the Grievance and Arbitration Procedure.

Mr. Willis like you, cannot reverse any decision(s) made by Mr. Thomas and has shown (through his silence) a refusal to meet with me within the time-frame specified by the Agreement and this, needless to say, requires me to move to Step 2 of the Procedure.

Accordingly, I'm asking that you consider this letter as the preliminary step to Article V, Section 3-B (Step 2) of the Agreement between the Bureau and the United Steelworkers of America.

Letter   —2—   4/4/91

Mr. Jerome A. Ferdinand
Chief, DAR Branch

A copy of this letter has been sent to Mr. Thomas in order to keep him abreast of recent developments.

Sincerely,

Liston Monsanto
Chief Shop Steward

cc: Mr. Edward E. Thomas
     Director

Having read a whole lot of books on mafia operations and underworld activities I could see right away the game Farrelly and his shadow cabinet were playing. Because of my honesty and willingness to do my work, I could not qualify as a member. On April 12, 1991, in an unctuous manner, Thomas sent me a copy of a letter that he had written to Ferdinand. His letter said: "Enclosed for your action is 'replacement' Grievance No. 1-19. As mentioned in my April 4, 1991 letter (copy attached) please hold the Step 2 Hearing as required by Article V of our Collective Bargaining Agreement."

My representatives in the Union (Tito Morales and Cephus Rogers) because of their close ties with Farrelly and certain members of the shadow cabinet, remained silent not wanting to intervene in a matter that needed their immediate attention. Willis and I were both members of a Union that was being treated roughly by Farrelly and his evildoers and yet there was no immediate help.

On April 15, 1991, still representing myself, I wrote to Thomas using as my lead-in a passage taken from Farrelly's inaugural address which said:

April 15, 1991

Mr. Edward E. Thomas
Director
V.I. Bureau of Internal Revenue
St. Thomas, Virgin Islands 00802

> "We should all join together and climb on the train of progress, the train of freedom, the train of fairness. The Government of the Virgin Islands, however, is a train out of control, heading downward, and down the tracks pretending not to know the dangers of derailment that lie ahead."
>
> —Gov. Alexander A. Farrelly

Dear Mr. Thomas:

While Secretary of State James A. Baker III is winding up his Mideast peace mission on a positive note with encouraging words from Syria and Jordan that they are open to face-to-face talks with Israel, you have rejected my friendly advice to achieve a cessation of hostilities between us, and to promote in the Virgin Islands Bureau of Internal Revenue a state of inner quiet, free from disturbance and strife.

Prompted by the everyday occurrences in the Bureau, the Sidewalk Analysts have made a survey of past events and experiences therein, and already they are saying that from your position of Director defacto during the Anthony P. Olive years, your latent power played a major role in the daily affairs and decision-making process in the Virgin Islands Bureau of Internal Revenue.

It is being said that Mr. Olive, who was really a figure head, shielded you from being attacked and/or ridiculed by our Bargaining Unit of which your wife —who works with us is a member.

But now that Olive is gone from the Bureau and you (in your genuine position of Director) are no longer lying hidden behind anyone, you have started out on the wrong foot by failing to protect the Bureaucracy and doing the same unlawful things that your intimate and trusted friend Mr. Anthony P. Olive was guilty of doing.

And although I've made an earnest effort to repress the impulse to address you, your modus operandi demands upon my time, and forces me to write with deliberate speed once again.

383

Mr. Edward E. Thomas
Director

On January 18, 1991, you were told that Olive's departure from the Bureau, gave me valid reasons to believe that the prime barrier against putting me to work in the position for which I am qualified (see the records at the Division of Personnel) was gone, and that under your stewardship, things would be different.

What's more, with you as our new Director, I was looking with great hope and expectation for you to amend your ways from your hidden role of Director de-facto, where you regularly flouted the law, to a more respected position among the scarce vanguard of leaders who stand for fairness in our tiny Virgin Islands community.

It was my firm conviction that cavalier statements such as the one you made in your letter to Mr. Luis "Tito" Morales on May 26, 1988 which described Mr. Louis Willis as a college graduate were behind us, and that the systematic punishment which had been perpetrated against Liston Monsanto would be a distant memory.

Hope however, springs eternal in the battered ear drums of man (or something like that) because sadly to say, my hopes did not end in fruition. Through your bland smile and your unctuous manner of operation you have maintained the same posture of defiant innnocence in the face of overwhelming evidence to the contrary.

A bird's-eye view of the aforementioned evidence appears below. It shows that it is either through a holier than thou attitude or a feeling of contempt for the Court's orders that you have shown open disrespect for the rules and decisions of the Courts and other decision-making Tribunals, by refusing to do what they have ordered you to do.

1. Opinion No. 81-1434 - An outgrowth of attempts to maliciously prosecute and ostracize Liston Monsanto. The Bureau and the less-than-professional governmental system are still smarting from this landmark decision. The vicarious punishment imposed on Liston Monsanto and your vindictiveness serve as evidence. History has shown us however, that vindictive acts rarely do much good.

2. The reinstatement of Mr. Levi Farrell (Enforcement Officer) to his lawful position following his acquittal in Territorial Court and the subsequent payment of his past due salary checks. Kindly do what's right. Put the man to work.

3. The Territorial Court's decision of July 18, 1990, which dismissed the Bureau's Petition for Writ of Review in the matter of Grievance 2-87 (Callender vs Attidore or Pay Disparity Case). To date (nine months following the Court's order) you have not done what you were told to do.

In continuing to flaunt your authority you have done a military about-face. You are now operating on the thesis that far-away talent is better than home-developed talent. Tell me, why do you have to import a person to do work for which a local person is qualified? Didn't you become Reviewer/Classifier because of my efforts to discontinue this unfair practice?

Letter   -3-   4/15/91

Mr. Edward E. Thomas
Director

       Noteworthy at this juncture is the fact that there are still a number of Grievances which were inherited by you and which need your immediate attention. Among them are the cases of Paulette Rawlins and Liburd etal., which I hasten to add is similar to the Pay Disparity Case.

       But in order to keep the context in perspective, let me continue by saying that I can vividly recall that whenever your predecessors were called upon to recruit people from outside the Virgin Islands, they always -keeping in mind that we live in an environment where loyalty is more important than honesty, looked for people who were to tough to be honest and to weak to lead their potential subordinates.

       It is further my recollection and something that I'd like to share with you that a manager once told me. He said: "The boss who attempts to impress employees with his knowledge of intricate details has lost sight of his final objective".

       This letter would pass unnoticed if I did not mention the following quotation from Governor Alexander A. Farrelly: "The state of the territorial government is deplorable. I believe it is charitable to describe the government that I now head as being in a shambles: bankrupt in its legal meaning, dispirited, often in violation of law, and operating often without rhyme or reason, benefiting neither the persons for whom services are to be provided nor fairly and fully compensating those who are to provide the services".

       Sometimes in order to hold on to what we've got, we have to let go. I'm fully behind the Governor of the Virgin Islands. In addition, I'm ready to get on the train in order to provide the services of which the Governor speaks. Please do not try to shut me out from participating and contributing to the Administration's success.

                                    Sincerely,

                                    Liston B. Monsanto
                                    Chief Shop Steward

c.c. Mr. Luis "Tito" Morales
       President - Local 8249

       Acquiescing to Thomas' instructions to discuss my Grievance, Ferdinand wrote to me on April 15, 1991. He said: "Reference is being made to your letter dated April 4, 1991 and Grievance Report No. 1-91 dated March 11, 1991 as replaced by Grievance Report No. 1-91 dated April 10, 1991. You are hereby notified that a "Step 2 Hearing" will be held on April 18, 1991 at 10:00 a.m. in the Bureau's conference room to discuss your grievance. This hearing is in accordance with Article V, Section 3-B of our Collective Bargaining Agreement." I called Ferdinand immediately (via the telephone) and told him that his letter did not meet the requirements of our agreement and I therefore would not meet with him. Now Thomas was frustrated. For some reason he did not entertain the thought that the employees of the Bureau of Internal Revenue had certain rights. The way he was carrying on, he honestly thought that the employees were children working for his own personal empire. He wasn't man enough to face me, instead he wrote to Tito Morales believing he had been appointed Arbitrator to hear my case. Here's what he wrote on April 15, 1991:

GOVERNMENT OF
THE VIRGIN ISLANDS OF THE UNITED STATES

VIRGIN ISLANDS
BUREAU OF INTERNAL REVENUE

Lockharts Garden No. 1A
Charlotte Amalie, St. Thomas, U.S.V.I. 00802

RECEIVED
APR 1 6 1991
Ans'd...........

April 15, 1991

Mr. Luis A. "Tito" Morales
President, Local Union 8249
St. Thomas, V. I. 00802

Dear Mr. Morales:

I am sending to you Grievance No. 2-91 filed by your union representative Liston Monsanto on his own behalf.

The grievance is not timely in accordance with Section 6 of Article V of our Collective Bargaining Agreement. The "Collection Plan" and Mr. Monsanto's assignment were given to him on Friday, March 22, 1991. Ten (10) working days thereafter is April 10, 1991.

I also consider this grievance to be frivolous and filed with the sole intention of tying up management's time. You know that Article IV of our Collective Bargaining Agreement gives management the exclusive right among other things, direct and supervise the employees of the unit; and determine "methods, means and personnel by which the Employer's operations are to be conducted".

We know that, in accordance with the contract, we have to provide the "tools' (cars, ferry tickets to St. John, overtime pay if necessary, etc.)

You and I have pledged to work harmoniously in the administration of our Contract. I acknowledge that there will be areas of disagreement, but this "grievance" is total nonsense. If management cannot decide how best to carry out its work, then it should close its doors.

Sincerely,

Edward E. Thomas
Director

386

The man was a snake in the grass. Every time I saw an opening I'd write to him. Who did he think he was? On May 1, 1991 I wrote to Thomas. I said:

May 2, 1991

Mr. Edward E. Thomas
Director
V.I. Bureau of Internal Revenue
St. Thomas, V.I.   00802

Dear Mr. Thomas:

"Blessed are they that go around in circles for they shall be called wheels."

I thought it appropriate to use the above quotation as the preliminary part of my letter for the reason that here in the Virgin Islands Bureau of Internal Revenue, we have continued to move in an orbit around the workplace from Director to Director.

This being the case, I'd like to begin by saying that on August 24, 1979, Mr. Leroy A. Quinn (former Director of the Virgin Islands Bureau of Internal Revenue) disregarding commonly accepted rules and principles and working with unbridled anger and vindictiveness, initiated dismissal proceedings against me, thereby forcing me to appeal to the Virgin Islands Government Employees Service Commission (GESC) pursuant to 3 Virgin Islands Code Section 530(a).

The Government Employees Service Commission (a body of citizens appointed by then Governor Juan-Luis - the Chief Executive at whose pleasure Mr. Quinn was also serving) met and pretending to be sympathetic to my cause, ordered a ninety day suspension without pay. They rejected Mr. Quinn's request for my termination.

But knowing that I was not guilty of Mr. Quinn's charges in any way, shape or form, and realizing that there was a conspiracy of Virgin Islands Government Officials afoot, I appealed the Government Employees Service Commission's decision to the United States Court of Appeals for the Third Circuit which is located away from the United States Virgin Islands in Philadelphia, Pennsylvania, where I was completely vindicated.

Of prime importance is the fact that in the period of time between the Government Employees Service Commission's order and the Third Circuit Court's Ruling, Mr. Quinn - still smarting from the slap on the wrist (ninety day suspension) given me by the Government Employees Service Commission and still feeling the sting of despair, began using what little savoir-faire he possessed by soliciting the assistance of a surreptitious Mr. Robert L. Parkhurst (an Auditor from from the United States Internal Revenue Service), who underhandedly (amid rampant rumors of payoffs and kickpacks akin to the same rumors that are rife today) proceeded to discredit and defame my character based only on unrealistic and imparctical notions conveyed to him by the Bureau's top Toady - Mr. Anthony P. Olive.

In spite of their machinations, however, the plot to deprive me of my civil rights and full employment failed due largely to the events listed in the foregoing paragraphs. These events - I hasten to add, had conspired to ruin Quinn and his henchmen including Robert L. Parkhurst, whom I never saw again.

Today – through a series of organized activities and a devious plan to bring a statesider into a brand-new environment, where he would operate incoginto so as to avoid being called Chief of the Delinquent Accounts and Returns Branch while watching over Liston Monsanto, you appear to be working in concert with many of the same people, who are exercised in some form of conspicuous consumption and whose only desire is to see you as leader of an inferior tax system in these United States Virgin Islands.

You have become so abjectly afraid to approach the task of confronting Liston Monsanto in an employer/employee kind of way that you must either ridicule him by means of a lampoon (see your letter of April 15, 1991 to Luis "Tito" Morales) or bring another Robert L. Parkhurst from outside of the Virgin Islands as an intermediary.

I have come to regard your actions as preposterous. What's more, I refuse to be sidetracked by someone's unreasonableness, especially someone who is not being honest about his feelings.

But as we patiently await the arrival of the new man, whose loyalty must be to your office, you and most of the higher level Revenue Officers continue to take grossly unfair advantage of Mr. Louis Willis, who because of his vanity and ingratitude has to do whatever he is told to do, without adequate directions or knowledge.

As far as my Grievances are concerned, there is no need to distance yourself from them. Forget your day dreams and start dealing with reality. Rather than trying to get the better of or defeating me by trickery, I ask that we join together in working for a better Bureau where all can share in the glory.

Sincerely,

Liston Monsanto
Chief Shop Steward

cc: Mr. Luis "Tito" Morales
     President, Local 8249

Ferdinand had seen the error of his ways. He knew that I was being victimized. He also knew that because of my ability to defend myself against all comers that he could not win and so on May 3, 1991 he bowed out.

There was no way that Thomas was going to put me in the position vacated by Ferdinand. He wanted a person that he could use to do his dirty work. Nevertheless, in the interest of consistency, I had to apply for the job even if it meant poking fun at him. I wrote to him on May 8, 1991. I said:

May 8, 1991

Mr. Edward E. Thomas
·Director
V.I. Bureau of Internal Revenue
Charlotte Amalie
St. Thomas, Virgin Islands 00802

Dear Mr. Thomas:

As a former Chief of the Delinquent Accounts and Returns Branch and one familiar with the everyday operations of the collection activity-by virtue of my more than thirty years of satisfactory service, I'd like to (once again) apply my knowledge and overall expertise in helping to bring about or further the growth of the Delinquent Accounts and Returns Branch.

I therefore ask that you consider this letter my application for employment as Chief of the Delinquent Accounts and Returns Branch.

My name has been on the Division of Personnel's eligible list long before Mr. Jerome Ferdinand, whose resignation became effective on May 3, 1991, and many others joined our organization.

Sincerely,

Liston B. Monsanto
Internal Revenue Officer

c.c. Mr. Luis "Tito" Morales
Pres. Local Union 8249

Gov. Alexander A. Farrelly

RECEIVED
DIRECTOR'S OFFICE
MAY 8 1991
V.I. BUREAU OF INT. REV.
ST. THOMAS. V.I.

On May 16, 1991 Thomas wrote to the employees of the Bureau of Internal Revenue telling them, among other things, that he was being sworn in as the Director. Here's what he wrote:

GOVERNMENT OF
THE VIRGIN ISLANDS OF THE UNITED STATES

VIRGIN ISLANDS
BUREAU OF INTERNAL REVENUE

Lockharts Garden No. 1A
Charlotte Amalie, St. Thomas, U.S.V.I. 00802

May 16, 1991

<u>MEMORANDUM</u>

TO : All Employees

FROM : Mr. Edward E. Thomas
      Director

Today, I am being sworn in as the Director of the Bureau of Internal Revenue in the Farrelly administration.

I look forward to a most productive four years with you and certainly anticipate good cooperation from all levels of activity.

Basically I have a two-year plan in mind and one of my first acts in February was to ask the Governor to sign an extension of our Interior Grant. This Grant provides for the IRS and Bureau to jointly work toward:

 a. designing and implementing a modern tax information system;
 b. improving the management and operation of the DAR Branch
 c. training revenue agents in large case audits; and
 d. improving taxpayer service.

Over the next two years you will see a number of advisors from the IRS in our offices. They will include a Project Manager, two Data Processing Advisors, a Collection Advisor, and an Examination Advisor. In addition there will be a number of short-term Code and Edit and Data Entry Specialists assisting in our tax processing operations.

I have given the authority to the Management Staff to fully implement programs as outlined by me. I will hold their "feet to the fire" to insure success.

The non-managerial employees are the ones that actually carry out our managerial initiatives. It is definitely important that this important group make the same commitment to succeed.

I will be issuing a number of guidelines and directives as the months go by with the sole purpose of increasing our efficiency, productivity and professionalism. I start by directing that each employee remain at his assigned duty station during his hours of work. Mingling at another's work station means that there are at least two employees in an unproductive mode. Managers will be asked to monitor this area closely and take appropriate action.

Again, let's move ahead together, good luck and God's richest blessings to each and every employee.

Edward E. Thomas
Director

Six days later, May 22, 1991, Farrelly had the effrontery to send me some documents relating to horse racing in the Territory asking for my input. The man was insulting what ever little intelligence I possessed. I wrote him a letter saying: "I very much appreciate your thoughtfulness in sending me a copy of your message (together with its attachments) concerning the 'Horse Racing Industry Reform Act of 1991.' It is fascinating reading and a storehouse of information. Undoubtedly, your actions were taken in furtherance of some higher good, like getting a new Reform Act together of which we all can be proud. But whereas you have remained sincere in your efforts to improve horse racing in the Territory and whereas my involvement in horse racing extends only to the sporadic calling of races at the Clinton Phipps race track on St. Thomas, you have, on the other hand, been inordinately quiet about righting the many wrongs at the Virgin Islands Bureau of Internal Revenue where I'm permanently employed. There may be some other very thoughtful people who would think of sending me a copy of the subject message, but very few who would actually follow-up the thought with action. Thank you so very much."

Louis "Lolo" Willis, as Assistant Chief of the Delinquent Accounts and Returns Branch was being rewarded for the part that he played in our job action of 1986. He was a novice who had no idea at all what supervisory responsibility was all about. I had filed a Grievance asking for his removal from the position, but he continued his stupid ways of trying to supervise my activities. On May 30, 1991, he sent me a memorandum which said: "On Thursday, June 6, 1991, at 2:00 p.m., you are hereby ordered to meet with me in my office with your entire inventory so that I can review your cases with you."

Thomas himself didn't know what to do with me. Every time he'd address a memorandum to me he would begin: "To: Liston Monsanto via Mr. Louis Willis and Mr. Graciano Belardo From: Mr. Edward E. Thomas." He came up with the stupid idea of a special assignment similar to Reuben Wheatley. He wrote to me on June 4, 1991 saying:

GOVERNMENT OF
THE VIRGIN ISLANDS OF THE UNITED STATES

◆

VIRGIN ISLANDS
BUREAU OF INTERNAL REVENUE

◆

Lockharts Garden No. 1A
Charlotte Amalle, St. Thomas, U.S.V.I. 00802

June 4, 1991

MEMORANDUM

TO   : Mr. Liston Monsanto
            Internal Revenue Officer IV

VIA   : Mr. Louis M. Willis
            Asst. Chief, DARB

            Mr. Graciano Belardo
            Deputy Director

FROM   : Mr. Edward E. Thomas
            Director

RE   : Port Authority Contracts

Attached is an article published in a recent article of the St. Croix Avis which speaks to numerous contracts let by the Port Authority in recent years. Because of the recent interest in VIPA and possible investigations it behooves us to review the tax status of these projects.

Your tasks are as follows:

1. Contact Mr. Eugen Gottlieb at the Port Authority and ascertain the status of each of the contracts awarded for St. Thomas.

2. Ascertain the tax status of each of the companies in the St. Thomas district. Your report must analyze by company whether each one is current in withholding, gross receipts and income taxes.

3. If any company is delinquent, then you must make contact immediately and bring to a current status.

4. I am specifically interested in the contracts for the Betteroads Company. They employ a lot of transients and we must be certain that the withholding taxes on wages are paid currently.

You will present your findings and report to the Assistant Chief, DAR, Mr. Louis M. Willis and Deputy Director Graciano Belardo on Monday, July 1, 1991 at 10:00 A.M. at the Conference Room in St. Thomas.

Edward E. Thomas
Edward E. Thomas
Director

I had become a thorn in their sides. Through a spate of worrisome letters I was trying to educate both Willis and Thomas. The advice they were getting from me spoke volumes about their law-breaking ways. On June 6, 1991, I addressed a letter to Willis with a quotation from Police Chief Ray Hyndman. I wrote:

RECEIVED
DAR BRANCH

JUN 6 1991

V. I. Bureau of Internal Revenue   June 6, 1991

Mr. Louis M. Willis
Delinquent Accounts & Returns Branch
V.I. Bureau of Internal Revenue
St. Thomas, Virgin Islands 00802

                                        "There is lawlessness in this
                                        place. We have a lawless com-
                                        munity."
                                          -Police Chief Ray Hyndman

Dear Mr. Willis:

        During this period when your employment status is unclear and our chances of appearing before Mr. David Helfeld continues to grow, extreme care should be taken so as to avoid acting like a ruffian, especially when it comes to dealing with an aggrieved Liston Monsanto.

        Because you are being less than assidious in your desperate attempts to order me around, it behooves me to repeat my contention that no Junior Revenue Officer can legitimately order a Senior Revenue Officer to do anything.

        The failure of Mr. Edward E. Thomas to produce your appointment papers (not a NOPA) signed by Governor Farrelly, has made the relationship between a prospective supervisor and a prospective subordinate a bit tenuous.

        In addition, the absence of appointment papers tend to make me believe that there is a secret agreement between you and somebody else to commit a wrong or harmful act against me.

        And speaking of wrong and harmful acts, I'd like to interject at this juncture, that the Bureau's unwillingness to conduct a matching operation of Taxpayer Delinquent Accounts against the Unit Ledger Cards could translate into your participation in a fraud or some kind of deceit. Be careful.

        I'd further like to say that the same political wisdom and the same departmental policies which have been protecting Mr. Anthony Attidore, Mrs. Janis Callendar and yourself, are the same assets protecting Liston Monsanto today as he awaits the final word on his grievance.

        Your malicious memorandum of May 30, 1991, (coming in the wake of my letter to Mr. Edward Thomas, which openly criticized you) indicates to me that you feel ready and willing to take issue with me over the several delinquent accounts in my inventory. Had you written a similar memorandum to Mrs. Lucia Thomas (wife of Mr. Edward Thomas) you may have been fired. "Monkey know wah tree to climb."

It is not my intention to decapitate the Bureau's leadership, but inasmuch as I have filed a grievance challenging your unlawful appointment, I'm of the belief that you should excercise caution while being more discreet in conducting the day to day operations of the Delinquent Accounts and Returns Branch.

Liston Monsanto is a law-abiding person, who does not have to be ordered around. His primary reason for being with the Bureau for as long as he has is because he respects law and authority. Furthermore, Liston Monsanto is in full agreement with the Police Chief regarding lawlessness in our community. You are part of that lawlessness. Check the records.

A simple request from you is all that I need in order to make available to you (or anyone else in authority for that matter) the accounts in my inventory. They are being forwarded to you herewith in the enclosed box.

Please use a Prescribing Directive and the appropriate forms in making your review, thereby making it easy for me to review your handiwork.

Finally, it must be noted that I am not the one holding your "feet to the fire'.' So in order to assist you in better understanding our system of government, I have attached hereto a photo-copy of a letter, which is dated February 9, 1984 and addressed to Mr. Kenneth C. Hansen.

Keep your shirt on.

Liston B. Monsanto
Chief Shop Steward

c.c. Mr. Edward E. Thomas

February 9, 1984

Mr. Kenneth C. Hansen
Chief, D.A.R. Branch
V.I. Bureau of Intenral Revenue
St. Thomas, V.I. 00801

Dear Mr. Hansen:

In the United States Virgin Islands (an area of 132 square miles where just about everybody-is by blood or through marriage related) Governor Juan Luis – a politician, heads the executive branch of government and structually, the Bureau of Internal Revenue as well.

Commissioners and Directors who require senate confirmation are appointed by the Governor and serve at his pleasure.

Money is a major source of political power and taxpayers – many of whom are in the private business sector of our community, donate money and have sponsored a number of worthwhile programs and projects in the territory. Many of them are also responsible for financing the political campaign of a number of Virgin Islands politicians, who are not required to make their contributions public. Through this maze of confusion, we in the Bureau of Internal Revenue are being asked to exhibit a professional attitude.

In exchange for their time and money, many of the aforementioned taxpayers resort to the quid pro quo operation that exists in the Virgin Islands. The last thing on their minds, is the so-called "mirror theory", the Internal Revenue Code, or the Internal Revenue Manual. Some of them came here to get away from the United States Federal Tax System after which you've said we are mirrored.

From time to time, some of these taxpayers become indebted to the Virgin Islands Government in a variety of ways, one of which is taxes; and yes, these are the same taxpayers on whom we are required to make demands for payment. What a predicament!

Even an under-achiever or a ranked amateur – based on the information that you have, would understand the way our governmental system works – a system fought successfully by me through the Third Circuit Court of Appeals. For reasons better known to you however, you prefer to carry out your duties reminiscent of a salmon swimming up stream, while Mr. Olive observes.

There now, for the final time, you've gotten a concise report on life in the Virgin Islands Bureau of Intenrnal Revenue.

Sincerely,

Liston B. Monsanto

Thomas also received a letter on the anniversary of "D-Day" (June 6, 1991). In Thomas' letter I wrote:

June 6, 1991

R E C E I V E D

JUN 6

VIRGIN ISLANDS BUREAU OF
INTERNAL REVENUE
St. Thomas, V.I.

Mr. Edward E. Thomas
Director
Virgin Islands Bureau of Internal Revenue
Lockhart's Garden #1-A
St. Thomas, Virgin Islands 00802

"The consent of the governed is
basic to American Democracy. If
the governed are misled, if
they are not told the truth, or
if through official secrecy and
deception they lack information
on which to base intelligent decisions, the system may go on –
but not as a Democracy."

-David Wise

Dear Mr. Thomas:

In response to my inquiries of May 3, 1988, Mr. Anthony P. Olive waited until May 11, 1988 to tell me that Mrs. Diane Tyrell - with you playing a major role,
had been suspended from duty based on the findings of an investigation by the Criminal Investigation Division, which recommended prosecution on two counts for her alleged unauthorized disclosure of tax information pursuant to Title 33, Section 1532
of the Virgin Islands Code.

I have preserved the memory of this event for it was a most improper and
hurtful treatment given to an uninformed employee. Moreover, Mr. Olive's tenden-
cies to remain in a fixed condition without change, served as a vivid description
of Mr. Leroy A. Quinn's attempts to rid the Bureau of Liston Monsanto.

Mr. Quinn tried desperately to restrict and prevent me from airing my views
on the many problems in the then Tax Division pursuant to the same disclosure law
cited in paragraph one of this letter.

But thanks to the United States Court of Appeals for the Third Circuit, and
many thanks also to the fact that incorruptible Judges cannot be bribed, he received
a result opposite to that expected. Now you, your family, and everyone else (under
the American Flag) can use Opinion No. 81-1434 whenever it becomes necessary to do so.

But just as dikes protect the lowland from incursions of the sea, the disclosure law and an uninformed workforce have protected you in a like manner for many years.
You have relied on it and used it as a sword of Damocles in silencing many of your internal critics – even in matters not covered by the law.

At the moment I'm not about to take the wind out of your sails nor am I (from my lowly position) suddenly about to take away any advantage that you now enjoy.

The truth of the matter is, that being an Internal Revenue Officer and an altruistic Shop Steward in the Virgin Islands Bureau of Internal Revenue is not an easy task. Sometimes I find myself wearing three or more hats in protecting the Government's interest and implicitly defending the members of our Bargaining Unit. These jobs—I hasten to add, necessitate a lot of complex and laborious work.

A classic example of this work may be found in my tactful reaction to an irate Taxpayer, who was on his way to Senator Elmo D. Roebuck's office with his discovery of a secret document (Revenue Officer's Daily Report of Collection Activity) prepared by Mrs. Lucia Thomas (your wife) on September 2, 1987 showing a partial payment made by Governor Alexander A. Farrelly on his delinquent account.

Being a "no nonsense person" like yourself and a man of unquestioned veracity, I have decided to include herewith, the report for your review.

As the Carrier delivering this report to you and as one who knows that the position of Chief-Delinquent Accounts and Returns Branch is not extensible to him, I am not about to evince my dislikes for anybody, nor am I about to ignore you the way that you've ignored me through your isolationist policy.

Had I not used the art of persuasion in prevailing upon the finder of the subject document to surrender it, who knows, he may have used it to expose Mr. Farrelly's delinquency and ultimately hurt the Governor's chances for re-election in the 1990 gubernatorial race.

Although a matter of this magnitude carries great and serious consequences (in the manner of Diane Tyrell's suspension), in defusing a potentially explosive situation (bear in mind that the Governor had declared publicly that his account had been fully paid) I had to choose between an investigation by the Criminal Investigation Division, which at the time came under the helpful influence of Mr. Olive (the Juan Luis appointee, who was being carried over reluctantly by Governor Farrelly) and a gubernatorial expose' by Mr. Roebuck-neither of which would work, without detriment to the Governor.

Nevertheless, taking everything into account including the latitude given you in carrying out your duties, I've come to realize that there is nothing doubtful about your appointment to the Directorship. And although no person has the right to be Judge, Jury, and Executioner, you have become such a trusted subordinate that I'm of the belief (based on your testimony before the Rules Committee of the Senate) that you are the only person qualified enough to resolve this sensitive matter.

Letter
Mr. Edward E. Thomas   —3—   June 6, 1991

You may not be a Machiavellian, but whether you do it consciously or overtly, unlike Olive and Quinn you seem able to use your prestige and authority to exert influence on Mr. Luis "Tito" Morales (President-Local Union 8249) and many of the people called upon to make important decisions from their positions of Arbitrator, etc.

With you in the "cat bird seat", there will be no jockeying around (by anyone except your wife?) to find the best way to embarass our Branch. Yet, the subject disclosure law doesn't mean two cents if powerful people such as yourself don't like it and there's no one to enforce it.

Incidentally, a governmental appointment which must be signed by the Governor as the appointing authority, and a NOPA which can be signed by the Governor's delegate are two different documents. You have yet to produce the appointment papers of Mr. Louis M. Willis.

Finally, it is distressing to note that your intransigence and overall attitude towards me is delaying my retirement. If you are truly a "no nonsense person" (a quality similar to that of Liston Monsanto) who honestly want to get the job done as you have expressed in your letter of April 15, 1991 to Mr. Luis "Tito" Morales, then I ask that we discuss my future with the Virgin Islands Bureau of Internal Revenue, keeping in mind the following: "Those who corrupt the public's mind are just as evil as those who steal from the public's purse".

Sincerely,

Liston B. Monsanto
Chief Shop Steward

Thomas was in the process of reading my letter when suddenly Willis sent me a memorandum on the same date which said: "On May 30, 1991, you were instructed by a written memo to meet with me in my office at 2:00 p.m. with your inventory so that I can review your cases in your presence. However, during the course of the working hours prior to 2:00 p.m. while I was in the Processing Branch area, you chose to leave your inventory in a box along with a letter in my office. I will not review your inventory without your presence. I am rescheduling another meeting with you for June 7, 1991 at 2:00 p.m. If you fail to comply with this new set date, I will have no other alternative but to take appropriate action." The memorandum is presented here in the exact language used by Willis. He didn't faze me, however. I couldn't repress the urge to laugh when I received Willis' memorandum. Here was a college graduate, as Thomas had referred to him in placing him in the position who had difficulty conveying his thoughts in writing.

On June 10, 1991 I wrote to Thomas once again. My lead-in was taken from Charles Caleb Colton and it said:

Liston B. Monsanto, Sr.

June 10, 1991

Mr. Edward E. Thomas
Director-V.I. Bureau Internal Revenue
Lockhart's Garden #1-A
St. Thomas, Virgin Islands 00802

> It is easier to pretend to be what
> you are not than to hide what you
> really are; but he that can accom-
> plish both has little to learn in
> hypocrisy.
> —Charles Caleb Colton

Dear Mr. Thomas:

Because you have brought into existence what appears to be a deliberate suspension of my judgement, and because I find myself caught between two fires (i.e. an overzealous Louis Willis and a vindictive Edward Thomas) pretending to be very good and religious in a Virgin Islands corrupted society, I find it most fitting and proper to respond in a measure to your memorandum of June 4, 1991.

1. Whereas Liston Monsanto has been kicked out of the Virgin Islands Bureau of Internal Revenue on numerous occasions for using the Internal Revenue Code, the Internal Revenue Manual, the Internal Revenue Rules and Regulations along with the Virgin Islands Code.

2. Whereas three Judges (Sloviter, Hunter, and VanDusen) in the Third Circuit Court scolded and reprimanded the Bureau's management for the harsh and cruel treatment meted out to Liston Monsanto.

3. Whereas Mr. Edward Thomas (Director of the Bureau) by virtue of his appointment serves at the pleasure of a Politician.

4. Whereas Mr. Edward E. Thomas is little bound by the love of truth.

5. Whereas Liston Monsanto (a model of decorum) arouses anger in Mr. and Mrs. Edward E. Thomas and consequently, continues to be persecuted.

6. Whereas Liston Monsanto desirous of working in a manner reflective of his training and ability has been asking for guidelines since 1979.

7. Whereas the Virgin Islands Bureau of Internal Revenue through Mr. Edward E. Thomas deceives and confuses Liston Monsanto by failing to update its Instructions, Policies, and Director's Memoranda.

8. Whereas the Federal Standards being different to the Bureau's the guidelines of the U.S. Internal Revenue Service are used only when it suits the Bureau's purpose.

400

9. Whereas Liston Monsanto has been told not to disturb the Business Community owing to Governor Farrelly's declaration that he's pro business.

10. Whereas Mr. Edward E. Thomas, who has a vested interest in the status quo favors reaction as evidenced by his swift response to the St. Croix Avis' story on VIPA contracts.

11. Whereas Mr. Edward E. Thomas' memorandum of June 4, 1991 was sent in haste and anger on June 5, 1991 in order to coincide with the fire at VIPA and Mr. Eugen Gottlieb's absence from the Island.

12. Whereas a routine investigation has disclosed that the VIPA assignment was neither discussed with Mr. Louis Willis nor collated with the other accounts in the Delinquent Accounts and Returns Branch so as to avoid a duplication of assignment.

13. Whereas a Virgin Islands Revenue Officer, who relies on arbitrary power in a less-that-professional governmental system cannot be temporarily assigned from the Virgin Islands to the U.S. mainland to assist in emergencies.

14. Whereas a Stateside Revenue Officer's goal is to be respected, trusted and believed, popularity is a Virgin Islands Revenue Officer's goal in an inferior Tax System.

15. Whereas Liston Monsanto is willing to carry out the Bureau's "managerial initiatives" as long as he knows the Bureau's Standard Operating Procedures.

Now therefore I Liston Monsanto seeing that Mr. Edward E. Thomas is not willing to give the Devil his due although the Devil (Liston Monsanto) is willing to cooperate in the Port Authority assignment, thereby carrying his share of the burden while relying on the foregoing statements of fact as a basis for his concerns, submit them to Mr. Thomas - as they are either nuisances or blessings in disguise contributing to Liston Monsanto's displeasure.

Additionally, Liston Monsanto realizes that a lack of initiative or resourcefulness on his part could defeat the purpose of the Delinquent Accounts and Returns Branch (especially during this period when there is much

talk of arson and suppression of evidence at VIPA) and has therefore begun
work on the assignment.

Liston Monsanto has been bitten once and consequently he has become
twice shy. However he feels certain (because of Mr. Thomas' "no nonsense"
attitude) that this letter will result in the much-needed guidelines.

Sincerely,

Liston B. Monsanto
Internal Revenue Officer
Chief Shop Steward

Thomas answered on June 11, 1991 with a memorandum to me which said:

GOVERNMENT OF
THE VIRGIN ISLANDS OF THE UNITED STATES

---o---

VIRGIN ISLANDS
BUREAU OF INTERNAL REVENUE

---o---

Lockharts Garden No. 1A
Charlotte Amalie, St. Thomas, U.S.V.I. 00802

June 11, 1991

MEMORANDUM

TO : Mr. Liston Monsanto
Revenue Officer IV

VIA : Mr. Louis M. Willis
Asst. Chief, DARB

Mr. Graciano Belardo
Deputy Director

FROM : Mr. Edward E. Thomas
Director

RE : Review of your inventory

    I have read the correspondence between you and your immediate supervisor, Mr. Willis, Asst. Chief, DAR Branch.

    As you know, you are already scheduled to meet with Mr. Belardo, Deputy Director and Mr. Willis on Monday, July 1, 1991 to review and analyze with them the status of the "Port Authority" projects. That meeting is scheduled for 10:00 A.M.

    You will now bring to that meeting also your complete inventory of cases for review by Mr. Belardo and Mr. Willis.

Edward E. Thomas
Director

    These gentlemen, like the others before them, had brought a duck to a cock fight. They were operating arbitrarily and didn't even know it. I shot back at Thomas on June 12, 1991. I wrote:

403

Liston B. Monsanto, Sr.

June 12, 1991

Mr. Edward E. Thomas
Director
V.I. Bureau of Internal Revenue
St. Thomas, Virgin Islands 00802

Dear Mr. Thomas:

Your memorandum of June 11, 1991, has been declared paradoxical and consequently raises several questions:

1. Where are the appointment papers designating Mr. Willis Assistant Chief?

2. What happened to the guidelines that I've been relentlessly asking for?

3. Didn't Mr. Willis get my inventory on June 6, 1991?

4. Would you have Mr. Willis cite his authority for a Revenue Officer being present at a review of accounts?

5. Don't we have forms designed for the purpose of conducting reviews?

6. Is the messenger or someone going to make himself available to move the accounts?

7. Is this some form of harassment?

Mr. Willis is a person who has yet to earn my respect. He has great courage and strength which (according to the record) is used for the following reasons:

1. May 11, 1988 – In his role of gold-bricker, Mr. Willis admits to going home during duty hours for his day-time siesta.

2. September 16, 1988 – Mr. Willis threatens Liston Monsanto (who is not afraid of him) in full view of his potential subordinates.

3. September 14, 1989 – Mr. Willis leaves his office to assume a posture of attack against a lower echelon employee.

4. May 29, 1991 – Mr. Willis reports to work in his undershirt.

Letter   -2-   6/12/91

Mr. Edward Thomas

      I fully respect the office of Assistant Chief, Delinquent Accounts and Returns Branch and I'm furthermore willing to cooperate with you while awaiting the answers to the foregoing questions, but it should be noted that cooperation does not mean emasculation.

                               Sincerely,

                               Liston Monsanto
                               Internal Revenue Officer

cc: Mr. Belardo
       Deputy Director

       Mr. Louis Willis
       Asst. Chief, DAR Br.

     On June 27, 1991 Willis sent me my annual Employee Performance Report with the following comments: "Revenue Officer, Mr. Monsanto need to start utilizing more Collection forms (tools) such as forms 4183, 668W, 668B, 668A, 433B, 433A, 433D and 2159. These forms are used by Revenue Officers, but Revenue Officer Monsanto does not utilize them. Revenue Officer needs to produce more quality work. Revenue Officer's collection is disappointing and enforcement forms (tools) mentioned above are not utilized. Revenue Officer does not accept change or direction." There was no way I'd sign a stupid report like that. What I would do was write an attachment to the report which said:

Liston B. Monsanto, Sr.

GOVERNMENT OF THE U.S. VIRGIN ISLANDS

EMPLOYEE PERFOMANCE REPORT
(READ THE REVERSE SIDE BEFORE FILLING OUT)

EMPLOYEE NAME	JOB CLASSIFICATION Internal	DEPARTMENT
Liston Monsanto	Revenue Officer IV	Bur. of Int. Revenue St. Thomas, V.I.

REASON FOR EVALUATION DATE (1) _____ RATING PERIOD
(2) _____ FROM 6/17/90 TO: 6/17/91

PROBATION ☐ FINAL PROBATION ☐ ANNUAL ☒ SPECIAL (EXTENSIONS, ETC.) ☐

SECTION A—FACTOR CHECK LIST
Immediate Supervisor Must Check Each Factor in the Appropriate Column

	A Not Satisfactory	B Requires Improvement	C Meets Standards	D Exceeds Standards	E Does Not Apply
1 Observance of Work Hours		X			
2 Attendance			X		
3 Grooming and Dress			X		
4 Compliance With Rules		X			
5 Safety Practices			X		
6 Attitude Towards Public			X		
7 Attitude Towards Employees		X			
8 Knowledge of Work		X			
9 Work Judgments		X			
10 Planning and Organizing			X		
11 Job Skill Level		X			
12 Quality of Work	X				
13 Volume of Acceptable Work		X			
14 Meeting Deadlines		X			
15 Accepts Responsiblity		X			
16 Accepts Direction	X				
17 Accepts Change	X				
18 Effectiveness Under Stress			X		
19 Appearance of Work Station			X		
20 Operation and Care of Equipment			X		
21 Work Coordination			X		
22 Initiative		X			
23 (Additional Factors)					
24					
25					
26					
27					
28					
29					
FOR EMPLOYEES WHO SUPERVISE OTHERS					
30 Planning and Organizing					
31 Scheduling and Coordinating					
32 Training and Instructing					
33 Productivity					
34 Evaluating Subordinates					
35 Judgments and Decisions					
36 Ability to Motivate Employer					
37 Operational Economy					
38 Supervisory Control					
39 (Additional Factors)					
40					
41					

(PRELIMINARY EVALUATION)
RATED BY: _____ DATE: _____

DEPT. HEAD: _____ DATE: _____

SECTION B — Record job STRENGTHS and superior performance incidents.

SECTION C—Record PROGRESS ACHIEVED in attaining previou set goals for improved work performance, or career development

SECTION D—Record specific GOALS or IMPROVEMENT PROGRAMS to be undertaken during next evaluation period.

Revenue Officer, Mr. Monsanto need to start utilizing more collection forms (tools) such as forms 4183, 668W, 668B, 668A, 433B, 433A, 433D and 2159. These froms are used by revenue officers, but Revenue Officer Monsanto does not utilize them.

SECTION E—Record specific work performance DEFICIENCIES job behavior requiring improvement or correction. (Explain che in Column A.)

Revenue Officer needs to produce more qualit work. Revenue Officer's collection is disappointing and enforcement forms (tools) mentioned above are not utlized.
Revenue Officer does not accept change or direction.

SUMMARY EVALUATION— Check Overall Performance —

Satisfactory ( ) Not (X) Requires Improvement ( ) Effective Meets Stand.
( ) Exceeds Standards

RATER: I certify this report represents my best judgmer
( ) I do ( ) Do not Recommend this employee I granted permanent status.
(For Final probation reports only)

(Rater's Signature) _____ (Title) _____ (Date)

Department Head: Edward E. Thomas-Director

REVIEWER: (If None. So Indicate)
(Reviewer's Signature) _____ (Title) _____ (Date)

EMPLOYEE: I certify that this report has been discussed with I understand my signature does not necessarily ind agreement.

Comment _____

Attachment to Performance Report for the period 6/17/90 - 6/17/91

Title 24, Section 65 of the Virgin Islands Code says in part:"It shall be an unfair labor practice for an employer to -- (1) spy upon or keep under surveillance, whether directly or through agents or any other person, any activities of employees or their representatives in the exercise of the rights set forth in Section 64 of this Title".

As the wife of Director Edward E. Thomas, Mrs. Lucia Thomas (an Internal Revenue Officer working ostensibly under the supervision of Mr. Louis Willis and positioned on the side of labor) is directly affected by the provisions of the aforementioned Title.

A misguided Mr. Louis M. Willis (the rater) is completely unaware of the existence of Title 24, Section 65 of the Virgin Islands Code. In fact, his continued disregard for Virgin Islands Law is incredible.

Mr. Willis actually believes that the Virgin Islands Bureau of Internal Revenue belongs to Mr. and Mrs. Edward Thomas and consequently feels that Liston Monsanto (ala Louis Willis) must show some form of submissive respect to the husband and wife team, who because of their comfortable positions in the Bureau, have been reputed as absolute monarchs.

Monotonous as he is when it comes to doing unprincipled things, Mr. Willis works as a hireling and acts the part of a moslem fakir in order to hold on to a position which he unlawfully received as a token payment for helping to persecute Liston Monsanto.

He loves the high degree of office politics which is most prevalent "in a Virgin Islands environment where loyalty is more important than honesty, where the police are too sympathetic to wealthy criminals and where everyone is indifferent to corruption".

Because the Virgin Islands Bureau of Internal Revenue has the characteristics of a monarchy and because what it takes to impersonate Liston Monsanto (pride, honesty, intestinal fortitude, etc. as evidenced by Opinion 81-1434 of the Third Circuit Court) Mr. Louis Willis does not have, I am refusing to sign the attached Performance Report for the period June 17, 1990 to June 17, 1991.

June 27, 1991

On July 1, 1991, poking fun at Thomas and his frivolous assignment, I wrote him the following letter:

Liston B. Monsanto, Sr.

July 1, 1991

Mr. Edward E. Thomas
Director
V.I. Bureau of Internal Revenue
St. Thomas, V.I. 00802

Dear Mr. Thomas:

It is an axiom that stories of adventure fire the imagination, but who would have imagined that amid a fire at the Virgin Islands Port Authority on June 5, 1991, coupled with the fact that on that particular day Mr. Eugen Gottlieb (the Port Authority's Acting Executive Director) was off-island, that I would be assigned the arduous task (pursuant to a June 4, 1991, memorandum from your office, which was received by me on June 5, 1991) of conferring with Mr. Gottlieb for the sole purpose of securing much information on the Virgin Islands Port Authority contracts? Only a sycophant intrepid enough to go along with anything would have imagined that.

Anyway, trying to forget the past and seeking to get down to the more mundane problems facing the Virgin Islands Bureau of Internal Revenue, upon accepting the assignment I started out like a person full of fire and courage, and using the guidelines issued me in your memorandum as an essential first step towards a "new direction" in the Bureau, I immediately began work on the first phase of the Virgin Islands Port Authority assignment.

After prolonged interviews with Mrs. Grace James (secretary to Mr. Eugen Gottlieb) I met with Mr. Gottlieb, and together we thoroughly went over the several names appearing on the newspaper clipping which accompanied your memorandum and which had been taken from the St. Croix Avis.

This morning I welcome the opportunity of presenting to you the paper work designed to show you exactly what was done by Mr. Gottlieb in completing Phase I of the assignment.

Phase II got underway on June 21, 1991, when (in keeping with the Virgin Islands Government policy not to issue business licenses without first making a tax delinquency check) I sent a memorandum to Mr. Roy A. Vanterpool (Chief Processing and Accounts Branch) asking for a status report.

But unlike Mr. Eugen Gottlieb who was most cooperative, a hostile Mr. Roy Vanterpool - completely oblivious of the fact that our jobs are interrelated, and acting as if he was being ordered to do now what he had failed to do previously, evinced a bitter attitude and in a belligerent tone denied my request, thereby bringing the assignment to an unexpected ending.

Letter   -2-   7/1/91

Mr. Edward E. Thomas
Director

It is significant to note here that in the Virgin Islands Bureau of Internal Revenue our chief problem concerns our ability to project ourselves as professionals rather than ordinary people.

It must be noted also that as you continue to work - hell bent on determining a future course of action for the Virgin Islands Bureau of Internal Revenue, there should be no doubts in anyone's mind that you can only accomplish your objective through the usage of guidelines.

I too am in need of guidelines. "Let us be thankful for the tools; but for them the rest of us could not succeed."

                                    Sincerely,

                                    Liston Monsanto
                                    Internal Revenue Officer

cc: Mr. Graciano Belardo
    Deputy Director

    Mr. Louis M. Willis
    Asst. Chief, DAR Branch

VIPA contracts worth $92 million

By CHARLES FISHER
Avis Political Reporter

The dollar value of Virgin Island Port Authority contracts which involve its Engineering Division adds up to $92,038,296.

This is an acute financial fact considering this last week's discussions during committee of the whole hearings which were held on St. Thomas by the 19th Legislature.

Given the controversy surrounding public scrutiny, and alleged violations of the Sunshine Law by the VIPA Board—a list of contracted projects for services rendered through VIPA seem germane to the issue.

Below is a list of contracts that are alleged to be the result of VIPA Board decisions.

		COMPLETE	ON GOING
Acosta & Associates Foundations/ Bid Pkg. 2 Slab/CEKA $4,627,892		✓	
Addison Steel Structural Steel $4,311,398 CEKA Terminal		✓	
American Airlines Terminal Improvements VIPA (August 1990) (AHA). $1,183,000		✓	PENDING CLOSE. OUT
V.I. Port Authority AHA Terminal General Engineering Renovations $687,036		✓	
Bristol Childs/ Consultants - AHA Contracts & Amendments 8/88 Amendments 1-4 $326,739			✓
Betteroads Apron & Taxiways (Bid Pkg. 1) CEKA $6,144,467		✓	
Betteroads (6/90) Access Road $5,272,277 Parking Lot/CEKA			85%
Betteroads/Phase IV North G.A. Apron (12/89) T/W/CEKA $3,299,349		✓	
Betteroads/Phase V Completion of the remainder $16,897,632 /Airfield work Taxiways.			✓

The Extreme Test

Complete   On.Going

Parking lighting poles
T/W Guidance signs
J. P. Electric   R/W-T/W lighting syst n   ✓
$606,067
Maintenance Bldg.
(In-house)   ✓
$23,083
Meridian Engineering   Overlay-Existing T/W   ✓
$1,318,833
MSI   CFR Building   ✓
$123,883
ECS Electrical
Construction Specialist Replacement of Beacon &
Tower   ✓
$28,000
Tender Pier   Repair by in-house crew   ✓
$100,000
Zenon Construction   Replacement of Awning AHA ✓
$19,680
Zenon Construction   Removal of Debris from
Krause Lagoon   ✓
$13,260
APC Rentals   Rehanging of tiers Crown Bay   ✓
$17,295
Charley's Trucking   Repair of Groin/Gregerie   ✓
$50,000
Deeper Cheaper   Diving for tires Crown Bay   ✓
$3,000
William J. Demetree   Repair of Eleven Bldg.
& Company   ✓
$293,990
Tropical Shipping   Repair of Warehouse Bldg.   ✓
$8,890
           Total:$92,038,296

411

VIPA from page 3

COMPLETE | ON-GOING

Eastman, Ken $9,072	Soil Borings-Tortola Wharf STT		✓
Grenier Inc. 6/88 $2,350,000	Consultants AHA Terminal Building	✓	
Grenier Inc. 10/89 $261,987	Consultants Access Road parking lot, kiosks phasing plans, etc CEKA		✓
Island Developers $2,118,560	VIPA Office/STT		80%
Jaca & Sierra $495,265	Concrete Testing CEKA/Phases IV & V CEKA Airport Improvements		✓
Ocean Systems Research, Inc. $6,380	Frederiksted Pier Environmental Plan	✓	
Parsons (Original contract January 1977)+ 13 amendments to 12/92 $864,782	Consultants	✓	✓
Frank J. Rooney Bid Pkg.9 5/90 $2,190,000	Terminal Bldg. Signage Graphics, Baggage Handling System & SoundSystem/CEKA	✓	
Frank J. Rooney Bid Pkg.7 8/89 $17,276,183	Architectural/Mech/Electrical CEKA	✓	PENDING CLOSEOUT
Aggregate Construction Restoration of Electrical System $191,540	Containerport	✓	
Aggregte Construction (A/C Tropical Shipping) $103,650	Containerport	✓	
Balfour Beatty $3,111,680	Frederiksted Pier	✓	
Balfour Beatty $4,270,601	AHA R/W Extended Area	✓	
C/R General Contractors $429,027	National Guard Building	✓	
C/R General Contractors $51,143	St. Croix Aviation Building	✓	
C/R General Contractors $66,609	Purchasing Building	✓	
C/R General Contractors $108,464	Gallows Bay	✓	
Eastern Metro Hangar	Pending		
General Engineering $105,615	H & O Building	✓	
General Engineering $26,900	Installation of Apron floodlighting	✓	

Willis also received a letter from me on July 1, 1991. The letter stated:

July 1, 1991

Mr. Louis M. Willis
Delinquent Accounts & Returns Branch
V.I. Bureau of Internal Revenue
St. Thomas, Virgin Islands 00802

Dear Mr. Willis:

Your aberrant behavior and Mr. Edward E. Thomas' somewhat vituperative memorandum of June 11, 1991, show that the little latitude given you in
pretending to carry out the duties of your office, has completely reversed
your moral values to the point where you cannot interpret the language in Section 5, Article II of our Contract.

This being the case, I feel it an obligation to duty to respond succinctly in sympathy to wit: I know how little the words and acts of friends
can do to ease the pain that has come to you as an employee desirous of doing
a veracious person a wrongful act.

I can imagine the terrible pressures that have been brought upon
you by the many vessels of wrath (evil people) and fifth columnists who clan-
destinely pursue your cooperation while posing as your friend – only to
force you into doing a whole lot of ugly things you wouldn't normally do.

You may recall that on June 6, 1991, I forwarded my inventory of accounts to your office with a cover letter, which cautioned you in part against
the lawless life you have chosen to lead.

The accounts were returned to me presumably after they had been reviewed by you. Conspicuously missing however, were forms 5188 and 5188-A
(forms used by the U.S. Internal Revenue Service in analyzing a Revenue Officer's case assignment) and/or comments from your office.

I have always known that crime has its sequence of misery, but now
that I have reviewed the sequence of events—which took pains to do, I have
reached the sad conclusion that somehow you are not satisfied with being boss,
you instead want to be bossy.

Today, you are being misled by Mr. Edward E. Thomas, who was found
guilty (on March 22, 1991) of violating Section 5, Article II of our contract. Mr. Thomas knows that unlike Jerome Ferdinand you are a fopish person
who loves being built up and consequently, he's using you and others as in-
termediaries between Liston Monsantoand himself.

Liston B. Monsanto, Sr.

Maybe you ought to offer Mr. Thomas your help in easing the tensions in the Delinquent Accounts and Returns Branch. Let him know that there is much to be done in the Branch and that his acting like a perfect stranger to what is legally and morally right does nothing to improve our relationship.

Once again though, I'm making my inventory of accounts available to you for your review. They can be found in a box atop the filing cabinet in my office.

Keep your shirt on,

Liston B. Monsanto
Chief Shop Steward

c.c. Mr. Edward E. Thomas
     Mr. Graciano Belardo

Thomas had to keep me busy. He had to show Farrelly and everybody else that he and his law-breaking ways could handle Liston Monsanto. He had come to the realization that although he was asking me to write to Willis and/or Belardo, I had continued to write directly to him. On July 1, 1991 he wrote directly to me saying:

GOVERNMENT OF
THE VIRGIN ISLANDS OF THE UNITED STATES

——◇——

VIRGIN ISLANDS
BUREAU OF INTERNAL REVENUE

——◇——

Lockharts Garden No. 1A
Charlotte Amalie, St. Thomas, U.S.V.I. 00802

July 1, 1991

MEMORANDUM

TO   : Mr. Liston Monsanto
              Internal Revenue Officer IV

FROM   : Mr. Edward E. Thomas
              Director

RE   : Virgin Islands Port Authority

I acknowledge receipt of your memo dated July 1, 1991.

I am enclosing a copy of my June 4, 1991 memo to you for your review and update. You, not Mr. Vanterpool, are to determine the tax status of each of the contractors,.... then you will proceed to complete tasks 3 and 4.

Mr. Belardo could not be in St. Thomas today therefore the session with him and Mr. Willis is rescheduled for Monday, July 8, 1991 at the same time and place.

Edward E. Thomas
Director

EET/cef

cc: Mr. Graciano Belardo, Deputy Director
    Mr. Louis M. Willis, Asst. Chief, DARB

Liston B. Monsanto, Sr.

On July 8, 1991 I responded to his memorandum saying:

July 8, 1991

Mr. Edward E. Thomas
Director
V.I. Bureau of Internal Revenue
Lockhart's Gardens #1-A
St. Thomas, Virgin Islands 00802

Dear Mr. Thomas:

After reading your ambiguous memorandum of July 1, 1991, which serves to complicate an already puzzling situation, I have become dubious over your modus operandi and consequently, I have concluded that the Virgin Islands Port Authority assignment is nothing but an old idea in a new guise.

I have detected an undercurrent of remorse over the fact that you are now trying to countermand the order and guidelines issued me in your memorandum of June 4, 1991. Exceeding that however, and rising to the surface is the sad fact that your latest instructions are not counter to those given initially.

Unless something is hidden from my view, I would dare say that it was because of my training and experience that you assigned me the arduous task of making certain that the many Contractors contractually employed by the Virgin Islands Port Authority were meeting their tax obligations.

From all indications the assignment was important, but time-consuming. Using my training and experience, while at the same time seeking to avoid duplications, I started out to successfully meet the challenge through the cheapest and quickest means by doing my homework and sticking to the guidelines. I did not expect that Mr. Roy Vanterpool would use the assignment to make capital of your attitude towards me.

I (Liston Monsanto), not Roy Vanterpool (a fact corroborated by you in your memorandum of July 1, 1991) is charged with the responsibility of determining the tax status of each Contractor whose name appears on the newspaper clipping taken from the St. Croix Avis.

While the usage of good judgement and maximum utilization of time go hand in hand, cooperation and teamwork are most essential in making the work of an organization successful and effective.

In order to use the correct approach and explanation in carrying out his duties, a Revenue Officer must know what is legally due and owing from a taxpayer before contacting that taxpayer.

The Processing and Accounts Branch and not Mr. Roy Vanterpool was used as a source of information before going outside the organization in a blind way.

416

Letter   -2-   July 8, 1991
Mr. Edward Thomas

I have to speculate at Mr. Vanterpool"s motives for the reason that upon receiving the VIPA assignment (the gist of which was explained to me in your memorandum of June 4, 1991), I shifted my emphasis from taxpayer delinquent accounts and began work in earnest as I saw the assignment as an incentive and an inducement to action. Are you now trying to say that the guidelines which were issued to me on June 4, 1991, are unimportant and therefore useless?

If we are to overcome any dissatisfaction we may feel, we must not allow an uncooperative Mr. Vanterpool to counter my plans (which incidentally, were drawn up following your June 4th memorandum) with any of his own.

Let's face it! The tax records are maintained by the Processing and Accounts Branch. Internal Revenue Officers are enforcers whose job it is to get information from all sources—especially those sources at their finger tips. Fishing expeditions are not a Revenue Officer's forte.

Permit me to fulfill my responsibility to you through the carefully laid plans of Liston Monsanto which were made based on your guidelines. Unless the assignment is frivolous or mutable, we must not allow Mr. Roy Vanterpool to become an obstacle to it.

Sincerely,

Liston B. Monsanto
Internal Revenue Officer

c.c. Mr. Graciano Belardo

Mr. Louis Willis

Later in the day I wrote him another letter which said:

July 8, 1991

Mr. Edward E. Thomas
Director
V.I. Bureau of Internal Revenue
Lockhart's Gardens #1-A
St. Thomas, Virgin Islands 00802

Dear Mr. Thomas:

Delegating authority to a Revenue Officer without that Revenue Officer having a clear understanding of what he can do, invites chaos. Having been systematically dismissed from duty on several occasions, my primary reason for persistently begging for guidelines has been to avoid a recurrent mistake on your part.

Several years ago (with your respected input playing a major role), I was told by the powers that be in the Virgin Islands Bureau of Internal Revenue, that a Revenue Officer to whom responsibility was delegated could cite as the basis for his authority the language embodied in Section 6301 of the United States Internal Revenue Code of 1954.

It must be noted that in my great desire to do my work and collect taxes without arousing a sense of injustice, I relied on section 6301 together with section 7602 of the aforementioned code as my justification for carrying out my duties and was thereafter relieved of my responsibilities through a dismissal. In using the code, I had gone against management's unwritten law, which took precedence over the code.

Recently, a triumvirate led by Messrs. Thomas, Belardo, and Willis(who by and large is a marginal performer) delegated me the authority to make certain that Contractors contractually employed by the Virgin Islands Port Authority meet their tax obligations.

They did so through the issuance of a June 4, 1991 memorandum from your office, which told me exactly what to do.

I'm all for the assignment (see my reports relating to it, which serve as evidence of my cooperation in the matter), but having been bitten so many times for doing what was legally correct, I've become very shy.

I know for a fact that the Processing and Accounts Branch establishes and maintains all Tax Returns, Files, Unit Ledger Card Files, and furnishes information from the files requested.

Letter   -2-   July 8, 1991
Mr. Edward E. Thomas

I know for a fact also, that that Branch is also responsible for furnishing advice and testimony concerning filing, processing, coding and related markings on all Returns and documents.

Because a Revenue Officer has the authority to determine what kind of action he must take and because he has the added authority to take that action, a request was made (pursuant to your guidelines) to the Processing and Accounts Branch to more or less provide me with a starting point on the several taxpayers involved in the VIPA assignment. In short, a yardstick.

But Mr. Roy Vanterpool (Chief of the Processing and Accounts Branch) not wanting to cooperate, but instead wanting my Persecutors (see letter of November 26, 1985 and reports of December 4, 1989 and September 10, 1990 in your possession) to escalate the torture of hostility and isolation, played the role of Usurper wresting the power from your office, and with unexpected ease, suspended action on the assignment. Had he read your memorandum of July 1, 1991, he would have known that Liston Monsanto and not Roy Vanterpool is charged with the responsibility of determining the tax status of the Contractors.

We must not (because of Mr. Vanterpool) do anything that is contradictory to your memoranda and the Internal Revenue Code. You need not worry about my part in the assignment. I shall cooperate with you to the fullest and comply with any instructions as long as they are not conflicting.

Please tell Mr. Roy Vanterpool to "do what is right, for it will gratify some people and astonish the rest."

Sincerely,

Liston B. Monsanto
Internal Revenue Officer

c.c. Mr. Graciano Belardo

Mr. Louis Willis

On July 17, 1991 I wrote to Thomas and in that letter I told him that following my retirement I would write a book. Here's what I said in the letter:

Liston B. Monsanto, Sr.

July 17, 1991

Mr. Edward E. Thomas
Director
V.I. Bureau of Internal Revenue
St. Thomas, V.I. 00802

Dear Mr. Thomas:

Through this letter, I'm not asking that you take my word for gospel nor am I asking that you consider the contents a graceful speech, I'm instead asking that you review in chronological order the files, starting with my letter of January 18, 1991, to Governor Alexander A. Farrelly (a copy of which was received by you on that particular day).

A review of the subject documents would show that I have been trying desperately to point out to you that the Virgin Islands Bureau of Internal Revenue (through its leadership) is guilty of persecuting Liston Monsanto and violating the various laws and authorities which were intended to serve as guidelines for us to make judgements or determine a course of action.

The Bureau's pattern of operating has not changed since Mr. Anthony P. Olive was removed by the Governor for his less-than-satisfactory performance. And based on what's going on at the moment, it is highly unlikely that things will change.

Today I'm being asked to report to your office at 4:00 p.m., for a summit parley. Knowing, however, that there is hardly anything more for me to add to the contents of my letters, which would relate to working conditions in the Bureau puzzles me and makes me wonder why I'm being asked to attend.

Mr. Louis Willis (Assistant Chief?) who has indicated through a memorandum that he's looking forward to being on hand for the summit parley appears bewildered by what's going on in the Bureau.

On the one hand he continues to make excessive demands for my presence before him together with my inventory of accounts in order to show the world who's in charge, while on the other hand he tells the world through my performance rating for the period ending June 17, 1991 (which by the way was prepared through the usage of his psychic impressions) that he has reviewed my accounts and that I'm not up to the standards of a Virgin Islands fun-loving Revenue Officer.

The truth of the matter is, Mr. Willis has never reviewed my accounts which were made available to him and furthermore, had he taken the time to review my performance ratings for the periods ending June 17, 1989 and June 17, 1990 (both prepared by him) his credibility today would be beyond reproach. See what on-the-job-training can do for you?

420

Like former Governor Ralph M. Paiewonsky, I'm in the process of having my memoirs published so that a third party may be made aware of the injustices in the Virgin Islands Bureau of Internal Revenue.

Finally, Mr. Willis must be told that misrepresentation and lies have never resulted in a permanent benefit for anyone.

Sincerely,

Liston Monsanto
Internal Revenue Officer

My next letter to Edward Thomas which is dated July 18, 1991 briefly explains what happened in Thomas' office on the afternoon of July 17, 1991:

July 18, 1991

Mr. Edward E. Thomas
Director
V.I. Bureau of Internal Revenue
Lockhart's Garden #1-A
St. Thomas, Virgin Islands 00802

Dear Mr. Thomas:

Please let the record show that because of Mr. Louis Willis' belligerence and fondness for fighting (he became a most vociferous person in challenging me to do battle with him, and were it not for your person coming between us, we may have gotten into it in the same way that he and his subordinate Claude Maduro got involved in 1989) you were forced to adjourn our meeting of July 17, 1991.

Prior to the adjournment, a frustrated Mr. Willis—acting like a person who had risen to a higher place than he was fitted for, showed that he was without knowledge when I used the word "grandfather" in a figurative way. He's going to have to learn a lot more about supervisory responsibility. He's not savvy at all.

I'm not one to criticize anyone until I know all the circumstances, but it must be noted without reservations that because of his conduct Mr. Louis Willis always seems to be the object of my criticisms. You'd think he'd try to be a model of deportment as one of your supervisors.

Although our meeting started off having s quality of harshness and sharpness, as a matured person I must admit that during Mr. Willis' absence from the room we had kind of reconciled with each other. Yes, as the meeting progressed, I got the feeling that I was being given a cordial welcome back to the organization.

It is distressing to note that Mr. Willis' attitude and overall behavior is not conducive to the overall growth of the Virgin Islands Bureau of Internal Revenue—especially in his role as supervisor.

So in the interest of avoiding any animosity or repercussions I will not be meeting with Mr. Willis at anytime soon. I would like to take this opportunity however, to thank you for taking the time to meet with me face-to-face. Your face showed no signs of vexation over my retirement proposal.

I now look forward to hearing from you or even meeting with you for that matter.

Sincerely,

Liston B. Monsanto
Internal Revenue Officer

Then on July 19, 1991 I wrote directly to Willis as follows:

July 19, 1991

RECEIVED
DAR BRANCH

JUL 19 1991

V. I. Bureau of internal Revenue

Mr. Louis M. Willis
C/O V.I. Bureau of Internal Revenue
Lockhart Gardens #1-A
St. Thomas, V.I. 00802

Dear Mr. Willis:

Because of your disrespect for law and authority and because of your fondness for fighting plus the added fact that you honestly feel that your spurious relationship with many of the wrongdoers in positions of authority gives you the right to threaten and molest certain law-abiding people, I find it of the utmost importance to write directly to you — if only for the record.

On several occasions you have threatened me with violence (the last such threat coming before Mr. Edward E. Thomas in his office at about 4:55 p.m. on July 17, 1991) and immediately thereafter you have spread the news of these threats to many people — within and without of the Virgin Islands Bureau of Internal Revenue where we are both employed.

Admittedly I'm a coward, yet I'm not afraid of you. I'm very much afraid of what I might do to you in defense of myself. Here's hoping that I've made myself clear.

Copies of this letter are being sent to Mr. Edward E. Thomas, the Attorney General's Office and the Department of Public Safety whose Police Chief continues to talk about lawlessness in our community.

These people must be made aware of your continuing threats of violence against me.

Sincerely,

Liston Monsanto

P.O. Box 2763
St. Thomas, V.I. 00803

cc: Department of Justice

Department of Public Safety

Mr. Edward E. Thomas
Director

Farrelly had failed to be a leader and to bring a sense of discipline to the Virgin Islands Government. He was doing his last term in office and therefore should not have been courting the favor of the Virgin Islands people for votes. What was he going to do about the Virgin Islands Bureau of Internal Revenue. I addressed him on July 23, 1991:

Liston B. Monsanto, Sr.

July 23, 1991

Honorable Alexander A. Farrelly
Governor - U.S. Virgin Islands
Government House
St. Thomas, Virgin Islands 00801

Dear Governor Farrelly:

Included in my January 18, 1991 "letter of thanks" to you was much information on a belligerent Mr. Louis Willis, which showed that as an upstart with a fondness for fighting in the workplace, Mr. Willis was not yet ready to enter on the professional duties of the Acting Assistant Chief of the Delinquent Accounts and Returns Branch.

Furthermore, you were cautioned against entrusting Mr. Willis with the care and overall management of the Delinquent Accounts and Returns Branch. But because the power elite in the Virgin Islands Bureau of Internal Revenue feel threatened by anything coming from me, I was completely ignored.

Now that you have indicated through your actions that personnel recruiting in the Bureau is a triumph of hope over experience and that there is no room for me on the top rung of the Delinquent Accounts and Returns Branch, and now that Mr. Edward E. Thomas has expressed the feeling that I'm causing a great many people to distrust people with whom they've worked for years, I'd like to retire from the Virgin Islands Government only after a suitable retirement plan has been agreed upon.

Keeping the context in perspective however, it is significant to note here, that not only were my pleas of January 18, 1991 ignored, but the Bureau's management went on to compound their error when on March 11, 1991, they (pursuant to the authority given them from your office) appointed Mr. Willis to the position of Assistant Chief of the Delinquent Accounts and Returns Branch.

What I've written so far serves as a background of earlier conditions and events in the Virgin Islands Bureau of Internal Revenue as they relate to an inexperienced Mr. Louis Willis.

This background was used as my introduction so as to make it easy for you to understand the main part of this letter, which follows in the upcoming paragraphs.

At about 4:55 P.M. on Wednesday, July 17, 1991, (in the office of Mr. Edward E. Thomas) Mr. Louis Willis took a turn for the irrational worse, when he challenged me to do battle with him in the presence of Mr. Thomas, who had to come between us.

Mr. Willis (still feeling his oats and knowing full well that our governmental system does nothing by way of punishing white-collar criminals and wrongdoers), did a like thing on September 16, 1988, when he charged my desk (where I was sitting immersed in my work) with a chair over his head threatening-through the usage of obscenities, to use his fists and the chair on me.

Immediately thereafter I reported the incident to Mr. Anthony P. Olive (former Director) and the Department of Justice, where - due largely to the fact that I was involved, it fell on deaf ears. Had they done something positive then, it is very doubtful that what happened on July 17th would have occurred. How many young people in the Bureau may be encouraged or otherwise influenced by Mr. Willis' antics remains conjectural.

I am a coward, yet I'm not afraid of Mr. Willis. I am the type of coward who is terribly afraid of what I might do to him in defending myseelf. I've had it up to my neck with Mr. Willis.

Following the incident of July 17th, Mr. Willis began bragging to his friends and other people not connected with the Bureau, thereby forcing me to tell him in a letter the type of coward that I am. Incidentally, copies of the letter which is dated July 19, 1991, were sent to the Police Chief, the Department of Justice and Mr. Edward E. Thomas.

I was hired by the Virgin Islands Bureau of Internal Revenue to use my brain in carrying out my duties in conformity with the various laws and authorities of the Virgin Islands Government. Fighting in the workplace with another employee is not my forte.

In any organization there will always be one person who knows what is going on. This person must be fired.

So in order to allay any fears that anyone may have regarding my retirement, and in order to begin work on my memoirs, I have submitted a proposal to Mr. Edward E. Thomas for his review and consideration. If he decides to act on it favorably, I'll be leaving posthaste.

Sincerely yours,

Liston B. Monsanto
P.O. Box 2763
St. Thomas, V.I. 00803

For some time I had entertained thoughts of retiring from the service. With their amateurish ways, Farrelly, Thomas and Willis were not going to force me into doing what I did not want to do. Unlike the other people in our Branch, I was never going to accept Louis "Lolo" Willis as my Supervisor.

I was closing in on forty (40) years of governmental service and I thought I would submit a proposal to Thomas for his review. As mentioned before, most of the employees with whom I was required to work were contemporaries of my children, thereby making me a patriarch. They were sympathetic towards my cause, but living in a passive Virgin Islands society they could only operate through the passive obedience of slaves.

I wrote to Thomas on October 18, 1991, using as my lead-in a quotation from James G. Fleming which said:

Liston B. Monsanto, Sr.

RECEIVED
DIRECTOR'S OFFICE
OCT 18 1991
VIRGIN ISLANDS BUREAU OF
INTERNAL REVENUE
St. Thomas, V.I.

October 18, 1991

Mr. Edward E. Thomas
Director
V.I. Bureau of Internal Revenue
Lockhart's Garden #1-A
St. Thomas, Virgin Islands 00802

"Without compromise there would be no peace
treaties, no "happy marriages", no democratic governments, no community in neighborhoods. Compromise is not surrender or defeat.
Both sides-or all sides-win".

-James G. Fleming

Dear Mr. Thomas:

Whereas our paths diverged following our stormy meeting of July 17, 1991,
and whereas I'm having difficulty and trouble understanding why our meeting hasn't
given serious attention to my "still-to-be-considered" retirement proposal, I find
it of the utmost importance to express (in writing) my disapproval over the way
that I'm being treated while speaking out at the same time against your isolationist policies.

At the outset however, it must be stated that what will happen to Liston
Monsanto in the Virgin Islands Bureau of Internal Revenue is often problematic only because those whose zeal in some cause or movement, goes beyond reasonable limits.

By now you must know that Detective stories are my passion and to the extent that you've been told that I'm enthusiastic over my imminent retirement from
the Virgin Islands Government, I have concluded that your failure to think of something that would direct the movement or course of my retirement proposal is a despicable act designed only to isolate me from my co-workers, in the hope that such
action would systematically force me into an even earlier retirement.

What's more, your unwillingness to speak plainly in your steadfast aim
to have me mistake tact for fact is causing me to look at you with wonder. Pray
tell me, what can I do to further my cause with you?

It saddens me to think that my situation in the Virgin Islands Bureau
of Internal Revenue has become a perennial problem only because I have not forsaken or renounced my moral principles.

I have never ever been a person who takes pride or comfort in wasting
his breath on causes that are doomed for failure, and furthermore, as one who
suffers from terminal honesty, it is incredible for me to believe that you in
your position of Director of the Bureau of Internal Revenue and an official who
has shown clearly that he can promote an Internal Revenue Officer I (Mr. Louis
Willis) to the second highest level within the Delinquent Accounts and Returns
Branch (i.e. Assistant Chief) that you cannot now use your powerful influence

Letter   -2-   October 18. 1991
Mr. Edward E. Thomas

to persuade the powers that be to work on my retirement proposal. Lest you forget, the precedent was set sometime in 1981 when Mr. Robert Woods and Mr. John Ferrant were both employees of the Virgin Islands Bureau of Internal Revenue.

My retirement together with a decent pension could have a profound effect on my life, and I might add, that as anxious as you are to see me leave the Virgin Islands Bureau of Internal Revenue, so too am I anxious to depart.

"Even the United States of America became united only because of the many compromises forged at the Constitutional Convention in Philadelphia."

Sincerely yours,

Liston B. Monsanto
Internal Revenue Officer

c.c. Gov. Alexander A. Farrelly

Farrelly had been communicating with Thomas and the members of his shadow cabinet on a regular basis placing much emphasis on my situation. On October 18th he sent me a message through a mutual friend asking me to explain my impending retirement. I sent him a letter on October 23, 1991 which said:

RECEIVED

October 23, 1991

OCT 2 3 1991

OFFICE OF
THE GOVERNOR

Honorable Alexander A. Farrelly
Governor - U.S. Virgin Islands
Government House
St. Thomas, Virgin Islands 00801

Dear Governor Farrelly:

Inasmuch as I've been advised by our mutual friend to briefly state my thoughts to you as they relate to my retirement from the Virgin Islands Government, I have consented to forward to you the pertinent information having a connection with the matter at hand.

Before saying anything else however, I'd like to state in the most unambiguous terms that as a classified employee who has little concern with politics, it is neither my intention to wage a contentious campaign against Mr. Edward E. Thomas (Director of the Virgin Islands Bureau of Internal Revenue) nor is it my intention-in any way, shape or form, to seize the reins of the Virgin Islands Government. I'm completely exhausted and consequently, I have been making a determined effort to bow out graciously from the Virgin Islands Bureau of Internal Revenue.

In order to provide an account of events for my future use, I applied the law of evidence, thereby recording much information which now discloses that on July 17, 1991-in my impassioned plea for tolerance before Mr. Edward E. Thomas, that I submitted a retirement proposal for his review and consideration.

I repeated the same proposal to you in a letter dated July 23, 1991. And once again after a three month hiatus, I wrote to Mr. Thomas on October 18, 1991 expressing a fervent desire (with ample justification) to retire with a reasonably good pension.

It must be noted that during my tenure of service as a civil servant with the Virgin Islands Government, I have witnessed a great deal of trickery and deception. Now that I know for certain that the position of Chief-Delinquent Accounts and Returns Branch (although vacant) is not extensible to me, and now that I know that my moralistic behavior is not suited or appropriate for the Bureau of Internal Revenue and is therefore causing my Persecutors to escalate the torture of hostility and isolation against me, I'd very much like to depart.

Because we are not of the same opinion, Mr. Thomas sees me as a refractory. His equivocal answers to my questions have left me uncertain as to his real opinion on the matter of my retirement. He talks in a confused and meaningless way leading to discordant views.

Letter   -2-   October 23, 1991
Gov. Farrelly

        With the realization that Mr. Thomas has been imbued with the ambition
to succeed, I'm of the belief that my continued presence in the workplace as a
Shop Steward, etc. will serve only to create a gulf between his office, myself,
and the members of our Bargaining Unit in a manner such as it did during the
stewardship of his predecessors.

        As a person serving at your pleasure, Mr. Thomas is a most trusted dele-
gate and subordinate and this Governor, I wholeheartedly respect.

        Finally, the contents of this letter is private; it concerns nobody but
Mr. Thomas, you and myself. So in closing, I ask that you give my retirement proposal the legal stamp of authenticity that it deserves.

        My cause is just, my cause is moral, my cause is right.

                                With all due fondness and respect,

                                Liston B. Monsanto
                                P.O. Box 2763
                                St. Thomas, V.I. 00803

    On November 22, 1991 Thomas was at it again. He docked me four (4) hours leave without pay
causing me to file yet another Grievance. These fellows were very spiteful. I sent Thomas a letter
on November 22, 1991 which said:

Liston B. Monsanto, Sr.

November 22, 1991

Mr. Edward E. Thomas
Director
V.I. Bureau of Internal Revenue
St. Thomas, V.I. 00802

Dear Mr. Thomas:

Dejavu! Two (2) months ago – although you had been notified far in advance that I'd be on sick leave, you abused your discretionary power the way you usually do, and ordered the Bureau's payroll custodian to charge me leave without pay. Had I not returned from the State of Georgia with a Doctor's Certificate as required by law, you would have done to me then, exactly what you willfully and maliciously did to me on November 21, 1991 – docked me leave without pay.

Let's face it. In the past and up to now you have shown a strong inclination for disregarding the record while working with the help of the Virgin Islands political system against a law-abiding Liston Monsanto. This says much about you and the organization that you head. Mainly that you (apologies to Sam Cooke) don't know much about history – the history of Liston Monsanto that is.

Here in the Virgin Islands Bureau of Internal Revenue egoes have become far more important than a person's presumption of innocence. And now just when I've begun to think that the time has come for me to walk away from a negative person or situation, a negative person with a furtive manner looking at me with jaundiced eyes creates a negative situation leading to an interruption in his somewhat busy schedule and ultimately to a unilateral decision to maliciously dock me four (4) hours leave without pay.

Now that the U.S. Supreme Court has ruled that state officials who violate someone's rights while performing governmental duties may be sued and forced to pay monetary damages, a number of Commissioners, Directors, and Supervisory Personnel in the Virgin Islands Government who heretofore took great comfort in knowing that they were accountable but not culpable are finding themselves today not as politically bold as they were before the court's ruling.

Why you've decided to arbitrarily dock me four (4) hours leave without pay remains a mystery to me. It reminds me of General Raoul Cedras (leader of the coup in Haiti) who ousted Haitian President Jean-Bertrand Aristide and "Murdered Democracy" in the process.

"The consent of the governed is basic to American Democracy. If the governed are misled, if they are not told the truth, or if through official secrecy and deception they lack information on which to base intelligent decisions, the system may go on – but not as a democracy."

430

Letter   -2-   11/21/91

Mr. Edward E. Thomas
Director

Today I'm forced to file a grievance as a means of protecting myself from a person who appears to be hung up on tradition and obsessed by Opinion Number 81-1434 of the Third Circuit Court. Yes, Mr. Thomas nefarious acts such as illegally docking an employee four (4) hours leave without pay are permeating our society. Your success (I know) is measured by the work that you get your employees to do; its quality and quantity.

Sincerely,

Liston Monsanto
Chief Shop Steward

On November 27, 1991, writing in a euphoric manner, Thomas sent me a letter expressing his delight that I was no longer Shop Steward. Here's what he wrote:

GOVERNMENT OF
THE VIRGIN ISLANDS OF THE UNITED STATES

VIRGIN ISLANDS
BUREAU OF INTERNAL REVENUE

Lockharts Garden No. 1A
Charlotte Amalie, St. Thomas, U.S.V.I. 00802

November 27, 1991

Mr. Liston Monsanto
Internal Revenue Officer IV
Bureau of Internal Revenue
Lockhart Gardens No. 1A
St. Thomas, V.I. 00802

Dear Mr. Monsanto:

I am returning your grievance No. 3-91 filed November 22, 1991 as it does not meet the provisions of Step 3, Section 3, of Article V of the Collective Bargaining agreement that you cited. I take this position for the following reasons:

1.   The Union requested permission to post on the bulletin board located in the DAR Branch a notice of election of a shop steward.

2.   The day of the election Ms. Jacqueline Brown requested and received permission from Mr. Louis Willis, the Assistant Chief, to hold the election.

3.   Ms. Brown informed Mr. Willis and subsequently me that Mr. Alvin Swan was unanimously elected Shop Steward to replace you.

Since the above-stated provision of the agreement requires that the "Union" take the action, your shop steward or local president should file the grievance on your behalf.

Sincerely,

Edward E. Thomas
Director

pc: Mr. Alvin Swan, Shop Steward
DAR Branch

Mr. Louis A. "Titio" Morales
President - Local 8249

Mr. Randolph Allen
International Representative - USWA

Ms. Jacqueline Brown, Shop Steward
Mr. Louis M. Willis, Asst. Chief, DAR Branch

The man was a coward. He could only act the way he was because of his position. He had been a coward from the first day he had reported to work as an employees of the Virgin Islands Government. I wrote to him on November 29, 1991. I said:

November 29, 1991

Mr. Edward E. Thomas
Director-V.I. Bureau of Internal Revenue
Lockhart's Gardens #1-A
St. Thomas, Virgin Islands 00801

> "It is easier to pretend to be what
> you are not than to hide what you
> really are;but he that can accom-
> plish both has little to learn in
> hypocrisy."
> -Charles Caleb Colton

Dear Mr. Thomas:

Having written to you on so many occasions, I really did not know how to begin this letter. Then I overheard a number of employees saying that through a vacuous smile and a most peculiar way of acting, that you had belied their hopes.

That information served notice on me and consequently became my cue for taking a paragraph from my letter to you of March 25, 1991 which goes: "Because I would hate to think that what's happening under your stewardship is a pious fraud being committed by a charitable, humble, and devout christian, I have decided to write to you in the same fashion that I would want you to write to me if I were Director."

In relation to your letter of November 27, 1991, please take notice that everybody (including Liston Monsanto and the members of our Bargaining Unit) knows that you are the Director of the Virgin Islands Bureau of Internal Revenue.

The news of your nomination and subsequent confirmation reached the people of the Virgin Islands in a timely manner, leaving no doubt in anybody's mind (including Liston Monsanto) that you are legitimately the boss.

It appears however-and this is very important, that you have forgotten that lower echelon employees have rights and that your power as Director is not absolute.

Since your appointment to the Directorship, you have become very perceptive. As indicated in your letter, your perception of a change in shop stewards came in a flash.

For your information it is worth noting however, that because I was elected by a majority of the employees in the Bureau's Bargaining Unit, (not the employees of the Delinquent Accounts and Returns Branch) I'm the Chief Shop Steward. The employees wanted a person with leadership qualities - someone they knew that management would respect.

Ms Jacqueline Brown is to me what I am to you in my capacity of Internal Revenue Officer IV. She cannot legally take it upon herself to remove me from office. She is no more a Usurper than I am. So if it is your intention to divide and conquer us through inducements, I suggest you use another approach and explanation.

Lest you forget, our Union (USWA) in this democratic form of government, like the Bureau of Internal Revenue has a constitution and by-laws which serve as guidelines for us to follow. Your open intervention into the affairs of the Union, borders on an unfair labor practice. Frankly Mr. Thomas, I think that you are stretching your credibility when you write the things that you've written in your letter.

By now it has become obvious to everyone that you are firmly determined on keeping me at a distance. Like a wary fox you seem to be on the alert for danger or trouble whenever I'm around or whenever my name is called.

But if the Administration's slogan of "The best is yet to come" translates into getting rid of Liston Monsanto by devious means and ultimately busting the Union, I submit to the inevitable-retirement. Please approve my proposal. Busting the Union is a matter that will be given strict attention by Mr. Luis "Tito" Morales and Mr. Randolph Allen to whom copies of this letter are being sent.

You need not worry about danger or trouble coming from me. You are the one that's blocking my path to retirement. I wish you'd think about my proposal. I'm ready to leave.

As for grievance 3-91, I'm returning it herewith so that an Arbitrator (not a Mr. Edward E. Thomas playing the role of Judge, Jury, and Executioner) can decide on its validity. Your excuses for not processing our grievances have become threadbare.

There are many peninsulas in the human race, but no man is an island.

Sincerely yours,

Liston B. Monsanto
Chief Shop Steward

c.c.   Mr. Luis "Tito" Morales

Mr. Randolph Allen

Ms Jacqueline Brown
Mr. Alvin Swan
Mr. Louis M. Willis

On February 21, 1992 Mr. Louis Willis sent me a memorandum which said:

Internal Revenue Service
memorandum

date: February 21, 1992

to: Mr. Liston Monsanto
     Internal Revenue Officer

from: Louis M. Willis
     Asst. Chief, DAR Branch

subject: Annual Leave

I will be on Annual Leave from February 27, 1992 to March 6, 1992. In my absence I am deligating all authories to you.

Please respond to me at your earliest convenience, to let me know if you accept the responsibilities.

Your consideration in this matter will be greatly appreciated.

/ajl

cc: Mr. Edward E. Thomas, Director
     Ms. Claudette Farrington, Deputy Director

What was Willis doing? He had already rated me less than satisfactory and now he was going to put me in charge of the many employees with satisfactory ratings. I wrote back immediately on the afternoon of February 21, 1992. I said:

```
RECEIVED
DAR BRANCH

FEB 21 1992                          Februery 21, 1992

V, I, Bureau of Internal Revenue
```

```
Mr. Louis M. Willis
Assistant Chief DARB
V,I, Bureau Of Internal Revenue
St. Thomas, Virgin Islands 00802
```

Dear Mr. Willis:

Because the various laws and authorities by which I'm ostensibly guided are not-like the confluence of two rivers blending into one, I have concluded that your memorandum of today is a gigantic hoax designed only to taunt me into taking a dare.

Mr. Willis, you have become so loaded with guilt that you can hardly bear it. Is your memorandum an act of contrition?

A review of the document and a juxtaposition of what you are saying therein with a view towards its implementation against what has been going on in the Delinquent Accounts and Returns Branch since your designation as Acting Assistant Chief in May 1988, show that in your preparation of the document the following hindrances were completely ignored:

1. Liston Monsanto is at odds with the values of the power structure.

2. Liston Monsanto was bypassed for you because you are more to the system's liking.

3. Your aberrant behavior.

4. Your inability to cement good working relationships with Liston Monsanto.

5. Grievances filed by the Union on behalf of Liston Monsanto.

6. Liston Monsanto's Performance Reports together with their attachments.

7. Liston Monsanto's letter of May 8, 1991 to Mr. Edward E. Thomas wherein he applied (for the umpteenth time) for the vacant position of Chief - Delinquent Accounts and Returns Branch.

Really, I'm not desirous of making a big fuss over the issue, but even as I write, I'm hard pressed to think that you would choose me (without any oral discussions with the highest levels in the Bureau, etc.) to replace you during your absence when-as evidenced by my grievances, I have yet to accept your position in the Branch.

Your memorandum has conveyed to me however, that the Delinquent Accounts and Returns Branch is in pressing need of help. But at a time when Liston Monsanto - a victim of the Bureau's isolationist policies, receives no credit for his work, is denied training and is non-promotable, your paradoxical memorandum is hardly a panacea.

436

Letter   -2-   February 21, 1992
Mr. Louis Willis

       Liston Monsanto's "no nonsense attitude" (the same as Mr. Edward E. Thomas') would serve only to transform sheeplike employees into roaring Lions. This-I'm sure you would not like.

Sincerely yours,

Liston Monsanto
Shop Steward

c.c.   Mr. Edward E. Thomas - Director

        Ms. Claudette Farrington, Deputy Director

On March 13, 1992 Thomas asked me to submit my proposal for retirement to him. I did through a letter dated March 13, 1992 which said:

Liston B. Monsanto, Sr.

March 13, 1992

Mr. Edward E. Thomas
Director-V.I. Bureau of Internal Revenue
Lockhart Gardens #1-A
St. Thomas, Virgin Islands 00802

Dear Mr. Thomas:

Based on your request of this morning, I have decided to forward to you the following information for your review and consideration.

1.   Whereas the record shows that Mr. John Ferrant and Mr. Robert Woods were both Chiefs (at the same time) of the Delinquent Accounts and Returns Branch during calendar year 1981.

2.   Whereas Mr. Jerome A. Ferdinand - the man who succeeded Messrs. Ferrant, Woods and later Mr. Kenneth C. Hansen resigned from the position on May 3, 1991.

3.   Whereas Liston Monsanto has been a candidate for the position of Chief-Delinquent Accounts and Returns Branch for a much longer period than the aforementioned Chiefs.

4.   Whereas Liston Monsanto's latest application for the position of Chief-Delinquent Accounts and Returns Branch was submitted on May 8, 1991.

5.   Whereas in a spirit of compromise and in keeping with the provisions of Act Number 5522 Liston Monsanto seeks to retire with a resonably good pension.

6.   Whereas on March 5, 1992, Liston Monsanto was given an offer which was made through Mr. Luis "Tito" Morales (President Local 8249 United Steelworkers of America) by Mr. Edward E. Thomas that Mr. Thomas had consented to make Monsanto Chief-Delinquent Accounts and Returns Branch retroactive to Jerome A. Ferdinand's resignation provided that Monsanto retire immediately thereafter.

7.   Whereas Mr. Edward E. Thomas denies making any such offer to Mr. Luis "Tito" Morales.

8.   Whereas there are a number of grievances affecting Liston Monsanto and still unsettled.

9.   Whereas with the exception of Grievance 3-91 dated November 22, 1991, Liston Monsanto is willing to withdraw all other grievances.

10.   Whereas Liston Monsanto has been denied the opportunity of working in an atmosphere that reflects the environment in which he was trained.

Letter
Mr. Edward E. Thomas   -2-   March 13, 1992

    11.   Whereas Liston Monsanto has been told to submit a retirement proposal by Mr. Edward E. Thomas.

    Now therefore I Liston Monsanto knowing that I'm not wanted in the Virgin Islands Bureau of Internal Revenue where the rule of thumb is a commonplace, and desirous of bowing out graciously rather than vindictively, is willing to cooperate with the powers that be in an effort to ease the tensions that my presence creates in the workplace, by proposing that I be given the position of Chief-Delinquent Accounts and Returns Branch retroactive to calendar year 1988 with the proviso that I leave immediately and in conformity with Act No. 5522.

Sincerely,

Liston B. Monsanto
Internal Revenue Officer

That Thomas and Willis would torment me was no surprise. Lest you forget it was on May 26, 1988 that Thomas, in writing to Tito Morales, said: "I see no merit in your argument that Mr. Willis, a college graduate, employed as a Revenue Officer for almost five years, is not qualified to supervise the Secretary and Revenue Officers." Funny thing is, while he was saying that, Willis was writing to Olive saying this: "On May 10, 1988 I was designated as Acting Assistant Chief of the Delinquent Accounts and Returns Branch. Since that commencement date I have tried to do the job to my best of my ability permits me to do. But I have noticed that certain things within the DAR Branch would have to be rectified if the DAR Branch is to be more productive. In order for your Acting Assistant Chief to be more productive Mr. Olive I have to attend officer school. The schools that I have to attend are Revenue Officer School Phase II, Advance Training School Group Manager School and Special Procedure School. I feel by adding Special Procedure School I will be able to supervise Mrs. Santana and also can have that knowledge to better assist her. Mr. Olive I see these schools as an asset to my career so I can be an effective manager. The bottom line is that I need training to proform my job and I need training soon." Mr. Willis was begging Olive to do for him the very thing that had brought on our job-action in 1986. And by the way, the letter you have just read was copied verbatim.

The young man had been put in the position by Thomas with the blessings of Farrelly who didn't want him there but was forced to keep him in the position due largely to insincere flattery from Thomas. After all, somebody had to protect Mrs. Thomas from Monsanto – the big bad wolf.

On March 27, 1992 Thomas sent the employees a memorandum which caused widespread distress. Here's what he said:

C O R R E C T E D

GOVERNMENT OF
THE VIRGIN ISLANDS OF THE UNITED STATES
—◊—

**VIRGIN ISLANDS
BUREAU OF INTERNAL REVENUE**
—◊—

Lockharts Garden No. 1A
Charlotte Amalie, St. Thomas, U.S.V.I. 00802

March 27, 1992

MEMORANDUM

TO   :   All Employees – IRS (St. Thomas)

FROM   :   Mr. Edward E. Thomas
                 Director

RE   :   PERSONAL BELONGINGS

It has been brought to my attention that recently a large sum of money belonging to one of our employees "mysteriously disappeared". It is disheartening to think that such a despicable act has occurred in our midst. Needless to say, the employee who was victimized is extremely upset and now in a financial dilemma

The purpose of this memorandum is twofold. First, as head of this agency, I feel that it is very important to communicate this incident to you because we are all "potential victims of such occurrences. In short, in light of this incident, I am asking you to make every effort to secure and safeguard your personal belongings while in the workplace. Secondly, I am asking that anyone having any knowledge of this incident (involving the disappearance of the money) please contact the Director's Office and speak with me or Ms. Farrington during my absence. All information will be held strictly confidential. The concern here is to recover the money since one of our co-workers is really hurting, financially and emotionally from this monetary loss.

Again I am very disappointed to know that this incident has occurred. "Taking bread out of another person's mouth" cannot be an easy thing to do. All of us have to eat and all of us have our families to feed. This is a final plea to our sense of decency as human beings. If we have any conscience, at all, it is incumbent upon us to do the right thing.

If you or anyone you know have information about this incident, but do not wish to have your identity known, you can forward the information via the interoffice mail to the Director's office.

Any monies found in an envelope should be brought to the Director's Office. No questions will be asked.

440

Memorandum to all Employees
Page 2
March 27, 1992

   Thank you for being understanding, and also for your cooperation.

                              Edward E. Thomas
                                 Director

   On April 1, 1992, I responded. My lead-in was an extraction taken from the memorandum which
said:

Liston B. Monsanto, Sr.

April 1, 1992

Mr. Edward E. Thomas
Director - Bureau Internal Revenue
Lockharts Garden No. 1-A
St. Thomas, Virgin Islands 00802

> Again I am very disappointed to know that
> this incident has occurred. "Taking bread
> out of another person's mouth" cannot be
> an easy thing to do. All of us have to eat
> and all of us have families to feed. This
> is a final plea to our sense of decency as
> human beings. If we have any conscience, at
> all, it is incumbent upon us to <u>do the</u>
> <u>right thing"</u>
>   -Edward E. Thomas

Dear Mr. Thomas:

Sometimes life just isn't fair. Because I have spoken out to a sickening extreme (a fact corroborated by the Third Circuit Court of Appeals through Opinion No. 81-1434) over the fact that we are not doing the right thing in the Virgin Islands Bureau of Internal Revenue, management together with certain individuals and certain special interest groups have made several attempts to blacken my character through false gossip and trumped-up charges, wholly designed to "take bread out of my mouth".

Today as I read your memorandum of March 27, 1992, I'm exuding an air of optimism inasmuch as the document echoes my sentiments and simultaneously sends a clear message of altruism (see paragraph three (3) which appears as a quotation in the upper right hand corner of this letter) to those of us who sincerely care about life in the Virgin Islands Bureau of Internal Revenue.

Now, as I await your response to my letter of March 13, 1992, which speaks of my retirement proposal, I feel completely vindicated.

Finally, while I share and understand the feelings of the victim whose money "mysteriously disappeared", it bears repeating that your memorandum has given me new encouragement and makes me supremely happy to be a part of what appears to be a changing organization.

Sincerely,

Liston B. Monsanto
Internal Revenue Officer

On April 28, 1992, Mr. Willis, who obviously did not understand what was going on sent me a memorandum which said: "Mr. Thomas, our Director, along with you and myself will meet with the following taxpayers as listed below. A letter was already mailed to the taxpayers: #1 Automotive May 19, 1992 10:00 a.m. and Malco Drew May 19, 1992, 11:00 a.m. On that same day Willis' mentor, Edward Thomas, sent a memorandum to the Revenue Officers which stated: "Attached is an updated statement which defines our mission and your role. You should be guided by this document

442

in your day-to-day activities. You will receive detailed operating guidelines from your immediate managers. If you have any questions, please consult them."

I wrote back: "I acknowledge receipt of the 'updated statement' mentioned in your memorandum of April 29, 1992. The record shows (and it must be noted) that I was fired, suspended and removed from my classified position for using the information contained in the 'updated statement.' Re-read my letter of June 10, 1991, which talks to the crux of the matter. I do not want to make the mistake (once again) of disturbing the business community."

Thomas had brought in a retiree from the U.S. Mainland to supervise the activities of our Branch. We had come full circle. Thomas had complained to a disgusting degree about the importation of statesiders to do jobs for which locals were qualified when he was working on the employee level. Now that he was at the top of the organizational structure, he was condoning the very thing he had condemned.

On May 4, 1992, I wrote to Willis. My lead-in was a quotation from Abraham Lincoln, which said:

RECEIVED
DARBRANCH

MAY 4 1992

V.I. Bureau of Internal Revenue

May 4, 1992

Mr. Louis M. Willis
Assistant Chief
Delinquent Accounts & Returns Branch
V.I. Bureau of Internal Revenue
St. Thomas, Virgin Islands 00802

"If I were to try to read, much less answer
all the attacks made on me, this shop might
as well be closed for any other business. I
do the very best I know how-the very best I
can, and I mean to keep doing so until the
end. If the end brings me out all right,
what is said against me won't amount to anything. If the end brings me out wrong, ten
angels swearing I was right would make no
difference."
                              --Abraham Lincoln

Dear Mr. Willis:

Because of the many meetings and social functions that were held in the Bureau of Internal Revenue during calendar year 1991 plus the addition of Mr. Don Walsh
as a consultant in the Delinquent Accounts and Returns Branch, many of us were of the
opinion that calendar year 1992 would have ushered in changed attitudes in the workplace. Instead, we find ourselves filled with dismay as man's inhumanity to man continues unabated in the Virgin Islands Bureau of Internal Revenue.

When you made the effort (without any authority) to maneuver for some advantage, by pretending to leave me in charge of the Branch during your absence on February 21, 1992, I thought that my outright refusal and subsequent retirement proposal
would have brought to an end a long-standing problem plaguing the Bureau of Internal
Revenue. This was not the case, however.

Today I find myself questioning the authenticity of your memorandum of April 28, 1992 regarding scheduled conferences with #1 Automotive and Mr. Malco Drew,
as the document conjures a vision of my formal training by the United States Internal Revenue Service, and my vain attempts to do the very things (reflective of my
training) that both Mr. Edward Thomas and Mr. Don Walsh are trying to do today in
their quest to promote voluntary compliance.

Now, it is not my intention to forsake my allegiance to the Virgin Islands
Government nor is it -I hasten to add, any attempt on my part to forsake my just,
moral, and right cause. I am a civil servant who continues to be persecuted only because (a) I am right about the less-than-professional conditions in the Bureau of
Internal Revenue and (b) only because -unlike you, I realize that Mr. Thomas' equivocal behavior makes it virtually impossible for me to trust him. From my subordinate
position I'm forced to stay alert to every nuance of fakery and bluff.

Letter   -2-   May 4, 1992
Mr. Louis M. WIllis

The record shows that on the one hand Mr. Thomas declares his policies should not be regarded as a substitute for the law, while on the other hand he attempts to do quite the opposite. By overruling many of the laws and authorities, Mr. Thomas is telling all of us that there is only one right way – his way.

It should be noted nevertheless, that I once headed up the Delinquent Accounts and Returns Branch, where without the approval of management (who for some inexplicable reason continues to believe that far away talent-especially retired people who are not familiar with our inferior tax system, is better than home-developed talent), to accomplish anything in compliance with the various laws and authorities was futile.

I was kicked around, fired, suspended from duty, denied my advanced training and ultimately isolated from the rest of the employees. Ask Mr. Thomas. He has been a contributive contributor to my sad plight in the Bureau of Internal Revenue for many years. It appears as if he's having so much fun that he doesn't even want me to retire. By the way, wasn't it before Mr. Thomas (in his office) that you challenged me to a fight on the afternooon of July 17, 1991?

Are you now attempting to challenge me to another fight before the representative of #1 Automotive and Mr. Malco Drew by requesting my presence at the conferencea on May 19th?

Before asking that I sit with Mr. Thomas and yourself, you should have reviewed my letter of November 27, 1989 to Mr. Jerome Ferdinand and all the other letters that I've written to you and Mr. Thomas since his appointment as Director. You could have used them as a mile post in ignoring me completely from participating in your conferences and also as justification for showing a third party exactly what management intends to do (through the issuance of your memorandum) in circumventing Opinion No. 81-1434 of the Third Circuit Court.

Liston Monsanto knows that he cannot change the system. Can the system change him?

Sincerely yours,

Liston B. Monsanto
Internal Revenue Officer

c.c. Mr. Edward E. Thomas

Willis was acting dopey. He sent me a memorandum on May 6, 1992, under the subject: "Leave without pay." He wrote: "On Tuesday, May 5, 1992, you were informed by memorandum that there will be a meeting for all Revenue Officers and Paulette Rawlins (Revenue Representative) to attend at 9:00 a.m., May 6, 1992. At 9:05 a.m. this morning Mrs. John-Lewis called you on your extension reminding you of the meeting, you elected not to come. I am aware that every time I call a meeting you are never in attendance. To address this situation, I am charging you two hours leave without pay for the duration of that meeting. If you cannot correct this type of behavior, stronger measures will be taken to insure that you attend these meetings when they are announced."

Liston B. Monsanto, Sr.

The man was emoting. He didn't have a clue as to what supervisory responsibility was all about. Thomas was using him to the fullest. I wrote to him on May 6, 1992. Here's what I said:

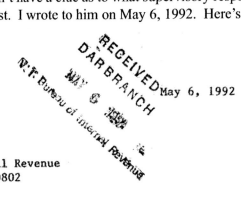

May 6, 1992

Mr. Louis M. Willis
Aasistant Chief DARB
Virgin Islands Bureau Internal Revenue
St. Thomas, Virgin Islands 00802

Dear Mr, Willis:

Your amazement is without cease! With the urgings of certain people in positions of authority (who have isolated me from the rest of the employees), you have continued adnauseam to confuse my methods with my objectives. I'm therefore not mortified (after numerous requests for guidelines, etc.) by your memorandum of today, which (put simply) tells me to attend meetings for the sole purpose of throwing a monkey wrench into the whole affair.

One does not have to be a soft-on-crime bleeding heart to detect the wrongs that are being inflicted on me in the Virgin Islands Bureau of Internal Revenue.

But in case anyone has any doubts about what's going on in the Bureau, they should ask for a copy of this letter.

The facts are disheartening:

(1) November 25, 1985 - Mr. Edward E. Thomas (Reviewer/Classifier) abuses his authority in the presence of the members of management's negotiating team threatening to "touch-up" Liston Monsanto.

(2) September 16, 1988 -Mr. Louis M. Willis threatens to destroy Liston Monsanto with a chair (which he held above his head) and his fists in full view before a number of employees.

(3) September 14, 1989 -Employees Claude Maduro and Louis Willis break the stillness in the office with a noisy quarrel wherein objects are thrown.

(4) September 22, 1989 -Part II of Maduro and Willis starts in the workplace and extends to the Grand Union Supermarket.

(5) September 22, 1989 -Mr. Edward Thomas threatens to blow Liston Monsanto's head off.

(6) July 17, 1991 - Mr. Louis M. WIllis verbally assaults Liston Monsanto (before Mr. Thomas - in his office) and challenges Monsanto to do battle with him.

(7) February 27, 1992 -Mr. Louis Willis while officially on annual leave uses the Government Vehicle (GT-575) to transport himself and luggage to the airport.

Letter   -2-   May 6, 1992
Mr. Louis M. Willis

You should be among the last persons to speak about an employee's behavior in the workplace. Not only are you guilty of the several facts listed on page one of this letter, you are also guilty of coming to work shirtless.

As far as docking me leave without pay, please be reminded that you have no authority whatsoever under the law to dock anybody leave without pay, especially when an employee reports for work.

Finally, unless there is a police or someone with the authority to arrest you when you begin your verbal assaults against me, I will not - and this was told to Mr. Edward E. Thomas on July 18, 1991, be meeting with you for some time.

Sincerely,

Liston B. Monsanto
Internal Revenue Officer

c.c. Mr. Edward E. Thomas

Willis was delirious. He knew that he was guilty of the items I had listed in the letter. What he did next is outlined in my letter of May 7, 1992 to Thomas. I wrote:

May 7, 1992

Mr. Edward E. Thomas
Director
V.I. Bureau of Internal Revenue
Lockhart Garden #1-A
St. Thomas, Virgin Islands 00802

NEWS ITEM: Proving that flighty people have volatile dispositions, Mr. Louis Willis reverted to savagery and shredded Liston Monsanto's letter of May 6, 1992 upon receiving it. He thereafter stormed out of the lobby, down the corridor towards Monsanto's office, where he made an illegal entry and promptly placed the fragments of the letter on Monsanto's desk.

Dear Mr. Thomas:

In our cordial meeting of March 13, 1992, you appeared as a most receptive person in asking that I submit a retirement proposal for your review. It was for that reason and the fact that I honestly want to retire from the Virgin Islands Government that I immediately submitted my proposal to you.

To date I have not received a response from you, and in the intervening time I find myself mired in a hostile environment due largely to Mr. Louis Willis' hostility. In order to protect myself I have been forced to resurrect many of the events that weigh heavily on my survival.

Noteworthy and of prime importance is the fact that I have never ever, and will never ever challenge your authority when it comes to legally directing the activities of the Virgin Islands Bureau of Internal Revenue.

As great as is my compassion for people, I cannot and will not subscribe to certain measures or even give support to anyone who tries to bully, cajole or intimidate me.

I'm a person who was raised to be fair and kind to everyone. I am one who can work in harmony with any individual or group provided that individual or group is readily and gladly willing to work with me. This attitude-I believe, is terribly important to my sense of fulfillment as a human being.

Presently, there are a number of grievances affecting me that are still unsetteled. If you are not going to work on my retirement proposal, I suggest that we start working on the grievances. My status-like everybody else's must be clarified.

Sincerely yours,

Liston B. Monsanto
Internal Revenue Officer

c.c. Mr. Luis "Tito" Morales
Mr. Randolph Allen

On May 8, 1992 I wrote to Governor Farrelly, I wrote:

RECEIVED

May 8, 1992

MAY 08 1992

OFFICE OF
THE GOVERNOR

Honorable Alexander A. Farrelly
Governor - U.S. Virgin Islands
Government House
St. Thomas, Virgin Islands 00801

Dear Governor Farrelly:

During your tenure of office I have written you several letters about my sad plight in the Virgin Islands Bureau of Internal Revenue, and although they have all been ignored, today I find it necessary to write to you once again.

Due largely to his rustic manners and inexperience, Mr. Louis M.Willis has become (for the lack of a better description) a problem child within the Virgin Islands Bureau of Internal Revenue.

His threats against me have been such that they have created a gulf between us and thrown a wet blanket over the entire Delinquent Accounts and Returns Branch.

On four (4) seperate occasions he has disturbed my train of thoughts and broken the stillness in our office by (a) menacing me with a chair (b) threatening to use his fist on me (c) challenging me to a fight in Mr. Edward Thomas' office - in front of Mr. Thomas and (d) making an illegal entry into my office in order to commit the farcical act of placing fragments of a letter (addressed to him) on my desk.

It is also a matter of record that in September of 1989 Mr. Willis left his office to do battle with Mr. Claude Maduro in the workplace.

As a rumor-monger he goes outside of our organization in his continued attempts to damage my reputation. He's been doing evil for so long that it does not occur to him that I'm guiltless.

Because of Mr. Willis' erratic behavior, I have declined respectfully to meet with him one on one or even in the presence of Mr. Edward Thomas.

I fully realize that everybody is difficult some of the time, but chances are there is at least one person who manages to get along with them, and who difficult people treat with extra care and respect. Mr. Willis however, appears to be an exception to the rule.

The fact that he continues to threaten me tells me one of two things: Either no one speaks to him about his behavior or he has instructions telling him to continue.

In any event, there is mutual hostility between him and me. So, in order to reduce the tensions between an uncontrollable man (who incidentally is occupying the position of Assistant Chief of the Delinquent Accounts and Returns Branch in an unlawful way) and myself, I'm asking that you confer with Mr. Edward Thomas for the purpose of considering my retirement proposal.

The Virgin Islands Bureau of Internal Revenue cannot continue to operate in a state of confusion. I'm willing to leave.

Sincerely yours,

Liston B. Monsanto
Internal Revenue Officer

c.c. Mr. Edward E. Thomas
     Director-Bureau Internal Revenue

On May 11, 1992 I wrote to Thomas using as my lead-in a quotation from Mark Twain which said:

204

May 11, 1992

Mr. Edward E. Thomas
Director-V.I. Bureau of Internal Revenue
Lockhart Gardens #1-A
St. Thomas, Virgin Islands 00802

> "Let us be thankful for the tools; but for them the rest of us could not succeed."
>
> —Mark Twain

Dear Mr. Thomas:

Your "updated statement" of April 29, 1992, (with its inordinate demands) transcends disbelief. Its presentation appears to be a specious act, which seemingly puts the cart before the horse.

As a person who was removed and subsequently fired from his job for doing work reflective of his training and ability, you are asking me to utilize that same outmoded training (bear in mind that unlike Jens Todman and your wife, I have never received my advanced training. What's more, it has been twenty-one years since I first received my basic training) to do the technical work required of a trained and up-to-date federal employee.

"Train and Retain": The battle cry of our strike in 1986, told the world that we were then, and still today clamoring for much-needed training in order to better perform our duties. Unlike most government employees, we did not strike for money. My main focus has always been in the area of training. With me, training remains a passionate issue. (Please read the attached letters which serve as evidence).

Messrs. Leroy Quinn, Anthony Olive and yourself ruined the Delinquent Accounts and Returns Branch out of spite. Flaunting your authority, you denied me my advanced training and unlawfully placed me under the supervision of a lower level Revenue Officer with an unstable mind.

So sunk in evil contemplation were you, that it never dawned on you that some day Liston Monsanto would need his advanced training in order to perform the technical duties outlined in your "updated statement", which—as you must know by now, is contrary to the fact.

In a related matter, Mr. Don Walsh — a man guided by an accepted system of professional ethics and a strong sense of public responsibility, is being called upon to act as a consultant in giving professional and technical advice to Revenue Officers whose only goal (as noted in my letter of June 10, 1991) is popularity.

At this juncture it is important to note for your edification that before the reorganization of the United States Internal Revenue Service in 1954, the position of Revenue Officer was filled mostly by political appointees. The year 1954 marked the beginning of a new day for both the Revenue Officer and the Revenue Agent, and today they occupy a position of pride and esteem in the United States Internal Revenue Service.

Having said that, it is safe to further say that Mr. Walsh's presence in the Delinquent Accounts and Returns Branch-his professionalism notwithstanding, creates a situation where you appear to be offering a cure where there is no disease.

Let's face it, Mr. Walsh can only give advice that's reflective of the environment in which he was trained. That environment-needless to say, is far removed in relationship to the Virgin Islands. In the Virgin Islands we are guided only by the rule of thumb.

Whether he knows it or not, Mr. Walsh has become the umpteenth in a series of consultants, who have worked in the Virgin Islands Bureau of Internal Revenue since the inception of my employment more than thirty years ago. Management in the Virgin Islands Bureau of Internal Revenue has been shamming for a very long time.

And speaking about shamming, please keep in mind that the Virgin Islands Bureau of Internal Revenue is not an autonomous agency. It works in conjunction with all the other departmental agencies of the executive branch under the auspices of the Governor's Office, where there is a high degree of politics.

The Governor-perhaps because of the prevailing quid pro quo, has made it known to all of us that he's pro-business. He knows that he cannot exist without our business people who operate like carpet-baggers.(Read my letter of February 9, 1984, which you have in your possession).

It is for reasons such as the above that a Virgin Islands Revenue Officer is denied the latitude given the Federal Revenue Officer in carrying out his duties. The Virgin Islander will always be at a disadvantage when a retiree from the United States Internal Revenue Service is brought in to review his work. Revenue Officers in the Virgin Islands are peerless.

Because of his unstableness and threat of war between us, I will not be attending any conferences called by Mr. Louis Willis unless a Policeman is in attendance. I want to be free from trouble, disturbance, violence and strife. Please start working on my retirement proposal. Again, I'm ready to leave.

Sincerely yours,

Liston B. Monsanto
Internal Revenue Officer

452

June 8, 1987

Mr. Anthony P. Olive
Director
Bureau of Internal Revenue
Lockhart Gardens #1A
St. Thomas, V. I.   00802

Dear Mr. Olive:

Trying to forget the past and seeking to get down to the more mundane problems facing the Government of the Virgin Islands, The Union-during our 1985-1986 negotiating sessions, broached the very important, but somewhat controversial subject of training.

Your strong exception to the subject, resulted in a Job-Action by the members of our Bargaining Unit, which forced management to enter into an agreement to send Unconditionally ("within twelve (12) months after acceptance") Newly-Promoted or Newly-Hired Employees to formal training conducted by United States Internal Revenue Instructors either on or off Island.

At this writing (10 days before the June 18th deadline), it appears as if our side was given a false sense of assurance inasmuch as you have either by omission, silence, or past practice, failed to live up to your promise. Maybe you felt that once the publicity of our Job-Action died down, we'd become apathetic.

This Sir is not the case. It is no secret (and records in your possession would corroborate this fact)that over the past several years I have spoken Ad-Nauseam about the poor working conditions under your Stewardship. These conditions-needless to say, have contributed immensely to the overall decline of our Government. In addition, They have caused the United States Internal Revenue Service (time after time) to entertain thoughts of collecting our taxes.

If we are to improve working conditions and increase productivity, like the Personnel in Management Employees of the Virgin Islands Bureau of Internal Revenue must be trained.

Since it is becoming increasingly apparent that you are once again attempting to violate the law, I must admonish you that a Breach of Contract on your part will result in still another grievance being filed by us. It therefore behooves you to ponder over the best way to get out of this scrape.

Liston B. Monsanto, Sr.

June 30, 1987

Honorable Alexander Farrelly
Governor - U.S. Virgin Islands
Office of the Governor
Charlotte Amalie
St. Thomas, Virgin Islands   00801

Dear Governor Farrelly:

After several years of service as an ombudsman in the Virgin Islands Bureau of Internal Revenue (formerly Tax Division), I took over the responsibility of Chief Shop Steward with the serious pledge to implicitly defend the members of our Bargaining Unit against the many injustices therein.

I assumed - what has become a most arduous responsibility, knowing full well that manifold problems - such as the ones in the Bureau of Internal Revenue, would not be solved by simply running away from them.

In addition, I discovered that if we were looking for perfection in our less than professional governmental system under your predecessor, we would not find it in the V.I. Bureau of Internal Revenue.

Striving for perfection, nevertheless, and knowing that no gains would be made without pains, during Calendar Year 1986 we negotiated with management a Bilateral Contract (which expires on September 30, 1987) placing emphasis on education and training.

For your edification, our Contract also contains a Grievance Procedure which from its inception has legitimately served as our authority to file a number of Grievances. This - I hasten to add, is to our good fortune inasmuch as disorder reigns so rampant in the Bureau of Internal Revenue that Mr. Anthony P. Olive (our Director) finds himself before an Arbitrator more often than any other department head in the Virgin Islands Government. Although our grievances have been valid, many of them were systematically resolved.

Inherited by your administration, the existing Contract stipulates - among other things, that newly-hired and newly-promoted employees must be given formal training by United States Internal Revenue Service Instructors on or before June 18, 1987. This was not done, thereby necessitating the filing of yet another grievance.

There are a number of ingrates and scoff-laws in management who are steadfastly opposed to fromal training for lower echelon employees. When it comes to our Contract, management has an innate tendency to believe that one cannot practice law by the books all of the time as sometimes there are extenuating circumstances.

Letter
Hon. Alexander Farrelly
Governor of the V.I.

Why management continues to violate our Bilateral Contract is among the Bureau's best kept secrets. Accordingly, the urgent intervention of your office has become necessary, and towards this end, I solicit your indulgence.

Sincerely,

Liston B. Monsanto
Shop Steward

cc: Luis "Tito" Morales
    President, Local 8249

    Mr. Cephus Rogers
    International Representative

Liston B. Monsanto, Sr.

July 17, 1987

Mr. Anthony P. Olive
Director
V.I. Bureau of Internal Revenue
St. Thomas, Virgin Islands 00801

Dear Mr. Olive:

Some members of our Bargaining Unit have become utterly miserable and puzzled over the very important matter of training - a topic excoriated by management in discussions with us and subsequently magnified in letters from me, which have served as the forerunner to Grievance Number 7-87 dated June 19, 1987.

For some inexplicable reason, Revenue Officers Martinez and Todman (two veterans) were selected to attend a training program somewhere in the United States on July 20, 1987.

We must have incurred the wrath of your office because unless these men were "newly promoted," there is absolutely no legitimate reason for their selection - especially since we have in our midst an untrained employee, who recently received her Masters Degree from the University of the Virgin Islands.

And speaking about training, by now it must be quite obvious to you that your latest act (see paragraph two) towards this critical issue has compounded your error, inasmuch as it borders on unfair labor practice. Frankly, I'm bemused.

Since you made the decision to send the two veterans to training, I have had numerous visits from concerned employees of our Bargaining Unit, who feel with good reason that you are still trying to divide and conquer them, while continuing to ignore our Contract.

For anyone to think otherwise is ludicrous. Furthermore, it is safe to say that with the emergence of the Bureau of Internal Revenue and all its broad powers, abuse of discretionary power became the eight deadly sin of the world.

It saddens me to see how things in this most sensitive area of our Government have gone awry under your stewardship. Allowing yourself to fall prey to the many vessels of wrath (internally and externally) after being highly recommended by me to fill the position of Tax Director is something that brings me strong regret. Your ambitions - I believe, have been subverted. You have so much to offer.

456

Letter   -2-   7/17/87
Mr. Anthony P. Olive
Director

In light of the foregoing, I politely request that you put the Labor/ Management Committee to work as agreed to in our Contract.

Kindly accede to my request.

Sincerely,

Liston B. Monsanto
Shop Steward

cc: Honorable Alexander Farrelly
      Governor of the Virgin Islands

      Mr. Kenneth C. Hansen
      Chief, Delinquent Accounts & Returns Branch

      Mr. Cephus Rogers
      International Representative

      Mr. Luis "Tito" Morales
      President Local 8249

      Mr. Jose McGregor
      Shop Steward (St. Croix)

Liston B. Monsanto, Sr.

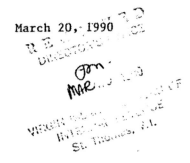

March 20, 1990

Mr. Anthony P. Olive
Director-V.I. Bureau of Internal Revenue
Lockharts Gardens #1-A
St. Thomas, Virgin Islands 00801

Dear Mr. Olive:

Over the past several years training has been a topic of much discussion and a matter of so much discontent that it has given most of our employees cause for complaining.

You may recall and as a matter of fact, the record shows that in 1986 there was a job action in the Virgin Islands Bureau of Internal Revenue to protest working conditions with the emphasis on training.

Governor Alexander Farrelly in a published report appearing in the Daily News of December 10, 1987 made his feelings known by voicing his displeasure with your attitude towards training.

Then frustrated and somewhat humiliated in his acting position, Mr. Louis M. Willis (a babe in the woods) sometime in 1989 made a preliminary sketch of a piece of writing (see the attached) wherein he begged you earnestly as a kindness or favor, to send him to his training program.

Hearing Mr. Willis' cries for help and knowing that the personnel in the Delinquent Accounts and Returns Branch needed to be trained so as to make them more proficient and qualified for their mission, I wrote to you on December 6, 1989 asking (once again) that Mr. Willis and his co-workers be sent to training.

Today as I write, I'm supremely happy to see that as a matured individual that you have made an adjustment of your mental activity in order to meet the unavoidable demands of our environment.

You are now facing the facts as they relate to the training provision of our contract and at the same time being practical rather than imaginative or visionary.

This attitude-needless to say, is a source of satisfaction to me and the others whose desire it is to see an improved Bureau of Internal Revenue.

Thanks very much for affording the untrained employees the opportunity to be trained.

Sincerely,

Liston B. Monsanto
Shop Steward

458

Mr. Anthony P. Oline
Director
Virgin Islands Bureau of Internal Revenue
Lockhart Garden #1A
St. Thomas V.I. 00801

On May 10, 1988, I was designated as Acting Assistant Chief of Delinquent Accounts and Returns Branch. Since that commencement date, I have tried to do the job to my best of my ability permits me to do.

But I have noticed that certain things within the DAR Branch have to be rectify if the DAR Branch will be to be more productive.

In order for your Acting Assistant Chief to be more productive, Mr. Oline I have to attend Officer School. The schools that I have to attend are Revenue Officer School Phase II, Advance Training, Group Manager School and Special Procedure School. I feel by going adding Special Procedure School I will be able to supervise the Santos and also run a case load that two R.O.

459

On May 14, 1992 Willis was complaining again about what he considered to be my "poor performance." He wrote:

Internal Revenue Service
memorandum

date: May 14, 1992

to: Mr. Liston Monsanto
Revenue Officer IV

from: Mr. Louis M. Willis
Asst. Chief, DAR Branch

subject: Poor Performance

Your work for the first seven (7) months of Fiscal year 1992 has been poor and unacceptable especially when compare with other senior officers (see attachment of comparision).

Why is it that Revenue Officers L. Thomas & Todman can close out 108 & 150, while you only manage to close out 6? Why is it that Revenue Officers L. Thomas & Todman can collect $571,106.06 & $736,549.91 while you only manage $13,587.04 in assessed amount collected? Why is it that these same Revenue Officers can serve 20 and 6 levies while you manage 0. What really caught my eyes making this comparison is that you close (6) accounts during this time and only $1.84 were collected in accurals, While other officers have collected $54,378.19 and $177,915.16. You have wrote more letters to management in the same period of time than you have close Taxpayer's Delinquent accounts!

Moreover, you have only collected $13,588.88 which include assessed amount and accural while officers L. Thomas and Todman have collected $625,484.79 and $914,465.07.

You are a senior officer with at least 30 years of service but your collection performance over the last 4 years (which I have been your supervisor) have been unsatisfactory.

It is a shame that you are one of the highest paid employee within the Bureau and your production is the least within the DAR Branch and probably the least within the Bureau of Internal Revenue.

Mr. Monsanto, you are are burn out and mentally drain of this job. You need to retire!

Something must be done to improve your collection performance, because I will not tolerate your past and present performance anymore. Furthermore, I am going to monitor your future collection performance diligently from hence forth.

Continued.......

Please give this your personal attention. We must resolve this problem.

LMW/ajl

cc: Mr. Edward E. Thomas
    Director

    Ms. Claudette Farrington
    Deputy Director of Operations

    Mr. Alvin Swan
    Shop Stewart

    Personal File

	Monsanto	L. Thomas	Todman
Month	October 1991	October 1991	October 1991
(a)	$6,486.93	$120,925.21	$150.472.21
(b)	3	55	40
(c)	0	$7,238.38	$94,837.67
(d)	0	1	5
(e)	$6,486.93	$128,163.59	$245.309.88
Month	November 1991	November 1991	November 1991
(a)	0	$46,312.92	$87,760.54
(b)	0	6	22
(c)	0	$2,649.91	$3,805.96
(d)	0	17	0
(e)	0	$48,962.83	$91,566.50
Month	December 1991	December 1991	December 1991
(a)	0	$20,545.19	$62,475.47
(b)	0	1	28
(c)	0	$4,562.77	$2,377.61
(d)	0	0	1
(e)	0	$25,107.96	$64,853.08
Month	January 1992	January 1992	January 1992
(a)	0	$55,076.05	$142.067.96
(b)	0	7	7
(c)	0	$6,452.32	$12,203.44
(d)	0	0	0
(e)	0	$61,528.37	$154,271.40
Month	February 1992	February 1992	February 1992
(a)	$1,804.45	$57,758.96	$108,182.70
(b)	1	7	34
(c)	0	$8,176.84	$36,838.47
(d)	0	2	0
(e)	$1,804.45	$65,935.80	$145,021.17
Month	March 1992	March 1992	March 1992
(a)	$3,108.00	$185,882.86	$12,698.36
(b)	1	24	14
(c)	0	$16,938.53	$12,698.36
(d)	0	0	0
(e)	$3,108.00	$202,821.39	$121,767.75

Preparing for my retirement and knowing that most of the people I had been called upon to represent in my capacity of Shop Steward were programmed to ignore the rule of law I decided to abdicate my position. I didn't need anybody to represent me as long as things continued the way they were.

On May 15, 1992 I answered Willis' memorandum. I said:

RECEIVED   May 15, 1992
DAR BRANCH

Mr. Louis M. Willis   MAY 15 1992
Delinquent Accounts & Returns Branch
V.I. Bureau of Internal Revenue   V.I. Bureau of Internal Revenue
St. Thomas, Virgin Islands 00802

Dear Mr. Willis:

Your memorandum of May 14, 1992 reminds me of a weird person bringing a duck to a cock fight. So weird is he, that it does not occur to him that unless the fight has been fixed, the poor bird (game as he may be) could never defeat a gamecock bred and trained for fighting.

Initially, I started to ignore the document, but then, not wanting to give a third party the false impression that you are finally correct about what you've called my poor performance, and following a cursory inspection of my records, which reveals that on February 21, 1992 you sent shock waves through me by asking me to run things in the Delinquent Accounts and Returns Branch during your absence from the office, I decided to answer posthaste.

At the outset I'd like to say that I've written several important letters to you - the contents of which piqued you so much that you shredded them. As a consequence, there is not a shred of evidence to explain the first paragraph of your memorandum.

Since it appears in paragraph two that you are more concerned with the volume of my letters than with their contents, I feel it an obligation to duty to let you know, that one of my reasons for stepping down as Shop Steward was because of the many Philistines that I represented. Through them, I finally learned that you cannot help people who don't want to help themselves.

Lest you forget, both Mrs. Thomas and Mr. Todman (by refusing to supervise the activities of the Delinquent Accounts & Returns Branch) are responsible for your unlawful placement from an Internal Revenue Officer I. Please fix the blame on the person who did the damage.

In paragraph three, you've gotten yourself into a bad fix. You are giving the reader the impression that the effect produced by the collection activity was based on the same accounts given to three different Revenue Officers.

Paragraph four does an injustice to the truth. Review my performance reports for the past four years. See what I mean? The credit procured by a lie lasts only till the truth comes out.

As for paragraph five, I repeat my contention as follows: What it takes to impersonate Liston Monsanto (honesty, decency, pride, intestinal fortitude, etc.) you haven't got.

I'm not qualified to answer paragraph six. I suggest you ask Mr. Edward E. Thomas our Director.

Paragraph seven tells me that even though your status remains unclear, you are now willing to promote the rule of law.

Much of my discontent with you and the Branch has been voiced in my letters to you and Mr. Edward Thomas. Judging from your reaction, they are apparently having an internal impact.

As far as your latest memorandum is concerned , I'm standing with Voltaire, who once said:"I may disagree with what you say, but I'd defend to the death your right to say it."

                                        Sincerely yours,

                                        Liston B. Monsanto
                                        Internal Revenue Officer

c.c. Mr. Edward E. Thomas

     Ms Claudette Farrington

On May 18, 1992 I wrote to Thomas. I said:

May 18, 1992

Mr. Edward E. Thomas
Director
V.I. Bureau of Internal Revenue
Lockhart's Garden #1-A
St. Thomas, Virgin Islands 00802

Dear Mr. Thomas:

Your heavyweight fighter (Mr. Louis M. WIllis) has taken a turn for the irrational worse. Owing to his failure to analyze the situation, he's gone into a quandary.

Like you, he has refused to welcome Opinion #81-1434 of the Third Circuit Court as a base on which to build needed reforms, and like you, he disagrees vehemently with the United States Internal Revenue Service, who upon accepting the Bureau's invitation to test the knowledge and review the qualifications of the personnel in the highest levels of the Delinquent Accounts and Returns Branch, said that because of Mr. Willis' inexperience and inability to establish harmonious work relations with several senior Revenue Officers, the situation in the Delinquent Accounts and Returns Branch had gotten out of control.

Mr. Willis continues to be long on emotion and short on reason. On May 14, 1992 - in a showy display, he sent me a memorandum accusing me-based only on an unfair comparison between two fully-trained Revenue Officers and myself, of being the villain in the Delinquent Accounts and Returns Branch.

Currently, the course of events show that Mr. Willis is trying everything in an effort to taunt me and show me who's in charge. Because he's influenced more by impulse than by reason, he feels (even though Mr. Jens Todman and your wife were sent to advanced training to prepare them for handling "the large dollar cases" and ultimately for supervisory responsibility),that I'm responsible for the Bureau's inability to reduce its receivables. With one foot in the grave, he fails to hear Mrs. Thomas and Mr. Todman singing:" Fools rush in where angels fear to tread".

One thing is certain however. When it comes to the operation of the Virgin Islands Bureau of Internal Revenue one never knows who's right, but he always knows who's in charge.

Little does Mr. Willis know that it was the games-man-ship of the wrongdoers to isolate and intentionally stop me from advancing within the Delinquent Accounts and Returns Branch that led to him being unlawfully placed in his present position. (Does Mr. Willis really believe that it's legal to move an Internal Revenue Officer I to the highest level in the Branch ahead of other Revenue Officers II's, III's, and IV's?) Maybe he should be told that my honesty and willingness to work are the foundation of my success.

He should also be told that negligence deserves the blame for many mistakes and that to this end, the Virgin Islands Bureau of Internal Revenue has neglected its work.

Sometime ago, a trip report and technical assistance workplan developed by the United States Internal Revenue Service for the Bureau of Internal Revenue, echoed many of the criticisms made by me in letters to you and everybody else. They ignored the "Stop Tax Evasion Program", however.

For your information, the "Stop Tax Evasion Program" has become a feature specific to reducing the Bureau's receivables, as it requires proof of tax payment before business licenses can be issued or renewed. This prime tool (important as it is) is not being used firmly and fairly on many of our delinquent taxpayers.

The Delinquent Accounts and Returns Branch is also guilty of being unkind to its untrained, lower level Revenue Officers. Caseload assignments are not being made based on a grade level system. In order to ensure that Revenue Officers I's, II's, III's, snd IV's do not get the same type accounts, they must be collated.

Finally, it is heavily suggested that you review the many letters that I've written. Please do this-if only for Mr. Willis' sake. You may want to begin with my letters of February 9, 1984, November 27, 1989 and May 2, 1991.

Sincerely,

Liston B. Monsanto
Internal Revenue Officer

c.c. Gov. Alexander A. Farrelly

Ms. Claudette Farrington

On May 19, 1992, at 8:10 .am., Willis walked into my office and threatened to "mash me up." I wrote an informal note to Thomas which said: "For the final time, I'm asking that you speak to Mr. Willis concerning his threats which have become unbearable." Thomas ignored my memorandum which told me that Willis had been given the green light by Farrelly and Edward Thomas to harass me into resigning. That would never happen.

On May 26, 1992, I wrote to Thomas saying:

RECEIVED
DIRECTOR'S OFFICE

MAY 26 1992

V.I. BUREAU OF INT. REV.
ST. THOMAS, V.I.

May 26, 1992

Mr. Edward E. Thomas
Director
V.I. Bureau of Internal Revenue
Lockhart's Gardens #1-A
St. Thomas, Virgin Islands 00802

Dear Mr. Thomas:

While you've continued to wrong me, I have maintained a magnanimous attitude and over the past several months I've written to you in a great variety of ways trying desperately to make you understand that (unlike many of our fearful employees) I cannot work in a state of confusion.

Today due largely to your intransigence, and to a lesser extent due to your denial of the right of a civil servant to differ, we've reached an impasse.

Because I'm fast approaching the end of my rope, a decision has to be made on whether or not I should make public the intolerable pain that I've been forced to endure amid hellish temperatures in the Virgin Islands Bureau of Internal Revenue. This decision-important as it is, hinges heavily on your choice between my retirement proposal (see my letter of March 13, 1992) and my aged grievances.

For your information here are the several reasons (not necessarily in order) for the impasse mentioned in paragraph two above:

1. Your outright refusal to welcome Opinion #81-1434 of the Third Circuit Court as a base on which to build needed reforms.

2. Ongoing litigation and the several grievances filed by me which show that I have never accepted Mr. Louis M. Willis as my supervisor.

3. Threats against me and my subsequent refusal to meet one on one with Mr. Willis or to even attend any conferences wherein the only participants are Messrs. Edward Thomas, Louis Willis and Liston Monsanto.

4. Offering a cure where there was no disease, you brought in Mr. Don Walsh (a retiree from the U.S. Internal Revenue Service) to serve as a consultant giving advice reflective of his training and experience-a move observers have described as being tantamount to communist China sending an emissary to the United States to give advice on democratizing our nation.

5. Your refusal to pay close attention to the comments made on the attachments to my performance reports.

6. Your mistake in reasoning that to train me while simultaneously issuing clear guidelines for the Virgin Islands District would result in a personal benefit for me.

7. You've tied my hands and rendered me ineffective.

The foregoing aside, it is important to note that in any democratic society where tolerance is practiced by an administration that advertises its purpose through a slogan loudly proclaiming "fairness for all", there is absolutely no way for an Internal Revenue Officer 1 - not even on the journey-man level, to legally come from the bottom rung of the career ladder (especially when as an Internal Revenue Officer that same Internal Revenue Officer 1 could not qualify for the higher level positions of Internal Revenue Officer 11, III, or IV) to the top rung.

That's why it became very easy for the federal auditors (who like Mr. Don Walsh were operating under federal guidelines) to immediately find that a sophomoric Louis Willis' inexperience and overall ability did not qualify him to be the Assistant Chief of the Delinquent Accounts and Returns Branch. Mr. Willis' appointment is contrary to everything that a well-run organization stands for.

The truth is, we did not need the federal auditors to tell us that Mr. Willis is a perfunctory supervisor. We already knew.

Mr. Thomas, as if you did not know, I'm going on my thirty ninth (39th) year of service with the Virgin Islands Government. To say that my record is unblemish is an understatement. Any person whatever can tell you that as a model of decorum I'm being persecuted because of my principles and beliefs.

My greatest wrong in the Virgin Islands Bureau of Internal Revenue is always being right. For that reason, it is safe to say that legally you cannot win in your quest to get rid of me.

I'm not one who would want to give the public the impression that I'm the pre-eminent person in the Virgin Islands Bureau of Internal Revenue. That's why I've asked you-time after time, to start work on my retirement proposal, which you asked me to submit for your review.

I'm very anxious to leave the unfriendly confines of the Virgin Islands Bureau of Internal Revenue, but not before something positive is done about my retirement proposal.

Letter
Mr. Edward Thomas   -3-   May 26, 1992

  Bewildered employees in our midst know that I'm not guilty of any wrong and are now asking, why does Mr. Thomas continue to treat Liston Monsanto like an outsider? Do you have an answer that's different to those listed herein?

             Sincerely, yours,

             Liston B. Monsanto
             Internal Revenue Officer

c.c. Governor Alexander A. Farrelly
   Ms Claudette Farrington
   Mr. Luis "Tito" Morales
   Mr. Randolph Allen

Liston B. Monsanto, Sr.

On June 5, 1992, I wrote to Willis. I said:

June 5, 1992

Mr. Louis M. Willis
Delinquent Accounts & Returns Branch
V.I. Bureau of Internal Revenue
St. Thomas, Virgin Islands 00802

Dear Mr. Willis:

I (Liston Monsanto) am not one of those government employees who enjoy re-ceiving a salary check for doing nothing, and although the record shows that I have not accepted you as the Assistant Chief of the Delinquent Accounts and Returns Branch, I stand fully aware of the fact that Mr. Edward E. Thomas' door is always open to you.

Consequently, I have decided to write you this letter (very slow, inasmuch as I know that you do not read very fast) in the hope that you'd be able to use whatever influence you posess in convincing Mr. Thomas that I'm in need of clear guidelines in order to get my work up to a professional level.

In the past and even now, when I deem it necessary to contact a delinquent taxpayer, I find myself resorting to the art of persuasion in trying to close out that taxpayer's account.

Knowing that the Governor relies heavily on his campaign contributions from our business people and has declared that he's pro-business, and aware of the fact that many of our practicing Accountants doing business with the Virgin Islands Bu-reau of Internal Revenue are critical of my aggressive approach to enforcing the Tax Laws, I must have a clear understanding from Mr. Thomas of exactly what is re-quired of me.

So I ask for the moment that you forget your antipathy towards me. Talk to Mr. Thomas to whom I'm sending a copy of this letter.

Tell him that although he's relentless in his efforts to force me out of the Virgin Islands Bureau of Internal Revenue that I'm as tired today as I was yesterday of reporting for work on a daily basis not knowing exactly what to do and not knowing what's going to be done about the position that you are now un-lawfully occupying.

Unlike a lot of apathetic government employees, I'm in need of a supervi-sor from whom I can learn. I'm desperately in need of work, and it is for this reason that I implore you to act on my behalf. Help me to earn my salary check!

Letter
Mr. Louis M. Willis   -2-   June 5, 1992

     A word of caution: As important as this letter is, I ask that you do not shred it.

                            Sincerely,

                            Liston B. Monsanto
                            Internal Revenue Officer

c.c. Mr. Edward E. Thomas
     Director-V.I. Bureau Int. Revenue

Liston B. Monsanto, Sr.

On June 11, 1992, I was forced to write to Thomas after noticing that I had been illegally charged with four hours of annual leave. I wrote:

Internal Revenue Service
memorandum

date: June 11, 1992

to: Mr. Edward E. Thomas
          Director-Bureau of Internal Revenue

from: Liston B. Monsanto
          Internal Revenue Officer

subject: Annual Leave Time

    A review of my salary check stubs for the pay periods ending May 16, 1992 and May 30, 1992 disclosed that I was charged with a total of four (4) hours annual leave for both pay periods.

    I do not recall taking annual leave during the pay periods mentioned above, nor is there any tangible evidence (except for the information appearing on the check stubs) to indicate annual leave taken by me.

    Believing that an error had been made on both occasions I approached Ms. Cecelia Hill regarding the matter and was told by her that she had gotten instructions from "my boss" to deduct two hours leave for the subject pay periods.

    I'm fully aware of the fact that under existing law no one other than a Department Head has the authority to deny an employee annual leave. I'm also aware of the fact that while a supervisor may recommend that an employee be charged with annual leave for reasons better known to that supervisor, that supervisor cannot take it upon himself to charge any employee with annual leave.

    I believe that an honest mistake was made and consequently, I'm asking that you use the power of your office to correct it.

    It would be highly appreciated if you'd let me know what's going on so that I may avoid a recurrence of the same problem in the future.

472

GOVERNMENT OF THE VIRGIN ISLANDS OF THE UNITED STATES

DEPT	EMPLOYEE NO
2714	209

SOCIAL SECURITY NO 580-01-2783
PERIOD ENDING 5/16/92 NO 18

EMPLOYEE NAME
LISTON MONSANTO
DELINQUENT ACCOUNTS

ACCRUED LEAVE BALANCE
ANNUAL LEAVE 254.10
SICK LEAVE 2245.00
UNAUDITED

EARNINGS	HRS UNITS	AMOUNT
REGULAR	78.00	1423.05
ANNUAL LV	2.00	36.49

DEDUCTIONS	
FICA	111.65
FED W/H	184.28
RETIRE. 8%	116.76
HEALTH INS	21.27
PERS LOAN	200.00
LOCAL 8249	18.57

YEAR TO DATE	
GROSS PAY	16054.94
FICA	1228.15
***TAX	2083.25
RET	1284.36
HLTH	212.70
RLOAN	2200.00
NET	8856.78

NET PAY 806.61

TOTAL EARNINGS 1459.54
TOTAL DEDUCTIONS 652.93

DIRECT DEPOSIT BANK AND ACCOUNT DESTINATION
841C143

GOVERNMENT OF THE VIRGIN ISLANDS OF THE UNITED STATES

DEPT	EMPLOYEE NO
2714	209

SOCIAL SECURITY NO 580-01-2783
PERIOD ENDING 5/30/92 NO 19

EMPLOYEE NAME
LISTON MONSANTO
DELINQUENT ACCOUNTS

ACCRUED LEAVE BALANCE
ANNUAL LEAVE 260.10
SICK LEAVE 2249.00
UNAUDITED

EARNINGS	HRS UNITS	AMOUNT
REGULAR	70.00	1277.10
ANNUAL LV	2.00	36.49
HOLIDAY	8.00	145.55

DEDUCTIONS	
FICA	111.65
FED W/H	184.28
RETIRE. 8%	116.76
HEALTH INS	21.27
PERS LOAN	200.00
LOCAL 8249	18.57

YEAR TO DATE	
GROSS PAY	17514.48
FICA	1339.80
***TAX	2267.53
RET	1401.12
HLTH	233.97
RLOAN	2400.00
NET	9663.39

NET PAY 806.61

TOTAL EARNINGS 1459.54
TOTAL DEDUCTIONS 652.93

Edward Thomas was behind it all. I knew it from the beginning but I had to set him up for this letter of June 17ᵗʰ. I wrote:

RECEIVED
DIRECTOR'S OFFICE
JUN 17 1992
V.I. BUREAU OF INT. REV.
ST. THOMAS, V.I.

June 17, 1992

Mr. Edward E. Thomas
Director-Bureau Internal Revenue
Lockhart Gardens #1-A
St. Thomas, Virgin Islands 00802

> "Self conceit may lead to self des-
> truction."
> —Aesop

Dear Mr. Thomas:

Since it has become axiomatic that crurrent events form the basis for future trends, your dastardly act of lampoonery - intended to be a clever ploy and
designed to cheat me out of four (4) hours annual leave, was - in retrospect an
excercise in utterly bad taste. Intuitively, I learned about it.

There is no fair-minded person in this whole wide world who would have done what you did. It was a flagrant error that requires yet another grievance.

I'm hard pressed to think that you'd take time out from your busy schedule
to abuse your discretionary power using spiteful reasons such as (a) your perception of me as the prototype of the legendary Swiss hero William Tell and (b) your
antipathy towards me.

In your little scheme to cheat me out of four hours annual leave however,
you completely forgot that the extent of your power was limited by law.

Mr. Thomas, I have no compunctions of being left alone in this abode of
devils referred to as the Virgin Islands Bureau of Internal Revenue. For your
information, I'm ready, willing and able to communicate with everybody (save the
ones previously noted in letters to you) for the conduct of business and nothing
else.

While on the job, I refuse to court your favor or to do anything contrary
to what's legitimate in our Virgin Islands Government of Laws.

Bigotry, Mr. Thomas, does not comport with the position of Director. A
Director must comport himself with dignity at all times.

To date - with the arrogant manners of a Dictator and using double standards, you have (among other things and without any notification to me) docked me
four hours leave without pay, thereby taking bread out of my mouth in the same
manner that you previously frowned upon taking bread out of someone's mouth in
your memorandum of March 27, 1992, and your latest act of willfully taking another four hours off my annual leave.

474

Letter   -2-   June 17, 1992
Mr. Edward E. Thomas

     You have on occasions threatened to "touch me up" and blow my head off. Additionally, you have treated as of little value the aberrant behavior of Mr. Louis M. Willis, and have furthermore been swept away by his emotional pleas to harass and intimidate me, while he continues to operate as a human shield for you from his unlawful position of Assistant Chief of the Delinquent Accounts and Returns Branch.

     As prosecutor, Judge and Jury in the Virgin Islands Bureau of Internal Revenue, you must know that Mr. Willis is a devious person, who refuses to submit to authority and office discipline. For proof, please look at the record.

     Finally, your procrastinating which is designed to delay action on my grievances, tells me that you've chosen the position that discretion is the better of valor; consequently, I'm preparing to make the prolongation of my persecution public beginning with my letter of reconcilliation to Governor Alexander A. Farrelly (copy to you), which is dated January 18, 1991. I really hate to incur your wrath, but enough is enough.

     As an afterthought it is worth noting that the moving of Mr. Louis M. Willis - a man without the required prerequisites from an Internal Revenue Officer I to Assistant Chief in violation of the Personnel Merit System, was an action that can serve as an example if an when you decide to act on my retirement proposal. I really want to leave this place.

                          Always respecting the Office of
                                Director

                                Liston B. Monsanto
                                Internal Revenue Officer

c.c. Governor Alexander A. Farrelly

    Ms. Claudette Farrington

    On June 17, 1992, Willis prepared and sent me my Performance Report for the period June 17, 1991 to June 17, 1992. Whether it was satisfactory or not I was never going to sign any Performance Report prepared by an unqualified person. I loved it when he sent me my performance Report inasmuch as it allowed me to write an attachment to it which would explain my reason for not signing the Report. So upon receiving the less-than-satisfactory rating, I attached the following:

Liston B. Monsanto, Sr.

GOVERNMENT OF THE U.S. VIRGIN ISLANDS
EMPLOYEE PERFOMANCE REPORT
(READ THE REVERSE SIDE BEFORE FILLING OUT)

EMPLOYEE NAME	JOB CLASSIFICATION	Internal	DEPARTMENT Bur. of Int. Revenue
Liston Monsanto	Revenue Officer IV		St. Thomas, V.I.

REASON FOR EVALUATION DATE (1)
(2)

RATING PERIOD

*PROBATION ☐   FINAL PROBATION ☐   ANNUAL XX   SPECIAL (EXTENSIONS, ETC.) ☐   FROM: 6/17/91   TO: 6/17/92

SECTION A—FACTOR CHECK LIST
Immediate Supervisor Must Check Each Factor in the Appropriate Column

	A Not Satisfactory	B Requires Improvement	C Meets Standards	D Exceeds Standards	E Does Not Apply
1 Observance of Work Hours		X			
2 Attendance			X		
3 Grooming and Dress			X		
4 Compliance With Rules		X			
5 Safety Practices			X		
6 Attitude Towards Public			X		
7 Attitude Towards Employees		X			
8 Knowledge of Work		X			
9 Work Judgments		X			
10 Planning and Organizing		X			
11 Job Skill Level		X			
12 Quality of Work		X			
13 Volume of Acceptable Work		X			
14 Meeting Deadlines		X			
15 Accepts Responsiblity		X			
16 Accepts. Direction		X			
17 Accepts Change		X			
18 Effectiveness Under Stress		X			
19 Appearance of Work Station			X		
20 Operation and Care of Equipment			X		
21 Work Coordination		X			
22 Initiative		X			
23 (Additional Factors)					
24					
25					
26					
27					
28					
29					

FOR EMPLOYEES WHO SUPERVISE OTHERS

30 Planning and Organizing					
31 Scheduling and Coordinating					
32 Training and Instructing					
33 Productivity					
34 Evaluating Subordinates					
35 Judgments and Decisions					
36 Ability to Motivate Employer					
37 Operational Economy					
38 Supervisory Control					
39 (Additional Factors)					
40					
41					

(PRELIMINARY EVALUATION)
RATED BY: DATE:

DEPT. HEAD: DATE:

SECTION B — Record job STRENGTHS and superior performance incidents.

SECTION C—Record PROGRESS ACHIEVED in attaining previously set goals for improved work performance, or career development.

SECTION D—Record specific GOALS or IMPROVEMENT PROGRAMS to be undertaken during next evaluation period.

SECTION E—Record specific work performance DEFICIENCIES or job behavior requiring improvement or correction. (Explain checks in Column A.)

SUMMARY EVALUATION— Check Overall Performance —
( ) Not Satisfactory   ( ) Requires Improvement   ( ) Effective Meets Standards
( ) Exceeds Standards

RATER: I certify this report represents my best judgment.
( ) I do ( ) Do not Recommend this employee be granted permanent status.
(For final probation reports only)

(Rater's Signature) _____ Asst Chief Dir (Title) ___ 6/17/92 (Date)

Department Head Edward E. Thomas, Director

REVIEWER: (If None. So Indicate)
(Reviewer's Signature)   (Title)   (Date)

EMPLOYEE: I certify that this report has been discussed with me. I understand my signature does not necessarily indicate agreement.
Comment   *SEE ATTACHED ATTACHMENT*

(Employee's Signature)   (Date)

Checks in Column (A) Must be explained in Section E

476

ATTACHMENT TO PERFORMANCE REPORT FOR THE PERIOD JUNE 17, 1991 TO JUNE 17, 1992

The Rater (Mr. Louis M. WIllis) who was unlawfully placed into his current position in order to block me from advancing to the top rung of the ladder in the Delinquent Accounts and Returns Branch, is a lackey without any compunctions about telling lies. With a servile disposition and little bound by the love of truth, he has become a personification of the puppet pinocchio whose nose grew longer every time he lied.

Aware of the fact that Mr. Willis feels that security and safety in numbers take precedence over lawfulness, an audit team from the United States Internal Revenue Service in criticising his woeful performance wrote that (because of his inexperience and the fact that he was illegally moved from an Internal Revenue Officer I past several higher level Revenue Officers to the position of Assistant Chief of the Delinquent Accounts and Returns Branch) he was not suitable for the position. I too (as evidenced by grievances filed challenging his appointment) have never accepted Mr. Willis as my supervisor. The gentleman is so naive that he doesn't know that were it not for my presence in the Delinquent Accounts and Returns Branch, someone else would be where he is today.

With a mind that's distorted by fear, Mr. Willis gets his pleasure from the psychological pain inflicted on him by the powers that be in the Virgin Islands Bureau of Internal Revenue. Frustrated and puzzled, he cannot distinguish good from evil.

As a scornful rumor-monger he enjoys going outside of the workplace spreading lies against me in his glaring attempts to harm and ruin my reputation. He fails to see that I'm not guilty of any wrong.

So lacking in experience and savoir-faire is Mr. Willis, that during the rating period (i.e. February 21st) he tried unsuccessfully to assign me the duties of supervisor over a number of employees good enough to be given satisfactory ratings by him. I was forced to refuse the assignment for the reason that accepting it would be the same as accepting as a reality his unlawful appointment to the position of Assistant Chief.

As has been the custom, I again refuse to sign the attached Performance Report. Furthermore, I refuse to sign any rating given me by a lower-echelon employee.

Liston B. Monsanto
Internal Revenue Officer

June 17, 1992

In masterminding my persecution and sicking Willis on me, Farrelly and Thomas had played right into my hands. I had never wanted to meet with Willis whom I knew was unqualified for the position he was filling and now I had defiantly declared that I would not join him in any meeting unless a policeman or some third party outside of the Bureau of Internal Revenue was present. And of course their disclosure law would not permit that.

Liston B. Monsanto, Sr.

On June 18, 1992, I wrote to Willis saying:

June 18, 1992

Mr. Louis M. Willis
Delinquent Accounts & Returns Branch
V.I. Bureau of Internal Revenue
St. Thomas, Virgin Islands 00802

Dear Mr. Willis:

With respect to my letter of June 5, 1992, I'd like to direct your attention to page 6 of Opinion #81-1434 of the Third Circuit Court of Appeals, where you'll find exactly what was said by the Government Employees Service Commission and other top people about my exemplary performance on the job.

I have always been a person who prides himself on working. Greater love hath no man for his work.

And this is precisely why I asked for your assistance in using your influence to tell Mr. Thomas that Liston Monsanto wants to work, but because of the absence of clear guidelines he cannot.

Again, I'm appealing to you to talk to Mr. Thomas. You might tell him that if he can find the time to dock me four hours leave without pay and then find additional time to cheat me out of four hours annual leave, surely he can find the time to issue me clear guidelines.

I do not want to be victimized by the business community with whom the Administration has an unholy alliance.

Sincerely,

Liston B. Monsanto
Internal Revenue Officer

In the Daily News of June 23, 1992, (see newspaper clipping attached to letter of June 26, 1992), under the headline, "Government is a Joke, Merchants Tell Senators." Business leaders blasted what they described as a bloated, lazy public sector that laid obstacles in front of business at every turn. From the mouth of Ann Abramson came these words: "I think this government should bow its head in shame. Government is a joke. A joke. They don't care." Abramson told those at the Christiansted meeting that the government, the largest employer in the Territory, is too large and characterized government jobs as "easy money." "They don't care," she repeated. Nobody wants to rock the boat. What have they (government employees) got to lose, when every other Thursday they can just go to pick up a check? It's all free this, free that, food stamps even if you have to lie to get it." This was the same Ann Abramson who had helped to persecute me for rocking the boat in the early seventies when Reuben Wheatley had removed me from the then Tax Division. Ann Abramson was failing to realize that she couldn't have it both ways.

Willis had been trying without any success to assign a number of delinquent accounts to me. This was the same Louis Willis who you may recall had written to Olive begging to be sent for training in both the Revenue Officer and Special Procedures Officer Programs. He had not been sent but all of a sudden without the required training he had become a pedant and was telling me who was far ahead of him in conducting the business of an office what was right and what was wrong. I wrote to him on June 26, 1992, using a lead-in from General Douglas MacArthur which said:

June 26, 1992

Mr. Louis M. WIllis
Delinquent Accounts & Returns Branch
V.I. Bureau of Internal Revenue
St. Thomas, Virgin Islands 00802

> "I am told in effect I must follow
> blindly the leader-keep silent-or
> take the bitter consequences".
>
> -Douglas MacArthur

Dear Mr. Willis:

Because I know that you do not read very fast, I've decided (once again) to write this letter very slow hoping to make you understand that I'm not your typical St. Thomas Revenue Officer, who favors reaction or believes in blind loyalty.

Your unlawful appointment to the classified position of Assistant Chief, was an event of great consequence for the two fully-trained Revenue Officers from whom you are now attempting to transfer several delinquent accounts. You seem to have forgotten that whereas love is opposed to hate, so too is the "real world"(where I was sent to be half-trained) opposed to fantasy. It goes without saying however, that some people refuse to grow with responsibility. They just puff up.

Why is it that in the wake of so many important letters (some asking for clear guidelines, others addressing the advanced training received by Mr. Thomas' wife and Mr. Jens Todman) would you waste valuable time to write me your memorandum of June 25th, 1992, which unilaterally attempts to assign me the work of two fully trained Revenue Officers? Incidentally, have you reviewed the attachments to my performance reports for the last four years? If you haven't, please do.

After reviewing the attachments, I ask that you turn your attention to my lettr of May 26, 1992, wherein I've spoken about our current impasse and the several reasons for it. This letter-important as it is, just cannot be ignored.

When one considers the fact that Revenue Officers are instructed to consistently perform in ways that convince the Taxpayer (or third parties) that they mean what they say, and say what they mean, why shouldn't I as a Revenue Officer be consistent with the things that I've said about conditions on the job while on the job? Are we neurotic? In order to be consistent, I must continue along the legal path that I've chosen (based on Opinion #81-1434 of the Third Circuit Court, etc.) until legal changes are made.

RECEIVED

DAR BRANCH

JUN 26 1992

V. I. Bureau of internal Revenue

479

Case in point: I cannot (see reason #3 on psge 1 of my letter of May 26, 1992) speak of recorded threats against me and then suddenly decide to make a bold appearance before you and Mr. Edward E. Thomas. (Don't you remember what happened on July 17, 1991 in Mr. Thomas' office when the three of us last met?) I'm terribly afraid to confer with you two in the same setting without a lawman being in attendance.

As for the accounts listed in your memorandum, I must say that you've received much advice from your Advisor with respect to the course of action to be taken on each account.

No consideration-it appears, was given to my right to reject the accounts nor was any given to the business bashing as outlined in the Daily News of June 23, 1992, and the Governor's declaration that he's pro-business. (This fact is magnified by the many businesses given special exemption from the "STEP" program. How else could they have gotten their business licenses?). Please re-read my letter of February 9, 1984 for more information on the business community.

Today, under the law of caveat emptor I've decided to reject the delinquent accounts listed in your memorandum of June 25, 1992. I will not (at this time) sign or initial the assignemnt slip as required for acceptance. Accounts (for your information) muat be collated before any assignments can be made.

If you are feeling a little jaded and do not want to review the letters written during the Olive years, I suggest you start with my letter of January 18, 1991 and chronologically work your way up to June 26, 1992, for an explanation regarding my status.

Your accounts are being returned herewith in order for you to do with them whatever you deem legally necessary.

Finally, looking at a person with jaundiced eyes and abusing discretionary power are not conducive to good management. "Example is not the main thing in influencing others. It is the only thing."

Sincerely,

Liston B. Monsanto
Internal Revenue Officer

480

'Government is a joke,' merchants tell senators

V.I., St. Croix economic woes get airing

By KAY JOHNSON
St. Croix Bureau

The problem with the V.I. economy is the local government, and radical reform is the solution, business people told senators Monday.

The battle over casino gambling expected at the Economic Development Committee meeting was only a skirmish, promising to be continued at second meeting tonight at the legislative building on St. Croix.

Business leaders blasted what they described as a bloated, lazy public sector that lays obstacles in front of business at every turn.

"I think this government should bow its head in shame," said Ann Abramson, owner of Tradewinds Building Supplies in Frederiksted. "Government is a joke. A joke. They don't care."

Abramson told those at the Christiansted meeting that the government — the largest employer in the territory — is too large and characterized government jobs as "easy money."

"They don't care," she repeated. "Nobody wants to rock the boat. What have they (government employees) got to lose, when every other Thursday they can just go to pick up a check? It's all free this, free that, food stamps even if you have to lie to get it."

Other speakers were less impassioned but repeated Abramson's complaints.

"We have a government that has become so huge in relation to the private sector, it leads to a very unhealthy situation. It stymies initiative, it stymies imagination," said Robert Bidelspacher of the St. Croix Board of Realtors.

James C. Savage, chairman of St. Croix 2000, urged senators to "stop the slide towards socialism."

Economic brainstorming

Highlights of the ideas to spur St. Croix's economy presented Monday at the Senate Economic Development Committee meeting:

✓ Spend money to market St. Croix as a tourist destination.
✓ Develop more tourist attractions, such as cultural fairs.
✓ Back or build projects, such as Hess Oil Virgin Islands Inc.'s catalytic cracker, to temporarily bring in new money.
✓ Allow casino gambling.
✓ Streamline permit approval for new buildings or enterprises, possibly granting pre-approval for certain projects.
✓ Identify sites for possible industrial plants.
✓ Restore deteriorating neighborhoods and landmarks in Frederiksted.
✓ Build a sports complex.
✓ Prisoner manufacturing for export.

"We believe the single most pressing issue is to foster the development of the free-enterprise system," he said. To accomplish this, government should provide direction and marketing aid for tourism and improve education.

William Roebuck, assistant commissioner in the Economic Development and Agriculture Department, told the committee that construction projects like the Hess Oil Virgin Islands Inc. catalytic cracker, Frederiksted pier and St. Croix Hospital could provide a "quick fix" for the economy.

But Roebuck said the island must bring in new investors and industries for lasting economic recovery.

Most at the meeting pleaded with senators not to deplete the Tourism Advertising Fund — which is fueled by the hotel-room tax.

"The marketing funds are des-

perately needed today," said Adam Hoover, representing the Hotel and Tourism Association. "We are outgunned in the world market. None of us individually is capable of stimulating the amount of business needed to sustain each one of us."

Roebuck said government obstacles to would-be investors include difficulty in obtaining building and operating permits.

"There has to be a quick, orderly process. It cannot drag out a year or nine months and just keep going around in circles."

For example, one prospective buyer for the closed Carambola resort considered expanding the facility to house a small convention center, Roebuck said.

"But after several months (of looking into permits), he decided it couldn't be done. When I last heard from him, he was considering Aruba."

To Edward Thomas, being Director of the Virgin Islands Bureau of Internal Revenue was about control, lies and dominance. He had goaded Willis into his unlawful position and could not afford to have me continuing, like a salmon, to swim against the tide. He would have to punish me, thereby showing Willis how absolute his power was. On June 26, 1992, he sent me a letter suspending me for thirty (30) days without pay. He was indicating to me in a way that he had not developed beyond a mental age of twenty-one (21) years. He was acting like an idiot due largely to the virus of fear, fear of Liston Monsanto. Here is what his letter said:

GOVERNMENT OF
THE VIRGIN ISLANDS OF THE UNITED STATES

VIRGIN ISLANDS
BUREAU OF INTERNAL REVENUE

Lockharts Garden No. 1A
Charlotte Amalie, St. Thomas, U.S.V.I. 00802

June 26, 1992

Mr. Liston Monsanto
Internal Revenue Officer IV
Lockharts Garden #1A
St. Thomas, Virgin Islands 00801

Dear Mr. Monsanto:

I am hereby suspending you effective at 5 p.m. today, June 26, 1992 for thirty (30) days <u>without pay</u> for gross insubordination.

Your willful failure to accept cases assigned to you by your immediate supervisor Mr. Louis Willis will not be tolerated by me. You have refused to attend meetings called for all revenue officers and you even refused to attend a meeting with taxpayers.

Every other employee in this Bureau carries out assignments directed by me through their group manager. No organization can run successfully unless a chain of command is in place and properly followed.

I am afraid that there really is no place for you in the Bureau since you refuse to follow directives.

Sincerely,

Edward E. Thomas
Director

EET/was

cc: Governor Alexander A. Farrelly
    Claudette Farrington, Deputy Director
    Louis Willis, Asst. Chief, DAR
    Alvin Swan, Shop Steward
    Luis "Tito" Morales, President USWA
    Cecilia Hill, Personnel Officer

I needed the vacation but I could not let him get away with such a despicable act. I filed a Grievance and while on suspension I wrote him a letter which I would use for my defense. The letter was dated July 10, 1992 and said:

July 10, 1992

Mr. Edward E. Thomas
Director
V.I. Bureau of Internal Revenue
Lockhart's Gardens #1-A
St. Thomas, Virgin Islands 00802

Dear Mr. Thomas:

To the extent that your opinionated letter of June 26, 1992, was formed without taking the time and care to judge my actions, and because I have suddenly become aware of the fact that after thirty eight years of satisfactory service you are trying desperately to tarnish my honor and hurt my feelings, by denying me my salary checks in flagrant violation of Article V, Section 11, of our contract, I made the decision (via this letter) to immediately correct your false allegations which ultimately led to my thirty (30) day suspension without so much as a hearing.

Firstly I'd like to say that what you've surmised to be my willful failure to accept cases assigned to me by my immediate supervisor Mr. Louis Willis is-to say the least, misleading and consequently deserves a detailed explanation.

As has continued to be the practice in the Delinquent Accounts and Returns Branch where I am assigned to work, more than thirty (30) years ago Mr. Jack Love of the New York district office and Mr. Guerrero of the Puerto Rico district office (Instructors assigned to formally train me in the collection activity) impressed in my memory that it was the right of a Revenue Officer (before initialling form 1976) to reject any account earmarked for assignment to that Revenue Officer.

Additionally, I learned in my training sessions (both on the job and in the classroom) that a collation of all accounts earmarked for assignment to Revenue Officers was most important-not only from an ethical standpoint, but also to avoid a duplication of assignments.

On February 4, 1971, the Commissioner of Finance as head of the Tax Division assigned me the arduous task of training several prospective Revenue Officers. Using my training, which I believe by now (more than twenty years later) has become outmoded, I proceeded to teach the trainees the same things that I was taught in my training program-including the fact that they too reserved the right to do what I did in rejecting certain accounts on June 26, 1992.

As their instructor, I imbued them with the ambition to succeed and reiterated the contention of my instructors that it would be a most unethical thing to accept an account of a family member, a friend, a relative, or any person or corporation with whom they were doing business.

For your information, many of the accounts that are earmarked for transfer among the Revenue Officers in our Delinquent Accounts and Returns Branch and even those initially assigned are rejected by Revenue Officers on a regular basis for one or more of the various reasons noted in the foregoing paragraph. (For more on the subject matter you may want to read the attached letter which was written by your wife Mrs. Lucia Thomas and is dated August 3, 1984. By the way, she was not suspended).

Because you've denied me my advanced training and/or a refresher's course, I'm unable to tell you whether or not any changes were made to affect the assignment of accounts within the last thirty (30) years.

Regarding your other remarks which are obviously calculated to "take bread out of my mouth", the record shows that Governor Alexander A. Farrelly, Mr. Edward E. Thomas, Mr. Louis M. Willis, the Attorney General, and the Police Chief were all told (from July 18, 1991 to the present) that I had declined respectfully to meet with Mr. Willis and/or Mr. Edward E. Thomas because of threats made against me. Why you did not say or do anything about my declination before now puzzles me.

The record also shows that you took it upon yourself to illegally charge me four hours annual leave for - as you put it, my failure to attend the same meetings of which you speak in paragraph two of your letter. Are you now trying to punish me twice for the same crime? Is this and other illegal actions on your part the reason that you have been dubbed absolute monarch in the Virgin Islands Bureau of Internal Revenue?

On May 26, 1992, when I told you that we'd reached an impasse, I thought that you had finally received my message. I guess you didn't. Please review the records.

You are treating me unfairly. The thirty (30) day suspension given me is an abuse of your discretionary power. As an employee with an unblemished record, who has served as Chief of the Delinquent Accounts and Returns Branch, and one who was asked as recent as February 27, 1992 to supervise the activities of the Delinquent Accounts and Returns Branch, why do you believe that I'd need to be told what you've said in paragraphs three and four of your letter?

Letter Mr. Edward E. Thomas   -3-   July 10, 1992

On June 5, 1992, and again on June 18th, I literally begged and pleaded with both you and Mr. Willis for clear guidelines in order to get my work up to a professional level. Your reaction to those two letters came on June 26th, when you willfully suspended me from duty.

I've said it before, but it bears repeating that I'm trying my best, but management is showing the whole world that they are capable of worst.

Sincerely,

Liston B. Monsanto
Internal Revenue Officer

c.c. Gov. Farrelly

Ms. Claudette Farrington

Mr. Luis "Tito" Morales

Mr. Randolph Allen

Ms. Cecelia Hill

GOVERNMENT OF
THE VIRGIN ISLANDS OF THE UNITED STATES

——o——

VIRGIN ISLANDS
BUREAU OF INTERNAL REVENUE
P. O. Box 3186
Charlotte Amalie, St. Thomas, U.S.V.I. 00801

August 3, 1984

Mr. Kenneth C. Hansen
Chief, Del. Accts & Returns Br
Charlotte Amalie
St. Thomas, V.I. 0801

Dear Mr. Hansen:

There are several cases which have been assigned to me for collection which the director, Mr. Anthony Olive, have met with their representatives and formulated certain plans.

As director, he is privileged to do so, however, being a senior revenue officer, it becomes increasingly difficult and frustrating to do the "correct thing" when these practitioners feel that I would take orders from them — given by Mr. Olive — while in the meantime, he gives you messages as to what should be done.

These cases are large dollar cases, and in the future, if I, as a senior revenue officer cannot be present at these meetings to secure "first hand information and instructions", the case can be transferred to someone else who might prefer such actions.

It would be noted that when Mr. Quinn received a request to meet with a practitioner to discuss a tax liability he always notified and requested us to brief him on the particular case. There were no second and third hand information given, therefore there was always a meeting of the minds.

This job can be very frustrating at times, but if there is cooperation between managers and their employees the work would flow smoothly and the collection process would be greatly enhanced.

Sincerely,

Lucia Thomas

cc: Mr. A. Olive
    Director

On July 28, 1992, as an afterthought, I wrote to Thomas once again. I said:

July 28, 1992

Mr. Edward E. Thomas
Director
V.I. Bureau of Internal Revenue
St. Thomas, Virgin Islands 00802

> "Officials who violate someone's rights
> while performing governmental duties
> may be sued and forced to pay monetary
> damages."
>   - U.S. Supreme Court 11/5/91

Dear Mr. Thomas:

As a postscript to my recent suspension, I'd like to say that over the past several years I've been an object of much harassment emanating from your office. Through the abuse of your discretionary power, you have violated my civil rights and unlawfully suspended me from duty without pay.

With thirty eight years of satisfactory service as a government employee, and one who is neither under obligation to anybody because of favors received, nor otherwise guilty of stealing or fighting in the workplace, my thirty day suspension which ended on July 26th was a dramatic event. Were it not for my effervescent personality, my spirits would have been so sad and gloomy, that I may have had a nervous breakdown.

Today as I write, my intuitive mind tells me that as Director of the Virgin Islands Bureau of Internal Revenue, you would not want to suffer the ignominy of being caught abusing your powers and harassing me.

So rather than allow your status as a member of the establishment (where you do not need a good reason or sound basis for doing wrong) to serve as your milestone in progress, I ask that you set your priorities giving full concentration to those grievances which call for the removal of Mr. Louis M. Willis from the classified position of Assistant Chief of the Delinquent Accounts and Returns Branch. Who knows, with your connections you might get a favorable decision.

With all my experiences (military and otherwise) I'm having difficulty understanding the methods by which you operate. A classic example of this difficulty is paragraph three of your letter of June 26, 1992. I just cannot discern its meaning.

We need a legitimate chain of command! Why you'd want to continue to play the roles of Prosecutor, Judge, Jury, and Executioner during this momentous period when there is no legitimate chain of command and with Mr. Willis' status unclear, overwhelms me.

Our Personnel Merit System precludes you from legally appointing anyone to the position of Assistant Chief of the Delinquent Accounts and Returns Branch as you've done with Mr. Willis. Bear in mind that the position is in the classified service and therefore outside of the political arena.

Currently, in his roles of psychologist and protector par excellence, a sophomoric Mr. Willis has told me that because I'm burnt out and mentally drained, that I need to retire. What a tactless thing to say! No self-respecting person would do the things Mr. Willis does.

And speaking of retirement, you have yet to respond to my retirement proposal - a proposal you asked me to submit for your review on March 13, 1992.

While many parents discipline their children for bad behavior, my purgatorial suspension designed to show me who's in charge (as if I did not know following your appointment and after more than thirty years of service) amounted to a showy display. There was no valid reason for the suspension. Absolutely none.

When it comes to my plight in the Virgin Islands Bureau of Internal Revenue, like an advocate of monarchical principles you continue to reason cleverly but falsely, especially in regard to right and wrong.

And it is because of your abrasive attitude that I'm contemplating a decision to sue both you and Mr. Louis M. Willis for violating my civil rights and harassing me.

As a paragon of efficiency I have always believed that little things accomplished are far better than big things talked about. I have never been a shirker - a fact corroborated by the record. Give me the tools (training, clear guidelines, etc.) and I'll always perform. A word of caution: Stop violating the laws and authorities.

                                         Sincerely,

                                         Liston B. Monsanto
                                         Internal Revenue Officer

c.c. Gov. Alexander A. Farrelly
     Ms. Claudette Farrington
     Ms. Cecelia Hill

On July 29, 1992, I appeared before Edward Thomas' kangaroo court for my hearing on the suspension. Did I expect him to reverse the unjust act? Of course not. The man was a little dictator. I wrote to him on July 30, 1992 using a lead-in from the Daily News which said:

July 30, 1992

Mr. Edward E. Thomas
Director
V.I. Bureau of Internal Revenue
Lockhart Garden #!_A
St. Thomas, Virgin Islands 00802

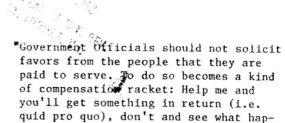

"Government Officials should not solicit
favors from the people that they are
paid to serve. To do so becomes a kind
of compensation racket: Help me and
you'll get something in return (i.e.
quid pro quo), don't and see what happens (use your imagination)."

 — V.I. Daily News

Dear Mr. Thomas:

In the Virgin Islands Bureau of Internal Revenue the phrase "law and order" has been much abused in recent years, but if "law and order" means anything,
it means that everyone — Rich man, Poor man, President, Governor, Judge, Senator,
Arbitrator, and Director of the Bureau of Internal Revenue obey the law; that the
law has no favorites; that before it all men stand equal.

When supreme power is formally vested in a single person or family (as is
the case in the Virgin Islands Bureau of Internal Revenue) we have a monarchy.
Operating from my subordinate position, one can clearly see that I'm no monarchist.
Nevertheless, after listening to you in our step 3 meeting of July 29, 1992, I was
reminded of a poem that I read as a child which started with the famous words, "I'm
monarch of all I survey."

Your attempts to judge my case which came about as a result of my being unlawfully suspended from duty by you, left me in a state of wonderment. The tone of
bitterness, which I believe stems from frustration — a frustration over your obses-
sion with the fact that Liston Monsanto continues to respect law and authority was
awesome. It was as if you were trying to use the power of your office to inspire
intense fear or fearful reverence.

You referred to me as an idiot and spoke about demoting and firing me. All
along, it never occurred to you that many of your senior Revenue Officers — now in-
sulated from me (this includes your wife, who may be Chief defacto) and who allowed
Mr. Louis M. Willis to be unlawfully placed in the classified position of Assistant
Chief of the Delinquent Accounts and Returns Branch, should have been demoted or
fired several years ago for their failure to challenge the unlawful action. Such
people cannot help our government, especially during this period when we are facing a forty million deficit.

A word to the wise: Double jeopardy is the jeopardy in which a defendant is placed by a second prosecution for the same offense or crime. It is prohibited by the U.S. Constitution.

Please do not allow your status as a member of "the establishment" (where you do not need a good reason or sound basis for doing wrong) to serve as your milestone in progress. Let's get an Arbitrator to hear my case. I'd like to tell him that whereas Mr. Edward E. Thomas cannot see that his wife's presence as an employee in the Delinquent Accounts and Returns Branch serves as a conflict of interest, Liston Monsanto can see a conflict of interest with many of the accounts earmarked for assignment to him.

Sincerely,

Liston B. Monsanto
Internal Revenue Officer

c.c. Ms. Claudette Farrington

Mr. Anthony Attidore

Mr. Luis "Tito" Morales

Ms. Cecelia Hill

I then wrote to Willis on August 3, 1992. I said:

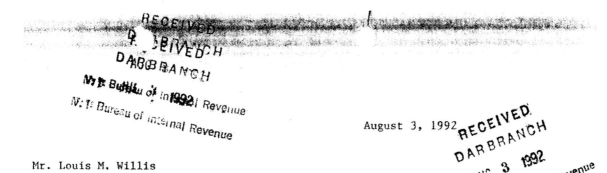

August 3, 1992

Mr. Louis M. Willis
Assistant Chief
Delinquent Accounts & Returns Branch
Lockhart Gardens #1-A
St. Thomas, Virgin Islands 00802

Dear Mr. Willis:

Our Director Edward E. Thomas remains an enigma. After more than thirty eight years of government service, he wants to dismiss me from the Virgin Islands Bureau of Internal Revenue for (of all things) agreeing with what is good, just, and lawful.

In his role of psychiatrist, he has reported that my mental capacity has deteriorated to the point of non-existence, and he has stated that even though he answers some of my letters, he doesn't read any of them.

As a Director with plenary powers, Mr. Thomas scheduled a meeting of the kangaroo court variety for July 29th, 1992 to hear what he already knew about the circumstances surrounding my unlawful thirty day suspension - a suspension put into effect by him on June 26, 1992.

Ranting and raving before messrs. Anthony Attidore, Luis "Tito" Morales, Alvin Swan, and myself, he was thwarted in his efforts to say anything about his glaring attempts to uphold what was, in effect, a unilateral decision made by him. It never occurred to him that much embarrassment could have been avoided if he'd held court on June 26, 1992 prior to my suspension.

As if suffering from a case of delirium, Mr. Thomas called me an idiot. Then through derisive laughter, he sought to exonerate himself from the threats he'd made against me by saying that such threats were made when he was not in the position of Director.

Flouting the law and seeing me as the pre-eminent person in the Virgin Islands Bureau of Internal Revenue, he appeared uneasy and ashamed in front of the assembled gathering.

As a charitable, humble, and devout christian, he finally admitted to making an offer through Mr. Luis "Tito" Morales to me on March 5, 1992,wherein he'd make me Chief of the Delinquent Accounts and Returns Branch retroactive to Mr. Jerome Ferdinand's resignation with the proviso that I retire immediately. He later reneged on his promise, however.

There is no record to show, and I cannot recall Mr. Edward E. Thomas ever attending classes in the Internal Revenue Officer Training Program. Yet the good gentleman has become so sophisticated that he knows the whole aspect of an Internal Revenue Officer's work.

As a member of "the establishment" he violates our contract with impunity. His latest act as a scoff-law came on June 26, 1992 when by way of ostentation, he willfully deleted my name from the payroll in clear violation of Article V, Section 11, of our contract.

So while our Police Chief continues to talk tough (with good reason) about lawlessness in our community Mr. Thomas continues to operate with reckless abandon in the Virgin Islands Bureau of Internal Revenue completely oblivious of the fact that ours is a government of laws.

Time after time I've stated my position to Mr. Thomas, and time after time he has refused to listen. Because I respect (very much) the several offices that make up the Virgin Islands Bureau of Internal Revenue, I've always been willing to cooperate to the fullest, but needless to say, cooperation does not mean emasculation.

Sincerely,

Liston B. Monsanto
Internal Revenue Officer

c.c. Mr. Anthony Attidore

Ms. Claudette Farrington

Ms. Cecelia Hill

Mr. Luis "Tito" Morales

Mr. Randolph Allen

Mr. Edward E. Thomas

As noted earlier, a retiree (Don Walsh) was brought in from the United States to do the very thing that the other retirees before him had failed to do. I felt sorry for him. At 8:45 a.m. on August 6, 1992, I received a memorandum from Willis which said: "This is a reminder to let you know about the lesson that is going to be conducted by Mr. Don Walsh, 8:30 a.m. in the conference room this morning." I had to answer him at once. I said: "At 8:45 this morning I was served with a 'reminder' about a scheduled meeting with Mr. Don Walsh at 8:30 a.m. in the conference room. I did not attend because (unlike a number of people) prior to being served with 'the reminder,' I was never notified about the meeting and what's more, my itinerary had been planned way in advance of the meeting."

On August 10, 1992, I wrote to Thomas using a lead-in from Thomas himself, which said:

August 10, 1992

Mr. Edward E. Thomas
Director
V.I. Bureau of Internal Revenue
St. Thomas, Virgin Islands 00802

> "Every other employee in this Bureau carries out assignments directed by me through their group manager."
> -Edward E. Thomas

Dear Mr. Thomas:

If you'd re-read paragraph nine (9) of my letter to Governor Alexander A. Farrelly, which is dated May 8, 1992, you'd find that the above quotation coincides with the assertions therein and offers circumstantial evidence to prove that you have directed Mr. Louis M. Willis to continue his threats of violence against me adinfinitum.

And although the record shows that you are a scoff-law, one has to wonder why (as a devoted christian) you'd want to lead Mr. Willis down the garden path. He's a young person whose potential - if he has any, can be developed in the best interest of the Virgin Islands Government.

In a related matter, I'd like to say that as you continue to use craft and ingenuity to get the better of the United Steelworkers of America in preventing my grievances from being heard, I'm willing (at this point in time and in the spirit of compromise) to have someone represent me before you for the purpose of discussing my imminent departure from the Virgin Islands Bureau of Internal Revenue.

At your kangaroo court on July 29th, your demeanor told all present that you wanted nothing better than my immediate departure from the Bureau.

Should you decide to entertain discussions on the matter, it would do you well to remember that I'm acting today (as I did yesterday) as a vicarious agent for you and a number of ingrates only in consideration of future generations of Virgin Islanders.

All things considered (including the hiring freeze being contemplated by the Governor), it is my honest belief that it would be a saving of precious time, money and much embarrassment for both sides to take a short cut.

c.c.   Mr. Randolph Allen
        Mr. Anthony Attidore
        Ms. Claudette Farrington
        Ms. Cecelia Hill
        Mr. Luis "Tito" Morales

Sincerely

Liston B. Monsanto
Internal Revenue Officer

493

On August 17, 1992, Willis, who was not writing on a regular basis, sent me a memorandum which read: "There will be a one hour training session from 9:00 a.m. to 10:00 a.m. in the conference room on Tuesday, August 18, 1992. The session will be on abatement of penalties for reasonable causes given by Mr. Don Walsh. It is expected that all Revenue Officers and Revenue Representatives attend." I answered right away. I said:

August 17, 1992

RECEIVED
D&R BRANCH

AUG 17 1992

V.I. Bureau of Internal R...

Mr. Louis M. Willis
Delinquent Accounts & Returns Branch
Charlotte Amalie
St. Thomas, Virgin Islands 00802

Dear Mr. Willis:

Your somewhat vague memorandum of this afternoon which speaks to a one hour training session to be given by Collection Advisor Don Walsh from 9:00 to 10:00 A.M. startled me.

First of all, it comes exactly three working hours before the session, and at a time when my itinerary for August 18, 1992 has already been prepared.

Inasmuch as Mr. Edward E. Thomas has said that his policies should not be regarded as substitutes for the law, in keeping with this declaration I'd like to direct your attention to Article XIX of our contract which says nothing about a Collection Advisor, who formerly worked for the U.S. Internal Revenue Service, conducting training sessions for the employees of the Delinquent Accounts and Returns Branch.

I have never been averse to attending meetings under normal conditions, nor am I averse. to cooperating with anyone in the best interest of the Virgin Islands Government.

Maybe you ought to read my letters of May 11, 1992 and May 26, 1992, for information relating to Mr. Don Walsh, who was introduced to me as Mr. Thomas' Collection Advisor.

Sincerely,

Liston B. Monsanto
Internal Revenue Officer

494

On August 20, 1992, I wrote to Thomas saying:

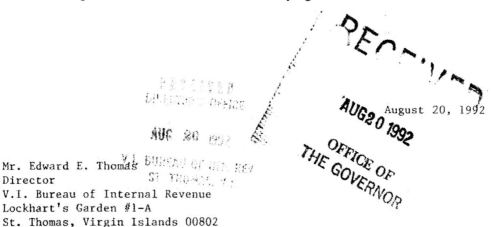

August 20, 1992

Mr. Edward E. Thomas
Director
V.I. Bureau of Internal Revenue
Lockhart's Garden #1-A
St. Thomas, Virgin Islands 00802

> "Esteem cannot be where there is no
> confidence; and there can be no con-
> fidence where there is no respect."
>
> -- Giles

Dear Mr. Thomas:

I've said it before, but it's worth repeating that as a member of "the establishment" (where you do not need a good reason or sound basis for doing wrong) working in concert with many of the wrongdoers in our Virgin Islands society, you've misused your power for many years in the name of office politics.

Amid my vicarious work, my endless persecution, and the many threats of violence against me from you and Mr. Louis M. Willis (who incidentally is trying desperately to curryfavor with you), I was called an idiot by you in a formal meeting which was also attended by Messrs. Anthony Attidore, Luis "Tito" Morales, and Alvin Swan on July 29, 1992. That, Mr. Thomas was as much as I could stand.

The record shows that since July 18, 1991, I've been telling both you and Governor Farrelly (among others) that because of management's disrespectfulness, I had decided against meeting with either you or Mr. Willis.

Willful and open disrespect should not be tolerated by any decent human being. How - in the pride of manhood, can you or Mr. Willis expect me to meet with either of you in the future?

No, I will not be attending any meeting(s) called by you and/or Mr. Willis unless the President of Local Union and/or the International Representative of the United Steelworkers of America together with a Policeman is on hand. I've taken too much abuse already.

In the past and even up to now I have been an object of much ridicule emanating from your office, and today mindful of your unethical behavior, I have envisioned myself as the laughing stock of the employees (most of whom are contemporaries of my children) of the entire Virgin Islands Bureau of Internal Revenue.

Doing things in the name of office politics that defy logic and common sense is not correct. My several years on earth coupled with more than thirty eight years of governmental service have taught me not to expect any change in your behavior. Your attitude towards me is really a flagrant crime of disrespect.

Sincerely,

Liston B. Monsanto
Internal Revenue Officer

c.c.   Gov. Alexander A. Farrelly

Mr. Anthony Attidore

Mr. Luis "Tito" Morales

Ms. Claudette Farrington

Mr. Randolph Allen

Ms. Cecelia Hill

Then I zeroed in on Willis on August 21st. I said:

RECEIVED

DAR BRANCH

August 21, 1992

AUG 21 1992

N. I. Bureau of Internal Revenue

Mr. Louis M. Willis
Delinquent Accounts & Returns Branch
V.I. Bureau of Internal Revenue
St. Thomas, VirginIslands 00802

Dear Mr.Willis:

As part of a dying breed of Virgin Islanders not desirous of remonstrating against Mr. Edward E. Thomas' law-breaking ways and overall hostile attitude, I'm once again reaching out to you for crystal clear guidelines using as your authority Article II, Section 5, and Article IV, Section 2, of our contract.

My continuing attempts to collect the delinquent taxes in my inventory through the simplest form of enforcement (see my letters of June 5, 1992 and June 18, for a better explanation) has become less than effective.

Relating to my formal training, I fully realize that one man with courage constitutes a majority, but speaking for myself, I'd like to say that I need to be trained in the manner agreed to by management when they negotiated our contract.

And speaking of training, I have never been told (please refer to the contract) that a Retiree from the United States Internal Revenue Service (as is the case with Mr. Don Walsh, who was introduced to me by Mr. Thomas as his Collection Advisor) was coming to the Virgin Islands to train me.

Failure to follow a contract was the underlying reason for Mr. Thomas being delegated the authority by Governor Alexander A. Farrelly to lead a team of individuals in collecting the 5.4 million dollars overpaid DeJongh/Williams. Why he'd want to violate our contract while enforcing the language in the contract between DeJongh/Williams and our government is an enigma.

Please do what is right, for it would gratify some people and astonish the rest.

Sincerely,

Liston B. Monsanto
Internal Revenue Officer

Thomas' abuse of authority had punctuated the Bureau's ability to do the job as required. The communication required from him down to his supervisory staff was missing. His only concern in the Bureau on Internal Revenue was Liston Monsanto.

Willis sent me several documents with a cover letter on September 14, 1992. His letter said: "Attached to this letter is a listing of suppliers and subcontractors that the Water and Power Authority had paid for service rendered or supplies bought for WAPA fiscal year ended June 20, 1992. I would like you to do a compliance check on these establishments." I wrote back immediately saying:

September 14, 1992

RECEIVED

DAR BRANCH

SEP 14 1992

Bureau of Internal Revenue

Mr. Louis M. Willis
Delinquent Accounts & Returns Branch
V.I. Bureau of Internal Revenue
St. Thomas, Virgin Islands 00802

Dear Mr. Willis:

Your memorandum of this morning, which speaks of Suppliers and Sub-Contractors doing business with the Virgin Islands Water and Power Authority is in facsimile with the Virgin Islands Port Authority assignment which was given to me by Mr. Edward E. Thomas on June 4, 1991.

Had you spoken to Mr. Thomas before issuing your memorandum, I'm sure that he would have told you the same thing. But since the proof of the pudding is in the eating, I have attached hereto three (3) letters (see paragraph 5 below) which contain the facts, admissions, and conclusions drawn from evidence which together operated to determine a verdict on the Virgin Islands Port Authority assignment.

I'm a very thorough person, who relies heavily on the various laws and authorities by which I'm guided in order to accomplish my objective and that of the Virgin Islands Bureau of Internal Revenue.

The "Stop Tax Evasion Program" which asks for the same "compliance check" of which you speak in your memorandum, falls under the auspices of our Processing and Accounts Branch.

In order to avoid duplications, etc. I suggest you re-read my letter of July 1, 1991 together with the other two letters which are both dated July 8, 1991. Because Mr. Thomas agreed with me then, it is safe to say that he'd agree with me now.

So before going outside of our organization in a blind way and in order to stop our whistling in the wind, I'm saying to you (with all the convictions at my command) that you consider doing exactly what I asked for in July 1991 as the kick-off point in the assignment. My feelings today are the same as they were on the Virgin Islands Port Authority assignment. Let's get to work!

Sincerely,

Liston B. Monsanto
Internal Revenue Officer

c.c. Mr. Edward E. Thomas
Ms. Claudette Farrington

July 1, 1991

Mr. Edward E. Thomas
Director
V.I. Bureau of Internal Revenue
St. Thomas, V.I. 00802

Dear Mr. Thomas:

It is an axiom that stories of adventure fire the imagination, but who would have imagined that amid a fire at the Virgin Islands Port Authority on June 5, 1991, coupled with the fact that on that particular day Mr. Eugen Gottlieb (the Port Authority's Acting Executive Director) was off-island, that I would be assigned the arduous task (pursuant to a June 4, 1991, memorandum from your office, which was received by me on June 5, 1991) of conferring with Mr. Gottlieb for the sole purpose of securing much information on the Virgin Islands Port Authority contracts? Only a sycophant intrepid enough to go along with anything would have imagined that.

Anyway, trying to forget the past and seeking to get down to the more mundane problems facing the Virgin Islands Bureau of Internal Revenue, upon accepting the assignment I started out like a person full of fire and courage, and using the guidelines issued me in your memorandum as an essential first step towards a "new direction" in the Bureau, I immediately began work on the first phase of the Virgin Islands Port Authority assignment.

After prolonged interviews with Mrs. Grace James (secretary to Mr. Eugen Gottlieb) I met with Mr. Gottlieb, and together we thoroughly went over the several names appearing on the newspaper clipping which accompanied your memorandum and which had been taken from the St. Croix Avis.

This morning I welcome the opportunity of presenting to you the paper work designed to show you exactly what was done by Mr. Gottlieb in completing Phase I of the assignment.

Phase II got underway on June 21, 1991, when (in keeping with the Virgin Islands Government policy not to issue business licenses without first making a tax delinquency check) I sent a memorandum to Mr. Roy A. Vanterpool (Chief Processing and Accounts Branch) asking for a status report.

But unlike Mr. Eugen Gottlieb who was most cooperative, a hostile Mr. Roy Vanterpool - completely oblivious of the fact that our jobs are interrelated, and acting as if he was being ordered to do now what he had failed to do previously, evinced a bitter attitude and in a belligerent tone denied my request, thereby bringing the assignment to an unexpected ending.

It is significant to note here that in the Virgin Islands Bureau of Internal Revenue our chief problem concerns our ability to project ourselves as professionals rather than ordinary people.

It must be noted also that as you continue to work — hell bent on determining a future course of action for the Virgin Islands Bureau of Internal Revenue, there should be no doubts in anyone's mind that you can only accomplish your objective through the usage of guidelines.

I too am in need of guidelines. "Let us be thankful for the tools; but for them the rest of us could not succeed."

Sincerely,

Liston Monsanto
Internal Revenue Officer

cc: Mr. Graciano Belardo
Deputy Director

Mr. Louis M. Willis
Asst. Chief, DAR Branch

Complete   On-Going

		Complete	On-Going
Parking lighting poles			
T/W Guidance signs			
J. P. Electric	R/W-T/W lighting syst n	✓	
$606,067			
Maintenance Bldg.			✓
(In-house)			
$23,083			
Meridian Engineering	Overlay-Existing T/W	✓	
$1,318,833			
MSI	CFR Building	✓	
$123,883			
ECS Electrical			
Construction Specialist	Replacement of Beacon &	✓	
Tower			
$28,000			
Tender Pier	Repair by in-house crew	✓	
$100,000			
Zenon Construction	Replacement of Awning AHA	✓	
$19,680			
Zenon Construction	Removal of Debris from	✓	
Krause Lagoon			
$13,260			
APC Rentals	Rehanging of tiers Crown Bay	✓	
$17,295			
Charley's Trucking	Repair of Groin/Gregerie	✓	
$50,000			
Deeper Cheaper	Diving for tires Crown Bay	✓	
$3,000			
William J. Demetree	Repair of Eleven Bldg.		
& Company		✓	
$293,990			
Tropical Shipping	Repair of Warehouse Bldg.	✓	
$8,890			

Total $92,038,296

501

VIPA from page 3

COMPLETE | ON-GOING

Eastman, Ken $9,072	Soil Borings-Tortola Wharf STT		✓
Grenier Inc. 6/88 $2,350,000	Consultants AHA Terminal Building	✓	
Grenier Inc. 10/89 $261,987	Consultants Access Road parking lot, kiosks phasing plans, etc CEKA		✓
Island Developers $2,118,560	VIPA Office/STT		80%
Jaca & Sierra $495,265	Concrete Testing CEKA/Phases IV & V CEKA Airport Improvements		✓
Ocean Systems Research, Inc. $6,380	Frederiksted Pier Environmental Plan	✓	
Parsons (Original contract January 1977)+ 13 amendments to 12/92 $864,782	Consultants	✓	✓
Frank J. Rooney Bid Pkg.9 5/90 $2,190,000	Terminal Bldg. Signage Graphics, Baggage Handling System & SoundSystem/CEKA	✓	
Frank J. Rooney Bid Pkg.7 8/89 $17,276,183	Architectural/Mech/Electrical CEKA	✓	PENDING CLOSEOUT
Aggregate Construction Restoration of Electrical System $191,540	Containerport		✓
Aggregte Construction (A/C Tropical Shipping) $103,650	Containerport		✓
Balfour Beatty $3,111,680	Frederiksted Pier		✓
Balfour Beatty $4,270,601	AHA R/W Extended Area		✓
C/R General Contractors $429,027	National Guard Building		✓
C/R General Contractors $51,143	St. Croix Aviation Building		✓
C/R General Contractors $66,609	Purchasing Building		✓
C/R General Contractors $108,464	Gallows Bay		✓
Eastern Metro Hangar General Engineering $105,615	Pending H & O Building		✓
General Engineering $26,900	Installation of Apron floodlighting		✓

July 8, 1991

Mr. Edward E. Thomas
Director
V.I. Bureau of Internal Revenue
Lockhart's Gardens #1-A
St. Thomas, Virgin Islands 00802

Dear Mr. Thomas:

After reading your ambiguous memorandum of July 1, 1991, which serves to complicate an already puzzling situation, I have become dubious over your modus operandi and consequently, I have concluded that the Virgin Islands Port Authority assignment is nothing but an old idea in a new guise.

I have detected an undercurrent of remorse over the fact that you are now trying to countermand the order and guidelines issued me in your memorandum of June 4, 1991. Exceeding that however, and rising to the surface is the sad fact that your latest instructions are not counter to those given initially.

Unless something is hidden from my view, I would dare say that it was because of my training and experience that you assigned me the arduous task of making certain that the many Contractors contractually employed by the Virgin Islands Port Authority were meeting their tax obligations.

From all indications the assignment was important, but time-consuming. Using my training and experience, while at the same time seeking to avoid duplications, I started out to successfully meet the challenge through the cheapest and quickest means by doing my homework and sticking to the guidelines. I did not expect that Mr. Roy Vanterpool would use the assignment to make capital of your attitude towards me.

I (Liston Monsanto), not Roy Vanterpool (a fact corroborated by you in your memorandum of July 1, 1991) is charged with the responsibility of determining the tax status of each Contractor whose name appears on the newspaper clipping taken from the St. Croix Avis.

While the usage of good judgement and maximum utilization of time go hand in hand, cooperation and teamwork are most essential in making the work of an organization successful and effective.

In order to use the correct approach and explanation in carrying out his duties, a Revenue Officer must know what is legally due and owing from a taxpayer before contacting that taxpayer.

The Processing and Accounts Branch and not Mr. Roy Vanterpool was used as a source of information before going outside the organization in a blind way.

I have to speculate at Mr. Vanterpool"s motives for the reason that upon receiving the VIPA assignment (the gist of which was explained to me in your memorandum of June 4, 1991), I shifted my emphasis from taxpayer delinquent accounts and began work in earnest as I saw the assignment as an incentive and an inducement to action. Are you now trying to say that the guidelines which were issued to me on June 4, 1991, are unimportant and therefore useless?

If we are to overcome any dissatisfaction we may feel, we must not allow an uncooperative Mr. Vanterpool to counter my plans (which incidentally, were drawn up following your June 4th memorandum) with any of his own.

Let's face it! The tax records are maintained by the Processing and Accounts Branch. Internal Revenue Officers are enforcers whose job it is to get information from all sources-especially those sources at their finger tips. Fishing expeditions are not a Revenue Officer's forte.

Permit me to fulfill my responsibility to you through the carefully laid plans of Liston Monsanto which were made based on your guidelines. Unless the assignment is frivolous or mutable, we must not allow Mr. Roy Vanterpool to become an obstacle to it.

Sincerely,

Liston B. Monsanto
Internal Revenue Officer

c.c. Mr. Graciano Belardo

Mr. Louis Willis

July 8, 1991

Mr. Edward E. Thomas
Director
V.I. Bureau of Internal Revenue
Lockhart's Gardens #1-A
St. Thomas, Virgin Islands 00802

Dear Mr. Thomas:

Delegating authority to a Revenue Officer without that Revenue Officer having a clear understanding of what he can do, invites chaos. Having been systematically dismissed from duty on several occasions, my primary reason for persistently begging for guidelines has been to avoid a recurrent mistake on your part.

Several years ago (with your respected input playing a major role), I was told by the powers that be in the Virgin Islands Bureau of Internal Revenue, that a Revenue Officer to whom responsibility was delegated could cite as the basis for his authority the language embodied in Section 6301 of the United States Internal Revenue Code of 1954.

It must be noted that in my great desire to do my work and collect taxes without arousing a sense of injustice, I relied on section 6301 together with section 7602 of the aforementioned code as my justification for carrying out my duties and was thereafter relieved of my responsibilities through a dismissal. In using the code, I had gone against management's unwritten law, which took precedence over the code.

Recently, a triumvirate led by Messrs. Thomas, Belardo, and Willis(who by and large is a marginal performer) delegated me the authority to make certain that Contractors contractually employed by the Virgin Islands Port Authority meet their tax obligations.

They did so through the issuance of a June 4, 1991 memorandum from your office, which told me exactly what to do.

I'm all for the assignment (see my reports relating to it, which serve as evidence of my cooperation in the matter), but having been bitten so many times for doing what was legally correct, I've become very shy.

I know for a fact that the Processing and Accounts Branch establishes and maintains all Tax Returns, Files, Unit Ledger Card Files, and furnishes information from the files requested.

I know for a fact also, that that Branch is also responsible for furnishing advice and testimony concerning filing, processing, coding and related markings on all Returns and documents.

Because a Revenue Officer has the authority to determine what kind of action he must take and because he has the added authority to take that action, a request was made (pursuant to your guidelines) to the Processing and Accounts Branch to more or less provide me with a starting point on the several taxpayers involved in the VIPA assignment. In short, a yardstick.

But Mr. Roy Vanterpool (Chief of the Processing and Accounts Branch) not wanting to cooperate, but instead wanting my Persecutors (see letter of November 26, 1985 and reports of December 4, 1989 and September 10, 1990 in your possession) to escalate the torture of hostility and isolation, played the role of Usurper wresting the power from your office, and with unexpected ease, suspended action on the assignment. Had he read your memorandum of July 1, 1991, he would have known that Liston Monsanto and not Roy Vanterpool is charged with the responsibility of determining the tax status of the Contractors.

We must not (because of Mr. Vanterpool) do anything that is contradictory to your memoranda and the Internal Revenue Code. You need not worry about my part in the assignment. I shall cooperate with you to the fullest and comply with any instructions as long as they are not conflicting.

Please tell Mr. Roy Vanterpool to "do what is right, for it will gratify some people and astonish the rest."

Sincerely,

Liston B. Monsanto
Internal Revenue Officer

c.c. Mr. Graciano Belardo

Mr. Louis Willis

On September 30, 1992, Willis sent me a memorandum which spoke of "mail handling." He said:

V.I. BUREAU OF INTERNAL REVENUE

memorandum

date: September 30, 1992

to: Liston Monsanto
Internal Revenue Officer

from: Louis M. Willis
Asst. Chief, DAR Branch

subject: Mail Handling

The purpose of this memo is to inform you that the procedures of opening mail was discussed in a staff meeting of the DAR Branch which was held on May 6, 1992 (copies attached), but as usual Liston Monsanto refused to attend.

If you had attended, you would have been informed like all other Revenue Officers and Revenue Representative of the procedures of opening mail.

Nevertheless, the procedures of opening mail was addressed on May 6, 1992 and was enacted on May 18, 1992. If you were accustomed to receiving mail, you would have realized this procedure a long time ago.

For your information, below you will find a listing of all incoming mails to this office that were opened by my secretary:

Employee Name	Number of Mail Received
J. Todman	65
L. Thomas	59
A. Swan	33
U. Vialet	31
OCF	264
* L. Monsanto	1

If you do not want your mail to be opened, please advise those people corresponding to you to indicate that on the outside of the envelope. Furthermore, all you personal mail must be addressed to P.O. Box 2763, St. Thomas, V.I.

* Received on September 29, 1992

cc: Mr. Edward Thomas
    Director

    Ms. Claudette Farrington
    Deputy Director – Operations

Internal Revenue Service
memorandum

date: May 5, 1992

to: All Revenue Officers & Paulette Rawlins
        (Revenue Representative)

from: Mr. Louis M. Willis
        Asst. Chief, DAR Branch

subject: Meeting

There will be a meeting for all Revenue Officers and
Paulette Rawlins (Revenue Representative) at 9:00 A.M. on
May 6, 1992.

Internal Revenue Service
memorandum

date: May 6, 1992

to: Mr. Liston Monsanto
Revenue Officer

from: Mr. Louis M. Willis
Asst. Chief, DAR Branch

subject: Leave Without Pay

On Tuesday May 5, 1992 you were informed by memorandum that there will be a meeting for all Revenue Officers and Paulette Rawlins (Revenue Representative) to attend at 9:00 A.M. May 6, 1992.

At 9:05 A.M. this morning Mrs. John-Lewis called you on your extension reminding you on the meeting, you elected not to come.

I am aware that everytime I call a meeting you are never in inattendance. To address this situation, I am charging you two hours leave without pay for the duration of that meeting.

If you cannot correct this type of behavior, stronger measures will be taken to insure that you attend these meetings when they are announce.

LMW/ajl

cc: Mr. Edward E. Thomas
Director

Mr. Alvin Swan
Shop Steward

I wrote to him at once. It never took me a protracted length of time to answer their correspondence.

Liston B. Monsanto, Sr.

When it came to dealing with them I became a clairvoyant. My letter dated September 30, 1992 using a quotation from Ching Ling, which said:

RECEIVED
DAR BRANCH

September 30, 1992

Mr. Louis M. Willis
Delinquent Accounts & Returns Branch
V.I. Bureau of Internal Revenue
St. Thomas, Virgin Islands 00802

"A college degree does not change a *fool*
a man - it merely disguises him."

- Ching Ling

Dear Mr. Willis:

Unlike you, I do not have the time while on the job to talk via the telephone about sports and cable television as you did at 9:17 on the morning of September 17, 1992 on the "Addie Ottley Show". I'm a victim of poetic justice.

Your memorandum of this morning which was written by way of repartee, tells me that it is perfectly okay for someone to open anybody's mail, while running the risk of being accused of taking something valuable from the envelope that was never there in the first place.

The minutes of your several meetings of which you spoke were never made available to me so that when I spoke of mail addressed to me being opened by someone else I relied on Mr. Edward E. Thomas' memorandum of March 27, 1992 wherein he spoke of "Personal Belongings" plus the standards of conduct and moral judgment as they apply to decent people.

Mr. Willis, I have never in my thirty nine years of governmental service used the Virgin Islands Government's post office box for the purpose of receiving mail. As a resident of St. Thomas, I have rented a box from the U.S. Postal Service for my own convenience.

On May 14, 1992, you told me that I was burnt out and mentally drained. Furthermore, you told me that I needed to retire. Now I ask, wouldn't it be (using your reasoning) an unfair thing for me to retire during this period when the Bureau must import retirees from the United States? Ponder that.

Sincerely,

Liston B. Monsanto
Internal Revenue Officer

c.c. Mr. Edward E. Thomas
Ms. Claudette Farrington

While Thomas had been delaying my retirement the Bureau had remained in a fixed condition. Either he thought I was needling him over my retirement or he was hoping that I would do something stupid so that he could show Farrelly and the other people with whom he was allied that he was indeed a crafty schemer. A tour through the workplace highlighted the fact that the Virgin Islands Bureau of Internal Revenue had become chaotic as its population of young people with an average age of twenty-eight mushroomed. I was serving as a distraction and therefore hoping to move past a feud, which had been carried on for over twenty years. I knew that I was going to write a book someday and in the process get Thomas on the rebound.

Within me was a desperate desire to put an end to the mess that had engulfed me for so long a period. I had become determined to retire from governmental service. It had become incumbent upon me to keep things in perspective and so I contacted Luis "Tito" Morales and asked him to speak to Thomas about working on my retirement proposal, which had been before him for several months.

Following a month of negotiations between the Union represented by Randolph Allen and Tito Morales and the Government represented by Joanne U. Barry and Edward Thomas, an agreement was reached and placed in the form of a Stipulation dated November 5, 1992. The Stipulation said:

UNITED STEELWORKERS OF AMERICA)
On behalf of LISTON MONSANTO.)
)
vs.)   RE: Grievance No. 1-91
)   Replacement   1-91
GOVERNMENT OF THE VIRGIN ISLANDS,)   Grievance No. 2-92
Bureau of Internal Revenue.)   Grievance No. 3-92
)

S T I P U L A T I O N

WHEREAS the Government of the Virgin Islands, Bureau of Internal Revenue and the United Steelworkers of America are parties to a Collective Bargaining AGreement made October 5, 1990 for the period of October 1, 1987 to September 30, 1991 and extended in a day to day basis on November 7, 1991; and

WHEREAS the Unites Steelworkers of America filed Grievance No. 1-91 on March 11, 1991; replacement Grievance No. 1-91 on April 10, 1991; Grievance No. 2-92 filed on June 29, 1992; and Grievance No. 3-92 filed on July 29, 1992, all filed on behalf of Liston Monsanto: and

WHEREAS in settlement of these grievances and any and all other claims arising therefrom, the parties hereby stipulate and agree as follows:

1.   Liston Monsanto will be appointed to the position of Chief, Delinquent and Accounts branch effective May 5, 1991, at a salary of $39,665 on the TX Schedule Range 13, Step 4.

2.   Concurrent with the signing hereof, Mr. Monsanto shall submit his retirement from the Bureau (attached) with an effective date of November 5, 1992.

3. All outstanding grievances shall be withdrawn within 5 days of the signing hereof.

4. The Bureau will pay Mr. Monsanto in full for 168 hours previously charged as Leave Without Pay at the rate of $18.24 per hour.

5. The Bureau shall transmit to the Division OF Personnel within 5 days of the signing hereof the NOPA for the appointment and the NOPA to effect the stated date of the retirement.

THIS STIPULATION IS NOT AN ADMISSION OF LIABILITY AND MAY NOT BE USED BY EITHER PARTY FOR ANY PURPOSE OTHER THAN THE RESOLUTION OF THE STATED MATTERS.

GOVERNMENT OF THE VIRGIN ISLANDS

BY: _____
JOANNE U. BARRY
Chief Negotiator

DATED: _Nov 4_____, 1992

BY: _____
EDWARD E. THOMAS, Director
Bureau of Internal Revenue

DATED: _Nov. 5___, 1992

UNITED STEELWORKERS OF AMERICA

BY: _____
RANDOLPH ALLEN
Staff Representative

DATED: _Nov 5_____, 1992

BY: _____
LUIS "Tito" MORALES
President, Local 8249

DATED: _Nov. 5____, 1992

BY: _____
LISTON MONSANTO

DATED: _11/5_____, 1992

In writing my letter of retirement to Thomas on the same day, I used a quotation from Angelo Patri which said: "The life of a soul on earth lasts longer than his departure; he lives on in your life and in the lives of all others who knew him." Then I continued with the letter as follows: "Because I have never been one to resign myself to failure, following discussions (from which a Stipulation dated November 5, 1992 arose) between the Office of Collective Bargaining, the United Steelworkers of America and the Virgin Islands Bureau of Internal Revenue, I made the decision to retire from the Government of the Virgin Islands to take effect immediately. The Stipulation mentioned in paragraph one above, serves as a tacit admission that I've always been free of blame and guilt in the Virgin Islands Bureau of Internal Revenue where, despite an unblemished record and based only on clever propaganda, a number of people have a very distorted view of me. The ties of nearly forty years have come to an end and although I'm leaving after being repeatedly persecuted for righteousness sake, magnanimously I continue to operate on the thesis that one should not say bad if he cannot say good. Moreover, I'm very enthusiastic over the notion that in this sinful world of ours, one must love his enemies just in case his friends turn out to be rotten."

There was an ecstatic look of pleasure on the face of Edward Thomas. He appeared to be coming from the depths of despair to the height of buoyancy with my departure from the Virgin Islands Bureau of Internal Revenue. As far as he was concerned, his dominance had not diminished. His empire was still intact. My retirement was not as courteous as would be expected. It was, put simply, unceremonious.

Retiring as Chief of the Delinquent Accounts and Returns Branch nevertheless meant that Louis "Lolo" Willis, the opportunistic man who due to circumstances had stepped up to a higher level for which he was not qualified, had become my subordinate in the end.

Twelve years later, as I look back on my ordeal, I cannot help but think that it was an attack against decency and humanity. No government employee in the course of human affairs in the United States Virgin Islands had ever been subjected to the nefarious acts perpetrated on Liston Monsanto, Sr. It was a thorough trial appropriately labeled the "Extreme Test." Anyone remotely familiar with the modus operandi of the exalted task masters who for many years took advantage of disadvantaged people and under whose supervision I was required to work will tell you today that there couldn't be a hole dug deep enough to bury them all.

"It takes courage for Government Employes to stick their necks out and blow the whistle in time to make a difference."

-Thomas Divine

Printed in the United States
48134LVS00006B/57-510

9 781420 849011